THE NALADIYAR
OR
FOUR HUNDRED QUATRAINS
IN TAMIL

THE NALADIYAR
OR
FOUR HUNDRED QUATRAINS
IN TAMIL

WITH

INTRODUCTION, TRANSLATION AND
NOTES CRITICAL, PHILOLOGICAL AND
EXPLANATORY
TO WHICH IS ADDED
A CONCORDANCE AND LEXICON

WITH AUTHORITIES FROM THE OLDEST TAMIL WRITERS

REV. G. U. POPE

GYAN

Published by

GYAN

Gyan Publishing House
5, Ansari Road
Daryaganj, New Delhi-110002
Phone: 011-47034999, 9811692060
E-mail: books@gyanbooks.com

Distribution Network
gyanbooks.com
India, USA, Canada, UK, Australia, France

ISBN : 978-81-212-3803-8 (PB)
First Published, 1893

2nd Impression 2020

Printed at: Gyan Press, Delhi.

The Naladiyar or Four Hundred Quatrains in Tamil
Author: Rev. G. U. Pope

முனிவர்

அருளிச்செய்த

நாலடியார்

THE NĀLAḌIYĀR

OR

FOUR HUNDRED QUATRAINS IN TAMIL

WITH

INTRODUCTION, TRANSLATION, AND NOTES CRITICAL, PHILOLOGICAL AND EXPLANATORY

TO WHICH IS ADDED

A Concordance and Lexicon

WITH AUTHORITIES FROM THE OLDEST TAMIL WRITERS

BY THE

REV. G. U. POPE, M.A., D.D.

SOMETIME FELLOW OF THE MADRAS UNIVERSITY
MEMBER OF THE ROYAL ASIATIC SOCIETY
AND OF
THE GERMAN ORIENTAL SOCIETY

Oxford
AT THE CLARENDON PRESS
1893

CONTENTS.

INVOCATION.

கடவுள் வாழ்த்து.

வானிடு வில்லின் வரவறியா வாய்மையாற்
கானிலந் தோயாக் கடவுளை—யாநிலஞ்
சென்னி உறவணங்கிச் சேர்தும் எம் முள்ளத்து
முன்னி யவைமுடிக என்று:

Knowing, like bow displayed in heav'n, man's advent here,
To earth my head I bow, to GOD in truth draw near,
Touch of whose foot earth never knew; thus what my mind
Conceives, I pray may happy consummation find.

This invocation is said to be by the commentator Pathumanār.

INTRODUCTION

TO

THE FOUR HUNDRED QUATRAINS

OR

NĀLAḌI-NĀNNŪRRU.

I. General Introduction.

THIS edition of a popular Tamil Classic was undertaken mainly with the view of assisting Europeans to acquire some acquaintance with classical Tamil. It is intended to be taken up after the study of the Second Catechism of Tamil Grammar[1], to which references are given throughout; and is a companion volume to the *Kurraḷ*[2]: these two great works serving as mutual commentaries, and together throwing a flood of light upon the whole ethical and social philosophy of the Tamil people.

I am not without a hope and belief that such editions of their great classics may find favour with some at least of the great multitude of young Tamil men who pursue with enthusiasm and fair success their English studies, but are, I apprehend, in some danger, alas! of neglecting their own wonderful language.

To avoid repetition, the student is referred to the introduction

[1] *First Lessons in Tamil;* or, An Introduction to the Common Dialect of that Language, for the use of foreigners learning Tamil and of Tamilians learning English, with *An Easy Catechism in Tamil* of both the Colloquial and Classical Dialects, by the Rev. G. U. Pope, M.A., D.D. Fifth Edition. Oxford: at the Clarendon Press. 1891.

[2] *The Sacred Kurraḷ* of Tiruvaḷḷuva-Nāyanār, with Metrical Translation, Notes, Grammar, Lexicon, and Concordance, by the Rev. G. U. Pope, M.A., D.D. London: Allen & Co.

to the *Kurral* for information on many matters connected with Tamil, and important to those who would thoroughly master the *Nālaḍi.*

This work is recommended to the student of Tamil for several weighty reasons.

These are not so much the originality of its teaching, as the peculiar terseness and vigour of its style; and the fidelity with which it reflects the thoughts and ideas of the great mass of the Tamil people, and indeed of the yeomanry of India; for, though composed most probably by Jains, it contains scarcely any traces of their peculiar tenets. [For these the student must read the *Jīvaga Chintāmaṇi*, and this is no easy task, though made easier by the publication of an admirable edition of it by Mr. Vē. Çāmināthaiyar. See p. xli.]

The *Nālaḍi-nānnūrru*, or 'Four Hundred Quatrains,' is often called the *Veḷḷāḷar-Vētham*, the 'Bible of the Cultivators of the soil.'

Not only is it one of the text-books prescribed for the Oriental Honour School of this University, but it is moreover a chief subject of examination in the Madras University; and is taught, in some shape, in every vernacular school in the Tamil country.

I have therefore in my official capacity prepared, under some disadvantages, this edition, with an extensive critical apparatus, in the hope of bringing at least a few European minds into closer contact with those of our Tamil fellow-subjects; and of inducing young Tamil students to bring the freer and more invigorating, though more laborious methods of European study to bear upon their own great classics.

The old method of continuous verbal commentary and paraphrase tends to paralyse the mind, and compels the student to go round and round in the mill of traditional interpretation.

A recent Tamil editor of the Nālaḍi begins his preface with these words, 'The Nālaḍiyār is one of the moral text-books emanating from the (Madura) Academy (சங்கம்), and, therefore, came into existence 4000 years ago!'

He also gives, with slight variations, the current tradition regarding the 400 quatrains. It is briefly this: 'Once on a time, 8000 Jain ascetics, driven by famine, came to a Pāṇḍiyan king and were supported by him. When the famine was over they prepared to return to their own country, though the king wished to retain the learned strangers who added lustre to his court. At last the poets were driven to depart secretly by night. In the morning it was found that each bard had left on his seat a quatrain. These were examined and found to differ widely from one another. The king then ordered them all to be thrown into the river Vaigai, when it was found that the palm-leaf scrolls containing these 400 quatrains ascended the river against the current, and came to the bank. To these the king gave the name of Nālaḍiyār (the quatrainists).' Some other verses reached the banks at various spots, and are found in two collections, called 'Old sayings' (பழமொழி) and 'The Essence of the way of virtue' (அறநெறிச்சாரம்)[1]. These latter works have never obtained the popularity enjoyed by the *Nālaḍiyār;* and I should regard them as mainly imitations due to a later period, though some of the verses are certainly more or less ancient.

These traditions point to a collection of popular verses made after the impalement of the Samaṇar (or *Amaṇar* = Jains, lit. 'naked ones'), perhaps in the time of Sundara Pāṇḍiyan (or *Kūn-P.*), who probably lived in the twelfth century A.D. [See C. D. G. pp. 132–140.]

These verses, mainly but not, I think, exclusively of Jain origin, were doubtless expurgated by the Çaivas, under whose chief guardianship Tamil literature has since remained.

They were re-edited, interpreted, arranged, and forced into a kind of parallelism to the *Kurraḷ* by *Pathumanār* (पद्म 'a lotus'), of whom nothing is really known. I have printed an elegant invocation ascribed to him. No other editor has done much for the quatrains.

The fact that to them exclusively the title of *Nālaḍi* (or quatrain) was given seems to render it probable that they constitute some of the earliest specimens of this elegant metre, the Alcaic of Tamil.

As might be expected from their history, no consistent and developed system of philosophy, religion, or morals can be deduced from them; and it may be said with truth that these utterances have too little sequence and connexion to admit of any scientific criticism. Yet it is a kind of merit to put a happy point upon a commonplace; and these epigrams, drawn sometimes from Sanskrit sources and oftener forming the ground

---

[1] Referred to as P. M. and A. N. Çā.

of ornate Sanskrit verses, written in imitation or rivalry, have become household words through all South India.

I am unwilling to enter here on any discussion of the date of this and other Tamil classics, since there are scarcely any ascertained facts or ancient inscriptions from which to reason. The discussion of these matters requires aptitude, leisure, and opportunity for archaeological research (and these I do not possess), in addition to a critical acquaintance with Tamil literature. The want of this last essential has rendered many otherwise profound researches almost valueless. A very careful consideration of many masterpieces of Tamil literature leads me to think that between A.D. 800 and 1200 the greatest of these works were composed [1]. Internal evidence, as far as I see, is all we have to rely on.

Hiouen-Thsang, the Buddhist pilgrim who visited the continent of India in 640 A.D., says that in *Malakūṭa* the people were not much addicted to the cultivation of literature, and only valued the pursuit of wealth; and mentions Jains as the most prominent sect. Now, this *Malakūṭa* must be = *Malakōṭṭa*, *Malaināḍu*, *Malaya*, *Malayāḷam*, and seems to have included the whole southern part of the Madras Presidency (Hultzsch, South-Indian Inscriptions, vol. ii. part i. p. 2 note): the Pāṇḍya and Çēra kingdoms.

The Jains were great students and copyists of books (Burnell, S. I. Palaeography, p. 88). We may feel quite sure that the seventh century A.D., at the latest, saw the beginning of Tamil literature under Jain auspices. Perhaps the Jains fostered the vernaculars partly out of opposition to the Brāhmans. Reformers and missionaries, who generally address themselves to the intelligent middle classes, have often been the most assiduous students and promoters of the vulgar tongues. Quatrain 243 of the Nālaḍi shows the feeling of hostility that existed between North and South: between Hindūs and Jains. The great antiquity of Tamil, which is the one worthy rival of Sanskrit, is abundantly plain.

The ancient grammatical works existing in Tamil, and its wonderful metrical system, prove its assiduous cultivation for long ages. An elaborate, scientific series of metres, such as Tamil glories in, adapted to every style and theme of composition, is the growth of centuries. Classical Tamil bears every

---

[1] To native scholars this field of research naturally belongs, and any reader of Mr. P. Sundaram Piḷḷai's able papers in the Madras Christian College Magazine (1891) will see that one of them at least is zealously and ably working in it.

mark of slow and natural evolution; but the subject is complicated by the number of works in circulation falsely attributed to old writers. The many really ridiculous forgeries of this kind bring discredit on all Tamil literature. Tamil scholars should banish, among other things, such spurious works as many of those attributed to Agastya, Avvai, Paṭṭaṇattu-piḷḷai, and others.

In regard to the teachings of these epigrams—philosophical, theological and ethical—I have little to add to what is said in the notes and analyses of chapters.

There is no mention of God in the Nālaḍi (save in the quite modern invocation) and no trace of religion. In this respect the quatrains differ from the *Kurraḷ*. There are indeed a few poetical references to certain deities, and allusions to popular beliefs and rites, but the bards evidently were not orthodox Hindūs.

As in most Hindū ethical and philosophical writings the ruling idea is that of Karma, which is discussed in pp. 66–69. A study of this is quite essential to the comprehension of all Hindū systems.

The misery of embodiment (பிறவி) in successive and infinitely varied forms, and the bliss of release (முத்தி) from all of these, are often expressed, and illustrated with every kind of figure. It is assumed that always, to all, conscious existence on earth, as well as in any heavens or hells, is an absolute evil. Here, of course, we find ourselves in antagonism.

Yet pervading these verses there seems to me to be a strong sense of moral obligation, an earnest aspiration after righteousness, a fervent and unselfish charity, and generally a loftiness of aim that are very impressive. I have felt sometimes as if there must be a blessing in store for a people that delight so utterly in compositions thus remarkably expressive of a hunger and thirst after righteousness. They are the foremost among the peoples of India, and the Kurraḷ and Nālaḍi have helped to make them so.

It is in vain to discuss elaborately the origin and possible sources of the work. The majority of the verses were almost certainly sung by Jain ascetics, yet there are a few that seem to be from the Mahābhārata, and undoubtedly many of the quatrains are fragments of the old ethical teaching which goes under the name of *Nīti-çāstra*[1]. The history of South India permits us

---

[1] See Sir M. Monier-Williams' *Indian Wisdom*, p. 55. How inferior the verses of Bhartṛihari are may be seen by examining the version given in Trübner's Series.

to expect to trace not only Buddhist, or Jain, but also Greek, Christian, and even Muhammadan influences in the early Tamil classics, as much almost as those inspired by Sanskrit writings.

When we examine each quatrain as an artistic whole—a kind of cameo—we find that there are several distinct and clearly marked types. Some of these may be conveniently arranged in classes.

1. There are the simply *didactic.*

Here the student must first master the third and fourth lines, in which is enunciated the truth, precept, or principle, of which the former part of the quatrain gives the proof or illustration. This is a prevailing type also in the *Kuṛṛaḷ*. A *Veṇbā* verse, like a sonnet, should have a very effective and striking finish.

This is seen in the first quatrain, where the aphorism is, 'worldly prosperity is a thing of no account.'

This axiom is illustrated by a matter of daily experience. The connective is எனின்='if this is an undeniable fact, then . . . .' Compare also 293.

2. One class of the didactic quatrain depends for its effectiveness chiefly on some apt and ingenious simile, illustration, or analogy. To us some of these seem forced and fanciful conceits, but we really are not always in a position to judge or rightly estimate them.

In 290 the aptness of the figure, the beauty of the expression, the wonderful terseness of the conclusion, together with the perfection of the form and rhythm, leave nothing to be desired.

3. In some of these the simile is simply thrown in, while the most prominent thing is the clear enunciation of a truth. Here the whole runs on like rhetorical prose. Examples of this are 8, 49, 87.

4. Some are cumulative, with or without a climax.

Thus in 65 we find three statements, with a thread of connexion: 'It is the difficulty of the achievement that makes it meritorious.' In 80 we have three precepts. In 100 there is a climax. See 4, 55, 88.

5. Others are enumerative, where the various parts and accessories of some idea are summed up. See 74, 81, 83, 84, 119.

6. A few are antithetic, suggesting a contrast with or without a simile; as, 48, 51, 52, 89.

7. A very few contain puns. So 39, 56.

If I am not deceived there is in many of these verses something far beyond mere technical skill. At times by a few happy touches an idea is expressed in such apt language, and illuminated by such a picturesque use and adaptation of familiar words, each chosen with truest and most accurate discrimination, that the quatrain becomes a group of life-like pictures, on which the mind is fain to linger long, and to which it recurs often. In this matchless verse [135]—

> கல்வி கரையில கற்பவர் நாள்சில
> மெல்ல நினைக்கிற் பிணிபல — தெள்ளிதின்
> ஆராய்ந் தமைவுடைய கற்பவே நீரொழியப்
> பாலுண் குருகிற் றெரிந்து—

not a syllable could be spared; while almost every word is common and easy, yet is the very fittest, and is used in its exact meaning. It is somewhat archaic;—has a fascinating air of mystery;—pleasantly exercises and amply rewards the student's ingenuity;—seems dark at first, but once lit up, sparkles for ever.

Thus கரை=*shore* suggests a metaphor: 'learning is a shore-less—infinite—ocean.'

Then comes the simple antithesis, 'the learners' days are few.' In Tamil the use of the same root twice (in கல்வி and கற்பவர்) and again in the third line (கற்பவே) imparts an added charm.

Into these perfectly (to Tamil ears) harmonious lines is compressed a whole chapter:

'The *subjects of study* (கல்வி with a plural verb) are infinitely numerous; but the learners' days are few; and if it be calmly thought out, men are liable to many diseases. [பிணி=natural infirmities or "bonds," that enfeeble and restrict.] Youthful enthusiasm may lead men to anticipate great and varied triumphs; *calm reflection* teaches them their natural weakness. So, men should learn with discrimination (தெள்ளிது), examining closely (ஆராய்) things befitting (அமை, "suit, satisfy, gladden") them, with intelligence (தெரிந்து) like that of the bird (the semi-divine *Hañça*), that drinks only the milk and leaves the water, when these mingled are presented to it.' Of course this last is received as a fact!

II. Grammatical Notes.

As to the grammar of the Nālaḍiyār, the Second Catechism is amply sufficient.

[In the IIIrd Grammar, which is much fuller, the *Nannūl* is given. This my late lamented friend Dr. Bower partly reprinted in 1876 (S. P. C. K. Press); and added a good translation of the *Nannūl* preface.] Here notes are added in which most of the poetical forms and difficulties in the text are explained, referring to the questions of the Grammar. These pages are in fact an appendix to that little manual.

It is, however, to the appended Lexicon and Concordance that the student should chiefly look for assistance. Notes, commentaries, and translations have their uses; but he who follows out a word through all its forms, and wherever it occurs, will soon gain a familiarity with the poetical style and diction which he will not easily obtain otherwise.

These grammatical notes follow the numbers of the Second Catechism.

G. 12. ĀYTHAM.

This is a letter which is not classed as vowel or consonant; so its other name is தனிநிலை (what stands alone). It is in effect an aspirate, equivalent to ह् in the middle of a word. Its name is, I think, from its shape, the trident (திரிசூலம், ஆயுதம்). It occurs in 39, where it simply lengthens the syllable, as the metre requires (– ᴗ ᴗ –). Exactly so in 61, 250; it is *h* or χ.

In 137 it seems an integral part of எஃகு = ĚHGU. [See Jī. Chin. i. 255.]

In 251 அஃதுடைமை must be (ᴗ ᴗ ᴗ ᴗ –); or ஃ = *ha* or *χa*.

So in 398 அஃதூஉம் must be (ᴗ ᴗ – –).

In 12 அஃகினர் is (– ᴗ ᴗ), i.e. ஃ = *h* or χ; so 17, வெஃகன்மின்.

Āytham must be preceded by a short vowel, and followed by either க, ச, ட, த, ப, or ற. *Nannūl*, 96.

G. 14.

அளபு or அளவு எடுத்தல் = 'prolongation of measure.'

1. This lengthening of vowels in *N.* is (1) to fill up the metre; (2) to emphasize the meaning (see 184); (3) to form a vocative case; or (4) in adverbial participles of certain verbs.

2. The most usual அளபெடை is when to a long syllable is subjoined its corresponding short. [So 'Ηέλιος for 'Ηλιος.]

Thus, உடாதும் (புளிமா / ᴗ ᴗ –) becomes உடா அதும் (கருவிளம் / ᴗ ᴗ ᴗ ᴗ), 10, 38, 94, 119, 127, 169, 199, 201, 254, 255, 310, 337.

கடா அய் = க. போம் becomes போ ஓம், 140.

3. Another kind first lengthens a syllable, and then extends it as above:

தொடி becomes தொடூ, and finally தொடூஇ. நின்றதும் becomes நின்றதூம், and finally நின்றதூஉம், 192, 235, 259, 314.

4. A third kind seems like அளபெடை, but is simply the omission of வ்: கூவும் becomes கூஉம், 140. கடா அய் = கடாவி, 258.

With this is found a real prolongation:

மருவு omits வ், and taking அளபு, becomes மரூஉ, 246, 285.

5. Another அளபெடை, found in certain adverbial participles, is made by taking the shortest root (மரு in மருவு; ஒரு in ஒருவு), forming adv. part. in இ, and prolonging: மருவு makes மரு, மரீ, மரீஇ.

So எழுந்து : எழு, எழீ, எழீஇ : 209. Comp. 85, 137, 213, 220, 239, 258, 399.

6. There is also a double அளபு. This is very picturesque in 184.

7. Some examples, as in 246, combine some of the above methods; but are poetic anomalies. [G. 137.]

G. 19–39.

A table is here given of sixteen orthographical changes. To this the student can refer throughout.

CONSPECTUS OF THE SIXTEEN DIFFERENT CHANGES OF LETTERS.

௧௬ பிரதான விகாரங்களின் சுருக்கமான அட்டவணை.

			விதி.
௧.	இ	யகரத்தின் முன்தோன்றும்	G. 24.
௨.	உ	குற்றியல் உகரம் உயிர் முன்கெடும்	24.
௩.	வ், ய்	சில உயிர் முன்தோன்றும்	23.
௪.	க், ச், த், ப்	உயிருக்குப்பின் இரட்டிக்கும்	27.
௫.	ம்	கெடும்; ங், ஞ், ந் ஆகத்திரியும்; இரட்டிக்கும் . . .	32, 33, 31.
௬.	ஞ் ந், ய்	இரட்டிக்கும்	31.
௭.	ட், ற்	மொழி அகத்து இரட்டிக்கும்	26.
௮.	. . .	மெய்கள் சுட்டின்பின்னும், வினாவின்பின்னும் இரட்டிக்கும் .	25.
௯. ௧௦.	ண் ள்	ட் ஆகத் திரியும் ட் ஆகத் திரியும் } [ண், ள் + க், ச், ப் = ட்க, ட்ச, ட்ப] .	34.
௧௧.	ள்	ண் ஆகத் திரியும் [ள் + ம் = ண்ம்]	36.
௧௨. ௧௩.	ன் ல்	ற் ஆகத் திரியும் ற் ஆகத் திரியும் } [ன், ல் + க், ச், ப் = ற்க, ற்ச, ற்ப] .	35.
௧௪.	ல்	ன் ஆகத் திரியும் [ல் + ம் = ன்ம்]	36.
௧௫.	த்	ட் ஆகத் திரியும் { ண் + த் = ட்ட், ண்ட் ; ள் + த் = ட்ட், ளிட், ட் } . . .	37.
		ற் ஆகத் திரியும் { ன் + த் = ற்ற், ன்ற் ; ல் + த் = ற்ற், லிற், ற் } . . .	38.
௧௬.	ந்	ன் ஆகத் திரியும் / கெடும் { ல் + ந் = ன்ன், ன் ; ன் + ந் = ன்ன், ன் } . . .	39.
		ண் ஆகத் திரியும் / கெடும் { ள் + ந் = ண்ண், ண் ; ண் + ந் = ண்ண், ண் } . . .	40.

See the Appendix on this subject in my H. B. Part II, pp. 41–44 (4th edition).

G. 24.

குற்றியலிகரம், i.e. இ shortened. Its quantity in verse is half a measure. See *Nannūl*, 93, 94.

When a word (other than a dissyllable, whose first syllable is short) ends in உ, that letter is short (குற்றியலுகரம்), and is cut off before the initial vowel of a following word. (In 1, அமர்ந்து + இல்லாள், சென்று + இருப்பர், ஒன்று + உண்டாக.) If, however, the following word begins with ய், the '*furtive*' உ is changed into furtive இ.

246 : செய்து + யார் (இ not reckoned as a syllable) in the metre (⏑ ⏑ – – | – – – | – – | ⏑ ⏑ –).

So 214 : நெஞ்சத்து + யாத்தாரோடு + யாத்ததொடர்பு : note the scansion!

G. 27.

This rule, with its exceptions, affects the pronunciation, decides not infrequently as to the meaning, and is very important.

The student should examine into the reason of every doubled consonant!

1. The following examples in regard to four ambiguous verbal forms will be found useful :—

(*a*) இகவா பிழைத்து, 6. Why is ப் not doubled? Because இகவா (இகவாது) is a *finite verb*. Comp. 88, 243. [G. 89.]

(*b*) தாழாத் தளராத் தலைநடுக்காத் . . . , 14. Here த் is thrice doubled, for these are positive adv. participles, and *after these* க, ச, த, ப *are always doubled*. [G. 86. (க)].

(*c*) தண்டாச்சிறப்பிற்று, 62 ; கல்லாப்புன்மாக்கள், 45. These are contracted negative adj. participles [G. 91] for தண்டாத, கல்லாத ; and *after such forms* க, ச, த, ப *are always doubled*.

(*d*) நில்லாநிலைபகலாம், 204. This is a negative adverbial participle for நில்லாமல். [G. 90.] *After these* க, ச, த, ப *are never doubled*. This discriminates them from (*b*).

2. In compounds of all sorts where the members are Tamil words, or quite naturalized, the initial of the second is generally doubled :

சகடக்கால், 2 ; சேனைத்தலைவர், 3 ; தீக்கூற்றம், 5 ; வாய்ச்சொல், 115 ; உறுத்தொழிலர், 128.

3. When there is an ellipsis of the sign of the 2nd case, க, ச, த, ப are not generally doubled, 203 ; but many exceptions are found. Thus after போல் (28) these are not doubled. For மின்னுப்போல் (8), see *Nannūl*, 217.

In 26 it is = ஈரினால். Exceptions are 393, புத்தொடு ; 24, தீக்கொண்டு ; 43, பூச்சூடு.

G. 55.

1. In Tamil poetry nouns may be declined as in prose ; but the normal method is to discard all case-endings, and to use the noun itself to express all relations. [G. 152.]

Thus in 1 the only (partially) inflected nouns are இடத்து and பாற்று. In 2, கூழ் and கால் are second cases.

2. The next step is to use the inflexional base (stem or crude form) to express any relation. [G. 66, 68, and § 18.] See இடத்து, 51 ; கலத்து, 12 ; களத்து, 16, 131, 132 ; காட்டு, 25.

3. This base is strengthened by addition of இன், அன், *etc.* [G. 65, 108.] In 12, வாழ்தலின் for 3rd case (வாழ்தலினால்). So அதன், 'its' [அது + அன் + (உடைய)], 20.

G. 56, 57.

1. Singular nominative endings : ஒன் : மடவோன், 273. அள் (fem.), comp. 93.

This leads to the consideration of the formation of new personal derivative nouns. [G. 93.]

2. A nominative is used like the Latin 'accusative of respect' : so 351, ஆண்டிளையர், 'young *in* years.' And சொல்வற்றும், 'will be mighty *in* speech,' 348. கண்ணகன்ற, 'wide *in* extent.' பேரும், 'even by name,' 200.

3. Words like ஆவது are used with the subject. Thus in 242 : அணிகலமாவது = 'it is (self-suppression) that forms their adornment.' [See H.B. § 151.]

G. 58.

1. The accusative, or direct object, often adds ஐ, 3.

In 273, for emphasis, the object is given thrice.

2. With இன் + ஐ : பறையினை, 24. With அன் + ஐ : அதனை.

3. Ellipsis is common : ஒன்றினை, 4, 255.

In ellipses of this case, க, ச, த, ப are not, as a rule, doubled ; but usage varies. See *Nannūl*, 255, and notes on G. 27.

4. A noun preceding a verb may be so joined to it as to form a compound verb, in which the meanings of the members are more or less modified. For these, see notes on G. 27.

G. 59.

1. The 3rd case expresses cause and connexion: WITH, BY. It also has the effect of an adverb often; compare படுதலால், வரிசையால், 18; வகையான், 71, 128, 179.

2. கொண்டு is used as a sign of the 4th case, 396. [H. B. § 239.]

3. = *Together with.* See 143. ஒடு = உடன், 214. நரம்பொடு, குணத்தோடு. See 2.

4. ஆல் and உடன் are found without any noun. See Lex. pp. 324, 332.

G. 60.

1. The Dative, or 4th case, is used as in prose: 13, 15, 202.

2. With இன், 121, 148.

3. Rare forms are அவற்கு = அவனுக்கு, 23. So 202, துன்பக்கு = துன்பத்துக்கு.

4. With என்று: மக்கட்கென்று, 'for,' 130. Comp. 134.

5. Note the remarkable ellipses in 145.

G. 61.

ஞானியில், தாரில் are 5th cases: 'from, commencing with,' 138. பொக்குளில், 'like,' 27. பித்தரில், 'like' or 'than,' 52, 154. செல்லின், 'than,' 133. மாக்களின், 'than,' 334. வாயில் for 3rd case, 156. கை|த்து = 'at *or* from the hands of,' 206. மருங்கில், '*by*,' 340.

The signs of the 7th case are sometimes used for the 5th: கண்: கல்லார் கட்டீர்வு, 'from,' 129.

G. 62. OF.

Genitive or Possessive relation.

1. This is oftenest expressed by a compound, analogous to the तत्पुरुष in Sanskrit.

மனையாறு, 'domestic life:' the way *of* the house, 54. மக்கண்மனம் = 'men's mind,' 127. See அறத்துப்பால் and the headings of most of the chapters.

The first member of the compound is the noun itself, or its inflexional base. Certain changed euphonic insertions are found. § 130, *etc.*

அறுசுவையுண்டி, 'food *of* six savours,' 1. சகடக்கால், 'a waggon's wheel,' 2; ம் is elided and க doubled. See *Nannūl*, 219.

This is sometimes neatly called இருபெயர் ஒட்டுப்பண்புத் தொகை. G. 154.

Thus வைக்கற்பால் in 1 is two nouns joined so that the former defines the latter: 'the category of placing.' This is then declined by G. 93: 'it belongs not to the category of things to be reckoned.'

2. உடைய as case-ending is shortened to உடை: 91, 274.

In this case a following க, ச, த, or ப is abnormally doubled.

3. இன். This euphonic insertion is found in சுரையின்காய், 116; சிறப்பின், 139.

N.B. இன் answers very constantly to the English 'OF of reference.'

4. தம் = 'their,' is inserted in 127. ஒருவர்தம் = ஒருவருடைய.

G. 63.

The 7th or Locative Ablative.

Its termination is இல், இன், 21, 207.

But a great number of nouns, used as adverbial particles, having an idea of place, time, or manner, may be used with, or instead of, இல்.

Each of these has its own shade of meaning. See Lex. Among these are (1) இடம், இடத்து, இடத்தில் = 'where, when,' 1, 11, 51, 160, 358. (2) உள், IN, AMONG, 24, 50, 121, 122, 188. (3) உழை, 159 [comp. 167], 353. (4) கண், கட்டு, 16, 121, 128, 158, 167, 186, 336. (5) சிழ், 3. (6) வாடு, வாட்டு, 2, 14, 161, 206, 207, 246. (7) மிசை, 21; மிசைமேல், 22. (8) முன், 51, 325, 326. (9) மேல், 27, 29, 186. (10) பின், 160, 398. (11) வயின், 400. (12) சாரல், 342 : கடற்றூர்தஞ்சாரல் = கடற்றூரிடத்தில். (13) போழ்து, 329.

The ellipsis of this case-ending in nouns in அம் [see under G. 55] is very common. 12, 16, 207, 398, கானத்து, 'through the *jungle.*'

G. 64.

The Vocative Case.

1. Here a finite verb in the second person is often used for a noun in the vocative case even as a nom.: thus (6, 7) வைத்தீர் = 'O you who have accumulated!'

So சார்ந்தோய்! 126.

2. There are ordinary forms: நெஞ்சே!

So சேர்ப்ப! நாட!

3. கண்ணாய்! may be voc. of கண்ணை = கண்ணுடையதீ! as பிச்சாய், பெய்வளாய்.

தொடீஇ! 111.

So நல்லாய் is formed as in G. 93.

G. 69.

Plural Nominative Endings are besides கள் (37)—

அர், ஆர், ஒர், இர், எம், நர், ஞர், ஆளர் for பலர்பால் (Epicenes); and அ, அவை for neuters. (1, 2, 4, 36, 194, 206, 320, 368.)

By *Nannūl* 159 no letters are doubled after any of the forms in ர்; thus, கொண்டார் கூற்றம் (35). This is an exception to G. 30.

By *Nannūl* 167 no letters are doubled after a neuter plural in அ.

The pluralizing particle is often suppressed.

கல் = கல்லுகள், 334.

G. 76.

☞ This root is not necessarily the philological root, or absolute பகாப்பதம். [G. 122.]

Various strengthening and modifying particles may be added to the original root (தாது). These the Lex. will show.

The root is used for the infinitive occasionally.

Thus விழைதக்க = விழையத்தக்க, 361; விய(க்க)த்தக்க, 325. Perhaps too நிறை for நிறைய, 360.

The root is used as an adjective in G. 157. See 350: கொய்புல், செய்தொழில். With தோறும்: மூத்தோறும், 'ever as they grow older,' 351.

G. 83.

Most of the forms of the past and future tenses as given in this table occur in the text. Note especially—

1. The aoristic future in ப.

எழுப, 'they will arise' (for எழுபர், எழுவர்).

☞ All South-Indian languages may reject the personal terminations of finite-verb forms. This has become the ordinary usage in Malayāḷam.

செய்பவோ, 'will they do?' 246. So துறப்பவோ, 62; எறிப, 24.

2. Poetical forms are: இருப்பன் = இருப்பேன், 276; அறிவாம், 19, 332; எமாந்தேம் = எமாந்தோம், 182, 385; என்றி = என்றாய், 398; தீர்ப்பேம், 27; செய்வது for செய்யும், 393.

அறி|திர், 106 = 'ye would know :' an ancient form.

அறி + த + இர். This may be compared with the Telugu *koṭṭ-iṭ-iri, koṭṭ-ed-aru, koṭṭ-ud-uru.* (A. D. Campbell, p. 103.)

போ|தி, 55, 376, is the sing. of the foregoing: 'goest thou,' or 'wilt go?' [Tel. *pō-ti-(vi)* : where the termination *vi* may be thrown away in poetry.]

வாழ்|தி, 32. நிற்றி (நில் + த் + இ), past for future : 'wilt thou remain?'

ஆதும், 'we shall prosper,' 181, 332, 336, 359, 372, 378, 385. [Comp. Telugu aorist, *avu-du-mu.*]

கழிந்தன்று = கழிந்தது, நீங்கியது, சென்றது, 55. This is கழி + ந்த் + அன் [G. 108] + து [G. 38].

G. 84.

The verbal root is the ordinary imperative, 2nd person singular.

காண் ! 'See!' 24.

Sometimes a termination is added, giving a form which is liable to be confounded with the negative. [G. 89.]

Thus, 241, காணாய்! 'See thou!' கேளாய்! 'Hear!' 207.

வழங்குமின்! 'Give ye!' 6. ஆகுமின்! 'Become ye!' 7, 36.

G. 85.

For optative in க, we meet with an elision, as in 326, போகென்னும்.

Optative in க: கொள்க, 28.

G. 86. [Comp. G. 140–142.] See *Nannūl*, 342–344.

1. The positive adv. participle in ஆ is a difficulty, as being liable to be mistaken for a negative form with the same termination. See 14.

In 250 உட்படா = உட்பட்டு; துவ்வா = துவ்வி; செய்யா = செய்து. See 366.

2. Of irregular forms [G. 86. (a)] note, போய் = போயி; ஆய் = ஆயி (ஆகி); விராஅய் = விரவி, 246; திரிதந்து for திரிந்து. See G. 351.

3. Adverbial participles in அ. G. 140.

செலிய, 399, 'in order to go,' about to go. The *paulo-post futurum.* Almost = செல்ல.

So அடிய, 332.

4. An elision of அ in கடக்கரும் = கடக்க = கடப்பதற்கு, 398.

In reduplication இறுகஇறுக becomes இறுகிறுக, and இறுகிஇறுகி becomes இறுகிறுகி, 328.

G. 87.

Adjectives, or Adjuncts, or Enlargements of Noun. Comp. H. B., Lesson XLIII, and G. 119, 121, 151–157.

The பெயர் எச்சம் or *adjectival participle* is so called because it gives no complete meaning by itself, requiring a noun as its complement. Take (218) செய்(யை) விளைக்கும் வாய்க்கால்; and note that

1. The future பெயர் எச்சம் is always liable to be taken as a finite verb. This may mean 'the watercourse will fertilize the field;' or 'the . . . which will . . .'

2. When it is taken as பெயர் எச்சம் it connects two nouns, one of which is its object (செய்) and the other its subject. What channel? The field-fertilizing one.

The குறிப்புப்பெயர் எச்சம் is a form analogous to the above, formed from a conjugated appellative [G. 93].

Thus உரி = proprietorship (உரி-மை), from which உரிய is formed, and may be—(1) the neuter plural = உரியவை(கள்) = 'things that pertain to;' or (2) the same taken as குறிப்பு முற்று = 'they pertain unto;' or (3) a பெயர் எச்சம், 'pertaining to.' (Comp. Lex.)

விரும்புதாளாண்மை for விரும்பும். G. 157.

முடிகிற்கும் = முடிக்கும், 62.

Commentator: 'who has power to carry out;' and one says கில் = 'power.' There is not, I feel sure, any authority for this. It is முடி + க்க, with இன் between க் and க்.

Telugu forms a few verbs so: *kōpagintsu.*

So தேர்கிற்கும் = தேரும், 352.

G. 89.

Finite Negative Verb.

See examples in 9, 10. ஆகா, 233. திரியாது, 244, 337. கழியான், 273. உண்ணேம் பெறேம், 366. செல்லார், 241. Comp. especially 338. சேரார், 378.

A negative aorist is formed with இல் and அல் added to the root, with or without கு or க்கு; or to other forms of the verb:

கண்	டு	இல்	அர்	'have they not seen?' 48.
செய்	க்	அல்	ஆர்	'they do not.'
எடு	க்க	அல்	அம்	'we do not (cannot, will not) support,' 203.
பிரி	ய்	அல்	அம்	'we sunder not,' 376.
ஈ	க்	அல்	ஆன்	'he giveth not,' 272, 338.
அறி	ந்து	இல்	இர்	'you know not,' 165.
எறி	கு	அல்	ஆ	'refrained from darting,' 395.
அறு	க்கு	இல்	ஆ	'will not rid themselves of,' 352.
உரை	ய்	அல்	க	'speak not,' 71.
வெஃகு		அல்	மின்	'desire ye not,' 17.
சேர்	க்	அல்	ஆ(ர்)	'that join not,' 121, 327.
ஒ	க்க	அல்	ஆ	'does not equal,' 236.
பூண்	க்	அல்	ஆ	'submits not to the yoke,' 350.
பொறு	க்க	அல்	ஆ	'that sustains not,' 203.
பரி	வது	இல்	அர்	'they grieve not,' 35, 157.
வை	ப்பது	இல்	அர்	'they will not reckon,' 50.
விழை	ந்த்	இல்	எம்	'we desire not,' 339.

G. 91.

செய்குறு = செய்யாத, 362 (செய் + கு + உறுத).

G. 92.

Negative Imperatives: Prohibitives.

உரையற்க, 'say not!' 71.
பரவன்மின், 'boast not!' 92.
பற்றன்மின், 'cling not,' 92.
கரவன்மின், 'hide not,' 92.

Here the negative auxiliary அல் [G. 125] is inserted between the root and the termination [G. 76, 84, 85].

உரையாதி, 'say thou not,' 390. கருதி, 388.

[In Jī. Chin. பிரியற்பீர், 'sever not!' அல் + ப் + ஈர்.]

G. 93.

This is *Nannūl* 321.

☞ From nouns expressive of (1) பொருள் (material), (2) இடம் (place), (3) காலம் (time), (4) சினை (member, component part), (5) குணம் (quality), and (6) தொழில் (function) may be derived other nouns, in a way analogous to verbal conjugation.

These have been called *conjugated appellatives, pronominals, etc.* The Tamil name is குறிப்புவினை, i.e. 'words which have a verbal indication.' They serve often as finite verbs, but always with the substantive verb (ஆ-கு) understood.

The following are references under the six classes. *Consult Lex.*

1. பொருள்: வில், பெயர், தார், பிணம், இழை.

தாரினன் (இன் often inserted): 3 sing. masc. 'he (who) wears a garland: the garlanded man,' 390. பிணத்த: 3 pl. neut. 'they (are) replete with corpses,' 121. பெய்வளாய்: 2nd pers. 'thou braceleted one,' for வளையாய்.

2. இடம்: நாடு, சேர்ப்பு, ஊர், காதம், அடுப்பு, உழை, கண், பக்கம். கண்ணது, 368. மெய்யது, 'pertaining to the body.' சேய்த்து in 218 is குறிப்பு வினைமுற்று, 'although *it is distant.*' சேய்+த்+து [G. 93] = 'that which is distant.' When thus used *there is really a substantive verb, expressed or understood.* Here சேய்த்து ஆனாலும், 'though it be (a thing) far off.'

3. காலம்: இளை; இளையம், 'we are young,' 19.

4. சினை: கண், 49. முலை, 85. கால், 122. நுதல், 387.

5. குணம்: நல், தீ, அர், உர, சிற, வல், அனை. தீது, 'what is evil,' or 'it is evil,' 51. மாட்சித்து, 'it (which) has the excellence,' 42, 382. வல்லை, 'thou art able,' 383, 398. அனையம், 'we are like,' 388. வற்று, 348. நல்ல, 'they are much better,' 334. அளித்து, 15.

6. தொழில்: உழவு, 356. மொழி.

The 3rd plural neuter in அ is considered to be a kind of குறிப்பு எச்சம் or participle. Thus அணியர், 218 = 'those close at hand:' அணியவர் from அணிய. See G. 87.

G. 94.

I. Negative Verbal Nouns are formed thus: √ + ஆ + மை. [H. B. § 154.]

கல்|ல|ா|மை, சொல்|ல|ா|மை, ஈ|ய|ா|மை (145); நிலை|ய|ா|மை; செய்யாமை (246).

1. The noun is occasionally used for adv. part.: மாற்றாமை = மாற்றாமல், மறக்காமல், 98.

2. The positive is found in 58, இகழ்ச்த|மை; and added to the root, புகழ்மை, சமழ்மை, 72.

II. Verbal Nouns in அல்.

See 334.

தகல், 'fitness,' 167. உயல் ஆகும், 'one may escape,' 90.

For வைக்கறபாற்று, see பால், which is often found with this form. It is appositive: comp. 97, 104.

With அரும், which may precede or follow: தவலரும், 'which scarce may fail,' 137; அரும்பெறல், 'hard to be attained,' 34.

These verbal nouns are used as optatives, as well positive as negative [G. 85]. But there is really an ellipsis of வேண்டும் and வேண்டாம், 75, 95.

Some verbs lengthen the root syllable in forming this noun: கோடல், 77. [கொள் + தல். G. 37.] See also கோள், பேறு, கேடு.

G. 95.

Participial Nouns.

In 24: செத்தார், சாவார். 25: உய்ப்பார்.

☞ It is often difficult to distinguish, in poetry, the finite verb. from the participial noun. (§§ 87, 88.)

In prose செத்தவன் is distinct from செத்தான். உணர்வார், 33.

வருவ, 'things that will come:' வருபவைகள். Comp. 4.

Almost any person of the finite verb may be used as a noun, in fact it becomes a true participial noun, losing none of its verbal habitudes and powers:

ஒழுகுவேன் (44, 45) is 'I who habitually comport myself.'

சார்தாய், சார்ந்தாய்|க்கு, சார்ந்தார்|கண், சார்ந்தேய், 126. Here சார்ந்தாய் can be rendered, 'thou hast attached thyself to;' or, as a voc. of a noun, 'O thou who hast . . .!'

நின்றது = 'that which has stood,' 192. Here it is so far a finite verb that ஆகி depends upon it = 'Even that which originally was a twig, that bending to every breeze, stood by the wayside.'

இருந்தைக்க, 79, seems for இருந்தைக்கு = 'to thee who hast been.' For final அ, see *Nannūl*, 318.

கொர்ந்தேன், இருந்தேன், 389.

Negative forms abound: செய்யாதார், 31.

G. 109.

1. போல் is used in comparison. But அன்னது, அற்று, உடைத்து are exclusively poetical: கண்டதுடைத்து, 'it is as if one saw.' See note on G. 143.

2. போல governs an accusative, but there is generally an ellipsis of case-ending, without doubling of க, ச, த, ப, 2.

G. 119.

This is explained in G. 87.

In 153 உள்ளம் எனும் நார், 'the cord OF the soul.' See ஆயர் in 216.

The use of உடை as nearly equivalent to உள் is worthy of study:

தகவு | உடை | யார், 241, 216.
இயல்பு | உடை | யார், 244.

The opposite is இல்:

தெளிவு | இல் | ஆர், 219.
மதுரம் | இல் | ஆளர், 211.

The use of அனை and அன் = 'such.' These sometimes take இன்:

கழுகு | அனை | அர், 216.
தெங்கு | {இன் + அனை} | ஆர், 216.

சார் = உள்ள [G. 153], 327.

கோட்டுப்பு (கோடு), 215. கயப்பு, 215.

Verbal roots become adjectives by G. 157. So கழி, 275. This is merely a contracted பெயர் எச்சம்.

G. 120.

Tamil has few real adverbs. See நனி, 200.

Nouns are used as adverbs: பெரிது, 'greatly;' நன்கு, 'well,' 200.

Some forms in ஆ are found (probably from G. 90): வாளா, 'silently,' 325. [Comp. சும்மா.]

ஏ added to a noun often converts it into an adverb. So அவத்தமே = 'in vain,' 327. உம் is often added as in 187: நகையேயும், 'even in jest.'

☞ Adverbial phrases of time, place, manner are in constant use. The noun is generally in the nominative case, often with உம் [G. 113], but sometimes in 3rd case.

இறும் அளவும், 'till they die,' 209. இயைந்த அளவினுல், 272. உளவரையால், 271. See under G. 143. ஆற்றுந்துணையும், 'to the extent of their power,' 196.

G. 121.

Adjectival prefixes. [See II. B. § 131.]

புன்குன்றநாட! (*Nannūl*, 200), 128. When பு becomes the first member of a compound a nasal is inserted.

புத்தோடு, 139. See புது. Note in the same verse நல், தொல், ஒள், நண்.

தீஞ்சுவை, 244. See தீ. In the sense of 'sweet,' ம் (ன், ஞ், ந்) is always inserted, hence தீம் TĪM = sweet.

இளம்பிறை, 241.

G. 124.

Many verbal forms are used in poetry when the original meaning is so nearly lost that they may be considered as merely symbolic. Such are—

1. என், என, என்று, என்றும். [G. 114.]

2. ஆகு, *etc.* ஆம் is often redundant.

3. தரு in திரி-த-ந்து for திரிந்து, 351.

4. சார் in 327. [See G. 119.]

5. உள், with its negatives இல், அல். Compare all the verbs in G. 125. From the *Lex.* it will be seen that these are partly examples of the regular வினைக்குறிப்பு, and partly irregular and defective verbs.

6. கூர், stronger than படு: 'feel the sting of.' இடும்பைகூர்நெஞ்சத்தார், 'those who suffer much affliction of soul.'

7. Examples of the true passive are found. H. B. § 92.

See Lex. படு and H. B. § 92; but the learner must weigh such examples as—

கற்றறிந்தாரைத்தலைநிலத்துவைக்கப்படும் (133), where வைக்க has அறிந்தாரை as its direct object, and படும் is impersonal = தகுதியாகும், 'it is befitting.'

In 103, அளந்தன is obviously = அளக்கப்பட்டன; but a subject is understood: 'enjoyments (போகங்கள்) are things which *the Creator* has assigned to each in due measure.'

In 197, தின்னப்பட்ட is passive.

G. 137. [*Nannūl*, 416–425.]

வழுவமைதி = 'permitted deviation from strict rule.'

These anomalies are the result in some cases of the poets' need requiring them to take a license (which in Tamil they sadly abuse); in other cases of corruptness in the tradition.

எவன் (masc.) is used for என், என்ன, 105.

கீழ், மேல், தலை, இடை, கடை, இல், and many other neuter nouns (அஃறிணை) are used for persons (உயர்திணை). This is a kind of synecdoche.

Personal subjects often have neuter predicates. This seems to indicate contempt often (242), though the form itself is of no gender or number.

G. 137*.

1. In regard to Case there is naturally much ambiguity. See note on G. 55.

(*a*) The noun itself may stand for any case.

(*b*) So may the inflexional base.

(*c*) So may the base with அத்து, இன், அன்.

2. Besides this, there are examples of one case being used for another.

Thus வாயில் (5) = வாயினால், 156, 157. வினையுள் = வினையால், 43. செம்மாப்பவரை for dative, 50.

G. 140.

1. This form comes nearest to an English infinitive mood. [§§ 41, 168–171.]

It is called அகர ஈற்றுவினை எச்சம், 'the adverbial participle in அ.'

2. Its use will be gathered from examples.

See 3. பொருவிய (so as to), உலப்ப (when), கோள (while).

In 61, இறக்க, பொறுக்க, 75, the infinitive is identical with the optative. G. 85.

We find கேட்ப, உவப்ப, which are a kind of future infinitive of purpose: 'so that men may hear: for (them) to hear.'

See 105, நினைப்பக்கிடந்தது, 'what is left for us to think?' Comp. 265.

In 162, தலைக்கூட seems direct object of பெற்று.

In 204, அறிய, தீர = 'openly and completely.' Used as adverbs.

In 5, உற, உய, 'so as to come into . . . so as to escape.'

Many infinitives are used as adverbs: so ஆ (for ஆக), *as*; அற, *without.*

G. 141.

CONDITION. Comp. G. 86 (2).

1. IF is expressed by எனின் (40), பெறின், ஆயின், ஆகின், வரின், செயின், which more or less lose their verbal signification.

2. These forms have three stems and three terminations in our text.

(*a*) Root + இல்: ஈர்க்கில், அடக்கில், பெய்யில், பழிக்கில், all in 26. [தோன்றில் or தோன்றின், 197.] ஆகில், 337. பொன்றில், 323.

(*b*) Root + இன்: எனின், 1. கூறின், 388.

(*c*) Past stem + ஆல்: உண்டால், 344 (see உள்). ஆனால், 42.

(*d*) Future stem + இன்: கொடுப்பின், உரைப்பின், நிற்பின், இமைப்பின், 361.

3. IF, WHEN, *etc.* are expressed as shown in note to G. 143. Note especially those in கால். See 35.

4. ஏல் = IF: perhaps from ஆகில், 9. அறிதிரேல் = 'if you would know,' 106.

5. The negative is used with கால். See 323.

G. 142.

CONCESSIVE. [See G. 86.]

கனியினும், 'though they ripen,' 244. எனினும், இடினும், 243.

சார்ந்தும், 'though they have been close to,' 245. விளியினும், 'though they perish,' 337.

1. உம் is added to past adverbial participles: PAST SUBJUNCTIVE: கேட்டும் (*and having heard*), 'although (they have) heard,' 364. கண்டும், 25, 39. ஓதியும், பெற்றும், ஓதாதும், இருந்தும், 323. குளித்தும், 90.

2. உம் is added to any of the forms in G. 141 (2): FUT. and AORISTIC: எனினும், 32. ஆயினும் (= ஆனும்), 38. அறினும், 41. வரினும், 79, 382. செயினும், நிற்பினும், தீற்றினும், கண்டாலும், 79. குளிப்பினும், ஒளிப்பினும், 90. ஊட்டினும், 396. செறிப்பினும், 358.

G. 143.

The use of adjective participles (or the root used for the participle, G. 153) with particles (really nouns) of place, time, or manner, to form adverbial phrases of every shade of meaning, or [G. 93] actual predicates, is a notable feature of Tamil poetry.

1. These particles are அற்று, அன்ன, அனைத்து, அனைய, ஆங்கு, இடம், இடத்து, உழி, வழி, ஆறு, கால், பொழுது, காறு, வரை, கடை, அளவு, துணை, தோறு, and the like.

2. The following are fair specimens. Comp. *Lex.*

☞ It is to be noted that final அ of the adjective participle is sometimes dropped; and that in other cases an initial க, ச, த, ப of the particle is *abnormally doubled.*

கண், 96, 97, 141. வரை, 271. வகை, 36.

அன்ன: உண்டன்ன, 16, 66. நக்கியன்னது, 87, 186. அள்ளிக் கொள்வன்ன, 262.

அற்று: வீழ்ந்தற்று, 17. போயற்றே, 136, 138, 211, 240, 254.

அனை: பெய்தனைத்து, 239. ஒறி அனையார், 270.

ஆங்கு: பயந்தாங்கு, 38, 51. ஊன்றி ஆங்கு, 97. உணராதாங்கு, 321, 322.

அளவு, 190. முடியுமளவு, 272. ஆறு: கெட்டாறு, 288. தகு, 302.

இடத்து: தேய்விடத்து, நீர்விடத்து, 51, 149, comp. 83. வழி: உறழ்வழி, 311.

உழி: செல்வுழி (செல் + வ் + உழி: செல்வு is an old future relative participle), 8, 230. வைப்புழி, 134. நின்றுழி, 284. இற்றுழி, 48. கண்டுழி, 62. உடைந்துழி, 284. பார்த்துழி, 26.

கால்: தோன்றியக்கால், 2, 'when:' 5, 26, 33. மலராக்கால், 282, 323.

காறு: பழிகாறும், 13. கடை: உழைந்தக்கடைத்தும், 147, 199, 236.

தோறு: செறுத்தோறு, 222. முத்தொறூஉம், 351. இசைதோறும், 60.

Ordinary forms:

உண்டாயபோழ்தின், 284. உண்டாம்போழ்தே, 19, 62, 238. திரிதருங்காலத்து, 284.

Consider 329: these particles form compounds with nouns.

Here it seems as if the வினை எச்சம் were systematically used for the பெயர் எச்சம்: நக்கி அன்னது for நக்கிய அன்னது. And in தோன்றியக்கால் for தோன்றியகால் there is a doubling of க், of which no certain explanation has been found.

[அடைந்தக்கால். Comp. Tel. *chēsinappuḍu.*]

நீண்டக்கடைத்தும், 291. Here the peculiarity is in the doubled க். I suppose it is for அடைந்து + அ + கால். The *Nannūl*, 343 (or rather the Commentator), makes these distinct forms of the adverbial participle. (H. B. § 123. *c.*)

The negative is frequent, and presents no anomaly: உறுக்கால்.

G. 150–157.

Compounds. These are called தொகைநிலை.

1. அறுசுவையுண்டி = 'food of six flavours.' Here the full expression is ஆறுவகுப்புள்ள சுவைகளை உடைய உண்டி. These quatrains exemplify every species of தொகைநிலை.

2. In அரிமா, 141, we have two nouns, of which the principal, மா, indicates the genus, and the accessory, அரி, the species: 'an animal of the lion kind.'

This is இருபெயர் ஒட்டுப் பண்புத்தொகை: an ellipsis of ஆகிய or என்னும்.

In the same verse கொடிப்புல்லு = 'grass of the creeping kind.'

In 149 பாய்பரிமா with வினைத்தொகை, 'a prancing charger.' Comp. 152.

In 339 தழங்குகுரல்பாய்திரை சூழ்வையம் we have G. 153 thrice, G. 157 once, and G. 15 once; and திரை = கடல் by G. 162.

உப்பீண்டுவரி (noun + verbal root + noun), 'brackish water saturated with salt:' '*salt-crowded-salt-water.*'

நறு[1] மலர்த்[2] தண்[3] கோதாய்[4]! [G. 93, 154, 157.]

Adj. + noun + adj. + noun.

'Thou who wearest a refreshing[3] wreath[4] of fragrant[1] flowers[2]!'

புலி[1] உகிர்[2] வாள்[3] புழுக்கல்[4]. [G. 152, 154, 155.]

Noun + noun + adj. + noun.

'White[3] rice[4] like the claw[2] of a tiger[1].'

யானை[1] + வரி[2] முகம்[3] புண்[4]படுக்கும்[5] வல்[6] + உகிர்[7] கோல்[8] + தாள்[9] அரி[10] + மா[11] மதுகை[12]யவர்[13], 'those[13] (possessed of) heroic strength[12], like the lion[10 11], whose paw[9] is mighty[8], and whose claws[7] are sharp[6], which inflicts[5] wounds[4] on the elephant's[1] spotted[2] face[3].'

G. 162.

1. Many words for a lady are by metonomy from her ornaments. தொடி is 'a bracelet,' and 'the lady who wears one,' 111. அம்மருங்கு = 'a lady with beautiful waist,' 396.

2. புல்வாய் = 'grass-mouth,' for மான்.

III. Metrical Introduction.

In my edition of the *Kurraḷ* (Introd. pp. xxv–xxviii) the peculiarities of the *Veṇbā* metre common to both that work and the *Nālaḍi* have been briefly explained.

A summary is given in G. 185–190; and the native authorities may be found in the IIIrd Grammar.

The *Veṇbā* (வெண், 'white, clear, bright,' + பா, 'verse') is the recognised metre for moral precepts and for all gnomic poetry.

The *Nālaḍi* quatrains are of two kinds, Nēriçai, (நேரிசை = regular) and Inniçai (இன்னிசை = euphonic).

Of the 400 verses we find that about 300 are *Nēriçai* quatrains, which consist of three lines of four feet, followed by a line of three feet, of which the last is one அசை, or metrical syllable. The fourth foot of the second line has the rhyme of the first and second lines, and is by some regarded as a distinct line, called தனிச்சொல் = *word that stands alone.* Thus the *Nēriçai* quatrain has been defined generally, 'two *Kurraḷs*, connected by a short line, or தனிச்சொல்' (G. 189); it must, however, be noted that the third foot of the second line is not the short foot that ends a *Kurraḷ*, but an ordinary foot.

The remaining 100 are called *Inniçai* (G. 190), being mainly like the *Nēriçai*, but without the rhyming தனிச்சொல். They have irregularities adopted for euphony. In general an *Inniçai Veṇbā* may be thus defined: 'a quatrain with three lines of four feet, followed by one of three feet,' as in the *Kurraḷ* couplet.

In order to scan and read these verses (and I would give to all students of *Nālaḍi* the advice of Bökh to readers of Pindar: *master the metre of each line before trying to construe it:* when you can intone your quatrain you will find the interpretation comparatively easy) it is necessary to consider (1) metrical syllables, (2) feet, (3) lines, (4) connexion of feet, and (5) rhyme and alliteration.

A. *Metrical Syllables.*

A single syllable is called a நேர், and always has the *arsis;* for Tamil metre *is not governed by quantity only.* (G. 169.)

Thus க (short open), கல் (short closed), கா (long open), கால் (long closed) may equally have the metrical *ictus*, and be 'long,' –. (G. 170.)

A pair of syllables, of which the former is short both by nature and by position, constitutes a நிரை or *pyrrhic*.

Thus கல, கலம், கலா, கலாம் are all metrically equal to ◡ ◡, and both syllables are unaccented.

B. *Metrical Feet* (G. 171).

Three kinds of feet (சீர்) are used in these quatrains:

அசைச்சீர் (single);
இயற்சீர் (double);
வெண்சீர் (treble or hypercatalectic).

1. A SINGLE foot consists of one அசை or measure; and may be a long syllable, whose mnemonic is நாள் (NĀḶ); a pair of short syllables, மலர் (MALAR); or either of these followed by shortened உ (காசு, பிறப்பு), (G. 15). These are only found as the last foot of a quatrain.

Ex. இல், 7. This is நாள்: a நேர். So பார், 11. ஆறு, 13, is= காசு: a நேர் with the very short உ.

விடும், 8, is மலர்: a நிரை.

உலகு: a நிரை with the very short உ: பிறப்பு, 15.

As a rule each foot consists of a single word, or of words closely connected; and it is generally thought inelegant to allow a word to be divided between two feet. Hence right scanning makes lines intelligible, while in most other languages it confuses. In this work I have generally separated the feet, a matter about which native usage is not uniform. Sometimes I have neglected this division for some special reason, or by oversight.

2. A DOUBLE foot consists of two metrical syllables; and is called இயற்சீர் (=natural). It may have four forms:

(1) நேர் + நேர், i. e. – –, spondee; for which the mnemonic தேமா is used;

(2) நேர் + நிரை, i. e. – ◡ ◡, dactyl: கூவிளம்;

(3) நிரை + நேர், i. e. ◡ ◡ –, anapaest: புளிமா;

(4) நிரை + நிரை, i. e. ◡ ◡ ◡ ◡, proceleusmaticus: கருவிளம்.

With regard to the combination of these in lines the law of sequence is (G. 179)

மாமுன் நிரையும்
விளம்முன் நேரும்:

☞ A. *A foot ending in –, (a long syllable,) must be followed by one beginning with ◡ ◡ (dactylic);* B. *and a foot ending in ◡ ◡ must be followed by one beginning with a long syllable (anapaestic).*

C. Whenever a proceleusmaticus (கருவிளம்) occurs, since it must by this law be preceded and followed by a long syllable, we have . . . –́ ◡ ◡ ◡ ◡ –́ . . ., that is an antispast, consisting of dactyl + anapaest.

The combinations of A, B, C constitute what is called the *balanced recitative rhythm.* [தூங்கிசைச் செப்பல். All *Veṇbā* verse is recited or chanted according to its scansion: this is செப்பல், and is of three kinds: (1) தூங்கிசைச் செப்பல் (தூங்கு, *v.* 'balance, swing')=the balanced (*lively*) rhythm; (2) எந்திசைச்செப்பல் (எந்து, *v.* 'be uplifted')=the sustained (*grave*) rhythm; and (3) ஒழுகிசைச்செப்பல் (ஒழுகு, *v.* 'flow on') = mixed, flowing (*easy*) rhythm.]

Few lines and still fewer verses consist only of these four feet in this threefold combination. Two complete quatrains (65, 89) only of this kind will be found in the *Nālaḍi.* These may be studied with advantage:

1	2	3	4
இளையான்	அடக்கம்	அடக்கம்	கிளைபொருள்
புளிமா	புளிமா	புளிமா	கருவிளம்
◡ ◡ – A	◡ ◡ – A	◡ ◡ – A	◡ ◡ ◡ ◡ B
5	**6**	**7**	**8**
இல்லான்	கொடையே	கொடைப்பயன்	எல்லாம்
தேமா	புளிமா	கருவிளம்	தேமா
– – A	◡ ◡ – A	◡ ◡ ◡ ◡ B	– – A
9	**10**	**11**	**12**
ஒறுக்கு'	மதுகை	உரனுடை	ஆளன்
புளிமா	புளிமா	கருவிளம்	தேமா
◡ ◡ – A	◡ ◡ – A	◡ ◡ ◡ ◡ B	– – A
13	**14**	**15**	
பொறுக்கு'	பொறையே	பொறை.	
புளிமா	புளிமா	மலர்.	
◡ ◡ – A	◡ ◡ – A	◡ ◡	

Here the rhythm is anapaestic. The three antispasts relieve the monotony. But the tune is decidedly lively and *lilting!*

So too,

1		2		3		4	
அம்பும்		அழலும்		அவிர்கதிர்		ஞாயிறும்	
தேமா		புளிமா		கருவிளம்		கூவிளம்	
— —	A	◡ ◡ —	A	◡ ◡ ◡ ◡	B	— ◡ ◡	B
5		6		7		8	
வெம்பிச்		சுடினும்		பறஞ்சுடும்		வெம்பிக்	
தேமா		புளிமா		கருவிளம்		தேமா	
— —	A	◡ ◡ —	A	◡ ◡ ◡ ◡	B	— —	A
9		10		11		12	
கவற்றி		மனத்தைச்		சுடுதலாற்		காமம்	
புளிமா		புளிமா		கருவிளம்		தேமா	
◡ ◡ —	A	◡ ◡ —	A	◡ ◡ ◡ ◡	B	— —	A
13		14		15			
அவற்றினும்		அஞ்சப்		படும்.			
கருவிளம்		தேமா		மலர்.			
◡ ◡ ◡ ◡	B	— —	A	◡ ◡			

3. The third kind of feet used in *Veṇbā* metre is called, for this reason, *Veṇçīr*. There are four of these formed by adding to each of the former a hypercatalectic syllable (called காய்), which may be any one of the four kinds of நேர், but is *always accented* or *metrically long*. And in a line this காய் must always be followed by a long (accented) syllable; or காய் முன் நேர்: ☞ KĀY is followed by a NĒR. (G. 179.)

This brings in another kind of antispast (. . . ´ | ´ . . .), and imparts dignity, sometimes heaviness, to the line. And this is the 'grave rhythm.' A few lines, but no entire quatrains, exhibit this unmixed gravity.

The verses almost always, and the lines very generally, contain a mixture of 'light' and 'grave,' which is the 'flowing' or 'easy' rhythm.

Examine the following, 139:

1	2	3	4
கல்லாரே	ஆயினுங்	கற்றாரைச்	சேர்ந்தொழுகின்
தேமாங்காய்	கூவிளம்	தேமாங்காய்	கூவிளங்காய்
— — —	— ◡ ◡	— — —	— ◡ ◡ —
5	6	7	8
நல்லறிவு	நாளுந்	தலைப்படுவர்	தொல்சிறப்பின்
கூவிளங்காய்	தேமா	கருவிளங்காய்	கூவிளங்காய்
— ◡ ◡ —	— —	◡ ◡ ◡ ◡ —	— ◡ ◡ —

9	10	11	12
ஒண்ணிறப்	பாதிரிப்பூச்	சேர்தலாற்	புத்தோடு
கூவிளம்	கூவிளங்காய்	கூவிளம்	தேமாங்காய்
— ◡ ◡	— ◡ ◡ —	— ◡ ◡	— — —
13	**14**	**15**	
தண்ணீர்க்குத்	தான்பயந்	தாங்கு.	
தேமாங்காய்	கூவிளம்	காசு.	
— — —	— ◡ ◡	◡ ◡̆	

This system may at first sight appear artificial, but its superiority to Sanskrit prosody is very striking. It is admirably adapted to the nature of the Tamil language, and seems naturally evolved from it. The great variety of the melody of *Veṇbā* verse is apparent from the fact that 512 types of the longer lines can be formed.

This variety is in effect much increased by the fact that a *Tēmā* may be really a spondee or a trochee; and a *Puḷimā* may be (◡ ◡ —, ◡ ◡ ◡, ◡ — —, or ◡ — ◡) anapaest, tribrach, bacchius, or cretic; and similarly the other feet.

I have analysed all the 900 full lines, and find about 300 varieties. This analysis is given as a curiosity of literature.

The fourth line admits of thirty-two types, of which thirty-one are found in our work.

These tables are subjoined. There are few lines in Pindar, or in any Greek chorus, which will not find a representative here.

Lines beginning with தேமா, – –. = 282.				
1	2	3	4	
தேமா, – –	புளிமா, ∪∪ –	∪∪ –	∪∪ –	1
		∪∪ –	∪∪∪∪	9
		∪∪ –	∪∪ – –	19
		∪∪ –	∪∪∪∪ –	9
		∪∪∪∪	– –	13
		∪∪∪∪	– ∪∪	8
		∪∪∪∪	– – –	24
		∪∪∪∪	– ∪∪ –	11
		∪∪ – –	– –	13
		∪∪ – –	– ∪∪	10
		∪∪ – –	– – –	16
		∪∪ – –	– ∪∪ –	7
		∪∪∪∪ –	– –	3
		∪∪∪∪ –	– ∪∪	3
		∪∪∪∪ –	– – –	13
		∪∪∪∪ –	– ∪∪ –	4
	கருவிளம், ∪∪∪∪	– –	∪∪ –	0
		– –	∪∪∪∪	3
		– –	∪∪ – –	5
		– –	∪∪∪∪ –	2
		– ∪∪	– –	2
		– ∪∪	– ∪∪	3
		– ∪∪	– – –	3
		– ∪∪	– ∪∪ –	1
		– – –	– –	5
		– – –	– ∪∪	1
		– – –	– – –	4
		– – –	– ∪∪ –	3
		– ∪∪ –	– –	1
		– ∪∪ –	– ∪∪	2
		– ∪∪ –	– – –	1
		– ∪∪ –	– ∪∪ –	1
	புளிமாங்காய், ∪∪ – –	– –	∪∪ –	0
		– –	∪∪∪∪	1
		– –	∪∪ – –	4
		– –	∪∪∪∪ –	1
		– ∪∪	– –	2
		– ∪∪	– ∪∪	1
		– ∪∪	– – –	5
		– ∪∪	– ∪∪ –	3
		– – –	– –	6
		– – –	– ∪∪	4
		– – –	– – –	5
		– – –	– ∪∪ –	4
		– ∪∪ –	– –	3
		– ∪∪ –	– ∪∪	7
		– ∪∪ –	– – –	2
		– ∪∪ –	– ∪∪ –	1
	கருவிளங்காய், ∪∪∪∪ –	– –	∪∪ –	0
		– –	∪∪∪∪	1
		– –	∪∪ – –	1
		– –	∪∪∪∪ –	4
		– ∪∪	– –	1
		– ∪∪	– ∪∪	1
		– ∪∪	– – –	9
		– ∪∪	– ∪∪ –	2
		– – –	– –	4
		– – –	– ∪∪	2
		– – –	– – –	4
		– – –	– ∪∪ –	0
		– ∪∪ –	– –	1
		– ∪∪ –	– ∪∪	2
		– ∪∪ –	– – –	1
		– ∪∪ –	– ∪∪ –	0

Lines beginning with கூவிளம், – ∪∪. = 172.				
1	2	3	4	
கூவிளம், – ∪∪.	தேமா, – –	∪∪ –	∪∪ –	0
		∪∪ –	∪∪∪∪	8
		∪∪ –	∪∪ – –	14
		∪∪ –	∪∪∪∪ –	6
		∪∪∪∪	– –	4
		∪∪∪∪	– ∪∪	5
		∪∪∪∪	– – –	7
		∪∪∪∪	– ∪∪ –	6
		∪∪ – –	– –	11
		∪∪ – –	– ∪∪	8
		∪∪ – –	– – –	6
		∪∪ – –	– ∪∪ –	5
		∪∪∪∪ –	– –	3
		∪∪∪∪ –	– ∪∪	7
		∪∪∪∪ –	– – –	5
		∪∪∪∪ –	– ∪∪ –	2
	கூவிளம், – ∪∪	– –	∪∪ –	0
		– –	∪∪∪∪	4
		– –	∪∪ – –	5
		– –	∪∪∪∪ –	1
		– ∪∪	– –	3
		– ∪∪	– ∪∪	1
		– ∪∪	– – –	1
		– ∪∪	– ∪∪ –	4
		– – –	– –	1
		– – –	– ∪∪	5
		– – –	– – –	2
		– – –	– ∪∪ –	1
		– ∪∪ –	– –	0
		– ∪∪ –	– ∪∪	2
		– ∪∪ –	– – –	0
		– ∪∪ –	– ∪∪ –	0
	தேமாங்காய், – – –	– –	∪∪ –	0
		– –	∪∪∪∪	1
		– –	∪∪ – –	2
		– –	∪∪∪∪ –	2
		– ∪∪	– –	2
		– ∪∪	– ∪∪	4
		– ∪∪	– – –	0
		– ∪∪	– ∪∪ –	1
		– – –	– –	2
		– – –	– ∪∪	3
		– – –	– – –	2
		– – –	– ∪∪ –	3
		– ∪∪ –	– –	1
		– ∪∪ –	– ∪∪	0
		– ∪∪ –	– – –	0
		– ∪∪ –	– ∪∪ –	1
	கூவிளங்காய், – ∪∪ –	– –	∪∪ –	0
		– –	∪∪∪∪	1
		– –	∪∪ – –	0
		– –	∪∪∪∪ –	1
		– ∪∪	– –	3
		– ∪∪	– ∪∪	2
		– ∪∪	– – –	3
		– ∪∪	– ∪∪ –	1
		– – –	– –	4
		– – –	– ∪∪	0
		– – –	– – –	1
		– – –	– ∪∪ –	1
		– ∪∪ –	– –	0
		– ∪∪ –	– ∪∪	0
		– ∪∪ –	– – –	0
		– ∪∪ –	– ∪∪ –	0

Lines beginning with புளிமா, ∪∪–. =156. 1	2	3	4	
புளிமா, ∪∪–	புளிமா, ∪∪–	∪∪–	∪∪– ∪∪∪∪ ∪∪–– ∪∪∪∪–	4 3 3 1
		∪∪∪∪	–– –∪∪ ––– –∪∪–	15 0 0 0
		∪∪––	–– –∪∪ ––– –∪∪–	10 0 0 0
		∪∪∪∪–	–– –∪∪ ––– –∪∪–	10 0 0 0
	கருவிளம், ∪∪∪∪	––	∪∪– ∪∪∪∪ ∪∪–– ∪∪∪∪–	9 8 4 5
		–∪∪	–– –∪∪ ––– –∪∪–	9 0 0 0
		–––	–– –∪∪ ––– –∪∪–	13 1 0 0
		–∪∪–	–– –∪∪ ––– –∪∪–	3 0 0 0
	புளிமாங்காய், ∪∪––	––	∪∪– ∪∪∪∪ ∪∪–– ∪∪∪∪–	14 3 3 2
		–∪∪	–– –∪∪ ––– –∪∪–	10 0 0 0
		–––	–– –∪∪ ––– –∪∪–	9 0 0 0
		–∪∪–	–– –∪∪ ––– –∪∪–	3 0 0 0
	கருவிளங்காய், ∪∪∪∪–	––	∪∪– ∪∪∪∪ ∪∪–– ∪∪∪∪–	4 0 0 2
		–∪∪	–– –∪∪ ––– –∪∪–	8 0 0 0
		–––	–– –∪∪ ––– –∪∪–	1 0 0 0
		–∪∪–	–– –∪∪ ––– –∪∪–	3 0 0 0

Lines beginning with கருவிளம், ∪∪∪∪. =154. 1	2	3	4	
கருவிளம், ∪∪∪∪	தேமா, ––	∪∪–	∪∪– ∪∪∪∪ ∪∪–– ∪∪∪∪–	5 8 6 3
		∪∪∪∪	–– –∪∪ ––– –∪∪–	10 0 0 0
		∪∪––	–– –∪∪ ––– –∪∪–	15 0 0 0
		∪∪∪∪–	–– –∪∪ ––– –∪∪–	6 0 0 0
	கூவிளம், –∪∪	––	∪∪– ∪∪∪∪ ∪∪–– ∪∪∪∪–	5 4 1 3
		–∪∪	–– –∪∪ ––– –∪∪–	7 0 0 0
		–––	–– –∪∪ ––– –∪∪–	5 0 0 0
		–∪∪–	–– –∪∪ ––– –∪∪–	2 0 0 0
	தேமாங்காய், –––	––	∪∪– ∪∪∪∪ ∪∪–– ∪∪∪∪–	12 3 1 6
		–∪∪	–– –∪∪ ––– –∪∪–	13 0 0 0
		–––	–– –∪∪ ––– –∪∪–	11 0 0 0
		–∪∪–	–– –∪∪ ––– –∪∪–	4 0 0 0
	கூவிளங்காய், –∪∪–	––	∪∪– ∪∪∪∪ ∪∪–– ∪∪∪∪–	3 2 3 5
		–∪∪	–– –∪∪ ––– –∪∪–	7 0 0 0
		–––	–– –∪∪ ––– –∪∪–	3 0 0 0
		–∪∪–	–– –∪∪ ––– –∪∪–	2 0 0 0

Lines beginning with தேமாங்காய், – – –. =171.

1	2	3	4	
தேமாங்காய், – – –	தேமா, – –	⏑ ⏑ –	⏑ ⏑ –	0
			⏑ ⏑ ⏑ ⏑	11
			⏑ ⏑ – –	12
			⏑ ⏑ ⏑ ⏑ –	11
		⏑ ⏑ ⏑ ⏑	– –	6
			– ⏑ ⏑	5
			– – –	24
			– ⏑ ⏑ –	2
		⏑ ⏑ – –	– –	10
			– ⏑ ⏑	9
			– – –	14
			– ⏑ ⏑ –	3
		⏑ ⏑ ⏑ ⏑ –	– –	1
			– ⏑ ⏑	3
			– – –	8
			– ⏑ ⏑ –	4
	கூவிளம், – ⏑ ⏑	– –	⏑ ⏑ –	0
			⏑ ⏑ ⏑ ⏑	1
			⏑ ⏑ – –	4
			⏑ ⏑ ⏑ ⏑ –	1
		– ⏑ ⏑	– –	5
			– ⏑ ⏑	1
			– – –	5
			– ⏑ ⏑ –	1
		– – –	– –	3
			– ⏑ ⏑	0
			– – –	8
			– ⏑ ⏑ –	4
		– ⏑ ⏑ –	– –	0
			– ⏑ ⏑	0
			– – –	2
			– ⏑ ⏑ –	0
	தேமாங்காய், – – –	– –	⏑ ⏑ –	0
			⏑ ⏑ ⏑ ⏑	1
			⏑ ⏑ – –	1
			⏑ ⏑ ⏑ ⏑ –	2
		– ⏑ ⏑	– –	1
			– ⏑ ⏑	2
			– – –	4
			– ⏑ ⏑ –	1
		– – –	– –	1
			– ⏑ ⏑	0
			– – –	3
			– ⏑ ⏑ –	1
		– ⏑ ⏑ –	– –	1
			– ⏑ ⏑	2
			– – –	2
			– ⏑ ⏑ –	0
	கூவிளங்காய், – ⏑ ⏑ –	– –	⏑ ⏑ –	0
			⏑ ⏑ ⏑ ⏑	0
			⏑ ⏑ – –	1
			⏑ ⏑ ⏑ ⏑ –	2
		– ⏑ ⏑	– –	0
			– ⏑ ⏑	2
			– – –	0
			– ⏑ ⏑ –	1
		– – –	– –	1
			– ⏑ ⏑	1
			– – –	1
			– ⏑ ⏑ –	2
		– ⏑ ⏑ –	– –	0
			– ⏑ ⏑	0
			– – –	0
			– ⏑ ⏑ –	0

Lines beginning with புளிமாங்காய், ⏑ ⏑ – –. =138.

1	2	3	4	
புளிமாங்காய், ⏑ ⏑ – –	தேமா, – –	⏑ ⏑ –	⏑ ⏑ –	8
			⏑ ⏑ ⏑ ⏑	2
			⏑ ⏑ – –	12
			⏑ ⏑ ⏑ ⏑ –	5
		⏑ ⏑ ⏑ ⏑	– –	5
			– ⏑ ⏑	0
			– – –	0
			– ⏑ ⏑ –	0
		⏑ ⏑ – –	– –	10
			– ⏑ ⏑	0
			– – –	0
			– ⏑ ⏑ –	0
		⏑ ⏑ ⏑ ⏑ –	– –	4
			– ⏑ ⏑	0
			– – –	0
			– ⏑ ⏑ –	0
	கூவிளம், – ⏑ ⏑	– –	⏑ ⏑ –	11
			⏑ ⏑ ⏑ ⏑	3
			⏑ ⏑ – –	7
			⏑ ⏑ ⏑ ⏑ –	0
		– ⏑ ⏑	– –	3
			– ⏑ ⏑	0
			– – –	0
			– ⏑ ⏑ –	0
		– – –	– –	12
			– ⏑ ⏑	0
			– – –	0
			– ⏑ ⏑ –	0
		– ⏑ ⏑ –	– –	2
			– ⏑ ⏑	0
			– – –	0
			– ⏑ ⏑ –	0
	தேமாங்காய், – – –	– –	⏑ ⏑ –	7
			⏑ ⏑ ⏑ ⏑	2
			⏑ ⏑ – –	8
			⏑ ⏑ ⏑ ⏑ –	0
		– ⏑ ⏑	– –	4
			– ⏑ ⏑	0
			– – –	0
			– ⏑ ⏑ –	0
		– – –	– –	7
			– ⏑ ⏑	0
			– – –	0
			– ⏑ ⏑ –	0
		– ⏑ ⏑ –	– –	7
			– ⏑ ⏑	0
			– – –	0
			– ⏑ ⏑ –	0
	கூவிளங்காய், – ⏑ ⏑ –	– –	⏑ ⏑ –	4
			⏑ ⏑ ⏑ ⏑	1
			⏑ ⏑ – –	2
			⏑ ⏑ ⏑ ⏑ –	1
		– ⏑ ⏑	– –	3
			– ⏑ ⏑	0
			– – –	0
			– ⏑ ⏑ –	0
		– – –	– –	6
			– ⏑ ⏑	0
			– – –	0
			– ⏑ ⏑ –	0
		– ⏑ ⏑ –	– –	2
			– ⏑ ⏑	0
			– – –	0
			– ⏑ ⏑ –	0

Lines beginning with கூவிளங்காய், − ◡ ◡ −. = 50.

1	2	3	4	
கூவிளங்காய், − ◡ ◡ −	தேமா, − −	◡ ◡ −	◡ ◡ −	1
			◡ ◡ ◡ ◡	2
			◡ ◡ − −	2
			◡ ◡ ◡ ◡ −	1
		◡ ◡ ◡ ◡	− −	2
			− ◡ ◡	0
			− − −	5
			− ◡ ◡ −	2
		◡ ◡ − −	− −	4
			− ◡ ◡	1
			− − −	3
			− ◡ ◡ −	3
		◡ ◡ ◡ ◡ −	− −	0
			− ◡ ◡	0
			− − −	1
			− ◡ ◡ −	3
	கூவிளம், − ◡ ◡	− −	◡ ◡ −	0
			◡ ◡ ◡ ◡	0
			◡ ◡ − −	1
			◡ ◡ ◡ ◡ −	3
		− ◡ ◡	− −	0
			− ◡ ◡	0
			− − −	0
			− ◡ ◡ −	0
		− − −	− −	0
			− ◡ ◡	1
			− − −	3
			− ◡ ◡ −	1
		− ◡ ◡ −	− −	0
			− ◡ ◡	0
			− − −	1
			− ◡ ◡ −	0
	தேமாங்காய், − − −	− −	◡ ◡ −	0
			◡ ◡ ◡ ◡	0
			◡ ◡ − −	0
			◡ ◡ ◡ ◡ −	1
		− ◡ ◡	− −	0
			− ◡ ◡	0
			− − −	0
			− ◡ ◡ −	1
		− − −	− −	0
			− ◡ ◡	0
			− − −	0
			− ◡ ◡ −	3
		− ◡ ◡ −	− −	0
			− ◡ ◡	0
			− − −	0
			− ◡ ◡ −	0
	கூவிளங்காய், − ◡ ◡ −	− −	◡ ◡ −	0
			◡ ◡ ◡ ◡	0
			◡ ◡ − −	0
			◡ ◡ ◡ ◡ −	0
		− ◡ ◡	− −	0
			− ◡ ◡	1
			− − −	3
			− ◡ ◡ −	1
		− − −	− −	0
			− ◡ ◡	0
			− − −	0
			− ◡ ◡ −	0
		− ◡ ◡ −	− −	0
			− ◡ ◡	1
			− − −	0
			− ◡ ◡ −	0

Lines beginning with கருவிளங்காய், ◡ ◡ ◡ ◡ −. = 73.

1	2	3	4	
கருவிளங்காய், ◡ ◡ ◡ ◡ −	தேமா, − −	◡ ◡ −	◡ ◡ −	5
			◡ ◡ ◡ ◡	0
			◡ ◡ − −	0
			◡ ◡ ◡ ◡ −	1
		◡ ◡ ◡ ◡	− −	5
			− ◡ ◡	0
			− − −	0
			− ◡ ◡ −	0
		◡ ◡ − −	− −	2
			− ◡ ◡	0
			− − −	0
			− ◡ ◡ −	0
		◡ ◡ ◡ ◡ −	− −	1
			− ◡ ◡	0
			− − −	0
			− ◡ ◡ −	0
	கூவிளம், − ◡ ◡	− −	◡ ◡ −	3
			◡ ◡ ◡ ◡	3
			◡ ◡ − −	2
			◡ ◡ ◡ ◡ −	2
		− ◡ ◡	− −	5
			− ◡ ◡	0
			− − −	0
			− ◡ ◡ −	0
		− − −	− −	2
			− ◡ ◡	0
			− − −	0
			− ◡ ◡ −	0
		− ◡ ◡ −	− −	3
			− ◡ ◡	0
			− − −	0
			− ◡ ◡ −	0
	தேமாங்காய், − − −	− −	◡ ◡ −	3
			◡ ◡ ◡ ◡	1
			◡ ◡ − −	2
			◡ ◡ ◡ ◡ −	5
		− ◡ ◡	− −	4
			− ◡ ◡	0
			− − −	0
			− ◡ ◡ −	0
		− − −	− −	3
			− ◡ ◡	0
			− − −	0
			− ◡ ◡ −	6
		− ◡ ◡ −	− −	2
			− ◡ ◡	0
			− − −	0
			− ◡ ◡ −	0
	கூவிளங்காய், − ◡ ◡ −	− −	◡ ◡ −	0
			◡ ◡ ◡ ◡	0
			◡ ◡ − −	0
			◡ ◡ ◡ ◡ −	0
		− ◡ ◡	− −	0
			− ◡ ◡	0
			− − −	0
			− ◡ ◡ −	0
		− − −	− −	2
			− ◡ ◡	0
			− − −	0
			− ◡ ◡ −	0
		− ◡ ◡ −	− −	0
			− ◡ ◡	0
			− − −	0
			− ◡ ◡ −	6

Of the fourth line, consisting of two full feet, with a catalectic third, there are thirty-one varieties in our text. (I cannot discover in Tamil verse the thirty-second : ⏑ ⏑ ⏑ ⏑ – | – – – | –.)
The most usual are —

1. – – – | – – | ⏑ ⏑ (of which I find forty-five).
   (– – ⏑) | (– ⏑) |

2. – – | ⏑ ⏑ – | ⏑ ⏑ (there are forty-two).
   (– ⏑) | ⏑ ⏑ ⏑ |
   | ⏑ – – |
   | ⏑ – ⏑ |

3. – ⏑ ⏑ | – – | ⏑ ⏑ (there are thirty-two).
   (– ⏑ –) |

4. ⏑ ⏑ – – | – – | ⏑ ⏑ (also thirty-two).

Ex.

1. உய்த்தீட்டுந் தேனீக் கரி, 10, 49, 50.
   (தேமாங்காய்—தேமா—மலர்.)

2. ஏகும் அளித்திவ் வுல்(கு), 15, 57, 170.
   (தேமா—புளிமா—பிறப்பு, பு is scarcely heard.)

3. சென்றன செய்வ துரை, 32, 179, 201.
   (கூவிளம்—தேமா—மலர்.)

4. முடைச்சாகா டச்சிற் றழி, 48, 207, 236.
   (புளிமாங்காய்—தேமா—மலர்.)

On rhyme and alliteration I have nothing to add to what is said in *Kurraḷ*, Introd. p. xxvi.

	Metres of 4th lines.			
	1	2	3	
I.	| |	◡ ◡ – ◡ ◡ ◡ ◡ ◡ ◡ – – ◡ ◡ ◡ ◡ –	◡ ◡ – – –	42 19 12 12
II.	ↄ ↄ |	– – – ◡ ◡ – – – – ◡ ◡ –	◡ ◡ – – –	32 9 7 8
III.	| ↄ ↄ	◡ ◡ – ◡ ◡ ◡ ◡ ◡ ◡ – – ◡ ◡ ◡ ◡ –	◡ ◡ – – –	18 10 8 3
IV.	ↄ ↄ ↄ ↄ	– – – ◡ ◡ – – – – ◡ ◡ –	◡ ◡ – – –	22 9 5 4
V.	| | |	– – – ◡ ◡ – – – – ◡ ◡ –	◡ ◡ – – –	45 9 6 4
VI.	| ↄ ↄ |	– – – ◡ ◡ – – – – ◡ ◡ –	◡ ◡ – – –	16 5 2 3
VII.	| | ↄ ↄ	– – – ◡ ◡ – – – – ◡ ◡ –	◡ ◡ – – –	32 7 9 3
VIII.	| ↄ ↄ ↄ ↄ	– – – ◡ ◡ – – – – ◡ ◡ –	◡ ◡ – – –	15 8 4 0

IV. Bibliographical References.

It will be of use to the student to have a list of some of the chief Authors quoted in this volume with a very brief account of their writings.

1.

A. V. R. P. அதிவீரராம பாண்டியன். Athi-vīra-rāma Pāṇḍiyaṉ, or Vallabha Dēva. See C. D. G. p. 144, *etc.* He lived in the sixteenth century. Many works, composed under his patronage, are now ascribed to him; but he was himself doubtless an elegant writer of verses. Three of his works are of especial interest: the *Naiḍatham*, *Kāçi-kāṇḍam*, and *Veṯṯi-vēl-kai.*

(A.) The *Naiḍatham* (நைடதம்), from S. नैषध, an epithet of the hero Naḷa, king of Nishaḍa. It is the story of Naḷa and Damayantī told in Tamil fashion in 28 chapters, and 1112 *Viruttam* quatrains. The following is parallel to *Nālaḍi* 285·*etc.* :—

கோற்றொடி ! செல்வர்பாற் குறையி ரந்துநின்
றேற்றயின் றுயிர்சுமந் திருத்தல் ஈறிலா
ஆற்றலு' மானமும் அறிவுங் கல்வியும்
மாற்றருஞ் சீர்த்தியு' மாற்றும் என்பவே.

[Metre: கூ́விளம் | கூ́ / கரு } விளம் | புளி / தே } மா́ | கூ́விளம்.]

'O (thou that wearest) bright armlets! To stand imploring aid for one's need, to receive alms and eat, and to endure (a dependant) life, will destroy a man's power though boundless, his honour, his wisdom, his learning, and his unchanging renown.'

(B.) காசிக்காண்டம், KĀÇI-KĀṆḌAM. See Taylor's Oriental MSS. vol. iii. pp. 112–115.

This is a translation of a portion (காண்டம்) of the Skandam, relating chiefly to Benares (காசி), in 101 chapters, and 2524 *Viruttam* quatrains.

(C.) வெற்றிவேற்கை, VEṮṮI-VĒL-KAI: 'the hand (that holds) the conquering dart.'

These are the first words of the verses, and are an epithet of the author. See Taylor's MSS. vol. ii. App. p. 21.

2.

AVV. AVVAIYĀR, அவ்வையார்.

The poetess *Avvaiyār* is currently said to have been a sister of *Tiruvaḷḷuvar*, though I feel sure she belongs to a later period. She composed two school-books, in universal use, in which a series of moral and prudential precepts are expressed in elegant and very condensed sentences, each beginning with a different letter of the alphabet [1]. Besides these, about fifty quatrains of great excellence are, on good grounds, attributed to her. Legends regarding her abound, most of them connected with miracles, which she is supposed to have wrought. All ascribe to her a quaint and highly original character. One story about her is amusing. The 'wonderful old woman' was sitting one day in the verandah of a small way-side temple, with her feet

[1] These are the ĀTTI-ÇŪḌI (ஆத்திசூடி) and KOṈṞAI-VENTHAN (கொன்றைவேந்தன்).

stretched out straight before her, a position not considered respectful in the presence of a superior. The priest of the temple rushed out with the question, 'Are you not ashamed to stretch out your feet in the presence of the *Çāmi* (idol or lord)?' To which she replied, 'Very true, sir, if you will show me where the *Çāmi* is not, I will stretch out my feet there!'

She was once asked, it is said, to compose some verses about the four great topics discussed by Hindū authors, 'virtue, wealth, pleasure, and heaven;' since Tiruvaḷḷuvar had sung his 1330 couplets on the three former. She replied in a quatrain:

ஈதல்அறம்; தீவினைவிட் டீட்டல் பொருள்; எஞ்ஞான்றும்
காதல் இருவர் கருத்துறவைத்—தாதரவு
பட்டதே இன்பம்; பரனைநினைந் திம்மூன்றும்
விட்டதே பேரின்ப வீடு!

'Giving is *virtue; wealth* what's gained eschewing sin;
And evermore 'tis *pleasure* when, their hearts at one,
Two live in love, sustaining and sustain'd. To leave
All three, heart fix'd on God, is perfect bliss of *heaven*.'

I am not sure, however, that these are her lines, though given to her by almost universal tradition. They savour of a later date and of a different school. There is no reason to doubt her authorship of the following:

சீரியர் கெட்டாலுஞ் சீரியர் சீரியரே!
அல்லாதார் கெட்டால் அங்கென்னாம்?—சீரிய
பொன்னின் குடம்உடைந்தாற் பொன்னாகும்; என்னாகும்
மண்ணின் குடம் உடைந்தக் கால்?

'Tho' worthy men be ruin'd, worthy men are still
Right worthy men; when worthless men are ruin'd, what
Are they? If vase of gold be broken, still 'tis gold!
What is there left, when shatter'd lies the earthen pot?'

3.

B. I. S. Indische Sprüche, by Dr. Otto Böhtlingk. 2nd edition. St. Petersburg, 1870.

The authorities cited are not seldom modern South-Indian writers. And these verses are presumably translated occasionally from the works of Tamil poets. It is of course peculiarly difficult to trace a proverb or an epigram to its source.

It would be possible, indeed, to find a close Sanskrit parallel to nearly every gnomic verse in Tamil poetry; but in many cases the beauty, spontaneity, and terseness of the Tamil stanza seem to prove its originality.

4.

Çi. ÇILAPPATHIGĀRAM, சிலப்பதிகாரம்: 'the chapter of the *Çilambu*.' [சிலம்பு is an anklet worn by dancers. It is hollow and filled with pebbles, which give forth a tinkling sound. S. शिला?]

This is an elegant, but little known composition, one of the five ancient Tamil poems [பஞ்சமகாகாவியம்], being a romantic story like 'The Lady of the Lake,' and not rising to the dignity of an epic. Only a small portion has been printed. Its author was *Çēramān*, of whose personal history absolutely nothing is known; but he was certainly a Jain.

The following is a specimen of its style. It is the dedication of the first canto:—

1.

திங்களைப் போற்றுதுந், திங்களைப் போற்றுதும்!
கொங்கலர்தார்ச் சென்னி குளிர்வெண் குடைபோன்றிவ்
வங்கண் உலகளித்த லான்.

2.

ஞாயிறு போற்றுது', ஞாயிறு போற்றுதும்!
காவிரி நாடன் றிகிரிபோற் பொற்கோட்டு
மேரு வலந்திரித லான்.

3.

மாமழை போற்றுது', மாமழை போற்றுதும்!
நாமநீர் வேலி உலகிற் கவன்அளிபோல்
மேனின்று தான்சுரத்த லான்.

4.

பூம்புகார் போற்றுதும், பூம்புகார் போற்றுதும்!
வீங்குநீர் வேலி உலகிற் கவன்குலத்தோ
டோங்கிப் பரந்தெழுத லான்.

'Praise we the moon! Praise we the moon! for, like the cool white umbrella over the fragrant-flower-garlanded head (of the king), it affords grace to the fair and spacious world.

Praise we the sun! Praise we the sun! for, like the chariot of the lord of Kāviri's domain, it wheels around Meru's golden heights.

Praise we the vast cloud! Praise we the vast cloud! for,

like his grace, it pours down blessings on the world begirt by the fearsome sea.

Praise we flowery *Pugār!* Praise we flowery *Pugār!* for it uplifts itself and spreads itself and grows together with his (*the king's*) clan, above all the world surrounded by the swelling ocean's tide.'

The metre of this is இன்னிசை சிந்தியல் வெண்பா, G. 185, *etc.* It consists of verses of three lines, being in fact *Kurraḷs* with an additional line prefixed. See Introd. to my *Kurraḷ*, p. xxv, *etc.*, and note on Quatrain 250.

5.

C. D. G. Dr. Caldwell's Dravidian Comparative Grammar. 2nd edition. Trübner. 1875.

A work of profound learning and research; but the grammatical portions are often founded on insufficient data.

6.

C. P. B. C. P. Brown's Telugu Dictionary.

Very unscientific, but full and accurate.

7.

Ēl. or Ēlā. ĒLĀTHI, ஏலாதி.

The name is S. एल, 'cardamom,' + आदि = *etc.* = a perfumed confection of ஏலம், 'cardamom,' கர்ப்பூரம், 'camphor,' எரிகாசு, 'an odorous wood,' சந்தனம், 'sandal,' and தேன், 'honey.'

This mingling of perfumes is used for the hair. The name is given to this collection of gnomic verses because each quatrain is supposed to combine, compare, and illustrate five or six things.

The work is of Jain origin. Its author's name is *Kaṇi-mēthaiyār*='he whose knowledge is appreciated (by all).' It is one of the eighteen lesser classics: சங்கச் செய்யுள். Of the author nothing is really known. He is styled a disciple of Makkāya-nār, son of Tamiṛ-āçiriyar, one of the Madura Academy. It is probably not of much later date than the *Nālaḍi* itself; and is once quoted by the Commentator on the Jī. Chin. The Madras edition of 1887 is referred to. Perhaps a careful study of *Ēlāthi* will, more than any other minor poet, help the learner to understand the *Nālaḍi*.

8.

Ellis. ELLIS, F. W. See Introd. to my *Kurraḷ*, page v.

Mr. Ellis' MSS. fell into the hands of the late eminent

orientalist, Sir Walter Elliot, who left them by will to me. They are now in the Bodleian Library. There are in them some unpublished translations. His texts were often incorrect, and his translations in general have not had the benefit of careful revision. See also Burnell's South-Indian Palaeography, p. 35.

9.

G. Ç. GŌVINDA-ÇATAKAM, கோவிந்தசதகம்.

102 choice proverbs, each illustrated by a quatrain. This is not at all a classic, but well worth studying.

It is by *Narāyaṇa-bhāratiyār*.

10.

G. My Second Catechism of Tamil Grammar; or IIIrd Grammar. [In 'First Lessons:' Clarendon Press.]

11.

Gu. Dr. Gundert's Malayāḷam and English Dictionary.

A very useful and scientific work. Mangalore, 1872.

12.

Jī. Chin. JĪVAGA-CHINTĀMAṆI, சீவக-சிந்தாமணி, S. जीवगचिन्तामणि. This is, on the whole, the greatest existing Tamil literary monument. My references are to the very admirable edition published by வே. சாமிநாதையர், of the Combaconam College, at the திராவிடரத்நாகரம் Press, Madras, 1887.

The late lamented Dr. Bower published an edition of the first book in 1868. To these indispensable works I must refer the student. A lexicon and concordance to this poem would afford a basis for a complete dictionary of Classical Tamil. All that is given as the history of the book rests on the very slenderest authority.

The author's name was *Tirutakka-dēvar* (திருத்தக்க-தேவர்), and he is said to have been born in Mayilāpūr or S. Thomé, now a suburb of Madras, where the author of the *Kuṟṟaḷ* also lived.

The work contains the life of *Jīvagan*, a king who governed Rāja-mā-puram, the capital of Yēmāñgadam (हेमाङ्गद = golden-limbed, a name of a Gandharva). A very minute examination of this poem leads me to conclude that it is somewhat later in date than much of the *Nālaḍi*. Meanwhile there is scarcely a word, phrase, or idea in the four hundred quatrains that is not in the epic.

The following (Jī. Chin. i. 325) compared with 289 will exemplify this:—

VIJAYAI IN THE WILDERNESS FORLORN.

(– ⏑ ⏑ | ⏓ ⏑ – | ⏓ ⏓ || ⏑ ⏑ ⏑ ⏑ | ⏓ ⏓ – | ⏓ ⏑ –)

பாலுடை அமிர்தம் பைம்பொற் கலத்திடை பாவை அன்ன
நூலடு நுசுப்பி னல்லார் ஏந்தவும் நேர்ந்து நோக்காச்
சேலடு கண்ணி காந்தட் டிருமணித் துடுப்பு முன்கை
வாலட கருளிச் செய்ய வனத்துறை தெய்வம் ஆனாள்.

'The lady, whose eyes excel the *Çēl* in brightness (395), did not deign even to glance at the ambrosial food mingled with milk which fair ones, like pictures, with waist slighter than a thread, presented in a vessel of pure gold; but feeding herself with a mess of simple herbs,—her hand,—beauteous as a *Kānthal* flower,—erewhile adorned with sacred gems,—serving as a ladle, became as a ruddy demoness dwelling in the woods.'

Tirutakka-dēvar has worked out in wonderful stories too diffusely what the *Nālaḍi* asserts in terse epigram. There is a tradition that before the composition of his epic, he had been the author of verses on the 'Instability of the Body,' the 'Transitory Nature of Wealth,' and kindred subjects. I feel inclined to believe, from careful consideration of style, that some of the earlier quatrains are not improbably his.

The great romantic epic, which is at once the Iliad and the Odyssey of the Tamil language, is said to have been composed in the early youth of the poet, when still residing with his teacher, or Āçiriyar. They had come, tradition says, to Madura, the great capital of the Pāṇḍiyan kingdom, and centre of religious activities, which was especially renowned as the seat of the Tamil Academy or *Çaṅgam*, founded by the god *Çivan* himself. (See Pope's *Kurraḷ*, Introd. p. iv.) Of this Academy he became a member, and in the freedom of social converse (the Tamil writer refers to *Nālaḍi* 137) some of the associated literati reproached him with ignorance of erotic works, which, they added, 'are so much esteemed.' This refers perhaps to the *Kali-togai* and similar compositions.

To this he replied, that he had never written poems on sensual subjects, because his fellow Jains held all such poetry in detestation, but that he could write amatory verses with the best of them if he chose to do so.

They ended by challenging him to produce a work which *should exhaust the whole subject of sensual. lustful indulgence.*

He accepted the challenge, and the *Chintāmaṇi* is the result. It was admitted on all sides that he had fully succeeded!

He makes his hero drink the cup of pleasure to the very dregs, and the poet carefully photographs everything, using words and giving details of unparalleled—as I suppose—grossness. Jīvagan does, indeed, at last renounce all; but without the faintest idea of repentance, or of the existence of any cause for penitence, and obtains a glorious 'release.'

I much wished to edit and publish some parts of this great poem, but found it impossible. If any native scholar could expurgate and condense it, not only removing the hopelessly licentious cantos, but bringing the epithets throughout into something like harmony with what we regard as higher and purer instincts, the very greatly diminished poem, like a cut and polished diamond, would shine the brighter for the operation.

A tradition exists that the Dēvar, on the production of his work, was quite naturally asked how he, from his childhood pledged to perfect purity, could compose a poem exhibiting such an unequalled familiarity with all that is connected with sensuality. 'You must be an habitual debauchee,' said they.

His reply was to take up a red-hot ball of iron with the words, 'May this burn me if I am not absolutely pure!' and he came out of the ordeal unscathed!

Certainly the poet of the Jīvaga Chintāmaṇi could not with Hippolytus speak of himself as *παρθένον ψυχὴν ἔχων*; though his work is one of the great epics of the world. I have mentioned all this in order that the Tamil idea of the character of the poem may be clear; and also to show from what species of traditions we have to glean the material for South-Indian Bibliography.

13.

K. T. (*கலித்.*) KALI-TOGAI, *கலித்தொகை.*

This is a collection (*தொகை*) of love songs in the *கலி* metre [G. 192]. The *கலிப்பா* (or '*resonant*') metre has what is called the *துள்ளல் ஓசை*, or '*saltatory*' rhythm. This is the result of its law of connexion of feet in the line, which is the reverse of that of the Veṇbā, i. e. மாமுன் நேர், விளம் முன் விளம், காய்முன் நிரை. (See p. xxviii).

But its connexion is often quite irregular.

The Kali-togai is by *Nallanthuvaṉār* (நல்லந்துவனார்), and is in five books, containing 150 lyrics, in which a series of somewhat disconnected stories of a pastoral and amatory kind are rather outlined than related; the imagery and accessories being confined in each book to one of the five kinds of country found in the Tamil land. A careful study of it will convince any one—

(1) That very much that is puerile, absurdly conventional, and even of an injurious character, is inextricably mingled up with these old Tamil bucolics;

(2) That with all this there is much of pathos, beauty, felicity of description, exquisite use of language, and even occasional sublimity;

(3) That a people possessing such a language and such gifts may, by throwing off some of these conventionalities, produce a literature not inferior to that of any age or country.

The commentator is Nachinārkkiniyār of Madura, the same great scholar that edited the Jīvaga Chintāmaṇi, and many other poems. Of its date and history absolutely nothing is known. It seems to me to be somewhat older than the *Nālaḍi*. See notes on ch. xl.

14.

K. Rām. கம்பராமாயணம், KAMBAN'S RĀMĀYAṆAM. See C. D. G. p. 134, and my H. B. pp. 4, 163.

Six books by K. and the seventh உத்தரகாண்டம் by a later author.

15.

Kit. Dr. Kittel's Canarese Dictionary.

A thoroughly satisfactory work.

16.

K. The 'Sacred' *Kurraḷ* of Tiruvaḷḷuvar: the Tamil Text, with Introduction, Grammar, English Translation, Notes, and a complete Lexicon and Concordance, by the Rev. G. U. Pope, M. A., D. D. Allen & Co. 1886.

17.

Mū. The *Mūthurai* or *Vākkuṇḍām.*

This consists of thirty quatrains (நேரிசைவெண்பா) on ethical and social topics, ascribed to *Avvaiyār.*

Many editions are in circulation. That published by சரவணப் பெருமாள் ஐயர் in 1833 is the *princeps.*

Several stanzas are identical in meaning with well-known Sanskrit verses. Much of it cannot be very ancient.

Mūthurai = 'old word;' the whole work being an exquisitely beautiful setting of old proverbial sayings.

Vākkuṇḍām is the beginning of a very modern invocation prefixed.

18.

N. M. K. NĀṈ-MAṆI-KAḌIGAI, நான்மணிக்கடிகை, 'the salver of four gems.'

This is a series of quatrains of the same metre and general character as the *Nālaḍi.* Their peculiarity, indicated by the title, is that in each stanza four things are somehow associated in the way of antithesis, comparison, or illustration. Thus (23):

> மொய்சிதைக்கும் ஒற்றுமை இன்மை; ஒருவனைப்
> பொய்சிதைக்கும் பொன்போனு' மேனியைப்;—பெய்த
> கலஞ்சிதைக்கும் பாலின் சுவையைக்;—குலஞ்சிதைக்கும்
> கூடார்கட் கூடி விடின்.

(As) 1. *Want of union* ruins society;

(and as) 2. *Falsehood* ruins even him whose form is resplendent as gold;

(and as) 3. The *vessel* into which one is poured ruins the flavour of milk;

(even so) 4. If you ally yourself to *those whose alliance is forbidden,* it will ruin your race. [See *Nāl.* ch. xxiii.]

A useful edition was published at the கலாரத்நாகரம் Press, with a good Tamil commentary, and (a poor) English translation. It is by *Viḷambiya Kāgaṉār* (விளம்பியகாகனார்), who probably lived in the fifteenth century.

The printed work contains 106 quatrains; but a MS., belonging to Mr. Stokes, gives only 101. Many are very modern; some are elegant; but more are rather rugged and pedantic. Parallel verses occur in Böhtlingk's Indische Sprüche. A work of this name is mentioned second in the list of சங்கச் செய்யுள், or poems that received the sanction of the Madura College.

This work is quoted or referred to in pp. 3, 5, 6, 37, 43, 44, 45, 61, 92, 120, 181, 187, 198, 222, 236, 237, 248, *etc.*

19.

N. N. NAṈ-ṈEṞṞI, நன்னெறி, 'the good way.'

This consists of forty quatrains by Çiva-piragāça-çuvāmi of Tuṟṟai-maṅgalam. They are printed in 'Minor Poets,' and separately. Though comparatively modern (seventeenth century) they are classical and of great value. Every verse has its apt, and often very ingenious simile.

20.

N. N. V. NĪTHI-NEṞṞI-VIḶAKKAM, நீதிநெறிவிளக்கம்.

This is an admirable series of 102 quatrains. An excellent edition with translations and much valuable information was published by H. Stokes, Esq., M. C. S.

The author was Kumāraguruparam, a Tambirān or Hindū monk. He was a native of Streevaiguntham in Tinnevelly, and lived about A. D. 1700.

21.

N. V. NALVAḶI, நல்வழி = 'the good way.'

This is another work ascribed to Avvaiyār, in the same metre. It contains forty quatrains. The following is quite in the style of the famous 'old lady:'

ஆண்டாண்டு தோறும் அழுது புரண்டாலும்
மாண்டார் வருவரோ, மாநிலத்தீர்?—வேண்டாம்!
நமக்கும் அதுவழியே. நாம்போம் அளவும்
எமக்கென்னென் றிட்டுண் டிரும்.

'O dwellers on this vast earth! Though ever, from year to year, you weep and roll on the ground, will the dead come back? Let be! That's our way too. And till we go, let us give and enjoy, saying, What's death to us?'

22.

NAṈṈŪL, நன்னூல்.

This is the most useful Tamil Grammar. In the edition printed in my IIIrd Grammar, the rules are numbered from

1 to 462. All that is necessary, or indeed useful, is given in the Catechism.

23.

T. TIRIKAḌUGAM, திரிகடுகம், from S. त्रिकटुकं='composed of three spices.'

These are dry ginger, long pepper, and black pepper (சுக்கு, திப்பிலி, மிளகு). Each stanza, of which there are 100, introduces three things for comparison, contrast, or illustration. A very fascinating little cento.

Thus wealth, science, and speech are introduced in 90:

> ஈதற்குச் செய்க பொருளை; அறநெறி
> சேர்தற்குச் செய்க பெருநூலை; யாது
> அருள்புரிந்து சொல்லுக சொல்லை: இம்மூன்றும்
> இருளுலகஞ் சேராத ஆறு.

'Acquire wealth in order to give;
Learn great works that you may walk in the way of virtue;
Speak every word with gracious purpose:
These are the paths that conduct not to the world of darkness.'

The author is *Nallāthaṉār* (நல்லாதனார்), of whom nothing is really known. It is impossible to assign an earlier date to this work than the fifteenth century.

Parallels to most of the verses will be found in Böhtlingk.

I have gratefully to acknowledge the liberal assistance of the Secretary of State for India in Council, as formerly in the case of the *Kurraḷ*. The Delegates of the Clarendon Press procured type especially for the book, and made the arrangements by which this Tamil classic is issued with a typographical accuracy hardly ever attained in a similar work. To them my most grateful thanks are due.

His Highness the Mahārāja of Travancore has also subscribed liberally to the work.

To the skill, patience, and unwearied zeal of Mr. Pembrey, Oriental reader at the Clarendon Press, it is mainly due that no table of errata is needed to a work so complicated and difficult.

It will be seen that the editor and translator has sought carefully and patiently to interpret his authors, and has avoided all controversy. His aim in this work has been simply to introduce Tamil thoughts to English students. We need to understand one another and love one another, if we are to be of any mutual benefit. He who knows and loves 'sweet' Tamil may come to know and love those to whom it is so dear, and thus to be known and loved by them.

G. U. P.

INDIAN INSTITUTE, OXFORD:
February, 1893.

ANALYSIS

OF THE

CHAPTERS OF THE NĀLAḌI.

நாலடிநானூற்றின்

அதிகார அடைவு.

PART I.

ON VIRTUE.

க-வது. அறத்துப்பால்.

PART II.

ON WEALTH.

உ-வது. பொருட்பால்.

PART III.

ON LOVE (OR PLEASURE).

௩-வது. காமத்துப்பால்.

NĀLAḌI.

I.

TEXT, ENGLISH TRANSLATION, AND NOTES.

PART I.

ON VIRTUE.

அறத்துப்பால்

[CH. I–XIII]

(= நூல்களில் விதித்தன செய்தலும் விலக்கியன ஒம்புதலுமாகிய அறத்தின் பகுதி).

The editor *Pathumanār* has arranged the 400 quatrains, in accordance with the *Kurraḷ*, into three parts, treating of Virtue, Wealth, and Pleasure. [See Pope's *Kurraḷ*, Introd. pp. vii–ix.]

Part I. அறம் (=virtue), thirteen chapters;
Part II. பொருள் (=wealth), ch. xiv–xxxix;
Part III. இன்பம் (=pleasure), ch. xl.

The titles of chapters are modern.

Of these ch. i–vi correspond roughly to ch. xxxiv–xxxvii of the *Kurraḷ*, being an introductory exposition of 'spiritual wisdom' (ஞானம்), which sees things as they are, and discerns their unreality and transitory character.

CHAPTER I.

THE INSTABILITY OF PROSPERITY.

அதிகாரம் க.

செல்வநிலையாமை

(=செல்வம் நில்லாது என்னுந் தன்மை).

The following (from N. M. K. 67) is a fitting motto for this chapter:

'கைத்துடையான் காமுற்ற துண்டாகும்;—வித்தின்
முளைக்குழா நீர்உண்டேல் உண்டாம்;—திருக்குழாம்
ஒண்செய்யாள் பார்த்துறின் உண்டாகும்;—மற்றவள்
துன்புறுவள் ஆகிற் கெடும்:

The desires of the wealthy will be gratified;—from the seeds a multitude of sprouts will arise, if there be water;—all riches will flow in, if the bright goddess of prosperity vouchsafe a favouring glance;—but all will perish, if she visit man with affliction.'

So (in N. M. K. 43):

' . . . . நல்லாள்
உடம்படிற் றானே பெருகும்;—கெடும் பொழுதில்
கண்டனவுங் காணாக் கெடும்:

(Wealth) will increase of itself, if the good goddess approve; when (that wealth) perishes, even what man has seen (*the desire of his eyes*) will vanish away!'

The analysis of the chapter is:

1. Wealth does not remain with men: there are vicissitudes of fortune. [1–3.]
2. Death, at any rate, robs men of their possessions; virtue alone survives. [4–8.]
3. How foolish then are misers! [9, 10.]

1.

பெருஞ் செல்வவாழ்க்கையரும் வறியராய் இரந்துண்பர்; ஆதலின் செல்வம் நிலைபேறுடையதன்று.

அறுசுவை உண்டி அமர்ந்தில்லாள் ஊட்ட
மறுசிகை நீக்கிஉண் டாரும்—வறிஞராய்ச்
சென்றிரப்பர் ஓரிடத்துக் கூழ்எனிற் செல்வம் ஒன்
றுண்டாக வைக்கற்பாற் றன்று.

Who to-day dine luxuriously to-morrow beg.

Those who ate erewhile, course after course, food of six flavours, supplied by their complaisant spouse, now roam as paupers and beg a mess of pottage here and there; if so, let wealth be counted as a thing of nought!

எழு: செல்வம்.—பயனி: அன்று.—அறு. G. 159. வறிஞர் = வறி-ஞ்-அர். ஞகரம் இடைநிலை. (G. 93. வறு.) இடத்து. G. 63.

The six flavours are—

கைப்பு (கச), bitterness,	உவர்ப்பு, saltness,
இனிப்பு, sweetness,	துவர்ப்பு, astringency,
புளிப்பு, sourness,	கார்ப்பு, pungency.

உண்டாரும், 'those even who were wont to eat.'

ஒன்று உண்டு ஆக, 'as though it were anything.'

வைக்கல் பாற்று அன்று (see பால், அல் in Lex.), 'it is not in the category of things to be considered.' G. 93. This quatrain seems to have been suggested by Jī. Chin. xiii. 25. 343. See Lex. கருணை.

For the idea, comp. K. 333, and the whole of ch. xxxiv. அமர்ந்த suggests the 'placens uxor' of Horace. In Tel. Vēmana i. 200 may be usefully compared.

For metre, see G. 189.

The எதுகை in third and fourth lines (சென்ற், உண்ட்) is இனவெதுகை. Intr. to K. p. xxvi.

2.

செல்வமானது யாவரிடத்தும் நிலைப்பதன்று; ஆதலால் அதுஉண்டான பொழுதே பாத்துண்க!

துகடீர் பெருஞ்செல்வந் தோன்றியக்காற் றொட்டுப்
பகடு நடந்தகூழ் பல்லாரோ டுண்க!
அகடுற யார்மாட்டு நில்லாது செல்வம்
சகடக்கால் போல வரும்.

Wealth abides not, share it and enjoy.

When you own ample wealth acquired by blameless means, with many sharing eat the grain that steers have trodden out! In centre poised prosperity stands with no man, but revolves like the waggon's wheel.

Ellis, p. 86.

எ: ஒருவன் (தொகை), செல்வம்.—ப: உண்க, வரும்.—யார்மாட்டும். G. 63. துகள், தீர். G. 37, 153.

For metre, see G. 190.

The transmutations of letters here are puzzling: ள் + த = ட்; G. 37. This is அல்வழிச் சந்தி, for தீர் does not govern துகள். G. 22. கால் + தொட்டு. G. 38.

தோன்றியக்கால் is past adj. participle, தோன்றிய for தோன்றின (G. 87), with கால்; but the doubling of க் is anomalous, since by G. 27 க், ச், த், ப் are not doubled after an adjective verbal form. It seems to be for தோன்றிய அக்கால், and to be emphatic: 'from the very time of its acquisition.' (Lex. கால், கடை.) K. ch. ix.

3.

நால்வகைச் சேனைகளை உடையவராய் வாழ்ந்த அரசர்களும் கெடுவர்.

யானை எருத்தம் பொலியக் குடைநிழற்கீழ்ச்
சேனைத் தலைவராய்ச் சென்றோரும் — ஏனை
வினைஉலப்ப வேறாகி வீழ்வர்தாம் கொண்ட
மனையாளை மாற்றார் கொள.

Mighty warriors fall.

Those who rode resplendent forth on the neck of an elephant, beneath the state umbrella's shade, as the leaders of the host, when '*other deeds*' destroy, shall change and fall, while foes lead away their wives as captives.

எ: சென்றோர்.—ப: வீழ்வர். Comp. 21.

A man's rank will not save him from vicissitudes of fortune (N. M. K. 42):

'திருவுந் திணைவகையானில்லா:
Nor will even Fortune on account of lineage abide.'

For பொலிய and கொள, see G. 140 (உ). Ellis, p. 86.

K. ch. xxxviii and ch. xi of this work must be studied for ஏனைவினை, which is the key of the whole. (See Pope's *Kurraḷ*, pp. 197, 248, etc.) The quatrain is a reminiscence of Jī. Chin. i. 298.

4.

செல்வம்நில்லாது ஆகலானும், மரணம் உண்மை ஆகலானும், விரைந்து அறஞ்செய்து உய்க!

நின்றன நின்றன நில்லா எனஉணர்ந்
தொன்றின ஒன்றின வல்லே செயிற் செய்க;
சென்றன சென்றன வாழ்நாள், செறுத்துடன்
வந்தது வந்தது கூற்று!

Do your duty, knowing the instability of all things. Time flies! Death comes!

The things of which you said, 'they stand, they stand,' stand not; mark this, and perform what befits, yea! what befits, with all your power! Your days are gone, are gone! and death close pressing on is come, is come!

எ: ஒருவர் (தொகை), வாழ்நாள், கூற்று.—ப: செய்க, சென்றன, வந்தது.

Comp. 52 and K. 331.

The past expresses 'swiftness and certainty.' G. 147, 8.

The repetition has the same effect. It is called அடுக்குத்தொடர். G. 126.

வல்லே செயிற் செய்க, 'do promptly what you design to do!'

Ellis, p. 86.

5.

யாதாயினும் ஒருபொருள் கிடைக்கின் அதுநில்லாது; ஆகலின் கிடைத்தபொழுதே அறஞ்செய்தவர் வீடுபெறுவர்.

என்னானும் ஒன்றுதங் கையுறப் பெற்றக்கால்
பின்னாவ தென்று பிடித்திரா,—முன்னே
கொடுத்தார் உயப்போவர் கோடிறீக் கூற்றம்
தொடுத்தாறு செல்லுஞ் சுரம்.

Give before death comes.

When you have gained and hold in hand any single thing, retain it not with the thought, 'This will serve some other day!' Those who have given betimes shall escape the desert road along which death, an unyielding foe, drags his captives away.

எ: கொடுத்தார்.—ப: போவர்.—செயப்: சுரம்.

Comp. Lex. கூற்றம், சுரம், ஆறு. A doubtful construction.

Curious and instructive is N. M. K. 69:

'பின்னவாம் முன்னறார்க்குப் பின்னதிர்க்குஞ் செய்வினை;
முன்னவாம் முன்னம் அறிந்தார்கட் கென்னும்
அவாவாம் அடைந்தார்கட் குள்ளந்—தவாவாம்
வரவிலார் செய்யும் வினை;

To those who think not beforehand events that cause a shudder follow after! To those that have been wise before, these things were (*foreseen and provided for*) before! Desire grows with acquisition! Firm will their mind be who in their poverty are virtuous!'

6.

தேகம் நில்லாது, ஆகலின் பொருளை இறுகப் பிடித்திராமல் இரப்போர்க்கீதல் வேண்டும்.

இழைத்தநாள் எல்லை இகவா; பிழைத்தொரீஇக்
கூற்றங் குதித்துய்ந்தார் ஈங்கில்லை;—ஆற்றப்
பெரும்பொருள் வைத்தீர், வழங்குமின்! நாளைத்
தழீஇந்தழீஇந் தண்ணம் படும்.

Death inevitable. Hoard not!

Man's days pass not their assigned bound. None here on earth have ever escaped death's power, made off and got free.

O hoarder of ample wealth, dispense it! On the morn the funeral drum will sound.

Comp. however *Nīti.* 51 with Mr. Stokes' note.

K. 269 is in direct contradiction to this : கூற்றங்குதித்தலுங் கைகூடும்.

In கந்தப்புராணம், அசுரகாண்டம், மார்க்கண்டப்படலம் the whole history of a victory over Yaman is given. See Lex. கூறு.

7.

மக்களாய்ப் பிறந்தோர் அடையும் பயன் அறம், அதலால் அதனைப் பொருள் உள்ள பொழுதே செய்துகொள்க.

தோற்றஞ்சான் ஞாயிறு நாழியா வைகலுங்
கூற்றம் அளந்துநுந் நாள்உண்ணும் ;—ஆற்ற
அறஞ்செய் தருளுடையீர் ஆகுமின் ; யாரும்
பிறந்தும் இறவாதா ரில்.

Death inevitable.

Death every day takes that fount of light the sun as a measure, metes out your days, and so devours. Do deeds of virtue full of kindly grace. Though all are born, none are exempt from death.

For தோற்றஞ்சால், comp. கலித், i. 17. 'தோற்றஞ்சா னெருபொருள், conspicuous store of wealth heaped up :'= விளக்கம் அமைந்த.

Ellis, p. 86. There is another reading in the last line : பிறவாதாரில் : '*they are to be reckoned* among those who have never been born.' It is ambiguous. Lex. பிற.

8.

அறிவிலார் செல்வம் பயன்படாது அழியும்.

'செல்வர் யாம்' என்றுதாஞ் செல்வுழி எண்ணாத
புல்லறி வாளர் பெருஞ்செல்வம்—எல்லிற்
கருங்கொண்மூ வாய்திறந்த மின்னுப்போற் றோன்றி
மருங்கறக் கெட்டு விடும்.

The wealth of the foolish like the lightning's flash.

The ample wealth of men of mean understanding, who say, 'We're rich,' yet ponder not their path and end, appears, and perishes, and leaves no trace; like the flash, when the black thunder-cloud by night opens its mouth.

எ: செல்வம்.—ப: விடும்.—செல்வுழி. (செல், வ், உழி.) G. 63, 153. புல். G. 119. Ellis, p. 86.

In T. 68 mention is made of 'இவ்வுலகினிலையாமையுள்ளும் நெறிப்பாடு: the habit of life that meditates this world's instability.'

The idea is given in neat proverbial form in *Ēlā.* 22:

'வளமை வலி இவை வாடும:
Wealth and strength—these fade.'

9.

ஒருவன் தானும் அநுபவியாமல் பிறர்க்குங் கொடாமல் பொருளைச் சேர்த்து வைத்திருப்பான் ஆயின், அவன் உலகத்தாரால் பொருளிழந்தவன் என்று சொல்லப்படுவான்.

உண்ணான், ஒளிநிறான், ஓங்கு புகழ் செய்யான்,
துன்னருங் கேளிர் துயர்களையான்,—கொன்னே
வழங்கான், பொருள்காத் திருப்பான் ஏல், அ ஆ!
இழந்தான்என் றெண்ணப் படும்.

The miser loses all.

He eats not, sheds no light of splendour around, performs no deeds that merit lofty praise, soothes no sorrow that choice friends feel, spends nought, but hoards his wealth in vain: 'Aha! he's lost it all,' shall men pronounce.

எ: அவன் (தொகை).—ப: படும்.—உண்ணான். G. 89. புகழ். (G. 162. காரிய ஆகுபெயர்.) துன், அருங்கேளிர். G. 153, 121.

Comp. 10, 273, 274, 277, and K. 228. The metre requires ஆஅ.

10.

அறஞ்செய்யாது பொருளைச் சேர்த்துவைத்தவர் அப்பொருளின்பயனை இழப்பர்.

உடாஅதும் உண்ணாதுந் தம்முடம்பு செற்றுங்
கெடாஅத நல்லறமுஞ் செய்யார்—கொடாஅது
வைத்தீட்டி னார்இழப்பர்,—வான்றோய் மலைநாட!—
உய்த்தீட்டுந் தேனீக் கரி.

The miser like the honey-bee.

Those who stint in clothes and food, and mortify their bodies, yet do not deeds of deathless virtue, and bestow nothing, hoarding shall suffer loss:—Lord of the cloud-capped hills!—this the hoarding honey-bee attests.

எ: ஈட்டினார், தேனீ.—ப: இழப்பர், கரி.—தேனீ. G. 152.

The Tamil Rhetoric (பொருளதிகாரம். See my III. Gr. 214–220) enumerates five kinds of land (ஐந்திணை).—These are குறிஞ்சி (hill-country); பாலை (desert); முல்லை (sylvan); மருதம் (cultivated); and நெய்தல் (maritime).—These quatrains are addressed occasionally to petty chieftains (நாடன்: this is also a title of Çōḷa kings). Here it is a hill-chief that is apostrophized (குறிஞ்சித்தலைவன்). Now, honey is one of the chief products of that region. Hence the simile. This harmony of thought, and appropriate local colouring (பொருத்தம்) is much esteemed in Tamil literature.

CHAPTER II.

YOUTH ABIDES NOT.

அதிகாரம் உ.

இளமை நிலையாமை

(= இளமைப்பருவம் நில்லாதென்னுந்தன்மை).

The transitoriness of youth. C. says 'from the age of 16 to 32 is the period of passionate excitation.'

Analysis :

1. Youth will give place to age and decrepitude. [11.]
2. Love and all joys of youth are fleeting. [12.]
3. 'Tis best to renounce earthly joys ere feeble old age comes. [13, 14, 15.]
4. The silly slaves of youthful lusts. [16.]
5. Your darling will become a decrepit, sightless crone. [17.]
6. Listen to courteous enquirers after your health ! [18.]
7. Death may take you off in your prime. Be wise betimes ! [19, 20.]

11.

இளமை நிலையன்று என்று கருதித் துறந்தோர் இன்புறுவர்.
இதனை நிலையென்று களித்தவர் பின்பு வருந்துவர்.

நரைவரும் என்றெண்ணி நல்லறி வாளர்
குழவி இடத்தே துறந்தார் ; — புரைதீரா
மன்னா இளமை மகிழ்ந்தாரே கோலூன்றி
இன்னாங் கெழுந்திருப் பார்.

Age will come. Be wise early.

'Grey eld will come,'—the wise remembering this renounce

the world even in tender age; but they who joy in youth, unstable, never free from fault, shall erewhile painfully rise up leaning on a staff.

எ: அறிவாளர், மகிழ்ந்தாரே.—ப: துறந்தார், இருப்பர்.—நீரர, மன்னு. G. 91.

Comp. K. 342.

In T. 14, இழுக்கல் இயல்பிற் றிளமை=இயல்பாக வழுவிப் போவது தான்பாலியம், 'to slip is the very nature of youth.'

Ēlā. 22:

> 'இளமை கழியும், பிணிமூப்பியையும:
> Youth will pass away, disease and eld will come!'

12.

நிலையற்ற இளமையை நிலை என்று கருதி வாழ்தலினால் துன்பமே அன்றி பயனில்லை.

நட்புநார் அற்றன; நல்லாரும் அஃகினர்;
அற்புத் தளையும் அவிழ்ந்தன;—உட்காணுய!
வாழ்தலின் ஊதியம் என்னுண்டாம? வந்ததே
ஆழ்கலத் தன்ன கலி.

All is vanity.

Severed are the ties of friendship; minished are the pleasant ones; love's bonds are loosened too; then look within and say, what profit is there in this joyous life of thine? The cry comes up as from a sinking ship!

அற்பு for அன்பு. G. 41.

13.

ஆசைவழியே ஒழுகும் அறிவினையுடையார்க்கு நன்னெறியில் நின்றொழுகும் வழி இல்லை.

சொற்றளர்ந்து கோலூன்றிச் சோர்ந்த நடையினராய்ப்
பற்கழன்று பண்டம் பழிகாறும்—இற்செறிந்து
காம நெறிபடருங் கண்ணினார்க் கில்லையே
ஏம நெறிபடரும் ஆறு.

Men are loath to give up bodily pleasures.

Speech falters, they lean on a staff, and walk tottering, their teeth fall out; yet, till the vessel (*the body*) is scorned by all, they linger in the house, still indulging fond desires; to these no way of safety opens out.

See காறு : பிறர் பழிக்கும் அளவும், 'until (others) revile the (filthy, unsightly) vessel.' எ: ஆறு.—ப: இல்லை.

14.

இளமையை நிலை எனக் கருதி இல்வாழ்க்கையை விரும்பினோர்க்குத் துன்பமே அன்றி இன்பம் இல்லை.

தாழாத் தளராத் தலைநடுக்காத் தண்டூன்றா
வீழா இறக்கும் இவண்மாட்டுங்—காழில்லா
மம்மர்கொண் மாந்தர்க் கணங்காகுந் தன்கைக்கோல்
அம்மனைக்கோல் ஆகிய ஞான்று.

The cherished wife of your youth.

To men that cherish weak desire for her that's doomed to droop and fail, supporting her palsied limbs with a staff, and then to fall and pass away, what anguish comes, when she grasps in her hands the staff her mother held!

எ: அணங்கு.—ப: ஆகும். To whom? (தா . . . மாந்தர்க்கு.) When? (தன் . . . ஞான்று.)

There are different interpretations of the latter half of the quatrain: 'When she becomes decrepit as her mother did before her.'

15.

இவ்வுலகில் பிறவித்துன்பம் மிகுதி.

எனக்குத்தாய் ஆகியாள் என்னைஈங் கிட்டுத்
தனக்குத்தாய் நாடியே சென்றாள்;—தனக்குத்தாய்
ஆகி யவளும் அதுவானாற் றாய்த்தாய்க்கொண்
டேகும் அளித்திவ் வுலகு.

Endless series of successive generations.

My mother bare me, left me here, and went to seek her mother, who in the selfsame manner has gone in search; and thus in ceaseless round goes on the mother-quest. Such is the grace this world affords!

For the last line, comp. K. 336, where பெருமை is used in the same ironical manner. But see அளி.

For அது = 'in like manner, just so,' comp. 276.

அளித்து (G. 93. வினைக்குறிப்புமுற்று).

16.

இளமை நிலைஅன்று, ஆதலால் அதினால் வரும் களிப்பு அறிவுடையாரிடத்தில் இல்லை.

வெறிஅயர் வெங்களத்து வேன்மகன் பாணி
முறிஆர் நறுங்கண்ணி முன்னர்த் தயங்க,
மறிகுள குண்டன்ன மன்று மகிழ்ச்சி
அறிவுடை யாளர்கண் இல்.

The lamb before the sacrificer.

The lamb in the ruddy slaughter-house will crop the fragrant shoots that dangle from the garland in the slayer's hand; such transient gladness of the thoughtless, youthful hour is never found amid the wise.

எ: மகிழ்ச்சி.—ப: இல்.

This pathetic verse illustrates the thoughtlessness of youth. The scene may often be witnessed in S. India, and not a syllable of the description is out of place.

The sacrifice of animals is common to many sects, though slaughter of living creatnres is forbidden.

Comp. *Nīti*. 97. வெறி seems to be the wild dance of the *Pūjāri* or hierophant; and so the whole line is literally: '*in the awful place where they perform devil dances*.'

17.

இளமை நிலை அன்று; ஆகலின், மாதர் போகத்தை விரும்பினோர் பின்னர் வருந்துவர்.

பனிபடு சோலைப் பயன்மரம் எல்லாம்
கனிஉதிர்ந்து வீழ்ந்தற் றிளமை ;—நனி பெரிதும்
வேற்கண்ணள் என்றிவளை வெஃகன்மின்; மற்றிவளும்
கோற்கண்ணள் ஆகுங் குனிந்து.

Fruit only ripens to fall. Youth leads to decay.

The sweet fruit from every tree that bears in the dewy grove must fall to earth. Thus youth decays. Desire not her whose eyes gleam bright as darts. Full soon she too will walk bent down, with a staff to aid her dim sight.

எ: இளமை, (நீவிர்), இவள்.—ப: அற்று, வெஃகன்மின், ஆகும். வேற்கண்ணள் (III. G. 205. 93).

18.

அறிவுடையோர் உடம்பின் தன்மையை ஒருபொருளாக மதியார்.

பருவம் எனைத்துள ? பல்லின்பால் ஏனை ?
இருசிகையும் உண்டீரோ ? என்று—வ்ரிசையால்
உண்ணாட்டங் கொள்ளப் படுதலால், யாக்கைக்கோள்
எண்ணார் அறிவுடை யார்.

Constant anxieties about health.

'How old are you?' 'How last your teeth?' and, 'Do you eat two courses yet?' men ask with kindly courtesy. By such close questions urged, the wise will learn to judge the body as a thing of nought.

எ: அறிவுடையார்.—ப: எண்ணார்.
Comp. 284.

19.

இளமை நிலை அன்று, மரணம் உண்மை; ஆகலின், பொருள் உண்டான போழ்தே அறஞ்செய்க.

'மற்றறிவா நல்வினை, யாம் இளையம்' என்னாது
கைத்துண்டாம் போழ்தே கரவா தறஞ்செய்ம்மின்;
முற்றி இருந்த கனியொழியத் தீவளியால்
நற்காய் உதிர்தலும் உண்டு.

Against procrastination.

Say not, 'in after time we'll learn virtue, we're young;' but while wealth is yours conceal it not; do virtuous deeds. When evil tempests rage, not the ripe fruit alone, but the unripe fruit's fair promise also falls.

எ: சீர் (தொகை), உதிர்தல்.—ப: செய்ம்மின், உண்டு.—இளையம். G. 93.

Comp. 17. The poet says, fruit ripens only to fall; but some falls even before it is ripe. The longest and most prosperous life must end in death; but in immature age also death often occurs. Tamil has a wealth of words which English lacks; thus, in its first stage, new from the blossom, the apple is a பிஞ்சு; developed, but still immature it is காய் (19); when fully ripe it is கனி (17): 'fruit' in general is பழம்; and 'produce' is பயன்.

20.

மரணம் உண்மை என்பதைமறவாது இளமையிலேயே அறஞ் செயல் வேண்டும்.

ஆட்பார்த் துழலும் அருளில்கூற் றுண்மையால்
தோட்கோப்புக் காலத்தாற் கொண்டுய்ம்மின்;—பீட்பிதுக்கிப்
பிள்ளையைத் தாய்அலறக் கோடலான் மற்றதன்
கள்ளங் கடைப்பிடித்த னன்று.

The infant slain by death.

Relentless death is roaming round, and eyes his man! 'Tis true. Take up your wallet, scape betimes. He bears away the new-born babe, while the mother sorely laments. It is good to bear in mind his guile.

எ: சீர் (தொகை), பிடித்தல்.—ப: உய்ம்மின், நன்று.

Comp. 328.

In Ji. Chin. xiii. 336, 'செல்கதிக்காற்றுணாப்பெறாத, not obtaining food for the way to the goal whither they are tending.'

ஆற்றுணா = ஆற்றுக்கு வேண்டிய உணவு = பொதிசோறு = தோட்கோப்பு.

CHAPTER III.

THE BODILY FRAME ENDURES NOT.

அதிகாரம் ௩.

யாக்கை நிலையாமை

(=தேகம் நிலையாது என்னுந்தன்மை).

The perishable nature of the bodily frame.

Analysis:

1. Reckon up the roll of the mighty : none have escaped death. [21.]
2. See how suns rise and set : measuring off your life. [22.]
3. The marriage drum beats for the funeral too. [23.]
4. 'The dying bear forth the dead.' [24, 25.]
5. How vile the body reft of soul ! [26.]
6. A bubble. [27.]
7. A cloud on the hillside. [28.]
8. A dewdrop on the blade of grass. [29.]
9. The corpse a deserted nest on the tree. [30.]

21.

குறைவற்ற செல்வம் உடையராய் வாழ்ந்த அரசரும் இறந்தார்; ஆதலால் சரீரம் நிலை அன்று.

மலைமிசைத் தோன்று மதியம்போல் யானைத்
தலைமிசைக் கொண்ட குடையர்—நிலைமிசைத்
துஞ்சினர் என்றெடுத்துத் தூற்றப்பட் டார் அல்லால்
எஞ்சினர் இவ்வுலகத் தில்.

Mighty kings die.

Even kings that rode on elephants beneath the state umbrella's shade, like the moon appearing over some hill, have had their names proclaimed on earth as dead;—not any in this world have escaped.

எ: குடையர், எஞ்சினர்.—ப: பட்டார், இல்.—மலைமிசை. G. 63. குடையர். G. 93.
Comp. 3.

22.

இவ்வுலகத்து இறத்தலின்றி நிக்கினோர் ஒருவரும்இல்லை ; ஆதலால், இறப்பதற்கு முன் அறஞ்செய்க !

வாழ்நாட் கலகாய் வயங்கொளி மண்டிலம்
வீழ்நாட் படாஅ தெழுதலால்,—வாழ்நாள்
உலவாமுன் ஒப்புர வாற்றுமின்! யாரும்
நிலவார் நிலமிசை மேல்.

Time is fleeting,—use it.

As the measure of your days the shining orb each day unfailing rises; so before your joyous days have passed away, perform ye 'fitting deeds of grace'; for none abide on earth.

எ: நீர் (தொகை), யாரும்.—ப: ஆற்றுமின், நிலவார். நாட்கு = நாளுக்கு. வயங்கொளி. (வயங்கு, ஒளி.) G. 153. நிலவார் = நிலையார். (இதில் நிலை என்னும் பகுதிக்குப்பதிலாக நில என்பது வந்தது.)
Comp. 7 and K. ch. 34.

23.

அறிவுடையோர் தேகம் நிலைப்பது அன்று என்றுகருதி நற்கருமங்களையே செய்வர்.

மன்றங் கறங்க மணப்பறை ஆயின
அன்றவற் காங்கே பிணப்பறையாய்ப்—பின்றை
ஒலித்தலும் உண்டாம், என் றுய்ந்துபோம் ஆறே
வலிக்கும்ஆம் மாண்டார் மனம்.

Mutability of earthly joys.

The marriage drums that sounded out in the festive hall, there and that very day have served for him as funeral drums! Men of lofty minds will note that thus it haps, and will strive to gain the way to escape.

எ: மனம்.—ப: வலிக்கும்.—செயப்படு: ஆற்றை. ஆம், அசைநிலை.

24.

தேகம் அநித்தம், உலகத்தின் இயற்கை இகழத்தக்கது.

சென்றே எறிப ஒருகால்; சிறுவரை
நின்றே எறிப பறையினை;—நன்றேகாண்!
முக்காலைக் கொட்டினுண் மூடித்தீக் கொண்டெழுவர்,—
செத்தாரைச் சாவார் சுமந்து.

The funeral.

They march and then strike once! A little while they wait, then strike the drum a second time. Behold, how fine! The third stroke sounds. They veil *it*, take the fire, and go forth:—the dying bear the dead!

எ: அவர் (தொகை), சாவார்.—ப: எறிப, எழுவர்.—எறிப. G. 83. பறையினை. G. 65. கொட்டினுள். G. 63.

முக்காலைக் கொட்டினுள்=‘within the time of the third stroke.’ I take கொட்டு as a noun.

25.

இல்வாழ்க்கையில் இன்பம் உண்டென்பது புத்தியீனம்.

கணங்கொண்டு சுற்றத்தார் கல்லென் றலறப்
பிணங்கொண்டு காட்டுய்ப்பார்க் கண்டும்,—மணங்கொண்டீண்
டுண்டுண்டுண் டென்னும் உணர்வினாற் சாற்றுமே
தொண்டொண்டொ டென்னும் பறை.

Death pours contempt on human joys.

To him, who, although he sees them bear the corpse to the burning ground, while friends in troops loudly lament, boldly asserts that wedded life is bliss on earth, the funeral drum speaks out, and mocks his vain utterance.

எ: பறை.—ப: சாற்றும். தொண்டொண் டொடு என்பன ஒலிக்குறிப்பாகிய அடுக்குமொழிகள்.

உணர்விநற்(ன்)=உணர்வினவனுக்கு=புல்லறிவாளனுக்கு G. 35, 152, 93. K. 331.

[He says:— *uṇḍ' uṇḍ' uṇḍu* = it is! it is! it is!
and it says, with mocking echo:—
toṇḍ' oṇḍ' oṇḍu!]

26.

உயிர்நீங்கிய உடலை யாதுசெய்யினும் பழிப்பன்று.

நார்தொடுத் தீர்க்கில்என், நன்றுய்த் தடக்கில்என்,
பார்த்துழிப் பெய்யில்என், பல்லோர் பழிக்கில்என்,
தோற்பையு ணின்று தொழிலறச் செய்தூட்டும்
கூத்தன் புறப்பட்டக் கால்?

The dead body.

When the '*soul*,' that, taking its stand in this skin-clad frame, has fully wrought its works and partaken of life's experiences, has gone forth, what matters it whether you attach ropes to the body and drag it away, or carefully bury it, or throw it aside in any place you light upon, or *if* many revile the departed?

எ: வருவது (தொகை).—ப: என் (ஆகும்).

The words தொழிலறச்செய்து ஊட்டும் கூத்தன் may mean 'the deity who in union with the soul causes it to experience the fruit of works so that they are consumed.' See note on வினை.

Comp. Chhāndogya Up. VI. xi. 3, xv. 3.

தொழில் அற admits of three interpretations: (1) taken with புறப்பட்ட, 'when the soul which . . . has departed so that life's work comes to an end;' (2) taking it with செய்து and ஊட்டும், 'feeding it with life's joys and sorrows and so doing life's appointed tasks thoroughly;' or (3) as in note above.

27.

சரீரம் நிலையுள்ளதன்று என்றுநினைத்து பிறவித்துன்பத்தினின்று நீங்குதற்கேற்ற நற்கருமங்களைச்செய்யும் மூதறிவுடையார்க்கு ஒப்பாவார் ஒருவரும் இல்லை.

படுமழை மொக்குளிற் பலகாலுந் தோன்றிக்
கெடும்இதோர் யாக்கைஎன் றெண்ணித்—தடுமாற்றந்
தீர்ப்பேம்யாம் என்றுணருந் திண்ணறி வாளரை
நேர்ப்பார்யார் நீணிலத்தின் மேல்?

The body a bubble.

'Like a bubble, that in pelting rain appears full oft, and disappears, is this our frame.' So sages have judged, steadfast in wisdom, and have decided to end this dubious strife. On this wide earth who equal these?

எ: யார்.—ப: சேர்ப்பார். K. 336. இல்=போல. G. 61. (ஒப்பு.)

Comp. *Niti.* 1:

‘நீரிற் குமிழி இளமை; நிறைசெல்வம்
நீரிற் சுருட்டு நெடுந் திரைகள்;—நீரில்
எழுத்தாகும் யாக்கை; நமரங்காள், என்னே
வழுத்தாத தெம்பிரான் மன்று?

Youth is a bubble on the water; wealth's plenitude is as long waves that roll on its surface; this well-knit frame is writing traced on the water. My friends, why bow we not within the courts of Him, our Lord?'

28.

தேகம் நில்லாதாகலின் அதனைப்பெற்றதனால் ஆய அறப்பயனை விரைவிற் செய்துகொள்க.

யாக்கையை யாப்புடைத்தாப் பெற்றவர் தாம்பெற்ற
யாக்கையால் ஆய பயன்கொள்க!—யாக்கை
மலை ஆடு மஞ்சுபோற் றோன்றிமற் றாங்கே
நிலையாது நீத்து விடும்.

The body like a cloud on the hillside.

Those who've gained and held fast by this well-knit frame (a human body) should take the gain the body they have gained is intended to yield. Like a cloud that wanders over the hills, the body here appears, and abiding not, departs leaving no trace behind.

எ: பெற்றவர், யாக்கை.—ப: கொள்க, விடும்.

Comp. K. ch. xxxiv. The attainment in the round of the metempsychosis of a human form is hard (Jī. Chin. xiii. 151-5). *Tiru-takka-dēvar* says, 'it is as difficult for a soul to escape the infinitely numerous matrices in the universe, and obtain a human mother, as it would be for a peg cast into the Southern Ocean, to reach and adjust itself in the centre of a yoke floating in the farthest Northern Ocean:

[Metre: . . மா | . . விளம் | விளம் | விளம | . . மா.]

பரவை வெண்டிரை வடகடற் படு நுகத் துளையுள்
திரைசெய் தென்கடல் இட்டதோர் நோன்கழி சிவணி,
அரச! அத்துளை அகவயிற் செறிந்தென அரிதாற்
பெரிய யோனிகள் பிழைத்திவண் மானிடம் பெறவே.'

Having then through the grace of Çivam obtained this favourable position, so live as to obtain *Mutti* at the end of this brief stage of existence.

Comp. 34.

29.

உடம்பு கணப் பொழுதாயினும் நிலைப்பதன்று, ஆதலால் விரைவில் அறஞ்செய்க.

புன்னுனிமே னீர்போ னிலையாமை என்றெண்ணி,
இன்னினியே செய்க அறவினை!—இன்னினியே
நின்றான் இருந்தான் கிடந்தான்றன் கேள் அலறச்
சென்றான் எனப்படுத லான்.

The body like dew on the tip of a blade of grass.

Considering that all things are transient as the dew-drop on the tip of a blade of grass, now, now at once, do virtuous deeds! 'Even now he stood, he sat, he fell,—while his kindred cried aloud he died:' such is man's history!

எ: ஒருவன் (தொகை).—ப: செய்க.—செயப்படு: அறவினையை. புன்னுனி மேனீர் போனிலை யாமை = புல் நுனி மேல் நீர் போல் நிலையாமை. G. 39. எனப்படுதலான். G. 124. (1.)

30.

இறக்குந்துணையும் தம்மாற் பாதுகாக்கப்பட்டு இறக்குநாளிற் சொல்லா திறக்குமவரை உறவினர் என்று கருதி வீணாள்கழியாது விரைவில் அறஞ் செய்க.

கேளாதே வந்து கிளைகளா இற்றோன்றி
வாளாதே போவரால் மாந்தர்கள்,—வாளாதே
சேக்கை மரன்ஒழியச் சேணீங்கு புட்போல
யாக்கை தமர்க்கொழிய நீத்து.

All human relationships merely temporary.

Unasked men come, appear in the home as kinsmen, and then silently go. As the bird silently deserts the tree where its nest yet remains, and goes far off, so these leave but their body to their friends.

எ: மாந்தர்கள்.—ப: போவர்.—இற்றோன்றி = வீட்டில் தோன்றி. (G. 152, 38.) மரன் = மரம். (G. 17.) 152 பாட்டையுங் காண்க.

Comp. K. 338.

There is an infinite pathos in the words with which *Çachanthan* consoles (but consolation there is none!) *Vijayai*, his too fondly loved queen, on the eve of their separation (Jī. Chin. 270):

[Metre: . . விளம் | . . மா | . . மா *bis.*]

‘தொல்லைநம் பிறவி எண்ணில்
  தொடுகடல் மணலும் ஆற்றா
எல்லைய; அவற்றுள் எல்லாம்
  ஏதிலம்; பிறந்து நீங்கிச்
செல்லும் அக் கதிகடம்முட்
  சேரலம்; சேர்ந்துநின்ற
இல்லினுள் இரண்டுநாளைச்
  சுற்றமே;—இரங்கல் வேண்டா!

Count up our births of old, their bound exceeds the sands dug out of ocean's bed.—Strangers through all of these were we; and in those homes, through which, departing hence, we pass reborn, we shall not join again. Two days we met, and in one house abode. Lament not thou because this brief relationship is ended thus!'

CHAPTER IV.

THE MIGHT OF VIRTUE.

அதிகாரம் ௪.

அறன் வலியுறுத்தல்

(=அறமானது பொருள் இன்பங்களினும் வலியுடைத்தென்பது).

The fourth chapter of K. has the same title. The one idea is, that virtue is all that makes life worth living. What virtue is does not appear so clearly here as in the *Kurraḷ*. But see chapter vi.

Analysis:

This is a discursive chapter, of which the theme is the necessity of employing all life in charity and asceticism.

1. All but the virtuous excluded from bliss. [31.]
2. Man must steadily regard the end and use of life. [32, 39.]
3. A man must not be hindered by afflictions: they come from former deeds. [33.]
4. Use your period of human existence to gain future bliss: this is the sugar-cane's juice, the body is the dry refuse. [34, 35, 37.]
5. Against procrastination. [36.]
6. Virtue gains infinite reward. [38.]
7. Death better than life protracted for a brief space by dishonour. [40.]

31.

தவஞ்செய்யாதார் வீட்டினுள் புகப்பெறாது கடைப்புறத்தைப்பற்றி நின்று வருந்தி இருப்பர்.

அகத்தாரே வாழ்வாரென் றண்ணாந்து நோக்கிப்
புகத்தாம் பெறாஅர், புறங்கடை பற்றி
மிகத்தாம் வருந்தி இருப்பரே, மேலைத்
தவத்தாற் றவஞ்செய்யா தார்.

The door closed. Too late.

'Yes, those within are blest,' so saying, they look up, but obtain no entrance; their place is at the outer gate. There will they suffer much, who thro' lack of former penitence do no penance now. [In a former state penance won for them a human shape. As *men* they have now failed.]

For தவத்தால் some editions read தவற்றால் 'through fault' in a former state (மேலை). Through காமம், வெகுளி மயக்கம்—the three faults that make virtue impossible—they omitted penance in the former birth, and so they have not power or inclination to perform it now. (K. 372.)

For metre, G. 188. K. Introd. p. xxvi.

அகத்தாரே may = அகத்துக்குள்ளவர்தாமே, 'those within the house;' or அகத்து யாரே = 'within the house who (are living happily)?'

32.

பொருளைத்தேடி வீண்பொழுதுபோக்காது நன்முயற்சிகளையே நாளுஞ்செய்ய வேண்டும்.

ஆவாநாம் ஆக்க நசைஇ அறமறந்து
போவாநாம் என்னாப் புலைநெஞ்சே!—ஓவாது
நின்றுஞற்றி வாழ்தி எனினுநின் வாழ்நாள்கள்
சென்றன செய்வ துரை!

What wilt thou do in the end thereof?

Say not, O silly soul, we will live desiring wealth and die forgetting virtue! We'll say that ceaselessly toiling thou shalt live long; but tell me, what wilt thou do when all thy happy days are over?

எ: நீ (தொகை).—ப: உரை. வாழ்தி = வாழ்வாய். G. 83. செய்வது is object. G. 129*.

This quatrain is of a very quaint archaic type. Thus ஆவாம், நசைஇ, போவாம் (G. 77, 83), என்னா, வாழ்தி are all ancient forms.

நசைஇ = நசைந்து. Verbs in ஐ may take அளபெடை (G. 14) instead of the middle particle of the past tense. என்னா is neg. adv. part. for imp. என்னாதே. G. 90, 92.

Ellis, p. 87.

33.

தீவினைப் பயனை வெறுப்பின்றி அநுபவிக்கும் அறிவுடையாரே துன்பத்தினின்று நீங்குவோர் ஆவர்.

வினைப்பயன் வந்தக்கால் வெய்ய உயிரா
மனத்தின் அழியுமாம் பேதை ;—நினைத்ததனைத்
தொலைய தென்றுணர் வாரே தடுமாற்றத்
தெல்லை இகந்தொருவு வார்.

The wise accept the sorrows of life as retributive.

When the 'fruit of deeds' is come, the fool sighs heavily, and all his soul dies out; but those who reflect and say, ''Tis old desert,' will pass beyond the bound of life's perplexity, and escape (by devoting themselves to virtue).

எ: பேதை, உணர்வார்.—ப: அழியும், ஒருவுவார்.

Ellis, p. 87.

In the *Jīvaga Chintāmaṇi*, when the king *Çachanthan* is on the point of losing his kingdom and his life, he says to his idolised queen, whom he is sending to a place of safety (I. 240):

[Metre: . . விளம் | . . மா | . . மா *bis.*]

'சாதலும் பிறத்த ருனுக் தம்வினைப் பயத்தின் ஆகும்;
ஆதலும் அழிவும் எல்லாம் அவை; பொருட் இயல்பு கண்டாய்!
சோதலும் பரிவும் எல்லா நுண்ணுணர் வின்மை, அன்றே?
பேதை! நீ பெரிதும் பொல்லாய், பெய்வளைத் தோளி! என்ருன்.

Death and birth, too, are the fruit of men's deeds; so, too, all prosperity and ruin. This is the natural course of things. All grief and desire are signs of want of refined understanding. Is it not so? O silly one, whose arms are adorned with bracelets, thou art greatly in fault, said he.'

34.

உயிர்நீங்கிய உடம்பு பயன்படாதழியும் ஆகலின், அஃதுள்ள பொழுதே அழியாது உயிருடன்
செல்லுதற்குரிய அறப்பயனைச் செய்து கொள்ள வேண்டும்.

அரும்பெறல் யாக்கையைப் பெற்ற பயத்தால்
பெரும்பயனும் ஆற்றவே கொள்க!—கரும்பூர்ந்த
சாறுபோற் சாலவும் பின்னுதவி; மற்றதன்
கோதுபோற் போகும் உடம்பு.

Virtue is the gain. The body mere refuse.

As the gain from the mortal frame now reached—and which is so hard to reach—with all thy might lay hold of virtue's lasting good. As the juice expressed from the sugar-cane 'twill afterwards be thine aid, when the body goes like refuse flung away.

Comp. 28, 37; K. 36, and my notes.
The simile is found also in the next quatrain.
For அரும் பெறல் யாக்கை, comp. கலித், I. 5:

> 'அந்நாள் கொண்டிறக்கும் இவள் அரும்பெறல் உயிரே:
> That day will bear away her *precious* life.'

35.

மக்கள் யாக்கையைப் பெற்றதனால் ஆய அறப்பயனைச்செய்து கொண்டவர் மரணத்துக்கு அஞ்சார்.

கரும்பாட்டிக் கட்டி சிறுகாலைக் கொண்டார்
துரும்பெழுந்து வேங்காற் றுயர்ஆண் டுழவார்;
வருந்தி உடம்பின் பயன்கொண்டார் கூற்றம்
வருங்காற் பரிவ திலர்.

The same. The body only sapless stalks.

Those who have pressed the sugar-cane, and early taken the juice, when the refuse heaped up burns, will suffer no grief: those who have toiled and gained the fruit won from embodied existence will feel no pangs when death shall come.

36.

செய்யக் கூடுமான அறங்களை விரவிற் செய்து கொள்ளவேண்டும்.

இன்றுகொல், அன்றுகொல், என்றுகொல், என்னாது
பின்றையே நின்றது கூற்றம்என் றெண்ணி,
ஒருவுமின் தீயவை, ஒல்லும் வகையான்
மருவுமின் மாண்டார் அறம்.

Death stands waiting behind you. Delay not!

'This day?' 'That day?' 'What day?' O question not the time! Bethink you death stands behind you ever waiting! Put from you every evil thing; and with all your powers embrace the virtue which sages teach.

எ: நீவிர் (தொகை).—ப: ஒருவுமின், மருவுமின்.
Ellis, p. 87.
Comp. K. My ed. p. 197.

37.

தேகபோஷணைக்குரிய அறங்களையே செய்தொழுகாது வீடுபெறுதற்கேற்ற அறங்களைமிகுதியுஞ் செய்க.

மக்களால் ஆய பெரும்பயனும் ஆயுங்கால்
எத்துணையும் ஆற்றப் பலஆனால்—தொக்க
உடம்பிற்கே ஒப்புரவு செய்தொழுகா தும்பர்க்
கிடந்துண்ணப் பண்ணப் படும்.

Use the body to gain the world to come.

When you examine closely the mighty gains to be acquired by birth in a human shape, if they seem manifold, perform not deeds which suit the body's frame alone, but deeds whose fruit is joy in the world to come!

ஒப்புரவு. K. ch. xxii.
Comp. 28, 34.

38.

ஒருவன் சற்பாத்திரத்தில் அறஞ்செய்யின் அவ்வறஞ் சிறியதாயினும் அவரது தகுதி அளவாகப் பெருகும்.

உறக்குந் துணையதோர் ஆலம்வித் தீண்டி
இறப்ப நிழற்பயந் தாஅங்—கறப்பயனுந்
தான்சிறி தாயினுந் தக்கார்கைப் பட்டக்கால்
வான்சிறிதாப் போர்த்து விடும்.

A benefit conferred by the worthy on the worthy.

The banyan seed, though it be minute as one might see in dreams, grows to a mighty tree of amplest shade; so gifts from a virtuous hand, received by a worthy hand, though small, will hide the diminish'd heavens.

எ: பயன்.—ப: விடும்.
Ellis, p. 84.

39.

நாள்தோறும் நாட்கழிதலைத் தம்மாயுள்கழிதலாக நினைத்து அறஞ்செய்யாது அறிவிலார் அதனைப் பொழுது போக்காக எண்ணி இன்புறுவர்.

வைகலும் வைகல் வரக்கண்டும் அஃதுணரார்;
வைகலும் வைகலை வைகும், என் றின்புறுவர்;
வைகலும் வைகற்றம் வாழ்நாண்மேல் வைகுதல்
வைகலை வைத்துணரா தார்.

Days pass.

Daily they see the passing day added to the sum of the days gone by, as a day that is spent from out the store of their days; yet daily, as they see day dawn, they say joyously, 'This day will abide with us till the close of day.'

எ: உணராதார்.—ப: இன்புறுவர்.
This curious verse exhausts the meanings of வைகல்.
The last line means: 'at least we are sure of this day.'

40.

நான் இழிவினால் இவ்வுடம்பை ஊட்டிய விடத்தும் நெடுங்காலம் நில்லாது, ஆதலால் நான் மானம் என்னும் அணியை நீக்கி இரந்து வாழ்வதில்லை.

மான அருங்கல நீக்கி இரவென்னும்
ஈன இளிவினால் வாழ்வேன்மன்,—ஈனத்தால்
ஊட்டியக் கண்ணும் உறுதிசேர்ந் திவ்வுடம்பு
நீட்டித்து நிற்கும் எனின்!

Why should man maintain the perishable body by dishonourable begging?

Parting with honour's jewel I might still consent to live a suppliant's life of shame, if when maintained by such disgrace, this body could abide in strength and last for length of days.

This is fitter for ch. xxx.

CHAPTER V.

IMPURITY.

அதிகாரம் ரு.

தூய்தன்மை

(=சரீரஞ் சுத்தமுடையதன்றுஎன்னுந்தன்மை).

The essential impurity (of the human frame).

Analysis:

Man cannot rely on externals (such as wealth, ch. i, புறக்காரியங்கள்); he himself waxes old (ch. ii); his bodily frame decays (ch. iii); virtue alone is his strength (ch. iv); but the body tempts to sin. To enable him to overcome the lusts of the flesh, let him consider *the essential vileness of the body*. And

1. The body is a festering mass of corruption. [41.]
2. The body is a bag of skin hiding loathsomeness. [42.]
3. And no perfumes disguise its foulness. [43.]
4. Consider the eye. [44.]
5. The teeth. [45.]
6. Its internal composition. [46.]
7. Its outlets. [47.]
8. See it on the burning ground. [48.]
9. Listen to the message of the skulls on the burning ground. [49, 50.]

Nothing can surpass the disgusting realism of this morbid chapter.

41.

அறிவீனர் தேகம் அசுத்தம் என்று உணராமல் மாதரைப் புகழ்ந்து வீடடைய முயலார்.

மாக்கேழ் மடநல்லாய் என்றரற்றுஞ் சான்றவர்
நோக்கார்கொ லொன்பதோர் புக்கிலே?—யாக்கைக்கோர்
ஈச்சிறகன்னதோர் தோல்அறினும், வேண்டுமே
காக்கை கடிவதோர் கோல்.

Any slight wound may fester, and reduce the fairest form to a loathsome state.

'O gentle maiden, fair and good!' These paragons that thus rave, know they not 'the heavenly home invisible?' Let a bit of skin be broken slight as an insect's wing, and you need the stick that drives away the crows!

எ: சான்றவர், கோல்.—ப: நோக்கார் கொல், வேண்டும்.—செயப்படு: புக்கில். ஈச்சிறகன்ன = ஈயினது சிறகு போன்றது. கொல் = ஐயப்பொருளில் வந்த இடைச்சொல். G. 116. கடிவது = ஓட்டுவதற்கு.

Comp. K. 340.

நோக்கார் கொல் நொய்யதோர்புக்கில் = (K. புக்கில் அமைந்தின்று கொல்லோ) = is it because they do not regard the etherial home? சான்றவர் is ironical.

There is no chapter corresponding to this in the *Kurraḷ;* but in Jī. Chin. xiii. 162–201 (very striking verses) we recognise the same spirit. Everything that can be said in disparagement of the 'body of humiliation' is heaped up there. This is a characteristic of Jain works. In *Çaiva* books the standpoint is somewhat different.

A foundation is laid in this and the preceding chapters, (which are introductory,) for the doctrine of Renunciation (துறவு).

The leading idea in the chapter is, that the body is a deception, skin-covered foulness, essential impurity clothed in a fascinating manner. You cannot cleanse the utterly unclean body by any external, ceremonial ablutions. Get rid of it! And then, how unreasonable is love (i. e. lust)!

42.

மாதருடம்பினைப் புறத்தேகண்டு மகிழாது அதன் அகத்தத்தைக் கண்டருவருக்கவேண்டும்.

தோற்போர்வை மேலுந் தொளைபலவாய்ப் பொய்ம்மறைக்கும்
மீப்போர்வை மாட்சித் துடம்பானால்—மீப்போர்வை
பொய்ம்மறையாக் காமம் புகலாது மற்றதனைப்
பைம்மறியாப் பார்க்கப் படும்.

The body's beauty only skin-deep.

If the body which, with a covering of skin above, possesses many apertures, owes its beauty only to that outward cloak that veils the false (*the inner foulness*), then is it fitting to say no word of lustful desire which hides the false from itself by the covering veil, but to regard that body as an undeveloped embryo.

பைம்மறி is ambiguous = 'a foal in a sac.'

Comp. 47. See படும் in Lex.

43.

உடம்பினைப்புறத்தே அழகுசெய்வதனால் அதனகத்துள்ள அசுத்தம் நீங்குவதன்று.

தக்கோலந் தின்று தலைநிறையப் பூச்சூடிப்
பொய்க்கோலஞ் செய்ப ஒழியுமே—எக்காலும்
உண்டி வினையுள் உறைக்கும் எனப்பெரியோர்
கண்டுகை விட்ட மயல்.

Outward adornment is not inward purification.

Will impurity ever cease from the worthless body which the great have abandoned, knowing it to be reeking with odours from processes connected with nutrition, though aromatics be chewed, the head covered with garlands, and the body adorned with false splendour?

The subj. is மயல், with which is understood அசுத்தம், 'the impurities of this vile body.' Pred. is ஒழியுமே, 'will they cease, be removed, pass away?'

44.

கீழோர் மாதரைப்புகழின் அறிவுடையார் மனநிலைதளரார்.

'தெண்ணீர்க் குவளை பொருகயல் வேல்' என்று
கண்ணில் புன்மாக்கள் கவற்ற விடுவேனோ,
உண்ணீர் களைந்தக்கா ணுங்குசூன் றிட்டன்ன
கண்ணீர்மை கண்டொழுகு வேன்.

Female eyes shall not bewilder me!

Shall I abandon (my ascetic purpose) because blind, low men worry me, saying (that woman's eye is like) the water-lily in the clear stream, or the warring carp, or a javelin? I will pursue my virtuous way as having seen (that) the eye's real nature (is), like (that of) the palm-tree fruit (which is) scooped out, after the water has been drained off!

எ: நான் (தொகை).—ப: விடுவேனோ. தெண்ணீர் = தெள், நீர். உண்ணீர் = உள்நீர். G. 39.

ஒழுகுவேன் in this and the next verse may be a finite verb = 'I will go on my way;' or it may be a participial noun = 'I who lead a well-ordered life.' G. 95.

45.

சுடுகாட்டின் உதிர்ந்துகிடக்கிற பற்களைக்கண்டு செல்கின்ற நான் அப்பற்களை முல்லையரும்பென்றும் முத்தென்றுஞ் சொல்லிப் புல்லிய மக்கள் என்மனத்தைக் கவலைப்படுத்தத் துறவை விட்டுநீங்குவேனோ?

முல்லை முகைமுறுவன் முத்தென் றிவைபிதற்றுங்
கல்லாப் புன்மாக்கள் கவற்ற விடுவெனோ?
எல்லாருங் காணப் புறங்காட் டுதிர்ந்துக்க
பல்லென்பு கண்டொழுகு வேன்.

The beauty of women's teeth shall not bewilder me.

Though worthless men untaught should fret my soul and rave of teeth like jasmine buds and pearls, shall I forego my fixed resolve, who have seen in the burning ground those bones—the fallen teeth—strewn round for all to see?

எ: யான் (தொகை).—ப: விடுவேனோ.
[Here ஒழுகுவேன் is taken as part. noun. See note to 44.]

46.

மூடர் காமநுகர்ச்சியை விரும்பி அசுத்தம் என்று அருவருக்காத மாதர் உருவங் கண்டு மகிழ்வர்.

குடருங் கொழுவுங் குருதியும் என்பும்
தொடரு நரம்பொடு தோலும்—இடையிடையே
வைத்த தடியும் வழும்பும்ஆம்; மற்றிவற்றுள்
எத்திறத்தாள் ஈர்ங்கோதை யாள்?

'This vile body.'

(The body) is entrails, and marrow, and blood, and bone, and connecting tendons, and skin, and here and there flesh interposed, and fat. In the midst of these, what sort of a being is she who wears the fresh garlands?

47.

உடம்பு யாவரும் வெறுக்கத்தக்க அசத்தமுடையது.

ஊறி உவர்த்தக்க ஒன்பது வாய்ப்புலனுங்
கோதிக் குழம்பலைக்குங் கும்பத்தைப்—பேதை,
'பெருந்தோளி,' 'பெய்வளாய்' என்னு மீப் போர்த்த
கருந்தோலாற் கண்விளக்கப் பட்டு.

The body disgusting.

The fool will address the earthen pot (the body), from which defilement oozes, which from nine disgusting outlets scatters pollution, and in which slimy liquids move to and fro,—and say, 'O thou of the rounded arms,' 'O thou with armlets decked,'—because it is made bright to his eyes by a covering of black skin.

எ: பேதை.—ப: என்னும்.—செ. ப: கும்பத்தை. Comp. 42.

48.

உடலின் அசுத்தத்தை அறியாத கீழோர் அதனைக் கலவைச்சாந்து முதலியவற்றால் அலங்கரித்து மகிழ்வர்.

பண்டம் அறியார், படுசாந்துங் கோதையுங்
கொண்டு பாராட்டுவார்; கண்டிலர் கொல்—மண்டிப்
பெடைச்சேவல் வன்கழுகு பேர்த்திட்டுக் குத்தும்,
முடைச்சாகா டச்சிற் றுழி?

The body a prey to corruption.

They know not what the body is; with sandal paste and flowers they make it fine. Have they not seen, I pray, the vultures and their mates in flocks with busy beaks devour the body foul when the chariot-axle is snapt?

Comp. Jī. Chin. xiii. 23, for the figure.

The பண்டி is the body; the அச்சு is the living, embodied soul, or உயிர்.

'உழந்தாலும் புத்தச்சொண் றிட்டேத றேற்று
திழந்தார் பலரால், இமைபகீர் யாற்றுள்
அழுந்துமால், அப்பண்டி அச்சிறு முன்னே
கொளுஞ்சிலங் கூலியாக் கொண்டேர்மின், பாகீர்!

Ye charioteers,—since many, toiling hard, and not finding it possible to obtain a new axle and ride on, have lost (their car); and, since in the river, whose stream is trouble, the car will be submerged,—before the axle of that car snap, take goodness, which is in your power, as your guerdon and drive on!'—(புத்தச்சு = புதிய அச்சு.)

49.

உடல்தூயதன்று, ஆதலின் தூய்மையாகிய வீட்டுநெறியில் நிற்க வேண்டும்.

கழிந்தார் இடுதலை கண்டார் நெஞ்சுட்கக்
குழிந்தாழ்ந்த கண்ணவாய்த் தோன்றி — ஒழிந்தாரைப்
போற்றி நெறிநின்மின் இற்றிதன் பண்பென்று
சாற்றுங்கொல் சாலச் சிரித்து.

The eyeless skulls teach.

The skulls of the dead, at the sight of which the gazer fears, with deep cavernous eyes appear, and grinning say to those who still survive, 'Guard well! In virtue's path stand fast. This is the body's grace and worth.'

எ: தலை.—ப: சாற்றும்.

50.

உடம்பு தூய்மையையுடையது அன்றென்று அறிந்த மேலோர் தம்மை ஒருபொருளாக மதியார்.

உயிர்போயார் வெண்டலை உட்கச் சிரித்துச்
செயிர்தீர்க்குஞ் செம்மாப் பவரை; — செயிர்தீர்ந்தார்
கண்டிற் றிதன்வண்ணம் என்பதனாற் றம்மைஓர்
பண்டத்துள் வைப்ப திலர்.

The sight of the skulls cures pride.

The skulls of the dead, grinning so as to excite disgust, cure the vain lovers of life of their folly. Those who are cured of this folly, seeing (the skulls in the burning ground), say 'such is this body,' and so value themselves as nothing.

Comp. Jī. Chin. xiii. 21, where வெண்டலை occurs:

'முருந்தனைய தாமுறுவன் முற்றிழையார் சேரி
இருந்திளமைக் கள்ளுண் டிடைதெரிதல் இன்றிக்
கருந்தலைகள் வெண்டலைகள் ஆய்க்கழியா முன்னே,
அருந்தவமுந் தானமும் ஆற்றுமினே, கண்டீர்!

Behold! perform ye rare penances and give gifts, before the dark heads become white heads (*skulls in the burning ground*, or *grey*), even while you still abide in the home of those whose teeth are pure white, like the young palm's shoot, drinking the intoxicating wine of youth, with no perception of aught else!'

CHAPTER VI.

RENUNCIATION.

அதிகாரம் ௬.

துறவு.

Comp. K. ch. xxxv and xxvii.

துறவு is defined: புறம்பாகிய செல்வத்தின் கண்ணும் அகமாகிய உடலின் கண்ணும் உண்டாகிய பற்றை அவற்றின் நிலையாமையை நோக்கி விடுதலாம்: 'the relinquishment of all attachment to worldly wealth without, and to the body within (the lusts of the flesh), in view of their impermanency.'

Convinced of the instability of all things without (புறம்) and within (அகம்); feeling that virtue alone has power; and made sensible of the innate impurity of the flesh, nothing remains but that man should betake himself to the highest form of virtue, asceticism (துறவறம்). This includes தவம், ascetic life, which is the real subject of the chapter.

But the student may here with advantage compare Jī. Chin. ch. xiii, § 26, verses 384, *etc.* There the author's real intention is unfolded. Queen Vijayai and her son have drunk deeply of the cup of all human enjoyment, and at last betake themselves to the desert.

The analysis is:

1. Light now dawns on the ascetic, and darkness flees away; [51]
2. but he must not be misled by vain philosophy. [52.]
3. Nor do the wise delay; for they discern [53]
4. the unreal and transitory character of pleasure. [54, 60.]
5. Yet the mind hesitates, loath to take the decisive step; [55] for
6. wife and home detain men. [56.]
7. Perseverance is the crowning virtue; [57]
8. and this must be accompanied by meekness and compassion, though themselves contemned. [58.]
9. Sensual desires must be thoroughly subdued. [59.]

It will be manifest that, as far as this book reveals it, the system takes no account of God. Man—the embodied living principle (உயிர்)—is in face of nature (இம்மை), of deeds of some former existence (ch. xi), and of a higher state or states which he may reach (அம்மை, மறுமை); and by ascetic virtue is to work his way, unaided, to some undefined goal. Existence has many painful stages (பிறப்பு), its prison-houses (நிரயம்), and its palaces (சுவர்க்கம்); but release from all sentiency (வீடு) is the prize to be ultimately won.

The poet (or poets) occasionally refers to gods and immortals, in a conventional way, as poetic machinery, but God is not alluded to in the whole of the 'Yeoman's Bible' (வெள்ளாளர்வேதம்). This is to be understood from the Jain point of view; but it differentiates the book from the *Kurral*, and renders it an inadequate exponent of South-Indian religious thought. Its literary value is nevertheless indisputable.

51.

துறந்துதவஞ்செய்வோர்க்குப் பாவமில்லை; செய்யாதார்க்குத்தீவினைசென்றடர்த்து நிற்கும்.

விளக்குப் புகஇருண் மாய்ந்தாங் கொருவன்
தவத்தின்முன் னில்லாதாம் பாவம்! — விளக்குநெய்
தேய்விடத்துச் சென்றிருள் பாய்ந்தாங்கு நல்வினை
தீர்விடத்து நிற்குமாந் தீது.

Penitence puts sin to flight.

As when a lamp enters darkness dies, so sin stands not before man's penitence. As, when in a lamp the oil wastes, darkness rushes in, so evil takes its stand where deeds of virtue cease.

52.

அறிவுடைய முதன்மையோர் நிலையாமையை உணர்ந்து துறந்து தவஞ்செய்வார். அறிவிலார் சத்தநூல் முதலியவை பொருளாக ஓதி வீண்பொழுது போக்குவார்.

நிலையாமை நோய்மூப்புச் சாக்காடென் றெண்ணித்
தலையாயார் தங்கருமஞ் செய்வார்; — தொலைவில்லாச்
சத்தமுஞ் சோதிடமும் என்றாங் கிவைபிதற்றும்
பித்தரிற் பேதையர் இல்.

Put away useless studies.

The chief of men reflect on change, disease, old age, and death, and do their needful work. Those who raving teach the endless round of sevenfold science, and the lore of stars, are maddest of the foolish throng.

Comp. K. ch. xxxiv, p. 243.

53.

அறிவுடையார் குடிப்பிறப்புமுதலிய யாவும் நிலையல்ல என்றுகருதி விரைவில் துறந்து வீடுபெறுவர்.

இல்லம் இளமை எழில்வனப்பு மீக்கூற்றம்
செல்வம் வலிஎன் றிவைஎல்லாம் — மெல்ல
நில்லாமை கண்டு நெடியார் துறப்பர்
தலையாயார் தாம்உய்யக் கொண்டு.

Renunciation at once.

The chief of men in quiet thought discern how house, and youth, and beauty's grace, and high estate, and wealth, and strength, all pass away; and thus, to save themselves, prolonging not the time, renounce all these.

The verses in Tamil which dwell on this theme are very numerous. Comp. *Ēlā.* 20;

> 'இளமை கழியும், பிணிமூப்பியையும்,
> வளமை வலியிவை வாடும்;
> உளநாளால்
> பாடே புரியாது, பால் போலுஞ் சொல்லினாய்!
> வீடே புரிதல் விதி:

Youth passes swiftly away, disease and eld draw nigh, bright flowers of wealth and strength fade fast. While life is thine, desire not earth's gifts, (thou whose words as milk are sweet!) desire release. The law is this.'

See N. M. K. 49, 59.

54.

அறிவிலார் அற்ப இன்பத்தைத் தருவதாகிய இல்வாழ்க்கையை இச்சிப்பர்; அறிவுடையார் அதனை விரும்பாது துறப்பர்.

துன்பம் பலநாள் உழந்தும் ஒருநாளை
இன்பமே காமுறுவர் ஏழையார்; — இன்பம்
இடைதெரிந் தின்னாமை நோக்கி மனையா
றடைவொழிந்தார் ஆன்றமைந் தார்.

Pleasure and pain.

Though wretched men suffer afflictions many a day, yet one day's delight they eagerly desire. The men of calm and full wisdom, in pleasure's core see pain, and quit the pleasant household paths.

Comp. K. 202; and 60, which seems another version.

55.

விடயங்களிற் சென்று வீணுள்கழித்தல் கலமன்று.

கொன்னே கழிந்தன் றிளமையும், இன்னே
பிணியொடு மூப்பும் வரும்ஆல்,—துணிவொன்றி
என்னொடு சூழா தெழுநெஞ்சே! போதியோ
நன்னெறி சேர நமக்கு?

Unreflecting soul, why not seek the way of peace?

In vain is my youth spent. Even now disease and old age will come. O soul! be bold; wrangle no more with me, but rise! Wilt thou not go where both thou and I may gain virtue's path?

ள: தீ.—ப: போதியோ.—போதியோ. G. 83.

56.

இல்வாழ்க்கையினுல் துன்பமே அன்றி, இன்பம் இல்லை; ஆதலால் அறிவுடையார் அதனைத்துறப்பர்.

மாண்ட குணத்தொடு மக்கட்பே றில்லெனினும்
பூண்டான் கழித்தற் கருமையால்,—பூண்ட
மிடிஎன்னுங் காரணத்தின் மேன்முறைக் கண்ணே
கடிஎன்றார் கற்றறிந் தார்.

Marriage to be dreaded.

Though your wife possess no excellence and bear no child, it is hard to get rid of the marriage bond. For this cause since he who weds puts sorrow on, in olden days the learned made *marriage* a synonym of *dread*.

[A play on கடி, which means, among many other things, 'marriage' and 'dread.']

57.

துறந்தோர் தாஞ்சென்ற நல்லொழுக்கவழியிலே தவறாது நிற்றல் வேண்டும்.

ஊக்கித்தாங் கொண்ட விரதங்கள் உள்ளுடையத்
தாக்கருந் துன்பங்க டாந்தலை வந்தக்கால்
நீக்கி நிறூஉம் உரவோரே நல்லொழுக்கம்
காக்குந் திருவத் தவர்.

Patience and perseverance.

When troubles arise, hard to resist, to cause them to break the vows which their lofty spirits have pledged, the men of power set griefs aside, and firmly fix their souls in right. These are the blessed, guarding '*decorum's*' rule.

For ஒழுக்கம் see *Kurral*, ch. xiv.

58.

துறந்த ஞானிகள் இகழ்ந்துபேசுவோரது அறியாமைக்கு இரங்குவார்.

தம்மை இகழ்ந்தமை தாம்பொறுப்ப தன்றிமற்
றெம்மை இகழ்ந்த வினைப்பயத்தால் — உம்மை
எரிவாய் நிரயத்து வீழ்வர்கொல், என்று
பரிவதூஉஞ் சான்றோர் கடன்.

Forbearance and pity for evil-doers.

To bear with those that speak contemptuous words; yea, more, to say, 'Ah, will these sink in the other world to hell, the place of fire, as fruit of their contemptuous words;' and to grieve, is duty of the perfect man.

T. 13: '. . . . . . வடுவின்றி
மாண்ட குணத்தான் தவசி:

He is a (true) ascetic who is faultless and possessed of eminently good qualities.'

59.

ஐந்தாசைகளையும் அறுத்தவன் வீடடைவான்.

மெய்வாய்கண் மூக்குச் செவிஎனப் பேர்பெற்ற
ஐவாய வேட்கை அவாவினைக்—கைவாய்
கலங்காமற் காத்துய்க்கும் ஆற்றலுடையான்
விலங்காது வீடு பெறும்.

Repression of sensuous emotions.

He who undisturbed, in the ordered way of right, has power to guard and guide the desires and lusts that find entrance by the five sense-gates, called 'body, mouth, eye, nose, and ear'—unfailing shall gain 'release.'

எ: உடையவன்.—ப: பெறும். G. 137.

Comp. T. 61, ஐ = ஐம்பொறி, 'five organs of sense.'

ஐவாய, 'which pertain to the five "ways" or "inlets":' வாய். This is குறிப்புவினைஎச்சம். G. 93. Such plural neuter forms in அ (நல்ல) are either (1) predicates, இவை நல்ல = 'these are good,' when they are குறிப்புவினைமுற்று; or (2) adjective enlargements, நல்ல மனிதர், when they are called குறிப்புவினை எச்சம், after the analogy of G. 87.

See K. ch. iii, and Ellis, p. 72. வேட்கை அவாவினை is either an example of G. 156, or of 154.

'ஐயறிவுந் தம்மை அடைய ஒழுகுதல்: the course of life in which knowledge of the five is under one's controul: when a man uses, but firmly controuls, his senses.' T. 61.

'செய்வகை செய்வான் தவசி: he is the true ascetic that fulfils—as they should be fulfilled—the obligations he has taken on himself.'

T. 43:

'. . . . . . பொய்யின்றி
நெஞ்சம் அடங்குதல் வீடாகும்:

The soul's yielding to moral discipline, in perfect truth, is *release*.'

And T. 80.

With regard to the doctrines here taught in relation to asceticism (தவம்), those who feel an interest in exploring the bye-paths of the history of quasi-religious thought, may compare the accounts of the Béguins (or Béguards), a sect of heretics or schismatics, that arose in the 13th century, in Germany and France, in the bosom of the church. Some of these still survive in the neighbourhood of Saint Etienne. These even taught the doctrine of the metempsychosis.

60.

கீழோர் உலக இன்பத்தையை விரும்புவார். மேலோர் வீட்டை விரும்புவார்.

துன்பமே மீதூரக் கண்டுந் துறவுள்ளார்
இன்பமே காமுறுவர் ஏழையார்; — இன்பம்
இசைதொறு' மற்றத னின்னுமை நோக்கிப்
பசைதல் பரியாதா' மேல்.

The bitter pleasures of life.

Though wretched men behold afflictions urge and press, *renunciation* is not in their thoughts; delight they eagerly desire. The great in every joy behold its pain, and seek it not.

எ: ஏழையார், மேல். — ப: காமுறுவர், பரியாது. — செ: இன்பம், பசைதல்.

Comp. 54.

CHAPTER VII.

THE ABSENCE OF ANGER: MEEKNESS.

அதிகாரம் எ.

சினமின்மை

(= கோபஞ்செய்யாதிருக்கை: வெகுளாமை).

The subject is patient endurance of reproaches, slights and injuries; and is essentially the same as ch. viii.

In the *Kurraḷ*, ch. xxxi, வெகுளாமை corresponds with this; but see also ch. xvi.

The practical part of the work begins here, the six preceding chapters having rather shown the necessity of virtue than explained its character.

Compared with the *Kurraḷ*, the present work is weak in its formal ethical teaching.

Here anger is forbidden; and in ch. viii, forbearance is inculcated: meekness and patience are the greatest virtues. In ch. ix, adultery and lust are condemned. Ch. x inculcates liberality. Ch. xi teaches submission to the decrees of destiny. Ch. xii insists on reality. Ch. xiii is on the fear of evil. This is the sum of the doctrine of virtue.

This chapter refers to all, but 'anger' seems to have been the 'last infirmity' of many ascetics, as Hindu stories testify. *Durvāsa* is a noted example.

The analysis of the chapter is:

1. Do not be concerned about the way the world treats you; [61]
2. nor renounce life in disgust; [62]
3. nor be provoked into the use of passionate words; but [63]
4. bear with composure angry words. [64.]
5. Forbearance is most excellent in the mightiest, and [65]
6. meekness is instinctive in noble minds. [66.]
7. Avoid all conflicts. [67.]
8. Good men's anger dies of itself. [68.]
9. The noble persist in goodness, even to the unthankful and evil. [69.]
10. An illustration: No one bitten by a dog bites it in return. [70.]

Comp. the following:

Ēlā. 61: 'பேணாச்சினம் = ungoverned wrath.'

Ēlā. 19: 'கடுங்கதம் = cruel rage.'

Ēlā. 21: 'கொள்ளோவெகுளான் = he yields not to causeless anger.'

N. M. K. 3: '. . . . . . உள்சுடினும்
சீறற்க சிற்றிற் பிறந்தாரை:

Be not wrath with low-born persons, tho' your heart be hot within you.'

N. M. K. 17: '. . . . . . வெல்வது
வேண்டின் வெகுளி விடல்:

If you would conquer, let go anger!'

N. M. K. 41: '. . . . . . முனியாதார்
முன்னிய செய்யுந் திரு:

Fortune will accomplish the desires of those who wax not angry.'

N. M. K. 61: 'இனியன் எனப்படுவான் யார்யார்க்கே யானும்
முனியா ஒழுக்கத் தவன்:

He whose way of life is freed from anger against any shall be called a pleasant man.'

N. M. K. 82: '. . . . . . கெடுப்பின்
வெகுளி கெடுத்து விடல்:

If a man will destroy anything, let him destroy anger!'

T. 14: '. . . . . . யாண்டும்
செறுவொடு நிற்குஞ் சிறுமை . . .:

Meanness ever abides with anger: the mean are implacable.'

Among vain things is reckoned (in T. 54)

'. . . . . . தாம்பயவா
நன்பயங் காய்வின்கட் கூறல்:

The utterance in heat of passion of great threats that come to nothing.' [Play on பயம=*fear*, and பய=*yield profit.*]

61.

தம்மை அவமதிக்குங் கீழோரைக் கோபியாதிருத்தலே அறிவுடையோர்க்கழகு.

மதித்திறப் பாரும் இறக்க! மதியா
மிதித்திறப் பாரும் இறக்க!—மிதித்தேறி
ஈயுந் தலைமேல் இருத்தலால் அஃதறிவார்
காயுங் கதமின்மை நன்று.

Disregard of the esteem or disesteem of men.

Who pass esteeming us, let them pass on! And those who contemn and trample on us as they pass, let them too pass on! If even a fly (*especially unclean*) should climb, trampling on their head, it is well that the wise who know its worth, should feel no wrath.

எ: கதமின்மை,—ப: நன்று. K. 130. இறக்க. C. 108.

62.

பிறவித்துன்பங்களை மனவெறுப்பின்றிப் பொறுப்பர் உயர்ந்தோர்.

தண்டாச் சிறப்பிற்றம் இன்னுயிரைத் தாங்காது
கண்டுழி எல்லாந் துறப்பவோ?—மண்டி
அடிபெயரா தாற்ற விளிவந்த போழ்தின்
முடிகிற்கும் உள்ளத் தவர்.

முடிகிற்கும்=முடிக்கும் (இன் inserted + கு). G. 108.

Resolute men bear meekly the evils of life.

Although disgraces throng thickly, and may not be repulsed, will those whose minds are set upon finishing the work begun, renounce sweet life's unfailing worth in their impatience, whenever they see (evils)?

சிறப்பின். G. 65, 38. எ: உள்ளத்தவர்.—ப: துறப்பவோ.

The question debated is, whether a good man may in angry impatience throw away his life, so losing the opportunities afforded by his birth as man: Hamlet's question, 'To be or not to be?' The idea of K. 970 seems opposed to this verse.

In N. M. K. 4 it is said,

'குறைபட வாழார் உரவோர்:

The magnanimous survive not disgrace;' and

'தனக்கொவ்வாச்சொற்பட்டாற் சாவதாஞ்சால்பு:

Greatness dies if subjected to unworthy reproach.'

The same idea, that a man should not survive the loss of his honour, is expressed in *Nîti.* 41:

'தம்முடை ஆற்றலும் மானமுந் தோற்றுத்தம்
இன்னுயிர் ஓம்பினும் ஓம்புக,—பின்னர்ச்
சிறுவரை ஆயினும் மன்ற தமக்காங்
கிறுவரை இல்லை எனின்:

If any would cherish sweet life, having incurred the loss of strength and honour, let them cherish it; if only they can be sure of immunity even for a little while from death.'

63.

அறிவுடையார் யாவரையுங்கோபித்துக் கடுஞ்சொற்சொல்லார்.

காவா தொருவன்றன் வாய்திறந்து சொல்லுஞ்சொல்
ஓவாதே தன்னைச் சுடுதலால்—ஓவாதே
ஆய்ந்தமைந்த கேள்வி அறிவுடையார் எஞ்ஞான்றும்
காய்ந்தமைந்த சொல்லார் கறுத்து.

Rashness in speech hurts one's self.

If a man open his mouth and speak unguarded words, his words will ceaselessly burn his soul. The wise who ceaselessly hear, and ponder well and calmly, even in their wrath, will never give utterance to words of fire.

எ: அறிவுடையார்.—ப: சொல்லார். Comp. my K. p. 220.

64.

மேலோர் பிறர்வைதவசையை எண்ணிக்கோபங்கொள்ளார்; கீழோர் அதைப்பலமுறை எண்ணி வருந்துவர்.

நேர்த்து நிகரல்லார் நீரல்ல சொல்லியக்கால்
வேர்த்து வெகுளார் விழுமியோர்,—ஓர்த்ததனை
உள்ளத்தான் உள்ளி உரைத்துராய் ஊர்கேட்பத்
துள்ளித்தூண் முட்டும் ஆங் கீழ்.

The good man's meekness. The low man's ungoverned fury.

When men who are beneath them confront them, and speak unseemly words, the excellent wax not hot with anger. The base man will brood over it, chafe and rave for all the town to hear, and leap, and dash his head against a post.

எ: விழுமியோர், கீழ்.—ப: வெகுளார், முட்டும்.—ஓர்த்து = ஓர்ந்து; நேர்த்து = நேர்ந்து. G. 41. உராய் = உராவி.

In N. M. K. 10: 'எல்லாம் வெகுண்டார் முற்றேன்றுக் கெடும், rage blinds men.'

65.

இளையான் அடக்கமும் வறியவன் கொடையும் ஆற்றலுடையான்பொறுமையும் உத்தமம்.

இளையான் அடக்கம் அடக்கம்; கிளைபொருள்
இல்லான் கொடையே கொடைப்பயன்?—எல்லாம்
ஒறுக்கு மதுகை உரனுடை யாளன்
பொறுக்கும் பொறையே பொறை.

Self-restraint in youth, gifts from the poor, and forbearance in the mighty are excellent.

The young man's self-restraint is self-restraint. The gift of him who owns no stores of wealth is gift indeed. When man has means and might to punish every fault, if he forbear, call him the patient man.

எ; அடக்கம், கொடை, பொறை. பயனிலையும் அவையே.—உரன் = உரம். G. 17.
Comp. K. 152, p. 223. This really belongs to the next chapter.
So Shakespeare on Mercy: *'tis mightiest in the mightiest.*

66.

நற்குடியிற் பிறந்தோர் பிறர்தம்மை இகழின் அவர் மேற் கோபங்கொள்ளார்.

கல்லெறிந் தன்ன கயவர்வாய் இன்னாச்சொல்
எல்லாருங்காணப் பொறுத்துய்ப்பர், — ஒல்லை
இடுநீற்றாற் பைஅவிந்த நாகம்போற் றத்தம்
குடிமையான் வாதிக்கப் பட்டு.

Noble instinct restrains.

As stones the base shower down their bitter words: the noble bear, in sight of all, and let them pass, by sense of noble worth constrained: like serpent's crest at once by touch of sacred ash subdued.

The idea is that sacred ashes sprinkled on a cobra lower its crest at once and subdue it. (See சைவவினாவிடை, p. 38.) நீறு (திருநீறு, விபூதி, பசிதம், பசுமம், க்ஷாரம், இரக்ஷை) is the ash from burnt cow-dung. For குடிமை, see K. ch. 96.
The subject is நற்குடியிற்பிறந்தோர்—'the noble'—understood.

67.

தீங்கு செய்தோர்க்கு எதிர்செய்யாமையே அறிவுடையார்க்கு அழகு.

மாற்றாராய் நின்றுதம் மாறேற்பார்க் கேலாமை
ஆற்றாமை என்னார் அறிவுடையார்; — ஆற்றாமை
நேர்த்தின்னா மற்றவர் செய்தக்காற் றாம்அவனைப்
பேர்த்தின்னா செய்யாமை நன்று.

Return not evil for evil.

When men stand forth as our enemies, and would begin the conflict, to decline the strife is not, in the language of the wise, lack of power. Even when men have confronted and done us intolerable evils, it is good not to do them evil in return.

எ: அறிவுடையார், செய்யாமை.—ப: என்னுர், நன்று.

Here an absolute peace policy is taught: 'to decline a challenge is no sign of weakness, and not to avenge oneself is virtue.' Comp. K. 861, which is less heroic in strain.

68.

இழிந்தோர் கோபந் தணியாது வளரும்; மேலோர் கோபந்தானேதணியும்.

நெடுங்காலம் ஓடினு நீசர் வெகுளி
கெடுங்காலம் இன்றிப் பரக்கும்;—அடுங்காலை
நீர்கொண்ட வெப்பம் போற் றானே தணியுமே
சீர்கொண்ட சான்றோர் சினம்.

The wrath of the base never expends itself. That of the good of itself dies out.

Long time though base men's wrath run on, it spreads abroad, and knows no time when heat is spent; as the heat of water, when boiled at cooking time, itself grows cool, the ire of perfect men of worth abates.

எ: வெகுளி, சினம்.—ப: பரக்கும், தணியும்.

For வெகுளி comp. K. 309. In T. 93, 95 வெகுள்வு is found.

69.

நற்குடியிற்பிறந்தோர் தமக்குத்தீங்குசெய்தார்மேற்சினங்கொண்டு தாம் அவர்க்குத்தீங்கு செய்யார்.

உபகாரஞ் செய்ததனை ஓராதே தங்கண்
அபகாரம் ஆற்றச் செயினும்,—உபகாரந்
தாஞ்செய்வ தல்லாற் றவற்றினுற் றீங்கூக்கல்
வான்றோய் குடிப்பிறந்தார்க் கில்.

It is not the way of the noble to do evil to those who injure them.

Though men think not of good received, and do much ill to men of family whose fame has touched the sky, these still do good; nor are they wont, provoked by faults, to render evil to the thankless ones.

எ : ஊக்கல்.—ப : இல்.

உபகாரஞ் செய்ததனை for செய்த உபகாரத்தை.

70.

கீழோர் இழிவான சொற்களைச் சொன்னால் மேலோர் அங்ஙனஞ் சொல்லார்.

கூர்த்துநாய் கௌவிக் கொளக்கண்டுந் தம்வாயாற்
பேர்த்துநாய் கௌவினார் ஈங்கில்லை;—நீர்த்தன்றிக்
கீழ்மக்கள் கீழாய சொல்லியக்காற் சொல்பவோ,
மேன்மக்க டம்வாயான் மீட்டு?

Return not railing for railing.

Though a dog, in rage, should lay hold of them, there are none in the world who, in return, would lay hold of it with their mouth; and thus, when low men speak, not what is fitting, but low words, will high-minded men, in reply, utter such words with their mouth?

எ : கௌவினர், மேன்மக்கள்.—ப : இல்லை, சொல்பவோ? G. 81. நீர்த்து = நீர்மையுள்ளது. G. 93. கீழாய = கீழ்மை ஆனவைகளை. G. 93, 87.

CHAPTER VIII.

PATIENCE.

அதிகாரம் அ.

பொறையுடைமை

(= ஒருவன்தம்மிடத்திற்குத் தீங்குசெய்த விடத்துத் தாமும் அதனை அவனிடத்துச் செய்யாது பொறுப்பது).

This is the subject of ch. xvi in K.; but here chapters vii and viii differ little.

Analysis:

I. Bear with folly.

1. Don't answer a low, ignorant wrangler. *Forbear* in silence. [71, 72.] K. 153, 159.

II. Bear with friends.

2. Bear and *forbear* when those you love use harsh words. [73.]
3. A *patient*, contented, disciplined life is free from sorrow. [74.]
4. How to deal with unfaithful friends. [75, 76, 77.]
   The idea is that *forbearance* is necessary to friendship.

III. Bear ills and trials of life.

5. *Bear* want. It is better to suffer and die in uncomplaining silence than to beg. [78.]
6. *Patiently* and unswervingly go on in the way of virtue. [79, 80.]
   Here patience (பொறை) is used in a very wide sense, for meekness, temperance, self-restraint, and magnanimous forbearance, nearly answering to அடக்கம், and so compare K. ch. xiii.

The connexion between this and the last chapter is thus very close.

In Sanskrit क्षमा = பொறுமை. Comp. B. I. S. 2495: 'क्षमा गुणवतां बलम्, forbearance is the strength of the virtuous.'

71.

அறிவிலாருக்கு அறங்கூறுதல் நன்றன்று.

கோதை அருவிக் குளிர்வரை நன்னாட!—
பேதையோ டியாதும் உரையற்க;—பேதை
உரைப்பிற் சிதைந்துரைக்கும்; ஒல்லும் வகையான்
வழுக்கிக் கழிதலே நன்று.

Don't argue with the foolish.

Lord of the pleasant land, where down the cool mountains the streams fall as garlands!—With a fool hold no converse. If you speak with him, in replying he will pervert your words. To slip away from him as best you can is well.

எ: கீ (தொகை), பேதை, கழிதல்.—ப: உரையற்க, உரைக்கும், நன்று. பேதையோடியாதும். G. 24. Comp. 325. [See K. p. 227.]

72.

தமக்கு நிகரல்லார் சொல்லுங் கடுஞ் சொற்களைப் பொறுத்தல் அறிவுடையோர்க்குப்புகழ்.

நேரல்லார் நீரல்ல சொல்லியக்கான் மற்றது
தாரித் திருத்த றகுதி ; மற் — றேரும்
புகழ்மையாக் கொள்ளாது பொங்குநீர் ஞாலம்
சமழ்மையாக் கொண்டு விடும்.

Insults from inferiors.

When persons not our equals say unfitting things, to bear and to be still is worthy conduct. The world girt by foaming waters regards not a contrary course as praiseworthy, but as discreditable.

சொல்லியக்கால். Comp. 86 = சொன்னால். See H. B. § 97 note.

The first மற்று and ஓரும் are called அசைகள், G. 116 ; but see Lex. The second மற்று is by Com. made to mean பொறுத்திராமையை! 'the contrary course of not forgiving;' but comp. B. I. S. 5614 : '**तस्मान्नित्यं क्षमा तात पण्डितैरपवादिता**, therefore ever by the wise, my dear, is forbearance blamed.' This is probably the meaning here. Constant forbearance is condemned, since it may be mistaken for weakness. But see also 67.

73.

அன்புடையார் சொல்லுங் கடுஞ்சொல்லை இன்சொல்லாகக் கொள்ள வேண்டும்.

காதலார் சொல்லுங் கடுஞ்சொல் லுவந்துரைக்கும்
ஏதிலார் இன்சொலிற் றீதாமோ,—போதெலாம்
மாதர்வண் டார்க்கு மலிகடற் றண்சேர்ப்ப!—
ஆவ தறிவார்ப் பெறின்?

Harsh words of those who love are better than complaisant words of foes.

Lord of the swelling sea's cool shore, where bright insects hum around every flower!—Are severe words from loving lips harder to bear, if men can only rightly estimate their result, than pleasant words that strangers courteously speak?

எ: கடுஞ்சொல்.—ப: ஆமோ?

Or, 'words of reproof.' Comp. Ps. cxli. 5, and K. 795.

74.

கிடைத்தமட்டில் திருப்தி அடைந்து அறஞ்செய்து பொறையுடையவராய் வாழ்வோர்க்கு என்றுந் துன்பம் இல்லை.

அறிவ தறிந்தடங்கி அஞ்சுவதஞ்சி
உறுவ துலகுவப்பச் செய்து—பெறுவதனால்
இன்புற்று வாழும் இயல்புடையார் எஞ்ஞான்றுந்
துன்புற்று வாழ்தல் அரிது.

The thoroughly disciplined and contented man is happy.

Those who know what should be known, and rule themselves thereby; who fear what should be feared; who use all their faculties to bless the world; and whose nature rejoices in all good gained: are for ever free from woes.

எ: வாழ்தல்.—ப: அரிது. K. p. 219.

This is Contentment, S. संतोष. Comp. B. I. S. 6800, which speaks of the blessedness of (संतोषामृततृप्तानां—शान्तचेतसाम्) 'those satisfied with the Ambrosia of Contentment, the men of quiet minds.'

75.

நட்டோர் இருவரில் ஒருவனிடத்துத் தீயவொழுக்கங்கள் உண்டாயின், அதனை மற்றொருவன்பொறுக்கும் அளவும் பொறுத்துப் பொறுக்கக் கூடாதபோது பிறர்க்குரையாது நட்பை விடல்வேண்டும்.

வேற்றுமை இன்றிக் கலந்திருவர் நட்டக்கால்
தேற்றா ஒழுக்கம் ஒருவன்கண் உண்டாயின்,
ஆற்றுந் துணையும் பொறுக்க! பொறான் ஆயில்
தூற்றாதே தூர விடல்.

If a friend act doubtfully, forgive or quietly withdraw.

When two with strict accord unite in friendship's bond, if one betray the other's confidence by unkind act, this latter should endure as best he may. And if he can't endure, he should not divulge it, but withdraw himself.

எ: ஒருவன் (தொகை).—ப: பொறுக்க, விடல்.

This seems better to fit ch. xxiii. Comp. 221, 229, and K. 807.

76.

நட்டோர் தீயன செய்யினும் சிநேகத்தை விடாதிருத்தல் வேண்டும்.

இன்னா செயினும் இனிய ஒழிகென்று
தன்னையே தானோவின், அல்லது—துன்னிக்
கலந்தாரைக் கைவிடுதல்,—கானக நாட!—
விலங்கிற்கும் விள்ளல் அரிது.

If a friend do evil to you, think it good, refrain from anger and blame yourself; but never forsake him.

Lord of the woodlands! Separation is hard even to beasts; therefore if friends do things that are unpleasant, think them pleasant, bid yourself cease (from wrath), and blame yourself alone; but forsake not those that have been joined to you in the intimacy of friendship.

எ: கைவிடுதல்.—ப: அரிது. நோவின் அல்லது = நோவதல்லாமல், இனிய ஒழிகு = அவை இனியவையாகும், சினத்தை விட்டுவிடு.

Comp. 223, and my K. p. 223.

77.

அறிவுடையார் தம்மொடு நட்டார் செய்த தீமையைப்பொறுத்துக் கொள்ளல்வேண்டும்.

பெரியார் பெருநட்புக் கோடலுஞ் செய்த
அரிய பொறுப்பஎன் றன்றோ?—அரியரோ—
ஒல்லென் அருவி உயர்வரை நன்னாட!
நல்ல செய்வார்க்குத் தமர்?

Forbearance cements friendship.

Is not the reason why the close friendship of the great is sought, that they will bear even with faults hard to endure? Lord of the good land of high mountains with resounding waterfalls!—to good people are intimate friends rare?

எ: தமர்.—ப: அரியரோ.

Comp. *Kamb. Rām.* I. x. 80:

'பிழைத்தன பொறுத்தல் என்றும்
பெரியவர் கடனே என்பர்:

Ever to bear with things done ill
is special duty of the great, they say.'

This seems to refer to the வெற்றிவேற்கை of King Athi-vīra-rāma Pāṇḍiyan:

'சிறியோர் செய்த சிறுபிழை எல்லாம்
பெரியோர் ஆயிற் பொறுப்பது கடனே:

All the little faults that little ones commit
it is the duty of men, if great, to bear with.'

78.

பொறையுடையார் தம்வறுமையைப்பிறர் அறியச்சொல்லார்.

வற்றிமற் றுற்றப் பசிப்பினும் பண்பிலார்க்
கற்றம் அறிய உரையற்க!—அற்றம்
மறைக்குந் துணையார்க் குரைப்பவே தம்மைத்
துறக்குந் துணிவிலா தார்.

Bear want.

Though sore wasted with hunger, let not men tell out their destitution to ungracious churls. Those indeed who lack resolution to deny themselves may tell their wants to those who are able and willing to save them from destitution.

எ: தோ.—எ: பொறையுடையார், துணிவிலாதார்.—ப: உரையற்க, உரைப்பவே.

The idea is, it is better to die than to beg. Comp. 292 and ch. xxxi; also K. 1051–1057.

79.

தீநெறியால் வரும் இன்பம் அப்பொழுதின்பம் ஆயினும் பின்புதுன்பந்தருவது.

இன்பம் பயந்தாங் கிழிவு தலைவரினும்,
இன்பத்தின் பக்கம் இரிந்தைக்க!—இன்பம்
ஒழியாமை கண்டாலும்,—ஓங்கருவி நாட!—
பழிஆகா ஆறே தலை.

Forsake pleasure that brings disgrace. To avoid guilt is the chief matter.

Although shameful things may present themselves as things that yield pleasure, flee from that pleasure's side! Though thou couldst see pleasures that cease not soon,—Lord of the land of fountains high!—the guiltless way is best.

எ: ஆறு.—ப: நிலே.

Pleasure that brings disgrace is to be shunned. It is transitory, and if it were not so, to keep innocence is best.

80.

தேகம் அழிந்தாலும் பாவஞ் செய்யற்க.

தான்கெடினுந் தக்கார்கே டெண்ணற்க; தன்னுடம்பின்
ஊன்கெடினும் உண்ணார்கைத்துண்ணற்க;—வான் கவிந்த
வையகம் எல்லாம் பெறினும் உரையற்க
பொய்யோ டிடைமிடைந்த சொல்!

Never desire evil, nor eat with improper persons, nor lie.

Though ruin seize you, plan not ruin to the just! Though body's flesh should waste, eat not from hands unfit! Though the whole earth o'er-arched by heaven accrue as gain, never speak word with falsehood mixed!

எ: ஒருவன் (தொகை).—ப: எண்ணற்க, உண்ணற்க, உரையற்க.—செ: கேட்டை, கைத்து, சொல்லே.

CHAPTER IX.

THE NOT DESIRING OTHER MEN'S WIVES.

அதிகாரம் ௯.

பிறர்மனை நயவாமை.

Comp. K. ch. xv (p. 221, *etc.*). நயவாமை = விழையாமை.

This chapter is naturally divided into two portions, of which verses 81–87 set forth the danger and disgrace of adultery, and 88–90 the evils of lust.

Analysis :

I. 1. Fear and many evils are caused by it. [81–84.]
   2. The punishment in another birth. [85.]
   3. The injustice of it. [86.]
   4. An illustration of its perils. [87.]

II. 5. The terrible torment of lust. [88–90.]

The use of the S. दार in 81, 82 points to a Sanskrit original. Many verses in B. I. S. (see Introduction) bear on this subject.

81.

பிறன் மனையாளிடத்தில் சேறலை அறிவுடையார் விரும்பார்.

அச்சம் பெரிதால் அதற்கின்பஞ் சிற்றளவால்
நிச்ச' நினையுங்கால் கோக்கொலையால்—நிச்சலும்
கும்பிக்கே கூர்த்த வினையாற் பிறன்றாரம்
நம்பற்க நாணுடை யார்.

Against adultery.

The fear it brings is great ; its pleasure is brief ; each day if it is divulged death threatens by the king's decree ; and ever it is a deed that tends to the pains of hell ; O shamefast men, desire not your neighbour's wife.

எ : நாணுடையார்.—ப : நம்பற்க.—செ : தாரம்.

See K. p. 221, and *Nīti.* 77.

There are coincidences in language between this and Jī. Chin. xiii. 171, which are worthy of note:

'காதலாள் [1]கவிந்து கையக் கடியவே கனைந்து கன்றி
ஏதிலான் றார நம்பி எளிதென [2]விறந்த பாவத்
தூதிலே [3]உருக வெந்த ஒள்ளழற் செப்புப் பாவை
ஆ, தகா தென்னப் புல்லி அலறுமால்,—யானை வேந்தே!

Lord of elephants! He who, while his wife is fading away with grief, utters bitter reproaches, hardens himself, and transgresses with another's wife, trusting in the easiness of the crime; for his sin shall shriekingly embrace a brazen image heated thoroughly in a blast furnace till it glows with fire, while men cry out, Ah, horrid sight!'

[1] *Or* கரிந்து. [2] *Or* வீழ்ந்த. [3] *Or* உருவ.

No copies of Jī. Chin. agree. The metre is ஆசிரியவிருத்தம், and the rhythm வி .. மா .. மா || வி .. மா .. மா.

82.

பிறன்மனைவியை விரும்புவோரிடத்துப்பகை பழிமுதலியவை அன்றி அறமுதலியன வந்தடையா.

அறம்புகழ் கேண்மை பெருமைஇந் நான்கும்
பிறன்றார' நச்சுவார்ச் சேரா;—பிறன்றாரம்
நச்சுவார்ச் சேரும் பகைபழி பாவமென்
றச்சத்தோ டிந்நாற் பொருள்.

The sinner forfeits much, and incurs much.

Virtue, praise, friendship, greatness, all these four draw not anigh the men who covet their neighbour's wife. Hatred, disgrace and guilt, with fear, these four possessions abide with men who covet their neighbour's wife.

Comp. my K. p. 222. *Nīti.* 79.
This seems to be K. 146. Which is the original? Or, are both from Sanskrit?

பகைபாவம் அச்சம் பழியென நான்கும்
இகவாவாம் இல்லிறப்பான் கண்.

83.

களவொழுக்கத்தினால் அச்சமே அன்றி இன்பமில்லை.

புக்கவிடத் தச்சம், போதரும் போதச்சம்,
துய்க்கும் இடத்தச்சம், தோன்றுமற் காப்பச்சம்,
எக்காலும் அச்சந் தருமால், எவன்கொலோ
உட்கான் பிறனில் புகல்?

Fear on every side.

In entering in there's fear; in home returning fear; during enjoyment is fear; in guarding the secret is fear; it evermore brings fear: why shuns he not with dread the entrance of neighbour's house?

84.

பிறன்மனையாளை விரும்புதலால் பலதீங்குகள் சேரும்.

காணிற் குடிப்பழிஆங், கைஉறிற் கால்குறையும்,
மாணின்மை செய்யுங்கால் அச்சம் ஆம்;—நீணிரயத்
துன்பம் பயக்குமாற் றுச்சாரி, நீகண்ட
இன்பம் எனக்கெனைத்தாற் கூறு!

The way of transgressors is hard.

If any one see, disgrace lights on the house; if any hand should seize, leg's maimed; in the doing of the shameful deed is dread; it yields as fruit vast hell's affliction: tell me, O profligate, what measure of delight is thine?

எ: நீ.—ப: கூறு.

85.

பிறன் மனையாளிடத்திற் சென்றோர் அநுபவிக்குந் தீமைகள்.

செம்மைஒன் றின்றிச் சிறியார் இனத்தராய்க்
கொம்மை வரிமுலையா டோண்மரீஇ—உம்மை
வலியாற் பிறர்மனைமேற் சென்றாரே இம்மை
அலியாகி ஆடிஉண் பார்.

Punishment of ravishers.

Those who, in a former state, without any regard to right, becoming associates of the mean, enjoyed the embraces of beautiful women, and by violence approached their neighbour's wife, in this state will become eunuchs, and dancing shall earn their bread.

86.

தனக்கு அன்புள்ளமனையாள் இருக்கப் பிறன்மனையாளைக்கண்ணாலே காணுதல் நன்றன்று.

பல்லார் அறியப் பறைஅறைந்து நாட்கேட்டுக்
கல்யாணஞ் செய்து கடிப்புக்க—மெல்லியல்
காதன் மனையாளும் இல்லாளா என்னொருவன்
ஏதின் மனையாளை நோக்கு?

Why should a man who has his own wife look at his neighbour's?

While his loving wife dwells in his home, the tender one whom he espoused,—seeking (out an auspicious) day, and sounding the drum, for many folks to know,—and whom he guards as his own,—what means a man's glance at another's wife?

நோக்கு = நோக்குதல். *Nīti*. 80.

87.

பிறன்மனையாளை அநுபவிக்கும் அநுபவம் தப்பாது தீமையைத் தரும்.

அம்பல் அயல்எடுப்ப அஞ்சித் தமர்பரீஇ
வம்பலன் பெண்மரீஇ மைந்துற்று—நம்பும்
நிலைமையி னெஞ்சத்தான் றுப்புரவு பாம்பின்
தலைநக்கி அன்ன துடைத்து.

Pleasure dearly purchased.

The enjoyment of the man of unstable heart, who under the influence of infatuation, approaches his neighbour's wife and sets his affections upon her, while neighbours spread abroad his guilt, and kinsmen dread and mourn, is like (that of the person who takes pleasure in) licking a serpent's head.

88.

அறிவுடையோரிடத்து ஓர்காலத்துக்காமம் எழும்பினாலும் அது விரைவிற்றணியும்.

பரவா வெளிப்படா பல்லோர்கட் டங்கா
உரவோர்கட் காமநோய், ஓஒ கொடிதே!
விரவாரு ணாணுப் படல்அஞ்சி யாதும்
உரையாதுள் ளாறி விடும்.

The passions of virtuous men are under controul.

The disease of lust in men mighty (in wisdom) gains not ascendancy, is not revealed, does not remain fixed on many objects.

O! it is a cruel conflict; but fearing to incur shame in the midst of their foes, they say nothing about it, and it is extinguished within them.

89.

காமம் அம்புமுதலியவற்றினுங் கொடியது.

அம்பும் அழலும் அவிர்கதிர் ஞாயிறும்
வெம்பிச் சுடினும் புறஞ்சுடும்;—வெம்பிக்
கவற்றி மனத்தைச் சுடுதலாற் காமம்
அவற்றினும் அஞ்சப் படும்.

Lust the most deadly enemy.

Arrow and fire and sun with glistening rays may rage and burn; but these burn the outer man alone. Lust rages and distracts and burns the mind, and is more to be feared than they.

Here only the feet called இயற்சீர் are used, and the unusual rhythm is called தூங்கிசைச்செப்பல். [K. Introd. p. xxviii.] *Nīti.* 79.

90.

காமந் தீயினுங் கொடியது.

ஊருள் எழுந்த உருகெழு செந்தீக்கு
நீருட் குளித்தும் உயலாகும்;—நீருள்
குளிப்பினுங் காமஞ் சுடுமேகுன் றேறி
ஒளிப்பினுங் காமஞ் சுடும்.

Fire and lust.

From the ruddy fire that fiercely rises in the village you may scape by bathing in water.—Although you bathe in water, lust will burn; and though you climb the hill and hide you there, still lust will burn!

உருகெழு is differently explained by commentators. Murugēça Muthaliyār says, உரு = வெப்பம் 'heat,' கெழு = மிகுந்த (வி. தொ. G. 153) 'abounding in' = '*fiercely raging.*' Older commentators say, உருகு = உட்கு = 'dread,' எழு 'arising' = '*which is a source of dread.*'

CHAPTER X.

LIBERALITY.

அதிகாரம் ௧௦.

ஈகை

(= வறியவருக்கு ஈதல்).

Chapter xxviii, which is headed ஈயாமை (illiberality: absence of charity), should be read with this. In K. this is chapter xxiii.

Comp. B. I. S. 2741–2768: 'दाने न तुल्यो निधिरस्ति अन्यः, no store like liberality.'

In Jī. Chin. xiii (§§ xvi, xvii) 225, 244 are two sections entitled தானம் and தானப்பயன் which may be studied. A great distinction is made between தலையானதானம் (=gifts to devotees) and இடையானதானம் (=gifts to ordinary persons: indiscriminate charity). The following is odd:

'அடங்கலர்க் கீந்த தானப் பயத்தினால் அலறு முந்நீர்த்
தடங்கட னடுவுட் டீவு பலவுள; அவற்றுட் டோன்றி
உடம்பொடு முகங்கள் ஒவ்வார்; ஊழ்கனி மாந்தி வாழ்வர்;—
மடங்கலஞ் சீற்றத் துப்பின் மானவேன் மன்னர் ஏறே!

O king, whose dart is dreadful as the angry might of a lion (or *Yama*)! In the wide sea whose waters ceaselessly rave are many islands. These are assigned as the abode of *those who give to the undisciplined.* In these they have human bodies, but faces of brutes, and eat the fruit of ancient deeds.'

There seems here, as in many parts of Jī. Chin., some Greek influence at work.

Analysis:

1. Under all circumstances cultivate a generous spirit: this opens heaven's door. [91. Comp. 271.]
2. Life has its vicissitudes: be generous while you may. [92.]
3. It is fate that enriches and impoverishes. Why spare? [93.]
4. It is churlishness in former life that brings poverty in this. [94.]
5. If you have nought to give, at least, beg not. [95.]
6. The generous and the churl like fruitful and sterile palms. [96.]
7. Even in time of poverty one must be generous. [97.]
8. Give to those that cannot make any return. [98.]
9. Little charities go to make a great sum. [99.]
10. Its praise fills all worlds. [100.]

This virtue is commended under the names of இடர்தீர்த்தல் ('removal of afflictions'), படர்தீர்த்தல் ('removal of wants'), and கொடை ('giving'), in *Ēlā.* 5, 7, 10, 16, 17, 21, 35, *etc.*

In T. 6 we find the praise of '. . . . அறவினையைக் காரான்மைபோல ஒழுகல், ... living in the exercise of charity like the beneficence of clouds.' [See கார், ஆர்.]

Connected with it is the much-lauded 'பாத்தூண்ணூர்தன்மை [Lex. பகு], the habit of sharing food with others.' (T. 10, 12, 31, 40.) [See K. 44.]

'வருவாயுட்கால்வழங்கி வாழ்தல், one fourth of a man's income should thus be spent.' (T. 21.)

This is 'தானங் கொடுக்குந் தகைமை, the excellent quality of giving gifts.' (T. 23.)

The delight of charity is expressed in N. M. K. 37: '. . . . சிறந்த அறக்கனி இல்லார்நர்க் கீயுமுற் றோன்றும், the exquisite gladness of charity will appear when you give to those that have nothing.' [Comp. K. 224.]

91.

ஈகை வீடுபேற்றைத்தரும்.

இல்லா இடத்தும் இயைந்த அளவினால்
உள்ள இடம்போற் பெரிதுவந்து—மெல்லக்
கொடையொடு பட்ட குணனுடை மாந்தர்க்
கடையாவாம் ஆண்டைக் கதவு.

Unchilled by adversity the good do good: heaven's gate is open to them.

Even in their adverse hour, up to the measure of their means, as in the prosperous times, with large rejoicing heart to give is their nature still. To such good men heaven's gate is never closed.

எ: கதவு.—ப: அடையாவாம். This must be compared with 271; and K. 218.

Comp. B. I. S. 1237. This is a favourite topic with both Tamil and Sanskrit moralists.

उदेति सविता ताम्रस्ताम्र एवास्तमेति च ।
सम्पत्तौ च विपत्तौ च महताम् एकरूपता ॥

'Red rises the sun, and red he sets: in prosperity and in adversity the great are the same.'

See also 112, 141, 150, 153, 212, 300, 343.

92.

பொருள் உண்டான காலத்து அதை இறுகப்பிடித்திராது யாவர்க்குங் கொடுத்துண்ணல் வேண்டும்.

முன்னரே சாநாள் முனிதக்க மூப்புள;
பின்னரும் பீடழிக்கு நோய்உள;—கொன்னே
பரவன்மின்! பற்றன்மின்! பாத்துண்மின்! யாதுங்
கரவன்மின்! கைத்துண்டாம் போழ்து.

Death, old age, disease stand round. Give!

Before (you) are death's day and age detestable; behind is disease that humbles pride. Discursive thoughts indulge not. Cling not to earth. Eat, sharing food; hide not your powers while wealth is in your hand.

எ: சாநாள், மூப்பு, நோய், நீர். — ப: உள, பரவன்மின் ஆதி. பாத்து = பகுத்து. G. 41. சாநாள். G. 153. Comp. 19.

93.

செல்வம் நீங்கும் ஆதலால் பிறர்க்கிட்டுண்க.

நடுக்குற்றுத் தற்சேர்ந்தார் துன்பந் துடையார்,
கொடுத்துத்தான் றுய்ப்பினும் ஈண்டுங்கால் ஈண்டும்;
மிடுக்குற்றுப் பற்றினு' நில்லாது செல்வம்,
விடுக்கும் வினை உலந்தக் கால்.

It is useless saving: fate gives and takes away.

Through dread of want they do not relieve the woes of men who as suppliants draw near! Yet although men enjoy and give, wealth grows in growing time: cling to it, and yet it flies when former deeds that brought wealth have lost their power.

விடுக்கும் is ambiguous. See Lex. விடு. This is K. 371, 376. Comp. ch. xi.

94.

முன்னர் கொடுத்துண்ணாதவர் பின்னர் இரந்துண்பர்.

இம்மி அரிசித் துணையானும் வைகலும்
நும்மில் இயைவ கொடுத்துண்மின்!—உம்மைக்
கொடாஅ தவரென்பர் குண்டுநீர் வையத்
தடாஅ அடுப்பி னவர்.

Give according to your power.

Daily having given somewhat, though but the fraction of a grain of rice, according to your ability, eat ye (your own food). Those who gave not in that world, men say, on this earth girt by deep waters are those on whose hearth nothing is cooked.

Those who give not in one birth become poor in the next.

95.

இரப்போர்க்கு ஈதல்வேண்டும் வறுமைக்காலத்து இரவாமைவேண்டும்.

மறுமையும் இம்மையு நோக்கி ஒருவற்
குறுமா றியைவ கொடுத்தல்;—வறுமையால்
ஈதல் இசையா தெனினும் இரவாமை
ஈதல் இரட்டி உறும்.

Do charity for the sake of this world and the future; and beg not.

Regarding the other world and this world, give to any suppliant, in fitting way, according to your ability. And if on account of poverty giving is not possible, yet refraining from begging is twice as meritorious as giving.

எ: இரவாமை.—ப: உறும்.

96.

ஈகைக்குணமுடையோர் பலர்க்கும் பயன்படுவர் அஃதில்லார் தமக்கும் பயன்படார்.

நடுவூருள் வேதிகைச் சுற்றுக்கோட் புக்க
படுபனை அன்னர் பலர்நச்ச வாழ்வார்;
குடி கொழுத்தக் கண்ணுங் கொடுத்துண்ணா மாக்கள்
இடுகாட்டுள் ஏற்றுப் பனை.

The fertile and sterile palms.

Those who live desired of many are as a fertile palm entered in the altar's enclosure, in midmost of the town. Those who, even when their house grows great, give not before they eat, are like the sterile palm in the burning ground.

எ: வாழ்வார், மாக்கள்.—ப: அன்னார், பனை. Comp. K. 216.

97.

உலகம் வாழ்தலிற்கு வேண்டியது மழையும் இகையும்.

பெயற்பான் மழைபெய்யாக் கண்ணும் உலகஞ்
செயற்பால செய்யா விடினுங்;—கயற்புலால்
புன்னை கடியும் பொருகடற் றண்சேர்ப்ப!—
என்னை உலகுய்யும் ஆறு?

In troublous time charity must not be omitted.

Even when the rain rains not in due season, if all the world should fail in virtuous actions that ought to be done, —Lord of the warring sea's cool shore, where acrid fume of fish in *Punnai's* perfume dies!—how scapes the world?

In times of adversity the good must still be charitable.
எ: ஆறு.—ப: என்னை. பெயற் பான் மழை = பெய்யவேண்டிய மழை. K. 218.

98.

இரப்போர்க்கீதலே ஈகை; மாறீவார்க்கீதல் கடன்கொடுத்தலோ டொக்கும்.

ஏற்றகை மாற்றாமை என்னுந் தாம்வரையா
ணாற்றாதார்க் கீவதாம் ஆண்கடன்—ஆற்றின்,—
மலிகடற் றண்சேர்ப்ப!—மாறீவார்க் கீதல்
பொலிகடன் என்னும் பெயர்த்து.

Give to him who cannot recompense thee.

Denying to no out-stretched hand, to give to needy men as he hath power, is duty of a man.—Lord of the swelling sea's cool shore!—A gift to those that can return the gift is usury!

எ: ஈவது, ஈதல்.—ப: கடன், பெயர்த்து. Comp. K. 211, 221. தாம் = தமது. Another reading is வரையாது. See Lex. வர்.

99.

ஒருவன் தன்னிடத்துள்ள பொருளளவுக் கேற்ப நாடோறுஞ் சிறிதாஞ் செய்ய வேண்டும்.

இறப்பச் சிறிதென்னா தில்லென்னா தென்றும்
அறப்பயன் யார்மாட்டுஞ் செய்க;—முறைப்புதவின்
ஐயம் புகூஉந் தவசி கடிஞைபோற்
பைய நிறைத்து விடும்.

Give though you have but little. The beggar's dish is filled in time.

Say not '’tis passing little,' nor '’tis nought I give;' on all confer thy boon of virtuous charity. Like the dish the mendicant presents from door to door, by frequent doles ’twill be filled full.

எ: அறப்பயன்.—ப: விடும்.—செ: அறப்பயனை.
Comp. K. 223. G. 90, 120.

100.

ஈகையால் வரும்புகழ் மூவுலகத்துஞ் சென்றுபரவும்.

கடிப்பிடு கண்முரசங் காதத்தோர் கேட்பர்;
இடித்து முழங்கியதோர் யோசனையோர் கேட்பர்;
அடுக்கிய மூவுலகுங் கேட்குமே சான்றோர்
கொடுத்தார் எனப்படுஞ் சொல்.

The fame of charitable deeds.

The sound of beaten drum a *kātham* off they'll hear; the thunder's voice through a whole *yōjanai* will reach men's ears; the three successive worlds will hear the word that says, '*Men excellent their gifts have given.*'

Comp. K. 233, 234. G. 93.

CHAPTER XI.

OLD DEEDS.

அதிகாரம் கக.

பழவினை

(= முன்செய்தவினையின்தன்மை).

This may be compared with K. ch. xxxviii, and my notes. The Tamil வினை is the equivalent of the S. कर्मन् (கன்மம்). இருவினை = 'twofold action,' = 'sinful and righteous deeds.' The words ஊழ், தொல்லை, பால், முறை (μοῖρα), உண்மை, தெய்வம், நியதி, விதி, பொறி are all used to express the effects of those deeds for which each individual is responsible, but which are supposed partly to have been performed in former states of existence, and partly to be an eternal possession or fated allotment of the living element or soul, antecedent to all embodiment.

It is not here man's responsibility for his actions merely, a belief in which is essential to morals; but chiefly, at least, an unmerited load of guilt and resulting suffering: the soul's sad destiny.

The theory propounded in this chapter lies at the foundation of every Hindū system of religious philosophy.

Every living principle (உயிர், *breath*, *life*, *soul*) obtains its peculiar embodiment in the almost infinite range of possible transmigrations, according to the necessity imposed upon it by an eternal accompt of merit and demerit (வினை), accumulated in an infinite series of previous embodied states (பிறப்பு).

The distinction between good and evil deeds is often confused in the manuals; but all action is in one sense treated as evil, and is to be deprecated, since it leads to birth, higher or lower, and so delays the desired emancipation from all embodied existence, which all sects alike seek, and call by the same names (வீடு, முத்தி); though the condition of the emancipated soul is variously conceived. Not only is man's present organization determined beforehand absolutely by these old deeds (பழவினை), but his present experiences, and even his faculties, physical, mental, and moral [108], are thus unalterably fixed; his being's whole history is imprinted on the sutures of his skull before his birth. [110.]

This is fate (விதி, தலைவிதி). But then what is man? And why prescribe to him duties? . . . .

The theory of the *Çaiva* system in regard to '*Old Deeds*' is illustrated in the four verses appended. It is briefly as follows:—At the beginning of each Aeon there are in existence (1) *Çiva*, the Supreme; (2) the aggregate of all souls, now disembodied; and (3) a threefold mass of what is called *Malam* (impurity): the three eternal categories of being (பதிபசுபாசம்). This *Malam* consists of (1) a veil of gross darkness (ஆணவம்); (2) a mass of deeds, somehow conceived of as actual objective existences; and (3) *Māyei* (மாயை), which is the material of all embodiment. The unconscious souls, shrouded in that primeval darkness, are responsible, in some inexplicable fashion, for these old—eternal—*deeds;* the fruit of which must be consumed by each at the time of its maturity, before the soul can attain by successive steps an eternal and blissful union with the Supreme, whose essence, though as yet they know it not, they share.

The eternal *Çivam*, full of gracious compassion for these darkened, alienated, and burdened souls, begins the work of their deliverance. This renders necessary the evolution from *Māyā* of the phenomenal universe, the clothing of these souls with bodies, in order to provide for them the means and opportunities of consuming the fruit of deeds, and of thus at length obtaining release from the necessity of future embodiment; and in order thus to prepare the way for *Mutti* (முத்தி), or final deliverance. Thus the nature and circumstances of each successive embodiment, the joys and sorrows of each birth, and all the destinies of every being, depend solely upon these 'old deeds.' With this preliminary explanation, the following verses from the *Çiva-Ñāna-piragāçam*, the great text-book of the *Çaiva-Siddhānta* system, will be intelligible, and may enable the student to grasp a subject, some idea of which is very necessary for all who would read the classics of South India, or enter into the feelings of the Tamil people.

[See also *Sarva-darśana-saṅgraha* (Bibliotheca Indica, Calcutta, 1858), pp. 80–90; and translated in Trübner's Series by Professors Cowell and Gough, pp. 112–127.]

கன்மம் (= கர்மம். S. कर्म.)

[1] கண்ணி இடும் உருவதனுக் கேது ஆகி
[2] நானா போகங்களாய் [3] நாசோற் பத்தி
பண்ணிவரும்; [4] ஆதலால் அநாதி ஆகிப்
[5] பலவாகி [6] அணுக்கடொறும் படர்வ தாகி
[7] எண்ணிவரு மனவாச கன்மத்தால் இயற்றும்
இயல்பினதாய் [8] மதிகதமாய் [9] இருபயனும் பாவ
புண்ணியமாய்ப் [10] புலர்காலே மாயை மேவிப்
பொருந்தும்; இது கன்மமலம் புகலும் ஆறே

[Translation with Commentator's notes.]

1 They (கன்மம், இருவினை) are the cause of the assumption (at the time of EVOLUTION, by souls) of the forms (body) to which these become united. (Souls are embodied that they may feed upon the fruit of 'old deeds.')

2 They give occasion to various experiences (of pleasure and pain).

3 They cause death and birth (one body succeeding another).

4 And therefore they are without beginning. (Every act of creation, or evolution, in each succeeding Aeon, presupposes the existence of 'deeds,' of which the fruit has to be consumed.)

5 They are many. (An infinite variety of forms are assumed, and in each of these an endless variety of pleasures and pains is experienced.)

6 They are spread over all souls. (அணு.)

7 Their nature is that they are done by the mind, speech, and body (they consist of thoughts, words, and deeds).

[8] Their seat is in the understanding (since all intellectual processes have action as their end).

[9] They exist as a twofold fruit of sin and merit (for desire of good, and aversion from evil having been brought into play, merit and sin accumulate, and the joys of paradise, or the sufferings of hell are experienced).

[10] In the time of INVOLUTION (சங்காரக்காலம், ஒடுக்குங்காலம், புலர்காலம் = 'the time when things fade away, when phenomena disappear') they are gathered into 'Causal Māyā' (together with the universe and all souls).

Thus is the 'taint of deeds' declared.

---

[1] கன்மநெறிதிரிவித'; நற்சாதி ஆயுட் போகக்
கடனதெனவரு'; [2] மூன்றும் உயிர் ஒன்றிற் கலத்தல்
தொன்மை; [3] அதூழல்லதணைவாகா; [4] தானுந்
தொடக்கடைவின் அடையாதே தோன்றுமாறித்
[5] தன்மைதரு தெய்விகம் முற்பவுதிகம் ஆன்மிகமாத்
தகையில் உறும், [6] அசேதனசேதனத்தாலுஞ்சாரும்;
[7] நன்மையொடுதீமை தருசேதனனுக் கிவணுறுநடில்
அதன் ஊழ்வினையா னணுகுந்தானே.

[1] The ways in which KANMAM operates are three: good 'genus' [= caste] (or low); (long or short) life, enjoyment (or suffering).

[2] These three from of old combine with each soul. (For when souls as the result of 'deeds' assume any body, that body must be of some genus, have some limit of life, and experience some joys or sorrows.)

[3] That experience arises from 'ancient deeds' (ஊழ்) and not otherwise. (For thus only can we account for vicissitudes, accidents, and strange experiences in life. The Commentator quotes K. 380.)

[4] And these (deeds) do not always present themselves (for the soul to eat their fruit) in the order in which they had their origin; but changing. (Thus when you sow, the recent seed, being softer, germinates earlier, and older seed, being harder, germinates later.)

[5] They assume the nature of DIVINE (inflictions) [pains of birth, death, hell, *etc.*: which come by visitation of God]; ELEMENTAL (inflictions) [pains from rain, cold, heat, from a material agency involving the five elements of earth, air, fire, water, ether]; and ESSENTIAL (inflictions) [pains, of mind or body].

[S. दैविक (from देव, 'god'), भूतिक, आत्मीक. Comp. *Sāṅkhya Kārikā*, Book I, Aphorism 1.]

[6] They proceed from unintelligent as well as intelligent agencies.

[7] If you enquire how the experiences of good and evil visit the sentient soul,—they draw nigh to it through the operation of 'old deeds.'

The three kinds and names of (கன்மம்) deeds.

(1) *Āgamiyam* [ஆகமியம். S. आगम्य = 'having arrived']. These are deeds done in the present state or birth; the deeds of good and evil, of which the man is the conscious doer.

(2) *Çañçitam* [சஞ்சிதம். S. सञ्चित = 'accumulated']. These are the store of deeds (eternal *a parte ante*) accumulated through the whole succession of infinite births; fruits which are ripening.

(3) *Pirārattam* [பிராரத்தம். S. प्रारब्ध = 'begun']. These are such of the last-mentioned store as are ripe for fruition, and cause the next birth with its twofold experience.

---

[1] மேலைக்கு வருவினையே தென்னில் ஆங்கண்
விருப்புவெறுப்பென அறி; [2] அவ்வினையும் எல்லாம்
மூலத்தவினை பயில்வாம் என்னின்மேன்
முற்றியதன் பயன் உனக்கு முளைக்கும் என்பர்.
[3] ஞாலத்துவினைகள் இருதிறன் ஆகும்: புந்தி
நண்ணாத வினை நணுகும் வினை என ஒன்றிரண்டாம்;
ஏலத்தான் இதம் அகிதமாம்; இதனால் வழுவா
தெய்தி இடும் புண்ணிய பாவங்கள் என்றே.

[1] If you enquire what is the cause of 'new deeds,' it is the desires and aversions which arise while the soul is experiencing the fruit of 'old deeds' (*pirārattam*). (These are the seeds of future birth).

[2] And if you say all those actions (with desires and aversions too) are the operation of the original deeds, (the wise) will reply 'the result of what we do afterwards (in the present birth) will grow for thee.' (This is *āgamiyam.*)

[3] Actions done in the earth are of two sorts, actions which are involuntary, and actions which are wilful. From the beginning these are also right (HITAM) and wrong (AHITAM). From these unfailingly men obtain *merit* and *sin.*

---

[1] உற்றதொழி லினைவுரையின் இருவினை உள்ளவாம்;
[2] ஒன்றொன்றால் அழியாதூண் ஒழியா துன்னின்;
[3] மற்றவற்றின் ஒருவினைக்கோர் வினையால் வீடு
வைதிகசை வம்பகரும்; மரபின் ஆற்றப்
பற்றியதுகழியும்; இது [4] விலையால் எற்கும்
பான்மையும் ஆம் பண்ணாது பலிக்கும்; [5] முன்னம்
சொற்றநூல் வழியின்வரின் மிகுதி சோரும்,
சோராதல் கருமேலைத் தொடர்ச்சி ஆமே.

[1] Twofold actions (merits and sins) are from deed, thought, and word.

[2] One of these is not destroyed by another. The participation of the fruit is not to be avoided by thee. [Good deeds and bad will not cancel one another. You must eat the fruit of each.]

[3] But the *Vaidic-Çaiva* system teaches that there is deliverance from the effect of (one) deed by means of (another) deed. If man act in conformity with the ordained method, deeds will pass away.

[4] This (expiation of the fault, guilt, evil result of deeds) is rendered possible by (paying) a price; and what you have not yourself done may avail for you. (You may hire a substitute to perform *Pirāyaççittam*, or expiatory rites.)

[5] If you do what the above-mentioned authorities enjoin, the heavier penalty is removed; and what is not so removed clings to you in a future birth.

Analysis:

1. Deeds unerringly come back to the doer. [101.]
2. Good deeds alone make life worth living. [102.]
3. Wishes are useless; man's condition is fixed by old deeds. [103, 104, 107, 109.]
4. Vicissitudes of life are the result of old deeds. [105.]
5. Death lets some men live, because they are not worth killing. [106.]
6. Men's vices too are the consequences of old deeds. [108.]
7. Men must accept their unalterable and inevitable destiny. [110.]

101.

இளங்கன்று தன்னை ஈன்றபசுவைப் பாலுண்ணுங்காலத்தில் தேடி அடைவதுபோல முன்னைவினை தன்னைச் செய்தவனையே அடையுங் காலத்தில் வந்தடையும்.

பல்லாவுள் உய்த்து விடினுங் குழக்கன்று
வல்லதாந் தாய்நாடிக் கோடலைத் — தொல்லைப்
பழவினையும் அன்ன தகைத்தேதற் செய்த
கிழவனை நாடிக் கொளற்கு.

Deeds come home to the doer.

Although you send forth the tender calf amid many cows, it has unerring skill to seek out its own mother. Deeds of old days have even so the power to search him out to whom their fruit pertains.

See K. 376 and notes. G. 142.

கோடல் = கொள்ளுதல். [Comp. சேறல், கோறல்.] The acc. of respect: 'hath power in regard to searching out for itself.'

தொல்லைப் பழவினை is ஒருபொருட்பன்மொழி, a compound where one word is redundant. G. 150.

So it is truly said, 'Your sin will find you out.' But this verse rather refers to deeds of a supposed former birth.

Comp. B. I. S. 5114 (from Mahā Bhā.):

'यथा धेनुसहस्रेषु वत्सो विन्दति मातरम् ।
तथा पूर्वकृतं कर्म कर्तारमनुगच्छति ॥

As amongst a thousand cows a calf knows its mother, so the deed done before finds out its doer.'

102.

அறஞ் சிறிதுஞ் செய்யாதான் பிறந்திறத்தலையே பயனாக உடையவன்.

உருவும் இளமையும் ஒண்பொருளும் உட்கும்
ஒருவழி நில்லாமை கண்டும் — ஒருவழி
ஒன்றேயும் இல்லாதான் வாழ்க்கை உடம்பிட்டு
நின்றுவீழ்ந் தக்க துடைத்து.

A merely animal life.

Beauty and youth, and glittering wealth and reverence abide not in one stay. To him who, though he sees this, does no single virtuous act in this one stage of being, life's joy stands with the body and falls with it.

The idea is that if a man accumulate no merit of good deeds during his human embodiment, his life is a merely animal existence; and so when he dies all the gain of his earthly sojourn perishes with him. Comp. 120. வீழ்ந் = வீழுந் = வீழும். G. 41, 143.

103.

வேண்டியவரே போகங்கள் அநுபவிக்கவாரா.

வளம்பட வேண்டாதார் யார்யாரும் இல்லை;
அளந்தன போகம் அவரவ ராற்றான்;
விளங்காய் திரட்டினார் இல்லைக் களங்கனியைக்
காரெனச் செய்தாரும் இல்.

Wishes are inoperative.

Who would not see Prosperity? All seek her gifts; but as men's ways are, so each man's enjoyments are meted out. Who made the *Viḷam's* apple round? Or who gave its dusky hue to the *Kaḷam* fruit?

This really is intended to affirm the doctrine of necessity, the ஆறு being 'his destined way;' but it admits of a more useful interpretation: indulge not in idle wishes for happiness, but try to deserve it. Comp. 109.

104.

யாவராலும் நல்வினைதீவினைப்பயன்களைத் தடுத்தல் கூடாது.

உறற்பால நீக்கல் உறுவர்க்கும் ஆகா;
பெறற்பால் அனையவும் அன்னவாம்; மாரி
வறப்பிற் றருவாரும் இல்லை; அதனைச்
சிறப்பிற் றணிப்பாரும் இல்.

What must be, must be.

Not even saints can drive away predestined ills; and all the fated gain must needs accrue. In time of drought who can bestow the rain? or who can check its rich abundance when it falls?

See Ellis, p. 98; *Hitō.* Pref. 61–64.

So *Mū.*:

'அடுத்துமுயன்றாலும் ஆகுநாளன்றி
எடுத்த கருமங்கள் ஆகா:

Though you use strenuous efforts, save in the favouring day, your undertakings come to nought.'

Comp. also B. I. S. 2486:

'तन्न भवति यद्भाव्यं भवति च भाव्यं विनापि यत्नेन ।
करतलगतमपि नश्यति यस्य तु भवितव्यता नास्ति ॥

What may not be is not; what is to be is without effort. What is in the very hand perishes, if it is not the man's destined possession.'

105.

கல்வி அறிவு கேள்வி முதலியவற்றுற் பெரியரும் மகிமை கெட்டுவாழ்தல் முன்செய்வினைப்பயனே ஆம்.

தினைத்துணையர் ஆகித்தந் தேசுள் ளடக்கிப்
பனைத்துணையார் வைகலும் பாடழிந்து வாழ்வர்,
நினைப்பக் கிடந்த தெவனுண்டா மேலை
வினைப்பய னல்லாற் பிற?

Vicissitudes of life are fate.

Those who rose like stately palms, when their greatness is gone, become small as the millet seed, hiding their glory within,—and so they pass their days. This is the fruit of deeds of former days: when you think of it, what other cause can there be?

106.

நல்லோர் இறத்தற்குந் தீயோர் வாழ்தற்குங் காரணம் வினைப்பயன்.

பல்லான்ற கேள்விப் பயனுணர்வார் வீபவும்
கல்லாதார் வாழ்வ தறிதிரேல் — கல்லாதார்
சேதனம் என்னும்அச் சேறகத் தின்மையால்
கோதென்று கொள்ளாதாங் கூற்று.

Why ignorant men live, while the wise die.

Those that know the fruit of varied and profound learning die off, while the unlearned joyously live on. Would you know the cause?—The unlearned possess within no 'sap of sapience;'—so death deems them refuse stalks, and takes them not!

107.

உலகத்துள் சிலர் வறியராய் இரந்துண்பதற்குக் காரணம்.

இடும்பைகூர் நெஞ்சத்தா ரெல்லாருங் காண
நெடுங்கடை நின்றுழல்வ தெல்லாம் — அடம்பம்பூ,
அன்னங் கிழிக்கும் அலைகடற் றண்சேர்ப்ப!
முன்னை வினையாய் விடும்.

Why some beg from door to door.

Lord of the sea's cool shore, where amid the wave swans sport, tearing to shreds the *Aḍambu* flowers! When those whose hearts are sore with urgent need stand begging, and wander through the long street, in sight of all, this is the fruit of former deeds.

108.

அறிவுடையார் சிலர் தீக்கருமங்களைச் செய்தற்குக் காரணம்.

அறியாரும் அல்லர் அறிவ தறிந்தும்
பழியோடு பட்டவை செய்தல்,—வளியோடி
நெய்த னறவுயிர்க்கு நீள்கடற் றண்சேர்ப்ப!—
செய்த வினையான் வரும்.

Why even wise men sin.

They are not ignorant; but, though what man should know they know, yet they do deeds that bring guilt to their souls.—Lord of the wide sea's pleasant shore, where breezes breathe the lily's fragrance round!—This comes from former deeds.

எ: செய்தல்.—ப: வரும்.
So in B. I. S. 1217:

'उत्पादयति लोकस्य प्रीतिं मलयमारुतः।
The Malayāḷam wind affords pleasure to the world.'

109.

அவரவர் செய்த நல்வினைதீவினைகளை அநுபவித்தால் அன்றி அவை ஒழியா.

ஈண்டுநீர் வையத்துள் எல்லாரும் எத்துணையும்
வேண்டார்மற் றீய, விழைபய னல்லவை;
வேண்டினும், வேண்டா விடினும், உறற்பால
தீண்டா விடுதல் அரிது.

Desires are unavailing.

On the earth begirt by gathering waters no men desire in anywise evil things, but choice fruit of good things. Yet whether they desire, or abhor, it is hard to shun the touch of what fate assigns.

This is against (விருப்பு வெறுப்புகள்) desires and aversions (see note at the beginning of this chapter), which are the cause of *āgamiyam*.

Comp. 103 as to wishes, and K. ch. xxxvii.

110.

இருவினைப்பயன்களை யாவரும் விருப்புவெறுப்பின்றி அநுபவிக்கவேண்டும்.

சிறுகா, பெருகா, முறைபிறழ்ந்து வாரா,
உறுகாலத் தூற்ருகா, ஆமிடத்தே யாகும்,
சிறுகாலைப் பட்ட பொறியும்; அதனுல்
இறுகாலத் தென்னை பரிவு?

Fate is unalterable. Why grieve?

The early fates diminish not, nor do they increase, they come not in order changed; help in troublous times is none; what haps will happen, there and then; and so, when all things fail, why grieve?

Comp. 117. G. 89.
This is B. I. S. 92:

अचोद्यमानानि यथा पुष्पाणि च फलानि च ।
स्वं कालं नातिवर्तन्ते तथा कर्म पुराकृतम् ॥

CHAPTER XII.

TRUTH: REALITY.

அதிகாரம் கஉ.

மெய்ம்மை

(= உண்மையினதுதன்மை).

In K. ch. xxx is entitled வாய்மை = மெய்ம்மை; but here it is not simply truth as opposed to falsehood that is treated of, but also reality, as opposed to what is in appearance only. In a world of feigning and folly a man must be true.

Comp. B. I.S. 1257:

'धर्मः सत्यपरो लोके मूलं सर्वस्य चोच्यते ।

Truth is chief among virtues in the world, and is called the root of all.'

Analysis:

1. Do not delude suppliants with vain hopes. [111.]
2. Be always the same. [112.]
3. Avoid the false friendship that cannot stand the test of adversity. [113.]
4. Wealth is essential alike to virtue and pleasure. [114.]
5. The poor man's words are unheeded. [115.]
6. The real nature changes not. [116.]
7. Scorn scorners. [117.]
8. Truth is one. Schools of thought many. [118.]
9. Make the best of things. [119.]
10. Nothing survives men but their deeds. [120.]

111.

தம்மை.ஒன்று கேட்டோருக்குத் தருவோம் என்றுகூறிப்பின்பு தராதவர்கள் மிகவும் குற்றமுடையவர்கள்.

இசையா வொருபொரு ளில்லென்றல் யார்க்கும்
வசைஅன்று வையத் தியற்கை — நசைபழுங்க
நின்றோடிப் பொய்த்த லிரைதொடீஇச் செய்ந்நன்றி
கொன்றாரிற் குற்றம் உடைத்து.

Broken promises.

O maid with many armlets graced! To answer 'no' disgraces no man, when the boon asked exceeds his means.

It is the world's course. But to delay and cheat the soul faint with desire is a sin like his who '*slays*' a benefit conferred.

எ: என்றல், பொய்த்தல்.—ப: அன்று, இயற்கை, உடைத்து. G. 91.

To 'kill a benefit' is a curious phrase; see K. 110. It means 'to pervert, turn good into evil.' Perhaps the idea of நசை *etc.* is 'while (the suppliant) is suffering from desire, the deceiving him by standing (as though about to give) and then running away from him.' This is a Sanskrit idiom too. See Lex.

112.

மேலோருங் கீழோரும் தம்மியற்கைக் குணத்தில் நின்றும் நீங்கார்.

தக்காருந் தக்கவர் அல்லாருந் தந்நீர்மை
எக்காலுங் குன்ற லிலராவர்;—அக்காரம்
யாவரே தின்னினுங் கையாதாங் கைக்குமாம்
தேவரே தின்னினும் வேம்பு.

Natures change not.

Men of worth, and men unworthy too, retain their natures ever unchanged. Whoever they be that eat it, sugar can never grow bitter; and *margosa* is bitter even when eaten by gods.

113.

செல்வர்க்கு யாரும் உறவினர்; வறியவர்க்குச்சிலர் உறவுடையோம் என்பர்.

காலாடு போழ்திற் கழிகிளைஞர் வானத்து
மேலாடு மீனிற் பலராவர்; ஏலா
இடரொருவர் உற்றக்கால்,—ஈர்ங்குன்ற நாட!—
தொடர்புடையேம் என்பார் சிலர்.

Friends in adverse and prosperous times.

When a man moves prosperously on, devoted kinsfolk are countless as shining stars that move in the upper heaven. But when grievous affliction haps,—Lord of the dripping hills!—few claim close alliance with him.

Comp. K. 752 and ch. xxix. ஈர்ங். G. 41. (அ.)

114.

பொருளுடையார் அறமின்பங்களை அடைவதும் அஃதில்லார் துன்பமுறுவதும் உண்மை.

வடுவிலா வையத்து மன்னிய மூன்றில்
நடுவணை தெய்த விருதலையும் எய்தும்;
நடுவணை தெய்தாதான் எய்தும் உலைப்பெய்
தடுவது போலுந் துயர்.

Wealth the essential thing. Virtue, wealth, and pleasure.

Of the three things that endure upon this faultless earth, he who gains the midmost gains the two extremes also. He who gains not the midmost gains the cruel smart that the turtle feels when put into the pot to boil.

தொ. எ: ஒருவன், எய்தாதான்.—ப: எய்தும்.—செ: இருதலை, துயர். Comp. 331. G. 137.

115.

செல்வர்சொல் வறியவர்சொல்.

நல்லாவின் கன்றாயி னாகும் விலைபெறாஉம்;
கல்லாரே ஆயினுஞ் செல்வர்வாய்ச் சொற்செல்லும்;
புல்லீரப் போழ்தி னுழவேபோன் மீதாடிச்
செல்லாவா நல்கூர்ந்தார் சொல்.

The words of the rich and of the poor.

A young heifer fetches a good price when it is the calf of a good cow; so the words of rich men, though unlearned, pass current. Poor men's words, like the plough when moisture is scanty, merely graze the surface and are of no avail.

எ: சொல்.—ப: செல்லும், செல்லாவாம். See K. 1046. G. 14.

116.

கல்வியால் இயற்கைக் குணம் மாறாமை.

இடம்பட மெய்ஞ்ஞானங் கற்பினும் என்றும்
அடங்காதார் என்றும் அடங்கார்;—தடங்கண்ணாய்!
உப்பொடு நெய்பா றயிர்காயம் பெய்தடினுங்
கைப்பறா பேய்ச்சுரையின் காய்.

Wisdom cannot benefit the undisciplined.

O wide-eyed one! though you cook the wild gourd, pouring in salt, ghee, milk, curds, and spices, it never loses its bitterness. So those who never discipline themselves, though they may learn extensive works of true wisdom, never become disciplined.

எ: அடங்காதார், காய்.—ப: அடங்கார், கைப்பரு. G. 31.
Addressed to a woman, the illustration is from her department.

117.

யாவருக்கும் வரத்தக்கது வந்தடைவது உண்மை, ஆதலால் இகழ்வாரை இகழ்க.

தம்மை இகழ்வாரைத் தாமவரின் முன்னிகழ்க!
என்னை அவரொடு பட்டது?—புன்னை
விறற்பூங் கமழ்கானல் வீங்குநீர்ச் சேர்ப்ப!—
உறற்பால யார்க்கும் உறும்.

Scorn the scorners.

When men scorn you, before their faces scorn them too! what has a man to do with them?—Lord of the shore where beauteous *Punnai*-flowers perfume the glades that surround the swelling tide,—what's fated comes to all!

118.

உண்மையைக்குருதமிடத்தச் சமயங்கள் பலவே அன்றி, அச்சமயங்கள் கூறும் அறநெறி ஒன்றே.

ஆவே றுருவின ஆயினும் ஆபயந்த
பால்வே றுருவின அல்லவாம்;—பால்போல்,
ஒருதன்மைத் தாகும் அறநெறி, ஆபோல்
உருவு பலகொளல் ஈங்கு.

Cows of many colours, milk always white. Virtue one—many sects.

Though cows in form are diverse, the milk they yield is not diverse. The way of virtue, like that milk, is one in nature, though the schools that teach it here are like those cows, of many forms.

எ: பால், அறநெறி, சமயங்கள் (தொகை).—ப: அல்லவாம், ஆகும், கொளல்.
So Vēm. i. 189: '*Pasula vanne vēru, pālellanokkaṭi:*
The colours of cows are diverse, the milk is one.'

119.

இவ்வுலகத்துப் புகழில்லாதாரும், முயற்சியால் வாழாதாரும், வசையில்லாரும், சாமளவும் செல்வம் அநுபவித்தாரும் இல்லை.

யாஅர் உலகத்தோர் சொல்லில்லார்? தேருங்கால்
யாஅர் உபாயத்தின் வாழாதார்?—யாஅர்
இடையாக இன்னாத தெய்தாதார்? யாஅர்
கடைபோகச் செல்வம் உய்த்தார்?

Four questions. The common lot.

Look well! of whom hath not the world found word to say?
And who have not by prudence prospered in life's way?
Ah! who in life's mid course no bitter grief have known?
Ah! who to end of life have kept their wealth their own?

This is evidently the same as B. I. S. 1606:

कस्य दोषः कुले नास्ति व्याधिना को न पीडितः।
व्यसनं केन न प्राप्तं कस्य सौख्यं निरन्तरम् ॥

சொல் is rendered by one Commentator as = புகழ், and by another as = நிந்தை: = 'none are faultless, so none escape *censure*.'

உபாயம் is used for 'means of success against an enemy.' These are சாமம், பேதம், தானம், and தண்டம், 'conciliation, division, bribery, and punishment.' Comp. *Hitōpadēçam*; and Jī. Chin. iii. 255, *etc.*

120.

இறக்கும் பொழுது உடன் செல்வது தாஞ் செய்தவினையே.

தாஞ்செய் வினையல்லாற் றம்மொடு செல்வதுமற்
றியாங்கணுந் தேரிற் பிறிதில்லை;—ஆங்குத்தாம்
போற்றிப் புனைந்த உடம்பும் பயமின்றே
கூற்றங்கொண் டோடும் பொழுது.

Nothing accompanies in death but deeds.

Save a man's deeds nought goes with him, search where you will. The body which men cherish so, and adorn, is itself profitless indeed when death shall seize and hurry off with it.

Comp. ch. xi, and 5.

CHAPTER XIII.

DREAD OF EVIL DEEDS.

அதிகாரம் கங.

தீவினையச்சம்

(=பாவஞ்செய்தற்கஞ்சுதல்).

In K. ch. xxi has the same title, but the subject is quite differently and more effectively treated there.

Analysis:

A virtuous man must dread the evils which would render his dedication of himself unfruitful; and these are here—

I. Cruelty to animals; [121–123]

1. by feeding on them; [121]
2. by imprisoning them in cages; [122]
3. especially by eating crabs;—[123]

II. Association with false friends; [124–129]

4. who pervert the righteous; [124]
5. whose pretended friendship will be as the waning moon; [125]
6. who will be as serpents; [126]
7. whose minds are inscrutable; [127]
8. who regard only their own interests; [128]
9. who will ruin you in both worlds;—[129] and

III. Addiction to worldly joys. [130.]

Comp. my K. pp. 241, 242.

121.

அறிவிலார் மிருகாதிகளைக்கொலை செய்து உண்டு துறவுநெறியிற் செல்லார்.

துக்கத்துட் டூங்கித் துறவின்கட் சேர்கலா
மக்கட் பிணத்த சுடுகாடு;—தொக்க
விலங்கிற்கும் புள்ளிற்குங் காடே புலன்கெட்ட
புல்லறி வாளர் வயிறு.

Men lead lives of self-indulgence.

The burning-ground is filled with the corpses of men that will not give themselves up to a self-renouncing life, but oscillate amid sorrows; and the maws of perverted foolish men are a mere burning-ground for beasts and birds.

எ: சுடுகாடு, காடு.—ப: பிணத்த, வயிறு.

122.

இக்கொடியவர் நரகம் அடைவர்.

இரும்பார்க்குங் காலராய் ஏதிலார்க் காளாய்க்
கரும்பார் கழனியுட் சேர்வர் — சுரும்பார்க்குங்
காட்டுளாய் வாழுஞ் சிவலுங் குறும்பூழுங்
கூட்டுளாய்க் கொண்டுவைப் பார்.

Penalty for imprisoning birds.

Their legs in iron bound, as slaves to alien lords, they will till the black and barren soil, who snared and kept in cages partridges and quails, that dwell in wilds where beetles hum amid the flowers.

எ: வைப்பார்.—ப: சேர்வர்.

Comp. K. 330. [Pope's K. p. 242.]

In Jī. Chin. xiii. 250–295 we have a striking illustration of this quatrain. *Jīvagan*, the hero of the poem, is met by a divine teacher, to whom he proposes the question, 'What is the history of my past transmigrations? What sin am I now expiating?' The *Guru* tells him the following story: 'In the country of *Dādaki*, in the city of *Bhūmimātilagam*, there was a king whose name was *Pavaṇamādēvan*. His wife was *Çayamati*. Their son's name was *Çōdaran*. *You are that son.* His parents married him to beautiful wives, and one day when he was sporting with them on the shore of a lake covered with lotus flowers, his wives begged him to cause some young cygnets to be caught and given them as pets. This he ordered his servants to do, and the ladies fed the young birds with milk and treated them with the utmost tenderness. One day the father of the young prince saw the captive birds, was horror-struck, and sending for his son, thus addressed him: "My son, those who separate birds and beasts from their kindred, and imprison them, will themselves in another birth be torn away from their kindred and reduced to captivity." [பூவைகிளிதோகை புணரன்ன மொடுபெண்மா னாவை அவைதங்கிளையினீங்கி அழ வாங்கிக் காவல் செய்துவைத்தவர்கடங்கிளையினீங்கிப் போவர் . . .] The prince hearing this, was sore afraid, and caused the birds to be released and restored to their flowery home on the lake. He afterwards, in due time, renounced the kingdom, performed penances, became the *Indra* of an *Aeon*, and was incarnate in your person. Your own exile, captivity, and conflicts have all been the consequences of that one sin!' *Jīvagan* was so impressed by this narrative, that he renounced the world, gave himself up to a life of penance, and at last obtained release.

123.

ஞெண்டுகொன்றுதின்பவர் வருந்துவர்.

அக்கேபோ லங்கை யொழிய விரலழுகித்
துக்கத் தொழுநோ யெழுபவே,—அக்கால்
அலவனைக் காதலித்துக் கான்முரித்துத் தின்ற
பழவினை வந்தடைந்தக் கால்.

The penalty incurred by crab-eaters.

Like fire their palms shall glow, their fingers rot away, who loved in other times on crabs to feed, and broke their joints, what time the guilt of 'olden deeds' comes home, and leprosy's fierce pangs assail.

Understand உண்டவர்கள் as subject to எழுப.

In Jī. Chin. xiii. § 10, verse 164 *etc.*, the punishments to be endured in different hells are described with terrible realism. See also *Kāçi-Kāṇḍam*, ch. viii. In Dante there is much that closely resembles these pictures, especially in the account of Malebolge.

அங்கை, see *Nannūl* 222.

124.

நல்லொழுக்கமுடையாருந் தீயொழுக்கமுடையாரைச் சேர்ந்தாற்கெடுவர்.

நெருப்பழற் சேர்ந்தக்கா னெய்போல் வதூஉம்
எரிப்பச்சுட் டெவ்வநோ யாக்கும்;—பரப்பக்
கொடுவினையர் ஆகுவர் கோடாருங் கோடிக்
கடுவினையர் ஆகியார்ச் சார்ந்து.

Bad companions.

Even things (soft and soothing) like *ghee*, when joined with the fierce heat of fire, will blaze and burn, and cause bitter anguish: so even upright men are perverted and give themselves up to deeds of utter evil, when they attach themselves to those whose deeds are evil.

. எ: போல்வது, கோடார்.—ப: ஆக்கும், ஆகுவர்.

அழல் becomes அழற் by poetic license. Comp. G. 35 and *Nan.* 255; also ch. xviii and xxiv, 171–180 and 231–240.

125.

தீவினைக்கு அஞ்சாத கேழோரதுநட்பு வளராததேயும்.

பெரியவர் கேண்மை பிறைபோல நாளும்
வரிசை வரிசையா நந்தும்;—வரிசையால்
வானூர் மதியம்போல் வைகலுந் தேயுமே
தானே சிறியார் தொடர்பு.

Friendships with great and mean.

Great men's intimate regard will daily grow in order due like the crescent moon. Mean men's alliance like the full moon that rides the sky daily by degrees dwindles away of itself.

Friendship of the great with the great. Comp. 138, 166. K. 782. வரிசையால். G. 137*.

126.

தகுதியில்லாத ஒருவரோடு நட்புக்கொள்ளின் தீதாய்முடியும்.

சான்றோர் எனமதித்துச் சார்ந்தாய்மற் சார்ந்தாய்க்குச்
சான்றாண்மை சார்ந்தார்க ணில்லாயின்,—சார்ந்தாய், கேள்!
சாந்தகத் துண்டென்று செப்புத் திறந்தொருவன்
பாம்பகத்துக் கண்ட துடைத்து!

Disappointment and danger from foolish attachments.

Thou didst attach thyself (to unworthy persons), saying, they are men of absolute integrity! If to thee who hast thus attached thyself, integrity in those thine intimates does not appear; hear, O thou who hast so attached thyself, it is as if one opened a casket, thinking it contained an odorous unguent, and saw a snake within.

எ: (அக).—ப: கண்டதுடைத்து.

127.

இவர் தீமைக்கஞ்சுவர், இவர் அஞ்சார் என்று ஒருவர் உள்ளக்கருத்தை அறிவது அரிது.

யாஅ ரொருவர் ஒருவர்தம் முள்ளத்தைத்
தேருந் துணைமை உடையவர்?—சாரல்
கனமணி நின்றிமைக்கு' நாட, கேண்!—மக்கள்
மனம்வேறு செய்கையும் வேறு.

Man cannot fathom other men's minds.

What single man has power to search and clearly know the inmost self of other men? Lord of the land where weighty gems glisten on mountain slope, O hear!—Men's minds are otherwise, and otherwise their deeds.

B. I. S.:

'सुदुःखं पुरुषज्ञानं चित्तं ह्येषां चलाचलम्।
It is very hard to know men, their minds are never in one stay.'

128.

தமக்கு ஒருபயன் கருதி நட்புக்கொள்பவர் சிநேகம் குற்றமுடையதாகும்.

உள்ளத்தா னள்ளா துறுதித் தொழிலராய்க்
கள்ளத்தா னட்டார் கழிகேண்மை — தெள்ளிப்
புனற்செதும்பு நின்றலைக்கும் பூங்குன்ற நாட!—
மனத்துக்கண் மாசாய் விடும்.

Friends from self-interest.

Lord of the flowery hilly land, where streams wash out and carry hither and thither (precious things) from the marshy land!—The effusive friendship of those who do not attach themselves (to us) in heart, but perform certain friendly acts merely to strengthen their own position, and who form friendships guilefully, will issue in disappointment to the minds (of those who are intimate with them).

உறுதித் தொழிலர் ஆகி = 'being persons of service which has strength.' This is quite ambiguous, but the context suggests the interpretation given. மனத்துக்கண்மாசாய் விடும் = 'will result faultily in the mind.' See உறு in Lex.

129.

தீவினைக்கஞ்சாதாரோடு கொள்ளும் நட்பு இருமைப்பயனையுங் கெடுக்கும்.

ஒக்கிய ஒள்வாடன் னொன்னார்கைப் பட்டக்கால்
ஊக்கம் அழிப்பதூஉ' மெய்யாகும்;— ஆக்கம்
இருமையுஞ் சென்று சுடுதலா னல்ல
கருமமே கல்லார்கட் டீர்வு.

Ruin from unfitting intimacies.

If the glittering sword a man brandishes (be allowed to) fall into the hands of his foes, it will assuredly come about that he will thus destroy also his own power of action. So wealth (bestowed on the foolish) will go and burn up (merit accruing in) both worlds, and therefore the really good thing is to keep clear of the foolish.

ஒக்கிய = ஒய்கிய (வலித்தல். G. 41). எ: தீர்வு.—ப: நல்லகருமமே (ஆகும்).

[His own carelessly-handled weapon will ruin him. If any one be the means of giving to evil men power, influence, and wealth (ஆக்கம்), he must be responsible here and hereafter for those men's abuse of these advantages.]

130.

தீவினைக்கஞ்சி அறஞ்செய்தோர்க்கு அதனினும் மிக்க பயனில்லை.

மனைப்பாசங் கைவிடாய்; மக்கட்கென் றேங்கி
எனைத்தூழி வாழ்தியோ, நெஞ்சே?—எனைத்தும்
சிறுவரையே ஆயினுஞ் செய்தநன் றல்லால்
உறுபயனே இல்லை உயிர்க்கு.

To do good is life's gain.

O mind! thou leavest not the bonds of home. How many cycles, pray, wilt thou live yearning still for children? Save the good he has done, however small its measure may be, there is no true result to any living soul.

END OF PART I.

PART II.

ON WEALTH.

இரண்டாவது: பொருட்பால்.

[CH. XIV–XXXIX.]

THIS division of the work treats of the good things of life, the way to obtain and enjoy them, and the evils that mar their enjoyment. The subjects are arranged in no very obvious logical order.

பொருள் = अर्थ. Beschi renders it curiously 'rerum proprietates;' Graul has 'de bonis,' 'vom Gute;' and Ariel, 'la fortune.' See my *Kurraḷ*, Introd. pp. vii, viii.

This book comprises twenty-six chapters, and may be thus subdivided:

§ I. Essentials of well-being: learning (xiv); good family (xv); magnanimity (xvi); tact in intercourse with superiors (xvii); good companions (xviii); moral greatness (xix).

§ II. Means to a happy life: energy (xx); family affection (xxi); suitable friendships (xxii–xxiv); prudence (xxv, xxvi).

§ III. Right use and estimate of wealth: benevolence (xxvii); liberality (xxviii); want (xxix).

§ IV. Qualities that give dignity: self-respect (xxx); independence (xxxi); skill in controversy (xxxii).

§ V. Things that degrade: folly and meanness (xxxiii–xxxvi).

§ VI. Domestic matters and miscellaneous: bad women and worthy matrons (xxxvii–xxxix).

The whole is a series of aphorisms full of homely proverbial philosophy connected with South-Indian middle-class life.

CHAPTER XIV.

LEARNING.

அதிகாரம் கச.

கல்வி

(= நூல்களைக்கற்றல்).

This is first among the means by which men obtain and rightly use 'the good things of life:' பொருள்.

The connection between this and civil government, which is maintained in the *Kurraḷ*, is here discarded.

Analysis:

1. Learning is the chief *ornament* of man; and this, because it gives a sense of equity, and enlightens his conscience. [131.]
2. It has four special advantages, and is the remedy for *unwisdom*. [132.]
3. It dignifies men whatever their place of birth. [133]
4. It has three special advantages, and is the best legacy a man can leave to his children. [134.]
5. It requires discrimination. [135.]
6. It is to be respected wherever found. [136.]
7. The pleasures of learned converse are surpassingly great; [137]
8. and these increase with enjoyment. [138.]
9. Association with the learned gives wisdom even to the foolish. [139.]
10. But not worldly knowledge merely is to be sought, true wisdom is needful. [140.]

With this comp. *Kurraḷ* 391–430, and the notes. *Nīti*, 2–25 are mainly on this topic.

131.

ஒருவற்குக் கல்வியழகே அழகன்றி ஆடை அணி முதலியவற்றான் வரும் அழகு அழகன்று.

குஞ்சி அழகுங் கொடுந்தானைக் கோட்டழகும்
மஞ்சள் அழகும் அழகல்ல;—நெஞ்சத்து
நல்லம்யாம் என்னு' நடுவு நிலைமையால்
கல்வி அழகே அழகு.

Learning, the only beauty.

Beauty of locks, beauty of circling garments' folds, beauty of saffron tint: these are not beauty true. Integrity of soul that brings the conscience peace is learning's gift: that only is beauty true!

Lit., by means of that impartiality that says 'we are good.'

Comp. K. ch. xii and Pope's K. p. 253. Only the thoroughly instructed man can be fair-minded and intelligently just. The line நல்லம்யாம், *etc.* = *mens conscia recti.* The kind of கல்வி is stated in 140. *Nīti.* 13.

நல்லம் is வினைக்குறிப்புமுற்று, pl. 1st pers. agreeing with யாம். G. 93. நெஞ்சத்து = நெஞ்சத்தில். G. 152.

An inferior version of this is found in *Ēlā.* 75:

'இடைவனப்புந் தோள்வனப்பும் ஈடின் வனப்பும்
நடைவனப்பு நாணின் வனப்பும்—புடைசால்
கழுத்தின்வனப்பும் வனப்பல்ல; எண்ணோ
டெழுத்தின் வனப்பே வனப்பு.

Beauty is not in waist, nor in arm, nor in strength, nor in deportment, nor in modesty, nor in a shapely neck: numbers and letters are beauty.' [K. 392, 407.]

Comp. B.I.S. 7609: 'विद्यैव भूषणं पुंसां, the adornment of men is knowledge.'

132.

அஞ்ஞானம் ஆகிய நோயை நீக்குதற்குக் கல்வியினுஞ் சிறந்த மருந்தில்லை.

இம்மை பயக்குமால், ஈயக் குறைவின்றால்,
தம்மை விளக்குமாற், றாம்உளராக் கேடின்றால்,
எம்மை உலகத்தும் யாங்காணேங் கல்விபோல்
மம்மர் அறுக்கு' மருந்து.

The remedy for bewilderment.

Since in this world it yields fruit; since given it grows not less; since it makes men illustrious; since it perishes not as long as (its possessors) themselves exist; in any world we see not any medicine that, like learning, removes the delusions of sense.

ஆல் occurs here four times. It is called by Tamil commentators அசைநிலை. See G. 116. But it is the sign of the instrumental case, and hence is equivalent to 'since, by cause that,' acting as a case-ending to the whole clause, considered as a noun.

The infin. ஈய and ஆ (= ஆக) make time-phrases, '*when* given,' '*while* they exist.' G. 140.

133.

கீழ்க்குலத்தில் பிறந்தோர் ஆயினும் கற்றறிந்தவரே சிறப்புடையவர் ஆவர்.

களர்நிலத்துப் பிறந்த உப்பினைச் சான்றோர்
விளைநிலத்து நெல்லின் விழுமிதாக் கொள்வர்;
கடைநிலத்தோர் ஆயினுங் கற்றறிந் தோரைத்
தலைநிலத்து வைக்கப் படும்.

The learned, though low-born, are first.

The excellent regard the salt produced in brackish *ground* as choicer than the *Nel* from fertile *soil.* It is fitting to place in the first *rank* the learned-wise, though (sprung) from the lowest *origin.*

The main word is நிலம், used in different senses. The first நிலத்து has ellipsis of 7th case; the second of the same, and of பிறந்த; the last of the 7th case. G. 152, 157.

கற்றறிந்தோரை is governed by வைக்க = வைத்தல், which is subj. G. 145. படும் is pred. = தகுதியாம். The two sentences may be connected by அதுபோல, 'in like manner.'

134.

ஒருவன்றன் புதல்வர்க்கு ஒன்றுனும் அழியாத கல்விப் பொருளையே தேடி வைக்கல் வேண்டும்.

வைப்புழிக் கோட்படா; வாய்த்தீயிற் கேடில்லை;
மிக்க சிறப்பின் அரசர் செறின் வவ்வார்;
எச்சம் எனஒருவன் மக்கட்குச் செய்வன
விச்சைமற் றல்ல பிற.

Learning, the best legacy.

It cannot be taken from its place of deposit; it does not perish anywhere by fire; if kings of surpassing grandeur are angry they cannot take it away; (and therefore) what any man should provide for his children as a legacy is learning. Other things are not (real wealth).

For உழி = place, see G. 63. படா. G. 89. என. G. 114. வாய்த்தீ. G. 153. வாயில் உள்ளதீ. எ: செய்வன. G. 95. ப: விச்சை. Comp. 280 and K. 67.

Comp. B. I. S. 3240:

'न चौरहार्यं न च राजहार्यं विदेशयाने न च भारकारि ।
एतद्धनं सर्वधनात्प्रधानं विद्याधनं यत्पुरुषा वहन्ति ॥

The wealth of learning, which men carry with them, is the best of all wealth; for it cannot be taken away by thieves, nor reft away by the king, nor is it burdensome in journeying from land to land.'

135.

வாழ்நாள்சில; அவற்றிலும் நோய்கள்பல; ஆதலால், யாவரும் இன்றியமையாத நூல்களையே கற்க வேண்டும்.

கல்வி கரையில, கற்பவர் நாள்சில,
மெல்ல நினைக்கிற் பிணிபல;—தெள்ளிதின்
ஆராய்ந் தமைவுடைய கற்பவே,—நீர்ஒழியப்
பால்உண் குருகிற் றெரிந்து!

Discriminating study.

Learning hath no bounds, the learner's days are few. If you think calmly diseases many wait around! With clear discrimination learn what is meet for you, like the swan that leaving the water drinks the milk.

See my K. p. 252. Note தனிச்சொல் in line 3.

Here are four sentences: subj. கல்வி, நாள், பிணி, and ஒருவன் (understood); pred. இல, சில, பல, கற்ப. கற்ப, G. 83, is poet. 3rd pl. = 'they will learn,' and is used as an optative, 'let learn.' குருகு + இல, G. 61, 'like the bird.'

The mythic *Hañça* (அன்னப்பட்சி) is said to have the faculty of drinking only the milk in any mixture offered to it. The following is suggestive:

THERE IS A SENSE BEYOND THE SENSES!

'நாக்கின் அறிப இனியசுவை; மூக்கினான்
மோந்தறிப எல்லா மலர்களும்;—நோக்குள்ளும்
கண்ணினாற் காண்ப அணியவற்றை; தொக்கிருந்
தெண்ணினான் எண்ணப் படும்.

By the tongue they know sweet flavours; by the nose they smell and know all flowers; by eyes that discern they see adornments; by thoughtful investigation of many combined (the truth of invisible realities) is thought out.'—[N. M. K. 78.]

Comp. B. I. S. 245 and 7605:

अनन्तशास्त्रं बहुलाश्च विद्याः स्वल्पश्च कालो बहुविघ्नता च ।
यत्सारभूतं तदुपासनीयं हंसो यथा क्षीरमिवाम्बुमिश्रम् ॥

Which is the original? Comp. also Vēm. i. 166:

Pāla nīru kramamu paraga hamsa yerungu.

136.

கல்விகற்றவனுடைய வருணத்தை நினைக்கவேண்டாம்.

தோணி இயக்குவான் றொல்லை வருணத்துக்
காணிற் கடைப்பட்டான் என்றிகழார்,—காணாய்!
அவன் றுணையா ஆறு போயற்றே, நூல்கற்ற
மகன்றுணையா நல்ல கொளல்!

Never mind the boatman's caste if he take you over!

As none contemn the ferryman, by old caste rule to lowest

rank assigned, but cross the stream by help he lends; so take thou teachings good and wise by help of him who is the learned man.

எ: ஒருவர். (தொகை.)—ப: இகழார், கொளல். G. 85. தோணி = தோணியை. அவன் = அவனையே. ஆறு = ஆற்றை. G. 152. போயற்று = போய் அற்று. இதில், போய் = போனல். G. 137. நல்ல கொளல் = நல்லவை கற்றுக்கொள்ளக்கடவாய். ரெல்லே. றுணை. G. 38.

137.

கற்றறிவுடையார்பலர் கூடி இருந்து அடையும் இன்பத்தினுஞ் மறுலோகத்திற்பஞ் சிறந்ததன்று.

தவலருந் தொல்கேள்வித் தன்மை யுடையார்
இகலிலர் எஃகுடையார் தம்முட் குழீஇ
நகலின் இனிதாயிற் காண்பாம்—அகல்வானத்
தும்பர் உறைவார் பதி.

The supreme enjoyment of the society of learned and amiable men.

We shall see whether any greater bliss is found in the city inhabited by the dwellers in the ample heaven than is felt when men of natures formed by old imperishable lore, from rivalries exempt, keen as tempered steel, meet together and laugh.

Comp. 233 and B. I. S. 5390. See தனிச்சொல் in line 3.

138.

கற்றூர், கல்லாதவர் கொள்ளும் நட்பின் இயல்பு.

கனைகடற் றண்சேர்ப்ப! கற்றறிந்தார் கேண்மை
நுனியிற் கரும்பு தின்றற்றே;—நுனிநீக்கித்
தூரிற்றின் றன்ன தகைத்தரோ பண்பிலா
ஈரம் இலாளர் தொடர்பு.

The friendship of the learned ever grows sweeter, that of the unlearned ever diminishes in sweetness.

Lord of the cool shore of the resounding sea! intimacy with learned people is like eating sugar-cane from the (tender, juicy) tip; association with graceless, sapless men is like leaving the (tender) tip and eating it from the (hard, dry) root.

எ: கேண்மை, தொடர்பு.—ப: தின்றற்று, தகைத்து. கனைகடற்றண் சேர்ப்ப. G. 153, 152, 50, 64. தின்றன்ன, தின்றற்றே = தின்றுற்போதும். G. 137. அரோ, அசைநிலை.

Comp. also 125, 166.

கேண்மை.

The enduring character of real friendship is a favourite topic with Tamil poets.

In Jī. Chin. xiii. 139 the fragrant unguent with which the queens anointed their hair is thus described:

[Metre: .. வி | .. மா | .. மா *bis*. G. 193.]

'ஒருபகல் பூசின் ஓராண் டொழிவின்றி விடாது நாறும்
பெரியவர் கேண்மை போலும் பெறற்கரும் வாச வெண்ணெய்.

Perfumed unguent rarely found, resembling the friendship of the great, yielding for a year unfailing fragrance, if it be used but for a single day!'

139.

கற்றவரின் சாவகாசம்.

கல்லாரே ஆயினுங் கற்றாரைச் சேர்ந்தொழுகின்
நல்லறிவு நாளுந் தலைப்படுவர்;—தொல்சிறப்பின்
ஒண்ணிறப் பாதிரிப்பூச் சேர்தலாற் புத்தோடு
தண்ணீர்க்குத் தான்பயந் தாங்கு.

The benefits of association with the learned. The pot impregnated with odour.

Though themselves unlearned, if men live in association with the learned they advance daily in excellent knowledge. The new vessel, by contact with the *Pādri*-flower of old renown and lustrous hue, imparts fragrance to the cold water it contains.

எ: மனிதர். (தொகை.)—ப: தலைப்படுவர். ஆயினும். G. 141. படுவர். G. 124. ஒண்ணிற = ஒள்ளிய நிறத்தையுடைய.

140.

அறநூல்களைக் கற்க வேண்டும்.

அலகுசால் கற்பின் அறிவுநூல் கல்லா
துலகநூல் ஓதுவ தெல்லாங்—கலகல
கூஉந் துணை அல்லாற், கொண்டு தடுமாற்றம்
போஒந் துணை அறிவார் இல்.

Books of wisdom are the best. Others cannot remove confusion of mind.

If men leaving works of wisdom, that contain well-weighed instruction, unstudied, devote themselves to the recitation of mere worldly literature, they will acquire a store of empty high-sounding words, but not that wisdom by means of which mental confusion (that treats unreal things as real) is removed.

எ: அறிவார்.—ப: இல். அலகு சால் = எண் அமைந்த நூல்களை. G. 157. கற்பின். G. 86. கூஉம், போஒம் = கூவும், போகும். G. 14, 87. Comp. K. 34.

CHAPTER XV.

HIGH BIRTH.

அதிகாரம் கரு.

குடிப்பிறப்பு

(= உயர்வாகிய குடியிற்பிறத்தல்).

This chapter can only be taken as a strong affirmation of the truth that nobility of heart and conduct is the only true nobility; without this the mere accident of birth in a noble family only renders the ignoble more conspicuously contemptible.

Analysis:

1. Adversity changes not the essentially noble man; [141, 147, 148, 149, 150]
2. nor does prosperity dignify the essentially ignoble. [142.]
3. True courtesy is nobility. [143.]
4. Essential nobility possesses: [144, 145, 146]
    - *a.* Instinctive perception of right and wrong; [144]
    - *b.* Sensitive dread of guilt; [145]
    - *c.* Fondness for good people, pleasant speech, liberality, and purity of soul. [146.]

With this K. ch. xcvi must be minutely compared.
The following (T. 92) is a fitting motto for the chapter:

'விழுத்துணைத் தோன்று தவனும்—எழுத்தினை
ஒன்றும் உணராத ஏழையும்—என்றும்
இறந்துரை காமுறு வானுமிம் மூவர்
பிறந்தும் பிறவா தவர்.

He who does not spring from virtuous ancestry; the wretched fellow who knows nothing of letters; he who delights in words that offend: these three though born among men are not men.'

141.

வறுமைக்காலத்தும் உயர்ந்தகுடியிற்பிறந்தோர் நல்லொழுக்கத்தினின்றுதவறார்.

உடுக்கை உலறி உடம்பழிந்தக் கண்ணும்
குடிப்பிறப் பாளர்தங் கொள்கையிற் குன்றார்;
இடுக்கண் டலைவந்தக் கண்ணும் அரிமா
கொடிப்புற் கறிக்குமோ மற்று?

In adversity noble men do not desert their principles.

Though their clothes may be old and their body worn with want, men of noble birth diminish nothing of their due observances. Will the lion nibble the creeping grass although sorest need should assail him?

Comp. K. ch. xcvii, and 148.

142.

மேன்மக்களின் இயல்பு.

சான்றாண்மை சாயல் ஒழுக்கம் இவைமூன்றும்
வான்றோய் குடிப்பிறந்தார்க் கல்லது,—வான்றோயும்
மைதவழ் வெற்ப!—படாஅ பெருஞ்செல்வம்
எய்தியக் கண்ணும் பிறர்க்கு.

The high-born only have perfect excellence, greatness, and good manners.

Lord of the hills traversed by clouds that touch the heavens! true excellence, and dignity, and good conduct,—these three things belong to men of race that touches heaven, and not to others, even though they may have acquired great wealth.

143.

மேன்மக்களின் ஒழுக்கம்.

இருக்கை எழலும் எதிர்செலவும் ஏனை
விடுப்ப ஒழிதலோ டின்ன,—குடிப்பிறந்தார்
குன்றா ஒழுக்கமாக் கொண்டார்; கயவரோ
டொன்றா உணரற்பாற் றன்று.

The noble only have an instinctive sense of propriety.

Rising from their seat (at the approach of worshipful persons), going forth to meet them, departing when they dismiss, and such-like things, the well-born maintain as invariable decorum. The low understand not one of these things. [Or, These are not to be confounded with the low.]

இருக்கை எழல் = இருக்கையை விட்டு எழுந்திருக்குதல். விடுப்ப ஒழிதல் = அவர்கள் அனுப்பிவிட்டால் உடனே போய் விடுதல். See Lex. ஒன்று.

144.

ஒருவர்க்கு நற்குடியிற்பிறத்தல் கூடுமாயின் அவருக்கு அதனினும் ஊதியம் இல்லை.

நல்லவை செய்யின் இயல்பாகுந் தீயவை
பல்லவர் தூற்றும் பழியாகும்;—எல்லாம்
உணருங் குடிப்பிறப்பின் ஊதியம் என்னே,
புணரும் ஒருவர்க் கெனின்?

Noble birth makes duty easy.

If men (of noble birth) do good things it is natural to them. As to evil things (to commit these is impossible to them); for this would be guilt which many would bruit abroad. What greater good then can accrue to men than high-birth, if it be their lot, to which the perception of all (these things) belongs!

This is identical with K. 951. Virtue is instinctive, and a sense of generous shame renders evil impossible. [செப்பம் and நாண்.] '*Noblesse oblige.*'

குடிப்பிறப்பின். (G. 61. ஒப்பு.)

In *Ēlā.* 4. தக்கார்க்கேல் அவம் அரிது ஆதல் எளிதாம் seems to throw light on this somewhat obscure verse: 'really worthy persons rarely fall and easily rise (since their nature is averse from what is low and evil and inclined to what is lofty and excellent).' அவம் from S. अव = 'what is faulty.'

145.

இழிகுடியிற் பிறந்தார் கல்லாமை முதலியவற்றிற்கஞ்சார்; ஆதலால் ஓரறிவுயிரினுங் கடை ஆவார்.

கல்லாமை அச்சங் கயவர் தொழில்அச்சஞ்,
சொல்லாமை உள்ளும்ஓர் சோர்வச்சம்,—எல்லாம்
இரப்பார்க்கொன் றீயாமை அச்சம்;—மரத்தார்இம்
மாணைக் குடிப்பிறந் தார்.

These four pious fears exist only among the really worthy.

Dread of unlearned ignorance; dread of the work that base men do; dread of forgetful slip in words which one must not utter; dread of not giving to those that ask: those who are born of a race not so distinguished by conscientious fears are as trees.

Those who have not this instinctive shrinking from all that entails disgrace are not worthy to be classed as human beings. But see Lex. மாணு. K. 600.

இம்மாணு = இவ்வகையான மாட்சிமையில்லாத, கல்லாமை *etc.* [G. 152. Fourth case.]

Note the தனிச்சொல் in line 3.

146.

இந்நான்கும் உயர்குடியிற் பிறந்தார்மாட்டே உளவாகும்.

இனநன்மை, இன்சொல், ஒன் றீதன்மற் றேனை
மனநன்மை, என்றிவை எல்லாம்,—கனமணி
முத்தோ டிமைக்கு' முழங்குவரித் தண்சேர்ப்ப!—
இற்பிறந்தார் கண்ணே உள.

The fine qualities of the high-born.

Lord of the roaring salt-sea's cool shore, where gleam rare gems with pearls! Association with the good, pleasant speech, a liberal hand, and purity of mind,—all these are only found among the nobly born.

Comp. K. 953, where the four are நகை, ஈகை, இன்சொல், இகழாமை.

147.

உயர்குடியிற்பிறந்தோர் வறுமையால் வருத்தம் உற்றகாலத்தும் செயத்தக்க அறங்களைச் செயாநிற்பர்.

செய்கை அழிந்து சிதன்மண்டிற் றூயினும்
பெய்யா ஒருசிறை பேரில் உடைத்தாகும்;
எவ்வம் உழந்தக் கடைத்துங் குடிப்பிறந்தார்
செய்வர் செயற்பா லவை.

High-born men do their duty always.

Though its frame-work has perished, and thronging white ants infest it, in a spacious mansion some room will still afford shelter from the rain. Thus, although want annoys them, the nobly born even yet will do what should be done.

This is K. 955. For the last line, comp. 153 and 185. Comp. S. कर्तव्यमेव कर्म.
ஏ: இல், குடிப்பிறந்தார்.—ப: உடைத்தாகும்.—செ: சிறை, பாலவை.

148.

பெரியவர் வறுமைக் காலத்தும் அறஞ்செய்தற்குத் தளர்ச்சி உறார்.

ஒருபுடை பாம்பு கொளினும் ஒருபுடை
அங்கண்மா ஞாலம் விளக்குறூஉந்—திங்கள்போல்
செல்லாமை செவ்வனேர் நிற்பினும் ஒப்புரவிற்
கொல்கார் குடிப்பிறந் தார்.

The moon when half in the serpent's mouth still gives light.

Like the moon which affords light to the fair and spacious earth with one side, while the dragon holds the other, the nobly born do not become remiss in works of seemly benevolence, though poverty (inability) stand fronting them.

Comp. 241.

149.

நற்குடியிற்பிறந்தார் வறுமைக்காலத்துஞ் செய்யும் அறத்தை மற்றையோர் செல்வமுற்றகாலத்துஞ் செய்யார்.

செல்லா இடத்துங் குடிபிறந்தார் செய்வன
செல்லிடத்துஞ் செய்யார் சிறியவர்;—புல்வாய்
பருமம் பொறுப்பினும் பாய்பரி மாபோல்
பொருமுரண் ஆற்றுதல் இன்று.

The deer becomes not a charger.

Men of mean descent, even when all goes well with them, will not perform the good deeds that the well-born will do, even when things do not go well with them.

Though the antelope should bear a pillion, it rushes not to war like the prancing charger.

Comp. 184, 358. See Lex. பருமம் for another interpretation.

150.

வறுமை உற்றகாலத்தில மேன்மக்களின் செயல்.

எற்றொன்றும் இல்லா இடத்துங் குடிப்பிறந்தார்
அற்றுத்தற் சேர்ந்தார்க் கசைவிடத் தூற்றுவர்;
அற்றக் கடைத்தும் அகல்யா றகழ்ந்தக்கால்
தெற்றெனத் தெண்ணீர் படும்.

The noble even in poverty afford aid to those who seek it.

The nobly born, even when destitute, are props in time of feebleness to the needy ones that draw nigh to them. So, when the wide river is dry, if you dig in its bed, forthwith clear waters gush out.

எ: குடிப்பிறந்தார்.—ப: ஊற்றுவர். Another reading is தண்ணீர்.

Comp. 185. Here ஊற்று = ஊன்றுகோல் = 'prop, support;' but it is also from *v.* ஊறு, 'a spring.'

CHAPTER XVI.

GREAT MEN.

அதிகாரம் கசு.

மேன்மக்கள்

(= மேலோரதுதன்மை).

Men of lofty mind.

The high-born spoken of in the last chapter should of course be great in character also; but they may be unworthy. This chapter treats of those who are great not merely by accident of birth, but by essential excellence: it is the picture of moral elevation (மேன்மை = மேல் + மை) or magnanimity (माहात्म्यं).

Analysis:

1. High-souled men cannot endure a stain: they must be without reproach, and are sensitively jealous of their honour. [151.]
2. They aim at noble ends, and do not care for present results alone. [152.]
3. No pressure of want induces them to sacrifice principle. [153.]
4. They at once recognise one who is worthy, and do not forsake him. [154, 159.]
5. They are distinguished by courteous forbearance in regard to the ignorant. [155.]
6. They are not easily provoked. [156.]
7. They are consistently virtuous. [157, 158.]
8. Their friendship is a mine of blessing. [160.]

151.

மேலோர் தம்மிடத்திற் சிறிதகுற்றமும் வரப் பொறர்.

அங்கண் விசும்பின் அகனிலாப் பாரிக்குந்
திங்களுஞ் சான்றோரும் ஒப்பர்மற் றிங்கண்
மறுவாற்றும்; சான்றோர்அஃ தாற்றார்,—தெருமந்து
தேய்வர் ஒருமா சுறின்.

The good cannot endure a stain.

The moon that diffuses light through heaven's fair realms, and truly worthy men are alike: yet *that* endures a spot, while the truly worthy endure it not;—perplexed and sad they pine away if but one stain appear.

Comp. K. 957. Note the second தனிச்சொல் in line 3.
Comp. also B.I.S. 2249; Pañch. i. 231: 'चन्द्रे लाञ्छनता, there are spots in the moon.'

152.

மேலோர் செய்ய இசைவதாயினும் இசையாதாயினும் பெருங்காரியங்களையே செய்ய எண்ணுவர்.

இசையும் எனினும், இசையா தெனினும்,
வசைதீர எண்ணுவர் சான்றோர்;—விசையின்
நரிமா உளங்கிழித்த அம்பினிற் றீதோ
அரிமாப் பிழைப்பெய்த கோல்?

Aim high! Better miss a lion, than hit a jackal.

Whether success attend, or do not attend the work, the excellent will ever ponder blameless ends.—Is the shaft that missed the lion worse than the arrow sent forth, that with its impulse pierced the jackal's heart?

பிழைப்பு = பிழைப்ப = பிழைக்க = 'so as to miss the mark.' தீர = நீங்கும்படி. G. 140.
Comp. K. 772, 596.

153.

மேன்மக்கள் வறுமையாற் றளர்ச்சியுற்ற காலத்துஞ் செய்யத்தக்க அறத்தையே செய்வார்.

நரம்பெழுந்து நல்கூர்ந்தார் ஆயினுஞ் சான்றோர்
குரம்பெழுந்து குற்றங்கொண் டேறார்;—உரங்கவறா
உள்ளமெனு நாரினாற் கட்டி—உளவரையால்
செய்வர் செயற்பா லவை.

The excellent are not led by want to commit evil.

The excellent, though emaciated and poor, do not transgress the limits of virtue and commit evil. With wisdom for the pillar, with perseverance as the band, they bind (the mind); and as long as they live they do what it behoves them to do.

Comp. 147. See கவறு in Lex. Note the second தனிச்சொல் in line 3.

154.

மேலோர் ஒருவரை ஒருநாள் காணினும் அவரைத் தொன்றுதொட்டு வந்த நட்பினராகக் கொள்வர்.

செல்வழிக் கண்ணொருநாட் காணினுஞ் சான்றவர்
தொல்வழிக் கேண்மையிற் றோன்றப் புரிந்தியாப்பர்;—
நல்வரை நாட!—சிலநா ளடிப்படின்,
கல்வரையும் உண்டா நெறி.

The good never forget even a casual acquaintance.

Lord of the land of goodly hills!—If trodden for a few days a path is formed over even the craggy hill; so, excellent persons, though they have seen (worthy) men only for one day, as they were travelling, will bind them to their soul, exhibiting all the marks of an ancient friendship.

கேண்மையில் (G. 6) = like : ஒப்பு.

155.

மேலோர் அறிவில்லார் பிழைபடக் கற்றவற்றைப் பிரசங்கிக்கினும் அவரை அவமதியாது அதனைக் கேட்பார்.

புல்லா எழுத்திற் பொருளில் வறுங்கோட்டி
கல்லா ஒருவன் உரைப்பவுங் கண்ணோடி
நல்லார் வருந்தியுங் கேட்பரே மற்றவன்
பல்லாரு ணாணல் பரிந்து.

The good listen with patient courtesy to the orations of the ignorant.

Even when one speaks who has an ungrammatical knowledge of the letter, but not of the meaning, who is of a low (empty) school, and is unlearned, the good with kindly compassion will listen, though it is pain to them, being grieved that he should be put to shame in the presence of many.

G. 190. ஒருவிகற்பம். One rhyme. Comp. 316.

156.

மேலோர் தம்மைக் கீழோர் மிகவையினும் தாம் அவரை வைதலிலர் ஆவர்.

கடித்துக் கரும்பினைக் கண்டகர நூறி
இடித்துநீர் கொள்ளினும் இன்சுவைதே ஆகும்;
வடுப்பட வைதிறந்தக் கண்ணுங்—குடிப்பிறந்தார்
கூறார்தம் வாயிற் சிதைந்து.

Sugar-cane, crush it as you will, is ever sweet.

Although you bite the sugar-cane, crush it till its joints are broken, grind it, and express its juice, it still will be sweet. The highly born, even when men have passed by abusing them so as to wound, never lose their self-respect so as to utter from their mouth (words of abuse).

But see சிதை in Lex. There is a தனிச்சொல் in line 3.

157.

மேலோர் மறந்துந் தீங்குசெய்யார்.

கள்ளார்கள் ளுண்ணார், கடிவ கடிந்தொரீஇ,
எள்ளிப் பிறரை இகழ்ந்துரையார்,—தள்ளியும்
வாயிற்பொய் கூறார், வடுவறு காட்சியார்
சாயிற் பரிவ திலர்.

The wise free from gross evils.

They defraud not, drink not palm-wine, shun what is forbidden, never despise and speak contemptuously of their neighbours, nor even forgetfully do they utter anything untrue with their mouth: these men of faultless vision grieve not though they fall into distress.

See K. 199, and note the use of காட்சி throughout.

158.

பிறர் இரகசியத்தைக் கேளாமை, அயலாருடைய மனைவியை விரும்பாமை, தீச்சொற்களைப் பேசாமை முதலிய நற்குணங்கள் மேன்மக்களிடத்தில் உண்டு.

பிறர்மறை யின்கட் செவிடாய்த்—திறனறிந்
தேதிலார் இற்கட் குருடனாய்த்—தீய
புறங்கூற்றின் மூகையாய் நிற்பானேல் யாதும்
அறங்கூற வேண்டா அவற்கு.

When a man should be deaf, blind, and dumb.

Deaf to others' secrets, blind to his neighbour's wife, dumb to evil backbiting—if, knowing what is befitting, a man thus abides, it is not necessary to teach him any virtuous precepts.

Comp. *Ēlā*. 20: 'பல்லார் மறையிற்செவியிலன்; தீச்சொற்கண்மூங்கை:
In regard to others' secrets without an ear, in regard to evil words dumb.'

So in *Ēlā*. 6, 15: 'அயல அயலவர்நூல், the ethical teaching of strangers is strange to him:' he needs no other teaching.

Note the rhymes in lines 1, 2.

159.

கீழோர் தம்மோடொருவர் நெடுநாட்பழகினும் அவரைநன்கு மதியார்: மேலோர் கண்ட அன்றுபோல் என்றும் நன்குமதிப்பார்.

பன்னாளுஞ் சென்றக்கால் பண்பிலார் தம்முழை
என்னானும் வேண்டுப என்றிகழ்ப;—என்னானும்
வேண்டினு நன்றுமற் றென்று விழுமியோர்
காண்டொறுஞ் செய்வர் சிறப்பு.

Seek the good, they are always kind.

They who are destitute of kindly courtesy, even after the lapse of many days, will contemn (those that visit them), saying, 'they will ask something of us.' The excellent will treat them with distinction whenever they see them, saying, 'if they ask something of us, it is well.'

160.

நற்குடியில் பிறந்தாரைச் சேர்ந்தொழுகுவோர் எல்லாநலமும் பெறுவர்.

உடையார் இவரென் றொருதலையாப் பற்றிக்
கடையாயார் பின்சென்று வாழ்வர்;—உடைய
பிலந்தலைப் பட்டது போலாதே நல்ல
குலந்தலைப் பட்ட விடத்து?

The treasure cave.

The lowest sort of men say, 'these are men of property,'—cling to them steadily, follow them, and so flourish. Is it not as when a mine of treasure has been found, when men of good lineage have become our friends?

This is ambiguous, and may be rendered: '(Some) follow the base, saying . . .; but is it? *etc.*' In போலாதே, ஏ is interrogative. G. 6.

CHAPTER XVII.

AVOIDANCE OF OFFENCE TO THE GREAT.

அதிகாரம் கஎ.

பெரியாரைப்பிழையாமை

(= பெரியோரை அவமதித்து நடவாமை).

The last verse of the preceding chapter prepares the way for this : such precious friendship is to be carefully guarded ; it must be a main object of life not to incur the forfeiture of the esteem and confidence of the morally great. This is ch. xc in K.

Analysis :

1. Presume not on the forbearance of the great. [161.]
2. Suffer not the rare privilege of such friendship to be fruitless. [162, 169.]
3. Value only the esteem of the good. [163, 165.]
4. Their anger is unendurable. [164.]
5. Their friendship alone is lasting. [166.]
6. It is not promiscuously given. [167.]
7. Miscellaneous. [168, 170.]

161.

பெரியோர்க்குச் சினந்தோன்றியபின் அதனைத் தடுத்தல் கூடாது ; ஆகலின் தீக்கருமங்களைச் செய்யாதிருத்தல் வேண்டும்.

பொறுப்பர்என் றெண்ணிப் புரைதீர்ந்தார் மாட்டும்
வெறுப்பன செய்யாமை வேண்டும் ;—வெறுத்தபின்—
ஆர்க்கும் அருவி அணிமலை நன்னாட!—
பேர்க்குதல் யார்க்கும் அரிது.

It is difficult to regain the forfeited favour of good men.

Lord of the pleasant land whose hills resounding water-falls adorn !—You may not even to faultless men do things that enkindle wrath ; for when their wrath is once kindled, it is hard for any one to change their mood.

எ ; செய்யாமை, பேர்க்குதல்.—ப ; வேண்டும், அரிது. K. 29.

162.

மெய் அறிவில்லாதவர் பெரியோரைச் சேர்ந்திருந்தும் தம் வாணாளை வீணாள் ஆக்குவர்.

பொன்னே கொடுத்தும் புணர்தற் கரியாரைக்
கொன்னே தலைக்கூடப் பெற்றிருந்தும்—அன்னோ
பயனில் பொழுதாக் கழிப்பரே நல்ல
நயமில் அறிவி னவர்!

Waste of golden opportunities.

Although those whose (pretended) wisdom is without moral excellence have gained access to men to whom approach is difficult even by gifts of gold, alas! they pass away (the precious moments) as mere waste time.

காலத்தை understood is the object of கழிப்பர்.

163.

பெரியோர் அவமதிக்கும் அவமானமும் புகழும்புகழ்ச்சியுமே பொருளாகக் கொள்ளப்படும்.

அவமதிப்பும் ஆன்ற மதிப்பும் இரண்டும்
மிகைமக்க ளான்மதிக்கற் பால; நயமுணராக்
கையறியா மாக்கள் இழிப்பும் எடுத்தேத்தும்
வையார் வடித்தநூ லார்.

Praise and dispraise of noble persons only of importance.

Both disesteem and thorough esteem are in the class of things that depend on the estimation of the great. Those who have a discriminating knowledge of true science, lay no stress on either the abuse or the fulsome praise of men who comprehend not moral principles, and know not the rules of propriety.

Comp. 294. Rhymes irregular.

164.

பெரியோரால் கோபிக்கப்பட்டார் தப்பாதுகெடுவர்.

விரிநிற நாகம் விடருள தேனும்
உருமின் கடுஞ்சினஞ் சேணின்றும் உட்கும்;
அருமை உடைய அரண்சேர்ந்தும் உய்யார்
பெருமை உடையார் செறின்.

None safe from the wrath of the great.

The serpent rich of hue, though it dwell in the mountain-cleft, from far is frighted by the thunderbolt's fierce wrath; so men escape not, though hid in strongholds hard to reach, when those great in virtue are wroth.

Comp. K. 25, 29, 900.

165.

பெரியோரால் மதிக்கப் படும் மதிப்பே ஒருவர்க்கு மதிப்பாவதன்றித் தம்மைத்தாமே மதிப்பது மதிப்பன்று.

எம்மை அறிந்திலிர் எம்போல்வார் இல்லென்று
தம்மைத்தாங் கொள்வது கோளன்று;—தம்மை
அரியரா நோக்கி அறனறியுஞ் சான்றோர்
பெரியராக் கொள்வது கோள்.

Self-praise is no commendation.

'You know not all our worth, for equals have we none:' when self thus estimates itself, this is not '*esteem!*' When perfect men, proficients in virtue, regard any as dear, and esteem them as great, this is '*esteem!*'

Comp. 340; *Nīti.* 18; and K. 439.

166.

சிறியோரோடுகொண்ட நட்புவளராது தேயும்; பெரியோரோடு கொண்டநட்பு வளர்ந்து பெருகும்.

நளிகடற் றண்சேர்ப்ப!—நாணிழற் போல
விளியுஞ் சிறியவர் கேண்மை;—விளிவின்றி
அல்கு நிழற்போல் அகன்றகன் றோடுமே
தொல்புக ழாளர் தொடர்பு.

Morning and evening shadows.

Lord of the great sea's cool margin!—Friendships formed with mean men dwindling die like shadows of the morn; friendship of men of old renown as shadows of the after-day will lengthen out and grow.

Comp. 125, 138.

See B. I. S. 1004:

'आरम्भगुर्वी क्षयिणी क्रमेण लघ्वी पुरा वृद्धिमती च पश्चात्।
दिनस्य पूर्वार्धपरार्धभिन्ना छायेव मैत्री खलसज्जनानाम्॥

The friendships with bad and good men are as the diverse shadows of the forenoon and afternoon of the day: that in the beginning is great and by degrees grows less; this at first is slight and afterwards grows.'

அல்கு = 'the diminishing (sc. day)' (दिनस्य परार्ध).

167.

அரசர்செல்வமும் மாதரின்பமும் நெருங்கினோர் பெறுவார்கள்.

மன்னர் திருவு மகளிர் எழினலமும்
துன்னியார் துய்ப்பர், தகல்வேண்டா,—துன்னிக்
குழைகொண்டு தாழ்ந்த குளிர்மரம் எல்லாம்
உழைதங்கட் சென்றார்க் கொருங்கு.

To those who cultivate them fruits accrue.

Those who press their suit, fitness apart, enjoy the wealth of kings, and the charms of maidens fair; so all the cool (shady) trees that droop earthward with thick foliage, give room to those that thronging seek their shelter.

உழை = இடம்ஆம். Comp. B. I. S. 1066:

'आसन्नमेव नृपतिर् भजते मनुष्यं विद्याविहीनम् अकुलीनम् असंगतं वा।
प्रायेण भूमिपतयः प्रमदा लताश्च यत्पार्श्वतोभवति तत्परिवेष्टयन्ति॥

A king attaches himself to the man who is near, though void of learning, of low caste or clownish. Princes, women, and creepers twine themselves round what is at hand.'

168.

யாரையுஞ் சிநேகியாமையே உத்தமம்.

தெரியத் தெரியுந் தெரிவிலார் கண்ணும்
பிரியப் பெரும்படர் நோய்செய்யும்;—பெரிய
உலவா இருங்கழிச் சேர்ப்ப!—யார் மாட்டும்
கலவாமை கோடி உறும்.

Friendship brings pangs of severance.

Severance from even those who have no understanding [lit. no understanding that understands (so as) to understand] causes great and spreading sorrow.—Lord of the shore of the great, unfailing, swelling bay!—To be intimate with none is ten million times the best.

கழி is an arm of the sea, a back-water. Its three enlargements here are பெரிய,

உலவா(த), and இரும். Many rivers are dry at certain seasons, but this is always full. பெரிய and இரும் mean much the same thing, but the former refers to the extent of the bay, and the latter to the abundance of water.

Comp. 247 for the construction of line 1.

Comp. B. I. S. 6624:

'संयोगाविप्रयोगान्ता जातानां प्राणनां ध्रुवम् ।
बुद्बुदा इव तोयेषु भवन्ति न भवन्ति च ॥

For all that are born it is certain that meetings end with partings. Like bubbles in the water they are and are not.'

169.

கல்விகற்றுமலும், பெரியோரைக் காணுமலும், தரித்திரருக்குக் கொடாமலும் ஓரபகலாயினும் இருக்கலாகாது.

கல்லாது போகிய நாளும், பெரியவர்கண்
செல்லாது வைகிய வைகலும்,—ஒல்வ
கொடாஅது தொழிந்த பகலும் உரைப்பின்
படாஅவாம் பண்புடையார் கண்.

No day unimproved.

Days gone by without learning, those passed without any intercourse with the great, those spent without giving what is fitting;—in the case of the excellent, if you tell them over, none such occur.

The form of this quatrain suggests T. 44. For பண்பு, see Pope's *Kurraḷ*, p. 312. போகிய = போன, § 58. Observe நாள், வைகல், பகல் are used with nice discrimination.

170.

பெரியவருக்குப் பணிவும், கல்விதசிறந்தவருக்கு அடக்கமும், செல்வர்க்கு ஈகையும் பெருமையைத்தரும்.

பெரியார் பெருமை சிறுதகைமை; ஒன்றிற்
குரியார் உரிமை அடக்கம்;—தெரியுங்கால்,
செல்வம் உடையாருஞ் செல்வரே தற்சேர்ந்தார்
அல்லல் களைப வெனின்.

Humility. Self-restraint. Charity.

The greatness of the great is [the quality of littleness (in their own sight), i.e.] humility; the (real) acquisition of those who have acquired (any) one (science) is modest self-restraint. If you rightly understand things, those possessors of wealth only are really wealthy who relieve the wants of those that approach them (as suppliants).

CHAPTER XVIII.

ASSOCIATION WITH THE GOOD.

அதிகாரம் கஅ.

நல்லினஞ்சேர்தல்

(= நல்லோர் இனத்தைச் சேர்ந்திருத்தல்).

With this chapter compare K. xlvi, and my notes, p. 257. There, however, the mean and low are to be shunned. See also ஏலாதி, 5.

The company of parasites and profligates will destroy all the benefits of good association; hence the position of the chapter.

Parimēlaragar says, 'சிறியவினமாவது, நில்லதிலே நன்மையும் தீயதிலே தீமையும் இல்லை என்போரும் விடருந் தூர்த்தரும் முதலாயினகூட்டம்: mean association is the company of those who say there is no goodness in what is good, and no evil in what is ill; and of panders and parasites and of such-like persons.' Here the obverse is given.

Analysis:

1. If a man leave the bad companions of his ignorant youth, and cling to the good, the sins of his early days will pass away like the early dew. [171.]
2. Six precepts: among them to detest the friendship of evil men, and to listen to the counsels of the morally great. [172.]
3. Associate with men who know the sorrows of life and will aid you in your struggle for emancipation. [173.]
4. Such communion makes even this life endurable. [174.]
5. A series of striking illustrations of the theme. [175–180.]

171.

ஒருவன் நல்லவரோடு சேரின் அறியாப்பருவத்துத் தீயவரோடுகூடித் தான் செய்த பாவம் அனைத்துந்தீரும்.

அறியாப் பருவத் தடங்காரோ டொன்றி
நெறியல்ல செய்தொழுகி யவ்வும் — நெறிஅறிந்த
நற்சார்வு சாரக் கெடுமே, வெயின்முறுகப்
புற்பனிப் பற்றுவிட் டாங்கு.

Good companionship cures the follies of youth.

In youth unwise, though men consort with haughty ones, and walk in lawless ways; yet, when they join with those that know the righteous path, their faults shall melt away as dew from off the grass when sunbeams scorch.

In ஒழுகியவும் there is duplication of க். [G. 41. ரு.]

So B. I. S. 6747: 'सत्सङ्गाद्भवति हि साधुता खलानां।

Even the base obtain excellence by connexion with the good.'

172.

அறநெறி அறிதலுங் கூற்றுவனுக்கு அஞ்சுதலும் பிறர் கடுஞ்சொல்லைப் பொறுத்தலும் பிறரை வஞ்சியாதிருத்தலுந் தீயவர் நட்பைவெறுத்தலும் பெரியார் சொல்லைப் பெறுதலும் வேண்டும்.

அறிமின் அறநெறி; அஞ்சுமின் கூற்றம்;
பொறுமின் பிறர்கடுஞ்சொல்; போற்றுமின் வஞ்சம்;
வெறுமின் வினைதீயார் கேண்மை; எஞ்ஞான்றும்
பெறுமின் பெரியார்வாய்ச் சொல்.

Six precepts.

Know virtue's path! Dread death! Bear others' words severe! Beware ye practise no deceit! Friendship detest with men of evil deeds! Daily get gain of words that fall from great men's lips!

எ: சீர். (தொகை.)—ப: ஐந்துவினைகளும். செயப்படுபொருள்: நெறியை, குற்றத்தை, சொல்லை, வஞ்சத்தை, கேண்மையை, சொல்லை.—அறிமின். G. 84. வினைதீயார் = தீவினையாருடைய. G. 152.

173.

பிறப்பிலுண்டாகுந் துன்பங்களைக்கண்டு ஞானிகளைச்சேர்தல் நன்மை.

அடைந்தார்ப் பிரிவும் அரும்பிணியுங் கேடும்
உடங்குடம்பு கொண்டார்க் குறலால்,—தொடங்கிப்
பிறப்பின்னா தென்றுணரும் பேரறிவி னாரை
உறப்புணர்க, அம்மாஎன் னெஞ்சு!

Life has many evils. Attach yourself to the wise.

Severance of close-joined friends and sore disease and death, all these combined hap to those that have assumed a human body: so the truly wise have felt that birth, from the very first, is bitterness. Ah! soul, cleave close to these!

174.

ஒருவன் மனதொத்த நல்லோருடைய கூட்டத்தைச்சேர்ந்து ஒழுகப்பெறின் வாழ்நாள் இனிதாம்.

இறப்ப நினையுங்கால் இன்னா தெனினும்
பிறப்பினை யாரு முனியார்—பிறப்பினுள்
பண்பாற்று நெஞ்சத் தவர்களோ டெஞ்ஞான்றும்
நண்பாற்றி நட்கப் பெறின்.

Friendship makes life endurable.

Though when you ponder it, it is surpassing bitterness, none hate (this mortal) birth, if in (this mortal) birth they ever perform friendly acts to men whose hearts are set on noble excellence, and gain their friendship.

எ : யாரும்.—ப : முனியார்.—செ : பிறப்பினை.
This is in some sort a reply to 173. இறப்ப is adv. to இன் in இன்னாது. Comp. 223. See பிற and நன் in Lex.

175.

சலதாரை நீரும் மிக்க நீரைச்சேர்ந்து தீர்த்தமாகும்; நல்லவர்கூட்டத்திற் சேரின் இழிந்தோரும் மேலோர் ஆவார்கள்.

ஊரங் கணைநீர் உரவுநீர் சேர்ந்தக்கால்
பேரும் பிறிதாகித் தீர்த்தமாம்;—ஓரும்,
குலமாட்சி இல்லாருங் குன்றுபோ னிற்பர்,
நலமாட்சி நல்லாரைச் சார்ந்து.

The water from the sewer becomes a sacred stream.

When water from the town-sewers has joined the great river its very name is changed, and it becomes a 'sacred stream.' Ponder well! Even those who have no greatness of clan, if they ally themselves with good men of goodly fame, shall stand firm as a hill.

எ : நீர், இல்லார்.—ப : ஆம், நிற்பர்.—ஊர், ஏழாம்வேற்றுமைத் தொகை. உரவுநீர் = ஆற்றுநீர். சேர்ந்தக்கால். G. 87.

This is the first of seven illustrations of the theme: (1) the sewer and the sacred stream; (2) the hare in the moon; (3) milk and water; (4) grass and the tree-stump; (5) good grain and good soil; (6) the boat in the tempest; (7) the sandal tree in the thicket. These are parables in the germ.

176.

பெரியோரைச் சேர்ந்த சிறியோருஞ் சிறப்படைவர்.

ஒண்கதிர் வாண்மதியஞ் சேர்தலா லோங்கிய
அங்கண் விசும்பின் முயலுந் தொழப்படூஉம்;
குன்றிய சீர்மைய ராயினுஞ் சீர்பெறுவர்,
குன்றன்னார் கேண்மை கொளின்.

The hare in the moon is worshipped.

Because it is in the bright-beamed moon the very hare in heaven's lofty fair expanse is worshipped. Though scant their worthiness, men obtain worth who share friendship with those firm as a hill.

Comp. 151. See B. I. S. 6304; Pañch. iii. 79.

'व्यापदेशेन महतां सिद्धिः संजायते परा।
शशिनो व्यपदेशेन वसन्ति शशकाः सुखं॥

By connection with the name of the great the best success is gained.
Hares live happily because of connexion with the moon.'

177.

பெரியோரைச் சேர்ந்த சிறியோர் இழிவு தோன்றாது.

பாலோ டளாயநீர் பாலாகும் அல்லது
நீராய் நிறந்தெரிந்து தோன்றாதாம்;—தேரின்,
சிறியார் சிறுமையுந் தோன்றாதா நல்ல
பெரியார் பெருமையைச் சார்ந்து.

Water with milk seems milk.

Commingled with milk water becomes milk; at least, it shows no more as water by its hue. Look close, the mean men's meanness shows not if they join themselves to greatness of the good and great.

அளாய, see அளாவு. Comp. Vēm. i. 13: 'Pālu galaya nīru pāleyai rājillu.'

178.

கல்வி அறிவு முதலியவை இல்லார் அவற்றையுடைய நல்லவர்களைச் சேரின் பகைவர்க்கஞ்சார்.

கொல்லை இரும்புனத்துக் குற்றி அடைந்தபுல்
ஒல்காவே ஆகும் உழவர் உழுபடைக்கு;
மெல்லியரே ஆயினு நற்சார்வு சார்ந்தார்மேல்
செல்லாவாஞ் செற்றார் சினம்.

The society of the good a protection.

Grass close around the stump in the field adjoining the house will not be destroyed by the ploughshare of the farmer; [thus] though men are weak, if they get under safe protection, the wrath of their foes will not reach them.

எ: புல், கிளை.—ப: ஆகும், ஆம்.—ஒல்கா, செல்லா, எதிர்மறை வினையெச்சம். G. 90. புனத்து = புனத்திலிடத்தில். G. 68, 152.

179.

நெல்லைப்போலத் தங்குலத்தினது நன்மையாற் சான்றவர் ஆவார்கள்; தீயவர்கூட்டத்திற் சேரின் நற்சால்புடைமை கெடும்.

நிலநலத்தா னந்திய நெல்லேபோற் றத்தம்
குலநலத்தா லாகுவர் சான்றோர்;—கலநலத்தைத்
தீவளி சென்றுசிதைத்தாங்குச் சான்றாண்மை
தீயினஞ் சேரக் கெடும்.

Good tribal associations maintain excellence, and evil ones wreck it.

As *Nel* that flourishes through the goodness of the soil, good men become illustrious by the excellence of their respective clanships.

Goodness perishes when it comes near evil associates, as the tornado advances and destroys the excellence of the ship.

180.

ஒருவர் நல்லவரோடு சேராது தீயவரோடுசேரின் தாமும் இகழப்படுவர்.

மனத்தான் மறுவிலர் ஏனுந்தாஞ் சேர்ந்த
இனத்தால் இகழப் படுவர்;—புனத்து
வெறிகமழ் சந்தனமும் வேங்கையும் வேமே,
எறிபுனந் தீப்பட்டக் கால்.

Evil association brings ruin.

Though themselves pure in mind, even good men incur contempt because of their associations. So in the woodland glade when a conflagration takes place (not the worthless brushwood only, but) the fragrant *Sandal* and *Vēngai* too are consumed.

மனத்தால் = மனதில். G. 137*. Comp. B. I. S. 758:

'शुष्केणार्द्रं दह्यते मिश्रभावान्नामिश्रः स्यात् पापकृद्भिः।

The green (grass) is burned up with the dry (stubble) because mixed up with it: let there be no mingling with men of sinful deeds.'

CHAPTER XIX.

(MORAL) GREATNESS.

அதிகாரம் கசு.

பெருமை

(= நற்குணங்களாற் சிறந்தவரதுபெருந்தன்மை).

This chapter exhibits the elements and indications of moral greatness, as the author conceives them.

Analysis:

1. Earthly desire (அவா) must be extinguished: the first test of greatness. [181.]
2. Worldly enjoyments must be despised: a further test. [182, 183.]
3. Even in adversity duties must be attended to: it is unaffected by adversity. [184, 185.]
4. Yet faults will exist, which will be more conspicuous in the great; therefore it shuns inconsistencies. [186.]
5. The enmity of such is more profitable than the friendship of the worthless. [187.]
6. A great man is all things to all:—adapts himself to his environment. [188.]
7. He is undisturbed by the strife of tongues. [189.]
8. His joy is in utterly unselfish charity. [190.]

With this must especially be compared K. ch. xcix-c, where பெருமை, சான்றாண்மை, and பண்பு are degrees of excellence.

In ch. xvi of this work, மேன்மக்கள் are 'the lofty-minded,' a somewhat different idea.

181.

ஆசைகளை விட்டுநீங்கி உயிருக்குறுதிபயக்கும் நன்னெறிக்கட் செல்வதே பெருமை.

ஈதல் இசையா திளமைசே ணீங்குதலால்
காத லவருங் கருத்தல்லர்,—காதலித்
தாதுநாம் என்னு அவாவினைக் கைவிட்டுப்
போவதே போலும் பொருள்.

Renunciation of desire is 'greatness.'

To give is no longer ours; and youth is gone far off; our once beloved ones think of us no more! To depart, having abandoned 'desire' that bids us love and hope for future joys, appears the thing that's meet.

Comp. 12. On desire (அவா), see K. ch. xxxvii. For போதும், see Lex.

182.

அறிவிலார் இல்வாழ்க்கைநிலை எனக்கருதி வீணாள் கழிப்பர்: அறிவுடையார் அதன் நிலையாமையை உணர்ந்து அதைவிரும்பார்.

இற்சார்வின் ஏமாந்தேம், ஈங்கமைந்தேம், என்றெண்ணிப்
பொச்சாந் தொழுகுவர் பேதையார்;—அச்சார்வு
நின்றன போன்று நிலையா எனவுணர்ந்தார்
என்றும் பரிவ திலர்.

Fools make their home in a changing world.

Fools thinking 'we have found joy in the *refuge* of home,' and 'we are here in perfect repose,' forgetful (of the instability of all things), go on their way.

Those who have felt that that 'refuge' is unstable, while it seems to stand fast, never fix their fond desire (on it).

எ: பேதையார், உணர்ந்தார்.—ப: ஒழுகுவர், இலர்.—பரிவதிலர். G. 95, 125. பரிவது + இலர். நின்றன. Comp. 4. The opposite here to (பெருமை) 'moral greatness,' is 'folly' (பேதைமை), that finds repose and sufficiency in earthly things. This is 'bewilderment' (மயல்) and 'meanness' (சிறுமை) in 183. சார்வு takes a plural (நின்றன), since it means 'home and all its joys.' (See சார்.)

183.

பெருமையுடையார் மறுமையின்பத்துக்குக்காரணமானவைகளைச் செய்துவாழ்வார்.

மறுமைக்கு வித்து மயலின்றிச் செய்து
சிறுமைப் படாதேநீர் வாழ்மின்—அறிஞராய்
நின்றுழி நின்றே, நிறம்வேறுங் காரணம்
இன்றிப் பலவும் உள.

Seek the unchanging. All things here change.

See that ye sow seed that in other world may germinate; free your lives from earth's bewilderment and meanness; stand in your lot as wise men; the changing hue of things shall without cause fade, and many things be new.

Comp. K. 24, p. 193, and Ellis, p. 65. I take அறிஞராய்நின்றுழி நின்று with வாழ்மின், 'standing as wise men where you have once taken your stand.' Understand இவற்றின், 'of these things,' before திறம். The whole admits of a wider and more poetical application than the C. recognises.

184.

பெரியோர் செய்தல்போல் சிறியோர் செய்தல் அரிது.

உறைப்பருங் காலத்தும் ஊற்றுநீர்க் கேணி
இறைத்துணினும் ஊராற்றும் என்பர்;—கொடைக்கடனும்
சாஅஅயக் கண்ணும் பெரியார்போன் மற்றையார்
ஆஅஅயக் கண்ணும் அரிது.

Good men are unfailing fountains of beneficence.

The well of springing water serves the town that draws and drinks, even in time when rains are scant; so great men in adverse hour dispense due gifts that others give not even in their best estate.

எ: செய்தல் (தொகை).—ப: அரிது.—உறைப்பருங் காலத்தும் = மழைபெய்தல் அரிய காலத்திலும். சாஅஅய = சாஇற. G. 87, 14. ஆஅஅய = ஆயிய. G. 87. (– ⏑ ⏑ –).
Comp. 149, 185, and 358; K. 975. உறைப்பு, see K. 559.

185.

செல்வம் அழிந்தாலும் பெரியோர் செய்யுந் தர்மங்களைச் செய்வார்.

உறுபுனறந்துலகூட்டி அறுமிடத்தும்
கல்லூற் றுழிஊறும் ஆறேபோற் செல்வம்
பலர்க்காற்றிக் கெட்டுலந்தக் கண்ணுஞ் சிலர்க்காற்றிச்
செய்வர் செயற்பா லவை.

Great men do not neglect duties because of poverty.

The river pours forth a mighty stream and feeds the world; and when it is dried up, if men dig in its bed, streams gush out! So good men, when rich, give to many; and, when ruined, give still at least to some, and do what should be done.

The figure of the river is found also in 150. புனல் + தந்து. G. 38.
The fourth line occurs in 147, 150, where the general idea is the same.
Each line has a தனிச்சொல் rhyming with the first foot.

186.

பெரியோர் செய்த குற்றங் காணப்படும்; சிறியோர் செய்த குற்றங் காணப்படாது.

பெருவரை நாட! பெரியோர்கட் டீமை
கருநரைமேற் சூடேபோற் றோன்றும்;—கருநரையைக்
கொன்றன்ன வின்னா செயினுஞ் சிறியார்மேல்
ஒன்றானுந் தோன்றா கெடும்.

Faults are conspicuous in great persons.

Lord of the lofty hills! Any evil in men of moral greatness shows like a brand on a mighty bull; but although mean men do painful deeds, like the slaughter of that same mighty bull, none of these attracts attention.

For சூடு, see Lex. Since தோன்றா = தோன்றாமல், க் is required by G. 27.

187.

சிறியவரிடத்திற் கொண்ட சிநேகந் துன்பமாம். பெரியவரிடத்திற் கொண்ட பகையும் பெருமைதரும்.

இசைந்த சிறுமை இயல்பிலா தார்கண்
பசைந்த துணையும் பரிவாம்;—அசைந்த
நகையேயும் வேண்டாத நல்லறிவி னார்கண்
பகையேயும் பாடு பெறும்.

Enmity of the wise better than friendship of the mean.

In proportion to the degree of one's intimacy with men essentially mean and without good qualities sorrow accrues;

but even the hostility of those who do not desire forbidden things even in jest will confer dignity.

The use of அசைந்த (= அசைந்தவைகள்), lit. 'shaky things,' is curious.

Comp. 219, and K. 816, 817. In N. M. K. 15 we have '... பசைந்தாரில் தீர்தலிற் றீப்புகுதனன்று, better to enter the fire than to separate from dear friends.'

188.

அவ்வவர்க்கேற்றபடி ஒழுகுதலே அறிவுடையோர்க்கழகு.

மெல்லிய நல்லாருண் மென்மை, அதுவிறந்
தொன்னாருட் கூற்றுட்கு முட்குடைமை, எல்லாம்
சலவருட் சாலச் சலமே, நலவருள்
நன்மை வரம்பாய் விடல்!

Be all things to all men.

With gentle fair ones use gentleness surpassing theirs; with foes display a wrath that death's self might dread; with persistent men show a persistency to match; amongst men of good do good; let the law of life be thus laid down.

விடல் is an optative. G. 85. Comp. *Nīti.* 98; and வரம்பு in Lex. and K. 714.

189.

ஒருவர் கடுங்குறளைகளைப்பேசித் தம்மை மயக்கினுஞ் சுத்தமுள்ளமனமுடையவர் விளக்கினுள் ஒள்ளியசுடரையே போல் திண்ணியராய் நிலைதளரார்.

கடுக்கி ஒருவன் கடுங்குறளை பேசி
மயக்கி விடினு மனப்பிரிப்பொன் றின்றித்
துளக்க மிலாதவர் தூயமனத்தார்,
விளக்கினுள் ஒண்சுடரே போன்று.

The great man is unmoved amid insults.

These are the pure in heart who, though any vex, and with use of slanderous words would fain perplex them, with calm unruffled mind abide unwavering, like the bright flame within the lamp.

எ: மனத்தார்.—ப: இலாதவர்; or எ: இல்லாதவர்.—ப: மனத்தார் (?).

190.

அறஞ் செய்யும் பெரியோருக்குக் குற்றம் நீங்கச் சாமளவும் இன்பம் உண்டாகும்.

முற்றுற்றுந் துற்றினை நாளும் அறஞ்செய்து
பிற்றுற்றுத் துற்றுவர் சான்றவர்;—அத்துற்று
முக்குற்ற நீக்கி முடியும் அளவெல்லாம்
துக்கத்து ணீக்கி விடும்.

Feeding the hungry.

The excellent will daily give to the needy in charity their first-served food; they themselves will eat what is served after: such good conduct removes the three faults, and from sorrow sets men free, through all the days, till comes the end.

In some copies துத்து is found for துற்று. See Lex.

The three faults inseparable from embodiment (பிறப்பு) are lust (காமம்), wrath (வெகுளி), and delusion (மயக்கம்). See K. 360.

The துக்கம் here is the நோய் of the K.

CHAPTER XX.

PERSEVERING ENERGY.

அதிகாரம் உ0.

தாளாண்மை

(= முயற்சியுடைமை).

Comp. B. I. S. 1200, *etc.*:

தாளாண்மை = ஊக்கம் = उत्थानं.

'उत्थानेनामृतं लब्धम्, by strenuous effort was ambrosia obtained.'

This subject is discussed by the author of the K. in chapters lx and lxii. His names for it are ஊக்கம், ஆள்வினை, முயற்சி, and தாளாண்மை. This is a fine, manly chapter.

The analysis is:

1. Independence: it is base to depend on relatives. [191.]
2. Self-reliance: a man must have a core! [192.]
3. Against false pride: a man must stoop to conquer. [193.]
4. Perseverance in the face of apparent failure: success is not the test. [194.]
5. Against caste-presumption: rank is nothing. [195.]
6. Self-suppression and acuteness. [196.]
7. Filial piety: also, a man may rise above any odium attaching to his kindred. [197.]
8. Endure poverty, not dishonour. [198.]
9. Do not rely on your rank and family: you must yourself make your name illustrious. [199.]
10. Food earned by energy is ambrosia. [200.]

Note the expressive and apt similes of the rice plants under the tank whose water is insufficient for the fields it has to irrigate [191]; the pliant shoot, waving with every breath, that grows into a sturdy inflexible tree [192]; the pendant branch-roots of the *banyan* tree [197]; and the flower that has lost its perfume [199].

191.

முயற்சி இல்லார் கெடுவர். முயற்சியுடையார் வாழ்வர்.

கோளாற்றக் கொள்ளாக் குளத்தின்கீழ்ப் பைங்கூழ்போல்
கேள்ஈவ துண்டு கிளைகளோ துஞ்சுப!
வாளாடு கூத்தியர் கண்போற் றடுமாறும்
தாளாளர்க் குண்டோ தவறு?

Active independence.

As for kindred that feed upon what relatives give them, they will die off like green grain below a tank, which does not hold a sufficient supply (of water).

Is failure possible to men of energy that are quick in movement as the eyes of those who perform the sword-dance?

Lazy persons exhaust—overtax—the resources of the family, and perish like green grain in fields dependent on tanks in which there is not a sufficient store of water. The alertness of the juggler averts danger and brings him rewards.

எ: கிளைகள், தவறு.—ப: துஞ்சப, உண்டேர.

192.

ஒருவன் இடைவிடாது நன்முயற்சி செய்வான் ஆயின் அவன்செல்வமுடையவன் ஆவதற்கு ஐயம் இன்று.

ஆடுகோ டாகி அதரிடை நின்றதூஉம்
காழ்கொண்ட கண்ணே களிறணைக்குங் கந்தாகும்;
வாழ்தலும் அன்ன தகைத்தே, ஒருவன்றான்
தாழ்வின்றித் தன்னைச் செயின்.

By energy a man makes himself.

What once stood by the wayside, a twig that bent to every touch, when its core is developed within, may become a stake to which they tie an elephant. Life too is thus, if man himself, unfailing make himself!

எ: நின்றதூஉம், வாழ்தல்.—ப: ஆகும், தகைத்தே.—அதரிடை. G. 63. Metre, G. 188:

'.... நட்டமைத்த
தூணின்க ணிற்குங் களிறு,
The elephant abides by the firmly-planted pillar.'

193.

ஒருவன் தனக்குக் கிடைத்த அற்பத்தொழிலை அவமதியாமற் செய்ய உடன்படுவானாயின் மேன்மையாகிய தொழிலுங் கிடைக்கப் பெறுவான்.

உறுபுலி ஊனிரை இன்றி ஒருநாள்
சிறுதேரை பற்றியுந் தின்னும்;—அறிவினால்
காற்றொழில் என்று கருதற்க, கையினால்
மேற்றொழிலும் ஆங்கே மிகும்!

Stoop to conquer.

The huge tiger, when lacking flesh for food one day, may even seize a little frog and eat it. Think not 'By (all my) knowledge I only gain menial tasks;' to the skilful hand nobler employments shall even there abound.

எ: மேற்றொழில்.—ப: மிகும்.—ஆங்கு, ஏ, அசைநிலைகள். G. 116.

By faithfulness in the performance of humble tasks, you prove your fitness for nobler things.

194.

தான் மேற்கொண்ட கருமஞ்செய்ய முடியாதாயினும் ஊக்கங்கெடாமல் அந்நிலையே நிற்பது ஆண்மகனுக்குரிய கடமை.

இசையா தெனினும் இயற்றிஓர் ஆற்றுல்
அசையாது நிற்பதாம் ஆண்மை;—இசையுங்கால்
கண்டறிரை அலேக்குங் கானல்அந் தண்சேர்ப்ப!—
பெண்டிரும் வாழாரோ மற்று?

Manliness is perseverance in spite of failure.

Manliness is working on, in no wise faltering, remaining stedfast though the matter succeed not. When all is successful,—Lord of the cool lovely shore, in whose groves the waves agitate the scented thorn,—will not even women live and flourish?

ஆண்மை (ஆள்) = தாளாண்மை, ஆள்வினை.

Comp. 152. The aim should be lofty, do not fret because of apparent failure. Comp. K. 618–620; and Jī. Chin. iii. 3:

'உமைை வினைநொந்து புலந்தூடல் உணர்வன்றே,
It is certainly not good sense to pout and sulk and lay the blame on *fate*.'

195.

உயர்ந்தசாதி என்றும் இழிவாகிய சாதிஎன்றுஞ் சொல்லுக்குப் பொருளில்லை; பொருள் முதலியவற்றினுல் மதிக்கவேண்டும்.

நல்ல குலமென்றுந் தீய குலமென்றும்
சொல்லள வல்லாற் பொருளில்லை—தொல்சிறப்பின்
ஒண்பொருள் ஒன்றோ தவங்கல்வி ஆள்வினை
என்றிவற்றுன் ஆகுங் குலம்.

What is good or bad caste?

When men speak of 'good *caste*' and 'bad *caste*' it is a mere form of speech, and has no real meaning. Not even by possessions, made splendid by ancient glories, but by self-denial, learning, and energy is *caste* determined.

எ: பொருள், குலம்.—ப: (சொல்லுக்)இல்லை, ஆகும்.

சொல்லளவு, 'are mere words.' ஒன்றோ, 'by that alone? not so.' Comp. B. I. S. 2160:

'गुणैरुत्तुङ्गतां याति न तु जाति प्रभावतः।

By good qualities a man attains to eminence, and not through greatness of birth.'

See also the curious கபிலர் அகவல். So 136.

196.

அறிவுடையார் தாம் மேற்கொண்டகருமம் முற்றுப்பெறும் அளவும் தம்முயற்சி யைப் பிறர்க்க அறியார்.

ஆற்றுந் துணையும் அறிவினை உள்ளடக்கி
ஊக்கம் உரையார் உணர்வுடையார்—ஊக்கம்
உறுப்பினால் ஆராயு மொண்மை உடையார்
குறிப்பின்கீழ்ப் பட்ட துலகு.

Reserve as to your own plans, and skill in detecting those of others.

Till the time for action comes men of understanding keep close within themselves their wisdom, and speak not of their designs (ஊக்கம் = what they are labouring to effect).

The world is subject to the nod of the brilliant (diplomatists), who search out (and know) men's designs from outward indications (lit. *from their members*, i.e. from eye, gesture, tone, expression, *etc.*).

So B. I. S. 5361:

'यस्य कृत्यं न जानन्ति मन्त्रं वा मन्त्रितं परे।
कृतमेवास्य जानन्ति स वै पण्डित उच्यते॥

He verily is called a wise man whose designed action and deliberate counsel others know not; but they know the action done.'

Comp. K. ch. lxxi, cx, and cxxviii. This quatrain seems unconnected with the rest of the chapter; but the power of self-suppression, and the acuteness of an accomplished diplomatist, are manifestations of (முயற்சி or தாளாண்மை) practical energy.

The idea of குறிப்பு is 'a wish expressed by a sign.' The following quatrain is given as 96 in T.; but I doubt its genuineness. The last line is identical with a celebrated line in the K. (55):

'கொண்டான் குறிப்பறிவாள் பெண்டாட்டி; கொண்டன
செய்வகை செய்வான் றவசி;—கொடிதொரீஇ
நல்லவை செய்வான் அரசன்; இவர்மூவர்
பெய்யெனப் பெய்யு மழை.

She is a wife who knows her husband's sign. He is an ascetic that does the things he has undertaken as they should be done. He is a king who eschews cruelty and does good. *It will rain when these three bid it!*'

197.

சிதலாலே தின்னப்பட்ட ஆலமரத்தைத் தன்விழுது பற்றாகத் தாங்கினாற் போலத் தந்தையிடத்தில் தளர்ச்சி தோன்றில் அவன்பெற்ற புதல்வன் பாதுகாக்கக் கெடும்.

சிதலை தினப்பட்ட ஆல மரத்தை
மதலையாய் மற்றதன் வீழூன்றி யாங்குக்
குதலைமை தந்தைகட் டோன்றிற்றான் பெற்ற
புதல்வன் மறைப்பக் கெடும்.

The worthy son conceals his sire's defects, and sustains his weakness.

If the *banyan's* trunk be eaten by the gnawing ant, its '*branch-root*' bears it up, like a buttress; even so, when decay appears in the sire, the son he has begotten shall hide it, and weakness is no more.

எ : குதலைமை—ப : கெடும். சிதலை = by ants. G. 152. ஒருவிகற்பத்தினால் வந்த நேரிசைவெண்பா. G. 190. ஊன்றி = ஊன்றின. Verb. part. for rel. part.

So in T. 33 : 'குடிதழீஇ ஆலம்வீழ்போலும் அமைச்சன், a minister who cherishing the people resembles the offshoot of the *banyan.*'

Comp. Jī. Chin. iii. 6 :

'தூங்குசிறைவாவல் உறை தொன்மரங்கள் என்ன
ஓங்குகுலமைய அதனுட் பிறந்த வீரர்
தாங்கல் கடனாகும் . . .

It is the duty of brave men to support the high family from which they sprang, when it is in decay, like as old (banyan) trees where bats dwell with drooping wing (are upheld by their subsidiary trunks).'

198.

அறிவுடைய மேலோர் வறுமைக்காலத்தும் பிறர்பழித்தற்கேதுவாகிய முயற்சிகளைச் செய்யார்.

ஈனமாய் இல்லிருந் தின்றி விளியினும்
மானந் தலைவருவ செய்பவோ,—யானை
வரிமுகம் புண்படுக்கும் வள்ளுகிர் நோன்றாள்
அரிமா மதுகை யவர்?

Poverty but not dishonour.

The lion's pointed claw and mighty foot will wound the spotted face of an elephant; those who have power like his,—though bereft of all, they die in want within their home,—will they do deeds that bring disgrace?

எ : மதுகையவர்.—ப : செய்பவோ ?—செ : வருவனவற்றை.

199.

முயற்சியில்லார்க்கு உயர்ந்த குடிப்பிறப்பினுற் பயனில்லை.

தீங்கரும் பீன்ற திரள்கால் உளைஅலரி
தேங்கமழ் நாற்றம் இழந்தாஅங்—கோங்கும்
உயர்குடி உட்பிறப்பின் என்னும், பெயர்பொறிக்கும்
பேராண்மை இல்லாக் கடை?

High birth useless without lofty energies.

Like the flowers on a rounded stalk, with hair-like filaments that sweet cane bare, when the sweet fragrance they breathed is lost, what gain accrues from birth in a lofty noble house when energy, that makes the name noteworthy, is wanting?

The metre is peculiar. In the third line உயர் rhymes with பெயர், and the fourth line has no rhyme; in fact, பெயர்பொறிக்கும் is a second தனிச்சொல்.

எ: என்.—ப: ஆம்.

200.

முயற்சியில்லாத கீழோர் மானமின்றி இரந்துண்பர்; முயற்சியுடையார் அதனுற்கிடைத்த நீரை ஆயினும் உண்டு மானங் கெடாது வாழ்வர்.

பெருமுத் தரையர் பெரிதுவந் தியும்
கருனைச்சோ றார்வர் கயவர்;—கருனையைப்
பேரும் அறியார் நனிவிரும்பு தாளாண்மை
நீரும் அமிழ்தாய் விடும்.

The scant fare of the laborious is the diet of the gods.

The base feed full of rice and savoury food, that men, great lords of the triple lands, with generous gladness give; but water won with willing strenuous toil by those who know not savoury food by name even, will turn to nectar.

எ: கயவர், நீரும்.—ப: ஆர்வர், விடும். G. 156.

பெருமுத்தர் ஐயர் may be பெரிய முத்தர் ஆகிய ஐயர்='persons of dignity who are great devotees;' or பெரிய மூன்று தரையிலுள்ளவர்கள்='dwellers in the three lands,' i.e. சோழனுடு, சேரனுடு, and பாண்டியனுடு. See Lex. தரை. Comp. also 268.

CHAPTER XXI.

THE SUPPORT OF KINDRED.

அதிகாரம் உக.

சுற்றந் தழால்

(=உறவின்முறையார் பாரம் எல்லாந்தமதுபாரமாகவே கொண்டு அவர்களைத்தழுவிக் கொண்டு போதல்).

With this comp. K. ch. lii, though the standpoint is different. These are especially one's kindred. The Tamil தன், 'one's own,' is very expressive, recalling the saying of the noble dame who declined patronage, for said she, 'I dwell among mine own people.'

Analysis:

1. The sight of one's sympathizing kindred is a comfort in trouble. [201.]
2. The desire to aid one's friends and dependants is a motive to exertion. [202.]
3. Magnanimous persons never refuse to bear family burdens. [203.]
4. Noble relationships endure. [204.]
5. The worthiest are they who claim all the needy as their kin. [205.]
6. The meanest fare partaken with one's kindred is preferable to a regal feast with uncongenial persons. [206, 207, 210.]
7. The fire of affliction tries friends. [208.]
8. Perfection is to share sorrows as well as joys. [209.]

201.

வறுமைமுதலியவற்றுன் எய்திய இடுக்கண் அன்புள்ள சுற்றத்தாரைக் காணிற்கெடும்.

வயாவும் வருத்தமும் ஈன்றக்கா ளோவும்
கவாஅன் மகற்கண்டு தாய்மறந் தாஅங்
கசாஅத்தான் உற்ற வருத்தம் உசாஅத்தன்
கேளிரைக் காணக் கெடும்.

Comfort from sympathy of kinsmen.

As a mother when she sees her son upon her lap forgets the languors, the pains, and the throes of birth ; so trouble arising from weakness will die when a man sees his sympathizing kinsmen around him.

எ : வருத்தம்.—ப : கெடும். கவான் = தொடையினிடத்தில். அசா = தளர்ச்சியால். G. 152. உசா = சூழ்ச்சியையுடைய. G. 152. மகற் = மகனை. மறந்து. G. 148.

See Ellis, p. 231. Rhyme as 199.

This is quoted by the commentator on Jī. Chin. i. 275, which shows that this stanza at least is as old as the commentary on that great work.

202.

முயற்சியால் வருந்துகிற உறவினர்பலரையும் பாதுகாத்தலே ஆண்மையையுடையவனுக் குரியகடன்.

அழன்மண்டு போழ்தின் அடைந்தவர்கட் கெல்லாம்
நிழன்மரம்போ னோர்ஒப்பத் தாங்கிப்—பழுமரம்போற்
பல்லார் பயன்றுய்ப்பத் தான்வருந்தி வாழ்வதே
நல்லாண் மகற்குக் கடன்.

Good friends like trees that afford both shade and fruit.

To yield ready protection alike to all, as a tree affords shade to those that seek its shelter when the heat grows fierce ; and to live toiling so that many may enjoy the gain, resembling thus a fruit-producing tree, is the duty of the manly man.

எ : வாழ்வது.—ப : கடன். மண்டு. G. 153.

As to நிழல், see 167.

Comp. B. I. S. 2307 :

'छायामन्यस्य कुर्वन्ति स्वयं तिष्ठन्ति चातपे।
फलन्तिच परार्थे च नात्महेतोर्महाद्रुमाः॥

Great trees afford shade to others, themselves standing in the sunshine ; and bear fruit for others, not for themselves.'

K. 216, 217. So B. I. S. 5921 :

'वदान्यः संविभागेन पूर्णं कुर्यादनुग्रहम्।
छाययाप्याययन्दद्यात्फलान्यपि महीरुहः॥

A generous man confers favours by completely sharing all : a tree not only affords profit by its shade, but it gives fruit also.'

203.

பெரியோர் தம்முறவினரைக் கைவிடார்.

அடுக்கன் மலைநாட!—தற்சேர்ந் தவரை
எடுக்கலம் என்னார் பெரியோர்;—அடுத்தடுத்து
வன்காய் பலபல காய்ப்பினும் இல்லையே
தன்காய் பொறுக்கலாக் கொம்பு.

The magnanimous never refuse to support their kindred. The bough sustains all its fruits.

Lord of the land where mountains piled on mountains rise! the great demur not to support their kith and kin;—there is no bough but will support the fruit it bears, though clustered thick great fruits and many cling thereon.

Comp. note on 10.

All along the Western Ghāts you see lines of hills rising one over another and stretching up to the central mountain like the clansmen (சுற்றம்) around their chieftain.

எ: பெரியோர், கொம்பு.—ப: என்னார், இல்லையே.—எடுக்கலம் = எடுக்கமாட்டோம். (எடு, கு, அலம். G. 93, 108, 135.) பொறுக்கலா = பொறுக்கமாட்டாத. See அல்.

So in common talk one hears it said:

'கோழி மிதிக்கக்குஞ்சு சாகுமா?
கொடிக்குச் சுரைக்காய் கனத்திருக்குமா?
குருவியை எற்காத கொம்புண்டா?

Will the chicken die from the tread of the hen?
Will its fruit be too heavy for the gourd?
Is there any branch that will not hold a bird?'

204.

மேலோரோடு சேர்ந்த உறவு நிலைக்கும்.

உலகறியத் தீரக் கலப்பினு நில்லா
சிலபகலாஞ் சிற்றினத்தார் கேண்மை;—நிலைதிரியா
நிற்கும் பெரியோர் நெறியடைய நின்றனைத்தால்
ஒற்கம் இலாளர் தொடர்பு.

The friendship of the great alone is lasting.

Though mingled in a complete intimacy so that all the world knows of it, the friendship of the little will last but little time. Connection with the firm unyielding men endures till the great ones' path, who never swerve, is reached.

The friendship we are privileged to form with (ஒத்கம் இலாளர் those who are firm, steady, good men, will last till the time when we and they gain the path trodden only by the great: i.e. till we obtain release. For ஒத்கம், K. 414, comp. K. 815.

The great ones we are to join hereafter and the friends we cherish now have one character, for நிலைதிரியா நிற்கும்பெரியோர் = ஒத்கமிலாளர்.

எ: கேண்மை, தொடர்பு.—ப: ஆம், அணைந்து.—ஆல் is redundant. Note the use of the infinitives, அறிய, தீர, அடைய. (G. 140.)

The following (*Ēlā.* 67) contains a striking description of this goal reached by the sage:

HEAVEN: மோட்சத்தின்சிறப்பு.

'பொய்தீர் புலவர் பொருள்புரிந் தாராய்ந்த
மைதீர் உயர்கதியின் மாண்புரைப்பின்—மைதீர்
சுடரின்று சொல்லின்று மாறின்று சோர்வின்
றிடரின் றினிதுயிலும் இன்று:

If one would tell of the excellence of the pure and lofty goal, which sages from falsehood free have sought out and desired as the only reality, (in that place) there is no light that dispels darkness, no speech, no change, no weariness, no suffering, no sweet sleep.'

[No light, since no darkness; no words; no increase or diminution of joy; . . . . no sweetness of repose, because no toil.]

205.

யாவரையும் உறவினராகக் கருதிக்காப்பவரே மேன்மக்கள் ஆவார்.

இன்னர் இனையர் எமர்பிறர் என்னுஞ்சொல்
என்னும் இலராம் இயல்பினால்—துன்னித்
தொலைமக்க டுன்பந்தீர்ப் பாரேயார் மாட்டும்
தலைமக்கள் ஆகற்பா லார்.

Universal benevolence.

'Such are they and so many;' 'these are ours; those strange:' those worthy to be classed as chief of men say nothing like this; so to speak is not their nature; for they relieve the distress of ALL that troubled come to them!

எ: தீர்ப்பார் (G. 95).—ப: பாலார். See பால்.

Comp. K. ch. lxxix, and especially 790. Ellis, p. 232. For the double use of என்னும் see Lex. என்.

Translate, 'through the innate goodness (இயல்பு), by which they are free from (இலர் ஆம) any trace of (என்னும்) that way of speaking (என்னுஞ்சொல்).'

தொலைமக்கள் = (செல்வம்) தொலைந்தவர்கள் = 'the unfortunate.' See in Lex. இன் and இனை. இன்னர் and இனையர் may mean 'good' and 'bad;' or 'such' and 'so many.'

206.

அன்பிலாரிடத்த இனியவை உணவில் அன்பரிடத்துக் கூழை உண்ணுதல் நன்று.

பொற்கலத்துப் பெய்த புலியுகிர் வான்புழக்கல்
அக்காரம் பாலோ டமரார்கைத் துண்டலின்
உப்பிலிப் புற்கை உயிர்போற் கிளைஞர்மாட்
டெக்கலத் தானும் இனிது.

Hard fare with kindred, better than a feast without love.

More sweet than rice, though white as tiger's claw, with milk and sugar served on plate of gold, by loveless hands, is any tasteless mess, in any dish, when shared with kindred dear as life.

For metre, G. 190; the rhyme is இனவெதுகை. Introd. to K. p. xxvi, § III. (v.)

The word அமரார் = நள்ளாதார், மேவாதார், விருப்பிலார், அன்பிலார், and பகைவர் in this connexion.

See K. 1065; and comp. here 207, 210, and 217; and Ellis, p. 232. அக்காரத்தோடும், பாலோடும். G. 156.

207.

பகைவரிடத்த இனியவை உண்ணலின் உறவினரிடத்து இலைக்கறியை உண்ணுதல் நன்று.

நாள்வாய்ப் பெறினுந்தந் நள்ளாதார் இல்லத்து
வேளாண்மை வெங்கருனை வேம்பாகும்;—கேளாய்!
அபராணப் போழ்தின் அடகிடுவர் ஏனும்
தமராயார் மாட்டே இனிது.

Any food with foes bitter, with friends sweet.

Most bitter (*margosa*) is the bounteous meal of dainty food at early dawn in house of those who love us not. Hear thou! though not till evening given, the mess of herbs when eaten with our own is sweet.

எ: கருனை, (உணவு).—ப: வேம்பாகும், இனிது.

நாள்வாய், இல்லத்து, போழ்தின், தமராயார்மாட்டு (G. 63) are all in the 7th case.

208.

ஒருவர் வறுமையால் துன்புற்றகாலத்துத் தாமும் துன்புற்று அவர் இறக்கின்கூட இறக்குமவர் உறவினர் ஆவர்.

முட்டிகை போல முனியாது வைகலும்
கொட்டி உண்பாருங் குறடுபோற் கைவிடுவர்;
சுட்டுக்கோல் போல எரியும் புகுவரே
நட்டார் எனப்படு வார்.

Interested and disinterested friends.

Even those who, like the artificer's small hammer [with slight strokes fashioning the jewel], gently (*முனியாது*), day by day, moulding their patron to their will, eat his food, will drop him (when poverty assails him), as the pincers do the gold put into the crucible. Those worthy to be called friends are like the artificer's rod which enters the fire with it.

K. 521. Ellis, p. 232, where the meaning is missed.

So the proverb:

'குறைவு வைட்டளவு தோன்றும்: in reduced circumstances appears the measure of friendship.' [குறை = வறுமை.]

209.

உறவினர் துன்புறுங்கால் துன்புறுதலும் இன்புறுங்கால் இன்புறுதலுமாகிய இவற்றினும் தாஞ்செய்யும் உதவி வேறே இல்லை.

நறுமலர்த் தண்கோதாய்! நட்டார்க்கு நட்டார்
மறுமையுஞ் செய்வதொன் றுண்டோ—இறுமளவும்
இன்புறுவ தின்புற் றெழீஇ, அவரோடு
துன்புறுவ துன்புறாக் கால்?

Sympathy in sorrow and in joy.

O maid adorned with fresh garlands of fragrant flowers! is there one thing that even in other world, friends may perform for friends, if till they die, their joys they share, but shun to share their griefs?

எ: ஒன்று.—ப: உண்டோ.

Ellis, p. 232.

The following rather rugged but interesting verse (*Ēlā.* 80) expresses a similar idea :

'சாக்காடு கேடு பகைதுன்பம் இன்பமே
நாக்காடு நாட்டறை போக்குமெனை—நாக்காட்ட
நட்டார்க் கியையிற், றமக்கியைந்த கூறுடம்
பட்டார்வாய்ப் பட்டது பண்பு;

Death, ruin, enmity, affliction, pleasure, evil and good report spoken through the land by busy tongues, when such as these their friends experience,—if men consent to regard these as their own experience [*if they feel their friends' joys and sorrows as their own*],—excellence dwells with them.

நாக்காடு, 'utter with the tongue.' நாடு + அறை + போக்கு, 'what goes spoken through the land.' நாக்காட்ட = சொல்லப்பட்ட இவைகள்.

See B. I. S. 1221 :

'उत्सवे व्यसने चैव दुर्भिक्षे शत्रुसंकटे।
राजद्वारे श्मशाने च यस्तिष्ठति स बान्धवः॥

He is a friend who stands by us in joy and in sorrow, in hunger, in affliction from enemies, at the door of the prince, and in the burning ground.'

210.

ஒருவர் தம்மாட்டு விருப்பமுடைய உறவினரில்லின்கண் புல்லரிசிக் கூழையேனும் உண்க!

விருப்பிலார் இல்லத்து வேறிருந் துண்ணும்
வெருக்குக்கண் வெங்கருனை வேம்பாம்;—விருப்புடைத்
தன்போல்வார் இல்லுட் டயங்குநீர்த் தண்புற்கை
என்போடியைந்த அமிழ்து.

Better fast with friends than feast with foes.

The savoury fried *curry*, (in colour) like a cat's eye, which one eats seated apart in the house of those who are without affection, will be bitter as margosa ; but cold gruel (weak and insipid), like clear water, in the house of affectionate equals, is ambrosia that cleaves to the bones.

எ : கருனை, புற்கை.—ப : வேம்பாம், அமிழ்து.

Comp. 206, 207, 217.

In K. 1065 we find தெண்ணீர் (அடுபுற்கை) = அமுத்தமில்லாமல் தெளிந்த நீர்போன்ற கூழ் = 'without consistency like clear water.'

வெருக்கு adj. form of வெருகு. (§ 131. G. 119.) The figure of the cat's eye indicates 'brightness and freshness.'

CHAPTER XXII.

SCRUTINY IN FORMING FRIENDSHIPS.

அதிகாரம் உஉ.

நட்பாராய்தல்

(= நட்புக் கொள்ளத்தக்காரை ஆராய்ந் தறிதல்).

Here K. ch. lxxx may be compared. Much stress is laid upon friendship by Tamil writers. Domestic life does not satisfy. A man wants more than his சுற்றம். Rosseau's saying, *L'amitié est l'amour sans le tumulte des sens*, 'friendship is love without the perturbations of passion,' gives one reason why it has been so esteemed by thoughtful men of all times.

Compare நட்பு, கேண்மை, தொடர்பு in Lex.

சிநேகம் and other Sanskrit words are not used here, or in K.

Analysis:

1. Worthy friendships grow more precious with lapse of time, and friendships with the unworthy grow less so. [211.]
2. A man's lineage is the best ground for admitting him as a friend. [212.]
3. Grateful and ungrateful hearts. [213.]
4. Congeniality in friendship. [214.]
5. Constancy. [215.]
6. Three grades of friends. [216.]
7. Faithful though poor. [217.]
8. Really helpful friends. [218.]
9. Friendship with trustworthy persons. [219.]
10. It is hard to drop a friend. This emphasizes the necessity of care in forming friendships. [220.]

211.

மூடர் நட்பு முன்னர் இனிதாய்ப் பின்னர் இன்னாதாம்.

கருத்துணர்ந்து கற்றறிந்தார் கேண்மை எஞ்ஞான்றும்
குருத்திற் கரும்புதின் றற்றே;—குருத்திற்
கெதிர்செலத்தின் றன்ன தகைத்தரோ என்றும்
மதுரம் இலாளர் தொடர்பு.

Satisfying friendships.

Intimacy with those who understand the real intention (of one's words), and who have acquired wisdom by learning, will at all times be like eating sweet cane from the tender shoots; but attachment to those who have no sweetness of disposition is like eating it in a direction opposite to the tender shoot (it grows harder and less sweet).

Here are two antithetical statements: எ: கேண்மை, தொடர்பு.—ப: அற்று, நகைத்து.

Ellis, p. 232. This is another version of 138. Comp. also 166 and 125, and K. 782, 783.

The definition of men of cultivated understanding is neat: கருத்தை உணர்ந்து கற்று அறிந்தவர்கள்.

So B. I. S. 1088; Pañch. ii. 37:

'इक्षोर् अग्रात् क्रमशः पर्वणि पर्वणि यथा रसविशेषः।
तद्वत् सज्जनमैत्री विपरीतानां तु विपरीता ॥

There is a different taste in the sap of the sugar-cane as you go gradually from the tip joint by joint (or month by month); even so friendship of the good is diverse from that of the evil.'

Here पर्वन् has a double meaning: 'joint' and 'change of the moon.' Thus the Tamil misses the play on the word. Comp. 138, 390, 156.

212.

நற்குடிப்பிறந்தவர் மாறமாட்டார் என்ற உறுதியாற் சிநேகிக்கவேண்டும். மனமறிவது அசாத்தியம்.

இற்பிறப் பெண்ணி இடைதிரியார் என்பதோர்
நற்புடைக் கொண்டமை; அல்லது,—பொற்கேழ்
புனல்ஒழுகப் புள்ளிரியும் பூங்குன்ற நாட!—
மனம்அறியப் பட்டதொன் றன்று.

Examine the lineage of a candidate for your friendship.

Lord of the land of flowery hills, where wild-fowl golden in hue fly, scared by the rush of the waterfall!

'*Regarding the nobility of their birth—these will not swerve:*'—To say thus is a good ground of confidence—(a good position to take up); but to say 'their minds are known,' is not any (i. e. real ground).

எ: அறியப்பட்டது.—ப: அன்று.—கொண்டமை. G. 94. பூங்குன்ற நாட = பொலிவையுடைய மலை நாடனே! G. 119, 64. ஒன்று = ஒருநற்புடை.

If you have ascertained that a man is of good family, you have good ground for believing that he will be faithful and unswerving in friendship; but you must not rely upon any supposed knowledge of his disposition. The two grounds of trust (புடை =பட்சம், 'hypothesis') are, 'they will act as becomes their birth,' and 'I know their hearts.' The former alone is நல்லபுடை, 'a tenable ground of confidence.'

Comp. K. 793, 794.

213.

நன்றி யறிந்தவரோடுதானே நட்புச்செய்ய வேண்டும்.

யானை அனையவர் நண்பொரீஇ—நாய்அனையார்
கேண்மை கெழீஇக் கொளல்வேண்டும் ;—யானை
அறிந்தறிந்தும் பாகனையே கொல்லும்,—எறிந்த வேல்
மெய்யதா வால்குழைக்கு நாய்.

The elephant and the dog, types of false and true friends.

Forsaking friendship with those who resemble the elephant, embrace and hold fast intimacy with those who are like the dog; for the elephant will slay even its keeper though it has long known him; but the dog will wag its tail when it has in its body the javelin (*hurled at it by its angry master*).

எ: ஒருவர் (தொகை), யானை, நாய்.—ப: வேண்டும், கொல்லும், குழைக்கும்—ஒரீஇ = ஒருவி. கெழீஇ = கெழுவி. G. 79. எறிந்தவேல். G. 143. மெய்யதா = மெய்யது + ஆ. இதில் மெய்யது எ—து ஏழாம் வேற்றுமை மயக்கமாகவந்த ஆறும் வேற்றுமை. G. 62, 137*. ஆ = ஆக. G. 140. = 'while it has the dart in its body.'

Ellis, p. 233. K. 814. Three தனிச்சொற்கள் in lines 1, 2, 3.

214.

மனங் கலந்து நட்புச்செய்தவர் தம்மைநெடு நாள் பிரிந்திருப்பினும் அவர் நட்பை அறிவுடையார் விடார்.

பலநாளும் பக்கத்தார் ஆயினு' நெஞ்சில்
சிலநாளும் ஒட்டாரோ டொட்டார் ;—பலநாளும்
நீத்தார் எனக்கை விடல்உண்டோ தந்நெஞ்சத்
தியாத்தாரோ டியாத்த தொடர்பு?

Friends are not to be forsaken because long severed.

Though men dwell side by side for many days, when their souls cleave not (are not congenial), for even a few days they retain not their friendship. But is it possible to let go attachment's well-knit ties, though those to whom one's soul is knit dwell many days afar?

No intimacy can render uncongenial friendships lasting; and no separation can annul a real friendship.

எ: அறிவுடையார், கைவிடல்.— ப: ஒட்டார், உண்டோ?— செய்: தொடர்பு.

Comp. 237, and Ellis, p. 233. See my K. p. 292.

Note குற்றியல் இகரம் twice in line 4. G. 24. It does not affect the metre.

215.

உயர்ந்தோரோடு ஒருநிலையே நட்பாக வேண்டும்.

கோட்டுப்பூப் போல மலர்ந்துபிற் கூம்பாது
வேட்டதே வேட்டதா நட்பாட்சி;—தோட்ட
கயப்பூப்போன் முன்மலர்ந்து பிற்கூம்பு வாரை
நயப்பாரு' நட்பாரும் இல்.

Tree-flowers and water-flowers.

The use and wont of friendship is that, what once it has loved it loves always,—like the flower on the tree-branch which having once unfolded afterwards closes not; but who will esteem, or make friends of, those who are like flowers on the surface of the excavated *tank*, which unfold and afterwards close themselves?

Comp. K. 425. Ellis, p. 233. The idea that there should be no fickle caprice in friendship is to be found also in 246. The lotus daily opens and shuts: the tree-flower blooms and remains in full bloom till it withers away!

கோட்டு from கோடு. § 131. தோட்ட for தோண்டின=தோண்டப்பட்ட; or from தொடு for தொட்ட. See Lex. For வேட்டதே வேட்டது ஆம் (√வேள்), comp. 216: இட்டஞான் றிட்டதே, 'what it once has given is given for ever.'

216.

கடை, இடை, தலையானவர் நட்பு இன்னது.

கடையாயார் நட்பிற் கமுகனையர்; ஏனை
இடையாயார் தெங்கின் அனையர்;—தலையாயார்
எண்ணரும் பெண்ணைபோன் றிட்டஞான் றிட்டதே
தொன்மை உடையார் தொடர்பு.

Three grades of friends.

The lowest sort of men in friendship are like the *Areca-nut* tree. The middle sort are like the *Cocoa-nut* tree. Attachments to the chief of men—who are old friends—is like the *Palmyra* tree of rare worth: what was given that first day was given once for all.

எ: கடையாயார், இடையாயார், தலையாயார்.—ப: அனையர், அனையர், இட்டதே. கடையாயார் = கடைவரிசையில் உள்ளார். ஆயார் = ஆனோர். G. 82. (7.) அனையர். G. 109. எண்ணரும் = எண்ணுதற்கரிய. G. 153, 121.

Read . . . தொடர்பு . . . போன்று . . . இட்டதேயாம்.

This quatrain is a riddle, and the latter half rather puzzles all the commentators. The meaning is this: Some men must be daily cultivated, or their friendship fails. Of these—the lowest type—the *Areca* is the emblem, for it requires daily care and irrigation. Others must be attentively considered for some time, till friendship has become a fixed habit. Of these—the medium type—the Cocoa-palm is the emblem, for it requires constant care in its earlier stages only. Others, once friends are friends for ever. Of these—the highest type—the Palmyra is the emblem. Planted in the sandy plain, it requires no care, and is of incalculable value (எண்ணரிது) to South India. Comp. B. I. S. 4249.

217.

அன்பினுடைய நட்பினர் இடும் இலைக்கறி அமிர்தம்; அன்பிலார் இடும் அறுசுவையோடுகூடிய உணவும் எட்டிக் காய் ஆகும்.

கழுநீருட் கார்அட கேனும்ஒருவன்
விழுமிதாக் கொள்ளின் அமிழ்தாம்;—விழுமிய
குய்த்துவையார் வெண்சோறே ஆயினு மேவாதார்
கைத்துண்டல் காஞ்சிரங் காய்.

A dinner of herbs with affection is ambrosia. The greatest delicacies without it, nux vomica.

If one receive you courteously, though what he gives is but rank herbs dressed in water in which rice had been washed, it is ambrosia. To eat from the hands of those who love us not, though it be white rice with rich spicy condiments, is nux vomica.

எ: அடகு, உண்டல்.—ப: ஆம், காய் (ஆகும்).—கார். G. 121, 154. விழுமிதா = விழுமியது + ஆ = ஆக. G. 93.

Comp. 206, 207, 210; and K. 1065. கைத்து may = பொருள், or be a kind of 7th case of கை = *at*, or *from their hand*. கழுநீர் = அரிசிகழுவியநீர். G. 153.

218.

சமீபத்திலிருந்தும் உதவிசெய்யாத நட்பாரலேபயனில்லை.

நாய்க்காற் சிறுவிரல்போ னன்கணியர் ஆயினும்
ஈக்காற் றுணையும் உதவாதார் நட்பென்னும்?
சேய்த்தானுஞ் சென்றுகொளல்வேண்டுஞ் செய்விளைக்கும்
வாய்க்கால் அனையார் தொடர்பு.

Friendship of those who though near aid not.

Of what value is the friendship of those who being very near, like the little claw on a dog's leg, afford not help as much as a fly's foot? Though you go far to seek it, lay hold of the friendship of those who are like the water-channel that causes the crops in the field to flourish.

எ: நட்பு, ஒருவர் (தொகை).—ப: என்னும், வேண்டும். செயப்படுபொருள்: தொடர்பை.—நாய்க்கால், ஈக்கால். G. 152.

Comp. 263.

219.

அறிவிலாரதுநட்புந் தீராப்பிணியும் இகழ்ச்சியும் இல்லாதகுணங்களைப்புகழ்தலுங் கொடியன.

தெளிவிலார் நட்பிற் பகைநன்று; சாதல்
விளியா வருநோயி னன்றால்;—அளிய
இகழ்தலிற் கோறல் இனிதே; மற் றில்ல
புகழ்தலின் வைதலே நன்று.

Four bad things.

Better hate than friendship of the *ignorant.*

Better death than disease which comes on yielding to no remedy.

Sweeter is killing than contempt that breaks the spirit.

Better abuse than undeserved praise.

எ: பகை, சாதல், கோறல், வைதல்.—ப: நன்று, நன்று, இனிது, நன்று.—நட்பில். (G. 61. ஒப்பு.) ஆல், ஏ, மற்று, அசைச்சொற்கள். அளிய. G. 140. கோறல்=கொல்லல். G. 41.

Comp. 187. Looking at K. 508–510, I would translate தெளிவிலார், 'persons unworthy of confidence.' K. 816.

In Tel.: *Avivēkitō snēhamu kannā*
Vivēkitō virōdhamu mēlu.

220.

கூடிப் பிரிதல் கூடாது; ஆதலால் தகுதியுடையாரையே நட்புக் கொள்ளல் வேண்டும்.

மரீஇப் பலரொடு பன்னாள் முயங்கிப்,
பொரீஇப் பொருட்டக்கார்க் கோடலே வேண்டும்;—
பரீஇ உயிர்செகுக்கும் பாம்பொடும் இன்னா
மரீஇப் பின்னைப் பிரிவு.

Never forsake a friend!

When men have formed an intimacy (மரீஇ), separation afterwards even from a snake which slays with its tooth (பரீஇ), causes affliction (இன்னா); therefore associate intimately with many, and for many days take them to your bosom, conform to their tastes and habits (பொரீஇ), and hold fast the really worthy ones.

எ: ஒருவர் (தொகை), பிரிவு.—ப: வேண்டும், இன்னா.—செயப்படு: தக்காரை.—ஏ-அசைநிலை. மரீஇ, பொரீஇ, பரீஇ. G. 79. பன்னாள் = பல்நாள். G. 39, 36. பொருட்டக்கார் = பொருளாகத் தக்கவர். G. 57, 37.

So *Avvaiyār*, கூடிப்பிரியேல!

This is corrupt. பரீஇ = பருவி is made for the rhyme.

The idea seems to be: 'Cultivate friendship on all sides, and even if you find some friends dangerous, try to make the best of the matter: *anything is better than dropping a friend!*'

மரீஇ in line 4 is bad metre. Perhaps we may read மரீஇய பின்னே பிரிவு.

See B. I. S. 5375 (also Pañch. ii. 60, iv. 60):

'यस्य न ज्ञायते शीलं न कुलं न च संश्रयः न तेन संगतिं कुर्यात्।

Form no friendship with him whose disposition, race, and connexions are unknown.'

CHAPTER XXIII.

BEARING AND FORBEARING IN FRIENDSHIP.

அதிகாரம் உ௩.

நட்பிற் பிழைபொறுத்தல்

(= நட்டோரிடத்துளவாகிய குற்றங்களைப்பொறுத்தல்).

There is no chapter with this title in K., though chapters lxxix-lxxxiii deal with friendship. Comp. also K. xvi. This is a very complete chapter in which there is nothing extraneous, and the verses bear the appearance of having been composed by one poet as a connected poem. The motto might be—

> 'I know not, I ask not, if guilt's in that heart,
> I know that I love thee whatever thou art.'

The whole subject of friendship is treated in this work and in the K. in a very earnest, enthusiastic, and real manner. It is a sacred, inviolable bond. Much of what western writers connect only with love between the sexes is here introduced.

Analysis :

1. None are perfect. We must hide in our bosom the faults of our friends. [221, 227, 229.]
2. Never dissolve a friendship, since friends are essentials of life! Tank, fire, hand! [222, 225, 226.]
3. The worth of forbearance. [223, 228.]
4. The pain of friends' unworthiness.—Ignore their faults. [224.]
5. The evil of suspecting friends, and seeking out their faults. [230.]

221.

சிநேகர் குற்றங்களைத் தம்முள்ளத்தில் மறைக்கவேண்டும்; குற்றமில்லாதவர் பூவுலகிலில்லை.

நல்லார் எனத்தா' நனிவிரும்பிக் கொண்டாரை
அல்லார் எனினும் அடக்கிக் கொளல்வேண்டும்!
நெல்லுக் குமிஉண்டு; நீர்க்கு நுரைஉண்டு;
புல்லிதழ் பூவிற்கும் உண்டு.

Bear with infirmities. None are perfect.

When those to whom with strong desire we clung as good, prove otherwise, keep the sad secret hid,—cling to them still! *The growing grain has husks; the water has its foam;* flowers too have scentless outer sheath of leaves.

எ: ஒருவர் (தொகை), உமி, நுரை, புல்லிதழ்.—ப: வேண்டும், உண்டு.—என. G. 114. தாம் + கனி = தாகனி. G. 33. கொண்டாரை. G. 124. (5.) புல்லிதழ். Comp. 266. G. 150. பூவிற்கும் = பூ + இன் + கு + உம். G. 23, 65, 35, 24. அடக்கி seems to govern குற்றங்களை understood, and கொள்ளல் governs கொண்டாரை. One commentator suggests that அடக்கிக் கொள்ளல் means 'trying to repress faults, and amend the erring ones.' But see also 229.

Comp. 75. Ellis, p. 233.

K. 807. So *Avvaiyār*, கொன்றைவேந்தன், 18. குற்றம்பார்க்கிற் சுற்றமில்லை, 'if you scrutinize faults you will have no friends.'

222.

நல்லோர் பிழை பொறுப்பர்.

செறுத்தோ றுடைப்பினுஞ் செம்புனலோ டோர்,
மறுத்துஞ் சிறைசெய்வர் நீர்நசை வாழ்நர்;
வெறுப்ப வெறுப்பச் செயினும்—பொறுப்பரே
தாம்வேண்டிக் கொண்டார் தொடர்பு!

Bear with your friends' faults, as the cultivator bears with the stream that often bursts its enclosure.

If, though they dam it up, the fresh flood should burst its bonds, men do not feel aggrieved; but straightway imprison it again, for by the precious stream they live: so though their friends again and again do very disagreeable things, men bear with those whose friendship is dear.

எ: வாழ்நர், கொண்டார்.—ப: செய்வர், பொறுப்பர்.—ஏ, அசைநிலை. செறுத்தோறும் = செறுக்குந்தோறும். G. 153. நீர் நசை = நீரை நசைந்து, அல்லது நீரின் நசையினால். G. 153. வாழ்நர். G. 95 = வாழ்வர்.

Comp. ch. viii, and especially 77.

The latter clause is difficult: '(men) will endure (even the disagreeables of) the attachment of those whom they have desired (=chosen).' Some take தாம் விரும்பித் தொடர்பு கொண்டாரைப் பொறுப்பர்.

For the repetition (அடுக்கு) see IIIrd G. 200. Here it is = 'exceedingly great and repeated offences.' Note the தனிச்சொல் in line 3.

223.

பொறுத்தல் நட்பை வளர்க்கும்.

இறப்பவே தீய செயினுந்தன் னட்டார்
பொறுத்த றகுவதொன் றன்றோ?—நிறக்கோங்
குருவவண் டார்க்கும் உயர்வரைநாட!
ஒருவர் பொறைஇருவர் நட்பு.

Bear all things!

Lord of the lofty hilly land, where the bees hum through all the flowery Gōngu-glade!—Though friends should work us surpassing ills, the only thing that is meet is forbearance: *Patience of one is friendship of the twain.*

எ: பொறுத்தல், பொறை.—ப: தகுவது, நட்பு (ஆகும்).—இறப்பவே. 'Though they do things so bad as to *pass* (the limits of forbearance).' G. 140. நிறக்கோங்கு உருவ வண்டு ஆர்க்கும் உயர் வரை நாட! = பொன்னிறத்த கோங்கம்பூவிலே அழகிய வண்டுகள் ஆர்ப்பரிக்கும் உயர்ந்த மலை நாடனே. G. 152, 162. ஒருவர், இருவர். G. 159. ல் + த = ற. G. 38. ந: this is அல்வழி.

224.

நட்டார் செய்த பிழையால் அதிக மனவருத்தம் உண்டாகும்.

மடிதிரை[1] தந்திட்ட வான்கதிர் முத்தங்
கடுவிசை நாவாய் கரைஅலைக்குஞ் சேர்ப்ப!
விடுதற் கரியார் இயல்பிலர்஡ல் நெஞ்சஞ்
சுடுதற்கு மூட்டிய தீ.

[1] '*Ever curling waves.*'

To be wroth with those we love, is like fire in the breast!

Lord of the shore where pearls of purest lustre are thrown up by circling waves, and where swift darting boats are borne through the surf!—When friends whom we may not leave have alien hearts, it is as a scorching fire enkindled in the soul.

எ: அரியார்.—ப: தீ (ஆவார்).—மடிதிரை. G. 153. தந்திட்ட. G. 124. (5.) கடு. G. 119.

☞ The student will recognise, in this and many other verses, a beautiful description of the old Pāṇḍiyan country, with its seaboard (சேர்ப்பு), its extensive forests, and limiting hills (வரை).

Some say உம் is understood: . . . முத்தங்களையும் . . . நாவாய்களையும். Others render: 'the strand where . . . ships toss up . . . pearls on the shore.'

Ellis, p. 233. K. 799, 809. The idea of the inviolability of friendship is expressed here and in 214, 225, 226 in similar phrases: விடுதற்கரியர், விடற்பாலரல்லார்.

225.

விடத்தகாத நட்பினர் தீமைகளைச்செய்தார் ஆயினும் அவரை நீங்குதல் நலம் அன்று.

இன்னா செயினும் விடற்பாலர் அல்லாரைப்
பொன்னன்னாய்—போற்றிக்கொள்ளல்வேண்டும்; பொன்னொடு
நல்லிற் சிதைத்ததீ நாடொறு' நாடித்தம்
இல்லத்தில் ஆக்குத லால்.

Forsake not friends though they wrong you.

Though those, from whom you may not part, do grievous things, O maid who art as Lakshmī! you must still cherish your chosen friends;—fire destroys men's wealth and happy homes, yet is it sought there and kindled every day.

The idea of fire is taken on from 224. Some read பொன்றுக='cherish them as gold.' Ellis, p. 233. K. 791.

Comp. B. I. S. p. 472:

'अप्रियाण्यपि कुर्वाणो यः प्रियः प्रिय एव सः ।
दग्धमन्दिरसारेऽपि कस्य वह्नावनादरः॥

He who is dear, remains dear even though he do unpleasing things.
Who ceases to honour fire though it has consumed the most precious things in the house?'

226.

நண்பரைப் பிழையின் பொருட்டுப் பிரியல் ஆகாது.

இன்னா செயினும் விடுதற் கரியாரைத்
துன்னத் துறத்த றகுவதோ?—துன்னருஞ்சீர்
விண்குத்து நீள்வரை வெற்ப!—களைபவோ
கண்குத்திற் றென்றுதங் கை?

Friends are not to be forsaken on account of their faults.

When those from whom it is hard to part do evil things should men at once renounce them?—Lord of the lengthening hills that pierce the sky, whence rarest gifts descend!—Do men cut off their hand because it pricked their eye?

எ: துறத்தல், மனிதர் (தொகை).—ப: தகுவதோ, களைபவோ.—துன்னருஞ் சீர் விண்குத்து நீள் வரை வெற்ப!=விட்டுதற்கு அரிய நன்மையை உடைய வானைப் பொருத்திய நீண்ட மலை நாடனே!

227.

சிநேகிதரை விட்டுப்பிரிந்தவர் பிழை செய்தவரிலுங் கடையர்.

இலங்குநீர்த் தண்சேர்ப்ப! இன்னா செயினுங்
கலந்து பழிகாணார் சான்றோர்;—கலந்தபிற்
றீமை எடுத்துரைக்குந் திண்ணறி வில்லாதார்
தாமும் அவரிற் கடை.

Those who forsake friends that have committed a fault are worse than they.

Lord of the cool shore of the shining sea! The perfect ones when they have contracted an intimacy with any, see no faults in them, even if they do things that cause pain. Those who, being without stable wisdom, take up and tell out men's evil deeds after contracting an intimacy with them, are themselves worse than they.

எ: சான்றோர், இல்லாதார்.—ப: காணார், கடை (ஆவர்).—செயப்படு: பழியை.—கலந்து = நட்புக் கொண்டபின். நட்பரைத்திருத்த வேண்டுமே அல்லாமல் அவர்களுடைய குற்றங்களைப் பலர்க்கு அறிவிக்கக் கூடாது. அவரில். G. 61.

The bond of a friendship once formed is indissoluble.

228.

நட்பினர்செய்த பிழையை உரிமையாற் செய்ததென்று கருதிப்பொறுத்துக் கொள்ள வேண்டும்.

ஏதிலார் செய்த திறப்பவே தீதெனினும்
நோதக்க தென்னுண்டா' நோக்குங்கால்—காதல்
கழுமியார் செய்த—கறங்கருவி நாட!
விழுமிதா நெஞ்சத்து ணின்று.

Faults in strangers and in friends.

Lord of the land of resounding waterfalls! Though what those alien to us have done may be surpassingly evil, what is there to be pained at, when you regard it?

Things done by affectionate friends, will be excellent when so regarded by the mind.

Bear patiently all unpleasing actions of men. If they are entire strangers, it must be fated, or it was all one could expect! If friends, regarded in a friendly spirit, all will be good.

Comp. K. ch. lxxxi, esp. 804, 805.

229.

கேளிர்தன் பிழைகளை வெளிப்படுத்தல் ஆகாது.

தமர்என்று தாங்கொள்ளப் பட்டவர் தம்மைத்
தமர்அன்மை தாம்அறிந்தார் ஆயின், அவரைத்
தமரினு' நன்கு மதித்துத் தமர்அன்மை
தம்முள் ளடக்கிக் கொளல்.

If friends prove unfaithful, love them the more, and keep the secret of their unfaithfulness in your own bosom.

If we perceive those we have accepted as our own to be not really ours, we must pay even more respect to them than to our own, and keep concealed in our own mind the fact that they are not really ours.

எ: ஒருவர் (தொகை).—ப: அடக்கிக்கொளல். தமர். G. 123. அன்மை. G. 94, 152. நன்கு. G. 120. கொளல். G. 85.

This is 221 with variations. There is a play on தம் throughout.

கொள்ள and பட்டவர் must be carefully separated in construction. தாம் is subject of கொள்ள. பட்டவர்தம்மை is object of அறிந்தார்.

230.

கேளிர் குற்றங்களை வெளிப்படத் தூற்றினவன் சாபம்.

குற்றமும் ஏனைக் குணமும் ஒருவனை
நட்டபி னாடித் திரிவேன்எல்—நட்டான்
மறைகாவா விட்டவன் செல்வுழிச் செல்க,
அறைகடல்சூழ் வைய நக.

He who pries into his friend's faults shares the punishment of the revealer of secrets.

If, after I have taken a man for my friend, I go about prying into his faults and virtues (other qualities), may I depart whither that man goes who has not kept his friend's secret, while the earth, begirt by the resounding sea, laughs.

எ: யான் (தொகை).—ப: செல்க.—காவா = காக்காமல். செல்வுழி = செல், வ், உழி. G. 153, 63, 152, 25. செல்க. G. 85.

Comp. Ellis, pp. 233, 234. See 238, 158.

[So in this more ancient verse:

‘பொருந்திய கேண்மையின் மறையுணர்ந் தம்மறை
பிரிந்தக்காற் பிறர்க்குரைக்கும் பீடிலார் தொடர்புபோல்:

Like the friendship of the dishonourable who learn your secret when joined in intimacy with you, and divulge it to others when separated from you.’—கலித். i. 25.]

CHAPTER XXIV.

UNREAL FRIENDSHIP.

அதிகாரம் உச.

கூடாநட்பு

(= உள்ளே கூடாதிருந்தே புறத்திலேகூடநட்பவர்நட்பு;—
பொருந்தாதசிநேகம்).

This is in K. நட்பு and கூடாநட்பு, chapters lxxxii, lxxxiii. The idea is of a seeming friendship without any bond of heartfelt affection.

Analysis:

1. False friends cling to you only so long as it serves their own interests to do so. [231.]
2. Contrast between friendships contracted with worthy and unworthy persons: 'Rain and drought;' 'Heaven and hell;' 'Honey and margosa.' [232, 233, 239.]
3. Friendship with men of unloving souls, blazes up suddenly, and as quickly dies down: 'Fire in the straw!' [234.]
4. Avoid men who glibly promise impossibilities, and yet delay to perform what is in their power. [235.]
5. Trust none on account of their birthplace and associations. [236.]
6. Flippant, irreverent people are bad friends. [237.]
7. A spirit of self-sacrifice is essential to friendship. [238.]
8. Pleasing exterior and worthless character. [240.]

231.

கூடாநட்பினர் தம்கருமம் முடியும் அளவும் ஒருவரைநட்புச் செய்து அது முற்றியபின் அவரை விட்டுநீங்குவார்.

செறிப்பில் பழங்கூரை சேறணை யாக
இறைத்துநீர் ஏற்றுங் கிடப்பர்;—கறைக்குன்றம்
பொங்கருவி தாழும் புனல்வரை நன்னாட!
தங்கரும முற்றுந் துணை.

Unreal friends cling to you till they have gained their desire.

Lord of the pleasant well-watered mountain land, where boiling waterfalls pour down from the dark hills! (Poor men) linger beneath the old roof that affords no shelter, baling out the water, and making mud embankments, and enduring the down-pour; (even so unreal friends stick by you) *till their purpose has been attained.*

எ: (வறியவர், or சிலர், or கூடாநட்பினர்).—ப: இடப்பர்.

This is very elliptical. This and the next verse are genuine reminiscences of the south-west monsoon season in the Tamil country.

K. 813. ஆக = ஆகச்செய்து.

In *Nannūl* 1, the idea of disinterested kindness is prettily illustrated:

'பூங்கை புகழவோ நாவிற்குதவு'கின்றது,

Is it for praise that the fair hand kindly serves the tongue?'

232.

நல்லோர் நட்பு மழையைப்போலும்; தீயோர் நட்பு வறட்சியைப்போலும்.

சீரியார் கேண்மை சிறந்த சிறப்பிற்றாய்
மாரிபோன் மாண்ட பயத்ததாம்;—மாரி
வறந்தக்காற் போலுமே,—வால்அருவி நாட!
சிறந்தக்காற் சீரிலார் நட்பு.

The friendship of the excellent like rain; of others like drought.

Lord of the land of pure (white, foaming) waterfalls! The friendship of the virtuous is of exceeding excellence, and yields glorious results—like (seasonable) rain; but the friendship of the vicious, even in the time of its exuberance, is as when the rain fails in the time of drought.

எ: கேண்மை, நட்பு.—ப: ஆம், போலும்.—எ, அசைநிலை. சீரியார் = சீரையுடையர். G. 93. சிறப்பிற்றாய் = (சிறப்பு + இன் + த + ஆய்) = சிறப்பினையுடையதாகி. G. 93. பயத்ததாம் = பயனையுடையதாம். G. 93.

Ellis, p. 234.

233.

அறிவுள்ளோர் சிநேகம் மோட்சத்தைப்போலவும்; அறிவில்லார் சிநேகம் நரகத்தைப் போலவும் ஆகும்.

நுண்ணுணர்வி னாரொடு கூடி நுகர்வுடைமை
விண்ணுலகே ஒக்கும் விழைவிற்றால்;—நுண்ணூல்
உணர்விலர் ஆகிய ஊதியம் இல்லார்ப்
புணர்த்த நிரயத்துள் ஒன்று.

Bliss enjoyed with the wise is heaven; association with the ignorant and worthless is hell.

Enjoyment of the society of men of refinement resembles the heavenly world in the pleasure it affords. Closest contact with those destitute of fine perception of the value of learned pursuits—men who gain no wisdom from you, nor you from them—is one of the hells.

எ: நுகர்வுடைமை.—ப: விழைவிற்று, ஒன்று (ஆகும்).—ஏ, ஆல், அசைநிலைகள். நுகர்வுடைமை (நுகர், வ், உடைமை). G. 153. விழைவிற்று=விழைவினது. G. 93. ஒக்கும். G. 125.

Ellis, p. 234. For the 'hells,' see Jī. Chin. xiii, § 10. நரககதித்துன்பம், 164–178.

234.

அன்பில்லாருடன் கொண்டநட்பு நிலைநில்லாது.

பெருகுவது போலத் தோன்றிவைத் தீப்போல்
ஒருபொழுதுஞ் செல்லாதே நந்தும்,—அருகெல்லாஞ்
சந்தனநீள் சோலைச் சாரன் மலைநாட!
பந்தம்இ லாளர் தொடர்பு.

Intimacy with those who have no sympathy is like fire in the stubble.

Lord of the land where wide groves of *sandal* cover the hilly slopes! Friendship with those who feel not its real obligation, like fire in the straw (suddenly) appears, seeming as though it would increase, but never advancing dies out.

எ: தொடர்பு.—ப: நந்தும்.—வைத்தீப்போல்=வைக்கோல் நெருப்பைப்போல். G. 132. நீள்=நீண்ட. G. 153.

Ellis, p. 234.

235.

செய்ய இயலாதவை செய்வோம் என்றலுஞ் செய்ய இயலும் காரியங்களைச்செய்யாது தாழ்த்தலும் கூடா நட்பின்குணம்.

செய்யாத செய்தும் நாம் என்றலுஞ் செய்வதனைச்
செய்யாது தாழ்த்துக்கொண் டோட்டலும்—மெய்யாக
இன்புறூஉம் பெற்றி இகழ்ந்தார்க்கும் அந்நிலையே
துன்புறூஉம் பெற்றி தரும்.

Boastings and delays.

The promising to do what cannot be done, and the putting off and leaving undone through delay things that could be done, will forthwith bring experience of sorrow even to those who have contemned truthfully the pleasant experiences of life (ascetics and saints).

As we say: 'These things would anger a saint.'

Comp. N.N.V. 71, where this verse is evidently quoted: 'செயக்கடவ அல்லனவுஞ் செய்தும் மன் என்பார், *they will promise to do anything, good or bad.*'

செய்தும் = செய்வோம். Tel. *chē-tu-mu*. G. 83.

பெற்றி is redundant: (Lex.) இன்புறூஉம்பெற்றி = இன்பம்.

236.

பெரியோருடன் நட்புக்கொண்டாலுங் கீழோர் நல்லோர் ஆகார்.

ஒருநீர்ப் பிறந்தொருங்கு நீண்டக் கடைத்தும்
விரிநீர்க் குவளையை ஆம்பல்ஒக் கல்லா;
பெருநீரார் கேண்மை கொளினுநீர் அல்லார்
கருமங்கள் வேறு படும்.

The water-lily does not become a lotus by being in the same tank with it: so evil persons will act in conformity with their natures.

The *Āmbal* (water-lily) does not equal the expanding *Kuvaḷai* though born and growing together with it in the same pool: though they attain to intimacy with those of generous instincts, the deeds of men in whom these instincts are lacking will be diverse.

எ: ஆம்பல், கருமங்கள்.—ப: அல்லா, வேறுபடும்.—செயப்படு: குவளையை.—நீர் = நீரிலே G. 152. கடைத்தும் = இடத்தை உடையன ஆயினும். G. 93, 113. ஒக்கல்லா = ஒக்க மாட்டாது (ஒக்கு + அல்லா). G. 125, 89. கொளினும் = கொண்டாலும். G. 86, 142.

There is a play on the two uses of நீர் = (1) *water*, (2) *nature*.

237.

மனக்கலப்பில்லார் நட்பு துன்பந்தருவதாகும்.

முற்றற் சிறுமந்தி முற்பட்ட தந்தையை
நெற்றுக்கண் டன்ன விரலான் ஞெமிர்த்திட்டுக்
குற்றிப் பறிக்கு மலைநாட!—இன்னாதே
ஒற்றுமை கொள்ளாதார் நட்பு.

Friendship with the uncongenial is bad.

Lord of the hilly land where the immature little monkey, with its finger like a bean-pod, will flip its father when it meets him, and poke him and snatch fruit from him! *Afflictive indeed is friendship with the uncongenial.*

எ: நட்பு.—ப: இன்னாது.—முற்றல் = முற்று + அல்லாத. G. 153.

As in other verses, the address to his patron harmonizes with the theme: the picture of the flippant little ape is intended as a satire upon the presumption of the young men whose forward behaviour in the learned assemblies and elsewhere was distasteful to him. Comp. ch. xxxii.

Comp. B.I.S. 3666:

'साम्याद्धि सख्यं भवति वैषम्यान्नोपपद्यते।

By congeniality friendship exists: by uncongeniality it grows not.'

· ஒற்றுமை = साम्यं.

238.

நண்பனது குறைதீராதவனுக்கு உறுஞ்சாபம்.

முட்டுற்ற போழ்தின் முடுகிஎன் னாருயிரை
நட்டான் ஒருவன்கை நீட்டேன்எல்—நட்டான்
கடிமனை கட்டழித்தான் செல்வுழிச் செல்க,
நெடுமொழி வைய நக.

The curse of him who does not offer his life for his friend.

If I hasten not to put forth my hand and offer my precious life to my friend when in distress, may I depart whither he goes who has violated the sanctity of his friend's wedded wife, while the far-famed world laughs!

எ: யான் (தொகை).—ப: செல்க. G. 85. ஆர். G. 121. செல்வுழி = செல் + வ் + உழி; இதில் வ் இடைநிலை. G. 153.

Ellis, p. 235. Comp. 230.

239.

கலவோர் நட்பு இனிது; மற்றோர் நட்பு கைப்பு.

ஆன்படு நெய்பெய் கலனுள் அதுகளைந்து,
வேம்படு நெய்பெய் தனைத்தரோ,—தேம்படு
நல்வரை நாட!—நயம்உணர்வார் நண்பொரீஇப்
புல்லறிவி னாரொடு நட்பு.

Bitter for sweet.

Lord of the land of goodly hills where honey flows! To forsake the friendship of those who know the right, and cultivate that of shallow pretenders to knowledge, is like emptying out cow's *ghee* from a vessel and pouring into it *margosa* oil.

எ: நட்பு (க்கொள்ளல்).—ப: அனைத்து. அரோ, அசைநிலை. G. 153. தேம்=தேன். பெய் தனைத்து=பெய்தாற்போலும். G. 137, 93. பெய்து=பெய்தால். ஓரீஇ=ஒருவி. G. 79.

240.

உருவுடையானிடத்து உபகாரியாந்தன்மையின்மையும் அறிவுடையார் தீயினத்தாராகுதலும் தீயன.

உருவிற் கமைந்தான்கண் ஊராண்மை இன்மை
பருகற் கமைந்தபா னீர்அளா யற்றே;
தெரிவுடையார் தீயினத்தர் ஆகுத லாகம்
விரிபெடையோ டாடிவிட் டற்று.

A specious outward appearance without a liberal spirit.

The absence of generosity in those whose exterior is pleasing, is like the mingling of water with the milk provided for food: when men of understanding take to bad company it is like the disporting of a *Cobra* with a female viper.

எ: இன்மை, ஆகுதல்.—ப: அளாயற்று, விட்டற்று.—அளாய்=அளாவி. அளாய், விட்டு, இவை அளாவினல், விட்டால் என்று பொருள் கொள்ளும். G. 117. பானீர்=பாலிலேநீரை. G. 152.

CHAPTER XXV.

THE POSSESSION OF PRACTICAL WISDOM.

அதிகாரம் உரு.

அறிவுடைமை

(=கல்விகேள்விகளானாய அறிவுடையனாதல்; or காரியாகாரியங்களைத் தெரிந்து கொள்ளும்புத்தி).

In Sanskrit ज्ञानं, यिवेकं, बुद्धि.

Chapter xliii of the *Kurraḷ* bears the same title, but there is little agreement. The wisdom here meant is sound, practical common sense.

Analysis:

1. Moderation and delicacy in treatment of vanquished enemies is enjoined: 'Parcere victis.' [241.]
2. Humility befits the poor. [242.]
3. Do not judge men by their place of birth. [243, 244, 245.]
4. Fickleness in friendship is to be shunned. [246.]
5. Pleasure arises from friendship of the truly wise, and pain from that of the foolish. [247.]
6. Man makes himself. [248.]
7. It is wisdom even for the learned to yield to necessity, and in the way of business to follow in the train of ignorant but necessary patrons. [249.]
8. The three essentials of a consummate life. [250.]

241.

அறிவுடையார் பகைவர்வலி குன்றியகாலம் அறிந்து போர்க்குச் செல்லார்.

பகைவர் பணிவிட நோக்கித்—தகவுடையார்
தாமேயு' நாணித் தலைச்செல்லார்;—காணாய்!
இளம்பிறை ஆயக்காற் றிங்களைச் சேரா
தணங்கருந் துப்பின் அரா.

Generosity to fallen foes.

Worthy men, when they behold where foes are foiled, themselves too feel sore abashed, and do not hasten on to crush them. Behold, the strong invulnerable dragon draws not near the moon (to swallow it) when it is in its tender crescent days!

எ: தகவுடையார் (தீ), அரா.—ப: செல்வர், கரறும், சோரது.

The rhymes are quite irregular.

See K. 773. This refers to *Rāhu* (இராகு), a Daitya, raised to the skies, who causes eclipses by his efforts to swallow his old enemies, the sun and moon. Eclipses do not occur when the moon is in its crescent stage, which is the occasion of the poet's quaint conceit.

அணங்கு அரும் துப்பின் அரா is doubtful: 'the dragon (possessed) of a strength which hardly (*suffers*) affliction;' or 'of a strength (which *inflicts*) sore affliction.'

So the proverb inculcates courtesy to foes:

'வல்லார் இளைத்தால் வந்திளைப்பாறும்
என்று சொல்லாதிரார்கள் சுத்தவீரர்கள்:

Perfect heroes will not refrain from inviting their wearied foes to take repose.' See G. Ç. 95.

242.

அடக்கத்தின் மாட்சி.

நளிகடற் றண்சேர்ப்ப!—நல்கூர்ந்த மக்கட்
கணிகலம் ஆவ தடக்கம்;—பணிவில்சீர்
மாத்திரை இன்றி நடக்குமேல் வாழும்ஊர்
கோத்திரங் கூறப் படும்.

Self-restraint an ornament.

Lord of the cool shore of the spreading sea! To men in poverty a modest self-restraint is the chiefest ornament. If a man live in unbending pride, and in a manner unbefitting his position, his fellow-townsmen will revile his race.

எ: அணிகலம், கோத்திரம்.—ப: அடக்கம், படும்.—ஊர் = ஊராராலே. G. 152, 162. Or ஊரிலே, *in the town where he dwells*, or *by his fellow-townsmen*.

But for his presumption the lowness of his origin might have been overlooked: he provokes men to look into it.

நடக்கும் = நடப்பான். This form = Tel. aor. *nadu-chu-nu*: it is used for all persons. So in 250 (probably) முடியும் = முடிக்கும் = முடிப்பான்.

243.

யாவரும் நல்லொழுக்கமுடைமையானன்றிப் பிறப்பிடத்தான் முத்திபெறார்.

எந்நிலத்து வித்திடினுங் காஞ்சிரங்காழ் தெங்காகா!
தென்னாட் டவருஞ் சுவர்க்கம் புகுதலால்
தன்னாற்றான் ஆகு’ மறுமை; வடதிசையும்
கொன்னாளர் சாலப் பலர்.

Character, not birthplace.

Whatever soil you sow it in, the *Strychnos* nut grows not into a cocoa-palm. Some of the Southern land have entered Paradise! It is man's way of life that decides his future state. Full many from the Northern land are denizens of hell.

வடதிசை = வடதிசையிற் பிறந்தாருள்ளும்.

This is doubtless a reminiscence of strife between Jains and Brāhmans, but is not quite in harmony with 212. Sanskrit is வடமொழி, ‘the northern speech,’ while Tamil is தென்மொழி, ‘the southern speech’ (தெம்மொழி, தமிழ்).

244.

அறிவுடையார் தீயாரோடு கூடினுந் தாந்தீயர் ஆகார்.

வேம்பி னிலையுட் கனியினும் வாழைதன்
தீங்சுவை யாதுந் திரியாதாம்;—ஆங்கே
இனந்தீ தெனினும் இயல்புடையார் கேண்மை
மனந்தீதாம் பக்கம் அரிது.

Good men not affected by corrupt influences.

Though ripened amid margosa leaves the fruit of the plantain loses no atom of its sweet flavour. Even so the friendship of men of noble mood, although their race be evil, can hardly work ill to the mind.

எ: வாழை, பக்கம்.—ப: திரியாது, அரிது.—மனம் = மனதிலே or மனதுக்கு. ? இலை or நிலை.

There is an ambiguity in the original. It seems to mean, ‘Noble men can hardly be corrupted even by friendships inadvertently formed with bad men.’

Perhaps we must understand திரியாது as pred. to கேண்மை, and so make three sentences. பக்கம் அரிது = ‘it is a rare case that.’

See G. Ç. 99: ‘வஞ்சகர்க்கெத்தனை வாஞ்சையாய் நடக்கினும்
நெஞ்சகந் தன்னில் நேசங் கொள்ளார்.

நெஞ்சார வஞ்சகர்க் கெத்தனை செய்யினு நேசங்கொள்ளார்
அஞ்சாயன் மென்குயின் முட்டையைத் தன்முட்டையாம் என்றெண்ணி
எஞ்சா தடைகிடந்துங் கருங்காகம் இகல்விளைக்கக்
குஞ்சாகிப் பூங்குயிலாம் . . . .

With whatever affection you treat treacherous persons they will never love you in their hearts.’

The illustration gives the obverse: ‘The *Kuyil* (bulbul), though hatched by a black crow, is a bright-plumaged *Kuyil* still.’

245.

ஒருவர் தம்மனத்தின் தன்மையால் நல்லர் தீயர் ஆவார்கள்.

கடல்சார்ந்தும் இன்னீர் பிறக்கும் மலைசார்ந்தும்
உப்பீண் டுவரி பிறத்தலாற் றத்தம்
இனத்தனையர் அல்லர்—எறிகடற்றண் சேர்ப்ப!
மனத்தனையர் மக்களென் பார்.

Not environment, but mind makes the man.

Though close by the sea, sweet waters ofttimes spring up there; on the hill-side the waters often gush out all brine! Thus men are not as their race.—Lord of the dashing sea's cool shore! Men are as their minds.

K. 595, p. 271; Ellis, p. 235. This seems to contradict 146.

The idea that 'the mind's the standard of the man,' is a favourite one in Tamil. But *Tiruvaḷḷuvar's* (595)

> '*With rising flood the rising lotus' stem unwinds;*
> *The height of men is measured by their minds,*'

is unequalled. It is curious to read in Landor's Gebir,

> 'The sea-bird rises as the billows rise;
> Not otherwise *when mountain floods descend*
> *Smiles the unsullied lotus glossy-haired.*'

B. I. S. 1831, 1832:

'कुलादपि वरं शीलं।
Good character is better than high birth.'

'कुलीनमकुलीनं वा वीरं पुरुषमानिनम्।
चारित्रमेव व्याख्याति शुचिं वा यदि वाशुचिम्॥

Whether a man is of high caste or not, whether he is a hero or a pretender, whether he is pure or impure, his conduct alone declares.'

246.

அறிவுடையார் ஒருவரோடு ஒருகாற்புணர்தலும் ஒருகாற்பிரிதலுமாக நட்புச்செய்யார்.

பராஅரைப் புன்னை படுகடற்றண் சேர்ப்ப!
ஒராஅலும் ஒட்டலுஞ் செய்பவோ, நல்ல
மருஉச்செய்தி யார்மாட்டுந் தங்கு மனத்தார்?
விராஅய்ச் செய்யாமை நன்று.

Against caprice.

Lord of the cool sea-shore, where flourishes the thick-stemmed laurel! Men whose minds are good (constant), and who adhere to whomsoever they have formed an intimacy with, will not sometimes avoid men, and at other times be intimate. It is good not to have fits of alternating warmth and indifference.

எ: மனத்தார்; செய்யாமை.—ப: செய்பவோ; நன்று.—செய்: இருவுதல், ஒட்டல்.

This is probably corrupt.

Comp. K. 425 and Nāl. 215; Ellis, p. 235.

The learned commentator on *Jī. Chin.* i. 191, quotes மருஉச்செய்து, and says it is parallel to கழூஉச்செய்து=கழுவி. This would lead us to translate 'clinging to'=மருவி. But see Lex. இ is குற்றியலிகரம். G. 24.

This is better than making செய்தி a noun, as several editors do, rendering 'even in the case of persons of seemly and good conduct.' Again Ellis and others translate விரவிச்செய்யாமை நன்று, 'it is better to contract no friendship.' See விரவு in Lex.

247.

உண்மையறிவுடையாரோடு கூடின் இன்பமும் அஃதில்லாரோடு கூடின் துன்பமும் உண்டாம்.

உணர உணரும் உணர்வுடை யாரைப்
புணரிற் புணருமாம் இன்பம்;—புணரின்
தெரியத் தெரியுந் தெரிவிலா தாரைப்
பிரியப் பிரியுமா' நோய்.

Good and bad associations.

Join the men who throughly feel true wisdom's inner sense, and forthwith joy joins you. Join yourself to men devoid of the accurate perception of knowledge, and then parting from them is parting from pain.

ஆம் is twice redundant. This resembles 168.

Comp. also K. 839; Ellis, p. 235.

248.

ஒருவன் தன்னை நன்னிலைக்க ணிறுத்துதல் முதலியவற்றிற்குத் தன்னறிவுடைமையே காரணம்.

நன்னிலைக்கட் டன்னை நிறுப்பானுந்—தன்னை
நிலைகலக்கிக் கீழிடு வானும்—நிலையினும்
மேன்மேல் உயர்த்து நிறுப்பானுந்—தன்னைத்
தலையாகச் செய்வானுந் தான்.

Man makes, unmakes, and ennobles himself.

He that establishes a man in good, and he that disturbs that good position and casts him down, and he that more and more exalts a man and establishes him, and he that makes a man head (among men) is (the MAN) HIMSELF.

தான் does all: for '*man is man, and master of his fate.*'

So, 'இம்மைக்கும் உம்மைக்குந் தம்மை உடைமைதலை: self-mastery is of primary importance for both worlds.'

The rhymes are altogether irregular.

B. I. S. 895:

'आत्मना विहितं दुखम्।
आत्मना विहितं सुखम्॥
By *oneself* is suffering fixed;
By *oneself* is happiness secured.'

B. I. S. 892:

'आत्मा ह्येवात्मनो बन्धुरात्मैवरिपुरात्मनः।
Each man is his own kinsman;
Each man is his own enemy.'

249.

அறிவுடையார் தாம் கருதிய கருமத்தை முடித்தற் பொருட்டுமூடர்பின் சேறல் அறிவின்மை அன்று.

கரும வரிசையாற் கல்லாதார் பின்னும்
பெருமை உடையாருஞ் சேறல்—அருமரபின்
ஓதம் அரற்றும் ஒலிகடற் றண்சேர்ப்ப!
பேதைமை அன்ற தறிவு.

It is prudent sometimes to sacrifice pride.

Lord of the cool shore of the sounding sea, where from old time the billows roar!—In the course of their affairs when even great men follow after the unlearned, this is not folly but wisdom.

It is wisdom (here = prudence) to serve fools, and to submit to them in the 'course of business (கர்மவரிசையால்).'

250.

பொருண்முயற்சியும் போகநுகர்ச்சியும் அறஞ் செய்கையும் ஆகிய இம்மூன்றும் முற்றும் ஆயின் அவனுக்கு அதனினும் ஊதியம் இல்லை.

கருமமும் உள்படாப் போகமுந் துவ்வாத்
தருமமுந் தக்கார்க்கே செய்யா—ஒருநிலையே
முட்டின்றி மூன்றும் முடியுமேல், அஃதென்ப
பட்டினம் பெற்ற கலம்.

A perfect life-voyage.

If a man has wrought all fitting works, enjoyed all seemly pleasures, done deeds of charity to worthy men: if he shall have accomplished all these three unchecked, in this one state, of him men will say: '*that is a ship that has gained the haven.*'

படா, துவ்வா, செய்யா. G. 86 (க).

Such have passed

'Through Death (இறப்பு) and Birth (பிறப்பு) to a diviner day.'

And this fittingly closes the chapter on Wisdom; for this is its consummate work.

The verse probably refers to *Kāviri-pūmpaṭṭinam* (Caveripattam: காவிரிப்பூம்பட்டினம் or புகார், where the hero of the famous poem, Çilappathigaram, lived. காவிரிபுகும்பட்டினம் = 'the town where the Caveri *enters* the sea'). This was one of the five chief cities of the Çōṟa kingdom. Here, the legend says, there lived a princely merchant named Panthan (? பாந்தன், S. पान्थ, and M. = a traveller: Sinbad, *the sailor*), of whose history this quatrain may well be a summary. A poem, of 100 quatrains, in his praise, absurdly ascribed to *Avvai*, exists under the title of Panthan-anthāthi.

CHAPTER XXVI.

THE LACK OF PRACTICAL WISDOM.

அதிகாரம் உசு.

அறிவின்மை

(= முற்கூறிய பகுத்தறிவில்லாமை).

Chapters xxxiii, xxxiv are on closely-allied subjects. Comp. K. also, chapters lxxxiv, lxxxv.

This treats of the absence of that plain, practical common sense which is extolled in chapter xxv.

The Jain devotees—or wandering bards of whatever class—are at their best when satirizing the world's folly, which they do contemptuously and with unfeeling bitterness. They give life-like cartoons exhibiting the fool in action.

Analysis:

1. Accurate perception is the one thing needful: mere ornament is nothing. [251.]
2. A learned man must not expect to be wealthy also: discontent is folly. [252.]
3. It is folly to neglect education. [253.]
4. An ignorant man is a dog in the learned assembly. [254.]
5. It is folly for a learned man to speak in an assembly of the ignorant. [255.]
6. It is folly to be always chattering. [256.]
7. It is folly to try to teach fools. [257–260.]

251.

ஒருவர்க்கு அறிவின்மை வறுமை ஆம்; அறிவுடைமை செல்வம் ஆம்.

நுண்ணுணர் வின்மை வறுமை; அஃதுடைமை
பண்ணப் பணைத்த பெருஞ்செல்வம்; எண்ணுங்கால்
பெண்ணவாய் ஆணிழந்த பேடி அணியாளோ
கண்ணவாத் தக்க கலம்?

Lack of accurate perception is poverty. Mere externals are nothing.

The want of refined knowledge is poverty, its possession is very great and abundant wealth. When one considers, will not a sexless creature, more woman than man, adorn herself with the jewels that her eye desires?

நுண்ணுணர்வு is that subtle, instinctive sense of what is fitting and right, which makes the virile mind despise mere outward ornament.

அவாய் = அவாவி. அவாத்தக்க = அவாவத்தக்க. See Lex. அவா.

This is K. 841.

A comparison of *Nannūl* 264, throws light on the (to us) strange illustration used by the poet. The பேடி may assume either masculine or feminine attire; but when its nature inclines to the feminine, and the masculine element is overborne, the creature naturally and instinctively puts on feminine ornaments, forfeits its place as male, and is styled பேடி. The regard for mere external adornments shows the prompting of a lower nature.

Comp. N.N.V. 24. For பண்ணை, *etc.*, see § 223, Lesson LXX.

252.

அறிவோர் வறியராகவும் அறிவில்லார் செல்வராகவும் இருப்பதற்குக் காரணம்.

பல்லான்ற கேள்விப் பயனுணர்வார் பாடழிந்
தல்லல் உழப்ப தறிதிரே!—தொல்சிறப்பின்
நாவின் கிழத்தி உறைதலாற் சேராளே
பூவின் கிழத்தி புலந்து.

Why the goddess Fortuna avoids the learned.

Men of vast and varied lore are seen in low estate, and suffer want. Would you know the reason? The anciently renowned 'Lady of the tongue' abides with them. 'The Lady of the flower' is jealous, and draws not near!

Sarasvatī, goddess of learning, and Lakshmī, goddess of wealth and good fortune. One dwells on the tongue, the other on the lotus. Comp. 266.

The first book of the *Jī. Chin.* is called நாமகளிலம்பகம் = 'Sarasvatī-Canto,' because it gives an account of the hero's education. See Nīti. 7, where she is styled கலைமகள்.

There are two readings here: அறிதிரேல் = 'if you would know,' or அறிதிரே = 'know ye.' உழப்பது is direct object: 'See the sufferings!' Comp. 106.

253.

கல்லாதவன் கற்றவர்சபையிலே அறிவின்மையால் அவமதிக்கப் படுவான்.

கல்லென்று தந்தை கழற அதனைஓர்
சொல்லென்று கொள்ளா திகழ்ந்தவன்—மெல்ல
எழுத்தோலை பல்லார்முன் னீட்ட விளியா
வழுக்கோலைக் கொண்டு விடும்.

Folly of refusing to learn in youth.

He who, when his father urgently bade him learn, did not take it as a serious matter, but contemned it; when, before many men, some one gently presents a written palm-leaf, will in anger fetch a stick to beat him as guilty of an insult.

This is an ambiguous verse: விளி is either 'call' or 'grow angry,' or இளி, 'contemn.' Commentators differ. I take it thus: the man cannot read, and when in an assembly some one quite courteously offers him a manuscript, he takes it as a reflection on his ignorance, and begins to belabour him. See வழு. வழுக்கோல் is either 'a stick faultily used,' or 'a stick that punishes a fault.'

Comp. *Mū.*:

'கவையாகிக் கொம்பாகிக் காட்டகத்தே நிற்கும்
அவைஎல்லாம் அல்ல மரங்கள்;—சவைநடுவே
நீட்டோலை வாசியா நின்றான் குறிப்பறிய
மாட்டா தவனே மரம்:

All that stand in the forest with forked branches and boughs are not *trees;* he that stands in the midst of the assembly unable to read the letter presented to him, and that cannot understand its meaning (or, *cannot take a hint*) is a tree.'

Comp. B. I. S. 3873:

'पठ पुत्र सदा नित्यमक्षरं हृदये कुरु।
Read, my son, ever, and take letters to thy heart.'

254.

கற்றறிவில்லான் கற்றோர் அவையில் வாளா இருக்கினும் ஒன்றை உரைக்கினும் பயனில்லை.

கல்லாது நீண்ட ஒருவன் உலகத்து
நல்லறி வாளர் இடைப்புக்கு,—மெல்ல
இருப்பினு' நாய்இருந் தற்றே, இராஅ
துரைப்பினு' நாய்குரைத் தற்று!

An ignorant man is a mere cur!

When a man who has grown up without learning enters the society of the wise, if he sit still, it is as if a dog sat there; and if he rise to speak, it is as though a dog barked.

எ: ஒருவன் இருப்பு (தொகை), உரைப்பு.—ப: அற்று.

இருந்தற்றே = இருந்த அற்று. See under அன். K. Introd. xxiv, § 10. This is a very favourite form with the author of the *Kurraḷ* also.

255.

அறிவுடையோர் மூடர் சபையில் தாங் கற்றவைகளைச் சொல்லார்.

புல்லாப்புன் கோட்டிப் புலவர் இடைப்புக்குக்
கல்லாத சொல்லுங் கடையெல்லாம்;—கற்ற
கடாஅ யினுஞ் சான்றவர் சொல்லார், பொருண்மேற்
படாஅ விடுபாக் கறிந்து.

Cast not pearls before swine.

All the baser sort consorting with scholars of a heterodox and low school, will utter illiterate rubbish; but men replete with learning, though urgently asked, utter not the results of their learning, knowing that (the askers) would fail to apply their minds to the import of what was said.

எ: கடை, சான்றவர்.—ப: சொல்லும், சொல்லார்.—செ: கல்லாத, கற்ற. G. 95. விடுபாக்கு. G. 86.

Comp. 314.

256.

அறிவுடையார் தம்மறதிக்கஞ்சி உரையார்; அறிவிலார் அஞ்சாதுரைப்பார்.

கற்றறிந்த நாவினர் சொல்லார்தஞ் சோர்வஞ்சி;
மற்றையர் ஆவார் பகர்வர்; பனையின்மேல்
வற்றிய ஓலை கலகலக்கும், எஞ்ஞான்றும்
பச்சோலைக் கில்லை ஒலி.

Modest silence.

Men of learned tongues are silent, fearing some slip; others (ignorant men) will speak out; on the Palmyra tree the dried-up leaves make a loud rustling noise; but evermore the green leaf gives forth no sound!

Comp. K. 642, and N. N. V. 23. பச்சு, see பசு (§ 131, G. 121).
See B. I. S. 1184:

'उत्तमो नातिवक्ता स्याद् अधमो बहुभाष्यकः।

The worthiest man should not be an excessive talker. The lowest is a man of many words.'

257.

அறிவிலார்க்கறநெறிகளைக்கூறின் பயன்படாது கெடும்.

பன்றிக்கூழ்ப் பத்தரிற் றேமா வடித்தற்றால்
நன்றறியா மாந்தர்க் கறத்தா றுரைக்குங்கால்,
குன்றின்மேற் கொட்டுந் தறிபோற் றலைதகர்ந்து
சென்றிசையா ஆகுஞ் செவிக்கு.

Good instruction thrown away on thankless people.

When you expound the way of virtue to ungrateful people,—which is like mashing up sweet mangoes for a pig in a food-trough,—those virtuous teachings lose all their force—have their point (தலை) broken (தகர்) by the obtuseness of the disciple—and do not enter into, or suit his ear,—like a stake which one would drive in on the side of a hill.

எ: அறத்தாறு.—ப: இசையா ஆகும்.

The union of two comparisons here is perplexing. First, good teaching is wasted on fools; secondly, it is like a wooden peg (or an axe) shivered by contact with a rocky mountain; i. e. its effect is lost through the obtuseness of the pupil. Arrange (அவ்வறத்தாறுனது) தகர்ந்து சென்று செவிக்கு இசையாது ஆகும்.

258.

நலஞ் செய்யாதவனுக்கு நல்லறிவுதரும் பொருள்களைக் கூறலாகாது.

பாலாற் கழீஇப் பலநாள் உணக்கினும்
வாலிதாம் பக்கம் இருந்தைக் கிருந்தன்று;
கோலாற் கடாஅய்க் குறினும் புகலொல்லா
நோலா உடம்பிற் கறிவு.

Learning requires discipline.

Though you wash it with milk for many days and dry it, charcoal on no hypothesis becomes white! So into the undisciplined body wisdom enters not, though you teach it, driving it in with a stick.

கடாஅய் = கடாவி.

இருந்தது + அன்று, 'it is not a thing that ever was:' contracted into இருந்ததன்று, இருந்தன்று. See அல். புகல் ஒல்லா = புகமாட்டாது, பிரவேசியாது. G. 89.

B. I. S. 7303:

'स्वभावो यादृशो यस्य न जहाति कदाचन।
अङ्गारः शतधौतेन मलिनत्वं न मुञ्चति॥

A man's innate disposition does not leave him ever! Wash charcoal a hundred times and its blackness leaves it not.'

Comp. also *Vēm.* ii. 52.

259.

அறிவிலார்க்கு அறிவுடையார் வாய்ச்சொற் பயன்படாது.

பொழிந்தினிது நாறினும் பூமிசைதல் செல்லா
திழிந்தவை காமுறூஉம் ஈப்போல்,—இழிந்தவை
தாங்கலந்த நெஞ்சினார்க் கென்னாகுந் தக்கார்வாய்த்
தேன்கலந்த தேற்றச்சொற் றேர்வு?

The fly desires not the fragrant honey. The base esteem not sweet and powerful words.

To those whose minds are full of foul things,—like the fly which goes not to feed on the flower that pours forth sweetness and breathes perfume, but fixes its eager desire on ordure,—what clear comprehension can there be of the lucid words full of honied sweetness that issue from the mouths of the worthy?

எ: தேர்வு.—ப: என்னாகும்?

பூமிசைதல்செல்லாது, 'not going to feast upon the sweet fragrant flowers.' தாம் is a mere expletive.

260.

அறிவிலான் கற்றோர்சொல்லும் நுட்பமாகிய பொருளைக் கேட்கவிரும்பான்.

கற்றூர் உரைக்குங் கசடறு நுண்கேள்வி
பற்றாது தன்னெஞ்சு தைத்தலான்—மற்றும்ஓர்
தன்போல் ஒருவன் முகநோக்கித் தானும்ஓர்
புன்கோட்டி கொள்ளும்ஆங் கீழ்.

The base man rejects the words of the learned, and seeks the assembly of congenial fools.

The base man does not apprehend the faultless words of accurate instruction which the learned utter. These pain his mind. He therefore looks in the face of some other one like himself (for encouragement), and convenes a wretched assembly of his own: i.e. *He finds one like-minded, and the two set up a sect.*

எ: கீழ்.—ப: கொள்ளும்.—செ: கோட்டியை.—ஆல், ஓர், அசைநிலைகள்.

Much of this chapter is an anticipation of ch. xxxii; and is the history of the 13th century in South India.

CHAPTER XXVII.

WEALTH THAT PROFITS NOT.

அதிகாரம் உள.

நன்றியில் செல்வம்

(= தேடியவர்க்கும் பிறர்க்கும் பயன்படாத செல்வத்தின் இயல்பு).

Pathumanār says it is wealth in the hands (1) of those who do not understand how to enjoy it; (2) of those who do not maintain their poor relations; (3) of those who give nothing to suppliants; and (4) of those who use it to injure others.

Comp. K. ch. ci.

Parimēlaragar says there is no (நன்றி) benefit from his wealth to himself or to others, so the fault of the man is ascribed to the wealth that he misuses.

Analysis:

1. No good to be got from churlish neighbours. [261, 262, 263.]
2. Merit goes for nothing! [264.]
3. Fortune is unjust. 'Tis fate! [265–267.]
4. Unequal conditions of life. [268.]
5. Foolish benefactions. [269.]
6. Men are not what they seem. [270.]

261.

பெருமையிலாதார் செல்வம் பிறரால் நச்சப்படுந் தன்மையையுடைத்தன்று.

அருகல தாகிப் பலப்பழுத்தக் கண்ணும்
பொரிதாள் விளவினை வாவல் குறுகா;
பெரிதணியர் ஆயினும் பீடிலார் செல்வங்
கருதுங் கடப்பாட்ட தன்று.

Useless neighbours: so near and yet so far.

The bat approaches not the *Feronia*, with its dry stem, though it be nigh at hand and bear abundant fruit; so, although mean people are very close at hand, their wealth is not a thing that can be counted upon.

Comp. 218. Here அருகலதாகி is doubtful. It has been rendered: (1) அருகு + அயலது + ஆகி = 'being what is adjacent to one's home:' அருகு = 'home,' அலது for அயலது. This is forced. (2) அருகல் + அது + ஆகி = 'being near:' அருகல் = 'contiguity.' (3) அருகு + அலது + ஆகி = 'being without diminution—abundance:' அருகு = 'diminution.' The context requires (2).

262.

கீழோர் பெருஞ்செல்வமுடையவர் ஆயினும் அவரை அறிவுடையோர் அணுகார்.

அள்ளிக்கொள் வன்ன குறுமுகிழ ஆயினுங்
கள்ளிமேற் கைநீட்டார், சூடும்பூ அன்மையால்:
செல்வம் பெரிதுடையர் ஆயினுங் கீழ்களை
நள்ளார் அறிவுடை யார்.

None pluck the Kaḷḷi flowers. The wise approach not the base.

Men reach not out their hand to the *Kaḷḷi* (*Cactus*), though it bears delicate round buds by the handful, because these are not flowers they can weave into a garland to crown themselves withal; so wise people form no friendships with the base, however great their wealth may be.

ள: அறிவுடையார்.—ப: நள்ளார்.—செ: கீழ்களை.—முகிழ. G. 93.
கொள்வ = கொள்பவைகள் = 'things that may be taken.' அ is elided. The singular is found in K. 1187.

263.

இரப்போர் நெடுந்தூரத்திலிருப்பவராகியகொடுப்போரிடத்திற் சென்று ஒன்றைப்பெற விரும்புவர்.

மல்கு திரைய கடற்கோட் டிருப்பினும்
வல்லூற் றுவர்இல் கிணற்றின்கட் சென்றுண்பர்:
செல்வம் பெரிதுடையர் ஆயினுஞ் சேட்சென்று
நல்குவார் கட்டே நசை.

Though living on the sea-shore, men go to the fresh spring to drink.

Though men live on the curved shore of the sea with its multitudinous waves, they go and drink at the well, with its perennial fountain of fresh water from the rock; so even if those (who are neighbours) are very wealthy, the desire (of the poor) is towards the liberal, though these may be far to seek.

எ: ஒருவர், நசை.—ப: உண்பர், ஆம் (தொகை).—திரைய = திரையையுடைய. நல்குவார் கட்டே = நல்குவாரினிடத்திலே.

Comp. *Mū.*:

'. . . . கடல்பெரிது
மண்ணீரும் ஆகாத' அதன்அருகே சிற்றூறல்
உண்ணீரும் ஆகி விடும்:
(மண்ணூ, உண்ணூ.)

The sea is great, but its water is not good even to wash in; the little runlet near affords water to drink also.'

வல் is a difficulty: வலிமை means *strength, hardness, force;* but seems to convey the idea of a well dug in the rock with effort; or 'ever trickling.' In 275 it is அறாச் சிறு . . . Comp. 218, 275.

Comp. B.I.S. 1271:

'प्रायः कूपस्तृषां हन्ति सततं नतु वारिधिः।
A well quenches thirst, but never the sea.'

And B.I.S. 7422:

'हेलोल्लासितकल्लोल धिक्सागर न लज्जसे।
यस्य तीरे तृषाक्रान्तः पान्थः पृच्छति कूपकाम्॥

Fie on thee ocean, with thy joyous tumult of waves, art thou not ashamed that the thirsty traveller on thy bank asks for a well?'

264.

புண்ணியத்திற்கு இம்மையில் பலனில்லை.

புணர்கடல்சூழ் வையத்துப் புண்ணியமோ வேறே!
உணர்வ துடையார் இருப்ப,—உணர்விலா
வட்டும் வழுதுணையும் போல்வாரும் வாழ்வரே
பட்டுந் துகிலும் உடுத்து.

The senseless dressed in silks! Virtue quite another matter.

In the world surrounded by the (all-)embracing sea, merit is quite an indifferent matter! Understanding ones are (poor); and even those of no understanding—who are like mere *palm tree tufts* and *brinjāls*—live prosperously, clad in silks and rich garments.

எ: புண்ணியம், போல்வார்.—ப: வேறே, வாழ்வரே.

This will give the meaning that prosperity does not in this world attend merit and good sense. Commentators say: 'Some other cause must be sought for the present prosperity of fools; that cause is the merit of good deeds done in former births.'

The next quatrain is closely parallel. Comp. also 368.

புணர். G. 153. வையத்து for 7th case. G. 152.

ஓ. G. 112. எ. உணர்வது=உணர்வு. இருப்ப. G. 86, 140, 'while they are (destitute).'

A similar ellipsis is found in 265, and in T. 12: 'விருந்திருக்க உண்ணாதான், who eats not while the stranger *waits without unfed*.'

265.

கீழோர் செல்வத்துக்குக்காரணம் அவரது அறிவுடைமை அன்று.

நல்லார் நயவர் இருப்ப நயமிலாக்
கல்லார்க்கொன் றாகிய காரணம்—தொல்லை
வினைப்பயன் அல்லது;—வேனெடுங் கண்ணாய்!
நினைப்ப வருவதொன் றில்.

Men fortunate who seem not to deserve it.

While pleasant folk and just abide (in poverty), you ponder why men unjust and ignorant have any joy. It is fruit of '*ancient deeds*,'—thou whose long eyes are darts:—to thoughtful mind no other cause occurs.

இருப்ப, see 264. ஒன்று=ஒருசெல்வம். வேனெடுங்கண்ணாய்! G. 39, 93, 121, 155, 162. நல்லார் நயவர் is ellipsis of உம் . . . உம் or of ஆகிய. See ch. xi.

266.

கீழோரிடத்துத் தோன்றியசெல்வம் அறிவுடையோரால் இகழப்படும்.

நாருத் தகடேபோ னன்மலர்மேற் பொற்பாவாய்!
நீருய் நிலத்து விளிஅரோ!—வேருய
புன்மக்கள் பக்கம் புகுவாய்நீ, பொன்போலும்
நன்மக்கள் பக்கந் துறந்து.

Fortune cursed.

O golden dame, that sittest like a scentless leaf on a beauteous flower! Die, and fall in ashes to the ground: thou enterest homes of worthless men of perverse mind, forsaking good men pure as gold.

Lakshmī, goddess of fortune, wife of Vishṇu, mother of Kāman. She is called Çrī (=Tam. திரு), and is represented as enthroned on the lotus. Comp. 252. பூவின்இழந்தி and K. 617. தாமரையினள்.

[See Wilson's Vish. P. pp. 60, 76, 78, 'Seated on a full-blown lotus, and holding a water-lily in her hand, the goddess Çrī, radiant with beauty, rose from the waves.']

267.

அறிவுடையாரிடத்துவறுமையும் அறிவிலாரிடத்துச்செல்வமும் யாவராலும் எண்ணப்படத்தக்கவை.

நயவார்க ணல்குரவு நாணின்று கொல்லோ?
பயவார்கட் செல்வம் பரம்பப்—பயின்கொல்?
வியவாய், காண், வேற்கண்ணாய்!—இவ்விரண்டும் ஆங்கே
நயவாது நிற்கு' நிலை.

Poverty with the good, and prosperity with the mean.

Has poverty, that bides with men of righteous souls, no shame? Does wealth to ungenerous men stick like glue? O thou of dart-like eye, with wonder see that thus, no just discernment made, these two abide!

எ: சீ.—ப: காண்.—செ: நிலை.

Perhaps it is still Lady Fortune that is apostrophized. பரம்ப, inf.='spreading on all sides.' Some say பரம்பர் = உறைகாரர், 'scabbard-makers.' Understand இருக்கும் with கண், 'who dwellest with.' வியவாய், காண் (*Nan.* 335)=Admire! 'Wondering see.'

268.

நாணமுடையார் வறுமைக்காலத்துத் தூரதேசத்திற் சென்றுவாழ்வர்; நாணமில்லாதார் தாமே உண்டு வாழ்வர்.

வலவைகள் அல்லாதார் காலாறு சென்று
கலவைகள் உண்டு கழிப்பர்;—வலவைகள்
காலாறுஞ் செல்லார், கருனையாற் றுய்ப்பவே
மேலாறு பாய விருந்து.

The self-denying and the self-indulgent.

Men who are not void of shame will travel forth on foot, and feed on scraps,—so pass their days; the shameless ones make no journeys on foot, but feed on dainties at home, perspiring over the feast.

கழிப்பர், understand *காலத்தை* as in 162. *செல்லார் . . . துய்ப்ப = செல்லாமல் . . . உண்பார்.* *கருனையால்* for *கருனையை.* G. 138*.

வலைவகள் = நாணிலிகள் says C. [See *இனியவைநாற்பது* 3.] Some say *வலைவகள் = வல்லமையுள்ளவர்!* Others *இடமினி காளிகளுக்கு ஊழியஞ்செய்பவர்* : Thugs?

269.

அறிவிலார் செல்வமுற்றகாலத்து வறியவர்க்குபயோகப்படுத்தாது செல்வர்கட்குபயோகப் படுத்துவர்.

பொன்னிறச் செந்நெற் பொதியொடு பீள்வாட
மின்னொளிர் வானங் கடலுள்ளுங் கான்றுகக்கும்;
வெண்மை உடையார் விழுச்செல்வம் எய்தியக்கால்
வண்மையும் அன்ன தகைத்து.

Misplaced liberality: rain on the sea.

While the red paddy's golden germ is parched within the ear and dies, the cloud gleaming with lightnings pours forth its treasures on the sea. When silly men gain ample wealth, even so are their liberal gifts bestowed!

Comp. K. ch. ii, especially 17, and see my K. pp. 190, 191.
Comp. '*As you like it:*'

> '. . . Thou mak'st a testament,
> As worldlings do, *giving thy sum of more*
> *To that which had too much.*'

So B. I. S. 4035:

> 'पाथोनिधिम् अधि पाथो वितरसि पाथोद किम् तेन।
>
> O cloud, thou pourest thy water on the sea. What good is that?'

And B. I. S. 6256:

> 'वृथा वृष्टिः समुद्रस्य तृप्तस्य भोजनं वृथा।
> वृथा दानं समृद्धस्य नीचस्य सुकृतं वृथा॥

Useless is *rain on the sea.* Useless is food to the satiated. Useless a gift to the wealthy. Useless a benefit conferred on the mean!'

270.

மூடர் கற்றுங்கல்லாதவர்; உணர்வுடையோர் கல்லாதும் கற்றவர்; இரவாத வறியவர் செல்வர் ஈயாத செல்வர் வறியர்.

ஓதியும் ஓதார் உணர்விலார்; ஓதாதும்
ஓதி அனையர் உணர்வுடையார்;—தூய்தாக
நல்கூர்ந்துஞ் செல்வர் இரவாதார்; செல்வரும்
நல்கூர்ந்தார் ஈயார் எனின்.

The unintelligent never learn; the intelligent perceive without learning.

Men void of understanding, though they learn, learn not! Men of understanding, though unlearned, are as men learned! They are rich, though utter paupers, who never beg; the rich are paupers if they bestow nothing!

எ: உணர்விலார், உணர்வுடையார், இரவாதார், செல்வர்.—ப: ஓதார், அனையர், செல்வர், நல்கூர்ந்தார்.—ஓதியும், ஓதாதும், நல்கூர்ந்தும். G. 141. ஓதி அனையர் = ஓதினாரோடு ஒப்பார். தூய்தாக. G. 93, 120. எனின். G. 86.

Comp. K. 89.

CHAPTER XXVIII.

ABSENCE OF CHARITY; OR, THE MISER.

அதிகாரம் உஅ.

ஈயாமை

(= கொடாதிருக்குந் தன்மை).

This is in S. लोभ = உலோபம்.
So B. I. S. 5883:

'लोभात्क्रोधः प्रभवति लोभात्कामः प्रजायते।
लोभान्मोहश्च नाशश्च लोभः पापस्य कारणम्॥
From avarice *wrath* proceeds!
From avarice *lust* is born!
From avarice come *mental confusion* and destruction!
Avarice is the Cause of Sin.'

Comp. 190: here are the முக்குற்றம், the three faults: வெகுளி, காமம், மயக்கம்.
There is no chapter with this title in K. Comp. ch. x on ஈகை; and K. ch. xxiii.

Analysis:

1. Charity alone makes the true householder. [271.]
2. Give though you have but little. [272, 275.]
3. The miseries of the miser. [273, 274, 276, 277, 278, 280.]
4. The man who gives only under compulsion. [279.]

271.

ஈகை யில்லார்க்கு வீடில்லை.

நட்டார்க்கு' நள்ளா தவர்க்கும் உளவரையால்
அட்டது பாத்துண்டல் அட்டுண்டல்;—அட்ட
தடைத்திருந் துண்டொழுகும் ஆவதின் மாக்கட்
கடைக்கும்ஆம் ஆண்டைக் கதவு.

Share your food with friends and foes. To the selfish heaven's gate is closed.

To eat your own meal, after sharing what you have cooked, to the extent of your ability, both with those who are friends and those who are not friends, is 'cooking and eating' (=*is real house-keeping*). To the good-for-nothing human beings whose habit of life it is to shut themselves up, and eat alone what they have cooked, the door of yonder world will be shut.

எ: பாத்துண்டல், கதவு.—ப: உண்டல், அடைக்கும்.—அடைக்கும் = அடைக்கப்படும். ஆவதின் மாக்கட்கு = ஆவது + இல் + மக்களுக்கு = பிறந்ததினால் ஆகியபயன் இல்லாத மனிதருக்கு.

If you *shut* yourself in to eat, heaven's gate will *shut* you out!

Comp. 91, 205; and K. 227, 229.

See also B. I. S. 2742:

'दातव्यं भोक्तव्यं सति विभवे संचयो न कर्तव्यः।
पश्येह मधुकराणां संचितमर्थं हरन्त्यन्ये ॥

While you have the means give and enjoy, but accumulate no store. See, others take the collected wealth of the honey-bees.' Comp. 10.

And B. I. S. 1343:

'एक एव न भुञ्जीत यदीच्छेत्सिद्धिमात्मनः।
द्वित्रिभिर्बहुभिः सार्धं भोजनं कारयेन्नरः ॥

He who regards his own welfare *should not eat alone*. With two or three or many let a man eat his meal.'

272.

ஈயார் மறுமையில் வீடுபெறுமையேயன்றி இம்மையிலும் இகழப்படுவர்.

எத்துணை யானும் இயைந்த அளவினால்
சிற்றறஞ் செய்தார் தலைப்படுவர்;—மற்றைப்
பெருஞ்செல்வம் எய்தியக்காற் பின்னறிதும் என்பார்
அழிந்தார் பழிகடலத் துள்.

Give what you can, when you can.

Whatever the measure be, those who do even lesser acts of charity to the measure of their power shall attain to excellence. But those who, when they have obtained great wealth, say 'we will be wise (*and give*) by and by,' are lost in a sea of guilt.

Or, 'we will see to it by and by, when we have accumulated great wealth.'
Comp. 19 and 36 as against procrastination.
இயைந்த அளவினல் - உளவரையால். 271. அழிந்தார். G. 148.

273.

ஈயாதானுக்குத் தான் தேடியபொருளான் இகழ்ச்சியே அன்றிப் புகழ்ச்சியில்லை.

துய்த்துக் கழியான் றுறவோர்க்கொன் றீகலான்
வைத்துக் கழியு' மடவோனை—வைத்த
பொருளும் அவனை நகுமே, உலகத்
தருளும் அவனை நகும்.

The miser contemptible.

The senseless man who spends not his time in enjoyment (of his wealth), and who gives nothing to pious devotees, but hoards and dies,—*him* his hoarded wealth derides; *him* all that is gracious in the world derides.

அருள் is personified as is அறம் in K. 77.
See B. I. S. 3067:

'धनेन किं यन्न ददाति नाश्नुते।
What is the use of wealth that one neither gives nor enjoys?'

274.

ஈயாதான் ஈட்டிய பொருளை அயலான் அனுபவிப்பான்.

கொடுத்தலுந் துய்த்தலுந் தேற்றா—இடுக்குடை
உள்ளத்தான் பெற்ற பெருஞ்செல்வம் இல்லத்
துருவுடைக் கன்னியரைப் போலப்—பருவத்தால்
ஏதிலான் றுய்க்கப் படும்.

The miser loses what he hoards.

The great wealth obtained by the man of straitened soul, who knows not how either to give or to enjoy, shall be enjoyed by a stranger, in due season—like lovely virgins remaining unmarried in the dwelling.

Comp. 10; and K. 228.

The first three lines have each a rhyming தனிச்சொல். G. 190. It is quite irregular. பருவத்தால், ஏதிலான் are 7th and 4th cases: 'in her maturity;' 'by a stranger.'

275.

ஈயாதார் செல்வத்திலும் ஈயும் நல்லோர் வறுமையே சிறந்தது.

எறிநீர்ப் பெருங்கடல் எய்தி இருந்தும்,
அறுநீர்ச் சிறுகிணற் றூறல்பார்த் துண்பர்;
மறுமை அறியாதார் ஆக்கத்திற் சான்றோர்
கழிநல் குரவே தலை!

Poverty better than the wealth of those who live for this world alone.

Though they have got the mighty sea with its dashing waves (to drink from), men wait for the stream slowly issuing from the little well, often dry, and drink there; so the exceeding poverty of the virtuous is preferable to the wealth of those who know not of the world to come.

எ: மனிதர் (தொகை). நல்குரவு.—ப: உண்பர். தலை. ஆக்கத்தின் = ஆக்கத்திலும்.

Commentators think the existence of two verses of the same import (in this case, and in others in the chapter) proof of a plurality of authors of *Nāladi*: it is certainly a proof of translation (probably by different hands) from Sanskrit.

Comp. 263, which is another version. அறுநீர்ச்சிறு = लघुरपि.

See B. I. S. 793:

'अस्ति जलम् जलराशौ क्षारं तत्किं विधीयते तेन।
लघुरपि वरं स कूपो यत्राकराठं पिबति॥

In the ocean is water which is salt. What can be done with it? This well, though small, of which men drink their fill, is better.'

276.

ஒருவன் அதை அனுபவியாமலும் ஈயாமலும் இருந்தால் அப்பொருள் அவனுக்குடைமையன்று.

எனதென தென்றிருக்கும் ஏழை பொருளை
எனதென தென்றிருப்பன் யானுந்—தனதாயிற்
றானும் அதனை வழங்கான், பயன்றுவ்வான்
யானும் அதனை அது.

Whose is the miser's wealth?

As to the property which the wretched churl claims, saying 'It is mine, it is mine,' I too chime in with 'It is mine, it is mine;' for if it is his, he himself spends it not, nor enjoys the benefit of it; and I, too, neither spend nor enjoy it!

எ: யானும், தானும்.—ப: இருப்பன், வழங்கான்.

The syntax is disjointed: Anacolouthon.

யானும் அதனை அது, 'and I too *treat* it in the same way:' அது = அப்படியே; understand செய்வேன்: அப்படியே வழங்கேன்.

This seems identical with B. I. S. 2189:

'गृहमध्यनिखातेन धनेन धनिनः यदि।
भवामः किम् न तेनैव धनेन धनिनो वयम्॥

If they are (called) wealthy because of wealth buried in their house, why are we not (esteemed) wealthy because of that same wealth?'

277.

ஈயாதசெல்வர் பொருளாற் பலவித இடுக்கண் எய்துவர்.

வழங்காத செல்வரி னல்கூர்ந்தார் உய்ந்தார்:
இழந்தார் எனப்படுதல் உய்ந்தார்;—உழந்ததனைக்
காப்புய்ந்தார்; கல்லுதலும் உய்ந்தார்;தங் கைநோவ
யாப்புய்ந்தார்;—உய்ந்த பல.

Poor men better off than churls.

The poor have escaped much from which rich men that dispense not suffer.

They have escaped the reputation of having lost (their substance). [Comp. 9, 10.]

They have escaped the toil of saving it. [280.]

They have escaped (the labour of) digging (to hide it).

They have escaped the ache of hands securing it from powerful plunderers.

Many are the (sorrows) they have escaped.

Comp. 280. எனப்படுதல், காப்பு, கல்லுதல், யாப்பு are examples of ellipsis of the 5th case, = 'they have been saved from.' செல்வரில், 5th case, = 'more than the wealthy.'

278.

செல்வர் பிறர்க்கீயாமைக்குக்காரணந் தமது லோபகுணமே அன்றி வேறொன்றும் இல்லை.

தனதாகத் தான்கொடான் ருயத் தவரும்
தமதாய போழ்தே கொடாஅர்;—தனதாக
முன்னே கொடுப்பின் அவர்கடியார், தான்கடியான்
பின்னே அவர்கொடுக்கும் போழ்து.

Nothing but his own churlishness hinders the churl from being liberal.

While it was his he gave not; and his heirs, now it is theirs, give not. Before, while it was his, if he had given, they would not have reproved (him); and afterwards, if they had given, he would not have reproved them! Men's own avarice is the sole reason for the lack of charity.

A commentator says, that this refers to some very notorious miser of those days.

279.

உலோபகுணமுடையசெல்வர் தம்மைத் தண்டிப்போர்க்கன்றி மற்றையோர்க்குதவார்.

இரவலர் கன்றாக ஈவார்ஆ வாக
விரகிற் சுரப்பதாம் வண்மை;—விரகின்றி
வல்லவர் ஊன்ற வடியாபோல் வாய்வைத்துக்
கொல்லச் சுரப்பதாங் கீழ்.

Those wanting in liberal instinct give only on compulsion.

Liberality is that which yields its gifts spontaneously (from good instinct), the askers being as the calf and the givers as the cow; meanness yields only when put into a strait and forced, as a cow with no good instinct gives a scanty supply (வடி) when strong ones press.

See 355 and K. 1078. See விரகு in Lex. வண்மை and கீழ் are contrasted, hence கீழ் = கீழ்மை, கயமை. Some read அடிஆ = 'a cow that kicks.' See வாய் in Lex.

280.

பெரும்பாலுஞ் செல்வருக்குப் பொருளாற் பலவகையினும் துன்பமே அன்றி இன்பம் இல்லே.

ஈட்டலுந் துன்பமற் றீட்டிய ஒண்பொருளைக்
காத்தலும் ஆங்கே கடுந்துன்பம்;—காத்தற்
குறைபடிற் றுன்பங் கெடிற்றுன்பந் துன்பக்
குறைபதி மற்றைப் பொருள்.

Wealth is the source of many sorrows.

Gathering it together is trouble, and even so the guarding of resplendent wealth is severe trouble. If the guarded heap diminish, it is trouble. If it perish, it is trouble. Wealth is trouble's very dwelling-place!

துன்பக்கு = துன்பத்திற்கு. [*Nan.* 243. விகற்பம்.]

Comp. 277; and B. I. S. 605 and 595:

'अर्थानामर्जने दुःखमर्जितानां च रक्षणे।
आये व्यये महद्दुःखं कथमर्थाः सुखावहाः॥

Trouble in acquisition of wealth; trouble in guarding acquisitions; great trouble in receipt and in disbursement: how can possessions bring happiness?'

The expression துன்பக்குறைபதி seems = सर्वदोषभूः, see B. I. S. 1052.

['. . . . ஒண்பொருள்
செய்வம் என்பார்க்குத்துயில் இல்லே, அப்பொருள்
காப்பார்க்கும் இல்லே துயில்:

No sleep to those bent on the acquisition of lustrous wealth!
No sleep to them that guard that wealth!'—N. M. K. 9.]

CHAPTER XXIX.

POVERTY.

அதிகாரம் உகூ.

இன்மை

(= இல்லாமையின் தன்மை).

This is ch. cv in K. நல்குரவு. See also ch. lxxvi.

Many words are used to express the idea. Comp. இன்மை, வறுமை, மிடப்பு, நல்குரவு. The S. தரித்திரம் is not found.

This chapter is wanting in arrangement.

Analysis:

1. Poverty renders life nugatory: caste, family, industry, learning are useless to a poor man. [281, 285, 287.]
2. Poverty makes a man a shameless, importunate mendicant: renders a man of light esteem. [282.]
3. The poor have no kinsmen. [283, 284, 290.]
4. A poor man loses his position in the town: had better go forth a mendicant. [286, 288.]
5. Poverty entails personal privations. [289.]

281.

இயல்வரும் பொருளுடைமையான் பெருமை எய்துவர்.

அத்திட்ட கூறை அரைச்சுற்றி வாழினும்
பத்தெட் டுடைமை பலருள்ளும் பாடெய்தும்;
ஒத்த குடிப்பிறந்தக் கண்ணும்ஒன் றில்லாதார்
செத்த பிணத்திற் கடை.

Money commands respect.

Though he wraps a cloth dyed red around his loins, a dozen coins or so, will gain (the wretch) respect among many men! The man devoid of wealth, though born of noble race, is viler (in the world's estimation) than a lifeless corpse!

பத்தெட்டு, i. e. eight or ten: a few pieces of money. பிணத்தின், 'than.' See B. I. S. 3047:

'विशेषं नाधिगच्छामि निर्धनस्य मृतस्य च।

I find no difference between a poor man and a dead man.'

And 2989:

'दौर्गत्यं देहिनां दुःखमवमानकरं परम्।
येन स्वैरपि मन्यते जीवन्तोऽपि मृता इव॥

Poverty is for all-embodied existences the greatest and most degrading affliction; for while alive the poor are regarded even by their own as dead.'

And 3056:

'धनवान् बलवान् लोके सर्वः सर्वत्र सर्वदा।

Every wealthy man everywhere in every time is mighty in the world.'

282.

வறுமையானது ஒருவனைப்பலவுந்திரும் நுண்ணிதாகச்செய்யும்.

நீரினு' நுண்ணிது நெய்என்பர்; நெய்யினும்
யாரும் அறிவர் புகைநுட்பம்;—தேரின்,
நிரப்பிடும்பை யாளன் புகுமே புகையும்
புகற்கரிய பூழை நுழைந்து.

The insinuating mendicant.

Where water cannot enter, the more insinuating *ghī* glides in; and smoke has a subtler power to penetrate than even *ghī*. If you look into it, the man debased by poverty will enter haunts where smoke scarce finds a way.

Comp. 107. There is not only an ironical reference to the importunity of the needy mendicant, but a subtle hint of the moral worthlessness—utter attenuation of all good—which poverty is apt to bring: the poor man is lighter than vanity itself!

Construe: புகையும் புகுவதற்கரிய பூழையில் நுழைந்து புகுவன்.

The neuter புகும் is used contemptuously.

This is an example of hyperbole: अतिशयोक्ति, அதிசயோக்தி (அதிசய உக்தி,.

283.

பொருளில்லார்க்கு உறவினர் இல்லை.

கல்லோங் குயர்வரைமேற் காந்தண் மலராக்கால்
செல்லாவாஞ் செம்பொறி வண்டினம்;—கொல்லைக்
கலாஅற் கிளிகடியுங் கானக நாட,—
இலாஅஅர்க் கில்லைத் தமர்!

All abandon the needy.

When on the high hill's crags the *Kānthal* blooms no more, the crimson-spotted beetle tribe seek not its boughs;—Lord of the hills wherefrom they scare parrots with stones!—*the needy have no kin.*

Another and finer version is given in 290.
See B. I. S. 2622:

'त्यजन्ति मित्राणि धनैर्विहीनं . . . ।
अर्थो हि लोके पुरुषस्य बन्धुः ॥
Friends forsake him who is bereft of wealth . . .;
Wealth only in the world is man's kinsman.'

284.

செல்வமுடையவர்க்கே யாவரும் உறவினவர்.

உண்டாய போழ்தின் உடைந்துழிக் காகம்போற்
றொண்டா யிரவர் தொகுபவே;—வண்டாய்த்
திரிதருங் காலத்துத் தீதிலரோ என்பார்
ஒருவரும் இவ்வுலகத் தில்.

Time-serving friends.

When wealth is there, obsequious myriads will assemble, like crows around the fallen corpse. When wealth, as the beetle wheels its flight, is gone, no one in all the world will ask, 'Is it well with you?'

எ: ஆயிரவர், என்பார்.—ப: தொகுப, இல்.
[See K. 752; Notes, p. 287.]
'Beetles circle around, sip here, taste there, and abide nowhere,' says *Nayanayappar*, 'so are the fortunes of men.'

With உண்டாய understand செல்வம். திரிதரும் for திரியும். [நா. G. 124. (ரு.)] உடைத்துழி for உடைத்த இடத்தில். இலீரோ = இல்லாதவர்களாயிருக்கிறீரோ. G. 125.

In regard to these friendly enquiries comp. 18, and B. I. S. 5867:

'लोकः पृच्छति सद्वार्त्तां शरीरे कुशलं तव।
कुतः कुशलम् अस्माकम् आयुर्याति दिने दिने॥

The world enquires after our well-being: Is thy body well? What weal for us whose life day by day departs?'

285.

வறியவர் குடிப்பிறப்புக் கல்விமுதலியவற்றாற் சிறப்பெய்தார்.

பிறந்த குல'மாயும், பேராண்மை மாயும்,
சிறந்ததங் கல்விய்' மாயும்;—கறங்கருவி
கன்மேற் கழூஉங் கணமலை நன்னாட!
இன்மை தழுவப்பட் டார்க்கு.

Nothing benefits the poor man.

Lord of the pleasant land of clustering hills whose crags are washed by sounding waterfalls!—Their race is nought, their manly prowess is nought, their rare learning is nought, when men are held in poverty's embrace.

[For மாயும் comp. N. M. K. 83: 'நலனும் இளமையும் நல்குரவின் கீழ்ச்சாம், beauty and youth perish beneath (the pressure of) poverty.']

See K. p. 317, and B. I. S. 4827:

'मानो वा दर्पो वा विज्ञानं विभ्रमः सुबुद्धिर्वा।
सर्वं प्रणश्यति समं वित्तविहीनो यदा पुरुषः॥

Honour and self-respect and knowledge and beauty and good sense, all perish together when a man is destitute of wealth.'

286.

வறுமையால் இரப்போர்க்கு உதவப்பெறாதவன் அயலூரிற்சென்று வாழ்தல் நன்று.

உள்கூர் பசியால் உழைநசைஇச் சென்றார்கட்
குள்ளூர் இருந்தும்ஒன் றாற்றாதான்—உள்ளூர்
இருந்துயிர் கொன்னே கழியாது தான்போய்
விருந்தினன் ஆதலே நன்று.

Let the churl become a guest of others!

Although he dwells within the village, and sees the poor draw nigh with hungry soul desiring aid, he yields them none: why then in the village does he vainly pass his days? It were better he went to be a guest himself!

With கூர் comp. Tel. KŪR, which answers to கூடு.

Comp. K. ch. ci; and 288. This seems rather to belong to ch. xxviii.

287.

வறியோர்மாட்டுள்ள நற்குணமுதலியன பயன்படுவனவல்ல.

நீர்மையே அன்றி நிரம்ப எழுந்ததம்
கூர்மையும் எல்லாம் ஒருங்கிழப்பர்;—கூர்மையின்
முல்லை அலைக்கும் எயிற்ருய்!—நிரப்பென்னும்
அல்லல் அடையப்பட் டார்.

Poverty ruins all.

O thou whose teeth vie in sharpness with jasmine buds!—When sharp distress of poverty assails, men lose all their attributes of goodness at once, with the mind's acuteness gained from amplest stores of wisdom.

Comp. 285. So B. I. S. 6506:

'सर्वं शून्यं दरिद्रस्य।

All is nought to the poor man.'

288.

வறியவன் தூரதேசத்திற் சென்று இரந்துண்டு வாழக்கடவன்.

இட்டாற்றுப் பட்டொன் றிரந்தவர்க் காற்ருது
முட்டாற்றுப் பட்டு முயன்றுள்ளுர் வாழ்தலின்
நெட்டாற்றுச் சென்று நிரைமனையிற் கைநீட்டும்
கெட்டாற்று வாழ்க்கையே நன்று.

The struggle with want.

Better indeed is the life that pertains to the ruinous course (கெட்ட ஆறு), that going far away (நெட்டாறு), stretches out (supplicating) hand at every door, than to dwell at home (உள்ளூர்) toiling, subject to (ஆற்றுப்பட்டு) obstacles (முட்டு), not giving aught to those that ask, because of straitened circumstances.

This is an elaborate series of puns on ஆறு.

Another version of 286. For the use of ஆறு = வழி, and especially as a comparative with படு, see Lex. under ஆறு and வழி.

So N.M.K. 16: 'இரவெழுஉம் இன்மைக்குழியில் விரைந்து, beggary will quickly grow in the bed of destitution.' குழி = பாத்தி.

289.

செல்வர் வறியோர் ஆகுவர்.

கடகஞ் செறிந்ததங் கைகளால் வாங்கி
அடகு பறித்துக்கொண் டட்டு—குடைகலனு
உப்பிலி வெந்தைதின் றுள்ளற்று வாழ்பவே
துப்புரவு சென்றுலந்தக் கால்.

Reverses.

The hands once loaded with golden bracelets now cull the forest-herb and cook the meal; and then eat the mess unseasoned, from a palm-leaf for a dish! Thus sad at heart they live, when fortune is gone and ruin come.

Comp. 1, *etc.* வெந்தை for வெந்ததை. [G. 41. அ.]
This is *Jī. Chin.* i. 325. See Introduction on that poem.

290.

வறியவருக்கு உறவாளர் ஒருவரும் இல்லை.

ஆர்த்த பொறிய அணிகிளர் வண்டினம்
பூத்தொழி கொம்பின்மேல் செல்லாவாம்;—நீர்த்தருவி
தாழா உயர்சிறப்பிற் றண்குன்ற நன்னாட,—
வாழாதார்க் கில்லைத் தமர்!

Interested friends.

The humming spotted beetle tribes all bright in hue gather not on the branch that has ceased to blow. Lord of the good cool hilly land, of high renown, whence bounteous streams flow down unceasingly,—*the unprosperous have no kin!*

Comp. 283. So B.I.S. 6245:

'वृक्षं क्षीणफलं त्यजन्ति विहगाः शुष्कंसरः सारसाः।
Birds abandon the tree that bears no fruit, and cranes the dry tank.'

CHAPTER XXX.

HONOUR (SELF-RESPECT).

அதிகாரம் ௩௰.

மானம்

(= தன்னிலையில் தாழ்வு படாமை).

This is the only chapter with a real Sanskrit title, except காமத்துப்பால், and it seems to be entirely from the Sanskrit. मान (from मन्) = (1) opinion; (2) self-conceit (अभिमान); (3) self-respect (गौरवं). Here it is used once (198) for अवमानं, and four times for honourable sensitiveness. Comp. K. 969, 970. Its Tamil equivalents are பெருந்தகைமை and பேராண்மை. மானி = 'a man of honour.' மானத்தாழ்வு, மானக்குறைவு, மானபங்கம், மானவீனம்: all equal அவமானம்.

The following is a motto for this chapter. B. I. S.:

'प्राणमेव परित्यज्य मानमेवाभिरक्षतु।
अनित्यो भवति प्राणो मान आचन्द्रतारकम्॥

Let a man preserve honour, even at the expense of life. Life is temporary. Honour abides as long as moon and stars.'

Comp. K. ch. xcvii. The place of this chapter, between இன்மை and இரவச்சம், throws light on its scope. See 292. A man may be destitute, and may lose all '*fors l'honneur;*' but as long as he is தன்னுடையான், 'lord of himself,' and refrains from mendicancy, he is worthy of honour.

Analysis:

1. The honourable mind burns with indignation against wealthy arrogance. [291, 298.]
2. The honourable prefer want, or even death, to loss of self-respect. [292, 293, 295.]
3. Honour is only from the honourable; and is a lasting possession. [294.]
4. Independence is in the highest degree honourable. [296.]
5. The honourable dread loss of reputation; [297, 299]
6. for the loss of which nothing compensates. [300.]

291.

செல்வமிகுதியாற் கீழோர் செய்யும் பெருமிதத்தைக் காணின் மானமுடையார் மனம்புழுங்குவர்.

திருமதுகை யாகத் திறனிலார் செய்யும்
பெருமிதங் கண்டக் கடைத்தும்—எரிமண்டிக்
கானந் தலைப்பட்ட தீப்போற் கனலுமே
மானம் உடையார் மனம்.

Honourable minds are wroth with wealthy arrogance.

The mind of those possessed of honourable feeling will kindle into flame, like the fire that has caught the forest when the conflagration rages, whenever they behold the haughty acts of those who are destitute of virtuous habits, and to whom their wealth is their only strength.

Comp. 298, for மண்டி 202, and for தீ 310.
திருமதுகையாக = 'with Lakshmī = fortune = *Çrī* as their strength.' பெருமிதம் (see Lex. பெர்) = செல்வச்செருக்கு, 'the arrogance of wealth:' மிதத்தற்கு மிஞ்சியது.

292.

மானமுடையார் தம்வறுமையைக் கீழோர்க்கு உரையார்.

என்பாய் உகினும் இயல்பிலார் பின்சென்று
தம்பா டுரைப்பரோ தம்முடையார்?—தம்பா
டுரையாமை முன்னுணரும் ஒண்மை உடையார்க்
குரையாரோ தாம்உற்ற நோய்?

High-minded men complain not to the unsympathizing.

Will (honourable men who are) 'masters of themselves' follow graceless men to tell of their sufferings, though fallen away to mere skeletons?

Do they not (rather) tell the pain they have felt to those enlightened souls that understand their sufferings before they speak?

The expression தம்முடையர் = 'owners of themselves,' gives the clue to the meaning of the whole chapter. There is no real, abiding, untarnished மானம் without அடக்கம்!

[The idea is that expressed in Tennyson's lyric address to fortune (Lakshmī, திரு, பூவின்கிழத்தி):

'Smile, and we smile the lords of many lands,
Frown, and we smile the lords of our own hands,
For man is man, and master of his fate.']

293.

தம்மை அவமதிக்குஞ் செல்வரை மானமுடையார் பின்செல்லார்.

யாம்ஆயின் எம்மில்லங் காட்டுதுந் — தாம்ஆயின்
காணவே கற்பழியும் என்பார்போல் — நாணிப்
புறங்கடை வைத்தீவர் சோறும், அதனால்
மறந்திடுக செல்வர் தொடர்பு.

Dependance on the wealthy destroys self-respect.

As for ourselves we would introduce them (these friends) to our household; but as regards them, they are ashamed (of us), as though they said, as soon as they (the ladies) saw them (the friends), it would be the destruction of their womanly reserve; and so they seat us at the back-door and give us rice! Therefore let us dismiss all thought of rich men's friendship.

This is rendered difficult by the pronouns. The idea is: 'Accept no hospitalities from those who will not fully and frankly admit you into their dwellings.'

See K. 966. சோறும், '*even* the food (civilities withheld) is served out at their back-door.'

294.

மானமுடையார் இம்மையிற் புகழும் மறுமையில் வீடும் எய்துவர்.

இம்மையு' நன்றாம், இயனெறியுங் கைவிடா
தும்மையு' நல்ல பயத்தலால், — செம்மையின்
நானங் கமழுங் கதுப்பினாய்! — நன்றே, காண்,
மானம் உடையார் மதிப்பு.

The law of honour is that maintained by honourable men.

O thou whose locks diffuse the odour of pleasant musk! Behold, especially good is (it to cultivate) that which is esteemed by men of honourable mind; for in this world it is (obviously) good; and, since it leads to perseverance in the way of virtue, it will yield good things in yonder world also.

There may be a doubt as to மதிப்பு: lit. 'the estimation;' either 'their esteem,' or 'that which they prescribe as the code of honour.'

இயல் + நெறி. G. 39.

295.

பழிபாவங்களுக் கேதுவாகிய தீக்கர்மங்கள் சாவினுங் கேடுள்ளவை.

பாவமும் ஏனைப் பழியும் படவருவ
சாயினுஞ் சான்றவர் செய்கலார்;—சாதல்
ஒருநாள் ஒருபொழுதைத் துன்பம், அவைபோல்
அருநவை ஆற்றுதல் இன்று.

Dishonour worse than death.

The men 'fulfilled of excellence,' though death were the alternative, do not deeds that entail sin and guilt.

Death is an affliction for one day, and for a little while. There is nothing that works irreparable ill like those (deeds).

For சாயினும், see T. 27. Comp. 40. வருவ = வருவனற்றை, object of செய்கலார்.
See B. I. S. 5978:

'वरं प्राणपरित्यागो न मानपरिखण्डनम्।
मृत्युः स्यात्क्षणिकं दुःखं मानभङ्गो दिने दिने॥

Better relinquishment of life than loss of honour;
Death is a momentary affliction, dishonour a daily sorrow.'

K. 968, 1017. N. N. V. 41.

So B. I. S. 40:

'अकृत्यं नैव कर्तव्यं प्राणत्यागेऽपि संस्थिते।
न च कृत्यं परित्याज्यं धर्म एष सनातनः॥

What should not be done must not be done; what should be done must not be left undone, even if loss of life impend! This is the everlasting law.'

296.

ஈயாதவர்வறியர் ; இரவாதார் செல்வர்.

மல்லன்மா ஞாலத்து வாழ்பவ ருள்எல்லாஞ்
செல்வர் எனினுங் கொடாதவர்—நல்கூர்ந்தார் ;
நல்கூர்ந்தக் கண்ணும் பெருமுத் தரையரே
செல்வரைச் சென்றிரவா தார்.

The wealthy and the poor.

Poor are the men that give not, even though deemed wealthiest of all that flourish on the teeming ample earth! They who even when they are poor seek not as suppliants wealthy men are 'Lords of the three mighty lands.'

பெரும் முத்தரை, i.e. சோழ சேர பாண்டியமண்டலம் : the *Çōṛa* land, the *Çēra* land, and the *Pāṇḍiya* land: all South India. The boundaries of these are given in lines ascribed to *Avvaiyār*. [See Lex. முத்தரையர்.]

297.

கீழோர் பசிநோய்க்கும் இடையாயோர் துன்பத்திற்கும் மானமுடையோர் பழிச்சொல்லுக்கும் அஞ்சுவர்.

கடையெலாங் காப்பசி அஞ்சு'மற் றேனை
இடையெலாம் இன்னாமை அஞ்சும்;—புடைபரந்த
விற்புருவ வேனுடுங் கண்ணாய்!—தலையெல்லாம்
சொற்பழி அஞ்சி விடும்.

The honourable dread most the loss of reputation.

Thou who hast long dart-like eyes with eye-brows extending far, like a bow! the lowest class of men dread burning hunger; the other (or middle class) dread what is unpleasant; all the chief of men fear words that impute crime.

The idea is of almond-shaped eyes, with well-arched brows, reaching almost from ear to ear.

சொற்பழி = scandal, (deserved) reproach : लोकपवाद. The threefold division of கடை, இடை, தலை, 'last, middle, head,' is the S. अधम (अन्त्य), मध्यम, उत्तम.

See B. I. S. 701 :

'अवृत्तेर्भयम् अन्त्यानां मध्यानां मरणाद्भयम्।
उत्तमानां तु मर्त्यानाम् अवमानात् परं भयम्॥

The lowest of men have fear of want ; the middle sort have fear of death ; the best of mortals have especial fear of dishonour.' Whichever may be considered the older, the Tamil is a fine quatrain. See N. M. K. 4.

298.

மானமுடையார் தம்மை அவமதிக்குஞ் செல்வரைக் காணின் மனம் புழுங்குவர்.

நல்லர் பெரிதளியர் நல்கூர்ந்தார் என்றெள்ளிச்
செல்வர் சிறுநோக்கு நோக்குங்கால்—கொல்லன்
உலைஊதுந் தீயேபோல் உள்கனலுங் கொல்லோ
தலையாய சான்றோர் மனம்.

The rich man's contemptuous pity.

When the very worthy and thoroughly learned see the rich men's glance of disparagement, as they say contemptuously, 'These are good people—persons in greatly reduced circumstances—poor folks,' does not their mind kindle into flame within them, like the fire by the breath of the bellows on the blacksmith's forge?

These are not words of kindly compassion, but of contempt.
Comp. 291, 301; and K. 1057.

299.

பகைவர் செய்தவற்றைச் சொல்லாமலிருப்பது வெட்கம்.

நச்சியார்க் கீயாமை நாணன்று; நாணும்
அச்சத்தா னாணுத னாணன்றாம்;—எச்சத்தின்
மெல்லியர் ஆகித்தம் மேலாயார் செய்தது
சொல்லா திருப்பது நாண்!

What is dishonouring.

It is no *shame* (*disgrace*) not to (be able to) give to those who desire it of us. The shrinking on account of fear (felt) day by day is not *shame* (modesty). But to become reduced in other ways, and not to [dare to] tell what injuries those who love us not have inflicted on us is *shame* (*disgrace*, or *self-respect*).

K. 1011. The whole is a play on the word நாண்.
The verse is very ambiguous. Comp. each word in Lex. The idea may be: (1) 'Nothing is so shameful (disgraceful, degrading, dishonouring) as to be compelled

to bear in uncomplaining silence the rich man's contumely;' or (2) 'Real self-respect (generous shame) is the keeping from the knowledge of every one the insults to which we have been subjected.'

ஆயார் either = 'those who have been foes,' with பகை understood [ஆகு]; or from ஆய், 'investigate' = 'the thoughtless.'

எச்சத்தின் = 'in regard to other things.' Either this applies to ஆயார் = 'foes in all respects save wealth our inferiors;' or to தாம், as in my rendering.

300.

மானிகள் விண்ணுலகுந் தம்மானங்கெடக் கிடைப்பதாயின் அதனைவிரும்பார்.

கடமா தொலைச்சிய கானுறை வேங்கை
இடம்வீழ்ந்த துண்ணா திறக்கும்;—இடமுடைய
வானகங் கையுறினும் வேண்டார் விழுமியோர்
மானம் அழுங்க வரின்.

Heaven itself must not be sought at the expense of honour.

The jungle-haunting tiger that slays the wild cow, refuses to eat and passes by what has fallen (of itself) in its path (i. e. carrion); so the excellent, though the wide realms of heaven were within their reach, would not desire them, if to be obtained (only) by the loss of honour.

The subject to வரின் is அது = வானகம் understood. Some say இடம் is here 'on the left side,' as being unlucky. Observe ச்ச in the formation of causal verbs (§ 160).

CHAPTER XXXI.

THE DREAD OF MENDICANCY.

அதிகாரம் ௩௧.

இரவச்சம்

(= மானங் கெடுதற்கு ஏதுவாகிய இரத்தலுக்கஞ்சுதல்).

Comp. K. ch. cvii.

In the preceding two chapters the chief topics are the degradation of poverty, the mortifications a poor man suffers, and the spirit in which the poor man of honourable mind is to face the evils of poverty. The same subject meets us in this chapter.

The Jains were not wandering mendicants!

Analysis:

1. The condescending, supercilious patron is again satirised. [301. Comp. 298.]
2. Want better than base compliance: life is but as the twinkling of an eye. [302.]
3. Ask only of the courteous. [303.]
4. No reverses make the lofty spirit truckle to the avaricious. [304.]
5. Mendicancy to be dreaded, whether from relatives [305], friends [310], or strangers. [306, 307, 308, 309.]

There is nothing original, or striking in sentiment or expression here; but the bitter emphasis reveals the fact that the poet was poor, and angrily discontented with his lot.

301.

அறிவுடையார் அறிவீனரைச் சென்றிரவார்.

நம்மாலே ஆவர்இந் நல்கூர்ந்தார், என்ஞான்றும்
தம்மாலாம் ஆக்கம் இலர்என்று—தம்மை
மருண்ட மனத்தார்பின் செல்பவோ தாமும்
தெருண்ட அறிவி னவர்?

Ignorant condescending patrons.

Will men themselves possessed of clear discerning knowledge follow after those who have yielded themselves up to mental bewilderment, and who (erroneously) say (of suppliants), 'These poor folks depend entirely on us, evermore are they without resources in themselves?'

தம்மால் ஆம் ஆக்கம் இலர், 'they are persons without any resources of their own.' தாமும் seems merely expletive.

Comp. 53 and 298 for the real position and character of the man whose poverty is voluntary.

Here மருள் and தெருள் are contrasted. The one (மருள்) regards earthly life as real, and does not know that the pious mendicant, by his renunciation, which is the result of the other (தெருள்), is gaining an eternal immunity from births and deaths. See the words in *K. Lex.*

The giver is in truth the dependant one: he obtains merit only through the pious mendicant!

Comp. on the whole subject, B. I. S. 3655 and 3656.

'नावज्ञया प्रदातव्यं किंचिद्वा केनचित्क्वचित्।
अवज्ञया हि यद्दत्तं दातुस्तद्दोषमावहेत्॥

No man should ever accompany his gifts with disrespectful treatment: gifts so given bring fault on the giver.'

302.

ஒருவன் வறுமையால் பிறர்பாற் சென்றிரப்பதினும் இறத்தல் நன்று.

இழித்தக்க செய்தொருவன் ஆர உணலின்
பழித்தக்க செய்யான் பசித்தல் தவறே?
விழித்திமைக்கு' மாத்திரை அன்றே ஒருவன்
அழித்துப் பிறக்கும் பிறப்பு?

Honest hunger and dishonest fulness of food.

Is not a man's dying and birth again measured by the twinkling of an eye? Is it then a fault if a man rather choose to suffer hunger, doing no blameworthy actions, than to feed full, doing things that entail disgrace?

Can you find fault with a man if, considering the momentary character of human existence, he prefer hunger with honour to satiety with disgrace?

செய்யான் = செய்யாதவன் ஆகி. அழித்து = அழிந்து. G. 41 (க).

See 55, and K. 1064.

303.

மேலோர் உபசரிப்பவரிடத்தன்றி மற்றையோரிடத்துச் சென்றிரவார்.

இல்லாமை கந்தா இரவு துணிந்தொருவர்
செல்லாரும் அல்லர் சிறுநெறி;—புல்லா
அகம்புகுமின், உண்ணுமின் என்பவர்மாட் டல்லால்
முகம்புகுதல் ஆற்றுமோ மேல்?

Ask only of the courteous.

There will never be wanting those who, with their destitution as their support (*making it their excuse*), will venture upon mendicancy, and tread the way of humiliation; but will the noble-minded man enter (*as a suppliant*) the presence of any save of those who will embrace him and say, 'Enter my dwelling, eat of my food?'

இல்லாமை = இன்மை. Ch. xxix.—புல்லா [G. 86 (க)] = புல்லி. A verbal form in ஆ is ambiguous. [Comp. G. 89, 90, 91.]

எ: ஒருவர், மேல்.—ப: அல்லர், மேல்.

Comp. 293. ஒருவர் செல்லாரும் அல்லர் seems an awkward way of saying ஒருவருஞ் செல்லாதவர் அல்ல, 'all go.'

304.

மேலோர் உலோபரிடத்துச் சென்றிரத்தற்கஞ்சுவர்.

திருத்தன்னை நீப்பினுந் தெய்வஞ் செறினும்
உருத்த மனத்தோ டுயர்வுள்ளின் அல்லால்
அருத்தஞ் செறிக்கும் அறிவிலார் பின்சென்
றெருத்திறைஞ்சி நில்லாதார் மேல்.

No reverses bend the noble spirit.

Though fortune forsake him, and fate frown, the man of lofty soul, dwelling with steadfast mind on things above, disdains to stand with bending neck in the train of the foolish who hoard their wealth.

ஏ: மேல்.—பி: நில்லாது.—ஆம் is redundant.

The subjunctive form with அல்லா(ம)ல் is = 'he will *or* may think . . . but not stand.'

For சீப்பினும் and செறினும், see § 100, and G. 141, 142.

The definition of दैवं in B. I. S. 1567 is instructive. Comp. also ch. xi.

'कर्मान्यजन्मनि कृतं सदसच्च दैवम्।

Deeds done in another birth—good or not good—are *daivam*.'

305.

மனமொத்தவரிடத்தும் இரப்பாகாது.

கரவாத திண்ணன்பிற் கண்ணன்னார் கண்ணும்
இரவாது வாழ்வதாம் வாழ்க்கை;—இரவினை
உள்ளுங்கால் உள்ளம் உருகும்ஆல், என்கொலோ
கொள்ளுங்காற் கொள்வார் குறிப்பு?

Mendicancy is always painful.

To live asking naught even from those dear as an eye, whose love is sure, and who never refuse, is happy life. Since the mind dissolves in shame at the very thought of beggary,—when men receive alms, what are the receivers' thoughts, I pray?

Comp. N. M. K.: 'இன்னாமை வேண்டின் இரவெழுக, if you desire affliction, go a begging;' and K. 1066, 1069, இரவாதவாழ்வது ஆம் வாழ்க்கை = இரவாமல் வாழ்வதுதானே நல்ல வாழ்வு ஆகும். Here ஆல் = ஆனால் = 'since.' The very thought of begging causes a sense of overpowering shame; what must be the feeling of actually taking a man's gift from his hand? Must it not be a feeling of utter degradation?

306.

பொருளின்கண் பற்றுடையாரன்றிப் பற்றிலாதார் பிறர்பாற் சென்றிரவார்.

இன்னா இயைக இனிய ஒழிகென்று
தன்னையே தான்இரப்பத் தீர்வதற்—கென்னைகொல்
காதல் கவற்று’ மனத்தினாற் கண்பாழ்பட்
டேதி லவரை இரவு?

Contentment better than mendicancy.

When a man himself begs of himself, saying, 'Let troubles come, let joys depart!' the sting of poverty is extracted; why then, for this purpose, should any one, his mind agitated with desire, and his eye wasted with weeping, beg of strangers?

ஒழிகென்று for ஒழிக வென்று. நிரப்ப is found in some copies: 'When a man fills—satisfies—contents himself, saying . . .;' but the antithesis of தன்னையே இரப்ப with எதிலவரை இரவு is of the essence of the verse.

இரப்பத்தீர்வதற்கு = for, or, in regard to, that which is removed when a man so begs of himself, why should a man beg of others?

Good doctrine! When aversion and desire cease, want is not felt. Who limits his desires, enlarges his possessions. 'Godliness *with contentment* is great gain.'

Comp. K. 1063; and B. I. S. 5436:

'याचना हि पुरुषस्य महत्त्वं नाशयत्यखिलमेव तथाहि।
Begging destroys utterly a man's greatness.'

307.

இரப்போரைப் பழியாதார் உலகத்தில் இல்லை.

என்றும் புதியார் பிறப்பினும் இவ்வுலகத்
தென்றும் அவனே பிறக்கலான்,—குன்றின்
பரப்பெலாம் பொன்னொழுகும் பாய்அருவி நாட!—
இரப்பாரை எள்ளா மகன்.

Beggars are universally despised.

Lord of the land where gold is borne down by rushing waterfalls from every hilly slope!—Though in this world new (kinds of) men are continually born, that very man is never born that does not scorn mendicants.

This is capable of a double interpretation: 'He who scorns no suppliant escapes all future births;' or, 'No man will ever be found among those born of women who does not despise mendicants.'

எ: மகன்.—ப: பிறக்கலான்.

[In T. 'இல்லெனக் கொன்றீ கென்பவனை நகுவான்: he who ridicules the man that says, "Give, I have nought."']

308.

இரத்தலினுந் தீயது ஒன்றும் இல்லை.

புறத்துத்தன் னின்மை நலிய—அகத்துத்தன்
நன்ஞான' நீக்கி நிறீஇ ஒருவனை
ஈயாய் எனக்கென் றிரப்பானேல் அந்நிலையே
மாயானோ மாற்றி விடின்?

Mendicancy is unmitigated misery.

Want wastes his outward frame; he lays aside wisdom, his inward being's good; and so resolving, begs of some stranger, saying, 'Give to me.'—If then the boon be refused, must he not that very instant die?

See K. 1069, 1070. The எதுகை in lines 1 and 2 is irregular. நிறீஇ for நிறுவி. Comp. B. I. S. 5955:

'देहीति कृपणं वचः।
The piteous utterance, "Give."'

309.

பிறர்பாற் சென்றிரவாது துறத்தல் நன்று.

ஒருவர் ஒருவரைச் சார்ந்தொழுகல் ஆற்றி
வழிபடுதல் வல்லுதல் அல்லால்—பரிசழிந்து
செய்யீரோ என்னும் என்னுஞ்சொற் கின்னாதே
பையத்தான் செல்லு' நெறி?

A hermitage preferable to mendicancy.

Men form close intimacies with others and live as their dependants, and this is permissible; but is it more painful quietly to go one's way (*to the hermitage*) than, lost to all sense of personal dignity, to say, 'Will ye not do aught for me?'

சொற்கு for 'than the utterance.' (G. 137*.) ஏ = ஆ. (G. 6.) Comp. 53, 55.
[For சார்ந்தொழுகு, see T. 51, 'live in close intimacy.]

310.

ஒருவர் பழமைபற்றி வந்தால் அவருக்குத் தக்கதேதாகிலும் உதவிசெய்யவேண்டும்.

பழமைகந் தாகப் பசைந்த வழியே
கிழமைதான் யாதானுஞ் செய்க!—கிழமை
பொறுஅர் அவர்என்னிற் பொத்தித்தந் நெஞ்சத்
தறுஅச் சுடுவதோர் தீ.

Relieve the wants of old friends, though they shrink from it.

Relying on old friendship, in an affectionate manner, render such assistance as your intimacy warrants. If he will not endure (the assistance), will it not be a fire heaped up and burning in his bosom?

I do not see any other meaning. The latter clause is ambiguous as to தம் (his): in whose bosom, and why? I think the intention is: 'If you allow your old friend to feel that your help has not been what was befitting your intimacy, *you* will feel remorse afterwards;' or, possibly, '*he* will feel deep and lasting pain.'

Comp. 286, 288. This verse suggests K. ch. lxxxi. Especially 801 gives the sense of பழமை and கிழமை.

CHAPTER XXXII.

THE KNOWLEDGE OF THE ASSEMBLY.

அதிகாரம் ௩௨.

அவையறிதல்

(= சபையின் இயல்பை அறிதல்).

The word அவை (S. सभा, சபை, அவை) is not used in this chapter. See Lex. அவை, கோட்டி. Of course the authors are not responsible for the titles.

In K. chapters lxxii, lxxiii it is the 'council' that is chiefly meant. Here it is the assembly of the learned (கோட்டி). Many such conferences were held when Jains, Buddhists, and Çaivas of several sects were contending in the South. For the character of these, the student may refer to the வாதவூர் புராணம், ch. vi, where Māṇikka Vāçagar's defeat of the Buddhists is related. He may also consult the பெரியபுராணம், Book V, for the history of the Çaiva saint *Ñāna-sambandha Mūrtti*, and other champions.

Much prudence, courage, dialectic skill, absolute conviction, and unscrupulous energy were often exhibited in those conflicts.

There was also the *Çaṅgam* (சங்கம்) or Academy at Madura, to which every new Tamil work was submitted. The literati had their assemblies with prescriptive rights and privileges in every petty court, and at many temples. Thus every work should have a verse or two in the preface, called அவையடக்கம், 'submission to the assembly,' in which criticism is humbly deprecated.

Comp. திருவிளையாடற்புராணம் (62, 63, *etc.*). See also Taylor's Oriental Historical MSS. vol. i. p. 53 *etc.*; Pope's *Kurraḷ*, Introd. p. iv.

Any new work claiming to be classical had to be first read in such an assembly. This was called அரங்கேற்றல் (அரங்கு = रङ्ग = சபை, அவை); and the author was required to bear and answer criticism.

This quaint, interesting chapter is rather discursive, but seems to consist of three sections:—

I. Satirical sketches of assemblies to be shunned:

1. Heretical; [311]
2. Violent; [312]
3. Unscrupulous. [315.]

II. The characteristics of vain praters who infest such assemblies:

1. Utter ignorance; [313]
2. Shamelessness; [314]
3. Superficiality. [316.]

III. The way to become fit to enter and take part in meetings of the learned:

1. Real perception; [317]
2. Study—not mere bibliomania; [318]
3. Scientific and exhaustive analysis of authorities; [319]
4. Dignified and candid mind. [320.]

There is much here to remind the student of Bacon. East and West have much in common.

311.

அறிவுடையார் அறிவில்லார்க் சபையில் ஒன்றனையுஞ் சொல்லல் ஆகாது.

மெய்ஞ்ஞானக் கோட்டி உறழ்வழி விட்டாங்கோர்
அஞ்ஞானந் தந்திட் டதுவாங் கறத்துழாய்க்
கைஞ்ஞானங் கொண்டொழுகுங் காரறி வாளர்முன்
சொன்ஞானஞ் சோர விடல்!

Cast not pearls before swine.

Decline entirely to utter *words of wisdom* before heretics (காரறிவாளர் = men of darkened knowledge,—men who professing to be wise, have their understanding darkened), who having forsaken the way pertaining to the assemblies of *true wisdom*, have there laid down propositions of *unwisdom*, and propagating them diligently, live in accordance with their own *shallow wisdom!*

எ: (நீவிர்).—ப: விடல் = விடுக (G. 85).—செ: சொன் ஞானம்.

The main idea is in கார் அறிவாளர்முன்.

There is a play on the word ஞானம்.

In கைஞ்ஞானம் (lit. 'hand-wisdom') there is a double meaning. It is either, 'mere hand-to-mouth-wisdom,' or '*fistycuff*-wisdom,' alluding possibly to the hand-to-hand encounters that often took place in those days.

Comp. 255, 256; and K. 719, 720.

312.

தீப்புலவன் தோற்பின் இகழ்ந்துரைப்பதும் அன்றிப்போருக்கு எழுவன், ஆதலால் அவனைச்சேரல் ஆகாது.

நாப்பாடஞ் சொல்லி நயமுணர்வார் போற்செறிக்கும்
தீப்புலவற் சேரார் செறிவுடையார்;—தீப்புலவன்
கோட்டியுட் குன்றக் குடிப்பழிக்கும், அல்லாக்கால்
தோட்புடைக் கொள்ளா எழும்.

Avoid the angry violent disputant.

Well-disciplined men come not near the heretic (=man of evil learning, the teacher of an evil system), who stores up (in his memory certain formulas, comp. 304), as though he understood their worth, and repeats them by rote (lit. *as a tongue-lesson*).

The heretic, if worsted in the assembly, will abuse the family (of his opponents); or he will spring up and challenge them to fight.

இப்புலவன் is the காரறிவாளன் of 311. கொள்ளா = கொண்டு. G. 86 (அ).

தோள் புடைக் கொள்ளா = 'he will grasp his own shoulders'—clasping his left upper arm with the right hand, and his right upper arm with his left hand: the attitude of a Tamil pugilist ready for an encounter.

313.

கற்றவர் சபையில் பயனில்லாதனவற்றையே கூறும் புன்கல்விமாக்கள் பலர் உளர்.

சொற்றுற்றுக் கொண்டு சுனைத்தெழுதல் காமுறுவர்,
கற்றுற்றல் வன்மையுந் தாந்தேறார்,—கற்ற
செலவுரைக்கும் ஆறறியார், தோற்ப தறியார்,
பலவுரைக்கு' மாந்தர் பலர்.

Vain babblers.

Many are the men that utter many things,—who long to rise up (in debate), from mere love of talking and an itching tongue; who do not themselves apprehend the power and might of learning; who know not the way to utter with penetrating force what they have learnt; and who know not what defeat means.

கற்ற = தாம் கற்றவற்றை. உறுவர் = உறுவர்களுமாய்; and so தேறார், அறியார், தோற்பதறியார் . . . . Understand இருந்து before பலவுரைக்கும்.

K. 649. See Lex. சொல்.

314.

கற்றவர்சபையில் புல்லறிவினோர் வாளா இராது வாய்திறக்கின் அவமதிப்படைவர்.

கற்றதூஉம் இன்றிக் கணக்காயர் பாடத்தால்
பெற்றதாம் பேதையோர் சூத்திரம்;—மற்றதனை
நல்லார் இடைப்புக்கு நாணாது சொல்லித்தன்
புல்லறிவு காட்டி விடும்.

The neophyte.

Without any learning of his own, the fool has obtained one formula from overhearing the lessons of a tutor (who was teaching others), yet unabashed he enters the circle of the good, speaks it out, and makes exhibition of his mean understanding.

எ: பேதை (அவன்).—ப: பெற்றது, காட்டிவிடும்.—செ: சூத்திரம், புல்லறிவு.
Comp. K. 649, 402.

315.

அறிவுடையார் புல்லறிவாளர்க்குத்தமது சொல் வன்மையை அறிவிக்கத்தொடங்கின் துன்பம் அடைவர்.

வென்றிப் பொருட்டால் விலங்கொத்து மெய்கொள்ளார்
கன்றிக் கறுத்தெழுந்து காய்வாரோ—டொன்றி
உரைவித் தகம்எழுவார் காண்பவே கையுள்
சுரைவித்துப் போலுந்தம் பல்!

Convincing arguments.

They who arise to utter words of wisdom, having associated themselves with the assembly of those who rage and burn and fume with anger, like beasts, for the mere sake of victory, not understanding the truth, shall see their own teeth like pumpkin seeds in their hands!

எ: எழுவர்.—ப: காண்ப.—செ: பல்.

உரைவித்தகம் எழுவார் is curious. Three interpretations are possible: (1) 'Those who rise to propound their opinions as wisdom.' Here உரை = 'word, opinion,' with காட்ட understood, and வித்தகம(ாக) = 'as decisive words of wisdom.' (2) Comparing உரைவித்தகம் with சொன்ஞானம் (311), we may translate 'Those who rise to utter (உரைக்க understood) words of wisdom.' (3) The metre suggests உரைவித்து அகம் எழுவார் = 'Those who rise in the place to speak.' But there are serious difficulties.

316.

புல்லறிவினர் கற்றவர் சபையின்கண் வெறுக்கத்தக்கவற்றையே கூறுவர்.

பாடமே ஓதிப் பயன்றெரித றேற்றாத
மூடர் முனிதக்க சொல்லுங்கால்—கேடருஞ்சீர்ச்
சான்றோர் சமழ்த்தனர் நிற்பவே மற்றவரை
ஈன்றாட் கிறப்பப் பரிந்து.

Fools disgrace themselves in the assembly of the learned.

When foolish men chaunt their lesson, not knowing the fruit that lesson yields, but uttering words that gender wrath, the learned ones, whose fame dies not, will stand by ashamed, sorely pitying the mother that bare them.

Comp. 155. சமழ்த்தினர்=சமழ்த்தினவராக: சமழ்த்தி . . . பரிந்து . . . நிற்பார்.

317.

நூற்பொருளை அறிபவரே அறிவுடையோர்.

பெறுவது கொள்பவர் தோள்போ னெறிப்பட்டுக்
கற்பவர்க் கெல்லாம் எளியநூன்; மற்றம்
முறிபுரை மேனியர் உள்ளம்போன் றியார்க்கும்
அறிதற் கரிய பொருள்.

The letter easy, the meaning hard.

Like the charms of those who sell their love for what they gain, the sacred texts are easy to those who rightly learn them; but like the minds of these whose forms are soft as tender shoots, the meaning is hard to all.

எ: நூல், பொருள்.—ப: எளிய, அரிய.
Read மற்று முறியை புரையும் அம்மேனியர் (உடைய) உள்ளத்தைப் போலே.

318.

நூற்பொருளறியும் அறிவுடையோரும் நூல்களை வீடுமுழுவதும் பரப்பிவைத்துக் கொண்டிருப் போரும் தம்மிலே வேறாவர்.

புத்தகமே சாலத் தொகுத்தும் பொருடெரியார்
உய்த்தகம் எல்லா' நிறைப்பினும்—மற்றவற்றைப்
போற்றும் புலவரும் வேறே, பொருடெரிந்து
தேற்றும் புலவரும் வேறு.

Book collectors and scholars.

Although men gather together books in abundance, and, not understanding their contents, fill the whole house with them; the *sages* who merely take care of books are of one sort, and the *sages* who understand their contents, and make them clear to others, are of another sort.

On the whole subject of study, the *Nannūl* (1–46; pp. 111–116, in my IIIrd Gr.) is of interest.

319.

நூலிற்குப் புல்லறிவினுர் கூறும் உரை உரையாகா.

பொழிப்பகல' நுட்டநூல் எச்சமிந் நான்கின்
கொழித்தகலங் காட்டாதார் சொற்கள்—பழிப்பின்
நிரையாமா சேர்க்கு' நெடுங்குன்ற நாட!—
உரையாமோ நூலிற்கு நன்கு?

A perfect commentary.

Lord of the land of long chains of hills where the wild cattle assemble in herds!

Is that a good commentary to a faultless composition, which consists of the words of those who do not sift it thoroughly, in the four divisions of *summary*, *amplification*, *minute exposition*, and *supplementary information*, and thus exhibit the full import?

Comp. *Nannūl* 21–23, where however only two kinds of commentary are treated of.

A perfect specimen of what is here taught is to be found in the edition of சிவப்பிரகாசம் by சிவப்பிரகாசத்தம்பிரான் of Madura. [Madras, 1872. தத்தவபோதினி Press.]

பொழிப்பு: a concise summary of the author's meaning; called sometimes பிண்டம். पिण्ड. An abstract.

அகலம்: an amplification, paraphrase: விருத்தி.

நுட்பம் takes up minute points, in the manner of an excursus. Critical notes on the text. (நுண்.)

எச்சம் gives additional matter. (எஞ்ச.)

The Tamil commentators are inferior to none. Parimēlaḻagar's splendid work on the Kurraḷ, and Nachinārkkiniyār's on the Jīvaga Chintāmaṇi, are models of profound and acute criticism and lucid exposition.

320.

கற்றறிவுடையோர் கல்லாதார் புல்லறிவினைக் காணினும் காணார் போல் இருப்பர்.

இற்பிறப் பில்லார் எனைத்துநூல் கற்பினும்
சொற்பிறரைக் காக்குங் கருவியரோ? — இற்பிறந்த
நல்லறி வாளர் நவின்றநூ றேற்றுதார்
புல்லறிவு தாமறிவ தில்.

Critics.

Will those who are not of high family, however they may study learned works, be fit instruments to guard others from faults of speech? And men of good family who are well learned will not (seem to) be aware of the deficiencies of those who do not comprehend the works they talk of.

The low-bred are incompetent censors; and the high-born, from courtesy, or sheer disgust, decline the task.

சொல், 'as regard niceties of expression and elegancies of style.' தேற்றுதாருடைய ஈனமான அறிவைத் தாமே அறியமாட்டார்கள் = 'will decline to meddle with the inanities of empty-headed sciolists.'

CHAPTER XXXIII.

INSUFFICIENT KNOWLEDGE.

அதிகாரம் ௩௩.

புல்லறிவாண்மை

(=புல்லிய அறிவை அருந்தன்மை).

There is no precise equivalent in English. See *Lex.* புல்.

Analysis:

1. The men of insufficient, imperfect, scanty, low degree of knowledge (புல்லறிவு) lose both worlds; for they have not good sense or taste or right feeling to appreciate the higher things here; [321, 324]
2. nor have they the foreseeing wisdom that prepares for the world to come. [328, 329.]
3. They are as 'the beasts that perish.' [322.]
4. They do no good in life: leave no gap when they die. [323, 326.]
5. Abuse is their element. [325.]
6. Their's are wasted lives. [327, 330.]

Their epigraph is:

'Some with lives that came to nothing, some with deeds as well undone,
Death stepped tacitly and took them where they never see the sun.'

The subject is more akin to those discussed in Part I (அறப்பால்).

There are degrees of Unwisdom. Comp. chapters xxvi and xxxiv. See also K. lxxxiv, lxxxv. Unteachableness is the prominent fault.

The epithets used here to indicate these shallow pretenders may be compared with advantage: பொருளல்லா ஏழைகள், செல்வியர் அல்லார், நாணின்மடமக்கள், புல்லறிவினர், பேதையார், and சிற்றறிவினர்.

321.

அன்புடையார் சொல்லும் அறநெறிகளை அறிவுடையார் அன்றி அறிவிலார் பயனுள்ளதாகக் கொள்ளார்.

அருளின் அறம்உரைக்கும் அன்புடையார் வாய்ச்சொற்
பொருளாகக் கொள்வர் புலவர்;—பொருள்அல்லா
ஏழை அதனை இகழ்ந்துரைக்கும்: பாற்கூழை
மூழை சுவைஉணரா தாங்கு.

Only the wise value the wise.

Men of sense receive as a reality the words from the mouth of the loving ones who graciously teach virtue. The (ignorant) wretch, himself unreal, speaks (of virtue) with contempt. Just so the ladle distinguishes not the flavour of the rice boiled in milk.

எ: புலவர், எழை.—ப: கொள்வர், உரைக்கும். G. 149. உணராதாங்கு = அறியாததுபோலும். Comp. in Lex. அற்று, அன்னது. This idiom is found in 322, தேற்றுதாங்கு.

உணர் governs சுவையை; and கூழை is for கூழின்: 'perceives not the flavour of the milk-pap.' Comp. in 322, சோற்றின். See Lex. முறை.

Comp. B. I. S. 350:

'अन्तः सारविहीनानाम् उपदेशो न जायते।
You cannot teach those destitute of inner sense.'

See 106: சேதனம் என்னும் அச்சேறு, *etc.*

322.

மேலோர் கூறும் நன்னெறிகளைக் கீழோர் கேளாதிகழுவார்.

அவ்வியம் இல்லார் அறத்தா றுரைக்குங்காற்
செவ்வியர் அல்லார் செவிகொடுத்துங் கேட்கலார்:
கவ்வித்தோ றின்னுங் குணங்கர்நாய் பாற்சோற்றின்
செவ்வி கொளறேற்று தாங்கு.

Foolish people hearing hear not.

When men of ungrudging soul declare the way of virtue, those who are not rightly disposed, although they give ear, hear not.

Even so the currier's dog seizes on and devours leather, not appreciating the flavour of milk and rice.

எ: அல்லார்.—ப: கேடகலார்.

கேட்கலார்: கேள் + கு + அலார் = கேளார்.

In 321 it was natural incapacity (the ladle made of a cocoa-nut shell); here it is absorption of the degraded soul in congenial mean pursuits (the currier's dog gnawing filthy skins) that forms the barrier to the attainment of true wisdom. Those were பொருளல்லா ஏழைகள் = 'essentially worthless persons;' these are செவ்வியர் அல்லார் = 'those who are not in the right path.'

323.

அறநெறிகளை அறியுமறிவிலாத கீழோர் இருக்கினும் இறப்பினும் பயனில்லை.

இமைக்கும் அளவிற்றம் இன்னுயிர்போ' மார்க்கம்
எனைத்தானுந் தாங்கண் டிருந்தும்—தினைத்துணையும்
நன்றி புரிகல்லா நாணின் மடமாக்கள்
பொன்றிலென், பொன்றாக்கால் என்?

Useless in life and unmourned in death.

What matters it whether they live or die—the shameless stupid people who do no good, not even as much as a grain of millet, though they see by every species of example the way in which their life so sweet to them, passes away in the twinkling of an eye?

More literally and word for word:

The twinkle of an eye is their sweet life's measure. This they every way discern, yet shameless stupid men no act of virtue do, though small as millet seed! What boots it if these live or die?

Comp. B. I. S. 3732:

'निमेशमात्रमपि हि वयो गच्छन्न तिष्ठति।
स्वसरीरेष्वनित्येषु नित्यं किमनुचिन्तयेत्॥

Life stays not in its course even for the twinkling of an eye. Why should men be eternally thinking of their bodies which are not eternal?'

And K. 331, 337.

324.

புல்லறிவினோன் பலரோடும் பகைகொள்ளுவன்.

உளநாள் சிலவால் உயிர்க்கேமம் இன்றால்
பலர்மன்னுந் தூற்றும் பழியால்—பலருள்ளும்
கண்டாரோ டெல்லா' நகாஅது தெவன்ஒருவன்
தண்டித் தனிப்பகை கோள்?

Misanthropy: against ἀκηδία.

Since being's days are few, and life no safeguard owns, and guilt by many blamed is rife, mid many men, why, laughing not with all they see, should any sulk apart, and nurse a sullen hate?

The days are few and evil; be genial! Comp. 338.

The Tamil poet contemplated men like those whom Dante heard making their confession from out the 'tristo ruscel:'

'. . . . Tristi fummo
Nell' aer dolce che dal sol s' allegra,
Portando dentro accidioso fumo.'

'. . . . We sullen were
In the sweet air, which by the sun is gladdened,
Bearing within ourselves the sluggish reek.'

Inf. vii. 121–123.

See Longfellow's note. Comp. the striking K. 999.

325.

புல்லறிவினோன் பிறரை இகழ்ந்து பேசுவதையே தனக்குப் பயனாகக் கொள்வான்.

எய்தி இருந்த அவைமுன்னர்ச் சென்றெள்ளி
வைதான் ஒருவன் ஒருவனை;—வைய
வயப்பட்டான் வாளா இருப்பானேல், வைதான்
வியத்தக்கான் வாழும் எனின்.

The evil tongue.

A man has gone before the assembly that had gathered together, and contemning another has reviled him. Now, if the reviled one remain silent, the reviler is to be wondered at if he survive; (for abuse is his very life, and the patience of the reviled one has closed his mouth.)

This seems to belong to ch. xxxii. It also illustrates the benefit of patience. See 64, 71, *etc.*

எ: வயப்பட்டான். — ப: வியத்தக்கான்.

326.

அறநெறிகளை உட்கொள்ளாத புல்லறிவினோன் வெள்ளாட்டியாலும் இகழப்படுவோன்.

மூப்புமேல் வாராமை முன்னே அறவினையை
ஊக்கி அதன்கண் முயலாதான்—நூக்கிப்
புறத்திரு போகென்னும் இன்னாச்சொல் இல்லுள்
தொழுத்தையாற் கூறப் படும்.

Dishonoured old age.

He who before old age comes, has not undertaken and zealously carried out works of virtue, will be pushed about in the house, addressed in harsh language, and bidden to get on one side or to go out, by even the maid-servants[1].

Comp. ch. vi, esp. 52. வாராமைமுன்னே = வாராமுன், 'before it come,' lit. 'before it comes not.'

எ : முயலாதவன்.— ப : படும் (= படுவான்).

[1] So Menander:

'Πικρὸν ἔστι χρῆμα γέρων ἐν οἰκίᾳ μένων :
An old man is a troublesome thing in a house.'

327.

புல்லறிவினர் நற்கருமங்களைச்செய்யாது செல்வப்பெருக்கத்தினால் மதிமயங்கி வீணாள் கழிப்பர்.

தாமேயும் இன்புறார், தக்கார்க்கு நன்றாற்றார்,
ஏமஞ்சார் நன்னெறியுஞ் சேர்கலார்,—தாமயங்கி
ஆக்கத்துட் டூங்கி அவத்தமே வாழ்நாளைப்
போக்குவார் புல்லறிவி னார்.

Wasted lives.

Men of scanty wisdom are those who do not themselves enjoy any sweets of life, bestow no benefactions on worthy persons, draw not nigh the good path that safeguards (the soul), but infatuated and absorbed in the acquisition of wealth, pass away their days of life in vain.

This gives the definition of புல்லறிவு: it is that which produces this life: தமது வாணாளை வீணாக்குவர்.

Comp. 273, 338.

சேர் + கு + அலார் = சேரார்.

328.

புல்லறிவாளர் தேடிய பொருள் தமக்கும் பிறருக்கும் பயன்படாதழியும்.

சிறுகாலை யேதமக்குச் செல்வழி வல்சி
இறுகிறுகத் தோட்கோப்புக் கொள்ளார்,—இறுகிறுகிப்
பின்னறிவாம் என்றிருக்கும் பேதையார் கைகாட்டும்
பொன்னும் புளிவிளங்காய் ஆம்.

The miser's death-bed.

In the very earliest time (*in early youth*) they take not food for the journey which they must make (*into another world*), tying tightly the wallet on their shoulders; but tying tightly (*their treasure bags*), they say, 'In after days we will learn wisdom:' the gold these idiots will indicate with their hands (as legacies, when they are speechless, and in the grasp of death) will be as sour *viḷam* fruit.

They have not speech to tell survivors where the wealth that they themselves have not used lies buried. It is like the sour, sapless wood-apple. (261.)

கொள்ளார் = கொள்ளாதவர்களாய்.

எ: பொன்.— பி: ஆம்.

See B.I.S. 5515:

'युवैव धर्मशीलः स्यादनित्यं खलु जीवितम्।

As a young man let him be virtuous, for life is evidently not eternal.'

329.

புல்லறிவினர் இம்மையிற் செல்வம் உண்டாகிய பொழுது மறுமையைச் சிந்தியார்.

வெறுமை இடத்தும் விழுப்பிணிப் போழ்தும்
மறுமை மனத்தாரே ஆகி—மறுமையை
ஐந்தை அனைத்தானும் ஆற்றிய காலத்துச்
சிந்தியார் சிற்றறிவி னார்.

Saints when they suffer, sinners when they prosper.

When poor, or when disease's deadly grasp they feel, to other world alone their minds are given; but when wealth grows, no thought, small as a grain of mustard seed, give they to other world—these souls unwise!

Comp. the following:

'பெறுதிக்கட் பொச்சாந் துரைத்தல், உயிரை
இறுதிக்கண் யாமிழந்தேம் என்றல்,—மறுவந்து
தன்னுடம்பு கன்றுங்கா னாணுதல்: இம்மூன்றும்
மன்னா உடம்பின் குறி.

To speak thoughtlessly about life while it is enjoyed; to say "we've lost it" when the end is nigh; and to feel shame (for sins) when disease comes and the body fails: these three are characteristics of short-lived mortals.'—T. 91.

அனைத்து (√அன்), *so-much*: 'Even so much as.' Here இடத்து, போழ்து, காலத்து are equivalents.

330.

புல்லறிவினோர் அறஞ்செய்யாது தமது வாழுநாளை வீணாள் ஆக்குவர்.

என்னைமற் றிவ்வுடம்பு பெற்றும் அறநினையார்,
கொன்னே கழிப்பர்தம் வாழ்நாளை,—அன்னோ!
அளவிறந்த காதற்றம் ஆருயிர் அன்னார்க்
கொளவிழைக்குங் கூற்றமுங் கண்டு?

Friends hurried away; the unwise heed it not.

Though they have gained a human frame, of virtue think they not! In vain they spend their days. Alas! and yet they see death eagerly hasting to snatch away those infinitely dear, like to their very souls! Why is this so?

Comp. especially 20 and 28; also 32, 34, 37.

அறிவில்லார் is the understood subject.

The warning is in vain. And men are foolish who hoard for their families. All are doomed.

காதல் = *அன்பினையுடைய* = 'beloving and beloved.' *அன்னார்* is object of *கொள*. G. 30 (உ). *கண்டு* = *கண்டிருந்தும்*. Some read *விழை*, but *இழை* = *சூழ்*, 'contrive, plan,' is better.

CHAPTER XXXIV.

UTTER FOLLY.

அதிகாரம் ௩௪.

பேதைமை

(= யாதோன்றினையும் அறியாமை).

The subject is mainly that of the last chapter, but special follies also are satirized. This relates to மயக்கம், as ch. vii to குரோதம், and ch. ix to காமம்: the *three faults*. See 190.

Analysis:

1. The folly of absorption in worldly pursuits. [331.]
2. The folly of procrastination. [332.]
3. The folly of ignoring wise teaching. [333.]
4. The folly of insensate apathy. [334.]
5. The folly of an abusive tongue. [335.]
6. The folly of trying to influence uncongenial spirits. [336.]
7. The folly of subserviency to avaricious and unfriendly men of wealth. [337, 339.]
8. The folly of a querulous temper. [338.]
9. The folly of self-glorification. [340.]

The comparisons of the turtle exulting in getting into the water again, the bathers waiting for the surf-waves to be silent, the stone of more account than the fool, and the ants round the neck of the closed oil-jar, are noteworthy.

331.

உலகவின்பத்தையே பொருள் என்றுகொண்டு மறுமை குறியாமை பேதைமை.

கொலைஞர் உலையேற்றித் தீமடுப்ப ஆமை
நிலையறியா தந்நீர் படிந்தாடி யற்றே,
கொலைவல் பெருங்கூற்றங் கோட்பார்ப்ப ஈண்டை
வலையகத்துச் செம்மாப்பார் மாண்பு.

Men disport themselves in the very meshes of death's net.

While the turtle's murderers have put it into the pot, and kindled fire beneath, it sports unconscious of its fate: such is their worth who joy entangled in life's *net*, while death, the mighty murderer, waits to seize them.

எ: மாண்பு.—ப: அற்று.

This is the great folly. This verse repeats the affirmation that it is folly to forget virtue and the life to come, while absorbed in the pursuit of transitory things. The illustration of the turtle—famous in Greek too—is very apt. It points to an early existence of turtle-soup, where it is not supposed to be! See K. 348, p. 246.

கொலை + ஞர்: அர் and euphonic insertion ஞ். Thus அன், யன், வன், நன், and ஞன் added to roots, *make nouns of agency*, equal to *er*, *or*: murderer. கொலைவல் பெருங்கூற்றம் = 'Great Yaman, strong in slaying.' Comp. உலை and வலை in Lex.

332.

இல்வாழ்க்கைக்கு வேண்டுவனவற்றையே செய்து அறஞ்செய்யாமை அறிவின்மை.

பெருங்கடல் ஆடிய சென்றார்—'ஒருங்குடன்
ஓசை அவிந்தபின் ஆடுதும்'—என்றற்றால்,
'இற்செய் குறைவினை நீக்கி அறவினை
மற்றறிவாம்'—என்றிருப்பார் மாண்பு.

Postponing virtuous action to a time that never arrives.

They went to bathe in the great sea, but cried, 'we will wait till all its roar is hushed, then bathe!' Such is their worth who say, 'we will get rid of all our household toils and cares and then we will practise virtue and be wise.'

எ: மாண்பு.—ப: அற்று.—ஆல் is redundant: அசை.

Comp. 19, 328. This is an oriental form of 'rusticus expectat,' K. (my edition) p. 244.

ஆடிய (G. 86. உ) a gerundial infinitive of purpose: 'in order to bathe.' இல்செய் குறைவினை = 'works remaining for me to do for my household.' (G. 157, 153.)

333.

குலம் முதலியவை ஒருவனுக்கமைந்தும் உலகநடை அறியாதிருப்பது சாரமற்றபால் சோறு போல் ஆகும்.

குலந்தவங் கல்வி குடிமைமூப் பைந்தும்
விலங்காமல் எய்தியக் கண்ணும்—நலஞ்சான்ற
மையறு தொல்சீர் உலகம் அறியாமை
நெய்யிலாப் பாற்சோற்றி னேர்.

A high tone of manners and morals.

Though a man be of good *caste*, have performed deeds of ascetic virtue, acquired learning, is of good family, and attained a ripe old age, so that in these five points he is faultless; yet his ignorance of what is thoroughly good, without stain, sanctioned by ancient precedent, and of good renown in the world's ways, will render all his advantages like thin, watery milk with boiled rice.

எ: அறியாமை = அறியாமல் (இருப்பது).—ப: நேர் = ஒப்பாகும். We have here good examples of every species of ellipsis. G. 151, *etc.*

Ghī (நெய்), 'butter oil,' is in India what butter, lard, and suet are in England, and olive oil in Italy. Here நெய்யிலாப் பால் is *milk without any rich element:* 'skimmed milk.' This would be an insipid condiment with plain boiled rice!

விலக்காமல் = தப்பாமல, 'without a flaw.'

Comp. K. 426.

334.

பிறர்க்குப் பயன்படாதார் கல்லினுங் கடை ஆவர்.

கன்னனி நல்ல கடையாய மாக்களின்;
சொன்னனி தாமுணரா ஆயினும் — இன்னினியே
நிற்றல் இருத்தல் கிடத்தல் இயங்குதல்என்
றுற்றவர்க்குத் தாம்உதவ லான்.

Stones and senseless men.

Stones are much better than low men; since, though those (too) are utterly without apprehension of your words, yet they (stones) are of assistance to those that employ them, inasmuch as they at once stand (where they are fixed), remain (where they are put), lie (where they are laid), and remove (when they are moved).

Or, '*men can stand, sit and lie on them, or walk over them.*' Low men are absolutely good for nothing!

எ: கல்.—ப: நல்ல = நல்லன, நல்லவை. G. 93. கன்னனி = கல்நனி. G. 39. மாக்களின் (G. 61, ஒப்பு).

335.

பயனில்லாமல் மூடன் கொடுஞ்சொற்களைச் சொல்லா விடில் அவனது நாவைத் தினவு தின்னும்:—அவனுக்குத் திருப்தி இல்லை.

பெறுவதொன் றின்றியும் பெற்றானே போலக்
கறுவுகொண் டேலாதார் மாட்டுங்—கறுவினாற்
கோத்தின்னா கூறி உரையாக்காற் பேதைக்கு
நாத்தின்னு' நல்ல சுனைத்து.

A fool angry without cause, longs to abuse.

If the fool, though nothing is to be gained (by such conduct), acting as though he had gained something, waxing wroth against those who disdain (*or* are unable) to contend with him, cannot say and utter forth in his wrath a string of evil words, a grievous itching will gnaw his tongue.

எ: ஏ.—ப: தின்னும்.—இன்றியும். G. 141. மாட்டும். G. 63, 68, 113. உரையா. G. 91. நல்ல. G. 120. சுனைத்து. G. 133.
Comp. 325.

336.

அறிவிலிகளை வசப்படுத்துதல் யாவர்க்கும் அரிது.

தங்கண் மரபில்லார் பின்சென்று தாம்அவரை
எங்கண் வணக்குதும் என்பவர்—புன்கேண்மை,—
நற்றளிர்ப் புன்னை மலருங் கடற்சேர்ப்ப!—
கற்கிள்ளிக் கையிழந் தற்று.

It is a hard, thankless task to bend the worthless to our will.

Lord of the sea-shore where the laurel with its bright foliage flowers! The poor (pretence of) intimacy enjoyed by those who follow after (wealthy but) utterly uncongenial men, and say 'we will bend them to our will,' is like losing one's hand while digging into a rock.

எ: கேண்மை.—ப: இழந்தற்று.

They will not succeed in obtaining any of the benefits of a real, fitting, congenial friendship, though they sacrifice both independence and honesty.

337.

பொருளுடையார் உலுத்தர் ஆயினும் அவரை யாவரும் மொய்த்துக்கொண்டிருப்பர்.

ஆகா தெனினும், அகத்துநெய் உண்டாகின்
போகா தெறும்பு புறஞ்சுற்றும்;—யாதும்
கொடாஅர் எனினும், உடையாரைப் பற்றி
விடாஅர் உலகத் தவர்.

Ants around the neck of the closed oil-jar.

If there be *ghī* in the pot, though they cannot get at it, the ants will swarm without ceasing around the outside; and so the people of the world will cling to and not leave the possessors of wealth, though these give them nothing.

The அளபெடை in கொடாஅர் and விடாஅர் emphasizes the tenacity on the one side and the pertinacity on the other. So Telugu lengthens its vowels: *koṭṭuṭū* = 'continuing to strike.' G. 14.

உலகத்தவர் (உலகத்தார்). II. B. § 180.

338.

அறிவிலார் வீணுள் கழிப்பர்.

நல்லவை நாடொறும் எய்தார்; அறஞ்செய்யார்;
இல்லாதார்க் கியாதொன்றும் ஈகலார்;—எல்லாம்
இனியார்தோள் சேரார்; இசைபட வாழார்:
முனியார்கொ ளும்வாழு' நாள்?

Fools make all life sad for themselves.

No good each day they gain; nor deed of virtue do; nothing to needy men impart; nor know they joy of loved ones' sweet embrace; devoid of fame they live: do such not loathe the days they live?

Comp. 324 and note. This ἀκηδία seems to have no name in English.

K. 140, 833, and 999.

In இயாதொன்றும் the இ is 'furtive இ.' G. 24. It is not reckoned in the metre, which is (– – – | – – – | – ᴗ ᴗ̄). Comp. *Kārigai* iii. 1.

339.

பேதையர் நட்புப்பெரும் பயனைத் தருவதாயினுங் கொடிது.

விழைந்தொருவர் தம்மை வியப்ப ஒருவர்
விழைந்திலேம் என்றிருக்குங் கேண்மை,—தழங்குகுரல்
பாய்திரைசூழ் வையம் பயப்பினும், இன்னாதே
ஆய்நலம் இல்லாதார் மாட்டு.

Friendship without reciprocity.

Friendship with those who are destitute of exquisite goodness, and who, though you cultivate them with affectionate deference, (morosely) say 'we entertain affection for none,'— though it should yield as its fruit the earth, which the sea with its noisy chime of leaping billows girds around,— would be only affliction!

எ: கேண்மை.—ப: இன்னாதே.

This naturally belongs to ch. xxiv, and is like 237. Comp. K. 833: நாணின்மை.

என்றிருக்குங் கேண்மை, 'so-called friendship with those who say.' விழைந்து, 'with affection.' விழைந்திலேம், a neg. perfect, 'we have never regarded you with affection.' Here is a splendid compound of seven members: வையம் is 2nd case, object of பய. It has five roots for its enlargement. தழங்கு, பாய், சூழ் are verb roots (G. 153), adj. to குரல், திரை, and வையம் respectively. திரை = கடல். G. 162.

340.

ஒருவன் தன்புகழைத்தானே எடுத்துக் கூறுவது அறிவின்மை.

கற்றனவுங் கண்ணகன்ற சாயலும் இற்பிறப்பும்
பக்கத்தார் பாராட்டப் பாடெய்துந், தானுரைப்பின்
மைத்துனர் பல்கி மருந்திற் றணியாத
பித்தன்என் றெள்ளப் படும்.

Self-laudation.

The learning a man has acquired, his world-renowned excellence, and his nobility of birth, will gain for him respect when the bystanders celebrate them; but if he himself proclaim them, the young kinsmen crowding around will deride him as one afflicted with a mania not to be mitigated by any medicine.

Comp. 165; K. 439; and N. N. V. 18. Irregular எதுகை; see K. Introd. p. xxvi.

This recalls Horace's 'tribus Anticyris insanabile caput.'

In தணியாத பித்தன் = தணியாத + பித்து + அன்; தணியாத qualifies பித்து, 'an incurable mania.' படும் for படுவான், as a mark of contempt.

CHAPTER XXXV.

LOWNESS.

அதிகாரம் ௩௫.

கீழ்மை

(= கீழ்களின் தன்மை).

Comp. K. cviii.

The idea is that expressed in this verse (N. M. K. 100):

'மாசு படினும்' மணிதன்சீர் குன்றாவாம்;
பூசிக் கொளினும் இரும்பின்கண்—மாசேறும்;
பாசத்துள் இட்டு விளக்கினும் கீழ்தன்னை
மாசுடைமை காட்டி விடும்!

Though foulness light upon the pearl, its worth's the same;
Anoint it, yet will rust upon the iron spread;
In fetters bind the BASE, and give him light of lore,
He still will show his nature's stain!'

It is difficult to distinguish the subject of this chapter (கீழ்மை) from that of the next (கயமை). There appears here and there something of sectarian rancour in many of these verses. Those whom they could not convince and convert are abused. It was a time when the *odium theologicum* and *philosophicum* infected the air. Rival devotees were disputing under every bush.

Analysis:

1. Teaching is thrown away on these. [The fowl on the dunghill; and the dog.] [341, 345. Comp. 352, 321.]
2. They avoid improving society; [342, 349]
3. are incapable of elevation; [343, 346, 347, 350; so 358, 360]
4. are always ungrateful; [344; so 357]
5. and are utterly impracticable. [348.]

341.

கீழோர்க்கு நன்னெறிவிளங்க எடுத்துக்கூறினுந் தம்மனம் போனநெறியே செல்லுவர்.

கப்பி கடவதாக் காலைத்தன் வாய்ப்பெயினும்
குப்பை கிளைப்போவாக் கோழிபோன் மிக்க
கனம்பொதிந்த நூல்விரித்துக் காட்டினுங் கீழ்தன்
மனம்புரிந்த ஆறே மிகும்.

Teaching wasted.

The fowl, though each morning duly you scatter broken grain into its very mouth, will ceaselessly scratch in the refuse-heap; so, though you expound and show the base man works of learning, full of weighty wisdom, he will but the more resolutely go on in the way in which his mind finds delight.

Comp. K. 410.

In 254, 257, 258, 259, 279, 321, 322, 331, 341, 345, 347, 350, 351, 352, 355, 358, 360, and some others, the satiric poet (and these verses may well be the composition of one rather misanthropic bard, a Tamil Antisthenes) searches through nature, animate and inanimate, for types of the heretical, and *ipso facto* worthless man. Some of these similes are found in Sanskrit poetry, and in the proverbs current in all the vernaculars of India.

The low, ignorant man is like a *dog* in the assembly (254); and like a *dog* he takes delight in low things (322, 345).

The same low tastes are seen in the domestic *fowl* (341), in the *pig* (257), and in the *carrion-fly* (259).

And you cannot change these essentially low natures, as you cannot make *charcoal* white by washing it in milk (258); or make the most gorgeous of *slippers* anything but foot coverings (347); nor make *young unbroken bullocks* draw a chariot (350); nor wash away the sliminess of a *frog* (352); nor can you train them to do great things, as you cannot convert a tusked *boar* into a *war-elephant* by enringing its tusks (358); nor give moisture to the pith of the *water-rush* (360).

Men's short-sightedness is exemplified in the *turtle* (331).

The base man must be compelled to do any good he does, like a *chisel* that requires taps of the artist's mallet before it cuts (355); and like the *vicious cow* that must be milked by force (279).

The foolish man is like the unappreciative *ladle* (321); grows harder as he grows older, but is hollow to the last, like *reeds* (351).

342.

கீழோர் மேலோரிடத்துச் செல்ல விரும்பார்.

காழாய கொண்டு கசடற்றார் தஞ்சாரல்
தாழாது போவாம் எனஉரைப்பின்—கீழ்தான்
உறங்குவாம் என்றெழுந்து போமாம்; அஃ தன்றி
மறங்குமாம் மற்றொன் றுரைத்து.

The base will not seek the company of the wise and good.

If you say to the base man, 'Let us without delay go to seek refuge with faultless sages possessors of mature wisdom,' he will probably get up and make off, exclaiming, 'Let us go and slumber,' or he will perhaps demur, and change the subject.

The words காழாய கொண்டு கசடற்றார் are most expressive, but not easy of transference into English. Lit. 'those who are freed from doubt (and imperfection, error) through the reception of solid (crystal-pure) doctrines,' i.e. the instructed sage.

The low man is here invited to become the disciple of a worthy Guru.

ஆம் (= *it may be*) is redundant, or gives an idea of probability.

343.

மேலோர் பெருஞ் சிறப்பெய்தின் தந்தன்மை வேறுபடார்; கீழோர் எய்தின் அத்தன்மையராவர்:—திருந்தார்.

பெருநடை தாம்பெறினும் பெற்றி பிழையா
தொருநடையர் ஆகுவர் சான்றோர்;—பெருநடை
பெற்றக் கடைத்தும்,—பிறங்கருவி நன்னாட!—
வற்றாம் ஒருநடை கீழ்.

Promotion does not spoil the good nor improve the bad.

Lord of the goodly land of swelling torrents! If thoroughly worthy men gain some added dignity, their nature knows no deviation, but they go on in the same even path of virtue; and although the base obtain promotion, his conduct too changes not, (promotion betters him not.)

There is a play on நடை.

வற்று, see வல்: 'baseness is mighty only in its own base way.'

In T. 14, 'பழித்தவை சொல்லுதல் வற்றாகும் பேதைமை, folly is mighty in uttering forbidden things.'

அற்று is another reading, = அத்தன்மைத்து: 'the base is always the same.' But ஒருநடை seems then almost redundant.

Comp. K. 977–979.

344.

மேலோர்க்குச் சிறிய நன்றி செய்பினும் அதைப்பெரிதாக எண்ணுவர்; கீழோர்க்கு எத்தனை நன்றிகளைச் செய்யினும் அதை நன்றியாகக் கருதார்.

திணைஅனைத்தே ஆயினுஞ் செய்தநன் றுண்டாற்
பனைஅனைத்தா உள்ளுவர் சான்றோர்;—பனைஅனைத்
தென்றுஞ் செயினும்,—இலங்கருவி நன்னாட!—
நன்றில நன்றறியார் மாட்டு.

Small benefits seem great to the wise; and *vice versâ*.

Lord of the goodly land of glistening torrents! The excellent will deem any favour done them, though small as a grain of millet, to be large as a palm tree. You may constantly confer favours huge as a palm tree, but they are not benefits, when conferred on those who are not grateful.

எ: சான்றோர், நன்று.—ப: உள்ளுவர், இல.—இலங்கு, அருவி, நல், நாடு. G. 153–157; 93; 64. மாட்டு. G. 63.

This stanza is somewhat out of place here. Comp. 111, 357.

Comp. K. ch. xi with my notes, pp. 216–218; and Vēm. ii. 41. திணை and பனை rhyme so well, and the antithesis is so perfect, that this comparison is very often repeated in Tamil poetry. திணைத்துணையும் = *even a very little.*

345.

கீழோர் பிறர் தம்மை மதித்தற்கேற்றவாகிய நற்கருமங்களை ஒருபோதுஞ் செய்யார்.

பொற்கலத் தூட்டிப் புறந்தரினு' நாய்பிறர்
எச்சிற் கிமையாது பார்த்திருக்கும்;—அச்சீர்
பெருமை உடைத்தாக் கொளினுங்கீழ் செய்யும்
கருமங்கள் வேறு படும்.

The dog prefers to feed on refuse. Nature will out!

The dog, though you tend it with care, feeding it from a golden vessel, will watch, eye fixed, for others' *leavings;* even so, although you receive the base as if they were possessed of greatness, the deeds they do will be otherwise (=their real character will be seen by their conduct).

Comp. 322. But 213 does more justice to the noble animal. K. 410.

346.

கீழ்மக்களின் செருக்கு.

சக்கரச் செல்வம் பெறினும் விழுமியோர்
எக்காலுஞ் சொல்லார் மிகுதிச்சொல்;—எக்காலு'
முந்திரிமேற் காணி மிகுவதேற் கீழ்தன்னை
இந்திரனா எண்ணி விடும்.

The base intoxicated by some trivial gain.

Though they obtain imperial wealth, the excellent never utter a vaunting word; but if at any time the base see some small fraction added to his scanty store, he will deem himself great as *Indra.*

எ: விழுமியோர், கீழ்.—ப: சொல்லார், எண்ணிவிடும்.—செ: சொல்லை, தன்னை.—கீழ் = கீழானவன். G. 162. இந்திரனா = இந்திரனாக. G. 140.

முந்திரி, காணி, see H. B. part ii. App. To his $\frac{1}{320}$th he gains an accession of $\frac{1}{80}$th *of itself!*

He is a beggar on horseback! Comp. K. ch. liv, and notes, p. 265. This is பெரச்சாப்பு: that evil, giddy 'self-oblivion' that is apt to come with a sudden, undeserved elevation.

'அற்பருக்குப் பவிசு வந்தால் அர்த்தராத்திரியிலும் குடை பிடிக்கச் சொல்வார்: if mean people become well off, they will have a parasol borne over them even at midnight.' See G. Ç. 46.

347.

கீழோர் செல்வர் ஆனகாலத்தும் ஈனர் ஆவர்.

மைதீர் பசும்பொன்மேன் மாண்ட மணிஅழுத்திச்
செய்த தெனினுஞ் செருப்புத்தன் காற்கேஆம்;
எய்திய செல்வத்தர் ஆயினுங் கீழ்களைச்
செய்தொழிலாற் காணப் படும்.

The slipper.

Though made of faultless yellow gold, enwrought with choicest pearls, the slipper serves but for one's foot; though the base be deemed prosperous through the wealth they have gained, their baseness will be seen by their actions.

The same thesis in 350 with a different illustration. K. 1001.
Comp. B. I. S. 349:

'अन्तः सारविहीनानां सहायः किं करिष्यति।
मलयेऽपि स्थितो वेणुर्वेणुरेव न चन्दनः॥

What assistance can be rendered to those who have no inner worth?
The *bambu* on the Malaya hills is only a *bambu* and not a *sandal* tree.'

செய்தது = செய்யப்பட்டது.

348.

கீழோர் கடுஞ் சொற்சொல்லுதல் முதலிய தீச்செயல்களையே செய்தொழுகுவர்.

கடுக்கெனச் சொல்வற்றாங் கண்ணோட்டம் இன்றாம்;
இடுக்கண் பிறர்மாட் டுவக்கும்;—அடுத்தடுத்து
வேகம் உடைத்தாம்;—விறன்மலை நன்னாட,—
ஏகுமாம் எள்ளுமாங் கீழ்!

The base man's habit of life.

Victorious lord of the good mountain land! The base is mighty in bitter words, is destitute of kindliness, rejoices in others' sorrows, is ever and anon full of sudden wrath, will run up and down and pour contempt on all he meets.

Comp. கடுகி in 189. An exceedingly powerful verse in Tamil.

349.

மேலோர் தம்மொடு பலநாள் பழகினவரைப் பழையநட்பினர் என்று நன்குமதிப்பர்; கீழோர் அங்ஙனம் பழகினும் இகழுவர்.

பழையர் இவரென்று பன்னாட்பின் னிற்பின்
உழையினியர் ஆகுவர் சான்றோர்;—விழையாதே—
கள்ளுயிர்க்கு நெய்தற் கனைகடற் றண்சேர்ப்ப,—
எள்ளுவர் கீழா யவர்.

No intimacy possible with the base.

Lord of the resounding sea's cool shore, where the *Neythal* breathes honied fragrance round! The worthy, if men for many days stand waiting in their train, will say 'these are old acquaintance,' and will make the place pleasant to them; the base in such circumstances feel no affection, but simply despise them.

Comp. K. ch. lxxxi.

350.

கீழோர் செல்வத்தராய காலத்தும் நல்லொழுக்கத்தை மேற்கொண்டொழுகார்.

கொப்புற் கொடுத்துக் குறைத்தென்றுந் திற்றினும்
வையம்பூண் கல்லா சிறுகுண்டை ;—ஐய,கேள் !
எய்திய செல்வத்தர் ஆயினுங் கீழ்களைச்
செய்தொழிலாற் காணப் படும்.

Prosperity does not elevate the base.

Hear, O Sir! The little bullock-calves will not learn to bear the yoke and draw the chariot, though you give them cut grass, clip them, and constantly[1] rub them down ; so, though they have gained wealth, the base will be seen (*to be so*) by the deeds they do.

Comp. 347 for lines 3 and 4.

[1] But see Lex. for இற்று.

CHAPTER XXXVI.

BASENESS.

அதிகாரம் ௩௬.

கயமை

(= கயவரது தன்மை).

Analysis:

1. The base are essentially worthless; [351]
2. lack fine feeling; [352]
3. are detractors; [353]
4. vaunters of self; [354, 356]
5. give only from fear; [355]
6. are ungrateful and unforgiving. [357.]
7. Prosperity does not change their hearts. [358, 360.]
8. They are always hoping for some unattainable good. [359.]

The base are naturally and hopelessly evil. But this and the preceding chapter are really one.

351.

அறிவுடையோர் இளையர் ஆயினும் அடக்கமுடையர் ஆவார்; அறிவிலார் வயதின் முதியர் ஆயினும் அடங்கார்.

ஆர்த்த அறிவினர் ஆண்டிளையர் ஆயினும்
காத்தோம்பித் தம்மை அடக்குப;—மூத்தொறூஉம்
தீத்தொழிலே கன்றித் திரிதந் தெருவைபோல்
போத்தறார் புல்லறிவி னார்.

Age does not improve the essentially base.

The thoroughly wise, though young in years, will guard themselves in stern self-repression. The low unwise as age comes on, become mature in evil works, and are like reeds, wind-shaken, hollow still!

The reed, or *bambu*, grows very strong and hard, but is always hollow (பொக்கறை), and yields to every wind (திரிதரும்). அர்த்த is for ஆர்த்த by G. 41. (க); so பொத்து = பொந்து, and becomes போந்து by G. 41. (ங).

352.

கயவர் நூல்நெறி செல்லுதல் சிறிதும் இலர் ஆவர்.

செழும்பெரும் பொய்கையுள் வாழினும் என்றும்
வழும்பறுக்க கில்லாவாந் தேரை;—வழும்பில்சீர்
நூல்கற்றக் கண்ணும் நுணுக்கம்ஒன் றில்லாதார்
தேர்கிற்கும் பெற்றி அரிது.

Fine perception unattainable by the obtuse.

Though frogs flourish long in a rich large lake, they never rid themselves of their slime; so it is hard for those void of fine perception, even when they have learned pure and excellent text-books, to acquire the gift of clear understanding.

There are two irregular forms here: அறுக்கஇலா = அறுக்காத and தேர்கிற்கும் = தேரும். அறுக்கஇலா = அறுக்க + கு + இலா = 'powerless to remove:' கு is redundant. தேர்கிற்கும் = தேர் + கு + இன் + கு + உம், where the three inserted syllables are meaningless. G. 108.

353.

கீழோர் பிறருடைய குற்றத்தையே கூறுவர்.

கணமலை நன்னாட!—கண்ணின் றொருவர்
குணனேயுங் கூறற் கரிதாற்—குணன்அழுங்கக்
குற்றம் உழைநின்று கூறுஞ் சிறியவர்கட்
கெற்றால் இயன்றதோ நா?

Detraction easy only to the base.

Lord of the goodly land of mountain chains! It is hard to stand before a man, and publish even his praise. How then can mean men's tongues depreciate a man's good qualities and proclaim his faults while standing before him?

எ: நா.—ப: இயன்றதோ? ஆல், அசைச்சொல். குணன் = குணம். G. 17.
What is the tongue of the abusive man made of?

354.

கீழோர் தம்மைப் புகழ்ந்துபேசிப் பிறரை வஞ்சித்து அவர் பொருளைக் கவர்வர்.

கோடேந் தகலல்குற் பெண்டிர்தம் பெண்ணீர்மை
சேடியர் போலச் செயற்பாற்றார்;—கூடிப்
புதுப்பெருக்கம் போலத்தம் பெண்ணீர்மை காட்டி
மதித்திறப்பர் மற்றை யவர்.

Base men vaunt themselves like wantons.

Chaste women trick not out their charms of womanhood, as is the wont of the wanton. Like fountains ever fresh those others make display of every charm, and vaunt their beauty as they pass.

This is an unsavoury verse. The rendering gives the sense. No western language could literally translate it.

355.

கீழோர் துன்பஞ் செய்வோர்க்கன்றி மற்றையோர்க்கு ஒன்றும் உதவார்.

தளிர்மேலே நிற்பினுந் தட்டாமற் செல்லா
உளிநீரர் மாதோ கயவர்;—அளிநீரார்க்
கென்னானுஞ் செய்யார்; எனைத்தானுஞ் செய்பவே
இன்னாங்கு செய்வார்ப் பெறின்.

You must extort from the base what you want.

The base are like the chisel, that, though it is over the bud (to be sculptured), moves not without some one to strike it. On those who are courteous these confer no boon whatever. They will do everything for those who use violent means.

Comp. 279, and K. 1077.
Favour does nothing; fear alone is effective.

356.

நல்லோர் தமக்குச் செய்த நன்மையை நினைப்பர்; தீயோர் தம்மை நிந்தித்ததை நினைப்பர்.

மலைநலம் உள்ளுங் குறவன்; பயந்த
விளைநிலம் உள்ளும் உழவன்; சிறந்தொருவர்
செய்தநன் றுள்ளுவர் சான்றோர்; கயந்தன்னை
வைததை உள்ளி விடும்.

Each thinks upon his own favourite place. The good remember only benefits conferred on them; the bad only injuries.

The hill-man thinks upon the beauty of his hills; the farmer thinks upon his fields that have yielded him rich crops; the good think on the boons bestowed by worthy men; the base man's thoughts are fixed on abuse he has received.

எ: குறவன், உழவன், சான்றோர், கயம்.—ப: உள்ளும், உள்ளுவர், உள்ளி விடும்.—உள்ளும். G. 137. கயம் = கயவன். G. 162. விடும். G. 124. (5.)

K. p. 215.

So in T. 51: 'சர்ந்தகல்லிஸ்ஞக்கயவர், the evil base ones that are like the broken stone:' the fracture cannot be mended: they neither forgive nor forget.

Some have read தான்வைத்தே for வைததை, 'his thoughts are fixed on himself;' but this destroys the rhyme; and his base *rancour* is the idea.

357.

மேலோர் முன்பு ஒருஉதவிசெய்த பின்பு பல தீங்குகளைச் செய்யினும் பொறுப்பர்; இழிவோர் முன்பு பல நன்மைகளைச்செய்த பின்பு ஒரு தீங்குசெய்யின் பொறுக்க மாட்டார்.

ஒருநன்றி செய்தவர்க் கொன்றி எழுந்த
பிழைநூறுஞ் சான்றோர் பொறுப்பர்; கயவர்க்
கெழுநூறு நன்றிசெய் தொன்றுதீ தாயின்,
எழுநூறுந் தீதாய் விடும்.

The good are grateful; the base ungrateful and malignant.

The good attach themselves to those that have done them one act of kindness, and forgive a hundred wrongs that arise. The base receive seven hundred benefits, but one wrong will turn them all to evil.

எ: சான்றோர், எழுநூறு.—ப: பொறுப்பர், விடும்.—தீதாய். G. 120.

See K. p. 216. The K. 109 is one part of this.

358.

மேலோர் வறுமைக்காலத்தும் உதவுவார்; கீழோர் செல்வம் மிக்ககாலத்தும் உதவார்.

ஏட்டைப் பருவத்தும் இற்பிறந்தார் செய்வன
மோட்டிடத்துஞ் செய்யார் முழுமக்கள்;—கோட்டை
வைரஞ் செறிப்பினும்—வாட்கண்ணாய்!—பன்றி
செயிர்வேழம் ஆகுதல் இன்று.

Base men illiberal even in prosperity.

Worthless persons even in high estate do not the deeds that men of noble birth perform even in their poverty. O keen-eyed maid! Men may enring and arm the boar's tusks, but it will not even so become a warlike elephant.

Comp. 149, 184.
See the Telugu Vēmana ii. 6. Or, word for word:

O bright-eyed maid! The utterly debased do not
In zenith of prosperity what noble men
In penury perform! Enring the wild boar's tusk,
It doth not thus a warlike elephant become.

359.

கீழோர் நன்பயன்பெற முயலாது வீண்பெருமைபேசிக் கெடுவர்.

இன்றாதும், இன்னிலையே ஆதும், இனிச்சிறிது
நின்றாதும் என்று நினைத்திருந்—தொன்றி
உரையின் மகிழ்ந்துதம் உள்ளம்வே றாகி
மரையிலையின் மாய்ந்தார் பலர்.

Vain dreams. We fade as a leaf.

'To-day, at once, a little hence, we shall gain our end!' So many speak and think, and joyously tell it out among their friends; but soon their eager minds are changed; and they have perished like a lotus leaf.

எ : மாய்ந்தார்.—ப : பலர்.
Comp. K. 337, p. 244.
There is a pretty play on நிலை and இலை in this exquisite verse.

360.

சிலோர் மக்கட் பிறப்பினர் ஆயினும் உயிர்களிடத் தன்புடையர் ஆகார்.

நீருட் பிறந்து நிறம்பசிய தாயினும்
ஈரங் கிடையகத் தில்லாகும்; — ஒரும்
நிறைப்பெருஞ் செல்வத்து நின்றக் கடைத்தும்
அறைப்பெருங்கல் அன்னார் உடைத்து.

Wealth without heart.

Though born in the water, and its hue appear green, the *Neṭṭi's* pith knows no moisture; so in the world are men of amplest wealth whose hearts are hard as stones upon the rocky mountain fell.

See Lex. இடை. No moisture ever reaches the pith of the water-rush (Αἰσχυνομένη), though the plant grows in the water.

Comp. K. p. 320.

CHAPTER XXXVII.

MISCELLANEOUS TOPICS.

அதிகாரம் ௩௭.

பன்னெறி

(= பலவழி).

When *Pathumanār* had arranged the quatrains into chapters, he found ten remaining, to which, from the diversity of their subjects, he gave this title: 'Many topics.'

Analysis:

1. A house desolate without a wife. [361.] This contradicts 364.
2. A woman's honour her only safeguard. [362.]
3. The bad wife. [363.] Contrast to 382–384.
4. Marriage an evil. [364.]
5. Choice of life. [365, 366.]
6. Like father, like son. [367.]
7. Bad times. [368.] Better in ch. xxvii.
8. The misery of unfeeling selfishness. [369.] This is ch. xxiv.
9. The wanton. [370.] This belongs to ch. xxxviii.

361.

கற்புடை மனைவாளை இல்லாதான் இல்லம் எத்துணைச் சிறப்பிற்றாயினும் இடுகாடுபோலும்.

மழைதிளைக்கு' மாடமாய் மாண்டமைந்த காப்பாய்
இழைவிளக்கு நின்றிமைப்பின் என்னும்?—விழைதக்க
மாண்ட மனையாளை இல்லாதான் இல்லகம்
காண்டற் கரியதோர் காடு!

The wife.

The mansion meets the clouds. A stately band of warders keep watch around. Gems glisten therein like lamps. What then? *Where the owner has not a wife of dainty excellence, the house within is a waste, hard to explore.*

The verb இல் governs the 2nd case = 'to lack.'

எ: இல்லகம்.—ப: காடு (போலும்).—அரியது in apposition with காடு. என்னும், 'what good is it?'

The காடு is perhaps rather the desolate 'burning ground,' *painful to contemplate.* Comp. K. ch. vi, with மனைத்தக்கமாண்புடையாள்.

[Comp. N. M. K. 101:

'எண்ணொருக்குஞ் சான்றோர் மதியாரிற் றீராமை;
புண்ணொருக்கும் போற்றார் உடனுறைவு;—பண்ணமையி
யாழொக்கும் நட்டார் கழறுஞ்சொல்;—பாழொக்கும்
பண்புடையாள் இல்லா மனை.

Not to sever from the excellent—the wise—is as an education; to live with those who cherish us not is as a sore; the word uttered by friends is as the tuneful lute; the house without a courteous house-wife is as a waste.']

So B. I. S. 5387:

'यस्य भार्या गृहे नास्ति सध्वी च प्रियवादिनी।
अरण्यं तेन गन्तव्यं यथारण्यं तस्य गृहम्॥

In whose dwelling there is no wife true and of pleasant speech, let him go to the wilderness: his house is as a wilderness.'

362.

தற்பகத்தில்லாத மகளிர்க்குப் புறக்காவலாற்பயன் இன்று.

வழுக்கெனைத்தும் இல்லாத வாள்வாய்க் கிடந்தும்
இழுக்கினைத் தாம்பெறுவர் ஆயின்—இழுக்கெனைத்தும்
செய்குறுப் பாணி சிறிதேயச் சின்மொழியார்
கையுறுப் பாணி பெரிது.

Outward guards avail nothing.

Though compassed round with a faultless guard of swords, if once they gain freedom, in little time they are stained with every fault; and long is the time those soft-voiced ones spurn every law of right.

In Ellis' MSS. this is rendered:

'Though women of light conversation (!) be as strictly guarded as the blade of a sword is carefully preserved (!); yet, if by any relaxation of vigilance, an opportunity be offered to them, little of this time will be occupied by deeds which are not evil, and much of it by them.'

This awkward and foolish verse is corrupt. The original idea is found in Manu, lect. ix. 10–18.

Various readings are:

i. *For* வாள்வாய் *read* வாழ்வாய் = 'when . . . have lived in all happiness, *etc.*'

ii. *For* இன்மொழியார் *read* இறுமின்றூர் = 'young beauties.'

iii. *For* பெறுவர் *read* பெறார் = 'if they obtain not.'

Contrast this with K. 57.

If we read, as I prefer, ஆள், it is = 'though she has fallen into the hands of a perfectly faultless husband.'

இழுக்கு, 'carelessness in the watch'?

363.

நற்குணமில்லாதமகளிர் தங்கணவனைக் கொல்லும் வாளுக்கு ஒப்பாவர்.

எறிஎன் றெதிர்நிற்பாள் கூற்றம்; சிறுகாலை
அட்டில் புகாதாள் அரும்பிணி;—அட்டதனை
உண்டி உதவாதாள் இல்வாழ்பேய்;—இம்மூவர்
கொண்டானைக் கொல்லும் படை.

The evil qualities of a bad wife and their effects.

Death is the wife that stands and dares her spouse to strike! *Disease* is she who enters not the kitchen betimes! *Demon domestic* is she who cooks and gives no alms! These three are *swords* to slay their lords!

நிற்பாள், புகாள், உதவாதாள் = நிற்பவள், புகாதவள், உதவாதவள். All three subjects.

[So in N. M. K. 85:

'கல்லா ஒருவர்க்குத் தம்வாயிற் சொற்கூற்றம்;
மெல்லிய வாழைக்குத் தானீன்ற காய்கூற்றம்;
அல்லவை செய்வார்க் கறங்கூற்றம்; கூற்றமே
இல்லிருந்து தீங்கொழுகு வாள்.

To those not learned the words of their mouth are death; to tender *plantain* tree the fruit it has borne is death; to men who perform vicious deeds virtue is death; death sure is she that in the house doth evil deeds.'

The plantain is cut down as soon as it has fruited.]

364.

மணத்தைக் கடி என்னும் பெயராற் கடியவேண்டும் என்றுணராதார் அல்லற் படுவார்.

கடியெனக் கேட்டுங் கடியான்;—வெடிபட
ஆர்ப்பது கேட்டும் அதுதெளியான்;—பேர்த்துமோர்
இற்கொண் டினிதுறூஉம் ஏமுறுதல், என்பவே,
கற்கொண் டெறியுந் தவறு!

The second marriage.

He hears (that *marriage* is another name for) *dread*, and yet he dreads it not! He hears the fearful funeral drum, but it gives him no sense! Again to take a wife and to dwell bewildered amidst domestic enjoyments is a fault that merits stoning; so say (the wise).

Comp. K. p. 200.
There is a play on the √கடி; see Lex. and 56. The எதுகை is peculiar.—இற்கொள் = 'take a wife.' For கொண்டு in line 4, see H. B. § 239.

365.

தவத்தினும் சிறந்த கர்மம் இல்லை.

தலையே தவமுயன்று வாழ்தல்; ஒருவர்க்
கிடையே இனியார்கட் டங்கல்;—கடையே
புணராதென் றெண்ணிப் பொருணசையாற் றம்மை
உணரார்பின் சென்று நிலை.

Different modes of life.

The *best* thing is a life spent in penitential practices. The *middle* course is to live with dear ones around. The *worst* of all is, with the thought that we have not enough, through desire of wealth, subserviently to follow those who understand us not.

Comp. ch. vi, and 292, 309. The next is a variation of this.
Comp. K. p. 316.

366.

உத்தமர் கற்றுப்பொழுதுபோக்குவர்; மத்திமர் உண்டுபொழுதுபோக்குவர்; அதமர் பொருள் இல்லை என்று வெறுப்பாற் பொழுதுபோக்குவர்.

கல்லாக் கழிப்பர் தலையாயர்;— நல்லவை
துவ்வாக் கழிப்பர் இடைகள், கடைகள்
இனிதுணேம், ஆரப் பெறேம்யாம் என்னும்
முனிவினாற் கண்பா டிலர்!

Three kinds of men: those that learn, those that enjoy, and those that complain.

The men of noblest mood pass their time in learning. The middle sort pass their time in the enjoyment of good things. The last and lowest cry: 'Our food is not sweet,' 'We've not got our fill,' and in angry mood lie sleepless.

This is a somewhat different idea from 365.

Comp. 338. கல்லா, துவ்வா. H.B. § 97, *note.*=கற்று, துவ்வி. உணேம், பெறேம் are old forms. G. 77, 89. Line 3 is bad metre.

And B.I.S. 4090:

'दुःखं निरन्तरं पुंसाम् असंतोषवतां पुनः।
Discontented men suffer continual sorrow.'

367.

மகனுக்கு உளதாகிய அறிவு தந்தைக்கு உளதாகிய அறிவே ஆம்.

செந்நெல்லால் ஆய செழுமுளை மற்றும்அச்
செந்நெல்லே ஆகி விளைதலால்,—அந்நெல்
வயனிறையக் காய்க்கும் வளவயல் ஊர!—
மகனறிவு தந்தை அறிவு.

Like father, like son!

The red grain's swelling germ in after time grows up and yields that same red grain.—O fertile crofted village lord, whose fields are filled with ripening crops of that same grain!—*Wisdom of son is wisdom of the sire.*

So in French: '*tel père, tel fils*, like father, like son.'

And in S. यथा पिता तथा पुत्रः. Comp. also Manu ix. 40.

This chieftain rules a tract of cultivated land: மருதநிலம். Here the type of men hardly changes from generation to generation. Village communities are scarcely affected by political revolutions.

368.

உலகநடை எல்லாம் விபரீதம் உள்ளது.

உடைப்பெருஞ் செல்வருஞ் சான்றோருங் கெட்டுப்
புடைப்பெண்டிர் மக்களுங் கீழும் பெருகிக்
கடைக்கா றலைக்கண்ண தாகிக் குடைக்காற்போல்
கீழ்மேலாய் நிற்கும் உலகு.

Bad times.

The wealthy men of great possessions and the perfect have perished, while wantons' sons and base men multiply. The lowest takes chief place, and, like the umbrella's handle, this world is upside down!

எ: உலகு.—ப: நிற்கும்.
Comp. ch. xxvii, and especially 264, 266, 267.
Also B. I. S. 836:

'अहो वत महत्कष्टं विपरीतम् इदं जगत्।
येनापत्रपते साधुर् असाधुस्तेन तुष्यति॥

Alas, alas! very troublous is this world which is upside down. What shames the good gladdens the bad.'

369.

நட்பினர் வருத்தத்தை ஒழிக்காதார் உயிர்வாழ்தலினும் இறத்தல் நன்று.

இனியார்தந் நெஞ்சத்து நோயுரைப்ப அந்நோய்
தணியாத உள்ளம் உடையார்,—மணிவரன்றி
வீழும் அருவி விறன்மலை நன்னாட!—
வாழ்வின் வரைபாய்த னன்று.

Misery of unfeeling selfishness.

Lord of the good land of mighty hills whence streams descend sweeping along pearls!

Better men should jump down a precipice than live with a mind not disposed to assuage the pain of the dear ones who tell them of their heart's pain.

Comp. 209, 238.
Men may lack the ability to relieve, but not to have the *mind* (உள்ளம்) is intolerable!

370.

வேசையர் அன்பு பொருள் அற்றவிடத்தே நீங்கும்.

புதுப்புனலும் பூங்குழையார் நட்பும் இரண்டும்
விதுப்புற நாடின்வே றல்ல:—புதுப்புனலும்
மாரி அறவே அறுமே; அவர்அன்பும்
வாரி அறவே அறும்.

This belongs really to the next chapter, and is a variation of 371.

Ellis' MSS.:

'When rightly perpended the water of the freshes and the love of women adorned with ear-rings differ not; for the water of the freshes will be dried up when the rain ceaseth, and so will their love when the income faileth.'

More exactly:

'The mountain freshet, and the love of those adorned
With pendant jewels rare, examined calmly prove
To differ nought: *that* fails when rains that feed it fail;
And love of *these* fails too, when income fails!'

CHAPTER XXXVIII.

WANTONS.

அதிகாரம் ௩௮.

பொதுமகளிர்

(= வேசையாது தன்மை).

To this chapter must be added 370.

Analysis:

1. Their mercenary character. [370–374, 378.]
2. Their heartlessness. [375–377, 379.]
3. Lust blinds men. [380.]

See K. p. 304, ch. xcii.
This is a poor chapter.

371.

தைலம் வற்றிய பொழுது விளக்கின் ஒளி அற்றுப்போம். கைப்பொருள் நீங்கிய பொழுது வேசையர் அன்பு அற்றுப்போம்.

விளக்கொளியும் வேசையர் நட்பும் இரண்டும்
துளக்கற நாடின்வே றல்ல:—விளக்கொளியும்
நெய்யற்ற கண்ணே அறுமே; அவரன்பும்
கையற்ற கண்ணே அறும்.

The lamp's light and harlot's love examined well are seen to differ not a whit: the lamp's light goes out when the feeding oil is consumed; and the harlot's love is spent when the lavish hand has spent its wealth.

Comp. 370, of which this is a variation.

Ellis' MSS.:

'When rightly perpended the light of a lamp and the love of courtezans differ not; for the former is extinguished when the oil is dried up, and the latter estranged when the empty hand no longer contains money.'

372.

பரத்தையர் பொய்யன்பைக்காட்டிப் பொருள் பறிப்பர்.

அங்கோட் டகலல்குல் ஆயிழையா ணம்மொடு
செங்கோடு பாய்துமே என்றாண்மன்;—செங்கோட்டின்
மேற்காணம் இன்மையான் மேவா தொழிந்தாளே,
காற்காணோய் காட்டிக் கலுழ்ந்து.

The wanton's self-interested professions.

She (of enticing beauty), adorned with choice jewels, said forsooth, 'I will leap with you down the steep precipice;' but on the very brow of the precipice, because I had no money, she, weeping and pointing to her aching feet, withdrew and left me alone!

The first line is not literally rendered.

373.

பரத்தையர் பொருளிலாரை உபசரித்துப் புறப்படுத்துவர்.

அங்கண் விசும்பின் அமரர் தொழப்படும்
செங்கண்மால் ஆயினும் ஆகமன்,—தங்கைக்
கொடுப்பதொன் றில்லாரைக் கொய்தளிர் அன்னார்
விடுப்பர்தங் கையாற் றொழுது.

Though he be *Māl*, the fiery-eyed, whom in the heaven's fair homes immortals worship, if in hand he bring no gift, the women tender as the buds men cull, will straight dismiss him, bowing low with folded hands.

Comp. Vēm. ii. 25.

Ellis' MSS.:

'Let them have been even as liberal as Shenganmàl (*sic*) the goddess of prosperity, who is worshipped by the gods in the beauteous heavens, courtezans whose hands are tinted like opening buds, will forsake those who have no wealth to bestow upon them, reverentially saluting them with folded hands.'

Ellis must be wrong. See மால்.

The French says: 'Le beau Vichnou aux yeux rouges.'

374.

பரத்தையர் பொருளுடையார் இழிவினர் ஆயினும் அவரையே தமக்கினியராகக் கொள்வர்.

ஆணமி னெஞ்சத் தணிநீலக் கண்ணார்க்குக்
காணமில் லாதார் கடுவனையர்;—காணவே
செக்கூர்ந்து கொண்டாருஞ் செய்த பொருளுடையார்
அக்காரம் அன்னார் அவர்க்கு.

Money makes a man the wanton's darling.

To the damsels of loveless hearts, whose eyes are as beauteous as blue water-lilies, those who have no wealth are as poison! Even those who have turned the (oil-) press, in sight of all men, if they have wealth, are as sugar to them.

The oil-man is hardly dealt with. In Manu iii. 158 he is condemned; and so in iv. 84, 85 is the owner of an oil-press; while an oil-press is equal in impurity to ten slaughter-houses! It is hard to see the reason of this.

375.

அறிவில்லாரே வேசையரைச்சேர்வார்கள்.

பாம்பிற் கொருதலை காட்டி ஒருதலை
தேம்படு தெண்கயத்து மீன்காட்டும்—ஆங்கு
மலங்கன்ன செய்கை மகளிர்தோள் சேர்வார்
விலங்கன்ன வெள்ளறிவி னார்.

Wantons and their paramours.

The silly ones, who are as beasts, seek the embraces of women who are like the eel, which shows one head to the snake, and another head to the fish, in the sweet clear lake: (*are of a double and deceitful nature.*)

376.

பரத்தையர் பொருளற்ற விடத்து மாறுபடுவர்.

பொத்தநூற் கல்லும் புணர்பிரியா அன்றிலும்போல்
நித்தலு’ நம்மைப் பிரியலம் என்றுரைத்த
பொற்றொடியும் போர்த்தகர்கோ டாயினா ளென்னெஞ்சே!
நிற்றியோ, போதியோ, நீ?

Feigned love becomes open hostility.

'We will never part, like the precious stone strung on its thread, or the *Andril*,' said the damsel with golden bracelets: she has now become the horn of a fighting ram (*she angrily repels me*). Dear heart! dost linger still, or wilt thou go?

The French says, 'Mais elle s'est dérobée de plus en plus, ainsi que (va en diminuant) la corne du buffle de combat,' which is ingenious, but not the native idea. Comp. 378.

The pearls strung together sunder not. The *Andril* (see Lex.) dies if taken from its mate.

377.

வேசையர் அன்பை மெய்யென்று கருதி மகிழ்வோர் பலராலும் இகழப்படுவர்.

ஆமாபோ னக்கி அவர்கைப் பொருள்கொண்டு
சேமாபோற் கூப்புறாஉஞ் சில்லைக்க ணன்பினை
ஏமாந் தெமதென் றிருந்தார் பெறுபவே
தாமாம் பலரா னகை.

Ridiculous infatuation of the wanton's dupe.

Those who fondly reckon upon the devoted love of the worthless wanton, that, like the wild ox, licks the hand and despoils men of their wealth, and then, like the buffalo, bounds away, shall suffer the deserved ridicule of many.

The wild ox or *gayal* is fabled to kill by licking its victims.

378.

வீட்டுநெறியில் ஒழுகுவோர் வேசையர்தோள் சேரவிரும்பார்.

ஏமாந்த போழ்தி னினியார்போ னின்றாராய்த்
தாமார்ந்த போதே தகர்க்கோடாம்;—மானோக்கின்
தந்நெறிப் பெண்டிர் தடமுலை சேராரே
செந்நெறிச் சேர்தும்என் பார்.

Bought embraces.

Those whose avowed purpose it is to walk in the way of rectitude seek not the embrace of the fascinating, fawn-eyed damsels, who walk in a way of their own, who are pleasant when gratified with gifts, and when they are filled (=*when no more gifts are to be expected*) are like the horn of the fighting ram.

Comp. 376.

379.

பரத்தையாது பொய்யன்பைக் காமுகரே மெய் என்று மகிழ்வர்.

ஊறுசெய் நெஞ்சந்தம் உள்ளடக்கி ஒண்ணுதலார்
தேற மொழிந்த மொழிகேட்டுத்—தேறி
எமர்என்று கொள்வாருங் கொள்பவே! யார்க்கும்
தமரல்லார் தம்முடம்பி னார்.

Let him be deceived that will.

Let those accept (*wantons' false love*), who take them as their own, believing the words uttered to inspire belief, by the bright-browed ones, who keep concealed within the cruelty that lurks in their heart. Those whose bodies are their sole wealth belong to none, (i. e. *they have no souls to give!*)

380.

பாவிகள் பரத்தையாது கள்ளத்தை அறிந்தார் ஆயினும் அறியார்போற் கூடிமகிழ்வர்.

உள்ளம் ஒருவன் உழையதா ஒண்ணுதலார்
கள்ளத்தாற் செய்யுங் கருத்தெல்லாம்—தெள்ளி
அறிந்த விடத்தும் அறியார்ஆம் பாவம்
செறிந்த உடம்பி னவர்.

Lust blinds men.

Though the dupes clearly discern and know the guileful intentions entertained by the bright-browed ones, even where their minds are (*apparently*) set upon some person, they whose bodies are full of sin do not recognise it!

CHAPTER XXXIX.

CHASTE MATRONHOOD.

அதிகாரம் ௩௯.

கற்புடைமகளிர்

(= கற்பினையுடைய மாதராதுதன்மை).

In S. पति + व्रता = 'one who is faithful to her husband.'

The legends of *Sītā*, wife of Rāma-chandra; of *Damayantī*, wife of Nala; of *Chandramatī*, wife of Harischandra; of *Visākhā*, the Buddhist female saint (see Oldenberg: Buddha); and very many others, afford pictures of womanly excellence not surpassed in any literature. The authentic history of *Ahalyā Bāi*, the Mahratta queen, would be regarded as utterly incredible, if it were not established, in every detail, by irrefragable evidence. [See Pope's Text-book of Indian History, p. 193, 3rd edition, Allen & Co.] See also the introduction to my Kurraḷ.

The extent to which wifely submission may be carried, and the powers of the *Pativratā* may be seen in an absurd story told in the இரங்கேச வெண்பா (௯): the legend of Nalāgini.

Analysis:

1. These should be chaste, and not be exposed to solicitation. [381.]
2. They should be good housewives, equal to all emergencies. Other things are slipped in: gentleness of speech, and dignity. [382, 383.]
3. They should endear themselves to their husbands; and be [384]
4. possessed of innate purity. [385.]
5. Their worth. [386.]
6. Jealousy: of little interest. [387–400.]

Comp. K. ch. v, vi.

381.

கற்புடையாளுக்குப் பின்னிற்பார் இன்மையே நன்றும்.

அரும்பெறற் கற்பின் அயிராணி அன்ன
பெரும்பெயர்ப் பெண்டிர் எனினும்—விரும்பிப்
பெறுநசையாற் பின்னிற்பார் இன்மையே பேணும்
நறுநுதலா ளன்மைத் துணை.

Freedom from temptation.

Though women live famed as *Ayirāṇi* for rarest gift of chastity, absence of men that stand enamoured of their charms is a help in way of good to those of fragrant brow who guard themselves.

Ayirāṇi, the virtuous wife of *Indra*.

K. p. 206.

The commentator says, 'She who is without suitors is a good help-meet (to her husband);' making நுதலாள் the subject, and supplying கணவனுக்கு. I make இன்மை the subject, and take நுதலாள் = நுதலாட்கு.

A commentator remarks that there would be no followers, or waiting suitors (பின்னிற்பார்), without some kind of encouragement.

382.

வறுமைக்காலத்தும் விருந்தோம்பன் முதலிய கடமைகளைச் செய்பவளே மாட்சிமையையுடைய மனையாள்.

குடநீர்அட் டுண்ணும் இடுக்கட் பொழுதுங்
கடனீர் அறஉண்ணுங் கேளிர் வரினுங்
கடனீர்மை கைஆறுக் கொள்ளு' மடமொழி
மாதர் மனைமாட்சி யாள்.

A true wife, in time of poverty, if friends come in enough to drink up the sea, performs her duties with kindness of speech.

When in the straitened time they cook and eat with but one pot of water on the hearth,—if relatives arrive enough to drain the sea, the soft-voiced dame, the glory of her home, well fulfils each seemly duty.

எ: மாதர்.—ப: மாட்சியாள்.

[மடம் in N. M. K. 105:

'மனைக்கு விளக்கு மடவாள், the gentle, simple, guileless lady is the *light of the house*.']

Comp. K. p. 206.

383.

கற்புடைய மனையாள் வசிக்கும் இல்லமே இல்.

நாலாறும் ஆறாய் நனிசிறிதாய் எப்புறனும்
மேலாறு மேலுறை சோரினும்—மேலாய
வல்லாளாய் வாழும்ஊர் தற்புகழு' மாண்கற்பின்
இல்லாள் அமர்ந்ததே இல்.

The real home!

On every side the narrow dwelling lies open, on every part the rain drips down; yet, if the dame has noble gifts, praised by townsfolk for her modest worth, such a housewife's blest abode is indeed *a home!*

Comp. K. p. 206.

384.

கணவன் கருத்துக்கொத்து நடக்கும் கற்புடையவள் பெண்.

கட்கினியாள், காதலன் காதல் வகைபுனைவாள்,
உட்குடையாள், ஊர்நாண் இயல்பினள்,—உட்கி
இடனறிந் தூடி இனிதின் உணரும்
மடமொழி மாதராள், பெண்.

The wife: 'placens uxor.'

She is sweet to the eye, and adorned in the way that a lover loves; she enforces awe; her virtue shames the village folk; she is submissive; but in fitting place is stern, yet sweetly relents:—such a soft-voiced dame is *a wife.*

All Tamil poets regard it as an accomplishment in a woman to know how and when to assume an offended air (ஊடு, புல, பிணக்கு), and when to come to a good understanding with her spouse, and lay it aside (உணரு).

The idea is that of Terence:

'Amantium irae amoris integratio est.'

Comp. 391; K. ch. cxxxi, and K. p. 206.

385.

கற்புடைய மகளிரே அன்றிப் பரத்தையர் கணவரைக் காணின் நாணுர்.

எஞ்ஞான்றும் எங்கணவர் எந்தோண்மேற் சேர்ந்தெழினும்
அஞ்ஞான்று கண்டேம்போ ஞணுதுமால்—எஞ்ஞான்றும்
என்னை கெழீஇனர் கொல்லோ பொருணசையால்
பன்மார்பு சேர்ந்தொழுகு வார்?

The modest woman cannot understand shamelessness.

'Whenever our spouse takes us in his embrace, we feel a timid shame as if we saw him then for the first time; and they (wantons) daily, through desire of gain, submit to the embraces of many! How can this be?'

386.

நாணமுடைய மனைவி.

உள்ளத் துணர்வுடையான் ஓதிய நூல்அற்றுல்
வள்ளன்மை பூண்டான்கண் ஒண்பொருள்—தெள்ளிய
ஆண்மகன் கையில் அயில்வாள் அனைத்தரோ
நாணுடையாள் பெற்ற நலம்!

A modest wife like a javelin in the hand of a hero.

As the scroll that he reads, whose inmost heart well understands it, is goodly wealth with him who is graced by a generous spirit. As a keen weapon in the hand of a clear-souled hero, is the loveliness that a modest woman owns.

K. p. 206.

387.

ஒரு நாட்டுப்புறத்தான் கருங்கொள்ளையுஞ்
செங்கொள்ளையும் விலை வித்தியாசமின்றி வாங்கிக்
கொண்டானும்; அதுபோல, என்கணவன் பலமாதரைச்
சேர்ந்து என்னைச் சேர வருவான்.
தன்பொறுமையையுஞ் சத்தியையுங் கூறினள் போலும்.

கருங்கொள்ளுஞ் செங்கொள்ளுந் தூணிப் பதக்கென்
ஞெருங்கொப்பக் கொண்டானும் ஊரன்;—ஒருங்கொவ்வா
நன்னுதலார்த் தோய்ந்த வரைமார்ப னீராடா
தென்னையுந் தோய வரும்!

The injured wife to her confidante:

'The lord of the town has bought, it seems, black *gram* and red *gram*, a *tūṇi* and a *pathakku*, as if they were all the same! He, whose chest is broad as a mountain, having associated with the beautiful browed ones,—inferior to me!—*unpurified, seeks my society too!*'

The four stanzas 387–400 seem out of place, and are probably more recent.

388.

தன்றலைவன் செய்த அக்கிரமத்தைக்கூற வந்தபாணனுக்கு, சகியாமல் சொன்னது.
குலமகளிர் கணவன் தூஷணையைக் கேளார்கள்.

கொடியவை கூறுதி, பாண! நீ கூறின்
அடிபைய விட்டொதுங்கிச் சென்று—துடியின்
இடக்கண் ணனையம்யாம் ஊரற் கதனால்
வலக்கண் ணனையார்க் குரை.

The neglected wife.

'O minstrel, utter not cruel words, or if thou utter them, softly draw back thy step, and go to utter them to those who are like the lute's right side; for we, to the lord of the town, are as its left.'

The tambour has two hollow vessels (கண்); it is the right one that yields the music. (Comp. 390.) She will not hear of her husband's wrong doings; these are for other and fitter ears to hear.

கூறுதி, a negative imperative. In common Tamil it would be கூறுதே! (§ 121.)
கூறு (root) + ஆ (negative) + தி (sign of 2nd pers. sing.). [See G. 84.]

389.

மனநொக்கிரங்குவாளே அன்றி வெகுளாள்.

சாய்ப்பறிக்க நீர்திகழுந் தண்வயல் ஊரன்மீ
தீப்பறக்க நொந்தேனும் யானேமன்—தீப்பறக்கத்
தாக்கி முலைபொருத தண்சாந் தணியகலம்
நோக்கி இருந்தேனும் யான்.

Meek complainings (to her maid).

'I am she, forsooth, that felt a pang when a fly alighted on the lord of the town, surrounded by cool rice-fields over which the waters gleam, where they pluck the rich grass! And I am she who have lived to look upon his breast adorned with cool *sandal-wood* paste, which has been warmly embraced by others.

She is pained, not angry.

390.

௩௮௮ போல்.

அரும்பவிழ் தாரினான் எம்மருளும் என்று
பெரும்பொய் உரையாதி, பாண!—கரும்பின்
கடைக்கண் ணனைய’நாம் ஊரற் கதனால்
இடைக்கண் ணனையார்க் குரை.

'Minstrel, utter not a gross falsehood, saying that he who wears a garland of opening buds will favour us!

'To the lord of the town we are as the (*tasteless*) tip of the sugar-cane; therefore, tell (such a tale) to them who are like its middle (sweet, juicy) joints.'

Comp. 138, 211, 388.

END OF PART II.

PART III.

ON LOVE
(OR PLEASURE).
மூன்றாவது காமத்துப்பால்.

[CH. XL.]

Comp. K. ch. cix–cxxxiii, p. 322.

These are mere fragments, suggesting the main topics of the subject of இன்பம்.

The Tamil student may, if he please, see the whole subject dealt with in the கலித்தொகை [see Introduction].

CHAPTER XL.

THE CHARACTERISTICS OF LOVE.

அதிகாரம் ௪௦.

காமநுதலியல்

(= காமத்தைக்குறித்த இலக்கணம்).

Analysis:

1. It is full of alternations. [391.]
2. It brings pain in separation. [392–394, 397, 400.]
3. It fills the lover's soul with desire and fear. [395.]
4. It makes the tenderest strong to dare and endure. [396, 398.]
5. It supersedes all else. [399.]

Here are hints of a kind of drama, in which are introduced (1) the lover (தலைமகன்), (2) the lady (தலைவி), (3) his friend (பாங்கன்), (4) her confidante (தோழி), and (5) her mother (ஆய்).

391.

தலைமகனுக்குத் தோழி சொல்லியது.

முயங்காக்காற் பாயும் பசலை,மற் றாடி
உயங்காக்காற் உப்பின்றாங் காமம்;—வயங்கோதம்
நில்லாத் திரைஅலைக்கு' நீள்கழித் தண்சேர்ப்ப!—
புல்லாப் புலப்பதோர் ஆறு!

'The way of true love never did run smooth.'

'Lord of the cool shore of the deep bay, where the gleaming ocean's restless billows beat!

'If there be no fond embrace, a sickly hue will spread itself (over her face); and, if there be no lovers' quarrels, love will lack its zest.

'To embrace and disagree is the one way (of love).'

Comp. 384.

The confidante (தோழி) says this to the bridegroom or lover (தலைமகன்), in regard to the coyness (புலவி) of the bride (தலைவி) or mistress, after a period of estrangement.

ஓர் = 'is the only.' K. ch. cxxxi, cxxxii.

392.

ஆற்றாளாகிய தலைவி தோழிக்குச் சொல்லியது.

தம்மமர் காதலர் தார்சூழ் அணிஅகலம்
விம்ம முயங்குந் துணையில்லார்க்—கிம்மெனப்
பெய்ய எழிலி முழங்குந் திசையெல்லாம்
நெய்தல் அறைந்தன்ன நீர்த்து.

The lonely one.

'To those who were wont to strain in close embrace their own beloved, whose broad breast was girt with garlands, when the rains patter down, it is as though one beat the funeral drum through all the regions where the muttering of the thunder is heard from out the clouds; since they are deprived of their loved one's society.'

K. cxxiii.

393.

விடப்பட்ட தலைமகள் மாலைக்காலத்தில் உற்ற இடர்.

கம்மஞ்செய் மாக்கள் கருவி ஒடுக்கிய
மம்மர்கொண் மாலை மலர்ஆய்ந்து பூத்தொடுப்பாள்
கைம்மாலை இட்டுக் கலுழ்ந்தா டுணையில்லார்க்
கிம்மாலை என்செய்வ தென்று.

The forsaken one at eventide.

At wildering eventide, when workmen all put by their tools, she culled choice flowers, and wove a gay garland;—then let it fall from her hands, and wailed, 'What can this wreath avail to me who weep alone?'

See K. 1227.
Compare the following (Kalit. i. 5):—

THE LONELY ONE.

1. கல்லெனக் கவின்பெற்ற விழாவாற்றுப் படுத்தப்பிற்
புல்லென்ற களம்போலப் புலம்புகொண் டமைவாளோ?

Can she endure to bide alone, like some enclosure that once shone all beautiful when there they kept the hallowed feast, but now is desolate?

2. ஆள்பவர் கலக்குற அலைபெற்ற நாடுபோற்
பாழ்பட்ட முகத்தோடு பைதல்கொண் டமைவாளோ?

Can she endure to bide in grief, with sad despairing face, like a land oppressed, that endures affliction from its tyrant king?

3. ஓரிரா வைகலுட் டாமரைப் பொய்கைய
ணீர்நீத்த மலர்போல நீநீப்பின் வாழ்வாளோ?

Can she endure to live for one night's space forsaken by thee, like a flower in the lotus-lake from which the water has ebbed away?

394.

வினைமுற்றி மீண்ட தலைமகன் சொல்லியது:

செல்சுடர் நோக்கிச் சிதரரிக்கண் கொண்டநீர்
மெல்விரல் ஊழ்தெறியா விம்மித்தன்—மெல்விரலின்
நாள்வைத்து நங்குற்றம் எண்ணுங்கொல் அந்தோதன்
தோள்வைத் தணைமேற் கிடந்து?

The lover says to his friend (பாகன்) in regard to his forsaken bride:

'Regarding the setting sun, and wiping away one by one with her soft finger the tears that well up in her eyes, suffused with red, sobbing she lies resting her arms on the couch, setting off the days on those same tender fingers: alas! are they my faults she is counting up?'

395.

தலைமகன்றான் உற்றதைப்பாகனுக்குச் சொல்லியது.

கண்கயல் என்னுங் கருத்திறற் காதலி
பின்சென்ற தம்ம சிறுசிரல்;—பின்சென்றும்
ஊக்கி எழுந்தும் எறிகல்லா, ஒண்புருவம்
கோட்டிய வில்வாக் கறிந்து.

The lover in a figure praises the lustre of his beloved's eye, and the beauty of her arched brow; and indicates also his own timid reverence.

'The little kingfisher seeing the eyes of my beloved (*as she was disporting in the tank*) and taking them for carp, followed her; but though it followed, and poised itself aloft, it darted not down, recognising her gleaming brow bent above them as a bow.'

Reverential admiration is well shadowed forth. The comparison of the lady's eye to the carp flashing through the water is classical in Tamil.

396.

மகளைப் போக்கிய தாய் இரங்கியது.

அரக்காம்ப னாறும்வாய் அம்மருங்கிற் கன்னோ
பரற்கானம் ஆற்றின கொல்லோ,—அரக்கார்ந்த
பஞ்சிகொண் டூட்டினும் பையெனப் பையெனவென்
றஞ்சிப்பின் வாங்கும் அடி?

The mother bewails the hardships of the rough desert path over which her tender daughter will follow her beloved.

'When I applied the (softest) cotton soaked in the red dye to the foot of her whose waist is lovely, and whose mouth breathes the fragrance of the red water-lily, did she not cry "gently, gently," and shrinking draw it back? And oh! has it endured the stony, desert path?'

She sees what she foresees and dreads, as if it had already happened. The lady does not set out yet. See 398, 399.

I cannot refrain from citing a similar tender touch in Virgil:

'A, tibi ne teneras glacies secet aspera plantas.'

397.

தலைமகள் பிரிவுடன்படாமை.

ஓலைக் கணக்கர் ஒலிஅடங்கு' புன்செக்கர்
மாலைப் பொழுதின் மணந்தார் பிரிவுள்ளி
மாலை பரிந்திட் டழுதாள், வனமுலைமேல்
கோலஞ்செய் சாந்தந் திமிர்ந்து.

Grief of the deserted wife.

When those who con the palm-leaf scrolls had ceased, in eve's dim twilight hour, she thought of her absent spouse; and weeping plucked the flowers from out her wreath, and brushed the odorous sandal from her lovely breast!

See 393 and K. 1231.

398.

உடன்போக்குக்குப் பொருந்திய தலைமகள் தோழிக்குச் சொல்லியது:

கடக்கருங் கானத்துக் காளைபின் நாளை
நடக்கவும் வல்லையோ? என்றி,—சுடர்த்தொடீஇ!
பெற்றான் ஒருவன் பெருங்குதிரை, அந்நிலையே
கற்றான் அஃதூரும் ஆறு.

The confidante demands of the bride if she can endure to walk after her beloved through the desert, she replies:

'Thou hast said, O maiden with burnished bracelets! have you strength to walk on the morrow after your beloved? When one (*a warrior*) has obtained a splendid horse, that very instant he has learned how to ride it!' (*his enthusiasm teaches him.*)

I am afraid the lady was mistaken!

399.

மகளைப்போக்கியதாய் கவலையுற்றுச் சொல்லியது :

முலைக்கண்ணு’ முத்து’ முழுமெய்யும் புல்லும்
இலக்கணம் யாதும் அறியேன் ;—கலைக்கணம்
வேங்கை வெரூஉ’ நெறிசெலிய போலும்என்
பூம்பாவை செய்த குறி.

The mother now aware of her daughter's flight, says:

'My breast, my necklace of pearls, and my whole body she embraced! I knew not what it portended. It was the sign, it seems, made by my lovely one that she was about to set out on the path where the herds of antelopes flee in fright from the tiger.'

I did not know why she bade me good night with such clinging, lingering affection; but now I see the reason.

The chapter of K. (cxxviii) on *indications* must be consulted.

The following pretty song from Kalit. illustrates this quatrain:

THE MOTHER CONSOLED.

Sic vos non vobis.

[The daughter has gone away with her husband.]

1. பலவுறு நறுஞ்சாந்தம் படுப்பவர்க் கல்லதை
மலையுளே பிறப்பினு’ மலைக்கவைதாம் என்செய்யும்?
நினையுங்கா லும்மக ளுமக்கும் ஆங்கனையளே!

The sandal trees, source of much fragrance, profit those that use them; but though born on the hill, how profit they the hill? Bethink you, so is your daughter's case with you!

2. சீர்கெழு வெண்முத்தம் அணிபவர்க் கல்லதை
நீருளே பிறப்பினு’ நீர்க்கவைதாம் என்செய்யும்?
தேருங்கா லும்மக ளுமக்கும் ஆங்கனையளே!

The pearls of dazzling white profit those that wear them; but though born in the sea, how profit they the sea? Ponder it well, so is your daughter's case with you!

3. ஏழ்புணர் இன்னிசை முரல்பவர்க் கல்லதை
யாழுளே பிறப்பினும் யாழ்க்கவைதாம் என்செய்யும்?
சூழுங்கா லும்மக ளுமக்காங் கனையளே!

The sweet harmonies of the seven strings profit those that sing to their accompaniment; but though born in the lute, how profit they the lute? Search it out well, so is your daughter's case with you!

[முரல்(லு), § 56. (III.) 'sing to an accompaniment.']

400.

தலைமகள் பிரிவாற்றாமையைத் தோழிக்குச் சொல்லியது.

கண்மூன் றுடையானுங் காக்கையும் பையரவும்
என்னீன்ற ஆயும் பிழைத்ததென்? — பொன்னீன்ற
கோங்கரும் பன்ன முலையாய்! பொருள்வயின்
பாங்கனார் சென்ற நெறி.

The lady complains of her lover's long absence.

'The triple-eyed (*Çivan*), the crow, the hooded snake, the mother that bare me: what have these done amiss? Maiden whose bosom bears the *Goṅgu* buds, all gold! The way my lover went for wealth is my pain.'

'Çivan restored *Kāman* to life:—from him I suffer. The crow is foster-mother of the *Kuyil*:—its love-sick notes make me sad. The dragon restores the swallowed moon:—the moonlight afflicts me. My mother gave me life:—life to me is one long sorrow. But all these are nothing to the thought of how far my lover has gone from me in search of wealth.'

The third line is not to be quite literally set down. See Lex.

END OF PART III.

INDEX

OF

FIRST LINES OF THE QUATRAINS.

நாலடியார்

பாட்டு முதற்குறிப்பகராதி.

NĀLAḌI.

II.

LEXICON, CONCORDANCE, AND GENERAL INDEX.

*** THE Lexicon and Concordance appended is intended as a small contribution towards the preparation of a complete dictionary of the Tamil language. The author in his Third Grammar has done something of the same kind for the *Nannūl*, and in his edition of the *Kurraḷ* has attempted the same for that important classical work. It is only by an exhaustive examination of the great classics of the language that the lexicon, for which we have been waiting hitherto, can be finally made. Of course there are very excellent Tamil dictionaries already in existence; but they lack authority, are not arranged on philological principles, and therefore leave very much to be desired.

Those who use this Lexicon must not suppose that the writer has attempted to determine the exact theme of every word, or to settle its derivation and affinities. What has been done is to put together hints which may to some extent guide future students in that more complete investigation for which the material is not yet fully accumulated.

Many of the Tamil roots, which are always monosyllabic, seem to be closely allied to certain Sanskrit roots from which it is yet difficult to think that they are absolutely derived. But much is of Āryan origin that does not on the surface seem so; for it must ever be borne in mind that classical Tamil was elaborated mainly under the guidance of those who used Sanskrit (or Prākrit) very freely, but were anxious to disguise its origin. And as their system of verbal commentaries, and the exigencies of Tamil rhyme, rendered it possible, and almost necessary, to make new words *ad libitum*, to give them new meanings, and to modify their forms in a very arbitrary manner, I cannot but believe that a good deal of old Tamil is somewhat artificial and literary.

Of the Drāviḍian languages Tamil undoubtedly preserves more of the genuine fragments of the original speech than any other. The question of the origin of the cerebral letters (ட, ண, ள and ழ) is a very important one for Tamil lexicography. It may be that these are all forms of one letter, a hard L; since they are all often unquestionably interchangeable both in Tamil itself, and in the various dialects,—the Telugu, for example, using *ḍ* for the Tamil ழ. It seems probable that their use originated in an attempt to express in Tamil sounds existing in other languages such as Sanskrit, for which the Tamil itself had no characters. Tamil has neither aspirates nor sibilants; nor can it express in general a consonantal diphthong. Thus the Sanskrit श्री cannot possibly be written in Tamil, and is represented by திரு! The Sanskrit अस्रु or अश्रु is possibly the origin of the Tamil அழு, which in Telugu is *ēḍ*. So *Vishṇu* has become விண்டு. This opens the door to numberless speculations, which may be fanciful, but also may possibly throw light upon the origin of many Tamil forms. It is enough to indicate what is believed to be a very interesting line of investigation.

The student is advised to compare all the passages referred to, and to advance slowly—and so surely—in the study of Tamil verse. It is undoubtedly a somewhat difficult, though a very profitable task.

A

LEXICON AND CONCORDANCE

TO THE

NĀLAḌI.

The references in the Lexicon are as follows:—

The numbers refer to the verses of the Text.

§ refers to the Tamil Handbook, or First Lessons

G. is the Catechism of Tamil Grammar, No. 1, 2, or 3.

K. points to words in the Dictionary to the Kurraḷ.

S., T., M., C., Tu. for Sanskrit, Telugu, Malayāḷam, Canarese, and Tuluva.

For quotations, see Introduction, where a list of authors is given.

அ Ă.

அ Ă. [G. 2, 3, 5.] A demonstrative. [Comp. இ, உ, எ, ஆ, அவன், அது, அஃது, அன். H. B. §§ 25, 26.]

123, 171, 367, 369. In 171 அவ்வும் is for அவைகளும். Comp. இவ்வென உரைத்தும், we will describe. இவ்வு. Jī. Chin. xiii. 164.

1. Initial அ is often found in words of Sanskrit derivation beginning with R, L, or Y, since those letters cannot generally begin words in Tamil according to strict grammatical rules. Comp. *Nannūl*, 148, 149.

2. Since pure Tamil has neither aspirate nor sibilant, Sanskrit words beginning with H or S, often drop those letters: thus, S. हरि = அரி, and सभा = அவை. So also அமர் = சமர், அமையம் = சமையம். [See note under அரவு.]

3. Comp. அணுகு with நணுகு; நண்ணு with அண்ணு; நெருங்கு with அருங்கு; அரற்று with உரற்று; நளிர் with குளிர்; நிமை with இமை; நான் with யான் (अहं); நின் with உன்; நும் with உம். In Telugu *n* is much used euphonically. So in Tamil நர் or ஞர் = அர்: அறிஞர், உழுநர்.

4. அ (or அவ) prefixed to Sanskrit words is often privative: அமிர்தம், அவமானம்.

5. அ and ஆ are often = ఎ and ఏ in Telugu.

6. In words with அ in the final syllable, அ is nearly = எ. H. B. Introd. p. 16.

A very remarkable and extensive use of the pronominals அ, இ, உ, எ, ஒ can be traced in Tamil and the cognate languages. From them many verbs and nouns, besides other particles, are formed; and they are joined to stems as prefixes and suffixes constantly.

(1) அ (ஆ) points out, asserts, emphasises, connects. As a verb it is ஆ(கு) [T. A-vu]. As a pronoun அ-வன், அ-வர், அ-து. It belongs to the 3rd and 1st persons.

[என் and ஒம் = ஆன், ஆம், § 31.] As a *connective* it is a sign of the 6th case (G. 62); forms participles, etc. (G. 87); is a term. of neuter plurals, like *a* in Latin and α in Greek (G. 77); and takes ன், ல் to strengthen it. Thus அன், அல் arise. See ஆ|க்கு.

(2) இ (ஈ) has a similar office, but with an idea of nearness, closer connexion. As a verb it is ஈ(இடு), 'give.' As a pronoun இ-வன், இ-வள், இ-து. As a connective it takes ன், ல்: இன், இல். It belongs to the 2nd person, and fem. gen., where distinction is required. See ஈ|க்கு.

(3) உ in old Tamil is demonstrative, and indicates what stands between. உவன் = 'he who is between இவன் and அவன்.' It thus gets its connective force. With a nasal (ம் in Tam., N in T.) it is = 'and.' It is the root of words signifying 'possession, existence,' உள், உடை, etc.; and has been changed into ஊ (ஊடு = between), ஒ and ஓ (ஒடு, ஓடு).

(4) எ (ஏ, யா) is the particle of reference and interrogation; seeks out, brings up and exhibits the unseen; and so gives an idea of what is beyond, above. It is in all South-Indian languages at the basis of many words that indicate motion from a lower place to a higher. ஏ-டு, ஏ-று, எ-மும்பு [T. E-kku]. § 47.

(5) ஒ, ஓ have the idea of doubt, examination, comparison, unity. § 47. See verbal stem ஒ and numeral ஒன்று.

A comparison of verbal stems அ|டு, ஆ|டு, இ|டு, எ|டு, ஒ|டு, உ|டு, ஊ|டு, together with a multitude of other stems beginning with these pronominals, will show how much has grown out of them.

அஆ, alas! ஐயோ, 9. [Metre requires ஆஅ.]

K. அக AGA = *in*, உள்.

I. அகம், the interior. [T., M.] Comp. அங்கை (அகங்கை), அகடு. S. अहं = I.

= உள்ளம், within: அகத்து for 7th case [G. 152]; 106, 126, 331, 337, 360. Opposed to புறத்து,—'inwardly:' 308. = இல், house: 303; 318, all the house. அகத்தார் = those within, 31 [G. 93]. In வையகம் almost redundant: (see வை) 80; and in இல்லகம், 361.

II. அக|டு, centre: நடு.

அகடுற = நடுவுநிலைமையாக = சாயாமல்நடுவுற, so as to remain in one stay, firmly centred, 2. Nig. அகடென்ப நடுவே குக்ஷி.

In T., C., M. the word means 'insolence,' etc. (S. अघस्.)

III. அக|ல் = breadth, width, expanse.

(C., M. In T. *agalu* = *pagalu*, be broken.)

IV. அக|ல், அகலு, *v.* [§ 56. (III)] expand; be removed.

The causal is அகற்று. [§ 160, G. 103.]

அகன்று, spreading, 166 [G. 86]. அகன்ற, widely diffused: (see கண்) 340 [G. 87]. அகன்ற is often contracted into ஆன்ற, q. v. அகல்வானம், the wide heaven: 137 [G. 153], 150, 151 [G. 39], 354, 372. அகலம், *n.* 1. width; hence 2. the chest, breast (of a man), 389, 392. 3. A full, paraphrastic commentary, 319. Comp. *Nannūl*, 21–23: விரிவு, விரித்தியுரை, வர்த்தகம்.

V. அக|ழ், *v.* (§ 57) dig, extend by digging.

(Hence, by contraction, ஆழ், ஆழம், தாழ், and அழுத்து): 150.

அக்கு = அக்குமணி, சங்குமணி, armlets of conch-shell, 123.
Nig. அக்கென்ப விடைமுரிப்புஞ் சங்குமணியும் ஆகும்.

அங்கை = அகங்கை, palm of the hand, 123: உள்ளங்கை.
See *Nannūl*, 222.

அக்காரம், sugar, 112, 206, 374.

A cor. of S. शर्करा, sugar. In common Tamil சர்க்கரை and சக்கரை. It would almost seem, looking at S. meaning 'pebble, fragment,' as if கல்கண்டு were the same; but see S. खण्ड. 'Jaggery' = coarse sugar (வெல்லம்) is another form of the same. It is even softened into அமிரம், அமிர்.

Nig. அக்காரம் வெல்லம் புடைவை.

(1. Sugar; 2. cloth (S. अंशुक). T. *achchu, achchanamu.*)

K. அங்கணம், a gutter, drain, 175. [S. अंगण.]

K. அஃகு, diminish, 12. See அல்கு.

அஃது = அது, 39, 61, 250, 251, etc. [G. 12.]

அசா, feebleness, 201.

Seems = அசைவு = தளர்ச்சி, the affliction of poverty. [Comp. அசதி, அயர்தி, அயர்வு.]

K. அசை AÇAI = S. चल्, *agitation.*

[T. *asi;* C. *asiyu, asungu.* Comp. S. असि = a sword, and the idea of 191, 'vibrate as a sword.' This points to S. अस् = shine. So Lat. *mico.*]

அசை, *v.* = தளர், be unsteady, waver. (§ 57.)

அசைந்த [G. 95] = அசைந்தவை = தளர்ந்தசெய்திகள் = ஒழுக்கத்தின் வேறுபட்டன, things not fixed on the firm basis of virtue. [So 'shaky things.']

அசையாது = தளராமல், unwavering, 194.

அசை|வு = தளர்ச்சி, 150: 'in time of distress.' [G. 94.]

K. அச்சு, the axle (of a carriage), 48. [T., M., C.; S. अक्ष.]

K. அஞ்சு, அச்சு, AÑJ, ACH, AJ. [M., C., T. Comp. S. यज्, GR. ἄγ-, ἅζ-.]

அஞ்சு, fear, dread, shrink from. (§ 62.)

74, 87, 88, 172, 256, 297, 396. Generally with a moral idea. [Comp. பயம், உட்கு.]

அச்சம், dread, 145, 299; 81–84, guilty fear. (§ 190.)

S. அ|ஞ்|ஞானம், un-wisdom, folly, 311. See ஞானம்.

K. அட ADA, '*descent, repression, inclusion.*' See S. अधस्.

I. அட|ங்கு, learn self-restraint; subside, sink down; cease, 74, 116, 171.

II. அட|க்கு, repress, hide, bury. (§ 62.)

அடக்குப, 351, they will restrain, controul, repress. [G. 83.] 26, bury = புதை. [G. 86.] 105, 196; 221, keep it hidden; 229. Often with உள்.

III. அட|க்கம், self-restraint; modesty; humility; 65, 170, 242. Comp. ஒடுக்கம், செறிவு.

[With this root comp. அடி, அடு, அடை, உடை, ஒடு, ஒது|ங்கு, அணை; S. √धा with its compounds, and Lat. *con-do, ab-do,* etc. The Tamil ட often represents the S. ध.

In T. AḌ-agu, AḌ-aṅgu; AḌ-ampu, AḌ-apu; AḌ-akuva (or AṆ-akuva). Here √AṆ = AḌ, by interchange of cerebrals.

☞ In South-Indian languages the cerebrals are often interchangeable. The T. √ANA = Tamil அணை. In M. the √ is AḌU (comp. AṆA). In C. the √ is AḌA or AṆA.]

அட|கு, greens, vegetables: இலை(க்கறி) 207, 217, 289.
In this sense found in Tamil only = what is boiled.

அடம்பு [அடம் = wandering, + பூ], a kind of creeper: *convolvulus grandiflorus*. It has large white flowers, which the swans attack as rivals.

அடம்பம்பூ, its flower, 107. [M.]

K. அ|டு AḌ|U, *nearness*.

I. அடு, *v.* (§ 64) approach. [Comp. அண்டு, அண்டை.]
['அடுத்துமுயன்றாலும், though you do your best.' *Mū.*] அடுத்தடுத்து, with increasing vehemence, 203, 348.

II. அடு|க்கு, *v.* (§ 62) pile one upon another.
100, அடுக்கல், a piling up. [G. 94.] 203, mountains piled on mountains.

III. அடு, cook, kill: சமை. (§ 68.)
68, 114, 116, 271, 289, 363, 382. அடாஅ = அடாத, whose hearths are cold, 94.

அடு|ப்பு, hearth, 94.

அட்டில், cook-house. 363, = சமையல்வீடு. [அட்டு as *n.* = cooked food + இல், house.] [T., M., C.]

IV. அடை (§§ 57, 64) draw near; take shelter; attain unto; be closed.
[அடை used as a noun = இடம், இடை. The idea is seen in T. 89:

'அருளினை நெஞ்சத் தடைகொடா தான்,
The man who gives not a place in his soul to benevolence.']

அடையாவாம், are not *closed* against—with 4th case, 91. அடைக்குமாம், will *be closed* against—with 4th case, 271. Here transitive is used for intransitive. அல்லல் அடையப்பட்டார், those whose ill fate it was to see misfortune *draw nigh*, 287. When the guilt of the old deed *has come home*, 123. Intimate associates, friends that have gathered around, 173. Connected with, under the *shelter of*, 178. To those that have *taken shelter*, 202. Until they attain to, gain, reach, 204. அடை|வு, the *resorting* unto = அடைதல், 54. அடைத்திருந்து, with closed doors, 271.

அண் AṆ, *near; high*. [Comp. அண்ணு, அணுகு; நண்ணு, நணுகு.]

I. அணை, *v.* (§ 64) tie: கட்டு, சேர்த்துக்கட்டு, 192.
n. a dam: அணைக்கட்டு, 231. A pillow, mattress: மெத்தை, சயனம், 394.
Nig. அணை என்ப மெத்தை கரையே.

K. II. அண|ங்கு, *n.* = affliction, = துன்பம்: 14, 241.
Nig. அணங்கு நோய் அழகு தெய்வம் ஆசை பெண் கொலை வருத்தம்.

[Comp. S. अनङ्ग = काम. But the South-Indian √*aṇ* indicates hostile approach. In Jī. Chin. I. iv. 128 (p. 46) we find 'கச்சலாமுலையார்க்கணங்காகிய சச்சந்தன் . . . , J., who was as *kāman* (?) to women.']

K. III. அண் | ணு, *v.* [§§ 56 (I), 66] = மேனோக்கு, அங்கா, lift up the head to look.

With நோக்கி = gazing upwards, 31.

IV. அணி(மை), nearness.

அணியர், 218, 261, those who are near. Comp. அண்மு, அண்மை, அண்ணு, அண்டு, அண்டை, அணவு, அணை.

V. அணி, 'beauty' [for 'beautiful'].

1. *n.* 161. அழகிய. 290, 374, 392.
2. *v.* (§ 57) 251, put on, adorn oneself with: பூணு. [G. 89.]
389. [வி. தொ. G. 153.]

அணிகலம் = ஆபரணம்: 242. [கலம். Comp. மணி, and S. √अणि. In M. as in Tamil. In C. = '*order*.' K. 575. T. 52. N.N.V. 13.]

VI. அண் as a formative = இடம்: see நடுவண், 114.

K. அதர். [Comp. அகழ். S. अधर. In some uses from அதறு. Only in Tamil, but *dar|i*, *dār|i* in Telugu.] = வழி: path, public road, 192.

Nig. அதர் [1] வழி [2] புழுதி ஆட்டின் [3] அதரு நண் [4] மணைலும் ஆமே.

K. அது, அஃது. [√அ. G. 71.] அதன், 197. அதனை, 276, 363. அதனல், 110, 293. அதற்கு, 81. அதன்கண், 326. அது = அத்தன்மை, 15, 276. அவற்றினும், 89.

Observe அது as a termination forming neuter nouns, or quasi-verbs, from adjectives: தொல்லை = ancient; தொல்லை(ய)து = (it is) that which is ancient [G. 93]. In this use து or த்து is found for அது.

அத்து = துவர், சிவப்பு, a red dye, 281.

Nig. அத்தென்ப அரைஞாண் செம்மை அசைச்சொலோடி சைப்பு நாற்பேர்.

அந்தோ, alas! (See அன்னே.) = அதோ nasalized. [G. 117.] 394.

அபகாரம், injury, 69. [S. अप + कृ. Comp. உபகாரம்.]

அபராநம், அபராணம், afternoon: பிற்பகல், 207. [S. अपर + अह्न (अहन्) = பின்னேரம்.]

அமர் AMAR [= அமை. Both forms in M.—T. C. *amar*. Comp. சமர்], *rest.*

K. அமர், *v.* (§ 60).

Lovingly, 1. Where she delights to dwell, 383. Whom they fondly love [G. 153], 392. அமரார் = தம்மிடத்து விருப்பமில்லார், பகைவர், those who love us not, 206.

K. அமரர், immortals, gods, 373. [S. अ + मृ.]

Nig. அமரரே விபுதர் தெவ்வர்.

K. அமிழ்து = ambrosia, 200, 210, 217.

[S. अमृत, where ழ் = ऋ. In many forms. அமிழ்தம், அமிருதம், அமிர்தம், அமிர்து, அமுதம், அமுது, அமரி, மருந்து. Comp. K. 82, சாவா மருந்து.]

அமை AMAI, *satisfy*. [This seems a form of சமை=S. शम्, श्रम्. M. *amey*. Comp. அமர், a variation of it. Also சமி, சமழ். அமையம்=சமயம்.]

K. அமை, *v.* (§§ 57, 64).

ஆன்ற அமைந்தார், 54. With ஆய்ந்து and காய்ந்த=thoroughly, fully, 63. அமை|வு, fitness: things agreeable to one's profession, 135. We are utterly at rest, 182. One who is pleasing; provided for food, 240. Possessing in full measure, 361.

அம் AM.

K. அம்=அழகு, beauty. [Nig. அம்மழகசைச்சொனீராம்.]

அங்|கண் (மாஞாலம்), 148, 151, 176, 194, 373.

அம்|மருங்கு, 396 (? 14).

அங்|கோடு, 372: in all these அம்=beautiful.

அம்பல்=பழிமொழி, scandal, evil report. [? அம்பலம்.] 87.

Nig. அம்பலே பழிச்சொல் சில்லோர் அறிந்தலர் தூற்றலாமே.

K. அம்பு, an arrow: கணை, சரம், எவு, பாணம், 89, 152.

[T., M., and C. Nig. அம்பு நீர் புயல் வேய் எவரம். Here the first two meanings are from S. अम्बु, water; the other two seem to be the word for *bambu*, perhaps வம்பு.]

அம்ம, 395. [See *Nannūl*, 370.] A meaningless expletive. Probably a voc. of அம்மை. [G. 116.]

அம்மா, 173. Probably voc. of அம்மை, a stronger form of அம்ம: a particle indicating surprise or emotion: 'Ah, do so!' [G. 117.]

அம்மனை=தாய், அம்மை, அம்மன், அம்மாள், 14. [S. अम्बा. But it may be அம்+மனை=அழகுள்ள மனைவியினுடைய.]

அய் AY. [Comp. ஐ=subtileness.]

K. அயர்=செய் (§ 57) perform, 16. [G. 153.]

அயல்=adjacency.

அயன்மனை யிலுள்ளார், அயலார், the neighbours, 87.

[T. 10: 'பாத்தூண்ணுந் தன்மையிலாரயலிருப்பு, residence near those who do not share their food with guests.']

அயிராணி, the wife of Indra: இந்திரன்றேவி, 381.

The reference is to the story given in Muir's Sanskrit Texts, vol. i. p. 310, *etc.*

Cor. of S. इन्द्राणि: some confusion with அயிராவணம், Indra's white elephant.

அயில்=கூர்மை, keenness; keen-edged, 386.

Nig. அயில் என்ப வேலே கூர்மை.

K. அர் AR, *rare, precious*. [அரி, அரு, அரும், ஆர். M. Comp. S. अर्ह्. G. 121. H. B. § 131. *e*.]

K. அரு|ள், grace, favour, benevolence. தயை, கருணை, கிருபை: 7, 273, 321.

அருளில் கூற்று, merciless Yaman, 20.

அருளு, (*v.*) regard with favour, 390. [G. 137.]

அரு|ம், *hard to* (obtain, bear up against, *etc.*), 9, 34, 40, 57, 381. That *scarce* may (perish), 137, 226, 241, 249, 316. A *sore* (disease), 173, 295, 363.

அரி|யார், those whom it is *hard* to (abandon), 162, 224, 226.

அரி|து, 74, 76, 109, 161, 184, 244, 352, 353. (It *rarely* or *never* occurs.) அரியது, 361.

அரி|ய, (things) *hard* to . . ., 77, 282, 317.

அரி|யர், *hard* (to find), 77, 165=choice spirits.

அரு|மை, because of the *impossibility* of, 56. Impregnable, 164.

[N. M. K. 36: '. . . . . . தேரின்,—
அரிய அரியவற்றுற் கொள்ப—பெரிய
பெரியாரன் எய்தப் படும்.

If you look closely, precions things by precious things men buy; and *great things by the great are won!*']

ஆருயிர், dear life, precious life, 238, 330.

அரக்கு. Comp. அரத்தம்.

1. Red: செவ்விய, 396. 2. Gum-lac.

[Comp. S. रक्त = लक्त. M. *arukku.* T. *era.* C. *arugu.*]

Nig. அரக்கென்ப மெழுகு கள்ளின் விகற்பமுஞ் சிவப்பும் ஆகும்.

S. அரசன்=king, 134.

[S. राजन्. See K. under அரசு.]

Nig. அரசனே வியாழம் மன்னும்.

அரவு, 400. அரவம்.

K. அரண்=காவல், stronghold, 164. [Comp. S. शरणं; அரணம். Also அர்.]

Nig. அரணம் கவசங்காடே அணிமதில்வேலிராற்பேர்.

அரா, 241: a serpent: பாம்பு.

Nig. அரவம் நாபுரம் பாம்போசை.

Words which are undoubtedly identical in origin with Sanskrit words are often so changed in the South-Indian or 'Drāviḍian' languages, by the operation of well-ascertained phonetic laws, that they would hardly be recognised by any one unacquainted with the tendencies of the Tamil phonetic system.

Thus in Sanskrit we have सृप् (from सृ), सर्प्, and ultimately √सृ.

The verbal roots *çari*, *çar*, *çarru* are found in all the Drāviḍian dialects, in both ancient and modern forms, with the same original notion of 'gliding' and 'slipping.'

But the equivalents of the Sanskrit noun सर्प (*serpens*, *ἑρπετόν*) in Tamil are curious. These are *çarppam*, *çarubam*, *aravam*, *aravu*, *arā*, and *arai* (சர்ப்பம், சருபம், அரவம், அரவு, அரா, அரை).

The following principles are here illustrated :—

1. Tamil cannot tolerate, as a general rule, the sound of mute and liquid together. It rejects consonantal diphthongs : *rp* must become *rup*, *rap*, or *rip*.

2. When *k*, *t*, or *p* (any tenuis) begins any syllable of a word except the first, it becomes, in order, *g*, *th* (as in 'this'), or *b* (i.e. the *tenuis* is changed into its corresponding *media*): thus *çaruppam* becomes *çarubam*.

3. The Tamil has neither any real sibilant nor aspirate ; (ச is really a soft palatal :) thus *çarupam* may become *arubam ;* and through the influence of *u* we have *v* for *b* (so Sanskrit सभा is in Tamil *avai*). Sanskrit स may be dropped in Tamil, or ச may be used for it.

(In Canarese for 'serpent' we have *hāva ;* this is in Telugu *pāmu*, in Tamil *pāmbu*, and in Tuḍa *pāb.*)

4. Final *m* is constantly dropped in Tamil, and the remaining vowel is written *u*, but is pronounced very faintly. Thus *aravam* is now *aravŭ*.

5. By syncope and crasis *aravu* becomes *arā*, and final *ā* is often changed into *ai* or *a*. Thus *arai* is a Tamil form of S. सर्प.

அர | ற்று (§ 62) = இரற்று.

1. Cry : அழு. 2. Reiterate foolishly: கத்து, 41. 3. Reverberate: ஆரவாரி, 249. [Comp. S. रु. இரை, அலறு, அலட்டு ; அறை.]

Nig. அரற்றலே அழுகை ஓசை. (சத்தம், ஒலி.)

அரி = 1. சிங்கம், a lion. [S. हरि.]

அரிமா = a lion, 141, 152, 198. [See மா.] Nig. gives thirty-two meanings.

2. See under அர்.

அரிசி, rice unboiled, 94. [In M. *ari*. From √ARI, reap.]

அரு | கு, *n*. [for அருவு. M., C., T.], the neighbourhood. 234, அருகல், nearness + அது = what grows near: அணியது, 261.

[அரு | க்கு, diminish: T. 50: 'மழை அருக்குங் கோள், a star that lessens the rain.']

S. அருத்தம் = பொருள், wealth, 304.

Nig. அருத்தமே பொருள் பொன்பாதி.

It represents two Sanskrit words, अर्ध (= *half*) and अर्थ (= *substance*).

K. அரும்பு, a flower-bud. √அரு, 390, 400. [In K. also. அரும் + பூ.]

அரு | வி, a water-fall. [In M. Comp. S. रु, री, रव. The idea seems to be *that which resounds*.]

கோதையருவி, a cascade like a garland on the brow of the hill, 71. ஒல்லெனருவி, 77. ஓங்கருவி, 79. ஆர்க்குமருவி, 161. கறங்கருவி, 228, 285. பொங்கருவி, 231. வாலருவி, 232. நீர்த்தருவி, 290. பாயருவி, 307. பிறங்கருவி, 343. இலங்கருவி, 344. மணிவரன்றி வீழுமருவி, 369.

அருள், see அர்.

அரை, half, middle. [Comp. s. अर्ध. M. *ara*. T. *ara*. C. *arai*.]

Stem, trunk of a tree, 246. The waist, 281.

அரோ, a mere expletive: ர் is euphonic.

See *Nannūl*, 373. [G. 116.] 211, 239, 266, 386.

அல் AL.

அலகு=எண், computation. In this sense found only in T. Comp. அள.

எண்ணுங்கருவி, shells used in computation, 22.

அலகுசாற்கற்பு, infinite learning, 140.

Nig. அலகுகெற்கதிரோயாதி பலகறைநுளம் பெண்ணேதி.

அல|வன், a crab: ஞண்டு, நண்டு, ஞெண்டு; கர்க்கடம், கர்க்கடகம், கடகம், 123. The √ seems to be அல்= *night*.

Its meanings are four (='he of the night'): 1. a crab, coming out of its hole by night; 2. the sign cancer; 3. the moon; 4. a cat, having claws like a crab. See *Nannūl*, எழுத்தியல், 36—a curious old bit, worth study—

'ஆஅ அளிய அலவன்றன் பார்ப்பினோ
டூஇர் இரையுங்கொண் டீர் அளைப் பள்ளியுட்
டேக் திரை அலேப்பத் துஞ்சா திறைவன்றோண்
மேவ வலேப்பட்ட நம்போ னறுநுதால்!
இ ஓ உழக்குந் துயர்.

THE FORSAKEN WIFE.

Ah! the loving crab with its young ones, sharing its dripping food, in its wet hollow chamber, amid the buffeting of the foam-besprinkling waves, sleepless, agitated with desire for its lord's embrace, suffers affliction as I do,—Alas!—O thou of fragrant brow.'

அலறு [an imitative word: அல்+அல்+து. See 25. In M. Comp. அரற்று, அழு], lament aloud, 20, 25, 29.

அலரி=flower=அலர்=மலர், 199.

Nig. அலரி கண்வரி அருக்கன் அழகொருமரம் பூவாமே.

[It is from *v.* அலர்+இ='that which unfolds, expands, shines forth.' Hence 1. FLOWER; 2. the oleander; 3. the sun; 4. beauty-lines in the eye; and 5. beauty in general. See T. √ALAR.]

அலி=பேடி, an hermaphrodite, 85. [√அல்=not. The s. न|पुंस.]

K. அலே. [M., T., C. as noun and verb in many forms. Comp. அல|மரு, அல|மந்தேன்.]

(*n.*) a wave,=திரை, 107, *v.* (§ 64). Cause to wave, agitate, 47, 128, 194, 224, 391. Distress by rivalling, 287.

[T. 50: 'குடியலேக்கும் வேந்தன், a king who afflicts his people.']

அல், not. (§§ 43, 44.) See அன். Comp. K. and G. 125.

அல்லால் (அல்லாமல், அல்லது), 21, 69, 105, 120, 130, 140, 303, 304, 309 'except.' ['என்னையலாற் பிறர்கள்யாரே, who but me?' Jī. Chin. i. 230.] அன்றி (as if from √அன்று = 'exclude'), 58, 70 'besides,' 287, 342. அன்று, it is not, 1, 77, 143, 165, 212, 223, 249, 258, 261, 299, 302. அல்லது, 76, 142, 177, 212, 265 'except.' அல்ல, they are not, not, 118, 131, 134, 370, 371. As noun: 'things which are not,' 171. அல்லா, are not, 236, 395. அல்லா = அல்லாத, 321.

அல்லர், அல்லார், 108, 112, 181, 221, 225, 236, 303, 379.

அல்லாதார் is the full form, 268.

அனையரல்லர், 'they are not as . . .,' 245.

அலான், 273. அன் | மை, 229, 262, 'absence of.' Comp. இன்மை.

[Looking at the use of T. *gā-ka* = அல்லாமல், from *a-vu* = ஆகு, I feel inclined to think that அல் = ஆகல், employed in the negative mood: so that அன்று = ஆகாதது = T. *kāthu*. Neither அல் nor இல் has primarily a negative meaning. See இல்.]

அல் | கு, *v.* grow less: அஃகு.

அல்குநிழல், the shadows of declining day, 166.

அல்குல், an immodest word, 354, 372.

K. அல் | லல், suffering, want, privation:

வறுமை, poverty, 170, 252, 287.

S. அவத்தம் [for அபத்தம்] = பயனில்லாமல், unprofitably.

[S. अबद्ध = unbound. Confounded with அவம்.]

S. அவ | மதிப்பு = disrespect, 163. .

[S. अव + मन्, अवमत. See மதி.]

அவன் [அ + அன்], he, that man.

அவன், 155. அவனே, such a man, 307. அவனை, 273. அவற்கு, 23, 158. அவன், 136, அவர், அவரை, 67. அவரோடு, அவரின்முன், 117, 209. அவரவர், 103. அவரின், than, 227 (fifth case). அவர்க்கு, 374.

K. அவா AVĀ, an imitative word, from அஆ.

1. அவா (அவாவு) = ஆசை, வேட்கை, intense desire, 59, 181.

2. அவா | வு, *v.* (§ 62) desire.

அவாய் = அவாவி, *leaning to* the female side, 251.

அவாத்தக்க = அவாவத்தக்க, such as eyes covet, 251.

Comp. H. B. § 70*.

[*Ēlā.* 12: 'அவாவறுக்கலுற்றான் றளரான், அவ்வைந்தின்
அவாவறுப்பின் ஆற்ற அமையும; — அவாவறான்
ஆகும் அவன்; ஆயின், ஐங்களிற்றினூற்றுண்டு
போகும் புழையுட் புகுந்து.

He who has cut off desire stands fast! If he cut off desires of the five (senses) fully shall he be filled with good. He who cuts not off desire shall be subject to vanity! (அவன் from அவம், "vanity.") If so, dragged away by the fivefold elephant (five senses) he shall go to enter the abyss (hell).'

Jī. Chin. xiii. 14: 'கற்சிறை அழித்து வெள்ளங் கடற்கவாயாங்கு. (கடற்கு அவாய ஆங்கு.)
As the flood sweeping away the stone dam seeks the sea.']

அவி AVI, *soften.*

அவி, *v. n.* [and *a.*] (§ 56. I) =அடங்கு, soften, abate, become extinguished. Comp. அவிழ்.

Whose crest *has been lowered*, 66. After the roar *has died away*, 332.

K. அவிர், *v.* (§ 60) glisten; *glittering* rays, 89. [G. 153.]

Nig. அவிர்தலே யொளிபிறற்பேர்.

அவிழ், *v. n.* and *a.*, loosen, expand. [Comp. அவி.] (§ 56. I.)

Have been *loosed*, 12. [G. 83.] A garland of *opening* buds, 390. [G. 153.]

K. அவை=சபை (சவை in *Mū.*), assembly, 325. [S. सभा.] [See also அது.]

அவையறிதல, knowledge requisite for the அவை. Ch. xxxii.

In K. அவை is the 'council of state;' here it is the 'learned assembly.' Comp. கோட்டி.

K. அவ்வியம்=பொறாமை, மனக்கோட்டம், அழுக்காறு (ஔவியம்), the pure in heart, 322.

அழ் AṞ [=*perish.* In M. 'be expended,' see அழி, அழல், அணங்கு].

I. அழல், fire: நெருப்பு, அக்கினி, வெப்பம், heat, 89, 124, 202.

[Comp. அனல், அனலம், அழனம், தழல். S. अनल. Comp. अर्क. In M. T.]

II. அழ|கு, beauty: வனப்பு=adornment, 131. [√எர், எழில். Comp. EL, 2, 24, 75; and நீதி, 13. In M.—அழகு seems hardly a classical word=குழகு. Comp. अर्घ.]

K. அழி (§ 57) perish; go to ruin, 147, 272, 293 [கற்பு]. Lose, 105, 252, 309. Waste away, 141. Fall into despair, 33. Die, 302, for அழிந்து [G. 41]. (§ 64) destroy, 92, 129, 238 [கட்டு].

K. அழு (§ 60) weep aloud, 397.

[Comp. S. अश्रु, அலறு, கதறு. In M.]

அழு|ங்கு=1. அழுந்து, sink down; 2. கெடு, be injured, sullied, destroyed, 111, 300, 353. [Seems confounded with மழுங்கு.]

Comp. T. 95: 'அறிவழுக்கத் தின்னும் பசிநோயும், மாந்தர்
செறிவழுக்கத் தோன்றும் விழைவும் . . . .

The disease of hunger that eats so as to injure the intellect, and the avarice that destroys the attachment of men.'

அழு|கு (§ 62) rot away. Comp. அழி, அளி. 123. [In M.]

அழு|த்து=பதி (§ 64) set in, inlay (jewels in gold), 347.

[Comp. அகழ், ஆழ். § 160. K. has the intransitive form அழு|ந்து.]

அள் AḶ, *measure.* [M. In C. the idea is *contiguity.* Comp. அண்.]

K. அள, *v.* (§ 66) measure, 7, 103 (int. or pass.).

[Jī. Chin. i. 184: 'அளந்தன போகம் எல்லாம் அவரவர்க் கற்றை நாளே;
அளந்தன வாழு நாளும்:
On that self-same day all his enjoyments were meted out to each one; his days of life, too, were meted out.']

அள|வு, a measure, 81, 91, 323, 330.

இயைந்த அளவினல் in 272 = உளவரையால் in 271. Comp. 36.

சொல்லளவு, a mere empty name, 195.

With rel. part. = until, up to, 190, 209. (With எல்லாம், உம். See வரை, வகை.)

K. அளாவு, *v.* mingle. (Comp. அளை.)

அளாய = அளாவிய, commingled: a variation of அள, 177, 240.

K. அள்ளு, *v.* take by handfuls, 262. [M.]

K. அளி, tenderness, kindness, gentle-minded, 355.

[The root idea is *mellowness, softness*, decay. Comp. அழி, அழுகு, which in C. have *ḷ*. Comp. also அலி, எளி, எழ், இள; and S. ली.]

Commentator says அளி = எழுமை or எளிமை, 15; but அளி = அன்பு; and comp. K. 336.

அளியர், 'poor persons;' or, condescendingly, 'worthy good souls,' 298. அளி, *v.* (§ 57). அளிய, so that the hearer is crushed, 219: நெஞ்சுநோவ, நையும்படி.

Nig. அளியென்ப கறவும் வண்டும் அன்பொடு கொடையு(ம்) நாற்பேர்.

அற் ARR, *cut, cease.*

I. K. அறம் (அறன்), virtue, charity; [√ARR = *cut, decide.* In M. = law. In ancient C. *aravu* = justice = தருமம். See my *Kurraḷ*, p. 196.]

நல்லறம், 7, 10, 19, 32, 36, 82, 158, 165, 190, 321, 330, 338. அறவினை, 29, 326, 332. அறத்துப்பால், the part which treats of virtue; i.e. ch. i–xiii. அறன்வலியுறுத்தல், ch. iv. அறப்பயன், the aid of charity, 38, 99. சிற்றறம், 272. அறநெறி, 118, 172. அறத்தாறு, 257, 322: the path of virtue.

II. K. அறி, *v.* (§ 57) know. [T. *eru.* M. and C. *ari.* √ARR. Comp. அறு.]

அறிஞர் (ஞர் = உடையவர்), 183. அறிந்தார், 229. அறிவாம் [K. 36] [G. 83], we will know, attend to, do, 19, 328, 332. அறிதும் [G. 83] 272. அறிவது [G. 95], what one should know, 74, 108. அறிந்து [G. 86] 74, 158, 255, 384, 395. அறிய [G. 140] 78, 86, 204. அறியாமை, 333.

அறியா = { 1. அறிந்து [G. 86, H.B. § 97].
2. அறியாத [G. 91] 163, 171, 257.

அறியார், 313 = { 1. they know not, 48, 380.
2. those who know not, 108, 344.

அறிந்தும் [G. 141] 108, 213. அறிவார், those who know, 61, 73, 140. அறிவர், 282. அறியாதார், 275. அறியாது [G. 90] 331. அறிதிர், you would know [G. 83] 106, 252. அறி|தல்

[G. 94] 317. அவையறிதல், ch. xxxii. அறி|வு, wisdom [G. 94] 16, 139, 193, 196, 249, 258, 262, 367. அறிவாளர், 254. அறிவுநூல், books of wisdom, 140. அறிவினவர் [G. 93] 162, 187, 137, 301, 351. அறிவில்லார், 304. அறியேன், 399. அறிந்திலிர் (see இல்), 165. அறிந்த, 171, 380. அறியின் [G. 84] 172. அறியப்பட்டது, 212. அறிவின்மை, ch. xxvi. அறிவுடைமை, ch. xxv. With கல், 56, 133, 138, 211, 256. (See கல்.) திண்ணறிவு, 27, 227. சிற்றறிவு, 329. பேரறிவு, 173. நல்லறிவு, 11, 187, 254, 320. With நன்று, நன்றி, 257. புல்லறிவு, 8, 121, 239, 320, ch. xxxiii. காரறிவு, 311. வெள்ளறிவு, 375.

III. Adj. form of ஆறு, six [H. B. § 172], 1.

IV. (*v.* tr. § 64.) [Comp. வறு. From அல்; so இறு from இல். In M., C., T.] Sever, cut off. Remove, cut the bonds of, 132. அறுக்ககிலலாவாம், are destitute of power to divest themselves of, 352. [கு is inserted.]

V. (*v.* intr. § 68.) Be severed, cease, fail. [Opp. to உறு.]

[Comp. உறு and அறு in the following :

'அற்ற குளத்தின் அறுநீர்ப் பறவைபோல்
உற்றுழித் தீர்வார் உறவல்லர் ; அக்குளத்திற்
கொட்டியும் ஆம்பலும் நெய்தலும் போலவே
ஒட்டி உறுவார் உறவு.

Those are not *friends* who withdraw when you *suffer want*, like water-birds who forsake the tank when its waters *fail;* they are *friends* who stick by you, like the water-lilies in that tank.' *Mū.*]

அறுநீர், a failing spring [G. 153] 275 (=term. '*less*'), 157, 260, 333: with வழி, சுவழி, and மை. அறும் இடத்தும், even when it dries up, 185. (§ 85.) அறும், will fail, 370, 371. அற, when . . . fails, 370. In 371, அற்றகண்ணே; 150, அற்றக்கடைத்தும், even when it has failed. Added to noun = '*without*,' 8, 371. அறஉண்ணும், drink *up*, 382. அற = excessively, 311. Fully, 26. அற்றன, they have been severed, 12. (§ 70*.) அற்று, 150: 'in destitution.' அற்றார், 342. [Comp. 260.] அறினும், when it is severed, cut, = அற்றாலும் (§ 100), 41.

Neg. அறார், cease not to have, 351. அறு (= அறுது), 116; (= அறுமல்), 310.

VI. அற்றம் = வறுமை, destitution, poverty, 78.

VII. அறை, *v.* sound ; strike.

[S. रव = அரவம். Comp. அரற்று. √ARR, cut. T. has ARA = room. C. ARAI = அரை and அறை. M. ARRA.]

அறைகடல், the resounding sea [G. 153] 230. பறையறைந்து, having *struck* the drum, 86, 392. *n.* = பாறை, a rock, 360.

Nig. அறை முறை மோதல் பாறை திரை சிற்றின் மொழி ஆறுமே.

அற்பு for அன்பு, 12. [G. 41.]

[So in T. 86: 'அற்புப் பெருந்தளை யாப்பு நெகிழ்ந்தொழிதல் ;
The relaxation and rupture of the mighty bond of love.']

அற்று, see அன்.

அ|ன் AN, *such*. See அ.

K. அன், அனை [so இன், என் ; இனை, எனை ; these are treated as குறிப்புவினை. G. 93], such, of that kind.

அன்|னது, 41, 87. அன்|ன, 12. Like to, such = ஒத்த, 16, 44, 66, 101, 104, 138, 186, 192, 211, 237, 262, 269, 381, 392, 400. அன்னார், அன்னூர், 96, 176, 305, 330, 360, 373, 374, 375. அற்று is another form of அன்னது (அன் + து), 136. 8, 211, 240, 254, 257, 331, 332, 336, 386. These forms are added to the வினையெச்சம், used for the பெயரெச்சம்: thus இருந்தற்று, it is as though (a dog) seated itself. அன்|னும், thou who art as . . . , 225.

அனை is a strengthened form of அன் (but see K. lex.). அனைத்து = so much as, such-like, so, 239, 270, 329, 344, 374, 386, 390. மனைத்தனையர், இனைத்தனையர், 'they are as . . .,' 245. அனையவும், all, 104. அனையம், 'we are as . . .,' 388. அனையார், 'those who are like,' 213, 216, 218, 388. [For the construction see my *Kurraļ*, Introd. p. xxiv. § 10. Comp. use of T. *aṭṭu.*]

K. அன்பு, affection, love, 305, 321, 370, 371, 377.

In M. *ambu* or *anbu*. Seems connected with S. अम्बु = water. Comp. கரம் in both senses.

அன்|மை, see அல்.

அன்றில், a fabulous bird which is said never to survive its mate, 376. [அன்று + இல் = அதன்றால் இதுஇல்லை, *if that is not, this is not.*]

Nig. அன்றில் ஓர்புள்ளுமூல காவெள ஆம் இரண்டே.

அ|ன்று: I. see அல் = it is not.

II. = அந்நாள், on that day. So இன்று, என்று (பின்றை), 23, 36. (அ, இ, எ with ன் + று.)

அன்னம், 107. [S. हंस.] It is referred to in 135.

அன்றே. Comp. அந்தே. An interjection: *Alas!* 330. [G. 117.]

ஆ Ā.

ஆ Ā, see அ.

1. ஆ|கு, become, be, befit; profit. It is an auxiliary of very extensive use, often redundant.

[§ 58, *etc.* T. A-*vu* (KĀ). M. Tul. Ā|*pini.* C. A|*gu*, Ā|*p*, AH|*a*. Comp. S. आ + इ and या. Whatever may be the source of the word, its use in poetry has been influenced by the S. आयति = ஆகும்.]

1. *Inf.* ஆக = *as*, 1. Contracted into ஆ = as, 7, 28, 165. While there is, 86, 341, 344, 345, 346. ஒன்று, as though any one (of these faculties) existed, 143.

2. *Past adv. part.* ஆய் = ஆகி (§§ 40, 136, 137). 1, 3 = having become: 'as.' 23, 67, 122, 357, 361: though it be, or have, 367. ஆகி (§ 77), 329, 359.

3. *Adj. part.* ஆன (§ 74). ஆய = உண்டாகிய, 28, 37, 278, 334, 367. ஆஅய [G. 14] 184. ஆயக்கால், when it is: [கால், and § 97 *note*,] 241. ஆகிய, 14, 265.

4. *Verbal noun.* ஆதல், the becoming (§ 148), 286. ஆகல், 205. ஆகுதல், 240, 358.

5. *Future.* ஆவர், 112, 150; they will flourish (§ 72), 301. ஆகுவர், 124, 343, 349. ஆவார், 256. (Often such forms are redundant: § 151.) ஆவாம், we shall prosper, 32. ஆம், 73, 110, 347, 361. ஆம் redundant, 23, 112, 247, 348, 376, 380. ஆகும், 14, 17, 110, 129, 243, 257. ஆதும் (ஆதுாம், 181), 359. [G. 83. Comp. Telugu aorist, *avu-dunu.*] ஆவது, 5, it will serve; resulting benefit (§ 88), 17, 73, 242, 271.

6. *Past tense.* ஆயினள், she became, 376.

Past part. noun. ஆயின, things that became, 23. ஆயவர், 349. ஆகியான், ஆகியவர், ஆகியார் [G. 82, 95] 15, 124. ஆயார், those who are (foes), 52, 299. So ஆய = ஆனவை, 70.

7. ஆயின் (§ 95) if it be, 115, 229, 357, 362. The neg. is இல்லாயின், 126. யாம் ஆயின், for our part, 293. ஆனும், ஆயினும் (§ 100), 5, 38, 98, 115, 139, 147, 176, 186, 206, 329, 347, 350, 351, 355, 360. ஆனால், 15, 37.

8. *Imp.* ஆகுமின் [G. 84] 7.
9. *Neg.* ஆகா|த [G. 89] 104, 243, 337. ஆகா (= ஆகாத) 79.
10. With உண்டு (*which see*) 12, 337. With இல் (*which see*) 360. With உடைத்து 147.

II. ஆ|க்கு, *v. tr.* (§ 62) make, cause; kindle, 225; ஆக்கும், will cause, 124.

ஆக்கம், increase, 129, 301, 327. Wealth: செல்வம், 32, 275.

III. ஆ = a cow: ஆன், பசு, 101, 115, 118, 279. ஆமா, the wild cow [see மா], 319, 377. கற்று = கன்று + ஆ, a cow with a young calf. சேமா [see சே]. கடமா = காட்டுப்பசு or கட + மா = an elephant in rut, 300. [Comp. ஆவே, ஆன், மா, மான், மாடு.]

IV. ஆ is a direct interrogative [G. 6]. Sometimes யா (யார், யாது) = ஏ, 92.

V. ஆ is a neg. verb. term. இகவா [G. 91] 6, 97, 109, 110; and middle particle. Its use *in the negative* is fourfold: (1) finite verb: [G. 89] 4, 6, இகவா = இகவாது; (2) by apocope, for adv. part.: [G. 90] 5, 230, காவா = காவாமல்; (3) for adj. part.: [G. 91] 145, மாணா = மாணாத; (4) in verb. nouns (√ + ஆ + மை): 145.

VI. ஆ is a term. of positive adv. part. கல்லா = கற்று [G. 86] 14, 366.

VII. ஆ is an interjection. See அஆ, for ஆஅ, for ஆ! 9.

VIII. ஆ = ஆறு = way, manner. See I. 1.

IX. In the beginning of Sanskrit words ஆ (1) reverses the meaning, thus दा is *give*, and आदा is *take*; (2) expresses *up to*.

X. ஆ is a demonstrative. See அ.

(1) ஆ|ங்கு = அங்கே. [In T. *e*, *ē* are often used for *a*, *ā*: ĒL = ஆள், ĒḌ = அழு, ĒḌU = ஆண்டு, ERI = அறி, *etc.*]

There, 23, 193. There, then, and so, 28, 267. ஆங்கே = just so, 244. So, as, 38, 51, 79, 139, 179, 197, 280, 321, 322. [With neg. verb. part. உணராது for rel. part. உணராத. See K. Introd. p. xxiv. § 10.] Then, 120.

(2) ஆ|ண்டு = i. there, 35. [Comp. T. *vadda*.]

ஆ|ண்டை, adj. form of ஆண்டு: (see ஐ) 91, 271: 'the gate of Paradise.'

ii. a year, 351. [T. *ēḍu*. M. C. *ēḍu*, *ērru*.] iii. Comp. ஆள்.

ஆட் ĀḌ [see ஆள், ஆண்], *move*.

I. K. ஆடு, *v.* swing, oscillate; play, dance; move briskly. [§ 62. Comp. S. अट. M., T., C. Also in C. *māḍu*.]

மலை ஆடுமஞ்சு, a cloud *traversing* the hill-side, 28. இயங்கு. So மேல் ஆடு in 113. ஆடி உண்பா, will gain a subsistence by *dancing*: கூத்தாடு, 85, 191. கால் ஆடு, *be* actively *at work*, 113. மீது ஆடு, *move over—touch* lightly—superficially, 115. That *vibrates* at every touch, 192. As it *disports* itself, 240, 331. Bathe, ஆடிய [G. 86 = ஆடவிரும்பி, § 97] 332. ஆடுஉறும் = ஆடுவோம் [G. 83] 332, 387.

II. ஆட்டு (§ 160) grind in a mill, 35. [M. C. *āṭu*.]

ஆண், ஆண்மை, see ஆள்.

ஆணம் = love: அன்பு, 374. [Lit. *juice*. Comp. ஈரம் in its two uses. √ĀṆ, AṆ.]

['ஆணமில்பொருள் எமக்கு, to us lovelorn creatures.' *Kalit.* i.]

ஆம்பல், *n.* the red and white water-lily, 236, 396.

[Comp. S. अम्बु, water = ஆம். M., C.]

ஆமை, turtle, tortoise: கூர்மம், 331. [ஆம், comp. S. अम्बु. M. ĀMA. C. ĀME.]

ஆமை, ஆமல் [G. 90, 91].

எலாமை, 67, might be neg. verb. part., or neg. verb. noun (எலா + மை).

ஆய் ĀY. [Āy, āyi, āyu. M., C.]

I. See ஆ|கு.

II. Term. 2 pers. sing.: செய்த|ாய். G. 77.

III. Voc. ending, 126: பிள்ள|ாய். G. 64.

IV. *v.* (§ 57). Investigate, enquire closely, seek out, cull, care for. [Comp. √ ஐ, அய். M. = *cull*. C.] 26, 37, 63, 393. ஆய்நலம், *choice* excellence, [G. 153] 339. ஆய் இழை, an *exquisite* jewel, 372.

Hence ஆராய் [intensive of ஆய். M. ĀRĀY. C. ĀREI. See ஆர்] 135, 196. Ch. xxii. கட்பாராய்தல்.

V. (*n.*) Mother: தாய், 400. [C. ĀYI. Hind. *āyā*. M. *āya*.]

ஆயிரவர், thousands of persons, 284.

[ஆயிரம். S. सहस्र. § 172. M. C. SĀVIRA.]

ஆர் ĀR.

I. See அர், 238, 330: = அரும், அரிய, அருமையான.

II. Affix = அவர் = ஓர். [அ + அர்.] G. 93.

III. *v. n.* (§ 57). Become full = நிறை, நிரம்பு, 378, 396. [Comp. சால. S. पूर्. M. T. ĀR. C.] ஆர, fully, our fill, 302, 366. ஆர் [G. 153] 16, 217.

Hence ஆராய், seek out thoroughly. See ஆய். *v. a.* Fill themselves, feed full, 200.

IV. *v. a.* (§ 64). 1. Sound, resound, hum, 73, 122, 161, 223, 290, 364. [S. आ + रु, आरव, ஆரவம்.] 2. Bind, tie, 122. [M. ĀR|KKU. C.] ஆர்த்த [for ஆர்க்க by வலித்தல், G. 41], full, ripe, 351.

ஆல் ĀL. [M.]

I. Case ending [G. 59]: 'instrument.' For this ஆன் is also used. It is really the verbal root ஆ, and ல் or ன் added. [See C. D. G., p. 172.]

II. Verb. inflection [G. 86]: 'condition.'

III. *v. n.* Become full, complete (§ 70). [Comp. ஆர். This seems to be used for சால், அகல், and ஆகல், q.v., by மரூஉ, see III Gr. index.] ஆன்று, being full, 54: ஆன்ற = சான்ற or அகன்ற, 106, 163, 252.

IV. As a redundant syllable, filling up the metrical foot: அசைச்சொல் [G. 116]; but it generally seems = since, because: 30, 55, 81, 83, 84, 132, 305, 324, 386.

V. ஆல், ஆலம், a banyan tree, *Ficus Indica*. [C. probably from அகல = broad.] 38, 197. See Ainslie, vol. ii. p. 11. Its minute seeds are much used in medicine.

The Telugu version of 38 is:

'Chittaçuddhi galgi chēsina puṇyambu
Konchemainanadiyu koduva gādu;
Vittanambu marri vṛikshambunakunenta?

Any meritorious deed done with pure intention though small is not defective;—how large is the seed of the banyan tree?' *Vēm.* i. 67.

ஆழ் ĀṚ, *v.* (§ 57) sink. K. [From அகழ்.]

ஆழ்கலம், a sinking vessel, [G. 153] 12. With hollow, sunken eyes, 49.

['ஆழ்ச்சிப்பகெகும் அளறு, a hell that deep engulfs.' T. 24.]

[M. C. ĀḶA. A. C. ĀḶ | du. T. LŌ | tu, where LŌ = உள். Many words belong to this group: அழுந்து, தாழ், ஆழ், வீழ், விழு, குழ, குழி, இழ: ழ் = ள் seems to give an idea of 'depth.' Comp. S. गाध, अगाध, आगाध.]

ஆள் ĀḶ (ஆண் ĀṆ, ஆட் ĀḌ).

K. I. ஆள், *v.* [§ 56 (III)] rule; use. Comp. ஆடு.

[This is an old root. A Tuḍa says 'I am an ஆள்' = *a man*, in answer to a question regarding his tribe. T. ĒL. (*ē* in sense of 'elevation' = ஆ, உள.) K. ĀḶU. In some places ஆள் as a fem. termination = அவள்: இல்லாள் = இல்லவள். So ஆர் = அவர், *etc.*]

ஆள்|வினை = முயற்சி, manly effort, [G. 153] 195.

II. ஆள், *n.* a person, 20. [Here ஆட், *Nan.* 255.] A slave: அடிமை, 122.

III. ஆள் in terminations = அவள், *she.* [G. 77, 93, 95.] See இல், மனை, வல், *etc.*, 382, 383, 384, 386.

IV. ஆளன் (ஆள் + அன்), an affix of possession or agency = '*he who possesses* or *exercises*' = ஆன், உடையவன், உடையான்.

நல்ல அறிவாளர், the truly wise, 11.
திண்ணறிவாளர், men firm in wisdom, 27.
புல்லறிவாளர், men of trivial knowledge, 8.
இடும்பையாளன், one debased, 282.
உடையாளன், a possessor of, 16, 65.
இலாளர் = அற்றவர், those destitute of, 138.
கொன்னாளர், worthless persons: வீணர், 243.

V. ஆண், male; the masculine character: opp. பெண், 202, 251, 386.

[M., C. ? from ஆள், or, more probably, அண். See அண்ணன்.]

ஆண்கடன், the duty of a man, 98.

VI. ஆண்|மை [from (1) ஆள் and (2) ஆண்].

(1) The exercise or possession of anything. In C. = உடைமை. புல்லறிவாண்மை, ch. xxxiii, 'ignorance, stupidity.'

(2) Manliness, 194. Almost = '*ness*' in the four following:

பேராண்மை, 199; சான்றாண்மை (சால்), 126, 142;
ஊராண்மை (உரு), 240; தாளாண்மை, ch. xx, 200.

VII. ஆட்|சி, the use, mastery, practice, exercise of anything, 215.

K. ஆற் ĀRR. [Comp. அறு, cut.]

I. ஆறு, *n.* six, § 172. [M., T., C. TUḌA. TU. *āji.* C. D. G. p. 235.]

II. ஆறு, *n.* a way: வழி, மார்க்கம், நெறி: 194, holes in the roof, 383. [M. Comp. ஆடு.] அறத்தாறு, the way of virtue, 257, 322; கையாறு, decorously, 382. Manner, method: வகை, 13, 23, 97 (with rel. part. =*how?*), 313, 398. Way of life: ஒழுக்கம், 79; தன்னுற்றான், according to his conduct; or=தன்னு வேதானே, by himself alone, 243.

In 5 it seems best to take ஆறுசெல் as a comp.='go:' *the desert path along which Death takes his way.* Conduct: வினை, in 103.

மனையாறு = இல்லறம்: domestic life, or virtue. [Notice the close connexion between அறம் and ஆறு.] 54.

உறும்ஆறு = in every fitting way, 95.

In 98 ஆற்றின் may be (1) *by* (or *than*) *the river;* (2) *if you do* (or *give*); or (3) *in the ordained method.*

காலாறு, a journey on foot, pilgrimage, 268.

இட்டாறு, straitened circumstances, 288.

முட்டாறு, hindrance, difficulties, 288.

III. ஆறு, *n.* a river: நதி. Often written யாறு. [Comp. T. KĀRU, 'flow;' and *ērru.*] 136, 150, 185.

மேலாறு, a river of perspiration, 268.

IV. ஆறு, *n.* a direction: திசை: நாலாறும் ஆருய், open to every wind that blows, 383.

V. ஆறு, *v.* (§ 62) grow cool; become mitigated, healed, 88. [Comp. S. रुह्. M., T., C.]

VI. ஆற்று, *v.* (§ 62) do: செய், 22, 174, 185, 286, 288 (உதவி understood), 295, 303, 309; [T. *āṭu.* ? a variant of ஆட்டு. The idea is power active and passive.] Protect (காப்பு understood), 184; bear, 149; endure, 151, 396; be able, 329.

ஆற்றுந்துணை, as long as you can put up with it, 75.

ஆற்ற = மிக: much, 6, 7, 34, 62, 69, 78.

ஆற்றல் = வலி: power (of action and endurance), 59, 313.

ஆற்றாதார், the poor and helpless: தரித்திரர்: those unable to *do* anything in return, 98. [III Gr. 95.]

ஆற்றாமை, the absence of ஆற்றல். In 67, (1) weakness; (2) an intolerable injury.

ஆன், (1) a cow. See ஆ III. 239. = (2) ஆல், term. of 3rd case, 195.

ஆனும், 1. see ஆ|கு = ஆயினும், ஆனாலும், although, 329.
2. ஆன் + உம் [G. 59] = even by, 323.
3. ஒன்றானும், anything at all, 98, 159. Comp. 205.

ஆன்று, ஆன்ற, see ஆல் and அகல்.

இ Ĭ.

இ Ĭ.

1. இ is a demonstrative letter (see அ), = 'this.' A large number of pronouns, adverbs, *etc.* are formed from it.

2. இ is the termination of the adverbial part. of middle verbs. [G. 86.]

3. உ is changed into இ in certain forms: வறு, 'poor,' makes வறி + ஞர், 1; so பெரிய, சிறிய.

4. இ is used for ஆய் in verbal inflexions. See G. 83. So போகி, 55.

5. In C. *ĕ* (pronounced *yĕ*) is used for இ: *eḍam* = இடம்.

6. When final உ is cut off before initial ய, a short இ is introduced. [G. 24.] So in 71 பேதைபோடு + யாது = பேதைபோடியாது.

7. In 145 இ = இப்படி.

இவன், he, 'this male.'

இவள், she, 'this female:' 14, 17. (இ + அள்.)

இது, 49, this. இவை, 52, 53.

K. இக IGA, *pass.* [S. ई, या, गम्.]

I. இக, *v.* (§ 66. Comp. இற, இய), pass over, transcend, with எல்லை = கட, 6; leave behind: விடு, 33 [= நீங்கு in T. 30].

II. இக|ழ், *v.* (§ 57. ழ் is a formative, not radical. Comp. புகழ், மகிழ், அகழ், தாழ், ஆழ், கீழ். C. *eggu*. This is contracted into இழ், q. v.)

Despise: எள், அவமதி, நிந்தி, 58, 117, 136, 157, 159, 180, 219, 235, 321.

III. இக|ல், *n.* jealous rivalry, 137. [In M.=a fight. See K.]
Nig. இகல் பகை துலி போர் முப்பேர்.

K. **இசை** IÇAI, *agree.* [இயை. S. या. M. IYA. See இய.]

I. இசை, *v.* (§ 57)=இயை, இயலு, fall to the lot of, 60; be possible, 95, 111, 181; succeed, 152, 194 [comp. *Nīti.* 97]; be innate, 187; sound out [இசை=*harmony*], 257.

II. இசை, *n.* fame, 338. [S. यशस्.]

['இசை கெட்டான், one dead to fame.' *Kalit.* i. 10. See also *Nīti.* 2, 82.]
Nig. இசை புகழ் இசைவி பாட்டாம்.

இதழ் (அதழ்), lip; petal, outer scentless leaves, sheathe, 221. *பாளை; இலை, பூவிதழ்.* [M. ITHAḶ. S. अधर.]
Nig. இதழ்பனையேடு பூவின் இதழ் உதடென இம்மூப்பேர்.

இட் IḌ='place.' [M., C. *iḍe, eḍe.* T. *eḍa.*]

I. இடம் (*n.*)=இடன்.

1.=place: இடத்து, inf. base for 7th case; (with verbal roots) 51. [G. 153. து is euphonic]=where or when, 329.

இடம்பட, extensively, 116.

இடமுடைய, vast, 300.

2.=time: சமயம், 11, 91, 149, 384.

3.=the left side: 300, 388 (opp. வலம்). [In this signification it is probably=வடம், 'north.' So தக்கணம்='right hand' and 'south.' Comp. Schrader's Prehistoric Antiquities of the Aryan Peoples, by Jevons, p. 254.]

II. இடு, *v.* (§ 68) give, put: கொடு, தரு.

[This is ultimately from இ; and டு=place. Its other form is ஈ for இய்: comp. Tel. See also விடு. M., C., T. S. दा, धा.]

இடுவர், they will *give*, 207.

Used as an auxiliary. (§§ 254, 263.)

வித்திடு, sow, 243. மறந்திடுக, forget, 291.

கீழிடு, degrade, 248.

கடிப்பிடுகண், the place where they *apply* the drum-stick, 100.

இடு|தலை=left, abandoned in the burning ground, 49. With காடு, 96.

இடுநீறு, ashes of sprinkling, 66.

இட்டு (§ 77), *p. adv. part.* 'having given.'
=விட்டு, 15, 48.=போகிடு or போகவிடு, 393: '*let go.*'

இட்டன்ன (see அன்ன) redundant (=குன்றினல் போலும்), 44, 237.

இட்ட (§§ 74, 87) once given, given for ever, 216.

அத்திட்ட, *dyed* red, 281.

III. இடு has an idea of compression. [Comp. இடி. C., M. IḌUKKU.]

இட்டு, (*adj.*) small, narrow, poor.

இட்டாறு, straitened circumstances, 288.

K. இடுக்கண், want, straitened circumstances, 141, 348, 382. [Comp. கண். M. IḌAṄṄA.]

இடுக்கம், avarice: உலோபம், miserliness.

இடும்பை (ம்பு + ஐ = துன்பம் = T. *iḍumu*. Comp. உடம்பு and see ஐ), want, poverty; annoyance, 107, 282. [K. 1045. N. M. K. 97.

'The heart knows its own bitterness.'

கள்ளின் இடும்பை களிஅறியும்; நீரிடும்பை
புள்ளினுள் ஓங்கல் அறியும்; நிரப்பிடும்பை
பல்பெண்டிர் ஆளன் அறியும்; கரப்பிடும்பை
கள்வன் அறிந்து விடும்.

The trouble from *toddy* the drunkard knows;
The trouble from water the sea-gull among the birds knows;
The trouble from poverty the master of many wives knows;
The trouble of concealment knows the thief.]

இடர், affliction: the pinch of poverty, 113. [M., C.]

IV. இடி, *v. a.* 1. thunder, send forth bolts, 100. [§ 64.] 2. crush, pound in a mortar, 156. [Comp. அடி. M., C., T.]

V. இடை, (*n.*) = நடு: middle.

As a sign of 7th case. அதரிடை, by the wayside, 192. [G. 63.] இடையாக, meanwhile, before they die, 119. இடை, the middle course [a form of இடம்], not worthy of praise or blame, 365. இடை, the middle sort of people, not base (கடை) nor first rate (தலை), 297, 366. இடையிடையே, everywhere between, 46. இடைதெரிந்து, knowing (it) through and through, 54. இடைமிடை, commingle [மிடை], 80. இடைதிரி, change, deteriorate [திரி], 216. இடைப்புகு, go into the midst of, 254, 255, 314.

Nig. இடைநடு என்ப மற்றும் இடப்பெயர் நசப்பும் ஆமே.

இம் IM. [M. IMA; *chima;* TU. *sima*. C. *imĕ*. Comp. சிமிட்டு. S. निमिष्. நிமை.]

இமை, *n.* a twinkle of the eyes: நிமை.

(1) *v.* (§ 64) wink, close the eyes, 302, 323, 345.

(2) shine, twinkle as jewels, 127, 146, 361.

இம்மி (1) a very small fraction: $\frac{1}{1,075,200}$; an atom.

(2) *மத்தங்காய்ப்புல் அரிசி*, the small seed of a wild grass, 94. [M.]

[Jī. Chin. iii. 3: 'இம்மியன நுண்பொருள்களிட்டிநிதி ஆக்கி, accumulating a treasure by collecting minute gains.']

இம்மென், 392, 'with pattering sound'=so as to say IM. [H. B. § 273.]

இய் IY=இசை, *fit*. [S. या. இக.]

I. இயல், (*n.*)=nature: குணம்.

மெல்லியல், tender-(natured), 86.

இயனெறி=நல்லொழுக்கவழி, the path of natural piety, 294.

இயல்பு, nature: 74, 144, 205, 384=குணம்; goodness: 187, 224, 244, 292=சற்குணம்.

['இயல்பிற்றொழும்பு, an ill-conditioned servant.' T. 67.]

இயற்கை, 111=natural course.

II. இயலு, *v.* (§ 70) be possible [comp. ஒல், இயை, இசை. M.]; be composed of, 353.

இயற்று, *v.* (§ 160) use effort, bring about, 194.

III. இயை, *v.* (§ 57)=இசை, be practicable; combine, adhere to, 91, 210, 306.

இயைந்த=உள=ஒல்லும். Comp. 36, 271, and 272.

இயைவ=இசைந்தவை, what you can, 94, 95.

IV. இய {-க்கு / -ங்கு} *v.* [§§ 62, 160. S. ईं, இக, எகு]; (*tr.*) move: =நடத்து, 136; (*int.*) move:=நட, 334.

இர் IR [=உறு. In C. as in Tamil. M. *iri*. Not in Tel.; but *ira*='place.' Comp. S. अस्; Lat. *er-am*. Old Can. *iha*].

I. இரு, *v.* (§ 60) sit, 29, 254, 334; remain, 268; be, 61.

As an auxiliary: 5, 9, 19, 162, 323, 345. இருந்தேன், I who was, 389. [Comp. 126.] இருப்ப a future (aoristic) infinitive absolute: 'while they are left in poverty,' 264, 265. இருப்பினும், 254=இருந்தாலும் [G. 142. H. B. § 100]. இருந்தற்று, 254, 'as though he were;' see அற்று under அன். இருந்தன்று, see அன்று under அல். இருந்து is for இருந்தது, 'it is not a thing that ever was,' 258. இரு|க்கை, a seat, 143.

II. இர்='dark' [C. *ĕrĕ*. S. रात्रि]; only in derivatives. Hence இரும்|பு, iron, *black metal*. Comp. செம்|பு.

இருள், darkness (see உள்). [M., T. *irlu*.]

III. இரு, two=இரண்டு, ஈர்: 18. [§ 172.]

இரு|மை, two states, this world and the next, 129. இரண்டும், both. இரட்டி, *n.*=

twice as much:' as though from இரு, 'become double;' and இரட்டு, 'make double.' இருவர், two persons, 75.

IV. இரு, *adj.* great. [Comp. உரு, உறு, and இறை.] இரும் = பெரும், 168, 178.

இரிந்தைக்க, 79, is doubtful. See இரி.

In *Kalit.* i. 27 we find மறந்தைக்க = மறப்பாராக! *Naççinārkkiniyār* says this is வியங்கோட்திரிச்சொல், 'an anomalous form of the optative.' (G. 85.)

? இரிந்தை for இருந்தை = இருந்தாய், 'thou wert;' used as a noun = 'thou who wert.' (G. 77. See 126.) Then க்க for க்கு: a poetic license = 'to thee who wert (on pleasure's side).'

இர IRA, *beg.* [C. *ere.* M., T. *eruvu.*]

1. இர, *v.* (§ 66) = யாசி, பிச்சைகேள், beg, ask.

1, 145, 270. இரவாதார் = இரவாதவர், 296, 305, 306, 307, 308. Often found with கர, 'refuse.'

2. இர|வு, 40, 303, 305, 306, mendicity: யாசகம். Comp. கரவு.

இர|வச்சம், 'dread of mendicancy,' ch. xxxi. இர|வாமை, 95.

3. இர|வலர், mendicants, 279. [இரவல்.]

இரி, *v.* (§ 57) be driven away, take to flight, 212.

இரிந்தைக்க = ஒழிக, 'be it put away!' 79. But see இருந்தை under இரு. [Comp. இழி, இற, and S. रि.]

இரு|ந்தை (இருந்து), charcoal: கரி, 258 [? √IR = 'dark' (இருள்)].

இரு|ம்பு, iron, 122. (From இரு II.)

[T. *inumu.* M. and *irimbu.* Metals for which there are pure Drāviḍian names are பொன், வெள்ளி, இரும்பு, செம்பு, வெண்கலம்; all connected with colours: and இரசம், ஈயம், தகரம், பித்தளே, தாமரம், துத்தநாகம் (रस, सीस, पित्तल, ताम्र, तुत्थनाग).

Of these பொன் is the only real Tamil name, the others are epithets. Gold was found in the South in abundance from pre-historic times.]

இரை, (*n.*) = உணவு: food, fodder. Provender of animals; prey, 193.

[Comp. இறை|சி. C. ERE. M. IRA. T. ERA (*era* = *erra* = 'red').]

இல் IL = இன்.

This √ is found in Tel. in LĒ = *not*, formed from இல்|லே by apocope. So *rā|du* from வ|ராது; and *kā|du* from ஆ|காது (in French *le* and *la* from il|le, il|la). As noun = *illu* = house. As postposition *lo* = in.

In M. *il, oḷa.* In C. *il, im, inda.* Also *alli, illi, elli* seem to be from the same √. In Tuḍa it is *oṟ.*

Comp. உள், அல், உறு, உளி, உழி.

Considering that இல், as a verb, is chiefly found in the purely negative mood, may it not really be originally, in itself, positive and = உள், உறு, இரு? Is it connected with நில்? [See ன்.]

I. இல், அன், *an inflection* = in, at; from; than; like; of. A sign of the locative case. [G. 61, 63.] 8 = *in*, 99, 138, 359. [Comp. C. D. G. p. 197, *etc.*] 52, 219 = *than*: both இல் and இன்.

II. இல், இன் = 'if,' form a subjunctive mood, when added to the verbal root, with or without கு, க்கு, பு, *etc.* [G. 86. H. B. §§ 95–98.] This is allied to எல், q. v., 1, 4, 139. To this உம் is often added; and = 'although.' See ஆகினும், எனினும், 41, 56, 139, 320, 360, 383.

III. இன் (rarely இல், see note on 352) is a சாரியை or euphonic increment, often used for a case-ending, or to connect it with the crude form or stem. அன் is another form, 56.

IV. இல், *n.* (1) a house: மனை, 30, 198, 210, 225, 326, 363, 383.

(2) A housewife: இல்லாள், இல்லவள், மனையாள், தாரம், 1, 86, 158, 383.

(3) A noble house, or family: குடி, 146 (with பிற), 212, 320, 358.

(4) Domestic enjoyment: வாழ்வு, 13.

இல் | லம் = இல்: 53, 207, 210, 225, 274. In 293 = இல்லாள். அட் | டில் [அடு], cook-house: சமையல்வீடு, 363. புக் | கில் [புகு], refuge, 41. இல் | லகம், house, 361.

V. இல், *v.* (G. 125. Comp. அல்), used in negation of existence, or of possession, *when it governs an accusative case*.

1. (1) Root used absolutely in predication: opp. to உண்டு, 7, 16, 21, 52, 99, 140, 284, 320; (2) as வினைத்தொகை, 5, 242, ch. xxvii; (3) with ஆகும் redundant, 360.

2. இல் | லை (இல் + ஐ), 6, 13, 283.

3. இல் | லா, இல்லாத. Adj. part. opposed to உள்ள: 14, 52, 91, 138. இல் | லாதான், 281, 361.

4. As conj. noun, G. 93; or part. noun. இல்லான், 65. இலர், 35, 50, 284, those without, 157, 205. இல்லார் (= the destitute) 158, 210, 219, 283, 320, 336. இல, they are (things that are) not, 344. இல்ல, 219. இலிர், ye are not, 165; are ye free from, 284. இன் | றி [as though from v. இன்று], destitute, 68, 75, 198, 242, 250. இன் | று (இல் + து) = இல்லை, is not, 132, 324, 358. இன் | மை (இல் + மை. Comp. அன்மை, உண்மை), absence of, 61, 106, 251, 372, 381, ch. xxvi; poverty, destitution, ch. xxix, 308 [opp. உடைமை]. இல | ளர், 138 [see ஆர்].

இல ILA. [T. VELA. M. ILA. Comp. S. लघु, लष्, or वि + लस्. Allied to வில | ங்கு, விள | ங்கு. Comp. வெள், ஒள்.]

இல | ங்கு, *v.* (§ 62) glisten, shimmer, 227, 344.

[Ji. Chin. i. 237: 'வாள் எயிறிலங்க நக்கான், he laughed so that his bright teeth glistened.']

இலை, leaf, 244, 359. [M. ILA. C. ELE, RĀLE. Comp. ஓலை.]

இலக்கணம், sign, 399: குறி. [S. लक्षणं.]

இழ IẒ. [M. Comp. கழ, இற. T. eḷuvu = 'loss.']

1. இழ, *v.* (§ 66) lose: sacrifice, 9, 10, 199, 251, 277, 287, 336.

II. இழி, *v.* [C. IḶI. M. IṞI. Comp. இளி, இடி, விளி, விழு, இழ.] (§§ 57, 64) suffer degradation; degrade.

இழி|வு, disgrace; pain, 79. இழி|ப்பு, contemptuous treatment, 163. இழி|க்தவை, low, contemptible things, 259. இழி|த்தக்க [தகு], things worthy of contempt, 302. [Root இழி for இழிக்க.]

K. III. இழு|க்கு, (*n.*) fault, failure, 362. [Opp. ஒழு|க்கு. Comp. வழு. As *v.* 'slip.' T. 14.]

K. IV. இழை, *v.* 'determine.' [§ 64.]

[இழை=yarn, thread; (met.) jewel, jewelled lady.] Assign, spin the thread of destiny, 6. Plan, hasten on, 330. (Some read விழை.)

In 361, comm. says: 'with jewels glistening as lamps:' இழை=ஆபரணம். Better perhaps 'lamps hung in rows.' ஆயிழையாள், she who wears choice jewels, 372. [Comp. C. and see பக. M. IṞA. C. EḶE.]

இள் IḶ.

K. I. இள=குழ, tender. [Comp. இளே, இழ், இர். T. IL|A; LĒ|SU='light,' LĒ|TA='tender.' M. IḶ|A. C. EḶ-E. S. लू.]

இள|மை, இளமை, youth: இளமைப்பருவம், [காமக்] குழவிப்பருவம், from the age of 16 to 32, during which a man is called குமாரன் or விடலே. In S. युव, यौवन, whence Tam. எவ்வனம், இயவ்வனம், யௌவனம. பயன்படுமிளமை = எல்லா இன்பங்களேயும் அநுபவிப்பதற்குரிய இளமை. Also (S.) பாலியம். இளமைநிலேயாமை, the transitoriness of yonth, ch. ii, 11, 17, 53, 55, 102, 181. இளம்பிறை, the young (crescent) moon, 241. [H. B. § 131.*e.*]

II. இளே, see இள, a mere variation in spelling, 55.

இளேயான், a youth, 65.

இளே|யர், 351.

இளேயம், we are young, 19. [G. 93.]

III. இளி, disgrace: இழிவு, இளிவரவு. [Opp. ஒளி, இளிவு, 40, 62.]

[Comp. இழி, இழ, இசி, இற|க்கு, where the idea of *going down* is common. C., M. IḶ-I ='descend.' Anc. C. EḶA.]

இற் IṞṞ.

I. இற, *v.* (§ 66) pass on, by, away; die; surpass. Opp. பிற. [Many roots with ற்: அறு, பற, மற, துற, திற, கற, சிற.]

இறவாதார், those who have escaped death, 7, 14, 61, 156, 300, 354. இறப்ப, surpassingly, 38, 99, 174, 223, 228. அதனிறந்து, and beyond that, 188.

[Comp. இற-ங்கு, இற-க்கு, இறு; இச, இழ, *etc.* In M. S. ऋ.]

II. இறு, *v.* (§ 68) come to an end, die; be broken.

[Comp. இற, அறு. M.='drip.' C. √IṞṞ.]

இறுகாலத்து, in the time of death, *or* ruin, 110.

இறும் அளவும், till they die, 209.

இற்றுழி = இற்றவுழி, when it is broken, 48.

III. இறு|கு, *v.* (§ 62) become tight.

[M., C. IR-a(u, un, i)-ku. T. IR-u-ku. Comp. இரு.]

இறுகிறுக = சிக்கென, யாப்புற, tightly, 328.

இறுகிறுகி = பத்திரப்படுத்தி, சிக்கென்றிருந்து, tying tightly, 328.

K. IV. இறை|ஞ்சு, *v.* (§ 62) = வணங்கு, bow before, 304.

[T. VAN-CHU. இறை, a lord.]

V. இறை, *v. a.* (§ 64) draw and pour out, 184, 231.

இ(ன்) IN [இ demonstrative] = this, thus, here, now.

I. இன்னே, even now, 55.

இன்னினியே, this very instant, 29.

இன்று, to-day, 36. Comp. 350.

II. இனம், race, kind, family, genus: சுற்றம், 146, 180, 244, 245, 283, 290.

தீயினம், evil association, 179, 240.

நல்லினம், the good, ch. xviii.

சிற்றினத்தார், the mean, 204.

இனத்தர் (ஆர்), 85. [Comp. இணங்கு.]

III. இற்று [இன் + து], of this kind, thus, 49, 50.

IV. இஃது [இன் + து] = இது = இன்னது.

V. இன்|னர், suchlike persons, 205.

[Comp. B. I. S. 550:

'अयं निजः परो वेति गणना लघुचेतसाम्।
उदारचरितानां तु वसुधैव कुटुम्बकम्॥

"This man is ours, that is a stranger:" so reckon men of light mind; to men of liberal understanding all the world is as their own family.']

இன்ன, suchlike things, 143.

VI. இனை|யர், such, of such account, 205.

[இன் + ஐ an adj. affix. Comp. அனை, எனை, தனை.]

VII. இன் is a mere euphonic insertion in forms like நடையினர், 13. (G. 93, 108.)

[M. Comp. இணை, இணர். இன் has meaning of 'connexion.' See இல்.]

VIII. இன்றி, இன்று, இன்|மை, see இல்.

இன் IN, *sweet, pleasant,* தீ(ம்). [C. IM, IN. M., T.]

I. இன், *adj.* [H. B. § 131] sweet, precious, fresh (not *salt*), pleasant. [இனிமை is used to distinguish it from இன்மை (இல்).]

இன்சுவை, 156. இன்னுயிர், 62, 323. இன்னீர், 245. இன்சொல், 73, 146. As a குறிப்புவினை, G. 93. இனியான், 384. இனியார், 338, 365, 369. இனிது, 137, 207, 219, 259, 364, 384. இனிய, 76, 306.

II. இன்பு, இன்பம், pleasure, 54, 60, 79, 81, 84, 247.

With உறு, 'enjoy,' 39, 74, 209, 235, 327. [Comp. துன்பம, நுட்பம்.]

III. இன்|னா, the negative rel. part. of a verb இன்|னு = *be sweet*, *etc.* (G. 89–92) = bitter, evil.

இன்னாச்சொல், 66. இன்னா = இன்னாதவைகள், injuries, evils, 67, 76, 186, 225, 226, 227, 306, 335. இன்|னா|ர், enemies, 378. இன்|னா|து, 174, 237, 339. இன்னாதது, 119. இன்|னா|மை, affliction, 54, 60, 297. இன்|னாங்கு [comp. பொல்லாங்கு; M. *innaṅgam*], 11, 355, trouble.

ஈ Ī.

ஈ Ī.

I. A demonstrative letter, intensive of இ. Comp. அ, ஆ.

(1) ஈ|ங்கு, *adv.* here: [ங்|கு as in இங்கு, ஒருங்கு, *etc.*], 6, 15, 70, 182.

(2) ஈ|ண்டு, *adv.* here, in this world, 25. [Comp. ஆண்டு.]

ஈண்டை, *adj.* pertaining to this world [see ஐ], 331. ஈண்டு, *v.* grow; accumulate; abound: 38, 109, 245 (§ 62). ஈண்டுங்கால், the time when Divine Providence wills that a man's resources should develope, 93. [In K. ch. xxxviii it is ஆகூழ், ஆகுநாள், நன்றாங்கால்.] ஈட்டு, *v.* (§§ 62, 160) collect, store up, hoard, 10, 280. [The M. *īḍu*: nasalized.]

II. ஈ, *v.* (§ 57) give, [*as a superior to an inferior.* Comp. கொடு, தரு, இ|டு. C. *ī*, *ī-yu*, *ī-nu*. T. *ĭ*, *ī*. M.]

ஈ|தல், a bestowing in charity, 95, 98. ஈ|வது, ஈவார், 146, 181, 279. ஈ|ய, 132. ஈ|யும், 200. ஈ|யார், they bestow not, 270. ஈ|கலான், he gives not, 273. ஈ|யாய், 308, 'give!' or 'givest thou not?' ஈ|கை, a giving; a gift, दानं, ch. x. ஈ|யா|மை, a withholding, 145, 299, ch. xxviii.

III. ஈ, *n.* a fly, 61, 218, 259, 389. [T. *īga.*]

தேனீ, a honey-bee, 10.

ஈர் ĪR.

I. ஈர், *adj.* form of இரண்டு = இரு (§ 172).

II. ஈரம், *n.* [நீர், நாரம். S. नीर, नार. M. *īram* or *īrram.*]

'Moisture,' 115, 360; புல் ஈரப்போழ்து, 'a time of drought,' *by met.* 'coolness, pleasantness, favour, affection,' 138. [Comp. the double meaning of நாரம், நசை, குளிர்.] ஈர்ம் (adj. form), 46, 'cool, fresh, moist garland,' 113.

Nig. ஈரமே|குளிர்ச்சி|அன்பு. 1. = coolness. 2. = affection.

['ஈரமில்லா நெஞ்சத்தார், loveless souls.' *Mū.*]

III. ஈர், *v.* (§ 64) drag, 26. [Comp. இழு. C. *hīru.* A. C. *īḷu.* M. *iṟu, īṟ.* T. *īḍu.* S. हृ.]

IV. A termination of 2nd person plural in verbs, [இர், from நீர், நீவிர் (G. 77). In T. *ru, āru.* C. *iri, īri*], 6, 7, 18.

ஈனம் [S. हीन] 'absence of, lack of'=இன்மை, so='dishonour,' கனவீனம், 40, 198 [§ 133].

ஈன் ĪN.

ஈன்றாள், 'mother:' பெற்றதாய். [Comp. ஈ (ன் strengthens). T. Ī-nu (du, ta). C. Ī, *Īt.* M. Ī-*H*am, 'womb of animals.' The Eng. YEAN offers a tempting, but delusive, analogy.]

ஈன், (*v.*) bear, produce [§ 56 (III)], 199, 201, 400.

உ Ŭ.

உ Ŭ.

1. One of the demonstrative letters. See under அ. [G. 3, 5.] Comp. S. उद्. In old M., C., Tu.
2. It is used as a euphonic insertion [சாரியை. G. 108]. மனிதன் + உ + கு.
3. உ is cut off in certain cases. [G. 24.]
4. It is a termination of past adv. part. [G. 86.]
5. உ becomes very short in certain places, and is changed into a very short இ. [G. 15, 24.]
6. உ is put before Sanskrit words when beginning with *r, l,* introduced into Tamil: रूप = உருவம், लोक = உலகம்.
7. உ is a neuter termination, அது *etc.* In Telugu = *i.*
8. As a sign உ = 'two.'
9. In other dialects it is often replaced by *o;* and indeed this is a common vulgar pronunciation in Tamil.

உகிர் = நகம், nail (*of finger or toe*), claw, talon; finger, toe, 198, 206.

[C. *uguru;* M. *ugir.* In T. *gōru.* Comp. S. नख, नखर.]

K. உ|கு UGU. [Comp. உ|கிர். M. *ukku.* C. *ugi, ukku.* T. *u-ḍu-gu, ūchu.*]

1. உகு, fall down, be shed, *v. int.* § 68=உதிர்.
   உக்க, which have fallen, 45.
   உகினும், though it waste away, 292: இளை.

['வீய்ந்துகல், the perishing and dispersion.' *Ēl.* 11.]

II. Pour down, *v. act.* § 64 = சிந்து. கான்றுகுக்கும், that will pour down abundantly, 269. [This may be formed from √உ = 'down.' See under அ.]

உசா, உசாவு, உசாஅ, (*n.*) kindly sympathizing enquiry, 201.

Here the compound='his friends who crowd round to enquire, consult, and sympathize.' [Comp. वश् , उशि ; C. *ose*.]

[In *A. N. Ç.*

'உணர்ச்சி அச்சாக உசா வண்டியாக,

With wise apprehension as the axle,
mental investigation as the chariot . . .' Comp. 48.]

K. உஞற்று, *v.* (§ 62). [Comp. உடற்று, ஊங்.] =முயற்சிசெய், use effort, 32.

K. உட் UḌ, (உள்), உட, உடை.

I. உட. [Comp. உள். T. *odda, oḍa, tōḍu.* M. *uḍa, uḍan.* C. *ōḍa|nē.*]

உட|ன், a particle expressing *co-existence:* used as a post-position. H. B. § 240. =ஒடு, ஓடு, 332.

[Comp. தொடு, தோடு, தோழமை, தடீ], 'forthwith'=உடனே (*adv.*), 4. [உடன்படு= agree.]

உட|ங்கு, *adv.* (comp. ஒரு|ங்கு. ங்கு forms adverbs: அ|ங்கு), together with, altogether, 173.

['உடங்கு நீர்வேட்ட உடம்புயங்கியானை, elephants with suffering bodies seeking water in troops.' *Kalit.* i. 12.]

உட|ம்பு, body: தேகம், யாக்கை, சரீரம்.

[உடல். T., M., C. *oḍalu.* Contr. OḶḶ.U. ம்பு forms nouns: இரு|ம்பு.]
10, 34, 35, 37, 40, 42, 80, 102, 120, 141, 173, 330='person,' 258.

உடம்பினார், உடம்பினவர், those whose bodies are . . ., 379, 380.

II. உடை [C. *oḍave*].

உடை, possessions, =செல்வம், wealth.

உடைப்பெருஞ்செல்வர், those who have wealth of possessions. உடை for உடைய, 274, 368.

['உடைப் பெருஞ்செல் வத்துயர்ந்த பெருமை
அடக்கமி லுள்ளத்த னாகி நடக்கையின்
ஒள்ளிய னல்லான்மேல் வைத்தல் குரங்கின்கைக்
கொள்ளி கொடுத்து விடல்.

The putting upon a man of undisciplined mind and who is not virtuous in conduct, the lofty greatness of a wealthy estate, is like putting a firebrand into the hand of a monkey.' எ: வைத்தல்.—ப: விடல்.—செ. ப. பெ: பெருமை. P. M.]

உடையான், a possessor, 59, 264, 292. உடையா ன்=உடையான், 16. [T. *oḍayuḍu.* C. *oḍeya.* M. *uḍama.*] உடையார், men of property, 160, 337. உடையர், 262, 263. உடையீர், ye-possessed of, 7. [G. 93.] உடைத்து, it that has [G. 93], 28, 87, 102, 111, 147. உடைய, that possesses, 160. Hence a sign of 6th case. G. 62. உடைமை, possession, 233, 251, 281. [Opp. to இன்மை.]

III. உடு [M., C.], *v.* (§ 64) put on, wear, தரி, 264.

உடாஅது = உடுக்காமல், 10. [G. 90.]

உடுப்பு, உடுக்கை, உடை, 141 : ஆடை. [Comp. புடவை.]

IV. உடை. [Comp. ஒடி. M. *uḍe*, *uḍayu*. C. *uḍi*, *oḍi*, *oḍe*.] (*Int. v.* § 56) become broken, perish, 57, 284. (*Tr. v.* § 64) break, burst, 222.

உட்|கு UḌKU. [Comp. K. 921, 1088.]

I. உட்கு, *n.* reverence, 102. [Stronger than அச்சம்.]

உட்குடைமை, awe-inspiring mien, 188.

உட்குடையாள், one whose bearing compels respect, 384.

II. *v.* (§ 62) dread, reverence, அஞ்சு.

உட்க, நெஞ்சுட்க, so that their gorge rises, 49, 50, 164, 188, 384.

உட்கான், on what grounds, I wonder, does he not dread the entrance . . . ? 83.

[Comp. உக்கு and M. In *Nīti.* 8 : 'உட்குவருங்கல்வி, learning attended with *shyness*.']

உணா UṆA.

உணா (§ 66), -க்கு, *v. tr.*, -ங்கு, *v. int.*, make dry, 258. [Cog. உலர், புலர். M. Comp. S. उच्छुस्.]

K. உண் UṆ, see உள்.

K. I. I. உண், *v.* eat; drink; suck, imbibe; enjoy: அருந்து, நுகரு. [√உள், H. B. §§ 56 (III), 70, 265.]

Pr. உண், / உண்ணு } கிறேன், (Pa. உண்டேன். F. உண்பேன்), eat.

[C. *ūn.* M. UṆṆU.] உண், 135 [G. 153]. உண்மகோர், 18. உண்டார் [G. 82, 95] I. = உண்டவர்கள். உண்டு, having eaten, 191, 268, 271. உண்டன்ன, as though it ate, 16. [அன்ன.] உணினும், though they eat, 184. உண்பார், they will subsist, 85; those who eat, 235. உண்ணும், 7, 210, 382. உண்பர், 263. உண்க, 2 [G. 85]. உண்ணுமின், eat ye! 303. உண்மின், 94 [G. 84]. உண்ண, so as to enjoy [G. 140]. உண்டல் = உண்ணுதல், 206, 217, 271 [G. 94]. உணல், 302.

Neg. உண்ணான், 9, 80, 157. உண்ணோம், 366 [G. 89]. உண்ணாது, 10, 300 [G. 90]. உண்ணாத, 80 [G. 92]. உண்ணா(த), 96.

2. உண்|டி, food: (+இ. C. *uṇṇi*), 1, 43, 363 = உணவு. [It may be imperative = *eat!*]

3. ஊண், food. [So பேறு from பெறு. G. 96.] Hence

4. ஊட்டு, (§ 62) feed, supply with food; dye: [C. *ūḍu*], 1, 26, 40, 345, 396 [so சூட்டு from இடு].

ஊட்ட, 1, 185.

II. உணர்(௫). [Obs. many verbs are formed by addition to √ of அர், இர், று, இழ், ழு.]

1. *v.* (§ 56). Understand, feel the truth of . . ., appreciate, 4, 39, 106, 144, 182, 239, 247, 292, 321, 365. Come to an understanding, be reconciled, 384; resolve, 27. உணரற்பாற்றன்று, is not within their comprehension, 143.

2. உணர்|வு, *n.*=விஞ்ஞானம், this is higher than அறிவு which=ஞானம். [See Chhāndogya Up. vii. 11.]

உணர்வதுடையார் = உணர்வுடையர் (opp. உணர்விலார்), men of understanding hearts, 196, 264, 270, 386. உணரவுணருமுணர்வுடையார், men of thoroughly . . ., 247. நுண்ணுணர்வு, subtle, refined understanding, 233, 251. உணர்விலன், to him who fondly deems, 25.

உண்டு, see உண்=(1) 'having eaten;' or உள்=(2) உளது='it is;' or (3) வினையெச்சம் with ஆ.

உத் UT.

1. உதிர். [Comp. உகு, உதறு=வீழ், விழு, fall off, fall to the ground, 17, 19, 45.]

[In 17, perhaps for முதிர்ந்து. இர் may be a formative=று, ழ். C. *udir*, *udar*. M., T. *ūchu*. Comp. S. उद्+देर्.]

K. II. உத|வு, *v.* (§ 62). [M. UTAGU. T. ODA. C. ODA.]

Serve a purpose, help, be of use, serve out, 218, 334, 363. [*Nīti.* 8: 'அவைக்குதவாது, being of no service in the assembly.']

உத|வி, help, 34. [M.]

உபகாரம் [S. उपकार], benefit: நன்றி, (or better) செய்ந் நன்றி, 69.

உபாயம்=முயற்சி [S. उपाय. उप+इ], stratagem, prudence, method of treating an enemy, தந்திரம், 119.

K. உப்பு=லவணம். [Comp. உவர், உவரி. M., T. *uppu*='salt,' *ubbu*='swell;' as a *v.*='swell,' and so in C.]

Salt, 133. உப்பு சண்டு உவரி, brackish water saturated with salt, 245; zest, 391. உப்பிலி [இல்], insipid, 206, 289.

[Jī. Chin. xiii. 'உப்பிலிப்புழுக்கல், rice boiled without salt.']

உ|ம்மை, see உய்.

(1) See under நீ: for நும்மை.

(2) The other, some other world, or state: மறுமை. [Comp. உம்பர், இம்மை, *etc.*, 58, 85, 94.]

உ|ம்பர். [S. उपरि.]

[√ உ. Here ம் is euphonic, and அர் a plural termination. M. Comp. இம்பர், அம்பர், எம்பர்; and see note under அ.]

(1) The upper, celestial world, 37.

(2) The immortals, 137.

உமி, *n.* [M., C. *ummi.* T. *umoka, ūka.* Probably from உமிழ், 'spit out'], 'husk,' 221.

['உமிக்குத்திக் கைவருந்துவார், they will hurt their hands by beating husks in a mortar.' T. 28.]

K. உ|ய் U|Y. The real root is உ='up.' See அ.

I. உய், *v.* (§ 57) escape: பிழை. [M. UY.]

உய்ந்தார், 1. they have escaped, or been saved from, 277; 2. those that have escaped, 6. உய்ந்து=தப்பி, 23. உய்ந்த, neut. noun pl. nom. [G. 95] 277: the things from which they have escaped (are) many. உய, 5. உய்ம்மின், 'scape ye! 20. உய்ய, so as to escape, 53. உயல் ஆகும், 97. உய்யார், 164. [Comp. *Nīti.* 96.]

['புள்ளுவர் கையினும் உய்யும் புள்ளுள, there are birds that 'scape even from out the fowlers' hands!' Jī. Chin. xiii. 333. See *ib.* பதிகம், 36.]

II. உய், § 64. [Comp. C. ŬY, ŎY; and T. ŏS.] Cause to go together; collect, 10, 318.

உய்த்து, carry forth: செலுத்தி, 25. [In *Nīti.*='employ, expend, cause to go.'] உய்த்து விடினும், though you drive, 101. உய்ப்பர், they will dismiss, or direct their minds rightly, 66. உய்க்கும், guide, 59.=செலுத்த, 119.

K. III. உயிர்=S. पुरुष, ஜீவன், ஆன்மா. [In C. *usuru.* M.]

(1) *n.* life, 62, 206, 220, 323; living, being, 130; lifetime, 286.

ஆருயிர், dear, precious life, 238, 330. [See அர்.]

(2) *v. a. n.* (§ 64) breathe; emit, exhale.

உயிரா=உயிர்த்து, sighing, 33. [§ 97.]

உயிர்க்கும், wafting, breathing (odours), 108, 349.

IV. உய{க்கு / ங்கு}, *v.* (§§ 62, 160) afflict; suffer, 391.

V. உயர் [உசர்]. உயரு, *v. int.* (§ 60) rise, be lofty, 77, 223, 283.

உயர்குடி, a high family, 199. [G. 153.]

உயர்|த்து, *v. tr.* (§§ 62, 160) exalt, 248.

உயர்|வு, higher things, 304.

K. உரம், உரன், உரனை, உரவு, [comp. உரு (3). S. उरस्. M., C.] (*n.*) strength: வலி, 57, 65, 88, 153, 175.

உரவுநீர், 'the rushing torrent.' It is obviously a larger stream into which the sewer discharges itself, before becoming a தீர்த்தம். உரவு for உரம்='strength,' or for உலவு='undulate.'

[*Naiḍ.* xx. 13: '. . . . . உரவுநீர்க்கருங்கடலுலகுகாவலன்,
The ruler of the world (girt by) the black sea with its mighty waters.']

உராய், *v.* (§ 57) rub against.

[Comp. உரை, உரிஞு, உராய்ஞ்சு, உரைசு, உரைஞ்சு. M. *ura, urasu.* C. *orasu.*]

உர், உரி UR|I. The root idea is 'propriety, peculiar fitness.'

உரி|யர், possessors, 170. உரி|மை, possession, 170. [Comp. √உடை.]

உரு URU (உருவு, உருவம்). [From S. रूपं, *form, beauty.*]

I. (1) form: உரு, 118, 240. (2) beauty: அழகு, 102, 274. ? வெப்பம் in 90.

II. (3) *adj.* much, great. [S. Comp. இரு, உரம், and உறு.]

III. (4) *v.* (§ 64) உருத்த = எழுந்த, vigorous, 304.

[Hence உருப்பு, உருப்பம் = anything vehement, violent; heat. கலித். i. 16.]

உரு|கு, *v.* (§ 62) [M. Comp. C. *uri*] melt, 305.

[In 90 some read உருகு + எழ, making உருகு = உட்கு = 'dread.']

உருமு, a thunderbolt: இடி, 164. Often உருமேறு.

['ஊற்றுடை நெடுவரை உருமுடன்றிடித்தென, as though from a lofty hill, from whence fountains flow, an angry thunderbolt came crashing down.']

உருவ, 223. Either from *v.* உருவு = *pass through*; and so = (1) 'through, in, in the midst of;' or (2) from S. रूप; உருவம், and உருவ = 'beautiful.'

உரை URAI. [Syn. சொல், கூறு, அறை. M. C. ORE.]

1. உரை, *v.* (§ 64) speak, say, tell; explain, 32, 64, 71, 73, 78, 80, 88, 155, 157, 169, 196.

   உரையற்க, speak not, 71.

   உரைப்பில், if you speak = உரைத்தால், 227, 254, 257, 292, 313, 321, 322, 376.

   உரையாதி, say not, 390.

2. உரை, *n.* an explanation, commentary, 319. [See *Nan.* 21-23.]

உல் UL = *fail, waste away.*

I. உல, *v.* (§ 66) dry up: fail, perish [M. *ulayu.* C. *ole.* உலர், உலை, உலறு. Comp. புலர்] 93, 168, 185, 289.

உலவாமுன், before it perishes, 22. [G. 91. H. B. § 220.]

உலப்ப, 3. = கெடுக்க, வருத்த (= உலர்ப்ப), when they bring ruin.

II. உல|று, *v.* (§ 62) be worn out, 141.

III. உலை, *n.* [C. *ole.*]

1. A forge, 298. [*Nīti.* 56.] 2. Boiler, cooking pot, 114, 331. [As a verb = அலை.]

K. உலகு, உலகம். [S. लोक.]

1. A world; the world. 2. The universe. 3. The people in the world. 4. The wise, 15, 21, 74, 97, 100, 119, 132, 140, 185, 196, 204, 254, 273, 337, 368. விண்ணுலகு, heaven, 233.

உ|வ UVA, *swell.*

உவ, *v.* (§ 66)=மகிழ், be glad, 73, 74, 91, 200, 348.

[From உ with the idea of 'bearing up *or* away.'
Often written உக. In M. the first meaning is 'spring up.' Comp. *ubbu* in T. and C.]
Nig. உவப்பென்ப மகிழ்ச்சி மேடாம்.

உவகை and உவப்பு=களிப்பு, joy.

உவர் [comp. உப்பு; and √உவ. M. T. *ūdu, uppu.* S. ऊष. C. *ūdu, ūbu, uppu*].

n. brackishness, saltness; disgust, 263.
v. (§ 60) loathe [comp. வெறு, வெரு], 47 (for உவர். Comp. *Nannūl,* 224).

உவரி, the salt sea, 146; brackish water, 245. [M. உவர்.]

உழ் UṚ. [Comp. உள் and உறு.]

I. உழ, *v.* (§ 66) suffer, 35, 54, 147, 252, 277.

Once without complement; in other places with துயர், துன்பம், எவ்வம், and அல்லல். Note the variety.

II. உழு, *v.* (§ 60) plough, 178.

உழவு, ploughing, cultivation, 115.

உழவன், cultivator, 178, 356.

[M., C. *eru, āru, uṛu.* S. हल्. See C. D. G. p. 476. Comp. ஏர்.]

III. உழல், *v.* [§ 70. Comp. உழை, உழிதரல், அலை]=திரி, wander about, 20, 107.

IV. உழி=இடம், place. [Comp. உழை, வழி, and உள்.]

1. As sign of 7th case, 134 (G. 63), or better in composition with வைப்பு, 'a place of deposit,' K. 226.

2. With participles: கின்றுழி=கின்றநிலையில், 'without any warning,' 183. உடைந்துழி, 'where dead bodies lie,' 284.

செல்வுழி=[செல்+வ்+உழி] செல்லும் இடம், 8, 328. =கதி, 26, 48, 62, 154, 230. (Here செல்வழி is preferable.)

V. உழை=இடம். Comp. உழி. Used as sign of 7th case (§ 251. G. 63). Place, refuge, 167.

[M. *uṛa.* Especially a place about a king.]
Before his face, 159, 286, 353, 380.

K. உள் UḶ, *withịn.* [உண், உட். T. *un, lō.* M. C. Comp. இல். G. 63. See C. D. G. p. 500.]

I. உள், *n.* 1. place: இடம். [உழி, உழை.]

2. As a sign of the locative case=*in, among, within:* (§ 251), 24, 26, 88, 122, 155, 229, 269, 281.

3. The inside, the mind, 286; 289 [see அழு], lose heart.

4. In compounds; உள்ளாறு, be cured, 88. உள்ளூர், the heart of the town, 286.

உள்ளடக்கு, keep hidden within, 105, 196, 379. உள்படு, engage, succeed in, 250. உள்ளுடை, fail, 57 (see உடை). உட்காண், look into, 12. உண்ணோட்டம், minute enquiry, 18. உண்ணீர், the water it contains, 44.

II. உள் : a conjugated noun (G. 92).

உளது, உள்ளது, உண்டு (உள் + து), 'it (which) is,' or 'it is,' 25, 221.

உள, உள்ள, 'they (which) are,' or 'they are,' or 'that are,' 18, 91, 92, 146, 153, 271.

N.B. These are (1) nouns; (2) குறிப்புவினைமுற்று = *predicates*; or (3) குறிப்புபெயரெச்சம் = *quasi-adjective participles*.

உளர், persons existing, 132.

III. உள் : a defective verb, § 43, *exist*.

[It is as though it formed a past tense, உண்டேன், 'I existed;' an adv. part. உண்டு, 'existing,' or 'having existed;' and so உண்டாகில், 'if . . . . exist.' So in T., C., M.]

This உண்டு, as a வினையெச்சம், is used as an auxiliary to ஆகு and ஆக்கு:

உண்டாம், 19, 92, 154, 228. உண்டாயின், 'if (there) be,' 75. உண்டாக, 'as though (it) were,' 1. உண்டாகில், 'if (it) be,' 344.

IV. உள்|ளம் (உளம்) = அகம்.

1. Mind, thought (p. 1), 62, 64, 127, 128, 153, 274, 305, 317, 359, 380.

2. Breast, மார்பு, 152.

[Also used of '*property*.' Comp. Jī. Chin. பதி, 36. உள்ளமில்லவர் = 'the poor.']

V. உள்|ளு, *v.* (§ 62) think, 60, 64, 304, 305, 344, 356.

VI. உண்|மை, actual existence, truth, reality, certainty: வாய்மை, மெய்மை, 20.

[In Çaiva-Siddhānta books, 'esoteric doctrine' (விசேடவத்தம்) as opposed to (பொது = சாமானியம்) 'exoteric teaching.']

உளி, *n.* a chisel [√உள். M., C., T.], 355. [*Nīti.* 14.]

உளை, *n.* the mane; tufted flowers, in 199.

Nig. உளைபரிமீது கட்டுமயிர் பிறைமயிரும் ஓதும்.

K. உறு URRU. I. *v.* [§ 68. Comp. இரு and ஊறு. Opp. to அறு, இறு].

[On the whole = ஆகு, become; befall; befit. In 340 செய்குறு (suggesting செய்குது) might throw light on the origin of இறு as a tense formative. M. *urru-ga*. C. *urru*.]

உறும், will be, profit, hap, befall, 117, 168.

உறுமாறு, as befits, 95.

உறின், if it befall, 151, 300 (with கை, though it fall to his lot).

உறல், the befalling, 173.

உறற்பால, things fated to befall, 104, 109. [பெறல், of joys; உறல், of sorrows! 117. Comp. ஊறு and பேறு.]

உற்ற = பட்ட, 201. உற்றக்கால் (இடர்), 113.

உறு = இல்லாத, 362 [with செய் + கு for செய்கை; and கை, a noun].

உற்றவர், those who in sorrow seek their aid, 334.

உற, firmly, fast: = ஆக, 2, 173. 5, p. 1.
உறு, real (G. 153) 110; the fated time, 130. = 'mighty' in [comp. உர] 185, 193.
உறுவர், ascetics: முனிவர், 104.

☞ In compounds: = ஆகு or படு. மயறுதல, infatuation, 364. மைமருற்று, being infatuated, 87. நடுக்குற்று, மிடுக்குற்று, enfeebled, holding fast, 93. இன்புறுவர், they will enjoy life, 39. காம் (q. v.). குப்பு, 377. See 209, 235. முட்டுறு, suffer privations, 238.

II. உறு|த்து, cause to hap. (§§ 62, 160.)

In 148, 209, 235 உறூஉம் may = உறும் or உறுத்தும்.

III. ஊறு (as பேறு from பெறு, comp. 104) = துன்பம், 379. Comp. இடையூறு.

IV. உறு|ப்பு, member: அவயவம், 196. [? रूप.]

V. உறு|தி, stability, strength, certainty, 40, 128. [? உர.]

VI. உற{க்கு / ங்கு}, *v. n.* (§ 62) sleep, 38, 342.

VII. உறழ், *v.* (§ 56) suit, fit, appertain to, 311. [G. 153.]

VIII. உறை, *v.* (§ 57) abide, [strengthened form of உறு], 137. = வசி, 252, 280, 300.

IX. உறை, *v.* (§ 64) burn, be pungent or rank; cause smart; reek of, 43; *n.* rain, 383.

உறைப்பு, pungency, a copious penetrating rain, 184.

உன் = நின் from நீ: 'thy.'

ஊ Ū.

ஊ ū. This root expresses 'energy, increase.' [Comp. ஓ. From √உ. M.]

I. ஊ|க்கு, *v.* (§ 62) act with energy, do.

ஊக்கி, acting vigorously, 57, 326, 395.

ஊக்கல், 69.

K. ஊக்கம், strength, 129; power; aim, plan, effort, 196.

The use of this word in K. is as = முயற்சி, தாளாண்மை. [Comp. ஓதல்.]

[N. M. K. 87:

'ஒன்றூக்கல் பெண்டிர்த் தொழினலம்; என்றும் அறனூக்கல் அந்தணர் உள்ளம்,

The beauty of a wife's work is co-operation; ever the soul of the good strives after virtue.']

K. II. ஊ|டு, *v.* (§ 62) sulk, get impatient or angry with, 222, 384, 391.

[Comp. விடு. T. ūḍ|u, 'separate.' S. ऊहू. M. ūḍu, 'inside' (உள்). C. = URI|DU (urdu) = 'having burnt with rage:' S. उष्, उष्ण.]

ஊட்டு, see உண்.

ஊண், see உண்.

ஊது, *v.* (§ 62) blow, inflate.

[S. वात (ventus, wind). T. ŪD|U. C. ŪD|U, Ū|BU. Comp. உப்பு, உயிர். M. Tu.]

K. ஊதியம் (ஊதிபம்), profit, utility. *பயன், இலாபம், பிரயோசனம்*, 12, 144, 233.

[S. उदय (उद्+ई) = 'gain;' so in C. M. *ūdi.* T. *ūdibam.* Comp. ஆதாயம், ஆயம்.]

ஊர் ŪR.

[Comp. उरस्, वह्, ऊह्, उर. The ideas are (1) 'crawl;' (2) 'ride;' (3) 'town;' 'greatness.' M. C. (not as v.). T. in other uses = VĀR and ஊறு. Comp. ஊர்தி with उर्ध्व.]

I. ஊர், *v.* (§ 57) cause to go, drive: *ஆட்டு*, 374; ride a horse: *செலுத்து*, 398; circulate as sap, 34.

மீதூர, crowd on, prevail, 60.

வானூர் மதியம், the moon that rides the sky, 125.

[Jī. Chin. xiii. 371:

'. . . . தேரை வல்லான்
நேர்நிலத் தூரு மாயிடி னீடெல் காலஞ் செல்லும்;
ஊர்நிலம் அறிந் தேற்று தூரு மேன்முறிந்துவீழும்:

If a capable man drive the chariot on level ground, it will go far and long; if one drive it without knowing the proper driving ground, it will fall and be broken.']

II. (*n.*) town: *புரம்*, 64, 90, 96, 175, 184, 242.

ஊரன், head-man, 367, 387, 388, 389, 390.

[Perhaps from புரம், as ஊழ் from பழ்.] ஊரரன்மை, 240. [? உரு = magnanimity, munificence, great. See ஆள்.]

ஊழ் ŪḺ.

[From உழ் = வழ் = பழ் = ஒழ். The ideas are 'order, succession, age, destiny, labour, decay.' The group is extensive. M. C. *ūḻiga* = 'work.' Comp. T. VĀḌU, VĀḌIGE.]

K. I. ஊழ் [comp. பழ், வழ்] = what is in regular sequence; 394, one after the other.

K. II. ஊழி, an æon, age; eternity, 130.

ஊற் ŪRR, *ooze.* [Strengthened from உறு. M., C., T. ŪRU. Comp. S. स्रु.]

K. ஊறு, *v.* (§ 62) ooze out, flow, = கசி, சுர, 47, 185.

ஊறு, *n.*, see உறு.

ஊற்று, *n.* spring of water, 184, 185, 263. [S. कूप.]
In 150 note the play on words. [See ஊன்று.]

ஊன் ŪN=*lean on.*

ஊன்று (M. § 62, *v. tr.* and *intr.*)=தாங்கு, நிறுத்து; சார்.
[Comp. ஊற்று; are these connected? T. ŪN|U. C. ŪRRU. M. ŪN|NU. Comp. स्थूणा=தூண்.]

தண்டூன்றா [G. 87] supporting herself with a staff, 14.
கோலூன்றி, leaning on, 11, 13.
ஊன்றியாங்கு, as it supports, 197.
ஊற்று=ஊன்றுகோல், support, 110, 150. [T. ŪTA.]
[See under ஊறு and உறு.]

ஊன், *n.* flesh: தசை, மாமிசம், 80.=இறைச்சி, 193.

எ Ĕ.

1. G. 6. An interrogative letter; see அ. Always initial. [Comp. ஏ, யா.]
Often pronounced as யெ. So *ewe* in English.
2. In Sanskrit words used for அ: जप=செபம். So in T. for அ: அறி=ERI.

எஃகு=கூர்மை, keenness, 137. [C., T., M. *ukku, urku.*]
Nig. எஃகுகொடு வேலாயுதக் கூர்மை.
1. Steel; 2. javelin; 3. keenness.
Comp. G. 37, 38. It would seem that ஃ is for ல் or ள். Comp. Introd. p. xv.

எச்ச் ECH, 'be over and above, survive.' [C. *echchu*, 'increase;' *hechchu*; EG|U. T. EG; EKK. M. ECH.]=மிகு, மிஞ்சு, மிச்ச்.

K. I. எஞ்சு, *v. intr.* (§ 62) survive, escape, remain over, 21.

II. எச்சம், *n.* what is left over, or behind; what supplies a deficiency; complement.

134 [K. 1004]; 299, other things; 319, things omitted.
[M. Comp. அச்சம் from அஞ்சு.]

III. எச்சில், refuse of food, leavings, anything unclean: மிச்சில், சேஷம், உச்சிட்டம், 345. [M., C. *eñjal.*]

எஞ்ஞான்றும், always, 74, 174. See ஞான்று.

எட் EḌ=*lift.*

எடு, *v. a.* and *n.* (§ 56. III) acquire, gain a name; raise, lift up; support.

[√எ. Comp. பேர்|டு, சேர்|டு, *etc.* under அ. C. ETTU; EṬṬU. M. EḌU; ETTU. T. ETTU.]
21, 87, 227, take up and circulate as a report. 163, 203=பெயர், தாங்கு.

எட்டு, *v.* reach up to.

எட்டு, eight (§ 172) 281. [See எண்.]

எண் EṆ = *number*.

I. எண் (ணு), *v.* (§ 62) count, calculate.

[√எள் = *sesamum*. C., Tu. T. ENN. M.]

Duly estimate, ponder: கருது, 8, 9. எண்ணாத, that ponder not, 394. எண்ணி, 11, 29, 36, 182, 346. எண்ணரும், rarely precious, 216. எண்ணுர், 18, 80, 152.

II. 'Eight.' Adj. form of எட்டு (§ 172) 281. [C. D. G. pp. 237–240. M., C. EṆ. T. *enimidi*. Tu. *eṇma*.]

எதிர், *n.* what is opposite to.

[Only used here in these two compounds. C. ED|IR (*ar*, *ur*); IDIR. M. *edir*. T. √EDA.]

எதிர்செல், go to meet; go in an opposite direction, 143, 211.

எதிர்நில், stand up against, 363.

எம், எம்மை, எமர், see நான், our, us, 293, 385.

எம்மை, see மை, 132, what world?

[எ + மை = state, birth, world. எம்மையுலகத்தும், in all worlds.]

K. எய் EY [= எ. Comp. இயை, இசை, எ|வு, எய். M. *eyyu*. C. *ēy*, *ēsu*, *isu*. T. *vēyu*, *ēyu*. S. इ, या.]

K. I. எய், *v.* (§ 58) send forth, emit: பிரயோகி, தொடு, 152.

K. II. எய்|து, *v.* [§ 62 = *reach to*. M. *eythu*. து is a formative. Comp. எழு-து, பொரு-து, போ-து, ஓ-து, ஊ-து, *etc.* C.D.G. p. 98]. The idea is primarily of '*something coming to a person*:' வந்தடை; and then '*obtain*.'

1. Obtain: அடை, 114, 119, 142, 269. பாடெய்தும், will command respect, 281, 340.

2. Possess, 275, 347.

3. Assemble, 325. [Comp. பெய்.]

K. III. எயிறு = tooth: பல். எயிற்றுய், 287. [G. 93.]

[எய், 'anything *emitted*;' thence 'a porcupine.' M., C. and T. *vē*.

Ēl. 8: 'முருக்கேய்க்கும் முட்போல் எயிற்றிஞய்!

Those whose teeth are like thorns and like the soft roots of peafowls' feathers.']

எர் ER, *red*. [M. *eri*. T. *eri*. C., TU. *uri*.]

I. எரி, *n.* fire: தீ, 58, 208, 291. (*v. a.* § 64) consume, 124.

II. எருத்தம் = பிடரி, பிடர், மிடறு, புறங்கழுத்து, the nape of the neck, 3.

[Said of a swan : 'பொன்னிற எருத்தம் கோட்டு, curving its golden-hued neck.']

III. எருத்து=*neck* [from எருது, 'a bull;' *ere* in C.='red;' T. *era*], 'bend the neck as suppliants,' 304.

எருவை=கொறுக்கை, a kind of reed, 351. [Comp. C. ERE.]

---

1. எல் EL, (1) brightness; (2) sun; (3) day; (4) night.

[C. In T. *elli*, *elluṇḍi*, the √எல் is found. Comp. வெள், ஒள். T. *ella*. M. *ela*.]

I. எல்|லை, *n.* bound, limit, 6, 33. [C. D. G. p. 328.]

II. எல்|லில், in the night, 8.

[One comm. says பகலில், and the other இராக்காலத்தில்.
'எல்லுழந்து, labouring night and day.' *Ēl.* 53. 'எல்வளை, a lady with shining bracelets!' *Kalit.* i. 13.]

Nig. எல்லொளி பகல் இகழ்ச்சி இரவுடன் இரவி ஐம்பெயர்.

---

11. எல் EL, 'all:' the idea is *limit*.

[C. *ella*, *erru*. T. M. Comp. எல்லை, 'limit.' O. H. G. *al*; Eng. *all*.]

எல்லாம், 17. All along, 107. எல்லாரும், all persons, 45, 107.

எ|வ|ன்-ள்-து, who? which? [எ; comp. யா.]
எவன் for எது [G. 137], 83.

எவ்வம்=pain, affliction, 124, 147. [Prob. from வெ; qu. வெவ்வம்.]

எழு EṚU=*rise* [see எ, ஏ. M. *eṛu*. C.].

I. எழு, adj. form of எழு, 'seven,' 357. [M., C.]

II. எழு, *v. intr.* (§ 57, REG.) rise up, rise; rise and wander forth; stand out, arise, 11, 22, 24, 35, 55, 90, 123, 143, 153, 209, 287, 312, 313, 342, 357, 385, 395.

III. எழில், beauty, youthful grace, youth: அழகு, வனப்பு.

எழில் வனப்பு, grace, charm of beauty, 53, 167.

Nig. எழில் வண்ணம் இளமைக்கும்பேர்.

IV. எழிலி, a cloud: மேகம் [perh. 'the beauteous'], 392. [Comp. எழு|ம்பு, ஏறு, உயரு.]

V. எழு|து, *v.* (§ 62) write.

எழுத்து, a writing, 155, 253.

[For து, comp. பொரு|து, எய்|து. C. BARE=வரை. T. VRĀ. M. *eṛudu*.]

எள் EḶ. [Comp. இள, இளே, இழ, இழி, எழை. C. eḷ, eḷa, eḷe. M. eḷ, eḷi, iḷi. T. ela. S. लघु (=ἐλαφρός=levis) is in Tamil இலகு, இலேசு.]

I. எள், 'sesamum seed:' (very small and cheap.) [C.]

II. (G. 93.) எளிய, 317.

[எளிது—அரிது. *Ēl.* 40.

'சாவ தெளிதரிது சான்றாண்மை; நல்லது
மேவல் எளிதரிது மெய்போற்றல்;—ஆவதன்கண்
சேறல் எளிது நிலைஅரிது; தெள்ளியராய்
வேறல் எளிதரிது வீடு.

To die is easy; to attain perfection hard!
To desire good is easy; to put on truth hard!
To set out in pursuit of the right is easy; to be steadfast hard!
To gain triumphs as accomplished scholars is easy; to reach heaven hard!']

III. எள்ளு, *v.* (§ 62)=இகழ்: think lightly of, despise, 157, 298, 307, 325, 340, 348, 349.

Nig. எள்ளலே நகையிழிப்பாம் (=நகைப்பு, இழிவு).

எற் ERR. [M. *erri, ērru.* C. *erra.* Comp. எறு, எழ்.]

எறி, *v.* (§ 57) strike: அடி, 363.

Strike a drum: கொட்டு, 24; hurl stones, *etc.*, 66, 213, 364, 395; clear of rubbish, 180 [? எறிபுனம், the field where refuse is *thrown*]; throw up water, 245, 275.

In எறிபுனம் all comm. agree that எறி=வெட்டிய; but எறி='cast, throw.' May it not rather mean '*the field where rubbish is thrown:*' when the accumulations are burnt the sandal tree suffers?

எற்று, see என் (III). Comp. அற்று, இற்று.

என் EN̠. [T. AN-U. H. B. § 82. C. AN, EN.]

I. என், say.

என்ப, 250. என்பர், 282.

எனின், if (§ 95). என்னுது, 36, 99; not saying, 36.

என்னு(த), 32. என்னுர், they do not call it, 67.

என்றல், 235. என்று=having said, 229. [G. 114.]

என்னும், it will say, 25. எனினும், although, 32, 174, 228. (§ 100.)

II. Inflexional base of யான். [G. 72.]

என், me, my, 399, 400. [See நான்.]

எனக்கு, 84. எனது, 'tis mine, 276.

III. என் (எ). Interrogative pron. 'what?' 12, 26, 228, 361.

It is used as a conjugated noun. [G. 93.] Thus என் + து = எற்று, it is of what sort?
With உம்=anything, 150. என்ன is 3 pl. neut.
In 353 எற்றால்=by (of) what sort of material?=out of what?

என்னை, it is what? = யாது; for என் + ஐ. This is parallel to இல்லை. Why? 97, 110, 330.

எனை [comp. அனை, இனை, தனை, எனை. C. *eni|tu*. T. *enni*. M. *etra*], how much, many?

எனைத்து, 18, 84, 130, 320. எனைத்தும், all, each, every, 362. (H. B. § 126.)
என்னுனும், anything whatsoever. [ஆனும் = எனும் = ஆயினும். H. B. § 100.] 98, 159.
So என்னும் = ஏதாகிலும், 205.

K. என்|பு = எலும்பு, bone: அஸ்தி, அத்தி, 45, 46, 210, 292.
[√EL or EM. C. EL|U, EL|ABU, EL|AVU, IL|UVU, EM|IKE. T. EM|MU, EM|UKA. M. EL|UMBU.]

என்|று, what day? 36. See also under என்.
[Comp. இன்று, அன்று. C. *endu*. Tu. *ēni*, *ēpa*.]
என்றும் = எஞ்ஞான்றும், always, continually, 99, 116, 182, 307.

ஏ Ē.

ஏ Ē, see note under அ.

I. Used for எ, as an interrogative, as in Telugu.
ஏது = எது. So ஏனை = எனை. For this யா is also used. G. 6.
II. Emphatic, 4, 11, 13, 19, 306. Comp. G. 111.
III. Interrogative final.
IV. A verbal root, the main idea being 'elevation.'
V. For ஆ or ஓ, in termination. உண்கோம் = உண்கேனும், 339, 366.
So வாழ்கேன் = வாழ் + க் + (ய)ான்.
VI. Sign of vocative case, 32.

I. ஏ|கு, *v.* go: செல்லு, 15, 349. [S. एति. இக.]
II. ஏ|ங்கு (comp. எம்), pine, *v.* (§ 62) 130.

ஏட்டை, poverty: தரித்திரம், வறுமை, 358. [S. एष्.]
ஏதில், *n.* strangeness; vicinity: அன்னியம், அயல்.
ஏதின்மனையாள், another's *or* neighbour's wife, 86.
ஏதிலார், strangers, foes, neighbours (comp. Lat. *hostis*), 73, 122, 158, 228, 274.
ஏதிலவர், 306.

[From ஏது, 'what, any' (or S. हेतु, 'cause'), and இல். In M. Comp. எதிர். 'ஏதிலுட்டுறைபவர், those who abide in a strange land.' கலித். i. 26.]

ஏம் ĒM. I. For ஆம், or ஓம் as a verbal inflexion, 339, 366. (G. 77, 93.)

II. ஏமம். [This word represents S. क्षेम, हेम, or याम.]
1. Safety, protection, 13, 324, 327. 2. Intense delight.

ஏம் for ஏமம்.

ஏமுறுதல், sensual bewilderment, 364. [Comp. காமுறு.]

III. ஏமு|ா, v. n. (§ 66) delight in, 182, 377, 378.

[So ஏம்பு, ஏம்பல். *Naiḍ*. xx. 1.]

IV. ஏ|ந்து, v. intr. (§ 62) be raised, elevated: உயரு, 354. [Comp. ஏ|று.]

V. ஏ|த்து, v. (§ 62) extol, praise; n. praise, 163.

ஏல் ĒL. [=ஆயில்; from இயல்; from ஏற் in sense of hostility. C. ĒRR.]

I. ஏல், 'if:' may be contr. of ஆகில்.

With fut. makes a *conditional*=ஆல் or இல் [H. B. § 95], 9, 158, 230, 242, 250.

II. *v. n.* [§ 56 (III)] another form of இயல், q. v.=தகு, be fitting, 113.

III. *v. a.* [§ 70 as கல்] accept, receive, resist, meet in battle, ask alms with outstretched hands, 67, 98, 231, 335.

ஏலாமை from I or II.

1. Impossibility, incongruity. 2. Declining a challenge, 67.

மாறேற்பார், those who commence hostilities, 67. [Comp. K. 861.]

['. . . . அன்பின்றி

ஏற்றார்க்கியைவ கரப்பான் . . . . T. 45.

He who, without love, from those who implore aid withholds what he could well give.'

'மாறேற்கும் மன்னர், hostile kings.' T. 61.]

ஏழை, an ignorant man: அறிவிலான, 321.

ஏழை|யார், ignorant wretches, 54, 60.

[Comp. இளை, இழி, எள், எளிதம். C. ELIDA.]

ஏற்று, *adj.* of ஏறு=male, 96.

ஏற் ĒRR. [√ஏ IV. Comp. எழு. C. ĒRR (ēḻu) and ஏல்.]

I. ஏ|று, rise, ascend, climb, act presumptuously, 61, 90, 153.

II. ஏற்று (§§ 62, 160) lift up, put up into, 331.

[Comp. ஏல், ஏற்றே, ஏற்றம், in 231.]

ஏனும் a corr. of ஆயினும்; or from ஏன். [See ஆ and ஆனும். C. EN-UM.] 164, 180.

ஏ|னை [√ஏ=*what;* என். ஐ forms adjectives: நானை. Comp. ஏனை, எத்தனை.]

1. (Adj.) other, 230. 2. How many? 18. எவ்வளவு.

Besides, 143, 146, 216, 295.

ஏனை|வினை=தீவினை, '*other*,' i. e. deeds done *contrary* to அறம்; or, *in a former birth*, 3.

ஐ AI.

K. ஐ AI. [C. D. G. p. 230; often = அய், ஆயி.]

I. Adj. form of ஐ|ந்|து: 'five,' 59. [§ 172.]

II. What is small, minute. Hence ஐ|யம், 'alms,' 99. [M. *ayyam.*]

ஐ|ங்கை = சிறுகடுகு, small mustard seed, 329.

III. ஐயன், 'a father.' Comp. அய்யன். 350, voc. 'O Sire!'

IV. A sign of the direct object. It is probably an emphatic form of எ.

V. ஐ added to some few nouns forms an adjective: நாள் = 'day;' நாளை, 'current. [See 295.] ஆண்டு makes ஆண்டை, 191. என் makes எனை, முன்னைவினை, 107; மேலைவினை.

VI. ஐ added to some verbal root makes a passive noun: கொடு, 'give;' கொடை, 'what is given, a gift.' Here க் or க்க் is often inserted:

ஈ + க் + ஐ = ஈகை. நட + க்க் + ஐ = நடக்கை.

VII. ஐ = ஆய்: 2nd sing. வந்தாய் = வந்தை.

VIII. Sanskrit nouns in Ā, change Ā into ஐ in Tamil, and into Ă in Telugu:

S. विद्या = வித்தை = T. *vidya.* Comp. கிளை, சபை.

ஒ Ŏ.

ஒ ŏ: the idea is 'unity.' This is found in all the South-Indian languages with an astonishing number of derivatives.

[Comp. ஒன்று, ஒரு. Also *o|ḍu, oka.* M. C. T. ஒருக்கு. C. D. G. p. 216 *etc.*]

I. ஒ, *v.* (§ 64). [C. ONDU. M. OKKU.]

விலங்கொடுத்து, like a beast, 315. ஒத்த, befitting, respectable, 281.

ஒக்கும், it will equal, be like, 233. ஒக்கல்லா = ஒவ்வாது, will not equal, 236.

ஒவ்வா(த), totally diverse, 387. ஒப்பர், will be alike, 151.

II. ஒப்பு, *v.* (§ 62) agree. [C. *oppu.* T. *oppu, ōpu.* M.]

ஒப்ப, alike, 202, 387.

III. ஒ|ப்பு|ரவு = அறம் [comp. K. ch. xxii], befitting conduct, 22, 37, 148.

[Ancient C. *opp-aram* = 'pleasant.']

ஒ|ட்டு OḌḌU, *v.* (§ 62) cling to, join with, unite: நட்புக்கொள், பொரு, 214, 246. Opp. ஒருவு.

[Comp. ஒ, ஒரு, ஒன்று, ஒடு, ஒடு, உடன், தொடு, தொடர், தொடங்கு. C. *tuḍ, toḍ, oḍḍu.* M. T. *oṭṭu, odda.*]

ஒட்டார் = பொருத்தமில்லார், enemies.

ஒது OTH.

ஒது|ங்கு (§ 62). [Comp. ஒடுங்கு, அட|ங்கு, பது|ங்கு. T. ODU|*gu.* M. OTTU|*ṅṅu.*] *v. n.* retire; recede, 388.

ஒரு, adj. form of ஒன்று [C. D. G. p. 217], 250, 295.

ஒருவன்கண், 74.

ஒருவன்(ர்), (any) person, 127, 230, 308, 309.

K. ஒருவு ORUVU [G. 64] shun. [Comp. வெரு, வெறு. T. VERA. M. VERRU. S. वृज्.]

ஓரீஇ = ஒருவி, 6, 36, 157, 213, 239; transcend, 33 (? = விடு).

ஓரா அல், 246 (= ஒருவுதல்), abandonment.

ஒரு|ங்கு, altogether, at once, completely: உடன், 167, 236, 287, 332, 387.

ஒருங்குடன் is a pleonasm.

[An adverb in (ங்)கு from √O, OR. Comp. அ|ங்|கு, *etc.*]

K. I. ஒல் OL, *v. n.* be possible. (ஒல்|லு, § 62.) [Comp. √ஒ, இயல், வல்? M. In C. = be unwilling. In T. GAL.]

ஒல்|வ, things in your power, 169. [G. 95.]

ஒல்லும்வகை, by all possible means, 36, 71.

ஒல்லா, is impossible, 258. [G. 87.]

II. ஒல்|லை, promptitude. [From imitative word ஒல் + ஐ for எ.]

As adv. 'swiftly, at once,' 66.

ஒல்லென் (§ 273) either 'the swift,' or sounding,' 77.

III. ஒலி, *n.* sound; *v.* (§ 64) roar, resound, 249, 256, 397.

[Comp. கலி, உலை. M. Anc. C. *uli.*]

Nig. ஒலி என்ப இடியே காற்றே ஓசை என்றுகுமுப்பேர்.

ஒலித்தல் = சத்தித்தல் [G. 94] a sounding forth, 23.

K. IV. ஒல்|கு, be shaken, fail. [Comp. ஒழி, உலை. T. OLU-KU.]

ஒல்கா, is untroubled, 178. ஒல்கார், fail not, 148.

ஒற்கம் = தளர்ச்சி, feebleness, 204.

ஒழ் OṚ = *cease.*

I. ஒழி (§§ 57, 62) leave, leave behind, forsake, depart from, cease. [M., C. *ora-su.*]

ஒழிய, remain; be left, forsaken; left behind, 19, 30; *while it remains behind.*

ஒழியுமே, 43, 123, 135. ஒழிந்தார், 49, 54.

ஒழிகு = ஒழிக, 76, shun [G. 85] 306. ஒழிந்தாள், she forsook, 372.

ஒழியாமை, unfailing enjoyment, 79. ஒழிதல், departure, 143.

ஒழிந்த, that have passed, 169. பூத்தொழி [G. 153] that have done flowering, 290.

K. II. ஒழு|கு, *v.* (§ 62) flow on; pass; be in the *habit* of, act, behave, 311.

ஒழுகாது, 37. ஒழுகல், conduct, course of action, 309.
ஒழுகுவேன், 44, 45, = I who am wont to behave as one who . . . .
ஒழுகின், 139. ஒழுக, while it rushes on, 212.
ஒழுகிய, 171. ஒழுகுவர், 182, 385.
உண்டொழுகு, habitually eat, 271.

K. III. *n.* ஒழு|க்கம் = சீலம், ஆசாரம், habit.

ஆசார உபசாரங்கள். 57 with நல்; 142, 143, decorum, virtue.
75 with தேற்று, unmentionable evils. [Comp. √வழ். வாடிகை.]

ஒள் OḶ. [M., C., T. OLA|YU. Comp. விள், வெள், நல், மேல். The two ideas are (1) light; (2) concealment.]

I. ஒள் (ஒண், ஒட்) bright; good; beautiful, wise.

Adj. 'bright,' 129, 379; 'lustrous,' 395: of the brow, eyebrow, *etc.* 176 [here the change is anomalous. G. 34. ள் becomes ட், and then *metri gratiâ* is softened into ண் (G. 41, 42)], 189 [comp. here நள், விள், ஒள்].

ஒண்|மை, brightness, clearness of understanding, 196, 292.

ஒளி = மகிமை, glory, 9. = பரவரும் அறியமிற்றல், radiated light, emitted splendour. = பிரகாசம், splendour, 22; light, 371.

ஒண்|பொருள், 102, wealth that yields distinction, 195, 280, 386.

ஒண்|ணிற, bright-hued, 139. ஒளிர், *v. n.* (§ 60) emit light: ஒளிந, 269.

II. ஒளி, *v. a.* and *n.* (§ 64) hide: மறை, 90.

ஒறு ORR.

K. ஒறு (§ 64) punish, 65. [Comp. ஒடு.]

ஒன் ON = ஒ.

ஒன்|று [√ஒ, ஒன், ஒரு, ஓர். Comp. C. D. G. p. 216 *etc.*]

I. *n.* anything, 1, 5, 281.

ஒன்றனும், 186. ஒன்றேயும், any one virtue, 102.

II. *v.* (1) suit, fit: பொருந்து (§ 62).

ஒன்றின [G. 95] things befitting and necessary, 4. [Comp. ஒப்புரவு.]

(2) join: கூடு, 171, 315, 357, 359; agree, 55.

'ஒன்றினர் வாழ்க்கையே வாழ்க்கை, the life of the loving is life.' கலித். i. 18.

ஓர், *adj.* 1, 361. ஒரு, 357.

ஒன்|னர் = பகைவர், for ஒன்றார் [G. 88, 95] 129, 188.

ஒற்றுமை, oneness, union (ஒன்று + மை), 237.

ஒன்று in 143 is variously explained:

1. ஒன்று + ஆ, 'as though any one of these existed.'

2. As a finite verb = பொருந்தாவாம். Then உணரற்பாற்று = அறியுந்தன்மை: 'the perception (of these) is not (to them).'

3. It is not meet to consider them as in the same category with the base: = 'as one with.'

ஒன்பது, nine (§ 172) 47. [C. D. G. p. 241 *etc.* பது = *ten*; what is ஒன்? M. T. *tom-midi.* C. *ombattu.* See தொண்டு and ஒன்பான்.]

For this verse compare B. I. S. 3411:

'नवद्वारैः स्रवद्देहं दुर्गन्धमध्यमन्दिरम्।
मानयन्ति पलैस्तुङ्गं पशवस्ते न मानवाः॥

Those who esteem this body, oozing at nine avenues, this stall in the midst of foul odours, are beasts, not men.'

[Comp. N. N. 12: ஒன்பான்வாயிலுடம்பு.]

ஓ Ō.

K. ஓ Ō.

1. ஓ seems to be for அ + வ (வ becoming உ): கல்லவர் = கல்லோர்.
2. In 1st pl. செய்வோம் = செய் + வ + உம. Comp. C. D. G. p. 30.
3. In questions *etc.* G. 112. Is equivalent to a negative. = Lat. *num*.
4. See under அ.
5. Not often interchangeable with ஒ; but ஓடு = ஒடு = உடன். பொரு gives போர், and from கொள்ளு comes கோள்.

K. ஓ Ō. [Comp. ஊங்கு. ? From ஊ. M. ŌṄṄ.]

ஓ|ங்கு, ஓ|க்கு, *v.* (§§ 62, 160) '*rise above.*'

ஓங்கருவி, the lofty waterfall, 79. ஓங்கு(புகழ்) = சிறந்த, மிக்க, 9.

ஓங்குமுயர்குடி, an excellent family of lofty lineage, 199, 283. [ஓங்கு + உயர்.]

ஓங்கிய, 176. ஓக்கிய for ஓங்கிய, the uplifted, 129 [G. 41].

ஓ ஓ, *interj.* Ah! Oho! 88.

ஓசை, sound, 332. ஒலி, சத்தம். Comp. ஓதம், இசை.

ஓட் ŌḌ. [C. T. = lose, fail.]

I. ஓடு, *v.* (§ 62) run on, 68, 108, 111, 120, 166.

II. ஓட்டு, cause to run, spend, pass.

ஓட்டல் (ஓட்டம்) = கழித்தல், 235.

கண்ணோடு, look on graciously, 155.

கண்ணோட்டம், kindliness, 348. = தாக்ஷிணியம்.

[K. 575. So T. 52: 'கண்ணுக்கணிகலங் கண்ணோட்டம்,
Kindliness is the ornament of the eye: it wears no gems like ear and neck: *the eye's jewel is its gracious glance.*']

ஓடு = earthen pot, = மண்பாத்திரம், 139. [C. prop. 'a potsherd,' see ŌTTAI.]

ஓது ŌTH. [Comp. S. वद्, वच. उद्+गै. C., M., TU.]

ஓது (§ 62).

ஓதுவது, the studying, 140 [G. 95].

ஓதியும் [G. 141], ஓதார் [G. 189], ஓதாதும் [G. 141], ஓதியவினையர், 270. See notes.

ஓதிய, 386.

ஓதம், *n.* billow, surf wave; ocean.

ஓலம், 249, 391. See ஓலி.

ஓம் ŌM. [√ō in C.='be kind.' Comp. உவ. C. Ō|VU. M. ŌMB|U, ŌM|AN. T. ŌM|U.]

K. ஓம்|பு, cherish (§ 62).

This verb seems to intensify the meaning of that to which it is added, as a kind of auxiliary.

Thus, காத்தோம்பி, *carefully* guarding themselves, 351.

ஓம் is also a verbal inflexion of 1st person plural. G. 77. See எம், ஆம்.

ஓர் ŌR. [Comp. ஆர|ாய், தேர், உணர். C. ŌR|U. M. OR. T. ŌR|U ='endure.']

ஓர், *v.* (§ 57) search out, ponder.

ஓர்த்து for ஓர்ந்து [G. 41] 64. ஓராது, not regarding, 69.

ஓருங்குலம், a thoughtful, intelligent clan [G. 87] 175.

ஓரும் is called a poetic expletive, or அசைச்சொல் [G. 115, 116]; but it seems to retain the meaning of '*ponder this!*' 72, 360.

ஓர் = ஆர் = அவர். See 126, சான்றோர் = சான்றவர். [வ is vocalised, and அ + உ = ஓ.]

ஓர் = ஒரு: adj. form of ஒன்று, one, 41, 361.

[C. D. G. p. 217 *etc.* M. C. So ஈர் and இரு.]

ஓ|வு, *v.* (§ 62) = ஒழி, cease, 32. [In T. = *pōvu.* C. = ஓம்பு.]

க KA.

க KA = *k*, *kh*, *g*, *gh*, and *h*. See H. B. introd. Comp. C. D. G.

It is often interchanged with *ch*: the guttural sinks into the palatal; so *kirk* has become *church*. க of the Tamil is often = வ in Telugu [ஆகு = *avu*].

A sign of the optative mood, both numbers [G. 85] 4. செய்க.

கச KAÇA, see கை.

கச|ப்பு [= bitterness, disgust] = கைப்பு.

Fault: குற்றம், 260, 342. [T. KASA-ṬU, GASI. C. Comp. கயம்.]

கடகம். [S. कटकम्. Also கடையம்.] A bracelet, 289.

[Jī. Chin. xiii. 397: 'கடகக்கைவிரலை, a pair of jewelled hands.']

கட் KAḌ.

I. கட. [C. D. G. p. 455. M., C. *kaḍa.* T. *gaḍa.* Allied to கழி, and S. ह.]

(I.) கட, *v.* (§ 66) cross over, pass, 398.

K. கடல், sea, 73, 97, 98, 107, 108, 138, 166, 230, 242, 263, 264, 269, 275, 332, 349, 382.

Observe the variety of epithets, eight in all: மலி, நளி, அலை, கனை, பொரு, அறை, நீர், பெரு. See சேர்ப்பன். [Ancient C. KAḌALU.]

கடலம், 272. = சமுத்திரம்.

[The majority of commentators say கடலத்துள் = கடல்குழ்ந்தபூமிக்குள், and treat பழி as = 'will incur guilt!' This is traditional, but clearly untenable. The tenses must be noticed: while they say 'we *will afterwards* do virtuous deeds,' they *have already plunged* into an ocean of guilt and there perished. We should expect பழிக்கடலம்.]

(II.) கட (§ 140).

கடவது, what is due, 341: = as much as is needful.

கடன், obligation, duty, debt, 58, 98, 184, 202, 382.

['கற்புடையாள் பூண்ட கடன், duties undertaken by the true matron.' T. 64.]

K. கட|ப்பாடு, obligation; order, 261.

கட|வுள், God (p. 1). [Comp. இறை.]

(III.) S. கட|மா [see மா] 300.

கடம் [S. घड, कद]. 1. Elephant's frontal secretion: மதம். 2. Forest: காடு.

II. கடி [C., M., T. *kara.* S. गहे].

(I.) *v. trans.* (§ 57) rebuke, 157, 278; renounce, 157, 364; scare away, 41, 283; overpower and dispel, 97. [T. 46.]

(II.) *v.* (§ 64) bite: கறி, 156. [Comp. கத்தி.]

(III.) *n.* marriage, 56, 364 [S. कटि]; protection, guardianship, 86, 238.

கடி means at the same time '*marriage*' and 'renounce thou.'

Nig. கடி மணம் விரைவு கூர்மை காவல் பேய் விளக்கங்காப்பு வடி வச்சம்வாசம் ஐயம் வரைவுவிம்மிதம் எழாறும்.

[கடிமனை, home. Jī. Chin. iii. 91.]

(IV.) கடி|ஞை, a beggar's bowl, 99.

[கடி, கடிகை. S. गडु. For ஞை comp. ஞன். T. *kaḍi-v-eḍu* = a bowl-ful.]

(V.) See under கடு.

கடி|ப்பு, a drumstick: குணில், 100. குறுந்தடி. [Comp. கடி. C. KUḌUPU.]

III. [கடு, S. कटु. See கொடு].

(I.) (Adj. forms from கடுமை. [H. B. 131. *e.*])

கடும், harsh, 73; fierce, 164; severe, 280. Opp. to இன், 172, 189.

கடு, evil, 124 ; intense, 224. [Comp. கறி.]

(II.) கடு, *n.* poison, 374.

(III.) கடு-க்கு, *v.* (§ 62) enrage, 189.

(IV.) கட்டு, *v. a.* (§ 62) tie, 153.

n. bond, 238.

Used as a sign of the 7th case, from கண், 'place' (+ து) 263. (= இடத்ததன்னது.) G. 93.

(V.) கட்டி, *n.* inspissated juice, lump of sugar, 35. [T. 48.]

IV. கடை, a word indicating remote position in space, *or* time, 199. [Comp. இடை, தலை.] Hence,

1. What is last or lowest in state, place, condition, 133, 227, 281, 297, 334, 365, 368.

2. (Meton.) 'a low man' [see கயம் and கீழ்] 255, 366.

3. = கடையாயார், 160, 216 ; = கீழானவர்.

4. 'Street,' 107 : 'shop,' or 'bazaar.'

In comp.: கடைபோக, to the last (of life).

கடைப்பிடி, (1) keep in mind, 20. As கால், கண்.

கடைக்கண், tip, 390. கடைப்படு, be degraded, 136.

['கடைநாள் இதுவென்று அறிந்தாரும் இல்லை,

There are none who know which day shall be their last.' கலித். i. 12.]

புறக்கடை, outer gate, 31, 293. கடைத்தும், even when, *or* where, 147, 150, 236, 343, 360.

[Used as 7th case + உம் ; with rel. part., G. 63.]

(2) Persevere, go on to the end.

[Comp. T. 74, 94 : 'ஒழுக்கக் கடைப்பிடியா தார்,

Those who don't hold on to the end in the way of decorum.']

[T., M. KAḌ|A. C. KAḌ|E. S. कट.]

கடு|கு (§ 62) make haste [√கடு] 189.

கடுக்கி some say by poetical license for கடுகி ; more probably from a causal கடுக்கு, 'fret, urge.'

கடுக்கென, hasty, passionate, 348. [H. B. § 273.]

கட்டு, கட்டே, see கண்.

கணக்காயர், teachers of the Vedas, 314.

From கணக்கு, arithmetic ;—any learning ; the Vedas.

See ஆயர் = கணக்குமுதலியன ஓதுவிப்பார். T. 10. [S. गण्.] கணக்கர், 397.

கண் KAṆ. [Comp. S. कण, खण्ड्, गण. M., C., T. KAN, KANU.]

கண் [see காண், காட், காட்டு].

1. *n.* eye, 44, 46, 59, 191, 251, 305, 306, 373, 384, 394, 395, 400.

In 251, 'கண்ணைவாத்தக்க, that strike the eye.'

கண்ண, things with eyes, 13, 17, 49, 116, 265, 267, 297, 358, 374. [G. 93.]

கண்ணின்று [நில்] before a man's face, 353.

In 47 கண் = கண்களுக்கு [G. 152].

2. For கணு, a joint of *bambū etc.*, 156, 390; knot (*or* eye) in tree. [T. GAṆU-PU. C. GAṆI-KE. M. KAṆA. In S. पर्वन्.]

3. Place, 148. Comp. கடை, 326, 373. Used as an ending of 7th case, 16, 267, 305, 336. [Gr. 63.] கண்ணது, that which occupies the place, 368. கண்ணும், even in their case, 56, 69, 75.

4. It is used with adj. part. (க doubled!) as = கால், to form an adv. part. (G. 86) = 'even when, even if,' 141, 142, 184, 281. 261, 371 [க not doubled].

5. Centre of a drum, *or* tambourine: வாத்தியத் தின்கணிடம், 100, 388.

கண்படு, slumber; see படு, 366. Hence,

கண்பாடு, see பாடு.

முலைக்கண், nipple, 399.

கட்டே [கண் + து + ஏ] 'is upon—dwells on:' lit. '(is) indeed a thing (occupying) the place of.' [G. 63, 93.]

கணவர், husband, 385.

கண்டேம் *etc.*, see காணு, 385.

K. கண்ணோடு [ஓடு] be graciously disposed towards, 155.

K. கண்ணோட்டம், 348 [ஓடு].

[In comp. as second member = '*ness*.' See வன், இடு.]

Comp. N. M. K. 93:

'வன்கண் பெருகின் வலிபெருகும்; பான்மொழியார்
இன்கண் பெருகின் இனம்பெருகும்; சீர்சான்ற
மென்கண் பெருகின் அறம்பெருகும்; வன்கண்
கயம்பெருகின் பாவம் பெரிது.

If hardness (*fortitude*) increase, strength increases;
if sweetness increase in those whose words are as milk (*women*), the tribe increases;
if all-glorious meekness increase, virtue increases;
if the base element of hardness (*of heart*) increase, sin becomes great.'

Here கண் is a suffix = '*ness*' = மை = தனம். Observe வன்கண் in good and bad sense.

கணம் = கூட்டம், in troops, 25; troop (S. गण) 399.

கணமலை, a knot of hills, 285, 353.

கண்டல் = தாழை, Pandanus odoratissimus: scented thorn, 194. [M. S. करटक.]

Nig. கண்டல் கேதகை முள்ளிப்பேர்.

கண்டு *etc.*, see காண்.

கண்|ணி [கண். M.] garland: = மலர்மாலை, 16.

கந்து. [S. स्कन्ध.]

1. தறி, stake, 192.

2. பற்றுக்கோடு, support = relying on it, 303, 310.

கது KATH. [கதுவு = 'mix.' C. *kade*, 'join.' T. *kadi.*]

கதம் = wrath : சினம், மூர்க்கம், 61. (K. 130.) [C. *kati.* Comp. கதழ் (C. *gadaṛa*) = rage furiously. S. गर्त. M. *katham.*]

கதவு [கதவம், கபாடம்] (leaf of a) door, 91, 271. [C., M., T. Comp. கடை. S. कपाट.]

கதிர் = கிரணம் [comp. S. किरण] ray, 89, 176, 224. [M., C., T. *kadiru* = spindle.]

கதுப்பு, a woman's hair : கூந்தல். [C. *kad* = black. Comp. கவுள். S. गराड. Anc. C. *kadapu* = cheek. T. *kadubu* = crowd.]

Nig. கதுப்பே ஆண்மயிரும் பெண்பான்மயிரொடு கவுளும் முப்பேர்.

கதுப்பினும், O maid, whose hair is fragrant with precious musk ! 294 (G. 93).

கப்பி, grain ; coarse grits, 341.

[√கப்|பு = 'eat greedily.' M. Comp. T. GAB. An imitative word = 'gobble.']

கம் KAM, 'smithery.' [Cor. of S. कर्म. May be connected with S. क, ख, ग, घ, or ह. T. KAM|MU. S. कम्.]

கம்மம் [S. कंस. M. KAMMAN] 'smith's work,' 393.

கம் KAM. [S. कम्.]

I. கம|ழ், *v.* (§ 57) be diffused as odours, 117, 180, 199, 294.

[அம் is a formative. Comp. கந்தம் = fragrance. T. KAM|MU. C. KAM|PU, KAM|ARU, *etc.*]

II. கமுகு = பாக்குமரம், the Betel-nut palm : *Areca Catechu*, 216.

[M. S. क्रमुक = गुवाक. Der. doubtful.]

கய|ம். [S. क्षि, क्षय. Comp. கெடு, கீழ். T. KAYYA. M. = 'depth.']

1. What is low : கீழ்மை. கயம் = கீழாயினேன், a low fellow, 356.

K. கயமை, baseness. Ch. xxxvi.

கயவர், base, low men : கீழ்மக்கள், 66, 143, 145, 200, 355. = கீசர்.

[Opp. to குடிப்பிறந்தார் and to சான்றவர்.]

2. A tank—*excavated :* குளம், 215, 375. [*Mū.* நற்குமரைக்கயம், a tank with fair *lotuses.*]

கயல், any fish ; a special fish ;—carp : *Cyprinus*, L. கெண்டை, சேல்.

It is the favourite simile to express the liquid lustre of the female eye, 44, 395.

[M. See கயம் = குளம் = 'a tank.' S. कज = 'water-born.' For term. அல், comp. சாயல் from S. छाया ; மயல் for மயக்கம்.]

கர் KAR. [S. कृ, कर्, 'hand ;' 'black ;' 'embryo.']

I. கர, *v.* (§ 66) 'conceal :' ஒளி ; and so 'refuse,' 19, 92, 305.

[So கரவு = வஞ்சம், deceit.
In *Mū.* கரவுடையார் தம்மைக் கரப்பர்; கரவார் கரவில்லா நெஞ்சத் தவர்.]

II. கரு (='the embryo.' From s. गर्भ; from √ग्रह्).

(I.) கரு|து, *v.* (§ 62) regard, 193, 261.

(II.) கருத்து, *n.* regard; idea; purport, 181, 211, 380, 395.

(III.) கரு|வி, instrument, 320, 393. [? s. कृ. M. KAR-I, -IVI, -UVI.]

III. கரு [கரும், கரிய, கார். Comp. கறு].

1. Black, 8, 47, 387.

கரும்பார்க்கழனி, a field of black soil, 122, i.e. நரகம்; [or கரும்பு + ஆர், full of sugar-cane.] See கார், 103, 217, 311. [M. KAR-I, KAR-U, KĀR.]

2. Eminence: பெரு, 186; கருநரை = பெரியவெள்ளேறு.

K. கரி = சாட்சி, evidence, example, 10.

[Only Tamil in this sense.]

Nig. கரி என்பதிருக்தை சான்று கறையடி சேகுநாற்பேர்.

கருனை = பொரிக்கறி, anything fried, 200, 210, 268. (√கரு = black.)

வெங்|கருனை, 207, 210, = savoury food.

Jī. Chin. xiii. 25:

'முல்லை முகைசொரிந்தாற் போன்றிலிய
பாலடிசின் மகளிர் ஏந்த
நல்ல கருனையா னென்வாயும்
பொற்கலத்து நயந்துண் டார்கள்
அல்லல் அடைய அடகிடுமின்
ஓட்டகத்தென் றயில்வார்க் கண்டும்,
செல்வ நமரங்கா ளினையன்மின,
செய்தவமே நினைமின், கண்மீர்!

Having seen those who joyously ate every day sweet milk, and rice, white as though jasmine buds were showered down, off golden dishes, *served up by handmaidens*, with rich spiced food,—now, since affliction has visited them, saying, "Give me any coarse food in this sherd," and feeding so,—see that ye regard not wealth, my friends, regard penitence!'

கரும்பு, sugar-cane: கன்னல், *Saccharum Officinarum*, 34, 35, 138, 211, 390.

[C. *kabbu.* Anc. C. KARUM|BU. M. KARI|MBU.]

கரை [comp. கரு. M. KAR|A] a shore: bank, 135, 224.

முடிவு, எல்லை. [To be distinguished from சேர்ப்பு, where ships anchor.

'நுண்ணூற் பெருங்கேள்வி நூற்கரை கண்டான்,

He who has thoroughly mastered science by subtle thought and extensive investigation.' T. 35.

The verb கரை (§ 57) = melt away.]

கர்மம், கருமம், *n.* [S. कर्मन्. √कृ, कर् = 'do'].

1. தொழிலாகியதவம், ceremonial and ascetic observance, 52.

2. செய்கை, the (right) thing to be done, 129.
3. Affair, business, 231, 249, 250.
4. Action, 236, 345.

கல் KAL. [Comp. S. कल् and its derivatives. T. KALI and KALU-GU.]

I. கல், கலீர், கல|கல, imitative words, 25, 140, 256. [Comp. 66.]

With என்று, or as *v.*, § 66. H. B. § 273. Comp. கலுழ். C. *gala*.

II. கல், *n.* stone, rock, 360, 364. [M. KAL|LU. C.]

கல்வரை = கன்மலை, rocky mountain, 66, 154, 283 (*bis*), 285.

III. கன்று [கல் + து] *v.* (§ 62) become matured, hardened; become enraged, 315, 351, [for கனலு, q. v.]

IV. கன்று, *n.* calf, 101, 115, 279. [M. Adj. கற்று.]

V. கல்|லு, excavate; dig; bury, 185 [G. 153], 277.

VI. கல், *v.* (§ 70) = learn, 253, 398. [M., C. KALI. T. KARA-CHU.]

கற்ற, 255. [G. 95.] கற்றோர், 139, 260, 313, 314.
கற்பின், if you learn, 116, 140. கற்பவர், the learners, 135, 317.
கற்ப, they will learn, 135.
With அறி: கற்றறி(ந்தார்), the learned and wise, 56, 133, 138, 256.
The negative:
கல்லாது, 140, 169, 254. கல்லாத, 255. [G. 95.]
கல்லார், unlearned, 115, 129, 139. கல்லாதார், 106.
கல்லா, 45, 155, 366. கல்லாமை, ignorance, 145.

K. கல்|வி (G. 95) = வித்தை, ch. xiv, 131, 132, 135, 195, 333.
கற்|பு, learning (? 140) = கல்வி (or கற்பின்).

கல KALA, *mix.*

I. கல, *v.* (§ 66) mingle with, be intimate with, 75, 76, 168, 204, 227, 259.

II. கல|ங்கு, *v. int.* (§ 62) be confounded, perturbed, 59.
கல|க்கு, *v. tr.* (§§ 62, 160) 248.

[M. = 'mix.' C. Also கலவு and கலாவு: comp. அளாவு.]
கலவை, mixed things, i. e. leavings, broken food, 268.

கலி = குரல், cry, 12. [S. कलि.]

K. கலுழ், *v.* (§ 57) wail, 372, 393.

கலம், கலன், *n.* [G. 17]. [M. Comp. S. कलश. M., T.]

1. A vessel: பாத்திரம், 206, 239, 289. பொற்கலம், 206, 345.
2. A ship: மரக்கலம், நாவாய், மதலை, 179, 250. ஆழ்கலம் [G. 153] 12.
3. A jewel, 40, 251, 376.

மாணவருங்கலம் [மானம் என்கிற அரிய அணி] = honour that precious jewel.
அணிகலம் = ஆபரணம், 242.

கலை = மான், a stag, 399. [M.]
கல்யாணம், marriage, 86. [S. कल्याण.]

கவ் KAV. [S. गभ. The idea is of anything forked, split; hence anything bent, arched, hollow. C., T. *kava* = a pair. M. = a forked branch. Comp. கப்பு, கொம்பு, கேப்பு.]

I. கவான் = தொடை, lap, thigh, 201.

II. கவறு = இருபிளப்புள்ள பனமட்டை, a forked piece of palmyra wood: so, 153 = பற்றுக்கோடு, a fulcrum. [Or, some say, கவல் + தாவு + உள்ளம் = a mind that care assails?]

III. கவற்று, *v.* (§ 62) = கவலைப்படுத்து, cause trouble to, distract, 44, 45, 89, 306. [Comp. μέριμνα from μερίς: *curae divorse trahunt.*] From கவல், 'be anxious.' C. *kavalu.*

IV. கவி, *v.* (§§ 57, 64) overarch, cover as a canopy, 80. [Comp. கவிழ். M., C., T.]

V. கவ்வு, *v.* (§ 62) seize with eagerness, with open jaws. See கௌவு, 70, 322. [Comp. கவர்.]

கழ் KAṚ, *pass off.* [Comp. S. गल्. T. *gaḍ.* C. *kaḷ.* M. *kaḷ, kaṛ.* Connected with கட.]

I. கழி, *v.* (§ 57) pass off; die; slip away, 49, 71.

II. கழி, *v.* (§ 64) get rid of; spend time, 56, 162, 268, 273, 286, 330, 366.

கழி, *adv.* and *adj.* = மிக்க, many, much (G. 153) 113, 128, 275.

III. கழி, *n.* a back-water, creek, 168, 391.

['அல்கு கழியினுஞ் செல்லாதோ கடல்?
Does the sea not enter even a little creek?']

IV. கழ|ல்(லு), *v.* (§ 70) fall or slip out, 13.

V. கழ|று, *v.* (§ 62) urge, 253.

VI. கழுமியார் (with காதல், see கெழ்) those overflowing with affection, 228.

VII. கழு|வு, *v.* (§ 62) wash.

கழீஇ, having washed, 258. கழூஉம்=கழுவும், 285 (G. 14).

கழுநீர், water in which rice has been washed, 217 (G. 153).

VIII. கழு, கழு|கு, 'eagle:' here it must be the 'vulture,' 48. [M. S. गृध्र. Germ. *geier*.]

IX. கழ|னி=வயல், a cultivated field, 122: some say கருங் பார்கழனி=நரகம். [Comp. களம். M.]

கள் KAḶ. [Has meanings: 1. 'thorn;' 2. 'removal;' கழ்; 3. 'toddy;' 4. 'deceit.']

I. களங்கனி, 103.

Fruit of the களா (களம், களர் or களவு), a wild thorn. It is intensely black. *Carissa Carandas.* [M. *kalāvu*. T. *kalivi.*]

II. களிறு, a male elephant, 192. [√கள்=wild exhilaration. M.]

K. III. களர், brackish soil. [Comp. அளம், அளக்கர், அளறு.]

களர்நிலம்=உவர்நிலம், 133.

IV. கள்|ளி, a kind of shrub, with white acrid juice. *Euphorbia nereifolia* or *Tirukaḻḻi*: 'milk-hedge,' 262. [M.]

V. (I.) கள் (கள்ளு), *v.* [*past tense* கட்டேன்] steal; act treacherously, 157.

(II.) கள், *n.* toddy, any intoxicating juice, 157; honey, sweet fragrance, 349. [M.]

(III.) கள்|ளம்=வஞ்சனை, deceit, 20, 128, 380. [M.]

VI. களை, *v.* (§ 57) remove, cut off, 9, 44, 170, 226, 239. Comp. கழி.

K. VII. களம் (களன்), any open place. [S. खल.]

வெங்களத்து, in the cruel place, slaughter-house, 16.

[T. 10: 'அவைக்களன், an assembly.']

கற் KARR. [Comp. கர். M. KARRA. C. KARE. T. KARA.]

I. கறு, *v.* (§ 64) grow black [M. KARR|UKKA]; grow dark with anger, 63, 315.

கறு|வு, anger, 335. [T. 46.]

II. கறை, *n.* darkness; the dark mountains, 231. கறையடி = ஆனை.

III. கறி, *v.* (§ 64) bite, eat: கடி, 141. [T. KORUKU; KARU-CHU. C. KACHCHU.]

கறங்கு, *v.* (§ 62) sound: ஒலி, 23, 228, 285.

K. கற்பு. [S. कल्प.]

1. Chastity, 293, 381, 383. Ch. xxxix.
2. Learning: கல்வியறிவு, 140. [√கல்.] (T. 86.)

கன|ல் KANAL, 'fire:' நெருப்பு. [See அனல், அழல். S. अनल.]

கனலு, *v.* (§ 70) = கொதி, சொலி, 291, 298.

கனம் [S. घन] weight, value, 127, 146, 341.

கனி [கல், comp. கன்று :—கனி = கன்றி. M.]

1. *n.* = பழம், ripe, sweet fruit, 19, 103.
2. *v.* (§ 57) ripen, 244.

கனை, *n.* sound, roar: அறை. *v.* (§ 64) roar [M.] 138, 349.

கன்னி|யர், virgins, 274. [S. कन्या.]

கா KĀ, *guard.* [M., C., T. have KĀ, KĀ-PU, KĀY. Hindūstāni کاول from Turkish قراول. In common Tamil they say காத்து. Comp. S. धा, हा = கா.]

1. கா, *v.* (§ 64) = காப்பாற்று, ஓம்பு: guard, hoard, defend, restrain: அடக்கு, பாதுகா = S. रक्ष्, 9, 57, 59, 63, 230, 280, 320, 351.

II. கா|ப்பு, *n.* = காவல், defence, protection, 83, 277, 361.

காக்கை, காகம் [S. काक] crow, 41, 400.

காஞ்சிரம் = எட்டி, 217, 243.

Strychnos Nux Vomica. See Ainslie's Materia Med. i. 318.
The tree came from Cochin China, where its name is *Cay-cu-chi*, hence perhaps the name.

காடு [√கட், கடு as காடு from கடு. But comp. கா. M., C. *kāṛ*. T. Tu. S. कानन = கான், கானம், கானல், and काष्ठ] 'a wilderness, jungle,' 25, 122, 361.

With புறம், சுடு, இடு, it is 'the burning ground,' 45, 96, 121.

K. காட்சி, 157, = பார்வை. [See காண், கண்.]

'The vision and the faculty divine.' In K. Lex. = தரிசனம். [M. *kāṛcha.*]

காணம்=பொருள், பொன், wealth, gold, coin, 372, 374. [Comp. காணிக்கை. M. S. काञ्चन.]

காணி = $\frac{1}{80}$ (or $\frac{1}{64}$), 346. [H. B. pt. II. app. vi. T., M., C.]

காண் KĀṆ, *see*.

I. காண், *v.* (§ 70)=நோக்கு, 'see,' 24, 49, 84, 293. [See கண்.]

காண, in sight of all, 45, 66, 107, 374.

காணும் (not neg.), see! examine! 12, 136, 241. கண்டு, 43, 44, 45, 50, 53, 330.

கண்டும், though they have seen, 25, 39, 60.

கண்டுழி [see உழி] as soon as they see, 62.

கண்டிலர், persons who have not seen, 48; or=to a past tense, neg.=have they not seen?

கண்டாலும், காணினும், 79, 154. கண்டதுடைத்து, is as terrible as to see, 126.

காணேம், we know not, 132. காண்பாம், we shall see, 137.

காண்டல், 361, = காணுதல். காண்டொறும், 159. See தோறு.

காண்ப, they shall see, 315.

II. காட்டு, *v.* (§§ 62, 160) show: காண்பி, 293, 314, 319, 341, 372. [M., TU., C., T.]

காதம் = காவதம். [C., M., Tu., T.] An Indian league; here about 5 English miles (or ½ யோசனை), 100.

காதல், see காம்.

K. காம் KĀM. [S. कम्, काम.]

I. காமம், love; desire; lust, sexual passion: ஆசை, 13, 42, 88-90 (!), 391.

காமநோய், the torments of lust.

[Comp. K. Rām. I. xi. 80:

'ஆசைநோய்க்கு மருந்தும் உண்டங் கொலோ?

Is there any medicine for the disease of lust?']

காமத்துப்பால், see Introd. to ch. xl. காமநுதலியல், chapter treating of love.

II. காம் for காமம். [G. 41. So இன்புறு and துன்புறு.]

காமுறு, desire eagerly. இச்சி, 54, 60, 259, 313. (See உறு.) Here உறு=படு (§ 161).

III. காதல்=காமம், affection; desire, 86.

காதன்மனையாள், =a loving housewife, 228, 306, 330, 384.

காதல்வகை, so as to please his taste.

காதலன் (f. காதலி, pl. காதலவர்) one who fondly loves, 73, 181, 384, 392, 395.

IV. காதலி, *v.* (§ 64) desire, 123, 181.

காந்தள் = கார்த்திகைப்பூ, a flower plant, *Gloriosa superba*, 283. [S. कान्त, or कान्ताय?]

காய் KĀY. [M., C., TU., T. KĀ-GU, -YU, -CHU.]

I. காய், *n.* (1) fruit immature, 19, 203, 217, 328.

(2) Any nut or legume that does not grow soft or sweet by ripening. Thus தேங்காய், 103, 116.

II. *v. int.* (§ 57) wax hot, 61, 63, 297, 315.

III. *v. tr.* (§ 64) produce, 203, 367.

காயம், condiment, seasoning, hot spice, 116. [M. From verb காய் = be hot. Comp. காரம், காழ்ப்பு.]

கார் [see கர்] blackness.

கார் என = கருமையாக: (§ 273), 103: so that men say blackness. [Met. a cloud. Comp. T. 6.]

காரறிவு, darkened wisdom, i.e. ignorant folly, 311.

In 217 கார் = 'black, made of கார்நெல்,' or கார், *v.* (§ 64) = be acrid.

காரணம் [S. कारण] cause: ஏது, 56, 183, 265. [See காரியம்.]

கால் KĀL. [M., T., C., TU. Comp. கழல் or கவல்.]

I. See காலம், from the knee downward.

II. 1. A leg, foot; (க. வர்) 84, 123, 218, 268, 372.

காலர், persons having legs, 122.

காலாடு, be active, 113. காற்றொழில், menial work, 193.

2. A wheel, 2.

3. A place: கண்.

கடைக்கால், what rightly occupies the lowest place, 368.

4. A handle: காம்பு, கைப்பிடி, 368.

5. A stem: தாள், 199.

காலம் [S. काल] = time, 68.

காலத்து, when; in the time of [G. 152] 110, 184, 284, 329. = பொழுது, இடத்து, *etc.*

காலத்தால், early [G. 137] 20.

கால் = காலம் [G. 41] 24. அக்கால், then, 123.

பல்காலும், many a time, 27. எக்காலும், always, 43, 112.

காலை = காலம்; தரம் [see ஐ] 24, 68.

இருகாலே, before; early, 341; in the morning of youth; betimes: உதயம், 35, 110, 328, 363.

கால், as a verbal inflexion, = when [G. 86. H. B. § 97 note] 2, 5, 26, 33, 37, 38, 44, 57, 64, 67, 70, 113, 241, 391.

காலு, *v.* (§ 70) discharge, vomit: பெய், கக்கு, சொறி, 269. [? From கால் = channel, mouth; but comp. காறு = hawk up. M., C. *kārr.* M. *kār, kārr, kāl.* T. *kār.*]

காழ் KĀṚ, 'a seed, or stone.' [This seems a form of கல், and is the Tuḍa pronunciation of that word.] = திண்மை, hardness, core, kernel; ripe and solid wisdom.

காஞ்சிரங்காழ், 243. காழில்லா = முதறிவில்லாத, 14.

காழ்கொண்டகண்ணே = வயிரம், when it has grown into a strong tree, 192.

[T. 3: 'காழ்கொண்ட இல்லாள், a virtuous wife.']

காழாய = முதிர்ந்தநூலறிவு, 342. [Comp. கடு. C. KĀṚ. M. *kādal.*]

[T. 75: 'காழ்த்தமரம், a tree with a core.'

T. 24: 'காழ்த்த பகைவர், implacable enemies.'

T. 46: 'காழ்கடிந்து மேலூர்மை இல்லாத வெல்களிறு, the conquering elephant that uproots the tree (it is tied to) and is unsafe to mount.']

காளை, a young bullock; a youth; a bridegroom, 398. [M. *kāḷa.* Comp. S. काल.]

காறு = அளவு, காலவெல்லை, until. [கால் for காலம் + து.]

பழிகாறும், until it is abused, despised, 13 (G. 153).

கானல் = சோலை [S. गहन. கா, கான்], a grove on the sea-shore, 117, 194. நெய்தனிலத்துச் சோலை.

கான் [S. कानन. Comp. கா, 'a park,' and காடு].

கான், கானம், கானகம் = காடு, a desert: பாலைநிலம், 76, 283, 291, 300, 396, 398.

கிட் KIḌ, *hap.* [In C. KIḌ, 'perish,' = KEḌ. T. KEḌAYU. M. KIḌA. Comp. கிடத்து, கிடை, கிட்டு; Lat. *cad.*]

கிட, *v.* (§ 66) lie down, 29, 394.

Present itself; lie patent, 105. Remain, lie still; be, 231, 334, 362.

[T. 67: 'நொந்தார் செய்யக்கிடந்ததில், there is nothing the afflicted ones can do.']

உம்பர்க்கிடந்து, whilst reposing in the blissful regions, 37.

[கலித். i. 17: 'சென்றோர்முகப்பப் பொருளுங்கிடவாது, wealth does not lie stored for any passers-by to ladle in.'

See in *Mū.* வலிகிடக்கமாற்றம் = 'violent words,' and புலிகிடந்ததூறு, 'a thicket where a tiger lurks.']

கிடை, *n.* = சடை, நெட்டி, a kind of cork wood; *Aeschynomene*, 360.

கிணறு, a well, often கிணம், 263, 275.

Versions of one original. [Comp. கேணி, கிண்டு, கிள்; S. खन्. M.]

K. கிழ KIṚA. [The idea is 'old.' Comp. கீழ்.]

= உரிய, specially pertaining to. [Comp. கெழு, கேள். C. KEḶE.]

கிழவன், proprietor. = உரியவன், their old or former proprietor, 101.

[Comp. கலித். i. 21:

'கிழவர் இன்னோர் என்னாது பொருடான்
பழவினை மருங்கிற் பெயர்புபெயர் புறையும்:

Wealth says not these are my *rightful owners*, but according to old deeds changes continually its abode.' பெயர்பு. G. 86.]

நாவின்கிழத்தி, 'she whose ancient seat is the tongue:' Sarasvatī, 252.

பூவின்கிழத்தி, 'she whose ancient seat is the flower (lotus):' Lakshmī, 252.

So மனைக்கிழத்தி, 'mistress of the house.' T. 64.

[In Jī. Chin. i. 244: ஆருயிர்க்கிழத்தி, 'the mistress of his very soul.']

கிழமை, 310, = உரிமை, propriety, familiar friendship [Comp. K. ch. 81.]

கிழி, *v.* [§ 64. Comp. கீறு, கீழ். M. S. क्षि, खुर्=क्षुर्] tear, 107; rend, pierce, 151.

கிள் KIḶ. [The idea is 'rise, raise, put forth.' C. KEḶ|AR. M. KIḶ|A. T. KILL. Comp. √விள், கிளர், கிளறு.]

கிளி, a parrot, *Palaeorpis:* கிள்ளை, 283. [T., M., C. *giḷi, giṇi.* T. *chilaka.* Either an imitative word='the screamer,' or from கிள்.]

I. கிளை, *n.* branch. [Comp. கேள், கிழ, கெழு.]

உறவினர், kindred, 30, 191. கிளைஞர், 113, 206.

v. (§ 64). Comp. கிளர்.

1. Grow, be amplified, 65 (G. 153).

2. *v. tr.* scratch, as fowls, சீய், கிண்டு. Hence, கிளைப்பு, a scratching up, 341.

II. கிளர், *v.* (§ 57) shine, 290. [Comp. விள், வெள்.]

III. கிள்(ளு), *v.* (§ 62) pinch; dig out, 336. [M. Comp. கல்லு and T. KAL-LU.]

கீழ் KĪṚ. [The root is கிழ். ழ் sometimes=ண்; hence கீணர் (but comp. s. क्षि and क्षीण). See கிழ, கிட, கெட; கட, கடை, கய.]

(Used for கிழி, rend; and கீள். Comp. கிள்.) [M. KIṚ, KIṚI, KĪṚ: comp. இழி. C. KEḶ, KĒ; KIṚ, KĪ. See kin=கின், with which and S. किम् (used in a depreciatory sense) the root is mixed up. T. KIN|DA.]

I. கீழ், 'under,' sign of 7th case, 3, 191 [G. 63], 196.

கீழி, degrade, 248. கீழ்ப்படு, be subject to. கீழாய, 70, 349. [கீழ்+ஆணை.]

By metonymy [G. 162]: a low man, 64, 260, 262, 279, 341, and ch. XXXV *passim.*

கீழ்மக்கள், 70. = கயவர்.

II. கீழ்மை=கயமை: baseness, ch. XXXV.

கு KU (கூ KŪ).

1. An increment or சாரியை: really=க். G. 108. Comp. 350: புண்கல்லா,=புண்+கு+அல்லா.

2. A formative of verbs: ஆ|கு, போ|கு=பு, வு; *gu* (*ṅgu*) in intransitives, and *kku* in transitives.

3. Sign of 4th case. C. D. G. pp. 175–179. G. 60.

4. A termination of 1st sing. future. G. 81.

5. A Sanskrit prefix denoting 'inferiority.'

6. As the basis of pure Tamilian words it seems='point, direct, aim, sharpness, gathering into one:' கு+றி, கூ+ர், கூ+டு, கு+த்தி, கு+ம்பு (கூம்பு).

குட் KUḌ. [Connected with கூட். Comp. s. कुट्, 'be curved.' C. KUḌ (*koṅku*). M. KUḌ. See various words with KOḌ.]

I. குடி [comp. S. कुटि, and C. D. G. p. 456. T. *guḍi*].

குடி, family, noble family, 69, 84, 96, 141 *etc.*, 199, 281, 312.

குடி|ப்பிறப்பு, noble birth, ch. xv.

குடி|மை, high birth, 333; sense of nobility, 66.

[N. M. K. 6 : 'அறிவார்யார் நல்லான் பிறக்குங்குடி,
Who know from what family a good man will come forth?']

II. குடா|ர் (குடல். Both forms in M.) 46.

III. குடம்=கும்பம், a large earthern pot, 382.

IV. குடை=சத்திரம், *n.* umbrella [comp. கவி, கவிகை. M. *kuḍa*. T. *koḍugu*. C. *koḍe*] 3, 368.

[Jī. Chin. i. 233.] குடையர், those over whom an umbrella is borne, 21.
v. (§ 57) hollow out, bend. [C.]
குடை கலன், a vessel of leaves bent [G. 153] 289.

குணம், குணன் [S. गुण] quality, excellence, 56, 91, 230, 353.
குறுங்கர், low people, workers in leather : தோல் வினைஞர், 322.

குண்டு=depth. [S. कुण्ड. M.]

குண்டுநீர்வையம், earth (girt by) the deep sea, 94.

குண்டை=எருது, bullock, 350. [Comp. S. कुण्ड.]

I. குதலை, I. prattle : மழலை. 2. A simpleton : மூடன்.

[कु in S. compounds='inferiority;' but probably an imitative word: see கொதி, C. *kutakuta*.]
குதலை|மை, folly, 197. =தளர்ச்சி, அறியாமைக்குற்றம் (மழலைச்சொல்லின்தன்மை).

II. குதி, *v.* (§ 64). [A mixture of a word 'to boil,' 'to jump,' and 'heel.' Comp. கொதி. C., TU. *kudi*; *gudi*. T. *gudi|kālu*, 'heel.' S. घोटक.] Leap; elude, escape from, 6.

III. குதிரை, a horse, 398. [M. *kutira*. T. *gurramu*. C. *kudire*.]

K. IV. குத்து, *v.* (§ 62) peck, pierce, prick, 48, 226.

குத்தி or குற்றி=தறி, a log, 178.
In 237 'having snatched.' [Comp. கொத்து. T. KOṬṬ, கொட்டு. M., Tu., C.]
[=beat in a mortar : 'உமிக்குத்திக்கைவருந்த, to pain your hand by pounding chaff.' T. 28.]

குப் KUP. [Comp. கும், குவ், கொம். C. KUP|PE, GUP|PE. குப்பல், குப்பம், குவி, கும்பு. M. *kuppa*. T. *gub*, *kuppa*. The idea is 'anything rounded.']

I. குப்பை, a dunghill, refuse (in a heap), 341.

II. குப்புறு [see உறு], rush away (fall headlong), 377.

[Jī. Chin. xiii. 327 : 'குட்டநீர்குளத்தினல்லாற் குப்பைமேற்குவளைபூவா,
The *kuvaḷai* only flowers in the hollow tank, not on a dunghill.'
Also 'a heap.' T. 83 : 'உப்பின்பெருங்குப்பை, the huge heap of salt.']

கும்பம் = கடம், கலசம், pot, 47. [S. कुम्भ.]

கும்பி, hell : நரகம், 81. [S. कुम्भीपाक.]

There are seven chief hells.

[In *Kāçikh.* viii. 31, the duty of feeding the hungry is thus enforced :

உம்பர் வேதியர் விருந்தினரை ஊட்டிருகரார்
தம்பசிக்கனறணிப்ப கனிதுய்த்த இவரை
வெம்புகண்டகர் உளத்தின் மிகவெம்மை புரியும்
கும்பிபாகநரகத்திடை குளிப்ப எறிவாய்.

Yama points out certain persons and gives the order to an attendant :

'These did not eat, first feeding those above, Brahmans and guests,
But gorged themselves, assuaging hunger's fiery pang !
Hurl them in *Kumbī-pākam* hell to bathe,
Whose fires the souls of savage ones inflame.'

கும்பிபாகம் [S. pot-roasting] is one of the seven hells.]

குய் [comp. கொய், rare herbs culled] spice, seasoning, 217.

[Jī. Chin. xiii. 343 : 'குய்கடிம் அஞ்சலை அடிசில்,
Rice of pleasant savour redolent of spice.'
Jī. Chin. xiii. 373 : 'பொரியுங்குய்யும் வறைகளும்,
Fried curry, spiced condiments, and parched viands.']

குர் KUR. [Comp. குற், குழ், what is little, young, tender. M. KURU.]

I. குர|ம்பு, bank, limit : வரம்பு, எல்லை, 153. [See வரி, வரை, கரை. So அழுகு = கழுகு.]

II. குர|ல் = ஒலி, sound, 339. [See குரை, குயில், கூ, கூவு. S. कुर. M. *kura*, *kural*. C. *kural*, *kūral*. T. *kurru*.]

III. குரு|கு, a bird : குரு|வி, குரீஇ, 135. [M. *kuri|gil.*]

IV. குருடு, blindness. குருடன், 158. [M., C., T. *guddhi.*]

V. குருதி = இரத்தம், blood. [S. क्रूर. Lat. *cruor.* M. *kuruthi.*]

VI. குரு|த்து, young white tender leaves, buds, or shoots, 211. [Comp. 138 = நுனி.]

VII. குரை, *v.* (§ 64) = குலை, bark, 254. [See குரல். M. *kur|a* = barking ; *kur|ekka.* C. *kor|a.*]

Nig. குரை என்பதிடைச்சொல் ஓசை. See *Nannūl*, 373.

குலம் [S. कुल] family = குடி, 160, 175 ; race, 179, 285 ; caste, 195, 333.

['. . . . குலந்தீது
கொள்கை அழிந்தக்கடை,
One's caste (family, tribe) is evil when the virtues pertaining to it have perished.'
கொள்கை = ஆசாரம், ஒழுக்கம், நன்னடக்கை.]

குவளை = குவலயம், the water-lily; *Pontederia*, 44, 236. [S. कुवलय. M.]

In 236 the ஆம்பல் and குவளை are contrasted to the disadvantage of the former. Here குவளை is used for the lotus.

குழ் KUṚ. [Comp. குர், குற், குள். M. KUṚ|A = what is hollow. C. KUṆ|I, KUṚI, KOḌ|A. T. *kurra.*]

The √ seems to mean—1. tender; 2. hollow; 3. collection. S. कुल्.

I. குழ, tender, 101: இள.

II. குழ|வி, early youth: இளமை, 11.

III. குழ|ம்பு, mud, slime, 47: சேறு.

IV. குழி, *v.* (§ 57) be hollow, sunken, 49.

V. குழு, குழாம், society. [From குலம்?]

குழாம் [N. M. K. p. 3] collection of things.

குழுவு, *v.* (§ 62) unite, associate, 137. [குழுமு, கூடு.]

VI. குழை, *n.* 1. ear jewel, 370; 2. tender leaves, 167; *v.* (§ 64) bend, wag, 213.

குள் KUḶ.

I. குள|ம் = ஏரி, a tank, 191. [Comp. S. कूलम्. C. D. G. p. 456. M. *kuḷam.* C. *koṇa*, *koḷa*, as though from KOḶ = the holder.]

II. குளி, *v.* (§ 64) bathe, 90. [M.]

III. குளிர், *n.* coolness, 71.

குளிர், *v.* (§ 57) be cool, 167.

[இர், குறு, மு are formatives. Anc. C. M.
With குளிர் compare களிர், களி.]

K. குற் KUṞṞ, சிற், செற். [C. D. G. p. 479. M. KURR, ÇIRR, ÇERR. C. KURR, KIRR, *etc.* T. KUR|U, KIR|I. Germ. *kurz.* Lat. *curt.* Teut. SKORTA. GR. κειρ-, ξυρ-. S. क्षुर्, खुर्. In Breton KORR = dwarf: குறள்.]

I. குறடு = pincers, tongs, 208.

II. குறளை = கோள், slander. [M. *kuraḷa.*]

III. குறு, *adj.* small, 262. குறும், 122. (§ 131. *f.*) = குறிய.

[' குற்றேவல், mean behest.' *Nīti.* 12.]

IV. குறு|கு (§ 62) approach, 261.

['குறுகார் அறிவுடையார், the wise draw not near.' T. 14.]

V. குறை, *v.* (§§ 57, 64). [Comp. T. *koda, koduva.*]

1. *int.* grow less, be cut off, 84.

2. *tr.* cut short, trim, 350.

குறைவு, diminution, 132; what yet remains to do, 332.

Comp. proverb: கொடுத்தாற் குறைவராது. [கோவிந்தசதகம், 8.]

VI. குற்றம் = தவறு, பிழை, பாவம், defect, fault, 111, 153, 230, 353, 394.

VII. குன்று, 1. *v.* (§ 62) diminish: குறை, 141. [Nasalized.]

குன்ற = குன்றாத = unfailing; in reduced circumstances, 176.

குன்றல் = குறைதல், 112.

குன்ற = இளைத்தப்போக, when he is worsted, 312.

2. *n.* a hill: மலை, வரை, 90, 175, 176, 257, 290, 307; (= tapering, conical.) = குன்றம், 113, 128, 212, 231, 319. [T. *konda.* M. *kunnu.*] குறவன் = குன்றவன், a mountaineer, 356.

கு|றி, see கு, குறு, கூறு; *v.* (§ 64) point out. [M., C. *kurri, gurri.* T. *guri.*]

குறினும் = கூறினும், 258 [see கூறு].

குறிப்பு, sign; nod, beck, command; thought, 196, 305.

[Comp. Jī. Chin. i. 277 for குறிப்பு = will, mind.]

குறி, sign: இலக்கணம், அடையாளம், 399.

[குறி = sound sense, in T. 52.]

குற்றி, 1. a stump, 178. See குத்தி, குத்து. 2. Poetical license for குத்தி, 237.

குனி, *v.* (§ 57) stoop, 17. [Comp. S. कुण्. M. *kuni.* T. கூன்.]

குன்று, see குற்.

கூட் KŪḌ, see குட்.

கூடு, *v.* (§ 62) join; embrace, 354.

தலைக்கூடு, join the society of, 162.

கூடு, *n.* a cage, 122. [M., T. *gūḍu.* T. *kūr, kūḍu*; C.; M.; S. कुड.]

கூத்தன், dancer. [M. S. गूढ़.]

The performer, i. e. the soul, which pulls the strings of the puppet, the body, and exhibits the drama of life, 26. (From கூத்து, drama, dance.)

கூத்தியர் = நாடகக்கணிகையர், dancing girls, 191.

கூம்பு, *v.* (§ 62) [see கு, கொம்|பு; கும்|பு, குப்பை. M. *kūmbu* = 'a bud.' S. कुम्ब] close as flowers, 215.

கூர் KŪR, *sharp.* [Comp. கு, குர், குறி, and S. क्रूर. M. C. T. *kūr* = *kūḍ.*]

I. கூர், கூரிய.

கூர்|மை, sharpness, acuteness; keenness of intellect: கூரிய அறிவு, 287.

இடும்பைகூர்நெஞ்சத்தார், who suffer acutely in mind, 107; உள்கூர்பசி, hunger inwardly raging, 286. Here கூர் is the root of an auxiliary verb (§ 57) added to a noun: so, அன்புகூருகிறது.

கூர்த்த, tending directly to, 81; கூர்த்து, attacking furiously, 70. These are apparently conjugated forms (G. 93) from கூர் = point.

For நல்கூர், be poor, and நல்குரவு, poverty, see நல்.

II. A sloping, *pointed*, thatched roof; by metonomy = a house, 231. [M. *kūra.*]

கூ|வு KŪVU, *v.* (§ 62).

கூஉம் = கூவும், which will vociferate, 140. [T. KŪ, KŪ|YU. M. KŪ|RRU. C. KŪ-GU. An imitative word.]

கூழ் KŪḺ = உணவு. [Comp. S. कूर. C. *kūḷu.* M. It is connected with குழு. T. *kūḍu.*]

1. Grain, rice. 2. Growing corn, பைங்கூழ், 191. 3. Food, 257, 321.

பால்கூழ், 321.

[In T. 48: ‘நெய்பெய்த சோறென்று கூழை மதிப்பான்,

He who esteems *rice-water* as if it were rice mingled with *ghī*.’]

கூறு KŪṞṞ, *allot.* [See குறு, brief. M., C., T. κήρ = கூறு. As verb = κηρύσσω.]

I. கூறு, *v.* (§ 62) say, declare, proclaim: சொல்லு, 84, 156, 157, 158, 242, 326, 353.

கூறற்றி, say not! 388.

II. கூற்றம், கூற்று = word, in மீக்கூற்றம், praise, 53.

புறங்கூற்று, defamation, 158.

III. கூற்று, கூற்றம், Death, Yaman (*the divider, decider*), 4, 5, 6, 7, 20, 35, 36, 106, 120, 172, 188, 330, 331, 363.

[Comp. B. I. S. 1690:

‘कालक्षेपः न कर्तव्य श्चायुर्याति दिने दिने ।
निरीक्षति यमोराजा धर्मस्य विविधां गतिम् ॥

Make no delay. Life wastes day by day. King Yama observes the various paths of virtue.’

The god of death (S. यम: இயமன், எமன்; தருமன்; கூற்று, கூற்றம், கூற்றன், கூற்றவன்; காலன்; மறலி).

A full account of him and of the struggle in which *Markaṇḍēyar* defeated him is to be found in the மார்க்கண்டேப்படலம் of the அசுரகாண்டம் of the *Skanda-purāṇa.*

In காசிகாண்டம் viii his appearance and attributes are described. See also *Nīti.* 42.

The name கூற்று = arbiter, one who pronounces a sentence, or divider.

So Jī. Chin. xiii. 22:

‘உடற்றும் பிணித்தீ உடம்பின் உயிர்பெய்திட்
டடுத்துணர்வு நெய்யாக ஆற்ற றுலையாகக்
குடித்துண்ணும் கூற்றங் குடில்பிரியா முன்னே,—
கொடுத்துண்மின், கண்டீர்! குணம்புரிமின் கண்டீர்!

Before "The DIVIDER" (death) tears in pieces the hut (the body),—pouring out as rice the life of that body consumed with fire of diseases that afflict, adding your understanding as the *ghī*, and your faculties as the condiment, and devouring all,—see that ye share with others what ye eat! see that ye delight in virtue!'

And *Él.* 23, 38:

'வாள்அஞ்சான், வன்கண்மை அஞ்சான், வனப்பஞ்சான்,
ஆண்அஞ்சான், ஆயபொரு ளான்அஞ்சான்,—நாளெஞ்சாக்
காலன் வரவொழிதல் காணின்வீ டெய்திய
பாலினூல் எய்தப் படும்.

He fears not sword; dreads not bravery; respects not beauty; shrinks not from any hero; is not dismayed by any assemblage of resources; and fails not his day:—therefore, if you see death's coming imminent, you should betake yourself to the studies that relate to "*release*."'

'அழப்போகான், அஞ்சான், அலறினுந் கேளான்,
எழப்போகான், ஈடற்றார் என்று—தொழப்போகான்,
என்னேஇக் காலன்ச டோரார் தவமுயலார்?
கொன்னே இருத்தல் குறை!

He goes not away though one weep; he knows no dread; if one lament aloud he hears not; if one spring up he does not relinquish his hold; he does not depart, saying "these are helpless ones;" though one pay him reverence he goes not; why do men not ponder *death's* power, and labour in works of penitential expiation? To remain idle is surely a fault!']

கூறை = சீலை, ஆடை, garment, 281. [√கூறு = portion. M. KŪRRA.]

K. கெட் KEḌ. [S. खिद्. C. D. G. p. 471. M., TU., T. GEḌA, CHEḌ, CHER. C. KEḌ, KIḌ.]

I. கெடு, *v.* (§ 68) perish, disappear: அழி, மறை, நீங்கு, 8, 10, 27, 80, 171, 186, 197, 201, 368.

கெடினும், 80 [§ 100] = and in the perishing: = though yourself should perish.

கெட்ட = அற்ற, இல்லாத, senseless, 121. கெட்டு for கெட்ட, 288.

II. கேடு (as பேறு *etc.*), ruin, 80, 132, 134, 173, 316. [S. खेद्. GR. κῆδος.]

கெழ் KEṚ. [Comp. கிழ், கேழ், கேள். C. D. G. p. 479.]

v. கெழு (கெழுவு, கெழுமு, கழுமு), become familiar, accustomed to.

கெழீஇனர், 385. கெழீஇ, 213.

In 90 உருகெழு, as an epithet of fire, is doubtful.

உரு = heat, and கெழு = splendour: or கெழு = உள்ள.

கேணி KĒṆI [S. खनि. Comp. கிணறு. C. *kaṇi.* M. *kēṇi.* T. *khani*, *gani*] a temporary well; hole in the sand, 184.

'எடுத்தாலும் ஊறும், இறைத்தாலும் ஊறும், இடைநடுவே
மடுத்தால் மறிபடுமோ, மணற்கேணித் தண்ணீர்? அதுபோல்
அடுத்தாரை வாழ்விக்கக் கல்விஉண் டானவர் அன்புடனே
கொடுத்தாற் குறைவருமோ? . . . . G. 8.

The water of the well dug in the sand, though you draw it forth, gushes still; though you irrigate with it, it gushes still; dam it up, is it stayed?

Thus, if the learned lovingly make happy those who approach them, will their resources diminish?'

கேழ் KĒṚ = நிறம், hue, 41, 212.

[From கெழு-மை. Comp. with √கழ் = abound. In M. = a reddish deer.]

Nig. கேழ் நிறம் ஒளி ஒப்பாகும்.

K. கேள் KĒḶ. [Comp. கிழ, கெழு, உரி, கிளை. C. *keḷe, geṇe.*]

I. *Coll. noun*, kindred, 29, 191. உறவு, உறவினர், தமர், சுற்றத்தார்.
= கேளிர், 9, 201, 382.

கேண்மை, intimacy; friendship: நட்பு, தொடர்பு, உறவு [see K. கெழுதகைமை].
125, 128, 138, 154, 166, 172, 204, 211, 236. [S. स्नेह.]

II. *v.* (§ 70) [M. KĒḶ. C., Tu. KĒṆ. Comp. Lat. CLU, AUS-CUL-T-. Gr. κλυ. S. श्रु].

1. Ask, ask leave, enquire, 30, 86.
2. Hear, 64, 100, 126, 322, 364. [கேட்கலார்: கேள் + கு + அலார்.]

K. கேள்|வி [G. 96] traditional lore, 63, 106, 137, 260. [M.]

கை KAI. [As செய் : கை :: कृ : कर. T. *cheyi, kēlu.* C. *kai, key.* M. TU. See C. D. G. pp. 468, 503.]

I. (1) கை, *n.* hand, 5, 98, 193, 315, 386.

கைக்கோல், walking-stick, 14. கைகாட்டு, indicate with the hand, 328.
கை(க்)நீட்டு, stretch out hand (*to take, supplicate,* or *give*), 238, 262, 288.
கையுறு, come into hand of, 5, 84, 300.
கைப்படு, fall into the hands of, 38, 129.
கைவிடு, abandon, 43, 76, 130, 208, 214, 294.
கைம்மாலை, the wreath in (her) hand, 393.
கைத்து = கைப்பொருள், சொத்து, means, property: *what is in hand* (G. 63), 19, 80, 92, 206, 217. [N. M. K. p. 3.]

(2) Minuteness. கைஞ்ஞானம், trifling, unreal wisdom, 311.

[This puzzles the commentators. Three explanations are given: (1) கை = அற்ப; (2) கை = கசந்த, அருவருத்த; (3) கை = கைளால்குத்தி, i. e. 'fisticuff wisdom.']

(3) Propriety of conduct, நல்ஒழுக்கம், 59, 163, 362, 382.

(4) Money (in hand), 371 [= வாரி in 370]. கைப்பொருள், property, 376.

II. *v.* (§ 64) for கச, be bitter, 112. [M.]

கை|ப்பு = கசப்பு, 116.

கொ KO [கொட், கோட்], கொ|ம். The idea is anything round, bent, spherical.

[Considering the many verbs whose first syllable is கொ, it may be equivalent to SAM, *σύν*, *con*, *cum*, in Sanskrit, Greek, and Latin, and these verbs may be mostly compounds. Thus

கொ|டு (comp. வி-டு, ஆ-டு, இடு).

கொ|ள் (விள், ஆள்).

கொ|ல் (வில், ஆல், இல்).

கொ|ழு (விழ், ஆழ், இழ்).

கொ|ழி, கொ|ய், கொ|த்து, கொ|ட்டு, கொ|மி, *etc.*

Have we traces of compounds in verbs with initial கொ, வி, ஆ, இ?]

கொம்|பு, the bough of a tree, 203, 290. [Comp. கூம்பு, கூன். M., C., TU. T. *kommu*.]

கொம்|மை, rotundity, 85. [Comp. கொங்|கை.]

கொடு KOḌ. [Comp. S. √कुट्, कोट्. Hence we have கோடு also. Comp. கடு. M. KOḌ. T. *goḍa*, KAḌ|U, *gaḍu*. C. KAḌ.]

I. கொடு=curved, folded round.

Cruel, evil. கொடு, 124. கொடியவை, cruel things, 388.

கொடிது, 'tis hard! 88.

II. *v*. [§ 64. Comp. கொள், of which it is a *causal*. M., C., Tu. *korru*] give: ஈ, தா, 5, 10, 93, 274, 278, 296, 373.

கொடாது, 169. கொடை, *n*. a giving, gift, 65, 91, 184,=ஈகை.

III: கொட்டு, *v*. (§ 62)=எறி, strike, beat a drum, 24, 257.=கடாவு, drive in. பதஞ்செய், tap, gently manipulate, 208. [T. M. In C. from *koḍu*. Comp. கொல்=smite; கோல்.]

IV. கொடி [M. Perhaps from கொள்+இ=*what grasps*] a creeping plant.

கொடிப்புல், a creeping grass, 141.

கொய் KOY [C. KOY, KUY. M. T. KŌY-U. Comp. *καρπός*. Lat. *carp*. There seems to have been a √कर्प्] *v*. (§ 58) pluck, 374.

K. கொல் KOL. [Comp. கோல், கல், கொட்டு. The idea is 'stroke, blow.' M.; C.; T. KOL-A, 'kill, quell.' In Lithuanian *kalwis*; Lettish *kalleys*. Lat. *cell-*.]

I. கொல், smith's or any artisan's work.

கொல்லன், a smith, 298.

[Jī. Chin. i. 208: கொன்னெறி=கொற்றொழில்.]

II. *v*. கொல், கொல்(லு), (§ 70) 213, kill; 363.

[Jī. Chin. i. 251: 'உப்புடைய முந்நீர் உடன்றுகரைகொல்வ தொப்புடையதானை,

A host comparable to the salt sea that in its wrath *devastates* the shore.']

Forget—destroy the benefit of, 111. கொன்றன்ன=கொன்ற அன்ன, such as if one had slain, 186; torture, 279.

[See நன்றி and செய்ந்நன்றி. The Sanskrit expression कृतघ्न = 'an ungrateful man'— '*destroying*,' from हन् = கொல்.

Comp. B. I. S.:

'कुतः कृतघ्नस्य यशः कुतः स्थानं कुतः सुखम् ।
अश्रद्धेयः कृतघ्नो हि कृतघ्ने नास्ति निष्कृतिः ॥

How can "the destroyer of the thing done" obtain glory, station, or comfort? Untrustworthy is he, for him is no expiation.']

கொலை, murder, 81, 331.

கொலைஞர், murderers, 331.

K. கோறல் = கொல்லுதல், killing. [So சேறல், கோடல்.]

[N.M.K. 92: '.... கரப்பினுங்
கொன்றான் மேனிற்குங் கொலை,

Murder, though you conceal it, stands over the murderer: *murder will out*.']

III. An expletive, emphasizing a statement, or a question: = 'I pray, I wonder, now,' 36, 41, 48, 49, 58. = ஐ, 267. கொல்லோ, 298, 385, 394.

கொல்|லை. [The idea is 'retired nook.' Comp. M. *kolli* and C. *kolli, golli*.]

= புனம், தினைப்புனம், backyard, croft, 178, 283.
'பலவயல்கள் சேர்ந்தவொருநிலம்' = a farm.

கொழி KOṚI, *v.* (§ 64) sift; examine, 319. [Comp. கழ்.]

கொழு KOṚ, plumpness, luxuriance. *v.* (§ 64) wax fat; prosper, 96.

கொழு|வு = மூளை, fat, 46. [Comp. குழ. C. *kobbu, korbu*. M.]

கொள் KOḶ, *receive*. [கோள், கோ, கொண்ட். T. KON, KŌ, KU. Comp. கொடு. M.; C.]

I. கொள், *v.* [§ 56 (III)].

(I.) Take hold of, receive, get, buy, 21, 24, 106, 118, 120, 153, 236, 253, 260, 305, 387.

(II.) Take possession of, use, maintain, practise, 3, 18, 25, 35, 136, 143, 364, 377. கொண்டு = with, by means of.

(III.) Seize, hold fast, carry off, 148, 156, 330.

(IV.) Hold, contain, 191, 394. [Comp. குளம்.]

(V.) Marry, 3, 364. கொண்டான், a husband = கொண்டவன், 363.

(VI.) Hold in estimation, 25, 48, 72, 133, 165 [see கோள்], 379.

[For கொள் in the sense of 'accept, receive,' see T. 82:

'பாய்ந்தெழுந்து கொள்ளாருட் கொள்ளாத கூறாமை,

The not rising and rushing forward impetuously to say unacceptable things among those who do not esteem us.']

(VII.) In comp. with a noun. கணைக்கொண்டு, in troops, 25, 393. (கொள், G. 153.)

(VIII.) With ellipsis. = தேடிக்கொண்டு, seeking, 15, 20, 34, 53, 382 (செய்து), 57. = undertake, 28, 143.

(IX.) A mere auxiliary [H. B. § 106] 70, 262.

(X.) கொண்ட = உள்ள, 14, 68.

II. கொண்மூ, *n.* cloud, = மேகம், முகில், 8.

III. கொண்டமை, a ground, position taken up, 212.

கொள்|கை, tenet, principle, 141.

IV. கொள்ளு, horse-gram: காணம், *dolichos uniflorus:* of two kinds, black and red, 387. [M. H. *kulthi.*]

கொன் = vain, useless: வீண்.

I. *adv.* கொன்னே + வீணும், in vain, uselessly, gratuitously, 9, 55, 92, 162, 286, 330.

II. *n.* hell, 243.

கொன்னுளர், those who inhabit hell; those who are lost: *perditi.*

['கொன்னே இருத்தல்குறை (= சும்மா இருப்பது குற்றம்), to remain idle is a fault.' *Ēl.* 38.]

கோ KŌ [கோன். M. See கோல், கொழு. T. *kolu* = 'serve.' Comp. *khān.* 'King' is from *cyn* = 'tribe;' but consider S. गो].

I. *n.* = அரசன்: king, 81.

II. *v.* (§ 64) string together, 335, [for கோர்.] [C. M. T. KŪR|CHU = கட்டு.] Hence கோதை.

III. கோ|ப்பு (a wallet slung over the shoulder) = உணவு, உணு, ஆற்றுணா, கட்டுச்சோறு. பொதிசோறு, provisions, food for a journey, 20, 328.

[√கோ, § 64, string (beads *etc.*)]

Used with கோர். Hence 'wallet' is probably the real meaning.

கோங்கு, silk-cotton tree, *Bombax gossypinum,* 223, 400.

கோட் KŌḌ. [Comp. S. कुट्, कोट्ट, कोण, कूण, and கோணம்.]

I. கோடு, see கொடு.

n. 1. Flexure, plait, fold, 131.

2. Turning: கோடு இல் தீ கூற்றம், death inflexible and cruel, 5.

3. Rounded edge, border, 354, 372. கடற்கோடு, the sea-shore, 263.

4. A branch, flexible twig, small shrub, = கொம்பு, 192, 215.

5. A curved tusk, 358, 376, 378.

II. *v.* (§ 62) bend, diverge from right: கோணு, 124.

Also, in the same sense, கோட்டு: கோட்டிய = கோடிய = வளைந்த, bent, 395.

['கோல்கோடியவன், a tyrant.' கலித். i. 10.]

'நடைநனக்குக் கோடாமொழி வனப்பு,

Strict truthfulness is the beauty of conduct.' Ç. P.]

கோடல், see கோள்.

கோடி (=anything eminent) [S. कोटि] ten millions, 168.

கோட்டி [S. गोष्टि] an assembly, society, 155, 255, 260, 311, 312.

The root idea is 'cattle-stall.' Syn. சபை, or அவை, கூட்டம். See ch. xxxii.

கோத் KŌTH.

கோ|து, v. [கோது, adjust, trick out. M. *kōthu*, 'dress hair'].

கோ|தை = பூமாலே [comp. கொத்து and கோ].

I. A flower-wreath. By metonomy, 'a damsel wearing such a wreath.'

கோதாய், 209. கோதையார், 46, 48.

[*Ēl.* 2, பூங்கோதாய். G. 93, thou of the flowery garland.]

கோதையருவி, waterfalls like flower wreaths on the mountain's brow, 71.

II. Refuse, dregs. சக்கை, fault, 106. சாரமில்லாப்பொருள், stalks from which the juice has been expressed. கருப்பஞ் செத்தை, 34.

[Jī. Chin. i. 204: 'கோதியல்காமம், faulty lust.' S. कोघ (कुघ्).]

III. *v.* (§ 62) ferment, 47. Perhaps = கொதித்து.

கோத்திரம் [S. गोत्र] family, race, 242.

Here = 'the lowness of the arrogant upstart's origin.'

கோல் = தண்டு. [From T. KOLU, 'measure; serve.' Comp. கொல் and கோ. M., T., C.]

1. A staff, 11, 13, 14 (with ஊன்று).

கைக்கோல், (her) staff. அம்மனேக்கோல், (her) mother's staff.

கோற்கண்ணள், she who uses a staff for eyes, blind with age, 17.

[Comp. B. I. S. 80, which seems an imitation of 13.]

2. Any stick, 41, 253, 258. தண்டம்.

3. Arrow, 152.

கூட்டுக்கோல், a smith's poker, 208.

கோலம் = அழகு [M., C., T. *kōla;* comp. S. गोल] adornment [lines of paint *etc.*] 43, 397.

கோழி, domestic fowl, 341 [from கொழு, கொழு, or கொழி = the pampered one. C., M. *kōṟi*. Tu. *kōri*. T. *kō-ḍi*. S. कुक्कुट. C. D. G. p. 504. Comp. √கு, கூ, or கோ: குயில், கூவு, கோகம், கோகிலம்].

கோள் KŌḶ, see கொள்ளு. It is another form of கொள்ள or கொள்ளல். Vulgarly கோ. So in T. *ko* for *kona*.

I. கோள், infinitive.

கோட்படா = கொள்ளப்படாது, it cannot be carried off, 134.

II. Acquisition.

கொள்ளுதல் = கொள்ளல் = கோடல் = கோள், the incurring of, 77, 101, 220, 324. [See G. 37.]

III. கோள், n. = holding.

1. Contents: 'a tank that holds little,' 191. [In C. குளம் is *koḷa*, 'the holder,' from KOḶ. There is a play on the word.]

2. Estimation: மதிப்பு, 165: கோட்பாடு.

3. Quality (good) : குணம், தன்மை, 18.
4. Opportunity to seize, 331.
5. Enclosure, precincts : சுற்றுக்கோள், 96.
[T. 12 : 'கோளாளன் என்பான் மறவாதான்,
He may be styled a man of *comprehension* who forgets not !']

கொள்வு, *v.* (§ 62) seize, clutch, 70. Often கவ்வு. [Comp. கவர். S. ग्रह्.]

ச ÇA.

K. சகடம், cart : வண்டில், 2. [S. शकट. சகடை, சகடு. சாகாடு is another variant.]
சகடக்கால், a cart-wheel.
[B. I. S. 5710 :
'रथः शरीरं पुरूपस्य दृष्टम्।
Man's body appears as a chariot.']

சக்கரம் = a wheel. [S. चक्रम्.]
சக்கர as adj. = kingly, 346.
சத்தம், either S. शब्दम्, word, grammar ; or सप्तन्, seven.
The science of grammar (or the seven sciences), 52.
சந்தனம், sandal-tree : *santalam album*, 180, 234. [S. चन्दन.]

சமழ் ÇAMAṚ (§ 64) = நாணு, suffer shame or distress. [? S. घम्.]
Nig. சமழ்த்தலேவருத்த நாணம்.

சமழ்|த்தனர், have felt humiliated [G. 83] 316.
சமழ்|மை = தாழ்வு, something to be ashamed of, 72.

சலம் [S. छल] trickery, 188.
சலவர், tricksters, 188. [T. 51.]
[T. 50 : 'சலமொழிமாந்தர், men of deceitful words.']

சா ÇĀ. [Comp. சாய். S. ज्या, सो, सित ; क्षि. T. CHA, CHĀ. C. SĀ, *sattu*. M. CHĀ, *chattu*. TU. SAI. See சாயம், சவம்.]
சா, *v.* die (§ 58. சா-கிறேன், செத்-தேன், சா-வேன், சா-க, சாவ, சா) 24 [157 from சாய்] 219, 281, 295.
சாயினும் = செத்தாலும் [T. 27]. சாகான் (சாம்), 92.
சாக்காடு = மரணம், சாவு, death, 52. [காடு an affix.]

சா|காடு = வண்டி, இரதம், 48. See சகடம்.
சாந்து, சாந்தம் [Tadbh. of சந்தனம். Comp. also शान्त] fragrant unguents, 48, 126, 389, 397.

சாய் ÇĀY, *lean, fall, die.*

I. சாய், *v.* [§ 57. Comp. சா and சாக். C. CHĀ|CHU. M. T. CHĀGU, SĀGU] 157, 184, 295.

II. *n.* கோரை, grass, 389.

III. சாய|ல் [comp. S. छाया. M.] reflected image, form, beauty, dignity, excellence, 142, 340.

சார் ÇĀR. [Comp. சேர், சாய்.]

சார் (சாரு, § 57) join, be close to, rely on, be dependant on, 124, 171, 175, 177, 178, 245, 309, 327.

In 126 சார்ந்தாய், 'thou hast relied upon.' This is then taken as a noun, and declined: சார்ந்தாய்க்கு, 'to thee who hast relied upon.'

And in voc. சார்ந்தோய்! O thou *etc.!*

சார்ந்தார், those thou hast relied upon.

[N.B. 1. Almost any form of the finite verb may thus be used as a noun.

2. The context alone decides whether the form is to be taken in an active or a passive sense.]

சார்வு, that on which one relies, 182.=சார்பு, ஆதரவு.

சாரல், the side and slopes of a mountain range, 127, 234. [M.]

சால் ÇĀL, *abundance.* [M., T. CHĀL. Comp. S. जल्.]

I. சால், *v.* abound [§ 56 (III)].

தோற்றஞ் சான் ஞாயிறு, 7. The sun so gorgeous in his appearing, 140.

சால, 49 and 318. சாலவும், (*adv.*) much, 243.

[சால்பு, excellence. *Ēl.* 6: 'சாலும் பிறர்நூலின் சால்பு, he will fully possess the virtues of every system.']

K. II. சான்றவர், சான்றோர், the excellent: மேன்மக்கள், ch. xvi, 41, 58, 68, 126, 133, 151, 153, 356, 357, 368.

In 100 சான்றோர் may be (1) subject to சொரித்தார்; or (2) subject to என: சான்றோரால்; or (3) for சான்றோர்க்கு.

சான்றாண்மை [see ஆள்], excellence, 126, 142, 179. [Comp. S. सान्द्र. M. *sāndra.*]

சாறு ÇĀRRU.

சாற்று, *v.* (§ 62) [M. *chāttu.* Comp. சாட்டு, சாத்து] announce, 25, 49.

[The idea is (?) பறை சாற்று, strike the drum. An imitative word. Or √SĀL=சொல் (so சொற்று).]

சாறு=juice, 34. [S. सारम्.]

சி ÇI=*small.* [M. CHI|NNA, CHI|RRU, CHE|RRU, CHI|LA, CHI|L. T. CH|INNA, CHI|RI, CHI|RU, KINDA, KON. C. KI|RRU, CHI|KKA, KE|LA; CHI|RRU; KIṚ. TU. KI|NI. Comp. குறு; also கிழ், கீழ். S. किम्, छिन्न, कण.]

I. சில், சிற், சின் [opp. பல், பற், பன்].

சில, some, but a few, 135, 154, 204.
சிலர், some, a few, few, only a few, 113, 185.

II. சிறு (§ 131. *f*), சிற்று, சிறிய, சின்ன [opp. பெரு], *adj.* 24, 170, 237, 303, 395. = புல்.

சிறுநோக்கு, a glance of contempt: அலக்ஷியமாய்ப்பார்த்தல, 298.
சிறியவர், mean, low people, 149, 166, 353. சிறியார், 85, 125, 177, 186.
சிறுமை, 177, 183, 187. [T. 14.] இசைந்தசிறுமை = natural meanness.
சிறிது, a little thing, 38, 99; a little while, 359.
சிறுகாலே, early, betimes, 35, 110, 328, 363. சிற்றறிவினர் = புல்லறிவினர், 329.
சிற்|றினத்தார், 81, 204, 272. சின்மொழி, gentle speech, 362.

III. சிறு|கு, *v.* (§ 62) grow less, 110.

IV. சிறை, (1) captivity, 222. [Comp. செறி.] (2) room: அறை, 147.

['சிறியவன் செல்வம்போற் சேர்ந்தார்க்கு நிழலின்றி, affording no shade to those who draw near—like the mean man's wealth.' கலித். i. 10. Comp. 202.]

சிகை = உண்டிச்சிகை, course at a meal, 1, 18. [S. सिक्थ.]

சித ÇITH.

சிதர், *v.* (§ 57) diffuse, spread.

சிதர் அரிக்கண், eye suffused with red, 394. [G. 153.]
[From *n.* சிதர். Comp. சிதறு, சிதை, சிந்து. M. CHIDAR = dust. S. छिद्.]

சிதல், சிதலே = செல், ஈசெல், white ant: கறையான், 147, 197. [√சிதை. M. *chidal.* C. *gedalu.* T. *cheda, chada.* S. सित, *white*; श्वित.]

சிதை, *v.* (§§ 57, 64) destroy, 179, 225.

சிதைந்து, degenerating, losing their moral sense, 156. Perverting, 71. (Or = சிதைய, so that others may be injured; injurious words, curses.) [S. छिद्. Comp. கெட்சிதற. T. *chedu.*]

சிந்தி: நினை, *v.* (§ 64) think of, 329. [S. चित्, चिन्त्.]

சிரல், the kingfisher, சிச்சிலி, 395.

சிரி, *v.* (§ 64) grin, 49, 50. [M., C., T. KĒR.]

சில்லே from சில், an utterly worthless woman, 377. [C.]

சிவல் = கவுதாரி, a partridge: = *the red one*, 122. [√சிவ, செ.]

சிற் ÇIRR. [Comp. சீர். S. श्री. M.]

I. சிற, *v.* (§ 66) abound, 104, 232, 285, 356.

II. சிறப்பு, *n.* politeness, courtesy, 159. Excellence; splendour; renown, 134, 139, 195, 252, 290.

தண்டாச் சிறப்பிற்றம் இன் உயிரை, their pleasant lives, possessed of (இன்) unfailing worth, 62.

சிறகு [comp. இறகு] wing, 41. [M. C., T. *rekka*. Comp. S. शिर.]

சிறியவர், சிறை, சின், see சி.

K. சின|ம்=கோபம், anger, ch. vii, 68, 178: குரோதம், கதம், வெகுளி. [M. CHIN|AM. C. KIN|ISU. T. KIN|KA.]

சீர் ÇĪR. [Comp. சிற. S. श्री. M.]

சீர், *n.* position, dignity, 176, 232, 242. Excellence, 226, 316, 352. Virtuous conduct, நல்லொழுக்கம், 68.

சீர்மை=சிறப்பு, position, dignity, 176.

சீரியார்=மேலோர், 232.

அச்சீர், so, with such attention, 345.

[*Mū.*: ‘சீரியர் கெட்டாலுஞ் சீரியர் சீரியரே;
அல்லாதார் கெட்டால் அங் கென்னாகும்?—சீரிய
பொன்னின் குடம்உடைந்தாற் பொன்னாகும்! என்னாகும்
மண்ணின் குடம்உடைந்தக் கால்?

When men of real worth suffer reverses, the really worthy are really worthy still; when those not so are thus reduced what is there left? If a pot made of gold be broken, the gold remains! If a pot made of earth be broken, what is there left?’]

சீலம், ‘good conduct,’ p. 34 *note* [S. शील], is not used in K. or in this work, though a technical term in the Jain system for நல்லொழுக்கம். See Jī. Chin. xiii. 220–224.

சுட் (சுட்) ÇUḌ. [M. CHUḌ. T. CHŪḌ. Comp. S. शुष्.]

I. சுடு, *v.* (§ 68) burn, 63, 89, 90, 124, 129, 224, 310.

சுடுகாடு=இடுகாடு: சுடலை: மயானம், burning ground, 121.

II. சுடர்=(1) சூரியன், (2) ஒளி, 189, 394, 398. [Comp. S. सुर.]

[Jī. Chin. i. 260: ‘படுவெஞ்சுடரின் ஆண்டகை அவிந்தான்,
Like the setting sun the hero sank into darkness.’]

III. சுட்டுக்கோல், a poker, 208. [See சூடு. T. SŪḌU.]

சும, *v.* [§ 66. S. क्षम्. M. T. *mō-chu*] bear, carry, 24.

சுர, *v.* [§ 66. S. स्रु. Comp. சொரி, சோர். M.] gush forth, yield.

சுரும்பு, a beetle, bee, 122. [S. सुरभि?]

சுரம் = சுடுகாடு = burning ground, 5.

The meaning of சுரம் is '*a path through the* பாலைநிலம், *or arid jungle, desert land.*' [M. *churam.*] In Nigaṇḍu : சுரமருநெறிகானமார்க்கம்.

The following fine passage, கலித். i. 10, illustrates it:

'வறியவன் இளமைபோல் வாடிய சினையவாய்ச் ;
சிறியவன் செல்வம்போற் சேர்ந்தார்க்கு நிழலின்றி ;
யார்கண்ணும் இகந்துசெய் திசைகெட்டான் இறுதிபோல்
வேரொடு மரம்வெம்ப விரிகதிர் தெறுதலின் ;
அலைவுற்றுக் குடிகூவ ஆறின்றிப் பொருள்வெஃகிக்
கொலை அஞ்சா வினைவராற் கோல்கோடி யவனிழல்
உலகு போல் உலறிய உயர்மர வெஞ்சுரம் :

The parched *desert path* (சுரம்) abounding in lofty trees, which were

(1) full of withered offshoots,—like the poor man's youth ;

(2) that afforded no shade to those that drew near,—like the mean man's wealth ;

(3) that were perishing root and trunk, dried up by stroke of the sun's rays,—like the end of him who sins against his neighbour and dies to fame ;

(4) that were blasted,—like the world, when under the shadow of a tyrant-lord, who extorts money unjustly, with the aid of ministers that shrink not from murder, while oppressed subjects cry out.'

I take it to be for ஸ்வலம் [S. स्वल]='the blazing region.' It has many other meanings, answering to S. स्वर, ग्वर, *etc.*

சுரை [S. सुरा].

1. Toddy. 2. A bottle-shaped gourd, pumpkin. [M. *chura.*]

பேய்ச்சுரை, a very bitter gourd : *Cucumis Colocynthis*, 116, 315.

சுவர்க்கம் [S. स्वर्गम्] paradise, 243.

சுவை = உருசி, இரசம், flavour ; sweetness, 1. [Comp. S. स्वद्, स्वादस्. Gr. ἡδ-ύ-ς. Lat. *suav-is*, savour. M. *chuva.* T. *chavi.*]

With இன், 156 ; with இம், 244, 321.

Spelt செவ்வி, 322.

['பால் சுவையிற் குன்றாது, milk loses nothing of its sweetness.' *Mū.*]

சுற் ÇURR. [Imitative like *whirl.* Comp. சூழ், சுருள். M., T., C., TU. *suttu.*]

K. 1. சுற்று, *v.* (§ 62) surround, gird, 281.

2. சுற்று, *n.* circuit, limit, 96.

3. சுற்றம், kindred. [T. *chuṭṭamu.*]

சுற்றத்தார் = உறவினர், கேள், கேளிர், கிளைகள், கிளைஞர், தமர், 25.

சுற்றந்தழால், ch. xxi.

சுனை, *v.* (§ 64) = தினவுதின், tingle, itch : சொறி, 313, 335.

[This is properly சுனா. S. शुरड. In M. CHUNE|KKA = to be acrid ; CHUṆE|KKA = to be irritable. Another reading is தினைத்து.]

சூட் ÇŪḌ.

I. சூடு, *v.* [comp. சூழ், சுற்று. So சூட்டு = மாலை. S. चूड. M.; A. C.] = முடி, அணி (§ 62) wear as a wreath, put on flowers, *etc.*

பூச்சூடி, having put on a garland of flowers, 43.
சூடும்பூ, a flower fit to be worn, 262.

II. சூடு, brand, scar [சுடு, burn], 186.

Some commentators say சூடு = திமில், 'hump: the hump of a white bullock.' But there seems to be no authority for this use of the word; and the glaring ugliness of a branded mark on the exquisitely white sleek skin of a southern bullock is easily understood.

சூத்திரம் = நூல், பனுவல் [S. सूत्र. See *Nannūl*] doctrine, rule, formula, aphorism, 314.

சூல் ÇŪL.

சூல், *v.* [§ 56 (III), சூன்றினேன், சூலுவேன், சூல] scoop out, 44. = தோண்டி, எடு; சூப்பு. [S. चूष्. M.]

சூழ் ÇŪṚ. [Comp. சுற்று. M. T. CHŪ|ḌA, inf. = 'to see.']

சூழு, *v.* (§ 57) 1. surround, 230 (G. 153), 264, 392.

2. Deliberate, debate, hesitate, 55.

செ ÇE. [T. ERA = red = சே; KEM, *chem*, *chenna*. C. *chen*, *chan*, *chem*, *chey*, *chay*, *say*, *sey*, *kem*. M. *chem*.]

செம், சே, செவ், செய், சேய், சி, சிவ has the idea of

(1) *Red, bright yellow, golden;* met. *fiery*.

(2) *Right, good.* [S. श्री.]

செங்கண், bright, glowing eyes, 373. செக்|தீ, red, hot, glowing fire, 90.
செ|க்கர், ruddy colour, 397.
செக்|செல், 269, 367. So செங்கொல்லு, red or golden, 387.
செக்|நெறி, 378. செம்|மை, rectitude, 85; excellence, 294.
செம்மா, *v.* (in loco) exult, 331. செம்|புனல், the fresh, pure flood, 222.
செம்|பொறி, red spots, 283.
செங்|கோடு [see கோடு]. Here செம் = 'perpendicular, sheer,' 372.
செவ்|வியர், the good, 322. செவ்|வி for சுவை, 322.
செவ்|வன், directly, 148. (செவ்வையாக.)
செய்|யான் = நல்லாள், இலக்குமி, the goddess of prosperity; [N. M. K. p. 3.]
சே|மா, a bull: எருது, 377.

செது|ம்பு [see சிது|ம்பு, சிதை. S. छिद्, छेद] = அசம்பு, வழுக்குநிலம், marshy, boggy soil, 128.

[In *Kalit.* 48 : 'இன்னுரைச் செறும்பாற்றுஞ்செவ்வி,
The season when the foaming mountain torrent raves !' செறும்பு = அருவி.]

செ|கு, *v.* (§ 64) = அழி, kill, 220. [Comp. S. छिद्. செகு. T. *chedu.*]

செங்|கோடு, a precipitous mountain. See செ and கோடு, 372.

செக்கு, *n.* an oil-press, 374. [A Tadbhava of S. चक्र. M., C.]

செத், see சா.

செ|ப்பு, a casket, 126.

[From செம்பு = 'copper' (தாம்பிரம்), itself from செம் = *red*, as இரும்பு from இரும், *black.* M.]

செம்|மா, *v.* (§ 56 [1]) [comp. எ|மா, இறு|மா; and செ] exult, 331. செம்மாப்பு = இறுமாப்பு, exultation, 50.

செய் ÇEY.

செய், *v.* [comp. பண். M. In T. CHĒ (CHE|YYU). Comp. Tamil கை with T. *cheyyi* and C. *kai.* S. कृ, कर. See C. D. G. pp. 468, 469] do, perform, 4, 7, 19, 26, 37, 52, 67, 97, 147, 153, 185, 250, 272, 358; make into, 103, 192; acquire, merit, 9, 134; profit, be of use, 393; help, give, 309.

As auxiliary forming verbs from nouns :

சிறைசெய், confine, 222. செயற்பால, what should be done, 147, 153, 185.

செய்(ந்)நன்றி, a benefit conferred, 111. செய்வினை = கர்மம், a man's actual deeds, 120.

செய்கை, work = (roofing *etc.*), 127, 147. வேலைப் பாடுகள் கட்டடங்கள்.

செய்தி, deed, 246. [Either செய்தியார், 'those whose deeds are good and consistent;' or செய்து + யார். G. 24.]

செய்குறு, that doeth not, 362. [See உறு.]

செய்குநம் (= நாம் செய்தும், we will do), 235 [G. 83. Comp. T. *çētumu*].

செய்கலர், they do not, 295.

செய்யாத = செய்யாதவைகளே, 235; செய்வதற்கியலாதவை (G. 95).

செயினும், though men do, 69. செய்யாமை, 246.

K. செயிர் [comp. சீறு, செறு] = குற்றம்; கோபம், wrath, eager worldliness, 50.

செயிர் வேழம், a fierce elephant, 358.

[Nig. செயிர் என்ப சினங் குற்றப்பேர்.]

செய் = வயல், field, rice-field, 218. [T. CHE|NU. M. Comp. சே|று, நன்செய், புன்செய்.]

செருப்பு, leathern sandal, 347. [S. चर्म.]

செல் ÇEL. [Comp. S. चल्, चर्. T. *jaru-gu, chel, sel, chanu.* C. CHEL. M. *chel-ga.*]

1. செல், *v.* (செல்லு, § 70).

Go : போ, 1, 15, 51, 85, 120, 230 (செல்க, may I go! G. 85) 238, 263, 400; pass away, 4, 32; go forth, 24, 179, 259, 268; march by, 3; gain acceptance, 115, 313; reach to, affect, 178; accompany, associate with, 159, 169; approach, 296, 325.

With ஆற, go along, 5.
செல்லாமை = வறுமை; ஈடேறாமை, inability through poverty, 148.
செல்லிடம், when things go well; செல்லாஇடம், when things go ill, 149.
செல்வழி, a path; destined goal: கதி, 8, 154, 230, 238, 328.
செல்சுடர், the setting sun, 394.
செலிய (G. 85) 'in order to go,' here = 'as about to go,' 399.
சேறல் for செல்லுதல் [comp. கோறல், கோடல்] = செல் + தல் and எ lengthened as a compensation, 249.

Compounds: எதிர்செல, in the opposite direction, 211.
எதிர்செலவு, a courteous advance to meet any one, 143. [See வழிச்செலவு. T. 2.]
தலைச்செல், advance against, 241.
பின்செல், wait upon, follow, serve, 160, 292, 365.

II. செல்வம். [C. *chel-avu* (*chal*, *chan*) = 'beauty;' and so T., M.]

Wealth = ஐசுவரியம், தனம், பொருள், சம்பத்து, 1, 2, 8, 53, 93, 119, 170, 185, 251, 261, 267, 272, 274.
செல்வர், happy, prosperous, wealthy persons, 8, 115, 170, 270, 277, 296, 368.
செல்வம்பெரிதுடையார், those who own wealth largely, 262, 263.
செல்வநிலையாமை, ch. i. நன்றியில்செல்வம், ch. xxvii.
விழுச்செல்வம், 269. சக்கரச்செல்வம், 346.

செவி ÇEVI = காது [C. KIVI (KIMI). T. CHEVI. M. TU. KEBI. S. श्रव] ear, 59, 257.

செவிகொடு, give ear, 322.

செவி|டு, deafness, 158. [K. KIVA|ḌU; comp. குரு|டு. T. CHEV-UḌU, CHEM|UḌU.]

செவ்வன், see செ.
செவ்வி for சுவை, 322.

செழ் ÇEḶ.

செழ், செழு, செழும், செழிய, rich, fertile, luxuriant, 352, 367. [Comp. சிற, சீர், செ. A. M. Comp. also செல்வம்.]

செற் ÇERR. [M. CHER|I. Comp. சேர்.]

I. செறி, *v.* (§ 57) become dense; stick close to, cling to, be attached to, 13, 289, 380.

[செறிந்தவர்கள், intimate friends.]

II. செறி|வு, *n.* self-restraint: அடக்கம், 312.

But செறிவு in T. 95 = approach; confidence (?). [Comp. *Nīti*. 99.]

III. செறி, *v.* (§ 64)=கட்டு, fasten on; cling to; hoard, 304, 312, 358.

[In 312 commentators disagree: (1) பிறரைச்சேர்க்கிற; (2) சேமிக்கும் (செறு); (3) *insist upon.*]

செறிப்பு, fastening; enclosure; shelter, 231.

K. IV. செறு, *v.* (§ 68) afflict, restrain.

செற்றும், though they afflict (வருத்தியும், ஒடுக்கியும்), 222.

செற்றார், enemies, 178.

V. செறு, be wrath with [§§ 64 and 56 (II)]: செறுத்து, 4. செறின், 134, 164, 304.

['வரைவின்றிச் செறும்பொழுதில், when they are inordinately wrath.' கலித். i. 8.]
[செற்றம்=wrath.] [Comp. செயிர், சினம். Another form of சீறு. M. CHERRU.]

சென்னி, head: தலை, முடி. (p. 1.) [M., T. *chempa*. C. *kenne*. Comp. S. कर्ण.]

சே, see செ.

சே ÇĒ=*height*. [Comp. சேய். M.=*breadth etc.*]

I. சே|ண், *n.* remoteness, 30.=நெடுந்தூரம், far off, 263.

[Used as an adverb — ண் forms adverbs of place: அவண், இவண், perhaps for கண்.]

II. சே|ய், distance: தூரம். Opp. to அணி.

சேய்த்து, what is distant, 218.

சேக்கை (? சேர்க்கை) [M. CHEGU='roost.' A. C. KĒ='lie']=கூடு, (bird's) nest, 30.

சேடி|யர், maids, slaves, wenches, 354. [S. चेट. M., C., T. *chēḍiya*, *chēti*.]

சேதனம்=அறிவு, 106. [S. चेतन, चित्.]

சேர் ÇĒR. [சார், செறி. M. T. C. TU. Comp. चि, चर्.]

I. சேர்(ரு), *v.* (§ 57) [comp. the synonymes நண், அடை, சார்] join, attach (oneself) to; (p. 1) 55, 93, 179; acquire, 40; be acquired, fall to the lot of, 82; come to, approach, 122, 124, 139, 150, 175, 176, 252, 385.

நல்லினஞ்சேர்தல், ch. xviii. சேராது, it does not approach with hostile intent, 241.

சேர்கலா (+ கு + அல் + ஆ, G. 91)=சேராத, 121.

[சேரி (p. 35 *note*)=சேர்பு, சேர்வு, 'village, street, home:' hence *chēri* or *cherry* in names of places.]

II. சேர், *v.* (§ 56 III) gather, collect.

In 319 சேர்க்கும் = சேரும்.

III. சேர்|ப்பு, a harbour; shore, bank: துறை.

சேர்ப்பன், a chief whose capital was a sea-port: துறைவன். [See 250, and compare நாடன் and வெற்பன்.]

With தண், 73, 97, 98, 107, 108, 138, 146, 166, 194, 227, 242, 245, 246, 349; except in 117, 168, 336.

IV. சே|வல் [சே, செ, 'red,' or 'male'] a cock, 48. [M., C. Comp. √KĒ, *kēvu.*]

Nig. சேவலேகாவலோடு சேறுபுள்ளாண் முப்பேரே.

V. சே|று, 1. sweetness, 106. [For சாறு = சாரம். Comp. S. अन्तःसार.]

2. Mud; wet soil, 231.

[M. Comp. C. *kesaru.* Syn. in Tamil சேவல், சகதி, சிறுமியம், செதுக்கு, செதும்பு, செயல், செய்யல், சேய்தகம். See Kittel *in loc.* T. *jīrugu.*]

Nig. சேறென்பகும்பிசாரந் தித்திப்பு விழவுகள்ளே.

சேனை = தானை, படை, an army, 3. [S. शेना.]

சேறல், see செல்.

K. சொல் ÇOL = *word.* [M. CHOL. Old C. SOL. Comp. S. स्वन्, स्वर्, सुर.]

Nig. சொல் உரை கீர்த்தி செல்வரம்.

I. சொல், *n.* a word: உரை, மொழி, வார்த்தை, பேச்சு, ஓசை, 13, 63, 100, 115, 119 (may be நிந்தை or புகழ்: comp. வசை from वचस्), 253, 334.

கடுஞ்சொல், 73. இன்சொல், 73. இன்னுச்சொல், 66. சொற்பழி, blame, 297. சொன்ஞானம், words of wisdom, 311. மிகுதிச்சொல், 346.

[Words to be avoided are (1) பயனில்சொல் (असत्प्रलापं), *useless words;* (2) இன்னுச்சொல் (पारुष्यं), *harsh words;* (3) புறங்கூற்று (पैशुन्यं), *slanderous words;* and (4) பொய் (अनृतं), *false words.* See K. x, xix, xx.]

II. சொல்(லு), *v.* (§ 70) say, speak, utter: உரை, 63, 64, 70, 73, 256, 346.

சொல்|லாமை, 145 (§ 154).

சொல்|லிய = சொன்ன, 64, 70, 72.

In 313 there are two readings: சொற்ருற்று and சொற்ருற்றல், see தாற்று. சொற்று may = சொல்லி, from an old past tense சொற்றேன் = சொன்னேன்.

['. . . . சொல்லின்
அரில் அகற்றும் கேள்வியார் நட்பு . . . .:
Friendship with those whose learning banishes faults in use of words.' T. 1.
'சொல்வென்றி, a victory in argument.' T. 17.]

சோதிடம், astrology, 52. [S. ज्योतिषं.]

சோர் ÇŌR [s. शॄ and सृ. Comp. சரி, சொரி. M., C. SOR] v. (§ 60) for சொரி, flow down, slip, let slip, omit.

சோரினும், though it trickle in, 383; totter, 13: தள்ளாடு, forget, 311.

சோர்|வு (for சொரிவு) = மறதி, remissness, negligence, 145, 256. = தளர்ச்சி, பொச்சாப்பு.

சோலை = பூங்கா [comp. சாலை; s. शाला. M.] a grove, 17, 234.

சோறு = சாதம், அன்னம், boiled rice, 200, 217, 293.

[= *anything soft*: comp. சேறு, சொண்டி. M. C. *sōru* = 'tender.']

ஞ ÑA = ந.

ஞாயிறு, *n.* = நாயிறு, the sun, 7. [M. A. C. *nēsaru.*]

[Comp. B. I. S. 1204:

'आयुषः खण्डमादाय रविरस्तं गमिष्यति ।

When the sun sets it takes away a portion of life.' See also K. 334.]

ஞாலம் [from ஞால், hang, = நாலம். C. JŌL. M. NĀLU] earth, world, = பூமி, 72, 148, 296.

ஞானம் (ज्ञान), knowledge: அறிவு, 116, 308 (see மெய், அஞ்-, கை, சொல்).

ஞான்று = பொழுது.

எஞ்ஞான்றும் = always, ever, 14, 216, 256, 385.

[Comp. நான் + இ|ன்று + அ|ன்று + எ|ன்று. M. *ñānnu.*]

ஞெமிர், *v.* (§ 64) compress, bruise, 237. [Comp. நெரி, நெருக்கு.]

த TA.

1. த represents S. त, प, द, ध.

2. த is used for S. स्, श; as in மனது = मनस्, திரு = श्री.

3. த is the middle particle or sign of past time; II. B. § 15. Changing into த்த், ந்த, ற், ட், and ன்.

4. த், து is the termination of neuter singular (ஒன்றன்பால்): அது, செய்வது. Comp. S. तद्. Lat. *illud.* Gr. τό. Goth. *thata.* A. Sax. *that.*

5. து (த்து) forms neuter nouns: கை|த்து, உடை|த்து, 19, 126.

து is also a formative: எய்|து; and த்து of causal verbs, நடத்து (§ 160).

6. தி forms nouns: செய்-தி; and is an inflexion of 2nd pers. sing., G. 83, 84. உண்டி = உண் + தி.

தக் TAG. [With idea of *contact, order, fitness.* M., C., T. Compare with தங்கு (*tango*, ταγ, स्थग्), தாக்கு, தாங்கு, தகரு, தகை; T. *tagalu.*]

தகு, *v.* (§ 157) fit, be becoming.

தகல், fitness, 167. தக|வு, worth, 241.

தகுவது, a befitting thing, 223, 226.

தக்க with verbal roots: 'things *blameable, despicable,* worthy of . . .' [G. 153] 47, 92, 102 (for வீழும், *Nannūl,* 224), 228, 251 (அவாவ), 302, 316, 361.

தக்கார், the worthy, 38, 80, 112, 220, 250, 259, 327.

தக்கவால்லார், the unworthy, 112. வியத்தக்கான், he is a wonderful person, 325.

தகு|தி, a fitting, worthy course, 72. தகை = தன்மை.

சிறுதகைமை, humility, 170. தகைமை for தகுமை.

அன்னதகைத்தே, it is of just such a nature, 101, 138, 192, 211, 269.

தகடு = தட்டு, leaf, 266; outer petal := புறவிதழ். [M. *tagidu* = 'thin leaf of metal.' Comp. C. *tagaḍu.* T.]

தக|ர் TAG|AR [S. तक्. Comp. தகு, தாக்கு.]

I. தகர், *v.* (தகரு, § 57) be broken, shattered, 156, 257.

தலைதகர்ந்து, having its point broken, or blunted.

II. *n.* a ram: *the shatterer,* 376, 378. [C. M. T.]

தக்கோலம், *Clerodendrum inerme,* 43. See Gund. Mal. 'aromatic berries.' In T., C., M. S. कक्कोल and तक्कोल, *Pimenta acris.*

Some say தக்கோலம் = அடைகாய், i. e. *betel leaves and areca nut,* so commonly chewed. Another says, பஞ்சவாசத்தி லொன்று, 'one of the five fragrant aromatics:' *illicium anisatum.*

தங் TAṄG. [Root TAG, தக் with inserted nasal, as in Latin *frag* and *frang.* T. *takku,* 'remain.' C. *taṅgu.* M. *taṅṅu, tañju.*]

தங்கு, *v.* (§ 62) abide, be stable, 88, 246, 365.

தட் TAḌ [S. तट्].

I. தடம் [comp. தடு. T., C., M. *taḍa*].

As *adj.* தட, broad, full, swelling, 116, 378.

II. தட்டு, *n.* a flat plate. [Comp. தகடு. C. *taṭṭe.*]

III. தட்டு, *v.* (§ 62) tap, strike, 355. [C., T., M.]

IV. தடு|மாறு, be perplexed. [? From தடம் + மாறு.]

தடுமாறும் = புடைபெயர்கின்ற, that moves rapidly, 191.

தடுமாற்றம், perplexity, confusion, bewilderment, 27, 33, 140. See மம்மர். [T. *taḍabaṭṭu, taḍamāṭṭu.* C. *taḍa.*]

v. தடி, flesh, = உன், மாமிசம், தசை, சதை, 46.

[The meaning is, '*what is* தடம், *stout; robustness;*' hence 'staff, body;' and 'flesh.' M., C., T.]

தண் TAṆ. [M. C. Hind. *ṭhanḍ*. Comp. T. *tani-yu*.]

1. தண் = குளிர்ந்த, cool (சேர்ப்பு) 73, 97, 98, 138, 166, 194, 227, 242, 249, 391.

(கோது) 209, (புறவை) 210, (வயல், சாந்து) 389.

தண்ணீர் (நீர்), 139. [Some read தண்ணீர் for தெண்ணீர் in 150.]

II. தணி, *v.* (§ 57) be relieved, grow cool: ஆறு, 68.

v. (§ 64) cause to abate, *or* diminish, 104, 340, 369.

['இல்லோர்புன்கண் ஈகையிற்றணிக்க,

To relieve by gifts the suffering of the destitute.' *Kalit.* 47.]

III. தண்ணம் [an imitative word. C. *daṇa-daṇa*] 'drum with one head,' used at funerals: சாப்பறை, 6. Comp. 24, 25. = தண்ணுமை.

[Jī. Chin. i. 263:

'செந்தீகருந்துளைய தீங்குழல்யாழ்
தேத்தேம் என்னுமணிமுழவமும்
தந்தாங்கிளையார் மெல்விரல்கூடண்டத்
தாந்தாம் என்றிரங்குந் தண்ணுமைகளும்.

They bring sweet-voiced flutes with black holes burnt with red fire, and lute, and jewelled tambour that sounds Tēm Tēm; and while youths touch these with their fingers, drums wail out Tām Tām.']

தண்டு, 1. *n.* = கோல், staff, 14. [S. दण्ड; but comp. தட், தட, தடி, தடு.]

2. *v.* (§ 62) separate: பிரி.

தண்டாச்சிறப்பின், endowed with inalienable excellence, 62; live apart, mope, 324.

தந்தை, father: எந்தை, தகப்பன், பிதா, 197, 237, 253, 367. [T. *tanḍri*. M. *tanda*. C. *tande*. Comp. C. D. G. p. 293; but also S. तत, तात. See Kittel.]

தம், தமர், see தான். (G. 108.)

தய TAYA.

தய|ங்கு, *v.* (§ 62) shine; wave; hang: தளம்பு. [Comp. இயங்கு, இலங்கு, and S. दय्, दी; and *dangle*.]

தயங்குநீர், clear water, 210.

தயங்க = அசைந்து தோன்ற, appear dangling, 16.

தயிர், curdled milk, 116. [M. S. दधि.]

தருமம் [S. धर्म] charity : அறம், 250.

The use of this word is a mark of later date.

தரை [S. धरा] the earth, a land, 200. See முத்தரையர்.

தல் added to verbal stems. G. 94.

தல் TAL, *place*.

தலை [as நிலை from நில், and கலை from கல். M., T., C., TU. *tare*. In some uses it is akin to S. स्थल, तल, दल].

1. Place : இடம். And so as a postposition of 7th case. G. 63.

[Jī. Chin. i. 232 : 'நிலத்தலைத்திருவன்னாள், she who is like Lakshmī *upon earth*.']

தலைவரு, 57, 79, 141, 198 : சேர், சேர், come upon. தலைச்செல், attack, 241.

தலைக்கூடு, join, come into association with, 162.

தலைப்படு = attain unto, advance, rise, 139, 160, 272, 291.

2. Head, 14, 21, 43, 61, 87, 375.

இடுதலை, வெண்டலை, see இடு, வெள், 49, 50.

3. What is chief; highest, best [S. उत्तम] 52, 53, 133, 216, 248, 275, 297, 366 (= the first-class men, 'head-men'), 298, 365.

தலைமக்கள், 205. தலைவன் = நாயகன், இறைவன், பதி, 3.

தலைக்கண், topmost place, 368.

4. The extreme point, top, 257.

இருதலையும், both extremes, 114. ஒருதலையா, persistently and exclusively, 160.

['ஒருதலையான் வந்துறூஉ மூப்பும் புணர்ந்தார்க்
இருதலையும் இன்னாப் பிரிவும் . . .

Old age that *steadily* draws on, and separation of lovers bitter to *both parties*.' T. 18.]

K. தவ் TAV, *fail*. [Comp. S. दभ्.]

I. தவு, fail, perish : தவல், 137. = தவறல். [C.]

II. தவ|று, *n*. [comp. தவு, தவல், தபு, தப்பு, தப்பிதம், தவிர். C. *tavir*. T. *dabbaru*].

தவற்றினால், on account of their faults, 69; failure, 31; குறைவு, deficiency, 191; fault, 302, 364.

III. தவ|ழ், *v*. (§ 57) creep, crawl; traverse, 142 : உலவு.

K. தவம் [தபம், தபசு. S. तपस्] penance, 31, 51, 195, 333, 365.

தவசி, an ascetic, 99.

தழ் TAṞ.

I. தழு|வு, *v*. (§ 62) [C. *taṟkey*, *tabbu*. M. *taṟugu*] embrace, enfold, 285.

தழால் for தழுவுதல், the support of, ch. xxi.

II. தழ|ங்கு=முழ|ங்கு, *v.* (§ 62) roar [an imitative word, s. तरङ्ग] 339.

III. தழீ இம் an imitative word, for the sound of a drum, 6.

தள் TAḶ, *push.* [Comp. தளம்பு, துள, தள்ளு. M., C., T. *tallaḍa.* S. दल्.]

I. தள|ர்=கட்டவிழ், நெகிழ், சோம்பு, பலவீனப்படு, சோர், become relaxed, enfeebled.

தளரா=தளர்ந்து, tottering, 14. (G. 86.) [*Mū.* i. தளராமல்=without fail.]
சொற்றளர்ந்து, hesitating, or mumbling in speech, 13.
[Comp. *Iniyavai,* 8:

'குழவி தளர்நடைபைக் காண்டல் இனிதே,
Sweet is the sight of the infant's tottering walk.']

II. தளிர், a tender shoot, 336, 355, 373. [See துளிர். S. दल. M., C., T. *taliru.*]

III. தளை, *n.* bond:=பந்தம், பாசம், கட்டு, கயிறு, 12. [M. *taḷa.* C. *daḷe, taḷe.* Comp. G. 177–179.]

IV. தள்|ளு, *v.* (§ 62) [C., M.].
=மற, தமொழு; not even by a slip, =தவறியும், 157.

தறி, *n.* a wooden post: கட்டுந்தறி, 257. [M., C. Comp. S. तरि.]

தற் for தன், G. 35.

தன், தன்னை, தற், see தான்.

தா TĀ, த TA [see தரு, § 70, and வரு. M. *taru, tari.* C. *taru* = 'bring.' Comp. S. दा, धा, C. D. G. p. 113. T. in comp. *dā-konnu*].

K. தா, give, produce; bring, 83, 104, 235.

தந்து, having yielded, 185.

['தாளினுற் றந்த விழுநிதி, precious treasure the fruit of indnstry.' T. 47.]
தந்திட்ட=ஈன்ற, 224, 311.
As an auxiliary: திரிதரும்=திரியும், 284. போதரும்=போகும், 83.

தா TĀ, த TA; தான் TĀṈ, தன் TAṈ; தாம் TĀM, தம் TAM. [See C. D. G. pp. 290–297. In C., TU., T., M. Comp. S. स, सा, तद्.]

I. Reflexive pronoun='self,' § 108.

தான், 248, 278. தன்னை, 192. தன், 203.
தற்=தன்னை, 93, 101 [G. 35, 152] 203. தத்தம், each one's, 66.
தனக்கு, 15. தனது, his own, 278. தானே, of its self, spontaneously, 125.

தாம், 3, 8, 229. தமது, 278. தம், 5, 10, 229, 292.
தம்முடையார், those that are masters of themselves.

II. தமர் (§ 184) kindred, 30, 77, 87, 229, 283, 290, 379.
தமராயார்மாட்டு, with one's own people, 207.

III. தன்|மை, nature, 118; *selfhood*,=தத்துவம் (§ 184) 137.

IV. தனி, lonely, 324. [In C. and T. as *v.* 'thrive.']

தா|க்கு, *v.* (§ 62) strike, dash against, 389. [Comp. தகர். S. तक्. M., T. *tāku*. C. *tāku*, *tăṭu*.]

In 57 தாக்கரும்=தாங்கரும்=தாங்குதற்கரிய, hard to bear.

தா|ங்கு, *v.* (§ 62) support, endure, 62, 202. [Comp. தா|ரு. S. धा. C., M. *taṅṅu*.]

தாம், 1. See தான், 378. 2. Redundant in 377.

தாரம் [S. दारा] wife: மனைவி, 81, 82.

தா|ய்=ஆய், அன்னை [S. धा, धातृ. C., T. *talli*. See C. D. G. p. 293; but ?] mother; nurse, 15, 20, 101, 201.

தாயம். [S. दाय, an inheritance.]

தாயத்தவர், 278=தாயாதிகள், the heirs.

தார் TĀR from தர்.

I. தார்=மாலை, garland, 392. [M.='a flower.' S. तार.]

தாரினன், one who wears a garland, 390.

II. தார், *v.* (§ 64)=பொறு [comp. தாள். S. धृ, धार] bear, endure, 72.

தாழ் TĀṞ. [Comp. ஆழ், கீழ். M. C.]

I. தாழ், *v.* (§ 57) flow down, 231, 290.

தாழா=தாழ்ந்து, கூனி, being bowed down, 14 [G. 86]; bend, overshadow, 167.

II. தாழ், *v.* (§ 64) delay, 235.

தாழாது, without delay, 342 [G. 90].

III. தாழ்|வு, failure of energy, 191.

K. தாள் TĀḶ, *endure*. [Comp. தாழ். M. C. T. *tāl-chu*, *tāḷu*. Eng. *thole*. S. तुल्.]

தாள், *n.* 1. Endurance, energy: முயற்சி, ஆள்வினை [T. 47].

தாளாளர்=நன்முயற்சியுடையார், 191. தாளாண்மை=முயற்சியுடைமை, ch. XX, 200.

In K. ஊக்கம். (S. उत्थान, उत्साय.)

2. A trunk, stem, 261.

3. A foot, support, 198.

[T. 31: 'வல்லிதிற் றுனின் ஒருபொருள் ஆக்கல்,
The invention of something by ability and energy.'

T. 12: 'தாளாளன் என்பான் கடன்படா வாழ்பவன்,
He is the man of effort who lives without incurring debt.']

தாற் TĀṞṞ.

தாற்று, *v.* (§ 62) fan, sift. [Comp. தால் and தூற்று.]

n. a sifting: merely bandying words, 313.

[This is also read and explained as சொற்று ஆற்றல் கொண்டு, 'relying on the power of mere words.']

தானை = ஆடை, வஸ்திரம், சீலை, a cloth, robe, 131.

[Nig. தானையே சேனை யாடை படைக்கலம் தானும் ஆகும்.

In S. स्थाने = in place, suitable.

In sense of 'army' it is merely a form of சேனை; comp. தாளுபதி. तान = thread, तान्तव woven cloth.]

தான், self, 248. See தா.

திகழ் TIGAṚ.

திகழ், *v.* (§ 57) shine, glitter: விளங்கு, 389. [M. S. दह्.]

திங்கள் = சந்திரன், moon (நிலா, நிலவு = moonlight) 148, 151, 241. [C.]

திசை = திக்கு [S. दिशा] quarter, direction, 243, 392.

திண் [திட்] TIṆ. [Comp. திட. S. दृंह, दृढ. திட்பம், திண்மை. C., M. T. *tiṭṭamu*.]

திண், *adj.* firm, stedfast.

திண்ணறிவாளர் = முதறிவுடையார், 27, 227, 305.

திமிர், *v.* (§ 57) rub; rub off, 397. [C. *timir*, *tiguru*. M.]

திர் TIR, *turu*. [Comp. S. तृ, तिरस्; GR. τρεπ-; Old Lat. *trep*-. C. *tiri*, *tiru*. M., T. திரும்பு; திருத்து; திரள், திரை.]

I. திரி, *v.* (§ 57) = வேறுபடு, change, 204, 244.

திரிதந்து = திரிந்து, 284, 351 [தரு]; wander about, 230.

II. திரை = I. அலை, wave, 194, 224, 391.

திரையகடல், the billowy sea, 263.

2. By meton. 'sea,' 339. [S. तर. தரங்கம். T. *tera.* C. *tere.*]

[In Jī. Chin. iv. 7: 'திரைநீராடை இருநிலமடந்தை,
The goddess of the vast earth to whom the billowy sea is a garment.'
And, 'அலைநீராடை மலைமுலையாகத்
தாரப்பேரியாற்று மாரிக்கூந்தல்
கவின்பெறு கண் பரப்பின் மண்ணகமடந்தை:
The goddess of this vast expanding earth, whose garment is the billowy sea, the mountains her bosom, the mighty rivers the garlands around her form, and the clouds her locks.']

III. திர|ள், *n.* ball, globe; cluster. [M.]

v. [§ 56 (III)].

திரட்டு, *v.* (§§ 62, 160) make round, 103.

திரள்கால் = திரண்டகாம்பு, rounded stem, 199.

திரு [S. श्री] 'Lakshmī,' goddess of good fortune, 304; 'wealth,' 167, 291.

திருவத்தவர், 'blessed ones,' as though from a noun திருவம், 57.

திள் TIḶ.

திளை, *v.* (§ 64) gather thick around, boil up, rise up to, embrace. = தவழு; நெருங்கு. [M. *tiḷa, tiḷā.*]

மழைதிளைக்குமாடம், a mansion around whose top the clouds cluster, 361.

திற் TIṞṞ, *open.*

I. திற, *v.* (§ 66) [T. *tera.* C. *terra,* 'an opening'].

With வாய், 'open,' 8, 63, 126.

II. திறம் = sort: தன்மை [comp. தரம், திரம், திறல், திராணி. S. स्थिर. M., C. *terra*] good qualities: திறன், 291; goodness, 158; knowing what befits.

எத்திறத்தாள், what kind of a woman? 46.

தினை, millet, *Panicum Italicum*, L., 105.

[தினை பனை என்பன சிறுமைபெருமைகட்குக்காட்டிய அளவை] 323, 344. [M. Comp. S. तृण.]

தின் TIN̠, *gnaw.* [M., C., T. S. तृन.]

தின், *v.* [§ 56 (III)] eat: அருந்து, நுகர், 43, 112, 123, 138, 193, 197, 211, 289; itch, 335.

தீ TĪ. [M. TĪ, 'fire, evil.' Comp. தித்தி, தேம். C. TĪ, TĪYU. S.

दी 'shine;' दिन्, दीप् 'fire, burn;' धी 'wisdom.' T. TĪ-PI, 'sweetness.' TU. TŪ. In C. CĪ='sweet,' and 'be scorched.']

I. தீ, *n.* fire: நெருப்பு, அக்கினி. S. वह्नि [comp. தேசு] 24, 180, 224, 225, 234, 291, 298, 310; a spark, 389= தீப்பொறி.

செக்|தீக்கு, glowing fire, 90. தீ|மடு, kindle a fire, 331.

II. தீ, தீய, *adj.* evil, 351.

தீவினை = பாவம், sin. தீவினையச்சம், ch. xiii. Cruel, 5. தீவளி, temper, 19.

தீது, (what is) evil, 51, 73, 152, 228, 244, 284, 357 [G. 93].

தீய, (*pl.*) evil, evil things, 36, 109, 158, 195, 223 (*adj.*).

தீயார், evil persons, 172. தீமை = இன்னு, evil, 186, 227. தீங்கு, 66, 240. = தீமை.

தீப்புலவன் = டம்பக்காரனுனபுலவன், an heretical teacher, 312. [Opp. to நற்புலவன்.]

III. தீ, தீம், *adj.* sweet: மதுரமான, இனிய, 199, 244.

தீண்டு, *v.* (§ 62) [comp. தீற்று, தொடு, தைாத்து, தீட்டு, தீட்டு. M. TIṆḌ. C. *tīḍ*, TĪṬE. T. *tīṭṭa*. S. दिह्] touch, 109.

தீர்த்தம் = புண்ணியநீர், பரிசுத்தமானசலம், a sacred stream, 175. [S. तीर्थ.]

தீர் TĪR.

K. தீர், *v. tr.* and *int.* (§§ 57, 64)=நீ|க்கு, நீ|ங்கு [C., M., T., TU. S. तॄ] remove; get rid of; cure, 50, 161, 205.

தீர் [G. 153]=termination 'less,' 2, 347.

So தீரா as a termination='full, never free from,' 11.

வசைதீர், faultless observances, 152. தீர, absolutely, 204.

[தீர்ந்த = நீங்கின. Comp. S. तीर.

'வஞ்சத்திற் றீர்ந்த பொருள், a thing *free from* deceit.' T. 43.]

தீர்|ப்பேம் (G. 83) 27. தீர்வதற்கு, although want would be thus removed, 306.

தீர்|வு, 129=(கட்பு) நீங்குதல். தீர்விடத்து = தீர்ந்தபொழுது, 51 [G. 153].

தீற்று TĪṮṮU, *v.* (§ 62) [M., C. TĪḌ; see தீண்டு].

I. Rub, polish: தேய்.

II. Feed with the hand: ஊட்டு, 350. [M. Comp. தின், தீனி.]

['காய்த்தநெற்கவளந் தீற்றின், if you feed with mouthfuls of ripened *Nel*.' Jī. Chin. xiii. 309.]

K. து TU, துய் TU|Y, *enjoy*; [old C. *tuttu*='a mouthful.' Comp. K. 12. துறு, துத்து, துற்று.]

I. து, *v.* (§ 64) eat, enjoy: நுகர்.

து|ப்பு, power, 241.

துப்|புரவு, enjoyment; means of enjoyment: நகர்ச்சி, 87, 289. [See ஒப்புரவு *etc.*]

து|வை, spiced food, 217.

து|த்து, food, 190.

[Jī. Chin. xiii. 329: 'துத்தவிழ் ஈதல் செம்பொற்றுறக்கத்துக்கேணி ஆகும்: Giving a grain of rice (அவிழ்) from (your) food (துத்து) is the ladder to the bright golden paradise.']

II. துய், *v.* (§ 64)=து, 83, 93, 167, 202, 268, 273, 274.

III. து|த்து, *v.* (§ 62) 190.

IV. து|வ்வு, *v.* (§ 62)=து, 250, 276, 366.

[There is a conflict. In 190 the oldest copies have துற்று throughout.]

துகள்=குற்றம் [comp. தூள், so from தொகல், தோல். S. धूलि. M. *tugal*, 'skin of fruit;' see தோல். C. *tokku, togaḍu*. S. त्वक्] 2.

துகில்=சீலை [M. Comp. தொங்கு. S. दुकूलं] rich attire, 264.

துக்கம் [S. दुख, दुस्, दुर्. Comp. துன்பம், துயர்] 'sorrow:' used for 'sin, worldly pleasures; all that brings sorrow of heart:' संसार, 121, 123, 190.

துச்சரி, a licentious profligate, 84. [S. दुराचारि, *an evil-liver.* Though sometimes confounded with துச்சன=S. तुच्छ, *a worthless fellow.*]

துஞ்சு TUÑÇU, *v.* (§ 62) die, 21, 191. [Comp. தூ in தூங்கு. M. T. The idea is 'nodding, falling.']

துடி, a drum, 388. [From verb துடி, throb. M., T., C. *tuḍumu.*]

துடை, *v.* (§ 64) wipe off, do away with: துன்பம், 93. [M., C. TOḌAI, TOḶEI. T. TUḌU, TOḌU.]

See *Ēl.* 4, துன்பந்துடைத்தல்.

துணி TUṆI, *v.* (§ 57) resolve upon, 303. [M., C., T. *tuṇi.* Comp. துண்டி. S. तुड्, तुण्ड्. The meaning is (1) *cut;* (2) *decide;* (3) *venture, dare.*]

['அரியதுணிந்து வாழ்வர், they have set themselves a difficult task.' T. 73.]

துணி|வு, decision, determination, 55.

துணிவொன்றி, coming to the same conclusion.

துணை=a match, companion, *etc.* [M., C. TOṆE. S. द्वा, द्वन्द्व. Comp. தனை.]

1. உதவி, assistance, 78, 136, 381 *help-meet ;* partner, 392.

2. அளவு, measure, 37, 38, 94, 105, 140, 187, 218. 196, 231 = until. Comp. வரை, வகை, and தனை.

எத்துணையும், at all ; in any degree, 109, 272.

தினைத்துணையும், even so much as a grain of millet, 323.

தினைத்துணையர், } those who as to greatness were as . . ., 105. [See under தினை.]
பனைத்துணையர், }

[In T. 51 : 'தார்த்தொழுகிக் கண்ணுறுந் துணைக ளெனகளே,

Even when a man is in straitened circumstances relations are helps ; or (perhaps better), *a friend in need is a friend indeed.*']

துணை|மை = சாதகம், ability, 127.

துப்பு, see து.

துய், see து.

துயர் = துயரம் [comp. துன்பம். M. ; from S. दुर्] sorrow. = துன்பம், 35, 114. துயர்களையான், he does not relieve their sufferings, 9.
'ஆழ்துயர் உழப்ப, they will suffer the deepest sorrow.' Jī. Chin. xiii. 165.

துரும்பு = சக்கை, refuse stalks, 35.
[Comp. S. तृण. M. Like இரும்பு, அரும்பு, கரும்பு.]

துவ், see து.

துழ TUṚA = குழை, கல.

துழவு, துழாவு, *v.* (§ 62) mix, mingle up.

துழாய் = துராவி, 311. [பரப்பி.]

[In M. TUṚA, 'a paddle.' Comp. துளம்பு.]

துள் TUḶ.

I. துள|க்கு, துள|ங்கு, துள|க்கம் [comp. துழாய். M. *tulayu*] agitation, 189.

துளக்கற, calmly, 371. [துளங்கு in T. 41.]

II. துள்|ளு, *v.* (§ 62) leap, frisk, caper, 64. [Imitative. M., C., T.]

துற் TURR = *take refuge.*

I. துற, *v.* [§ 66. In M. = 'open' = திற. Comp. S. दूर ; hence துறை, a haven ; துறக்கம், heaven] renounce ; reject ; forsake, 11, 62, 78, 226, 266.

துறப்பர், 53.

II. துற|வு, ch. vi, 60, 121.

துற|வோர், ascetics, 273.

துற்று, see து.

துன், துர், துற் [S. दुर्. Comp. துயர்].

துன்|பம், affliction, 54, 57, 60, 84, 93, 205, 280, 295. [Comp. இன்பம். Aff. பு, பம்.]

துன்|பு = துன்பம், 74, 209, 235.

With உறு = படு. [Comp. Jl. Chin. xiii. 201.]

துன் TUṈ [C. TUR. T. TURU|MU. M. TURR, TUN].

துன்|ன், துன்னு, துன்று, துறு (§ 62) = கிட்டு, பொருந்து, பெறு, நெருங்கு, approximate, harmonize with; gain; be crowded, 76, 205.

துன்னருங் கேளிர், not easily gained, 9, 226.

துன்னி, being thick, close packed, 167.

துன்னியார் = அடைந்தோர், those who press close, 167. துன்னு, not adhering, 226.

K. **தூ** TŪ [M. TŪ. Comp. T. DŪ, and S. धू].

தூய், pure, 189.

தூய்து, that which is pure.

தூய்தாக, completely, utterly, *purely*, 270.

தூய்தன்மை, '(the body's) destitution of purity,' title of ch. v.]

தூங்|கு TŪṄKU, *v.* (§ 62) [comp. தொங்க, தூக்கு, தூக்கம், துஞ்சு. M. TŪṄṄ. T., C. TŪG. S. तूण्, तूल्] cling to, linger; hang on; nod, slumber, 121, 327. = தங்கு.

தூங்கிசை is the name given to the rhythm of verses when only

(– –, – ◡ ◡, ◡ ◡ –, ◡ ◡ ◡ ◡)

இயற்சீர் are employed, and a long syllable is followed by a short, or ◡ ◡ is followed by a long [G. 174, 179]. See Introd. p. xxviii.

தூணி [M.] a grain, measure, equal to four மரக்கால்; while a பதக்கு is = two மரக்கால்: hence தூணிப்பதக்கு = six மரக்கால், 387. [Seems a cor. of S. द्रोण.]

தூண், a pillar, 64. [S. स्थूणा.]

தூய், see தூ.

தூரம், distance. [S. दूर.]

தூரவிடு, keep at a distance.

தூர, *adv.* = away, 75.

தூர் = வேர், root, 138.

[As verb, T. 51, be in difficulties. S. स्थूल = स्थूर, see Benfey Lex. *in loc.*]

தூற் TŪṞṞ, *drizzle as rain.* [தூறு, தூற்று. Comp. தூ, தூ|வு. C. TŪR, DŪR. T. DŪR. M. TŪRR, TŪTTU, TŪGU.]

தூற்று, *v.* (§ 62) publish abroad, 21, 75, 144, 324.

தெங்கு [தேங்கு]=தெண்ணை, 216, 243.

[A corruption for தென்|கு. The cocoa palm, first introduced into the South of India, is தென்னமரம். C., M. *tenńu*. T. *tenkāya*. S. नारिकेर, B. I. S. 4249.]

தெர் TER, *clear*. [Comp. தேர், தேறு, தெள், திற. C. *terra*. M., C. *tiḷi*. T. *teli*.]

I. தெரி [sometimes impersonal, or *v. n.* or *v. a.*, § 57] be understood, clear; enquire, understand,=தேர், 135, 168, 170, 247, 316, 318. With இடை, 54.

தெரி|வு, understanding, 240, 247.

II. தெருள் (see பொருள், அருள், *etc.*), *v.* [§ 56 (III)] be clear, 301. [M., C.]

III. தெரு|மரு=கலங்கு, be perplexed, தெருமருகிறேன், தெருமந்தேன், 151.

[Comp. T., C. *teraḷu*. In T. *terupu|marupu*=‘wayward fits of folly:’ a reduplication. H. B. § 123. *g*.]

தெய்வம் [S. दैवं] the deity, 304.

தேவன், தேவர், 112. [S. देव.]

K. தெள் TEḶ, *clear*. (=தெருள்.) [Comp. தெர், தேர், தேற். C. TEḶ=‘fine, thin.’ T. *teli*.]

I. தெள், *adj.* clear: (தெண்.)

தெள்ளிது, what is clear: accurate knowledge; 5th for 3rd இன்=ஆல் [G. 137*] 135.

தெள்ளிய, 386.

தெண்|ணீர், 44, 150, 375.

K. II. தெளி, *v.* (§ 57) understand, 364.

[T. II: ‘தெளியாதான்கூரையுட்பல்காலுஞ் சேறல்,

The frequenting of the house of a man who trusts (you) not.’]

தெளி|வு=பகுத்தறிவு, விவேகம், clear understanding, 219.

III. தெள்ளு, *v.* (§ 62) sift out, throw up, 128; examine, 380.

தெறி TERRI. [Comp. நெரி, தெளி. M.]

தெறி, *v.* (§ 64) dash off, 394.

தெற்றென, ‘so as to say *tettu*,’ an imitative word=‘immediately;’ or ‘certainly’ (§ 82) 150.

தென், *adj.* southern, 243. [Comp. வட, மேல், கீழ். தென்=S. दक्षिण. See தெங். M. *ten*. So தெம்மொழி=தென்மொழி=Tamiṛ.]

தே TĒ, *sweet.* [Comp. தீ, தீம்.]

தே|ம், sweetness, honey, 199, 239, 375. [Comp. *Nannūl*, 214.]

தே|ன், honey, 10, 259.

தேனீ, the bee. Comp. *Vēmana* ii. 207.

தே|மா, sweet mango, 257.

[C. *jē, jēm, jēn*='honey.' M. *tēn.* T. *tēne.*]

தேசு, *n.* lustre, 105. [S. तेजस्. Comp. தீ.] =மகிமை, ஒளி.

தே|ய் TĒY, *waste.* [Comp. தேம்பு. M. *tēyu, tēmbu.* C. TĒ, TĒY. (T. *deyu.*) Comp. S. क्षि, क्षय.]

தேய், *v.* (§ 57) waste away, 51; wane, grow less, 125; pine away, 151.

தேர் TĒR. [Comp. தெர், தேறு.]

1. தேர், *v.* (§ 57) enquire, discriminate, 119, 120, 127, 177, 282. (தேரு, § 62.)

தேர்கிற்கும்=தேரும் (கு + இன் + கு), the discerning faculty, 352.

2. தேர்|வு, *n.* the searching out, comprehension, 259.

தே|ரை, a frog: தவளை, 193, 352. [M. *tēra*, 'a lean frog.']

தேற் TĒṞṞ. [See தெர், தேர், தெள், தெற்று, தெற்றெனவு=certainty. T. 54.]

I. தேறு, *v.* (§ 62) be sure, know clearly, 313; trust, 379. [M. C. *tēru.* T.]

II. தேற்று, *v.* (§ 62).

(*Int.*) know certainly, be quite clear about, 274, 316, 320, 322.

தேற்றா ஒழுக்கம், doubtful (*shady*) conduct, 75.

(*Tr.*) impart certainty, teach, 318.

III. தேற்றம், certainty, assurance, confidence, accuracy, 259. [T., C. *tēṭe*, 'clearness.']

தை TAI.

தை, *v.* (§ 64)=உருவிச்செல், penetrate, 260. [M. strike, sew.]

தொ TO = து in most words: the idea is *connexion*.

தொ|கு, *v.* (§ 68) collect, join, 284, 318. [M.]

தொக்க, gathered together, 121. [G. 82 (கூ), 87.] Compacted, 37. [So யாக்கை.]

தொடு TOḌ, *join*.

I. தொடு, *v.* (§ 68) touch. [T., M., C. துட is the older form. Comp. உட, ஒடு.]

Used as a particle = *from*, *thenceforward*, 2. [So in M. See H. B. § 230.]

II. Dig. [For this தோண்டு is used. T. √TAV, TRAV.]

சோட்ட for தொட்ட or தோண்டின, dug out, 215.

[T. 16: 'உண்ணுநர் கூவல்குறைவின்றித்தொட்டான்,

He who has dug a well with a copious supply of drinking water.'

Naiḍ. xx. 5: 'தொடு கடல் உடுத்த ஞாலம்,

Earth girt with the excavated sea.' See the story of Sāgara.]

III. தொடு, *v.* (§ 64) tie, connect [cause to touch], 5, 26, 393. [M.]

IV. தொடர், *v.* (§ 57) connect: துடர், 46. [T., C., M.]

தொடர்|பு, association, intimacy: நட்பு, 113, 125, 138, 166, 204, 211–218, 222, 234, 293. [தொடர்ச்சி is used in T. I; தொடர்கை and தொடர்ப்பாடு in K.]

V. தொட|ங்கு, *v.* (§ 62) begin; 173, from the beginning. [T.]

[ர், ற், ம் (with various connecting vowels) added to a root often form derivative verbs. From தொடு comes தொடர்; பகு, பகிர்.]

VI. தொடி, a bracelet, bangle, 111. By *meton.* 'a lady,' 376, 398. [C. *toḍige.*]

தொடீஇ, voc. case, G. 64.

VII. தொண்|டு = பழமை, slavery, a slave, = தொழும்பன், 284. [See தொல், தொழ், தொத்து, தொறு: a nasalized form of தொடு. C. *tottu*, *toṛt|tu*. M. *toṇḍan* = 'old man.' Comp. T. *totti*, *tonte*.]

VIII. தொண்டு an imitative word, 25.

தொல் TOL, *old*.

I. தொல், old: பழ, பழைய. [T. *tolu*, *toli*. C. *tom*. ?துடல், தொடல்.]

தொல்கேள்வி, traditionary lore, 137. தொல்சிறப்பு, ancient excellence, 139, 195, 252. தொல்சீர், of old renown, 333. தொல்வழி, tradition, old custom, 154. தொல்புகழ், ancient renown, 166. தொன்மை, old association, 216.

II. தொல்லை, antiquity; trouble, perplexity: பழைமை, ஊழ், 101, 136, 265. [M. *tolla.*]

தொல்லையது, it is the result of old deeds,—fate, 33.

III. தொலை, *v.* (§§ 57, 64) perish, destroy. [M. TOḶI, TULE. C. TOḶE. துலை, A. C., T. *tolagu.*]

தொலைமக்கள், the hopeless and helpless, 205.

தொலை|வு, effacement.

தொலைவில்லா, endless, countless, 52.

IV. தொலை|ச்சு, *v.* (§§ 62, 160) destroy, 300.

தொழ் TOṚ, [தொடு, துடு. Folding of hands in reverence. M. T. *dōyali.* C. TUṚ. Comp. S. द्वन्द, दण्ड ; தண்டன், தொண்டு.]

I. தொழு, *v.* (§ 60) pay homage: கும்பிடு, கைகுவி, வணங்கு, 176, 373.

II. தொழு, *n.* leprosy: குட்டம், 123. [Comp. தொத்து. C. *tonnu.* தினவு.]

III. தொழில், employment, work, service: வினை, 26, 128, 145. [C. *tuṛil.*]

காற்றொழில், menial service: அற்பச்செய்கை, 193.

செய்தொழில், *active* service, 347, 350.

மேற்றொழில், noble service, 193.

தீத்தொழில், evil works: கெட்டகாரியம், 351.

IV. தொழுத்தை, a slave girl, 326. [C. *toṛtu, tottu.* தொழு, a cow-stall.]

தொள் TOḶ. [C. *toṛe.* M. *toḷḷa.*]

தொளை (துளை) = துவாரம், hole, entrance, 42.

தொறு, (properly தோறு) a collection. [M. *tōrru* = 'appearance.' C. = 'seem' = தோன்று. T. *dōra,* 'heap.' The root also means *a fold, herd;* and *slavery.* Comp. தொழ்.]

தொறும், தோறும், தோறு, = 'every, whenever:' a distributive suffix.

1. With verbal root (க் doubled): மூத்தொறூஉம், just as (they) grow old, 60, 222, 351.
2. With noun, 159. நாடொறும், daily, 225.

தோணி = மரக்கலம், boat, 136. [S. द्रोणी ; but comp. *v.* தோண்டு, scoop out. T. *dōne.* Another form is தோண்டி.]

தோய் TŌY, *touch*. [Comp. தேய், தொடு, தடவு, துவை. T. *tō-chu*. M. S. तोयं.]

தோய் (p. 1) *v. n.* blend with, touch, 387, = கல; reach, 10, 69, 142.

[In sense of *close, intimate friendship*: 'தோய்ந்தாருட் டோய்ந்தான், a very intimate friend.' T. 82.]

தோல் TŌL. [C. *togalu, tokku*. M., T. *tōlu*. S. त्वच्, त्वक्.]

I. தோல், *n.* leather, 26; skin, 41, 42, 46, 47, 322.

II. தோல், *v.* (§ 70) தோற்கிறேன், தோற்றேன், தோற்பேன், தோற்க, be defeated, 313. (Opp. வெல்.) [Comp. தொல், தொலை. M. T. *tōlu*. C., TU. *sōlu*.]

தோள் [S. दोषन्, दोस्. M., C.] = shoulder, arm; person, 85, 312, 317, 338, 375, 385, 394.

தோளி, she whose shoulder is . . ., 47.

[*Ēl.* 7: 'வேயன்னதோளி, she whose shoulder is like the *bambu*.']

தோட் கோப்பு (G. 34), 20, 328.

In journeys the rice is carried in a bundle over the shoulder: கட்டசோறு.

தோற் TŌRR.

I. தோன்|று, தோற்|று, *v.* (§ 62) appear, 2, 8, 21, 27, 28, 30, 49, 83, 154, 177, 186, 197, 234. [C. TŌ-RU, TŌ|CHU. M. *tōrru, tōnnu*. T. TŌ-CHU. See தொறும்.]

II. தோற்றம், appearance; light, 7. Lit. 'the sun full of light.'

III. தோறும் (also தொறும். In M. TŌRR = 'appearance') = what appears, all, each, every; whenever pleasure is attained, 60.

ந NA.

ந NA = ஞ.

1. This letter is sometimes inserted euphonically: thus அறிவன் = அறிஞர் = அறிநன். See உழவர் = உழுநர்.

2. As a Sanskrit prefix ந = அ = 'not.'

3. It seems to have been prefixed to some words to strengthen them. Comp. அவிழ் and நவிழ்; அணுகு and நணுகு; ஈர் and நரம். It is uncertain whether the ந in நான் and நீ is radical.

நக் NAG. [C. NA|GE. M. T. NA|GU, NA|VU.]

நகு, *v.* (§ 68) shine; smile, deride: இகழ்.

நகை, a jewel ; a laugh, 377. நக, while . . . derides, 230, 238.
நகையேயும், even in sport, 187. [K. 871.] நகும், will laugh him to scorn, 273.
நகா அது, 324. நகல், joyous intercourse, 137.

Nig. நகை மகிழ் வெள்ளி சிரிப்பாம்.

நக்கு, *v.* (§ 62) lick, 87, 377. [Comp. நா, நாக்கு, நாவு. C. and T. NĀKKU. M.]

From நகு, 'laugh,' we find நக்கு, 'having laughed,' § 68.

நச் NAÇ, *desire.* [See நச்சு. M. NACHCHAM. In T. NACH-U= நம்பு: so in C. In A. C. NANNI=நசை, and NAÇE='pleasure.' Comp. நயம், நேசம், சிநேகம், நெய், and S. स्निह्, स्नेह. நசை='moisture:' comp. ஈரம் in both senses.]

I. நசை, *n.*=ஆசை, desire, hope, expectation, 111, 263, 365, 381, 385.

II. நசை, *v.* (§ 57), 222,=நசைந்து root for வினையெச்சம். [G. 153.]

நசைஇ=நசைந்து, desiring, 32, 286: நச்சி. [G. 86.]

[In T. 94 நசைக்கிழமை=அன்புரிமை, 'affection.' So நசையுநர்=விழைவுநர்.]

III. நச்சு, *v.* (§ 62) desire, lust after.

நச்சியார்க்கு, 299. நச்சுவார், those who lust after, 82.
பலர்நச்ச, so that many desire their favour, 96.
[*Ēl.* 13: 'நச்சாமைநோக்காமைநன்று, it is well neither to desire nor regard them.'
T. 30: 'தன்னைச்சிச்சென்றோர், those that seek them as suppliants.'
Kalit. i. 8: 'நிலையிலாப் பொருளைய நச்சுபவோ?
Will they *hanker* after wealth that abides not?']

நட் NAḌ, *fix.*

நட, *v.* (§ 68) tread, walk, live, 242, 398: =ஒழுகு, மிதி. [C. NAḌ|E. M. T. NAḌ|U. S. नड्. Seems from நட், நள்,='middle.']

நடை, walk ; action, walk in life, position, 13, 343.

பகடு நடந்தகூழ், grain *trodden* out by oxen, 2.

நடுக்கு, *v.* or *n.* shake. [C. M. S. नट्.]

நடுக்குற்று=suffering want, 93. [This admits of several renderings: நடுக்கு is a noun: see உறு.] (1) The needy who come to them for aid ; (2) fearing poverty for themselves if they give.

தலைநடுக்கா=தலைநடுக்கெடுத்து. [G. 87, 150.] Here தலை is what in Latin is 'acc. of respect:' trembling *as to* (her) head='with palsied head,' 14.

K. நடு, √நள், middle, 96. [C. M. T. NAḌI. Comp. நள், நண்.]

நடுவணது (நடு+அண்+அது), that which is in the middle, 114.
[அண்=கண்=இடம்: so அக்கண் (அங்கு+அண்), இக்கண், எக்கண்.]
நடுவு=நடு, 131. நடுவுநிலைமை=நடுநிலை, impartial justice.

நந்து NANTH.

(1) *நந்து*, grow; wax:=பெருகு, வளர், 125, 179. [Comp. S. नन्द्. T. NANA, 'a bud;' NANA|YU,='expand.' C. *nandu*, 'decay.']

(2) Die out, 234: =கெடு.

Nig. நந்தல் கேடெனே ஆக்கம்.

நம்பு=desire, 81, 87: விரும்பு, நச்சு. [T. NAM. C. NAMB; NACH. M.]

நய NAYA. [Comp. நசை, நேசம். S. नय. Sometimes=நியாயம்.]

I. நய, *v.* (§ 66) love: விரும்பு, 215.

நயவாது, not duly estimating (=? நீதிநியாயமின்றி), 267.

II. நயம், *n.* goodness; =நன்மை: wise decorum: நல்லொழுக்க, 162, 163, 239, 265, 312.

நயவர், pleasant people, 265, 267.

நர|ம்பு, tendon, 46, 153. [C. NARA. T. NARAM. M. From நார்+ம்பு affix: comp. பாம்பு.]

நரி, a jackal, 152: ஓரி, நரிமா. [M. C. T. NAKKA.]

நரை, grey hair; age. [Comp. S. जरा. M. NARA. C. T. NARI.] மூப்பு, II.

[As *v.* (§ 64) grow grey:
'மயிர்நரைப்பத்தின்னும், it will consume till the hair grows grey.' T. 67.]

நல் NAL. [நன், நற். In T. *nal*='black.' Perhaps S. सत्, सन् have been changed into நற், நன், நல் as Tamil has no स. M., C. Comp. நறு, நய.]

I. நல், *adj.* good, goodly, 115, 154, 202, 225, 239, 248, 266, 308, 336, 387.

With நாடு *passim*, a pleasant land, 71, 77, 231, 344, 353, 369.

With இனம், ch. xviii.

நல்|வினை (opp. தீவினை), 19, 51. நன்|னெறி (நெறி), 55, 327.
நற்|காய், the promising —, 19. நன்|னெஞ்ச, dear heart! (55), 376.
நல்|லறிவு, 11, 139, 254, 320. நல்|லறம், 10. நல்|லொழுக்கம், 57.
நற்|சார்வு, association with the good, 171, 178. நற்புடை, 212.

II. Inflected as a குறிப்புவினை. [G. 93.]

[These forms are precisely analogous to the declension of a Latin adjective: thus,

BON-us, -a, -um,
நல்-லன், -லள், -ல்லது,
-i, -ae, -a,
-லவர், -ல்ல.]

But the following is a kind of conjugated form:
நல்லம், we are good, 131. நல்லாள், the goddess Fortune, p. 3, N. M. K.
நலவர், 188. நல்லர், 155, 175, 221, 265, 298, 314. நல்லாய், (voc.) 41.
நல்லார், the good women, 12, 188.
நன்று, it is good, = நல்லது, 20, 24, 67, 71, 159, 219, 246, 286, 288, 294, 369.
A thing that is good, 294, 327, 344. A benefit, = நன்றி, 257, 327, 356.
நல்ல, good things, 77, 136, 246, 294, 334.
Good, 129, 160, 162, 177, 195. *Adv.* much, 335.
நல (= நல்ல), *adj.* good, 175. நல்லவை, 109, 144, 338, 366.

III. Derivatives.

நன்|கு, *adv.* well, 229; very, 218, 319.

நன்|றாய், *adv.* well.

நன்|றி, *n.* a benefit: நன்மை, உபகாரம் [நல் + தி. उपकार, कृतं], 111, 323, 357.

In 111, செய்ந்நன்றிகொன்றார், 'the ungrateful.' Comp. S. कृतघ्न = 'slaying a benefit,' from हन्, 'slay.' The coincidence of घ्न and கொன்ற is curious.

In நன்றறியா, 257, comp. S. कृतज्ञ, अकृतज्ञ, where the idea is the same.

நன்றியில்செல்வம், ch. xxvii. நன்|மை, 146, 188, 381.
நலம், = excellence, richness, 167, 179, 333, 339, 356, 386 'beauty.'
நல்|கூர், *v.* be poor, 115, 153, 242, 270, 277, 296, 298, 301. [நல்கு + ஊர் ?]
நல்|கு, *v.* grant, 263. (M.) The open-handed. நல்|குரவு, poverty, 267, 275.
[T. 72: 'நிறைநெஞ் சுடையானை நல்குரவஞ்சும்,
Poverty will fear to approach the man of mind sincere.']

நலி NALI.

v. tr. (§ 57) afflict, 308. [C. NALI, NAVI. T. NAL-I, NAVA. S. नल्. Comp. அலை, அளி.]

நவில் NAVIL. 1. Tell; teach. 2. Learn.

நவின்ற, taught, 320. [Not in cognate languages; but comp. நா.]

Nannūl, 13: 'நவின்றோர்க்கினிமை, sweetness to the students.'
Nig. நவிலல் சொல்லுதல் பண்ணற்பேர்.

நவை = குற்றம், fault, 295.
[Seems to be originally = 'a soft spot, decay.' Comp. நோ.]

நள் NAḶ, idea of *intensity; centre; plant.* [M. NAḶIR, NAṆ|ICHU. A. C. NAḶA = 'joy.' Comp. நட், நண்.]

1. நளி: பெரிய, 'great.' Another meaning is 'cold;' comp. நளிர், குளிர்.

Nig. நளிர்குளிர்பெருமைசெறிவு நாட்டியசெறிவு நாற்பேர்.
நளிகடல், 166, 242.
[கலித். i. 17: 'நாற்றஞ்சானளிபொய்கை, the *huge* tank full of fragrance.']

II. *நள்*, *v.* [§ 56 (III)], *நள்ளு* (§ 62) approach, join, contract friendship.

நட்க, cultivate friendship, 174.

நட்டான், friend, 128, 208, 209, 223, 230, 271, 338.

நட்பார், 215. *நட்ட*, 230.

நட்டக்கால், 75. *நள்ளாது*, 128.

நள்ளார், receive not as friends, 262.

நள்|ளாதார் = பகைவர், those who are not our friends, 207, 271.

III. *நட்பு*, 12. = *கேண்மை*, *தொடர்பு* [s. स्नेह. Ind. Sp. 7240 *etc.* सख्यं], 215, 216, 218, 219, 223, 232, 237, 337, 339, 370, 371.

நட்புக்கோடல், the forming of friendships, 77.

நட்பாராய்தல், examination of (candidates for) friendships, ch. xxii.

நட்பிற்பிழைபொறுத்தல், bearing with faults in friendship, ch. xxiii.

கூடாநட்பு, unreal friendship, ch. xxiv.

IV. *நண்பு*, 174, 213, 339.

[*Mu.*: 'நட்டாலும் நண்பல்லார் நண்பல்லர் :

Though you lavish affection on the unloving they are loveless.']

'கள்ளாமை வேண்டும் கடிய வருதலால் ;
தள்ளாமை வேண்டுந் தகுதி யுடையன ;
நள்ளாமை வேண்டுஞ் சிறியாரோ டியார்மாட்டும்
கொள்ளாமை வேண்டும் பகை.

It is necessary to abstain from theft, for it brings heavy penalties;
It is necessary not to abandon things of worthy virtue;
It is necessary not to contract friendship with mean people;
It is necessary not to conceive enmity against any.'

[See II. B. § 154.]

நறு NARR. [Hence *நாறு*, q. v. H. B. § 131.]

[We find *நறுமை*, *நறவம்*, *நறவு*, *நறு*, *நறை*, *நாறு*, *நாற்றம்*.]

நறு|ங்|கண்ணி, a fragrant garland, 16.

நறு|மலர், 209, 381.

நறவு = மணம், fragrance, 108.

[In C. and M. In common use for 'a bad smell.']

நனி = very. Much: *மிகுதியாக*, *மிக*, 17, 200, 221, 334, 383.

[This is one of the very few real Tamil adverbs. G. 120. *Nan.* 388. Comp. S. ननु.]

நா NĀ.

நா, tongue, 335, 353. [T., C. NĀLIGE. M. NĀKKU, NĀVU, NĀ. நாவு, நாக்கு. See நக்கு.]

நாவின்கிழத்தி = சரஸ்வதி, 252. The goddess of learning: சகலகலாவல்லி.

நாவினோர், 256.

நாப்பாடம், a mere lip-lesson, 312.

நாகம் [S. नाग] a serpent: பையரவு, 66, 164, 240.

நாகு, a heifer: the young one, 115. பசுவின்பெண்கன்று.
Nig. நாகுசங்கிளமை நத்தை.

K. நாடு NĀḌ [from நடு, plant, or middle; √நள்: as காடு from கடு; பாடு from படு, *etc.* M., C., T.] a land, country. It is *habitable*, as distinct from காடு; and *rural*, as distinguished from ஊர்: comp. நாட்டார், காட்டார், ஊரார்.

நாடன் = நாட்டரசன், lord of the land, 10, 71, 76, 77, 79, 113, 127, 128, 154, 161, 185, 203, 212, 223, 228, 231, 232, 234, 239, 283, 285, 290, 307, 319, 343, 344, 348, 353, 369. [See also சேர்ப்பன், வெற்பன்.]

தென்னாட்டவர், 243.

The 'LAND' of the *Nālaḍi* is a land of lofty hills, with many waterfalls, a goodly land, well-watered (சா), rich in gems (காசை, 75), with flowery glades and a wide sea-board. [See note to 10, and to தரை.]

நாடு, *v.* = தேடு: follow with the eyes, covet, seek, 15, 225, 370, 371, investigate; 230, seek out: ஆராய், 101.

[*Ēl.* 35: 'நாடுவர் விண்ணோர் நயந்து, the celestials will anxiously expect *his arrival.*']

நாட்டம், investigation, 18.

[Comp. நோ-க்கு. M. A. C.]

K. நா|ண் NĀṆ, *shame.* [C. M. T. NĀ|NA. TU. NĀ-CHU.]

I. நாண் (நாணம்), *n.* (1) modesty, a sense of shame, a shrinking from disgrace, self-respect, = மானம், 81, 267, 386.

(2) Shame, disgrace: வெட்கம், 89, 299, 323 = insensible to shame.

[Comp. வெட்கம், இலச்சை (लज्जा), கூச்சம், நாச்சம். The Gr. αἰδώς.]

II. நாணு, *v.* (§ 62) feel shame, 384, with இயல்பினாள், she whose virtues the townsmen reverence.

நாணி, feeling embarrassed, 241, 293.

நாணல், suffering shame, 155.

நாணுதல், a shrinking back, 299.

நாணுது, not feeling abashed, shamelessly, 314.

நாணுதும், we feel abashed, 385. [G. 83. T. *nān-udu-mu.*]

நாம் = யாம் [H. B. § 10] pl. of நான்.

செய்துநாம் = நாஞ்செய்வோம், 32, 235, 390. [Comp. T. CHĒ-TU-MU.]

நம்மால், 301. நம்மொடு, 372. நம்மை, 376. நம், 394. = எம், 390. நமக்கு, 55.
எமர், நமர், our own people : கேளிர், 205, 206.

நாய் NĀY. [C. NĀYI. M., TU., Tuḍa. Comp. நா, நக்கு. Not in K. or NĪ. In T. KUKKA.]

நாய், a dog : ஞமலி, 70, 213, 218, 254, 322, 345.

The dog is here the type of the கீழ்மகன், the man of low, depraved instincts ; but full justice is done him in 213 !

நார் NĀR, *fibre.* [Comp. நரம்பு. M. C. T.]

Nig. நார் என்ப கயிறன்பாவே.

= பாசம், கயிறு, 12, 26 ; cord, generally made of vegetable fibre, 153.

நட்புநார், the bonds of friendship, 12.

நால் NĀL, **நான்** NĀṈ. Root means '*hang.*'

நான்கு, four, 82, 319. [M. C. T. Tuḍa.]

நாவாய், a ship, = மரக்கலம், 224. [S. नौ.]

நாழி = அளக்குங்கருவி, a measure, 7. It means originally a hollow tube, generally a joint of *bambu.* [S. नाडि, नाळम्, नाळि. Comp. நாழிகை.]

நாள் NĀḶ [from நள் ; நாட், நாண். M. NĀḶ. Comp. √*naḍ, nal,* = 'middle.' C. *nāḷe.* T. *nāḍu*].

1. நாள், a day from sunrise to sunrise [= ஞான்று] 6, 7, 22, 54, 135, 154, 159, 169, 214, 258, 295, 324, 349, 394.

An auspicious day, 86. Forenoon, 166.
நாள்வாய், the forenoon, = முற்பகல், 207. [S. पूर्वाह्णः.]
சாநாள், 92 (சாம்), the day of death.
K. வாழ்நாள் = ஆயுள், life in this world, 4, 22, 32, 39 [G. 153], 327, 330, 338 (!).

II. நாளை, (1) to-morrow, 6. [C. *nāḷe.*] ? நாள் + எ emphatic. This எ in a final syllable is often lengthened by a kind of அளபெடை to ஐ, as though எ இ.

(2) Belonging to a day, 54.

நாளும் = தினமும், every day, 125, 139, 190. பன்னாள், 220.
நாடொறும், 225, 338. நாளுளும், 299.

நாறு, *v.* (§ 62) yield perfume: மண. [See நறு. C., M. NĀRU.]

நாறினும் (= மணக்கினும்), 259.

நாறு (= பரிமளியாத), possessing no fragrance, 266.

நாறும், 396.

நாற்றம், *n.* = மணம், வாசனை, fragrance, 98.

நான் NĀN̲, *I*, = யான். [A. C. *ān.* C. *nān.* M. *ñān.* TU. *yān.* G. 72.]

என் inflexional base, 'my,' 399; for 2nd case, 'me,' 400.

நானம், musk: கத்தூரி, 294. [Comp. நாறு. S. नाभि.]

நிகர் [comp. நேர், நீர்] one's inferiors, 64. Here = நேர்? Comp. 72. [Yet *nēr* in T. = 'know; be able.' Both roots are found in M. and C. *Nigar* in C. = 'stand erect,' as though from *nil.*]

நித்தலும், நிச்சம், நிச்சலும், ever, or assuredly, 81, 376. [M., C., T. Corruption of S. नित्य, निश्चय, निश्चलं.]

K. நிர|ப்பு = இரப்பு, = வறுமை, poverty; beggary, 282, 287. [Comp. S. निर्. In this sense it is not to be traced in cognate languages; perhaps a poetic invention to rhyme with இரப்பு, in fact another form of that word.]

நிர|ம்பு, *v.* (§ 62) = நிறை, become full.

நிரம்ப, abundantly, 287. [√NIRA. Comp. நிரல், நெறி, *etc.* M. T. NERA. C. NERI, NERE.]

நிரயம், hell, 58, 84, 233, = நரகம். [S. निरय. Comp. Jī. Chin. xiii. § x. 164–178; and T. 45.]

நிரை NIRAI = வரிசை. [Comp. நிர, நேர், நெறி. M. NIRA. T. NERI. C. NIRI.] Row, line, 111, 288, 319; herd, 319.

நில் NIL [நின், நிற்], *stand*. [See s. निली, निलय. C., T. M. √NIL. Perh. = இல்.]

I. நில், *v.* (§ 70) stand.

நின்றன [G. 95] those things stood fast, or things that stood, 4, 182.
நின்றான், 29. நின்றது, 36. நின்றனைத்து = நின்றதுபோல்வது, 204. நின்றக்கடைத்தும், 360.
நின்றுழி, while he stands (= நின்ற), 183. நிற்பர், 158, 175. நிற்ப, 316 [G. 83].
நிற்கும், it will stand, abide, 40, 51 (§ 72) 368. Future rel. part., 204, 267.
நிற்பான் = நிற்பவன், 363. நிற்பார், 381 [G. 95]. நிற்பின், 349 (§ 95).
நிற்பினும், 148, 355 (§ 100). நிற்பது, the standing, 194.
நின்று [G. 86] 24, 26, 32, 67, 102, 111, 127, 128, 183, 228, 353, 359, 361.
நின்றும், though it stand, be, 164 [G. 141]. நின்றது, that which has stood, 192.
நின்றுழிநின்றே, while things remain in apparent stability : நின்றுழி = நின்றநிலையிலே.
நில்லா [G. 89] they stand not, 4, 51. = நில்லாமல், 204, 391.
நில்லாது, it abides not, 93 ; stands not, 304. நில்லாமை, 102 (§ 154).
நிற்றல், 334 [G. 94]. நிற்றி = நிற்பாய், 376. நின்மின் = நில்லுங்கள், 49 [G. 84].
எதிர்நில், confront, 363.

II. நிறு (§ 56 III), நிறுவு, and நிறுத்து are causals of நில் = fix on a firm basis.

நிறீஇ = நிறுத்தி, setting up = making up his mind, 308.
நிறான், he fixes not, sets not up (a light of glory), 9.
நிறுப்பான், he who fixes firm, 248. நிறூஉம் = நிறுவும், will fix firm, 57.
[Hence 'நிறை, virtue.' *El.* 7.]

III. நிலை, (I) *n.* = காலம் ; state : நிலைமை, 131, 248, 267, 331, 365.

பிறப்பு, 250 ; firmness in virtue, 87. இந்நிலையே = இக்கணமே, 359.
அந்நிலையே, there and then, 235, 308, 398.
[*Ēl.* 3 : 'நிலைதிரி, swerve from integrity.']

(II) *v.* (§ 64) become fixed.

நிலையாமை [G. 94] 29 ; transitory nature, 52, 53, ch. i, ii, iii.
நிலையாது, 28, 182. நிலைதிரியா, 204.

IV. நிலம் [S. निलय].

1. Ground, soil, 133 ; களர்நிலம் (உவர்நிலம்), விளைநிலம், 179, 243, 356. (க. வா.)
2. Earth = பூமி ; 21, 22, 266. நீணிலம், 27.
3. Position, இடம், 133. [Comp. நிலை.] கடைநிலம், தலைநிலம்.

V. நிலவு, *v.* (§ 62) = நிலைபெறு, abide. நிலவார் = நிலைபெறார், 22.

VI. நிலா (நிலவு) = திங்கள், the moon ; moonlight, 151 ; that which is not stationary, the changing orb.

நிழ் NIṚ.

K. நிழ|ல், *n.* shade, 3, 38, 202 ; shadow, 166. [= छाया.]

அல்குநிழல் = the afternoon shadow.
நாணிழல் = the forenoon shadow.

[In *Naiḍ*. xx. 5 நிழலுமிழ்ந்து = பிரகாசம்.

In Nig. நிழல் செல்வம் குளிர்ச்சி சாயை: (1) wealth, (2) coolness, (3) shade.

In T. *nīḍa*. C. *neralu*, *neraḷu*, *neḷalu*. M. *niẓal*. Prob. √*neḍ* = *nīḍ*, 'lon spread out, diffused.']

நிற் NIRR [= நிர|ம்பு. M. T. *nirru* = 'very much'].

1. நிறம் = வருணம்; குணம், 183; colour (golden), 139, 164, 177, 223, 269, 360; the glow of youth: = 'purpureum lumen juventutis.'

[M. NIRRA = 'fulness.' Comp. நீர் = தன்மை. As 'colour' not to be traced. In K. நிறை is used as a noun, but not in *Nāl*. It is perhaps a variation of நிறை.]

K. II. நிறை, *v*. (§§ 57, 64) become full: நிரம்பு; fill: நிரப்பு, 318.

In 99 நிறைத்து may = நிறைந்து; or (such conduct) will fill up the measure (of your merit).

நிறைய = நிரம்ப, 43. நிறை, abundant [G. 153] 360. Not used here as a noun. See நில்.

நினை NIṈAI, *think*. [Comp. எண் and நெஞ்சம்.]

நினை, *v*. (§ 64) ponder, think over; reflect. ஆராய், சிந்தி, 33, 81, 330, 359.

நினைப்ப, 105, 265. நினைக்கில், 135.

நின் = உன், 32. See நீ.

நீ, thou, 84, 266, 376, 388. [C. D. G. p. 279.]

நீ NĪ, *remove*. [M. NĪ|KKU, NĪ|ṄṄU. T. NĪ|GU. C. NĪ|GU, NĪ|NGU. Comp. S. निस्.]

K. I. நீ, *v*. (§ 64) forsake.

நீத்து, having abandoned, 28, 30.

நீத்தார், 214.

நீப்பினும் = நீத்தாலும் [H. B. § 100] 304.

II. நீ|ங்கு (§ 62) remove, depart, 30, 181.

நீ|க்கு (§ 62) put away; rid oneself of, 40, 57, 138, 190, 308, 332.

நீக்கல், 104.

நீசர், 68, = கீழோர்: base men. [S. नीच.]

நீர் NĪR. [S. नीर. T. NĪRAMU, NĪRU. M. NĪRAM, NĪR. C. NĪRU. In some uses comp. ஈரம், நிர, நிறை, நிகர்.]

நீர், *n.* (1) 'Fluid, juice,' 44, 156, 175, 394.

(2) 'Water,' 29, 44, 68, 72, 90, 94, 109, 117, 135, 177, 184, 200, 210, 217, 221, 222, 231, 236, 240, 245, 275, 282, 331, 360, 382, 387, 389.

(3) 'Sea,' 227.

(4) 'Nature:' தன்மை, 236.
நீர்மை, 44, 112, 287, 382.
பெருநீரார், 236, 355.

(5) Hence, 'goodness, excellence,' as in குணம்.
நீரல்லார், 72, 236.
நீரல்ல, evil things, 64, 72.
நீர்த்து = what is proper, 70.
நீர்த்தருவி = நீர்த்த அருவி = excellent.

(6) Pron. pl. of நீ for நீவிர், 183. [See நீ.]

நீலம் [S. नील] blue (flower) = lotus: கருங்குவளை, 374.

நீள் NIḶ [நீளம், நீண், நீட். Comp. நெடு. M., C. NĪḶA, NIḌ, NIṬ. T. NIL].

I. நீள்(ளு), *v.* [§ 56 (III)] lengthen out, grow tall, extend.
நீணிலம் = நீண்டபூமி, 27. நீள்வரை, 226.
நீள்சோலை, the ample grove, 84, 108, 234, 391. நீண்ட, grown up, 236, 254.

II. நீட்டு (§ 62) protract, extend, lengthen out. [M. *nīṭṭu.*]
நீட்டேனேல், if I reach not forth to give, extend the hand (as giver), 238. [Comp. C. NĪḌU = 'give.']
நீட்ட, to reach forth, present, 253. நீட்டார், 262.
நீட்டல், extend the hand (as a suppliant), 288.

III. நீட்டி (§ 64) be prolonged, 40. [M. *nītti-kka.*]

நீறு = பொடி, சாம்பல், திருநீறு [M., T. NIRU. Perhaps = நூறு (q. v.) = 'crush'], ashes, 66, 266.
[So proverbially நீறுமேல்போர்த்தநெருப்பு = 'smouldering fire.']

நு NU [comp. நுண், நுட்].

I. நு|ரை, foam: பேணம், 221. [C. NORE. M. NURA. T. NURU-GU. C. NU-GGU.]

II. நு|ழை, enter, penetrate, 282. [M. NŪṞU¦GU, NURṞAYU. C. NURU, NUSI, NUSUḶU; NOḶE.]

III. நு|னி = நுதி, tip, 29, 138. [Comp. நொய், முனை, நுண். T. KONA.]

The first line of 29 is an imitation of the following:

'नलिनीदलगतजलवच्चरलं — जीवनं ।
Life is unstable, like water on a lotus leaf.'

நுக|ர், eat; experience. [C. NUṄGU, 'swallow.']

நுகர்|வு, enjoyment of society, 233.

நுங்|கு, palm fruit, unripe and gelatinous, 44. [T., M. NOṄṄU.]

நுட், see நுண்.

K. நு|ண் NUṆ [நுட்]. [√நு. Comp. நுழை, நூழை, நொய், நுனி, நுதி. M. NUṆMA. C. NUṆ. T. NUNU. It is opposed to திண், 'solid, substantial.']

நுண், *adj.* refined, subtle, 260.

நுண்|ணிது, insinuating, 282.

நுட்|பம் [opp. திட்பம்] subtility, 282.

உள்ளுறை நூலுக்கு நுட்பம் பொறிக்கும் மனதிற்கும் சாதாரணமாய் எட்டாதவைகளை அறிவிப்பது.
In a commentary, 'exposition of minute details,' 319. [Comp. *Nan.* 18–23.]

நுண்|ணுணர்வு, fine perception, 233, 251.

நுண்|ணூல், a work of accurate learning, 233.

நுணுக்கம் = நுட்பமான அறிவு, acumen, 352.

K. நுத|ல், forehead: நெற்றி, 379, 380.

Those whose brow is bright, 381.

நறுநுதலாள், she of the fragrant brow, 387.

[Comp. S. निटल. M. K. NOSALU. T. NUDURU, NOSALU.]

Nig. நுதல் என்ப நுருவ நெற்றி.

நும் = உம், comp. நீர், 7, 94. [See C. D. G. I think, on the whole, ந is merely euphonic.]

நூக்கு, *v.* (§ 62) shove, push, 326. [Another form of ஊக்கு.]

K. நூல் [comp. நுவல். So பனுவல் = 'cotton; literature.' T. NŪLU = 'cotton thread.' M. C. See நன்னூல், 24, 25. The word is used in imitation of S. सूत्र = 'thread'], 136, 317, 319, 320, 341, 352, 386.

அறிவுநூல், 'sacred books,' 140. Opposed to உலகுநூல், 'secular literature.'

நூலார், well-instructed persons, 163.

1. Thread, 376.
2. A system, or systematic treatise: learning. [Comp. T. 35. நூல் = எண்ணம்.]

நூறு, a hundred, 357. [C. T. M.]

நூறு, (*v. tr.*) crush=நெரி, 156. [C. *nuri, nurukku.* T. M. Comp. நீறு.]

K. நெஞ்சம், நெஞ்சு=உள்ளம், mind; soul, 32, 49, 55, 130, 131, 214, 260, 310, 369, 376, 379.

உள்ளம், மனம், 173. நெஞ்சத்தவர், 87, 174, 224, 228, 374. நெஞ்சினர், 259.

[√EN. நினை. I think there is metathesis and reduplication. C. Comp. √NEN. M. NEÑJA; NEṆṆU; NINA, 'think.' T. ENNU=என்னு.]

Nig. நெஞ்சென்ப மனமாரின்பேர்.

நெடி (§ 64) [comp. நீள், நீட், நீட்டி, நீட்டு] delay: தாமதி.

நெடியார் = நீட்டியார், they do not procrastinate, 53.

நெடு, wide, vast [நீள்], 238.

நெடும், 68, 265, 297, 319. நெட்டு, 288.

[See H. B. § 131. *f.* நெடுமை, நெடும், நெடு, நெடிய, *etc.* by the side of நீள், நீண்ட, நீடு, *etc.*]

நெய் [S. स्नेह, √स्निह्].

1. Oil (for a lamp), 51, 282, 371.
2. *Ghee*, butter-oil, 115, 124, 333, 337.

ஆன்படுநெய், ghee from the cow, 238.

T. 65: 'தந்நெய்யிற்றும்பொரியும் ஆறு, like frying anything in its own fat.'

நெய்தல், *n.* [K. NAIDILE. M. NEYTHAL.]

1. Maritime country. See note to 10.
2. A water flower, *Nymphaea Alba*, 108.
3. Death-drum: சாப்பறை, 392.

Nig. நெய்தலேகடற்சார்பூமி நெய்தற்பூச்சாப்பறைப்பேர்.

நெருப்பு, fire: தீ, தழல், அக்கினி, அங்காரம், 124 (where consider அழல் = வெம்மை = heat; எரி = burning heat; சுடு, inflame).

[T. NERAPU='spread, diffuse, illume;' NIPPU. So in C. NERAPU=நிறை, நிரப்பு. M. *nerippu* (or ñ). Is ந original? Comp. எரி.]

நெல், rice unhusked; the growing rice plant, 133, 179, 221, 269, 367.

[C. NEL|LU. M. (In T. *vari.*) √NEL=நில், q. d. *standing corn*? Paddy, = C. *bhatta.* Comp. நெற்று.]

நெறி=வழி; நீதி. [Comp. நேர், நிரை. M. NERRI. Comp. T. NERA, NĒR.]

Way, 154, 294, 309, 378, 399, 400.

Conduct; esp. நல்லொழுக்கவழி, the way of rectitude, 204.

காமநெறி, the way of sensual indulgence, 13.

நெறியல்ல, vicious acts, 171: = virtue, 49.

அறநெறி, the path of virtue, 171, with நல், 55, 118.

சிறுநெறி, the way of humiliation, 303.

இயனெறி, 294 [G. 39]=நல்லொழுக்கவழி, the way of natural piety.

நெறிபடு (=வழிபடு), be devoted to, be a close adherent of, 317.

Nig. நெறிவழி நீதி என்ப.

நெற்|று, dried pulse in pods, 237. [? நெல் + து=what has grains.]

நேர் NĒR.

I. நேர், *n.* [comp. நிகர், நீர், நிரை, நெறி], directness, comparison, rectitude, opposition; with ஒப்ப=all alike, 202.

நேரல்லார், inferiors, 72; is like, 333. ['நீர்மேல் எழுத்திற்கு நேர், it is like a writing on water.' *Mū.*] செவ்வனேர், right opposite, 148.

II. நேர், *v.* (§ 64).

நேர்ப்பார் [G. 95]=ஒப்பார், those who can compare with.

நேர்ந்து=நேர்ந்து as from (§ 57) opposing, confronting, 64, 67.

[T. NĒR='learn; be able.' A. C. NĒR|RU='be straight.' M.='agree, vow;' NĒR, NIGAR.]

நொந்த், see நோ.

நொய், minuteness: நுட்பம், சூட்சுமம். [M. NOYI. Comp. T. NŪ-KA. C. NU.]

நொய்யது, what is minute, transcendent; the spiritual (body), 41.

[N. N. 5: 'நொய்தாகும், will be small.']

நோ NŌ, *feel pain; complain of.* [§ 58. IRR. நொ. Comp. நோவ், நோன். C., M. In T. NŎ|CH, NŌ.]

நோதக்கது (=நோவ), anything to grieve at, 228. நோ|வு, pain, 201.

நோ|ய்=பிணி, pain, disease, 52, 88, 92, 123, 124, 168, 219, 247, 292, 369, 372.

நோவ, 277:=நோக.

நொந்தேன், I who felt aggrieved, 389; each person is used as a participial noun. Comp. 126.

நோவின், if you complain of, 76.

[Comp. B. I. S.:

'आत्मानम् अनुशोच त्वं किम् अन्यम् अनुशोचसि।

Blame thyself, why blamest thou another?'

T. 69: 'நொந்து நெறிமாறி வந்த விருந்து,

A guest who has lost his way, and has come to you *in distress.*'

T. 11: 'ஊர் எல்லாம் நோவதுடைத்து,

It is a thing all the world will *blame.*']

K. I. நோக்கு, *v.* (§ 62)=காண், see, behold, regard, contemplate, 41, 228, 260, 298. [M., C. NŌ-ḌU. T. NŌRU='mouth.' ? From S. लोक्=रुच् (Benfey).]

நோக்கி (§ 230) 31, 54, 60, 95, 165, 241, 389, 394.

II. நோக்கு, *n.* a glance, 378.=பார்வை, 86.

சிறுநோக்கு, a contemptuous glance, 298, 378.

K. நோல், நோன். [√நோ, நோய்.]

1. [*v.* § 70. நோற்றேன், நோற்பேன், endure; do penance.]
நோலா, 258 (=தவஞ்செய்யாத).

2. (*adj.*) mighty. நோன்றாள், mighty foot, 198.

[Jī. Chin. i. 253: 'நோனான்=நோலான், he endures it not:' பொருள்.
There are many derivatives from √NŌ. நோன்பு. T. NŌMU.
T. 28: 'நோன்பிலி, an undisciplined man.']

ப PA.

1. This represents S. प, फ, ब, भ, and often व. On the other hand, these letters often become வ: बहु=வெகு.

2. In modern Canarese ப் is often changed into H.

3. ப் is a middle particle of future, or aorist; often ப்ப் (to keep hard sound). See 3rd plural in என்ப *etc.*

பக் PAG, *divide.* [Comp. வகு, பகிரு, வகிரு. S. भज्, भञ्ज्, and प्र+कृ in प्रकृति=பகுதி. M. C. *bage; hakku.* (TU.) A. C. *pasu.* T. *pagalu; (vaga.)* See பால்=பகல்; பகுதி; பாதி; பங்கு. Lat. *frag.* A. Sax. *brec.* GR. ῥαγ, ῥηγ.]

I. பகு, *v.* (§ 64) divide, share.

பகுத்து is written பாத்து=sharing, 92, 271.

II. பகை, hatred (as வகை from வகு), 82, 187, 219.

பகைவர், foes, 241.

III. பகல்=நாள், day, 169, 204.

IV. பகர், *v.* (§ 57) say, speak, 256.

V. பக|டு, bullock, 2. [Comp. மா|டு, ஆடு.]=எருது, ஏறு.
[T.='pride:' பெருமை.]

பகடுநடந்தகூழ், grain trodden out by bullocks.

Nig. பகடிபம் பெருமை ஏறு பஃறியாண்மேதி ஐம்பேர்:
இபம் (elephant), பெருமை (greatness), ஏறு (bull), பஃறி (boat), மேதி (buffalo).

[In T. 69 the bullock seems to be stigmatized as lazy:
அருந்தொழில் ஆற்றும் பகடு, a bullock that will work hard' is spoken of as a rarity: அரியபொருள்.]

பக்கம் [S. पक्षं].

1. Side, 79, 266: a sign of local ablative = இடத்தில்.

பக்கத்தார், neighbours, 214.

2. An hypothesis, the case of a thing being thus or thus, 244, 258.

பச் PAÇ, *green; soft, tender.* [In T. *pasa*='bright, fine, golden.' Comp. S. भा, भास्. GR. φῶς. M. *paça, paya, pachu, pai*, 'green, young, fresh.' C. *hasu, pas, pach.* See also S. हरि.]

I. பச, பசம், பசிய், பச்ச, பைம், பாச (§ 131. *c*).

பசம்பொன், yellow (*pure*) gold, 347.

[This is = S. हिरण्य, which is from हरि (हिरि) = 'greenish yellow.' So அரி = பொன்.]

பச்சோலை, the green palm-leaf, 256.

பசியது, what is green, 360.

பைங்கூழ், the green grain, 191.

K. II. பசலை, sallowness, 391.

[Ji. Chin. xiii. 394: 'பசிழை (= yellow gem), a jewelled lady.']

III. பசை, *v.* (§ 57) cling to, 187, 310. [T. *pasa*='essence;' *pasa-badu*='be devoted to.' Comp. பாசம் from पश्. The root is பச. பசை='gum, glue.' C. *pasa.* M.]

பசைந்ததுணையும், in proportion as attachments have been formed, 187.

பசைதல், attachment, 60.

[N. M. K. 15: 'பசைந்தாரில் தீர்தலின் தீப்புகுதலன்று,
To commit suicide by leaping into the fire is better than withdrawal from attached friends.']

IV. பசி, hunger, 286. [M. *pai, payi.* C. *hasi, pasi.*]

பசித்தல், the suffering hunger, 302.

V. பஞ்சி, cotton, 396. [Nasalized. M. *paññi.* C. *hañji, añji.*]

K. பட் PAḌ. [Comp. S. पत्, पद्, बाध्. M., C., T. In M. often *peḍu.* See C. D. G. p. 482. Lat. PAT-IOR. GR. παθ-.]

I. படு, *v. n.* [§ 56 (II)] suffer, fall; be, abide: தங்கு, 17; fall into, 38; befall, 110, 295; pertain to.

படா is pred. = 'are not found in them,' 142; occur, 22, 169, 239; தேம்படு, sound out, 6; fix upon, 255; issue, 150, 239 (ஆக்கபடு), flourish, 246; concern, 117.

In 91 = generous disposition = உள்ள. So 108.
As an auxiliary forming a passive voice (§ 92, G. 124) 18, 21, 242, 340.
படும் = befits, should be: தகும், 9, 37, 89, 133.
With various nouns, see வெளி, 88; பாழ், 306; தலை, 291; புறம், 26; வழி, 309; உள், 250.
[In this use it is *peḍu* in M. Comp. *peṭṭu* in T.]
அடிப்படு, be trodden, 154. படுசாந்து, sandal besmeared, 48.
பட forms adverbial phrases: இடம்பட, abundantly, 116. வளம்பட, 103.

Hence (G. 96),—

K. பாடு, (1) dignity, 105, 187, 252, 281, 340. [C. *pāṭu*, *pāḍu*. T.]

(2) Suffering, 292. [Comp. பாழ். T. *pāḍu*.]

[கண்பாடு = துயில், *Kalit.* i. 16.]
Often a mere formative: கடப்பாடு, q. v., 261.

II. படு, *v. a.* (§ 64) cause: படுத்து. With புண், will inflict a wound, 198.

III. படு, *adj.* (S. पटु) violent: a heavy rain, 27.

IV. படு, *n.* cluster of fruit: குலை; படுபனை, a fruit-bearing palm, 96. [Comp. T. PAṆḌ.]

V. படி, *v.* (§ 57) sink down: முழுகு, 331. [M.]

VI. படர், *v.* (§ 57) proceed: செல், 13; spread, as a sore, 168. [M.]

[In கலித்தொகை i. 29 (p. 84): 'நின் றேமொழி படர்ந்தே,
Remembering—allowing the mind *to dwell on*—thy sweet words.']

VII. பட்டு (S. पट्ट) silk, 264.

VIII. பட்டினம் [S. पट्टनं, पत्तनं] a sea-port, 250.

[But see C. D. G. p. 458, and comp. பட்டி, பட்டணம், பெட்டை.
N. M. K. 86: 'பண்டத்தாற் பாடெய்தும் பட்டினம்,
A port gains greatness from its merchandise.']

K. IX. படை, 178, 363, = ஆயுதம், கருவி, instrument. [M. *paḍa* (not in this meaning).]

பண் PAṆ = 'harmony; service.' [In T. *pani* is 'service.' M. *paṇi*, 'service.' Comp. √பட், படி, படை, பள்; S. पण. As harmony from பா; so கண் from கா.]

1. பணி, *n.* service: பணிவிடை.

2. பணி, *v.* (§ 57) bow, bend: தாழ். [M.]

K. பணி|வு, humility, 241, 242.

பணிவிடம், the place where (foes) lie humiliated, 241.

K. 3. பண்|பு = nature; good qualities; excellence, 49, 138, 159, 169, 174.

4. *பணை*, *v.* (§ 64) flourish, grow thick, 251. [T. *pambu.*]

பணைப்பணைத்த is a reduplication for emphasis = 'very abundant' (§ 223). Though some say = செய்ய.

[*Naiḍ.* xx. 17: 'கல்லெனப்பணைத்துயர்கலைவத் தோளினன்,
He whose anointed shoulders were lofty and sturdy as a rocky hill.']

5. *பண்ணு*, *v.* (§ 64) = செய், make, do, 37. [M. T. *pannu.* A. C. GR. πόν-ος.]

K. *பண்|டம்* = பொருள், any vessel, utensil, thing, baggage, 13, 48, 50. [M. Comp. *பண்ணயம்*. See S. पण्, पण्ड्, पण्यं; but perhaps a corruption of भाण्ड = 'vessel.']

Quatrain 13 is probably the original of the following from B. I. S. 79:

'अङ्गंगलितं पलितं मुण्डं दन्तविहीनं जातं तुण्डं ।
करधृतकम्पितशोभितदण्डं तदपिनमुञ्चत्याशा भाण्डम् ॥

The body is shrunken, head is white, mouth is destitute of teeth; yet desire leaves not the FRAME of him with ornamented staff trembling in his hand.'

(Benfey would read भण्डम् = 'a buffoon;' but the Tamil fixes the meaning.)

This *Çlōka* (which is also in *Vēm.* i. 19) is found in the little poem attributed to *Çaṅkarāchārya*, and entitled Mōhamudgara (= *hammer of infatuation*). It was translated by Sir W. Jones (Works, vol. xiii. p. 382). Note the four rhymes.

பதக்கு, a dry measure of two *மரக்கால்*, being half a *தூணி*, 387.

K. *பதி*, city, 137; from *v.* *பதி* = fix. [M. So *பதிவு*. Comp. S. अमरावति, and *வார்பதி*, the extensive city.]

பத்தர் = சிறுதொட்டி, trough, 257.

பத்து, ten, 281. [§ 172. It takes forms *பது*, *பன்*, *பை*. In M., C., T., TU., *etc.* Comp. S. पङ्क्ति.]

பந்தம், real attachment, 234. [S. बन्धु.]

பந்தன், see note to 250.

பய PAYA (for *பசு*). [Three derivations are possible: (1) *பழ்* = what is mature; (2) फलं = fruit; (3) *பசு* = what is green and flourishing.]

I. *பயன்*, *பயம்*, *n.* fruit, 28, 38, 58, 65, 99; aid, 105, 106, 109, 130, 162, 202, 232, 252, 265, 276; meaning, 316.

பயன்மரம், fruit tree, 17.

II. *பய*, *v.* (§ 66) yield, 38, 79, 84, 118, 132, 139.

பயந்தாங்கு=பயந்ததுபோல, 267, 294, 356.

பயின்=பசின், glue, 267. [Comp. பசை. M.]

பர PARA [S. पर].

I. பர, *v.* (§ 66) spread; extol, 68, 88, 92, 297. [Hence பார், and பாரி, 151.]

II. பரல்=pebbles: பருக்கை, 396.

III. பர|ம்ப=மிக, 267.

பர|ப்ப=மிக, much, 124.

பரப்பு, table-land: அகன்றவிடம், 307.

IV. பரு (பரூஉ)=பெரு, great.

பரா=பரவு=பர, great, wide, 246. [G. 153.]

V. பரு|கு, *v.* (§ 62) drink, sip: உண்ணு, 240. [M., C., TU.]

பரி PARI. [Comp. S. पृ. C. *hari.*]

I. பரி, *v.* (§ 57) (1) grieve over: இரங்கு, 35, 58, 155, 157, 316. (Like S. பரிதபி.) (2) Love, desire, 60, 182. (3) Pull to pieces: பிரி, 397. [A. C. *pare, pari.*]

பரிவு, distress, 110, 187.

[Jī. Chin. iii. 91: 'பரிவுதீர்ந்து, his sorrows being ended.']

பரீஇ=பரிந்து, grieving, 87; desiring, or cutting with teeth, 220.

II. *n.* a horse, 149. [S. भृ, हरि.]

பரிசு=குணம், dignity, 309. [Comp. வரிசை. T. *para-su.* M.]

பருமம்=கல்லணை, பண், a saddle, pillion, 149. [S. वर्मन्. T. *pallamu.*]

One commentator takes பருமம் as equal to பெருமை, and adds 'some deer are as large as horses;' but comp. N. M. K. 5.

பருவம் [S. पर्वन्]=ஆயுள், ஆண்டு, காலம், age, 18, 171; season, 358; season of maturity, 274.

பல் PAL. [S. पुल्, पुलु, पुरु, पृ. GR. πολύ. A. Sax. *fela.* Goth. *filu.* Germ. *viel.* Lat. *plus.* Its opp. is சில், சின், சிற். C. *pala, hala.* M. *pala.* T. *palu* (comp. *balu*).]

I. பல் [பன், பற்], many, 101, 106, 118, 214, 258, 385.

பல்காலும், often, 27. பலர், 185, 281.

பல்லார், 2. Many (*friends*), 86, 88, 144. பல்லோர், many persons, 26.

பல, 37, 261.=பலவற்றை, 183. தொளைபலவாய், having many apertures, 42.

II. பல், tooth, 13, 18, 45, 315. [C. *hallu.* M. *pallu.* T. *palu.*]

III. பல்|கு, *v.* (§ 62) multiply; assemble, 340.

IV. பன்றி, a pig, 257 (=the tusker), 358. [M. *panni.* C. *handi, pandi.*]

பழ் PAṚ, *old.* [See பழம்; பண்டு, பண்டை; படு=fruit. Comp. S. फल् and C. D. G. p. 484. A. C. *paṇṇu* (*pala, phala*). T. *paṇḍu* (*pala, phala*). M. *paṇḍu.* Lat. *frug.*]

I. பழ, ancient. [C. *haḷa.*]

பழ|மை, ancient friendship, 310.

பழவினை=முன்செய்தவினை, ch. xi, 123.

II. பழை, *adj.* old, 123. [C. *paḷe, haḷe.*]

பழங், 231.

III. பழு, *v.* (§ 64) bear fruit, 202.

பழுத்தக்கண்ணும், even when they have yielded fruit, 261.

IV. பழி (§ 64) 13, 26, 84, 312. [A. C. *paḷi, haḷivu.*]

பழிப்பு, blame, revile, 319.

பழித்தக்க, blameworthy deeds, 302.

n. guilt, 79, 82, 108, 144, 227, 272, 295.

V. பாழ், desolation. படு, 306. [C. *hāḷu.*]

பற் PARR. [A strengthened form of பா. S. प्र. M. C. *hāru, pāru.* TU. T. *pāru.* In T. see *para|chu; para|gu, etc.*]

I. பற, *v.* (§ 66) fly, 389.

II. பறி, *v.* (§ 64) gather; pluck away, rob of: பிடுங்கு, 237, 289, 389. [M. S. हृ=भृ, see Benfey; अपहृ.]

III. பறை, a drum, 24, 25, 86. [M. *parra.* C. *pare.*]

பிணைப்பறை, மணப்பறை, 23.

K. IV. (1) பற்று, *v.* (§ 62) hold; occupy, 31, 92, 93, 160, 260; seize, 193. [M. T. *paṭṭu.* C. *pattu, hattu; pottu, hottu.* Tam. ஒற்று.]

K. (2) பற்று, *n.* adhesion, 171.

In பனிப்பற்று almost redundant: 'The dew looses its hold.'

[T. 22: 'பற்றென்னுபாசத்தளையும்பலவழியும்
பற்றறுதேரெம் அவாத் தேரும்,

The bond and tie called பற்று, and the chariot of desire that holds things on all sides with unfailing பற்று,' *grasp, hold, clinging.*]

பனி=இமம், குளிர்ச்சி, coolness; dew, 17, 171.

பனிபடுசோலை, the cool (dewy) grove. [M., C. *hani*= 'fine drop.' TU.]

Nig. பனி என்ப நடுக்கம் துன்பம் பயம் குளிர் இமம் ஐம்பேரே.

பனை, a palmyra tree: *Borassus flabelliformis*, 96, 105, 256.

[Comp. திணை. M. *pana*. T.='sheaf.' From பனி (='dripper') or S. பர்ணம்= பன்னம் (='the leafy'). Another form is பெண்ணை; and போந்தை seems older still. As the palm was introduced into South India, its name perhaps came with it. The radicals are P-N: curiously suggestive of φοῖν-ιξ.]

பாகன் (பாகு)=பாலன், பாலனன், an elephant-keeper, 213.

[S. पाल; but comp. M. *pāvan*='an elephant-trainer,' from *pāvu*='training;' *pāga*='stable' in T.]

பாங்கனர் (fem. பாங்கிமார்), [from பாங்கு a corr. of பக்கம், or பங்கு] lover: நண்பனர், 400.

[C. *pāṅgu*='good.' Comp. T. *bāgu*. M. *pāññu*; *pāññan*.]

பாசம் [S. पाश; पश्='bind'], 130: மனைப்பாசம் (பிணிப்பு, பற்று, விருப்பம்), the family tie, household bond.

பாடம் [S. पाट] a lesson, 312, 314, 316.

பாடு, see படி; and பாணன்.

பாணன் [comp. பா, பாடு, பண்: perhaps from S. भाव= 'emotion.' So கா, காடு, கண். M. *pāna*='a poem;' *pāṇan*. See S. वाण, बाण, 'a pipe'], minstrel, 388, 390.

பாணி [S. पाणि].

(1) =கை, hand, 16.

கலித். i. 12: 'இளமையுங் காமமுநின்பாணி நில்லா,
Youth and love abide not in thy hand.'

(2) =காலம், 362. [? *local*.]

பாத்து for பகுத்து: sharing, see பகு.

பாதிரி, the trumpet-flower tree: *Bignonia Chelonoides*: பாடலம். [S. पाटलि (पाट='broad'). M., C., T.] Its flower is very fragrant, 139.

பாய் PĀY. [Comp. பா|வு, வா|வு, பெய். M. PĀY|U|GA. C. PĀY|U, HĀY|U. T. PĀY|U, *pāru*.]

பா|ய், *v*. (§ 57) rush in, leap, 51, 307, 369, 372, 391; flow, 268.

பாய்பரி, a charger, 149. [G. 153.]

பா|ம்பு, a snake, 87, 126, 148, 220, 375. [√பாவு. C. *pāvu*, *hāvu*. M. *pāmbu*. T. *pāmu* (*pāku*='creep.')]

பார் PĀR. [Comp. நோக்கு, 'regard;' காண், 'see, look.' s. लोक्, 'see,' is from लोक, 'universe;' so பார், 'see,' from பார், 'the earth.' (So *Gundert*.)]

பாரி, *v.* (§ 64) = press, urge, diffuse: பரப்பு.

நிலாபாரிக்கும், will diffuse moonlight, 151.

[பார் = 'a layer,' from பர. M., C. *pāru*. Or பாரம் = 'weight : = augment.' Comp. K. 193. In Jī. Chin. i. 214, பாரித்தேன் = 'I have urged at length.']

பார், *v.* (§ 64) look out for, 20, 275; find, come upon, 26, 42. Earth, soil, 122. [s. पार्थिव.]

பாராட்டு, *v.* (= பாரில் ஆட செய்), 48; (§ 62) celebrate, make a parade of, 340. See ஆட்டு (அடு).

K. பால் (= பகல்), portion, category. See பகு. [C. *pālu*, *hālu*. M., T. Comp. C. D. G. pp. 472, 473.]

1. = பகுதி, state, condition, 18, 104; fitting season, 97.

பால, things that pertain to. உறற்பால, things that must befall, 97, 104, 109, 117, 163. = பாலவை, what should be done, 147, 153, 185.

பாலன்(ர்), பாலார், 205, 225.

பாற்று [= பாலது, G. 93] what may be classed among things that . . ., 1, 143.

ஆகற்பாலார், those worthy to be deemed, 205.

2. Milk, 116, 118, 177, 206, 240, 258. [Comp. s. पा and its derivatives.]

பாற்கூழ், boiled milk and rice, 321. [s. क्षीरान्नम्.]

[In T. 27, பால்பற்றிச்சொல்லுதல் = 'partiality.'
In *Ēl*. 14, பாற்பட்டார் கொண்டொழுகும்பண்பு, 'the good qualities which adorn the daily life of the *virtuous*.']

பாவம், sin: தீவினை, 51, 82, 295, 380. [s. पाप.]

பாவை = பிரதிமை, a puppet; a lady, 399.

பாவாய், (voc.) O lady fortune! 266 [G. 93. s. भावा].

பாழ், see பழ், *n.* desolation. With படு, become desolate, consumed, Ps. xxxi. 10.

பிடி PIḌI.

I. பிடி, *v.* (§ 64) hold fast, 5.

II. பிடி, *n.* a grasp, handfull, handle. [A. C. *piḍi*, *hiḍi*. M., T. Comp. பிடுங்கு and பிள், 'break up.']

கடைப்பிடித்தல், the bearing in mind, 20. [In *Ātti*. நன்மைகடைப்பிடி.]

பிணம், a corpse, 25, 281. [M. C. *heṇa, peṇa.* TU. *puṇa.* T. *pīnuga.* Comp. பிணி. ? Corruption of S. पिण्ड.]

பிணப்பறை = சாப்பறை, a funeral drum, 23.

பிணத்த, are (full) of the corpses of, 121 [G. 93]. (Here it is predicate.)

பிண் PIṆ = *tie.* [M. T. *pen.* C. *peṇe.* From பிணி = 'tie.']

பிணி, disease, (a bond, infliction) = நோய், 55, 135, 173, 329, 363.

பித் PIT [comp. பேதை].

I. பித்தர், fools, 52, 340. [S. पित्तं 'bile.' T. *pichcha.*]

II. பித|ற்று, *v.* (§ 62) blab, speak folly, 45, 52.

III. பிது|க்கு, *v.* (§ 62). [M. ? பிதிர், a drop.]

பிது|க்கி, having expressed, squeezed out, 20 [G. 103].

பிரி PIRI := (1) twist; (2) twist off, separate.

பிரி, *v.* (§§ 57, 64) sever: போழ், 168, 247, 376.

பிரி|வு, severance, 173, 220, 397.

பிரி|ப்பு, mental perturbation, 189.

[M., C. *piri, puri.* Root is புரி. T.]

பிலம், *n.* a cave; mine, 160. [S. बिलं. M.]

[N. M. K. 71: '. . . அகனீர்

பிலத்தியல்பு புக்கான் உரைக்கும் . . .

The nature of the spacious cavern he only who has entered it can tell:' *experientia docet:* against mere *à priori* reasonings.]

பிழ் PIḺ [M., T. *pora.* C. *piḷilu.* Comp. भ्रम्].

(1) Escape: தப்பு, 6.

(2) Miss, 152. பிழைப்பு = பிழைப்ப = so as to miss.

(3) Commit a fault, 400. *n.* a fault, 357. [Comp. புரை.]

(4) Fall short of, 343.

பிள்|ளை, a child, 20. [Comp. பீள், பிள். S. बाल. C. M. T. *biḍḍa* and *pilla.*]

பிற் PIRR. [பின், பிறகு, after. T. PIRRA, PERRU.]

1. பிற, *v.* (§ 56) [comp. பெறு. S. प्र, भू].

Be born, 7, 199, 281, 285, 302, 307.

Perhaps B. I. S. 6681 may illustrate 7:

'सजातो येन जातेन याति वंश समुन्नतिम् ।
परिवर्तिनि संसारे मृतः को वा न जायते ॥

He is really born by whose birth the family obtains distinction; who indeed in this whirl of worldly existence is not born (again) after death?'

Be produced, 133, 236, 245, 360.

பிறை, the crescent moon: the nascent one, 125, 241. [M. A. C. T. PINA = 'young, small.']

பிற|ப்பு, *n.* birth: *பிற|வி*, *சனனம்*, 302; human existence, life: *சமுசாரம்*, 173, 174.

குடிப்|பிற|ப்பு, ch. XV, 141–150.

குடிப்பிறப்பாளர், the high-born, 141.

இற்|பிற [இல்], 146, 320, 340.

II. *பிற*, *adj.* other, comp. *வேறு*. Other things [G. 93] = besides, 105, 134.

பிறன், another; one's neighbour: *ஏதில்*, *அயலான்*, *வம்பலன்*, 81 *etc.*, 142, 157, 158, 205, 320.

பிறர்மனை நயவாமை, ch. ix.

பிறிது, anything else, 120, 175 (where some read *பெரிது*).

III. *பிற|ங்கு*, *v.* (§ 62) swell, 343.

['*கல்பிறங்காரிடை*, the desert path where rocks rise on every side.' *Kalit.* i. 20.]

IV. *பிறழ்*, *v.* (§ 56. I) vary, 110. [For *ழ்*, see *இக*.]

பின் PIṈ, *after*. [M. T. *pina* = 'little;' VEN. C. BEN.]

(1) (*Adj.*) after, afterwards, 5, 190.

(2) Sign of case, 249, 398.

(3) In comp.: *பின்னில்*, wait on, follow, 381.

பின்செல், follow, 292, 395.

பின்வாங்கு, draw back, 396.

பின்றை [*பின்* + *து* + ஐ], behind, after, 23, 36. [Prop. an adj., comp. *இன்றை*.]

பின்னை, afterwards; see ஐ.

பின்னர், after, behind, 92.

பீடு = *பெருமை*, 92, 261. [S. पीठ, 'a pedestal.']

பீள் [G. 34] = *கரு* [comp. *பிள* and *பிள்ளை*].

The embryo, 20: *முற்றுக்கரு*.

The germ, 269 [comp. *பிழி*].

புக் PUG, *enter*.

I. புகு, *v.* (§ 68) enter: நுழை, 266, 282. [M., C. *hogu*. A. C. *pugu*, *pogu*.]

புக, 31, 51. புகல், 258, 282. புகுதல், an entering, 243, 303.
புக்கு, having entered, 254, 255, 314. புக்கவிடத்து, when (he) has entered, 83.
கடிப்புக்க, (she) who has come under the protection of, 86; 'is,' 96.
புகுஉம் = புகும், (an ascetic) who enters (houses to ask alms), 99, 282.
புகுவர், they will enter, 208. புகுமின், enter ye, 303.
With இடை? 255, 258, *etc.* புகாதார், 363.

புக்கில், a permanent abode, 41. [புகும் இல்.]

II. புகை, (what finds entrance), smoke, 282. [C. *hoge*. A. C. *poge*. M. *puga*. T. *poga*.]

III. புகலு [§ 56 (III)] declare [M.], 42: talk not of desire, but regard it as . . .

IV. புகழ், I. *n.* கீர்த்தி, இசை, renown, 9, 82. [M., C. *hogaḷu*. = S. कीर्ति.]

2. *v.* (§ 57) 383. [T. *pogaḍu*.]

புகழ்மை, a subject of praise, 72. புகழ்தல், 219.
See B. I. S. 767:

'असंभवगुणस्तुत्या जायते स्वात्मनस्त्रपा।

From praise for good qualities that do not belong to one comes shame to oneself.'
[*Ēl.* 2: சென்றபுகழ் = 'world-wide renown.']

புட் PUḌ.

புடை [comp. புறம். ஐ as in இடை, கடை. S. पुट. M.].

I. *n.* (1) பக்கம், side, 148, 297.

புடைப்பெண்டிர், loose women, 367.

(2) Hypothesis, 212: பக்கம்.

நற்புடை, see கொண்டமை. (? *A favourable hypothesis.*)

[ஒருபுடை உவமை is a comparison that holds in some respects only; and is so opposed to முற்றுவமை.
In T. 97, நற்புடையிலார் = 'those without good qualities.' நல்லபக்கம் = தர்மவகைகள்.
In Jī. Chin. i. 56, புடைகள் = 'suburbs:' சேரி; and is opposed to இடைகள்.]

2. *v.* (§ 64) (தோட்)புடைக்கொள் = தட்டிக்கொண்டு, strike the shoulder, as a mark of defiance, 312.

புண|ர் PUṆ, *combination*. [M. C. In old C. *poṇar*. See பூண். Perhaps from பொர் nasalized.]

புணர், *v.* join, unite: (§ 57) கூடு, சேர்.

Fall to one's lot, 144, 365; intimacy, 162, 233; associate oneself with, 173, 247.

புணர்கடல், the sea into which all the rivers flow: புணரி, 264.
புணர்பிரியா, that separates not from its mate, 376, where புணர் is a noun = இணை.

K. புண், a wound, 198. [M. C. *huṇṇu; puruvu.* T. *puṇḍu.* TU. *puḍi.*]

புண்ணியம், merit, 264. [S. पुण्यं.]

K. புதல்வன் = புத்திரன், son, 197. [See A. C. *pudu* = 'be born;' or S. पुत्र.]

புதவு, door: கதவு, 99. [M. = 'a cover.' See புதை. C. T. *podu.*]

புது PUTH [புதி, புத்து. M. A. C. *pudu.* C. *hosa*].

புது, new, 307; fresh, 370.

புத்தோடு, a new pot, 139. [H. B. § 131. *e.*]

புதியார் = new sorts of people, 307.

புத்து, see புது.

புத்தகம் [S. पुस्तक] book, 318.

புரி PURI.

புரி, *v.* (§ 57).

(1) Act: செய், 154; perform, do, 323.

(2) Desire, 341. [Comp. பரி.]

[*Ēl.* 3: 'sanction.']

புருவம், eyebrow, 297, 395. [S. भ्रू. M. *purigam.* Lat. *frons.* GR. ὀφρύς, 'brow.']

புரை (1) *n.* fault, 11, 161. [Comp. பிழை.]

(2) *v.* (§ 57) resemble: போல், 317. [*Nannūl.* C., T. *puruḍu.* பொரு.]

புல் (புன், புற்), PUL. [M. PUL. A. C. *hulu.* T. Comp. பொல்.]

I. புல், what is mean, 44, 45, 221, 255, 260.

II. புல், grass, 29, 171, 178. [M., C., T., TU. Comp. புதல்.]

கொடிப்புல், 141.

புல்லீரம், slight moisture, 115. புல்லறிவு, 8, 314, 320, 351.
புல்லறிவினோர், 121, 239, 327. புல்லறிவாண்மை, ch. xxxiii.
புன்செககர், the fading light, 397. புன்மக்கள், mean people, 266.
[In *Ēl.* 3, புலான் or புலான் = 'a degraded person.']
புலை, (*adj.*) silly, 32. [See ஐ.]

III. புற்|கை=கூழ், 206, 210. [Comp. புன்கம்.]

IV. புல்|வாய், a kind of deer: இரலை, 149.

V. புல|ால், stench, 97. [C. *hole.* T. *pola*, 'flesh.' S. पल.]

VI. புலி, a tiger, 193, 206. [M., T., C., TU. *pilli.*]

K. VII. புல்லு, *v.* (§ 62) join, agree, embrace, 155, 303, 391, 399. [M.]

புல்லாப்புன்கோட்டி, a low heterodox school, 255: =புணர்.

K. VIII. புல, *v.* (§ 66) pout, sulk, 252. [புலம். See M.]

[புலம்பு=தனிமை. கலித். i. 16.]

K. IX. புலம், a sense; sensation; learning.

புலவன், a learned man, 255, 312.

தீப்புலவன் (opp. நற்புலவன்), the mere pretender, 318. [M., T., C., TU. Comp. புலமை, ஐம்புலன்.]

அறிவுடையான், 318, 321.

புலன்கெட்ட, senseless, 121.

புலன்=place, 47.

புழுக்கல் [√புழு-க்கு. M. In C. *pulu*='rot.' Comp. அழுகு, பூழி].

=சோறு, parboiled rice; boiled rice, 206. [Jī. Chin. xiii. 386.]

புள் PUḶ. [M. T. *pulugu.* C. *huṛu*='insect.' Comp. புழு, பூழ்.]

புள், fowl, bird, 30, 121, 212.

Nig. புள்ளே வண்டவிட்டம் புட்பேர். (வண்டு, அவிட்டம், பறவை.)

புளி, acidity. [M., T. *puli.* C. *puḷi, huḷi.* A. C. *puṇiche* ='tamarind.']

புளிவிளங்காய், the sour wood-apple, 328.

புற் PURR. [Comp. S. द्वार, GR. θύρα, Lat. *foris*, Fr. *hors.*]

புறம், the back, or outside, opp. to அகம், 89. [M., C. *hora.* Comp. T. *pera, porugu.* TU. *pida.* Comp. also பிற.]

புறத்திரு, 323. எப்புறனும், on every side, 383.

புறந்தரு, 345=பாதுகா, defend, take care of.

[Comp. *Nīti.* 87. So புறஞ்செய். T. 64.]

புறக்கடை, the outer gate, 31, 293. புறப்படு, depart from, 26. [See படு.]

புறங்கூறு, (*n.*) slander, 158. Here the meaning may be either: (1) *not given to utter slander*; or, (2) *dumb when others slander him, not rendering railing for railing.*

புறங்காடு = சுடுகாடு, 45.

புனம் [from புல்; comp. புன்செய், புலம், பொலம், an upland plain fit for dry cultivation, and wooded, 178, 180. [M. = 'a jungle.']

புனல் [புல்], a stream, torrent, 128, 185, 212, 222 (370, 'freshet'). [M.; A. C. *ponalu.*]

புனை, *v.* (§ 57) adorn, 120, 384. [M. *punayu.* See பூண், and S. भूष्.]

புன்னை (பின்னை), the Alexandrian laurel: *Calyophyllum inophyllum*, 97, 117, 246. [M. *punna.* Ainslie's Mat. Med. Ind. vol. ii. p. 310.]

K. பூ, flower = மலர், 43, 107, 139, 215, 221, 252, 259, 262, 290, 393.

பூங் = பூம், *adj.* flowery, 117, 128, 212, 370, 399. [? From S. पुष्प, or √पू. See பூண். In M., T., C. *pū, puvvu* (*hū*).]

பூண் PŪṆ, *an adornment, jewel.* [M., C., T. *pūnu.* From S. भूषण.]

பூண், பூணு, [§ 56 (III)] put on, assume the yoke or harness.

பூண்டான், he who has taken the yoke of marriage on him, 56.

பூண்ட, 56.

The √ is taken as a noun in 350.

பூண்கல்லா, that learns not to draw in harness, or பூண் + கு + அல்லா, 386.

பூழை = வாயில் [a form of புழை. Comp. புதவு, புகு. See M. *pūṟippaḍi*], a wicket gate, smaller gate in a larger, 282.

பூழ், a quail, 122. [M. *pūṟān.* Comp. புள்.]

பெட், see பெள்.

பெண்ணை = பனை, palmyra tree, 216.

பெண், see பெள்.

பெய் PEY, *pour*. [Comp. பொழி. M. T., C. *poyyu*.]

பெய், *v*. (§ 58) rain; pour into; dispose of, throw carelessly; serve up in, 26, 97, 114, 116, 147, 206, 239, 341, 392.

பெய்வளை, bracelets adjusted, strung on; a lady having these, 47. [G. 93, 162.]

பெர் PER, [பெரும், பெரிய, பேர். H. B. § 131. G. 121. Comp. பரு; பல். M. PERU. TU. HER. In old C. C. HE|CHCHU. T. PE|DDA. S. पुरु, पुलु, बृह्, वर्ह्, पर, परि.]

I. பெரு, *adj*., 77, 186, 200, 236, 296.

பெரும், 2, 6, 8, 37, 47, 142, 168, 251, 274, 331, 332, 360, 368, 381, 390, 398.

பெரிது, it is great, 81. [G. 93.] An *adv*.=very, 17, 91, 200, 261, 262.

பெரிய, 168.

பெரியர், 165.
பெரியார், the great, 77, 170, 172, 177, 184, 186.
பெரியோர், 43.
பெரியவர், 125.
} Opp. சிறியவர்.

பெரியாரைப்பிழையாமை, ch. xvii.

II. பெரு|மை=மேம்பாடு, *n*. greatness, 82, 164, 170, 177, 249, ch. xix. (Opp. சிறு|மை.)

III. பெரு|கு, *v*. (§ 62) increase: வளர், 110, 234, 368.

பெருக்கம், a swelling flood: வெள்ளம், 354.

பெருமிதம்=இறுமாப்பு, மிகுதி, மேன்மை, 291.

[A corruption of S. परिमित. பெரு is confounded with S. परि in its intensive significations. மிதம்=the mean, moderation.]

IV. பேர், 147, 173. [In பெரு, உ is lost and எ lengthened by the law of compensation.]

பெள் PEḶ, பெண் PEṆ, பெட் PEḌ. [TU. *pon*. M., C. *heṇṇu*. T. *peṇṭi*, *peṇḍli*. See S. जनि = GR. γυνή = poet. βανά. Ir. BEN, 'hen.']

I. பெண், a woman, womanhood, 87, 251, 354, 384.

பெண்டிர், women, 194, 368, 381.

II. பெடை, a hen; any female, 48, 240. [M. *peḍa*.]

பெறு PERR, *get*. [M. C. TU. *ped*. Comp. T. PUṬṬU and பிற, பொறு, பேறு; and S. भज्, भुज्.]

K. I. பெறு, *v*. (§ 68) obtain, gain, possess, 5, 28, 34, 59, 73, 74, 80, 104, 162, 172, 174, 207, 274, 330, 381, 386, 398; bear (a name), 59; fetch (a price), 115; gain, attain to, 335, 343; beget, 197; enjoy, 381; reach (haven), 250; get by rote, 314.

பெறுப, they will incur, 377.

பெறுவது, what they can yet, 317.

ஆரப்பெறேம், we don't get our fill, 366.

அருபெறல், hard to find or obtain, 34, 381.

K. II. பெற்றி [பெற் + இ] = தன்மை, nature, acquired character: 'பெற்றிருக்குஞ்சற்குணத்துக்கு ஆகுபெயர்,' 235, 343, 352.

K. III. பேறு, gain; birth, bearing, 56. [G. 96. Comp. פְּרִי, בַּר, بار.]

பேசு, *v*. (§ 62) speak, utter, talk. [S. भाष्. M. *pēchu*. C., TU. *pēḷu*, *hēḷu*.]

பேடி [பேண் + இ], an hermaphrodite, 251. [M., A. C., T., TU. *hēḍi*.]

பேணு, *v*. (§ 62) guard, cherish, 381. [Comp. பென், பெட், பெண். M. *peṇṇu*, *pēṇu*.]

பேதை (+ மை + ஆர்), a simpleton, 33, 47, 52, 71; 182, 249, 314, 335. [? Connected with S. पित्र, भीत, or perhaps with பேய்.]

பேதை|மை, folly, ch. xxxiv.

பேய், a devil, 363. Used for 'wild, poisonous,' 116. [M. *pē*. S. पिशाच.]

பேர் (பெயர்) PĒR. [M. C. *hesaru*. T.]

I. பேர், பெயர், *v*. (§ 64) change, remove, turn over, 48, 161; 67, 70 'in return;' 'again,' 364.

பேர்த்து, பேர்த்தும், again.

II. பேர், *n*. a name: பெயர், 59, 98, 175, 199, 200, 381.

பேர், *adj*. great, 147. See பெரு.

போராண்மை, manly excellence, 199, 285. [ஆள்.]

பை PAI. [M. Comp. s. पेट. Used for வயிறு. ? Comp. with வை.]

I. பை, sack, bag; cobra's hood.

தோற்பை, a leathern bag, 26, 66, 400.

பைம்மறி, 42. This is very ambiguous. [Either பை refers to *the body*, *a snake's poison bag*, or *the womb*. See மறி.]

II. பைய, by degrees, slowly, softly, 99, 309, 388, = மெல்ல.
பையென, softly, 396.

பைங் (see பசு), 191.

பொங்க் POṄG. [Comp. புகை. The √ is பொகு nasalized. T. M. *poññu*; comp. *poḍu*. C.]

பொங்கு, *v.* (§ 62) swell, 72; foam, rage, 231.

[N. N. 18: 'பொங்காதழற் கதிரத்தண்ணென் கதிர்வர வரற்பொங்குங்கடல்,
The tides rise not under the influence of the (sun's) hot beams, but of the (moon's) cool rays.']

K. பொச்சா, *v.* (§ 66) = மற: forget, 182. [Comp. K. ch. liv.]

[பொச்சம் = குற்றம், 'fault.' Comp. பொத்து from பொந்து: √POD or PUD, C. = '*hide*.' For the form, see ஏமா.]

பொது POTH, *hide*. [See பொதி, √பொது or புது, புதை, = 'COVER.' Comp. பொச்சா, புதவு. C. *pud, pod, hud, hod;* A. C. *hore*. M. *pud, puḍ;* புடவை: T. POD.]

I. பொ, *v.* (§ 64) perforate, 376. [Comp. பொந்தி, பொத்தி, புதை. M. C. *poda, hoda*. T. *potti, poda*.]

II. பொ|தி, *v.* (§ 57) be full: நிறை, 341.
n. sheath, 269. [M. *podi*. C. *podc*.]

[In T. 24: 'தூண்டிலிலுட் பொதிந்த தேரை,
The frog which is put over (as a பொதி) to hide the hook.']

III. பொ|த்து, *v.* (§ 64) be hidden or stored up in; envelope, 310. [M. *pottu*. C. *pochchu*.]

பொய் POY. [M. *poyi, poli, poḷḷu;* புளுகு: S. फल्गु. C. *pusi, husi*. T. *bollu*.]

பொ|ய், *n.* a lie, falsity.

[Ji. Chin. xiii. 313: 'சொடியல் ஓரெழுத்தும் பொய்ம்மை, utter not a letter that is false.']

As *adj.* false, unreal, 42, 43, 80, 157, 390.

பொய்த்தல், the deceiving, 111. [G. 94.]
பொய்|கை, a tank: குளம். [M. *poyga.*]

பொர் POR. [T. *pŏr;* M.; A. C. So *poṇar* from புணர். T. *porayu, pondu, ponchu.* M. *porunnu.*]

I. பொரி, *v.* (§ 57) be parched, dry, shrivelled, 261. [G. 153. M., T. *poranṭu; podu.* A. C. *puri.* Comp. பொறி.]

II. பொரு, *v.* (§ 58) fight; dash against, 44, 97, 149, 389.

III. பொருவு, *v.* (§ 62) fit, agree.

பொரீஇ=பொருவி, agreeing, 220.

K. IV. பொருள், what belongs: property; reality; meaning, 6, 9, 65, 82, 111, 155, 181, 195, 220, 255, 273, 276, 280, 317, 318, 321, 365, 385, 386, 400. [M.; A. C. *puruḷu.*]

ஒண்பொருள் (பலருள்ளும் தன்னுடையானுக்கு ஒளியைத்தரவல்லதாதலால்), 102.
கைப்பொருள், money in hand, 377.
பொருட்டு=நிமித்தம் (§ 157) for the sake of, 315.

பொல் (see பொன்) POL, *shine.*

பொலி, *v.* (§ 57) be conspicuous; increase. [M. T. VALI.]

பொலிகடன், interest, 98.
பொலிய=பொலிவுபெற, விளங்க, 3.

K. பொழ் POṞ='go forth:' a strengthened form of போ.

I. பொழி, *v.* (§ 57)=சொரி, pour, 259. [M. C. *hoy*, PŪ. T. PŌY. Comp. S. वाह्, and வார், பெய், போழ்.]

II. பொழிப்பு, *n.* 319,=பிண்டவுரை, தொகுத்துரை: an epitome in plain easy prose. (See உரை.) [பொழிப்பெனப் படுவது பொருந்திய் பொருளைப் பிண்டமாகக்கொண்டுரைப் பதுவே.]

III. பொழுது, *n.* (1) 'time:' காலம், 115, 162, 207, 329, 382. (போழ்து, போது, போ.) [M.='sun.' T. *proddu, poddu, puḍu: podalu*='shine.' C. *pottu, hottu: v.*='kindle,' பற்று. TU. *portu.* Comp. S. प्रातर्, πρωΐ.]

ஒருபொழுதைத்துன்பம், temporary afflictions. [ஐ seems adjectival; see நாளை], 295.

(2) = 'when,' with a relative participle, 19, 62, 83, 92, 120, 202, 378. [Comp. கால், கடை, கண், இடம், உழி, *etc.*]

(3) போது, a flower on the point of expansion, 73. [K. 1227.]

Nig. போதுதான் காலம் பூவாம்.

பொற் PORR, *bear*. [M., C. *poru*, *horu*. T. *ōru*. S. भृ; φερ; *fer*; Goth. *bair*; A. Sax. *bere*. பெறு, பேறு, பிற.]

I. பொறு, *v.* (§ 64) bear, carry; sustain; bear patiently with, 58, 65, 66, 75, 77, 149, 172, 203, ch. xxiii, 222, 223, 310, 357.

II. பொறை, *n.* patience: பொறுமை, சாத்விதம், 65, 223. [S. क्षमा, सहिष्णुता.] Ch. viii. So பொருமை = envy.

பொறி (= பொறி), 1. *n.* spot, mark, writing: எழுத்து = இலிபி. S. लिपि. Comp. ब्रह्मलेख = 'fate:' what was inscribed on the cranium before a man's birth; destiny, 110, 283, 290.

2. *v.* (§ 64) distinguish, 199.

[T. 15: 'பொய்வழக்கி வாழும் பொறியறை, the luckless man who lives by lies.']

பொன், gold, 162, 206, 212, 269, 307, 328, 345, 347, 400. [M., C. *honnu*. T., TU. √பொல் = 'shining.' Equivalent to स्वर्ण = சுவர்ணம்.] So பொலம், பொலன்.

பொன்னன்னாய், thou who art like Lakshmī! 225. (அன்.)

பொற்பாவாய், O golden puppet! (voc. of பாவை), 266. [G. 64.]

பொற்றொடி, O thou with golden bracelets! 376. [G. 162.]

K. பொன்று, *v.* (§ 62) die, perish, 323. [A nasalized form of போ? Comp. T. *polayu*.]

போ PŌ. [M. C. T. TU. GR. βα-; Lat. VA; S. गा.]

1. போ [H. B. § 58] go, pass, perish, 5, 30, 32, 55, 136, 181, 376.

போயார் = போயினோர், போனவர்கள், those whose life has passed away, 50. (§ 87.)

போகும் = அழியும், 34.

போம், 23, 140, 323. (§ 72.)

போகிய, 169, = போன (as from போகு inflected as in §§ 62, 70*).

போ|கு, go thou! 326.

போக used in adverbial phrases: கடைபோக, 'to the end,' 119.

II. போதரு, return, 83. [தரு = வரு. G. 124. ௫.]

III. போக்கு, *v.* (§ 62) pass (anything) away, 327.

போகம் [S. भोग, भुज्] enjoyment, 103, 250.

போது, see போழ்.

போத்து = பொந்து, hollowness: உட்புரை, 351. Comp. K. 468. [வலித்தல் and நீட்டல் (G. 41).]

[See T. 75: 'பொத்தின்றிக்காழ்த்தமரம், a tree without a hollow, well matured.']

போர் [from பொரு; so பேறு from பெறு. G. 96].

I. *n.* war, 376.

II. *v.* (§ 64) envelope, 38, 47.

[So proverbially, நீறுமேற் போர்த்த நெருப்பு = 'a smouldering fire.']

போர்|வை, an outer garment, 42.

போல் PŌL, *like.* [Comp. பொலி. M. PŌL. A. C. PŌL|U; C. *hōlike.* Comp. also T. POL|U = 'seem;' PŌL|U; VAL|E.]

போல is a very useful particle of comparison, 2. (G. 109.)

போல், *v.* (§ 70) resemble, 2, 114, 124, 160, 165, 399.

போலும், will appear to be, 181.

போன்று, (having been) like unto, 182, 216.

[This is considered to be a redundant particle: அசைச்சொல், G. 116; *Nannūl*, 373.]

போல் = like, 8, 21, 28, 115, 202, 335, 376, 377. (H. B. § 227.)

போலி [G. 17].

போல்வார், one's equals, 210; those who resemble, 264.

போழ்து, see பொழு, 202. = கோடைக்காலம்.

போற்று PŌTT. [M. T. *prōchu*, *brōdi.* Comp. S. पुष्, पोष.]

போற்று, *v.* (§ 62) guard; make much of; cherish, 49, 120, 225, 318; guard against, 172.

ம MA.

1. ம் is often equivalent to வ: வாணம் = மாணம்.
2. ம் is a pluralising particle: compare கள் with காம்; மார்; தம்.

மக் MAG. [TUḌA *mach.* C. *maga.* M. T. *maga*=' male.']

I. மக=a child.

மக்கள், children; men, 37, 56, 121, 127, 130, 134, 205, 242. [மகார் is also found.]

கீழ்மக்கள், the low, 70.

மேன்மக்கள், the noble, 70.

II. மகன்=மனிதன், son, man, 136, 201, 307, 367.

வேன்மகன்=' spear-*man*,' 16.

ஆண்மகன், a male, husband, hero, 202, 386. [Comp. ஆண், ஆள்.]

III. மகளிர், women, 167, 375 [ch. xxxviii, xxxix].

IV. மாக்கள், men, 44, 45, 242, 323, 393. [Corruption and confusion of மக்கள் and மாந்தர்.]

மகிழ், *v.* (§ 57)=rejoice, exult, 11, 359.

மகிழ்|ச்சி=களிப்பு, (youthful) gladness, 16. [Comp. S. मंगल.]

மஞ்சள் [S. √मञ्ज्] turmeric, Indian saffron (used to beautify the face), 131. *Curcuma longa.* [T. *pasapu.* M. *maññol.*]

மஞ்சு=மேகம் [S. मञ्ज्] a cloud, 28.

மடம் [S. मथ्, मद्. It combines the ideas of these roots. M. There is a confusion of *matam*, *madam*, and *maḍam*] ignorance, stupidity, folly; artless simplicity, 41, 323, 382, 384.

மட|மொழிமாதர், women of guileless speech.

மட|வோன், 273.

[*El.* 9: ' மடம்படான், he does not become infatuated.']

மட் MAḌ, *fold.* [M., T., C., TU. Comp. மட, மடு, மண்டு; and S. मरद्.]

I. மடி, *v.* (§§ 57, 64) bend, fold, curl, 224.

II. மடு, *v.* (§ 64)=மூட்டு, kindle, 331.

மண MAṆA. [M. C. 'fragrance,' *maduve* (வதுவை). T. *manuvu* (மரு, மருகன்).]

I. மண|ம், *n.* marriage, 25.

மணப்பறை, the marriage drum, 23.

II. மண, *v.* (§ 68) wed, 397.

மணந்தார், a husband.

மண்டு, *v.* (§ 62), [S. मण्ड्. மடு. M.='run.' T. 'blaze'] swarm, collect together; grow vehement, wax fierce, 48, 62, 147, 202, 291.

மணி [S. मणि] a gem, 127, 146, 347, 369.

[N. M. K. 5: 'மண்ணி அறிப மணி நலம்,

Men know the worth of a gem after washing it.'

மண்ணு = சுத்திசெய்.]

மண்டிலம் = சூரியன் [S. मण्डल] sun, 22.

K. மதலை = தூண், பற்றுக்கோடு, support, 197.

[In Jī. Chin. = மரக்கலம், 'a ship.']

மதி MATI. [S. मन्, मति.]

I. மதி, *v.* (§ 64) estimate; esteem, 61, 354.

மதி|ப்பு, estimation, 126, 163, 229, 294.

அவ|மதிப்பு, disesteem, 163.

II. மதியம் = நிறைமதி, சந்திரன் (opp. to பிறை), the full moon, 21, 125, 176. [Comp. S. मास, from मा, or मन्, मद्. M. அறுமதி = 'six months.']

மதுகை [comp. मधुक and மதம்] strength: பலம், வலி, 65, 198, 291.

[*Kalit.* 47: 'உலகம் புரப்பான் போல்வதோர் மதுகையுடையவன்,

Possessor of might as of one who guards the universe.']

மதுரம் [S. मधुर] sweetness, 211.

மந்தி = குரங்கு, a monkey, 237. [M.]

மம்மர் = மயக்கம், delusion, 132, 393.

மம்மர்கொண் மாந்தர், mortals that cherish delusions, 14.

This seems allied to many words. Especially to மம்மதை [S. ममता = 'mineness,' the habit of mind that claims things of earth as its own]. See root மை or மய [மையல், மயல், *etc.*]. Its equivalent is தமொற்றம் in 140. See also in K. மருள், மைந்து. This is அஞ்ஞானம், the புல்லறிவாண்மை of K. 331.

மய [= மை] MAYA. [See S. माया; மை, மழு; T. *masa*.]

I. மய|ங்கு, *v.* (§ 62) be bewildered, 327.

II. மய|க்கு, *v.* cause bewilderment, 189.

III. மயல் = மயக்கம், confusion; dried sticks and leaves, rubbish, 43, 183.

Nig. மயல் செத்தை மயக்கம் பேயாரம்.

[Comp. B. I. S. 1257:

'उद्वर्तितमपि बहुधानुलिप्तमपि चन्दनागुरुरसाद्यैः ।
भजति तथापि शरीरं दौर्गन्ध्यं तत्र को हेतुः ॥

Though perfumed oft and anointed with sandal, Agil and other fragrant spices, the body even then has a foul odour. What is the cause of this?'

This illustrates 43: மயல் = சரீரம்: அதற்குக் காரணமாகிய உடம்புக்கு ஆகுபெயர்.]

மர MARA.

I. மர பு = முறைமை, course; what is sanctioned by custom; line, 249, 336. [G. 163. Comp. வழு, பழு, முறை. T. *maragu*.]

II. மர|ம், மரன், tree: விருட்சம், தரு, 30, 197. [TU. MAR|A (*ō*). M., C., T. *mrānu*, *mānu*.]

பயன்|மரம், 17.

நிழன்|மரம், பழு|மரம், 202.

மரத்தார், persons irrational as trees, 145. [மரம் + அத்து + ஆர். G. 93.]

மரு MARU [S. मरु].

I. மரு|ங்கு = side, limit, 8; '*trace*' (?). [M. *maruṅṅu*. C. *maggal*. T. *marugu*. ? மறு.]

மருங்கற, *without 'a wrack behind.'*

[*Kalit.* 48: 'மருங்கறி வரரா மலையினும் பெரிது,
Greater than a trackless (boundless) mountain.'

K. Rām. I. x. 79: 'கருங்கலாய் மருங்கு வீழ்வாள்,
She fell a black stone by his *side*.']

II. மரு|வு, *v.* (§ 62) embrace, = சேர், 36. [M.]

மருஉச்செய்து (for *n.* மருவு?), having formed an intimacy; [but see செய்தி. G. 153.]

மரீஇ = மருவி, approaching, 220; defiling, 85, 87.

மருஉ = மருவு, union, 246.

III. மருள்(ளு), *v.* [§ 56 (III). From *n.* மரு|ள். Comp. இரு|ள், பொருள், *etc.*; and மறம்] = மயங்கு, be bewildered, 301.

மரை for தாமரை=lotus, 358.
மருந்து, medicine, 132, 340. [Corruption of s. अमृत; or √மரு. M., C., TU. T. *mandu*.]

மல் MAL. [=வல், வள், பல். S. बल्, मल्. M., T., C. The idea is 'strength, expansion, abundance:' வளமை, வலிமை.]

I. மல|ங்கு, an eel,=விலாங்கு, 375. [T. *malu-ga*. *Malu-ku* is a 'slip-knot' in T. and C., hence 'the slippery one.' Comp. வழு.]

K. II. மல|ர், *n.* a full-blown flower: அலர் [C. Comp. போது, அரும்பு], 209, 266, 393.
v. (§ 57) bloom, flower, 215, 283.

K. III. மலை, a mountain [S. मलय. T., C., M.], 10, 21, 28, 203, 237, 245, 285, 353, 356, 369. [Comp. வரை, வெற்பு, குன்று, கிரி.]

K. IV. மல்|லல்=வளப்பம், abundance, fertility, 296.

V. மல்|கு, *v.* (§ 62) abound, swell: பெருகு, 263.

VI. மலி, *v.* (§ 57) be full: நிறை, 73, 98. With கடல்.

மழ் MAṚ, *dull*. [M., C. Comp. மருள், மாரி, வாரி. S. वृष् and मसि.]

K. மழை, *n.* rain, cloud, 27, 97, 361.
[T. 83: 'செப்பமுடையர் மழையனையர், the just are like the rain.']

மறு MARR,='other, back again, change:' the strengthened forms are மற்று and மாறு. Comp. வேறு.

I. மற, *v.* (§ 68. M., C., T., TU.) forget, 32, 201, 293.

II. மறு|க்கு, *v.* (§ 62) refuse, find fault; grumble, 342. [Comp. மறம்=anger.]

III. மறி, the young of any quadruped. [M., C., TU. Comp. மறம், மறு, மறி (*v.*): the idea is 'motion, frisking.']
A lamb, 16. A foal, 42 (?).

[மறி as verb means 'arrest; turn; invert.' Here it is said to be used as a noun = மறிப்பு; and then பைமறியா='as though the bag (body) were inverted.' Another commentator makes பை to be the poison bag of a serpent: 'as though the poison were poured from the fangs of a snake.']

IV. மறு, I. *adj.* other, 1, 95, 183, 209, 243, 275, 329.
For மறுமை, see மை.

2. *n.* a spot, stain: மாசு, மச்சு, 151, 180. ['Something differing from the rest.' M.]

3. *v.* (§ 64) repeat; deny, refuse: மாற்று, கர.
மறுத்தும், again, 222.

V. மறை [a screen].

(1) *n.* a secret, 158, 230. [M., T., C., TU. S. मर्मन्.]

[T. 55:
'அருமறை காவாத நட்பு,
Friendship that guards not the profound secret.'

B. I. S. 3942:
'परस्परस्य मर्माणि ये न रक्षन्ति जन्तवः त एव निधनं यान्ति . . . ।
People who guard not one another's secrets go to death.'

The revealing of secrets (மறை) is one of the primary sins. Comp. K. 1076.

B. I. S. 5722:
'रहस्यभेदो याच्ञा च नैष्ठुर्यं चलचित्तता ।
क्रोधो निःसत्यता द्यूतमेतन्मित्रस्य दूषणम् ॥
Revelation of secrets, mendicancy, harshness, fickleness, wrath, untruthfulness, gambling: these are faults in a friend.']

(2) *v.* (§ 64) hide.
மறையா = மறைத்து (G. 86. க.) 42 (?), 78, 197.

VI. மற்று, = but, besides [T. KĀNI] 17, 20, 60, 67, 72, 141. Some other time: பின்னே, 19.

An அசைநிலை, G. 116; *Nannūl*, 365. It seems to have more or less of an adversative force always = 'but, on the other hand,' 330.

மற்றையார், others, 184, 256.

மனம் [S. मनस्, Lat. *mens*] mind, 23, 33, 89, 127, 128, 146, 212, 244, 245, 291, 298.

மனப்பிரிப்பு, distraction of mind, 189.

மனத்தார், 189, 246, 329.

மனத்தான் for மனத்தில், 180. [G. 137*.]

[ஐந்தறிவின்மேல் அதிகமாமனமே, *the mind is above the five senses.*]

மன் MAN, *permanence.* [S. मन्; GR. μεν-; Lat. *man-*; M., T., C., TU. Comp. மல்.]

I. மன், as a particle = indeed, forsooth. See *Nannūl*, 364, where its uses are said to be six: (1) redundant; (2) indicative of ellipsis; (3) increase; (4) excess; (5) certainty; (6) permanence, 40 (2), 109 (5), 372 (1), 389 (1).

II. மன்|னன் = அரசன்: a king, 167. [M. S. मनु.]

III. மனை, (1) a mansion, house: இல், 382. [M. T. C. TU.]
(2) Wife: மனைவி, மனையாள், 85, ch. ix, 238.
மனை|யாள் (மனையாட்டியாள்), 3, 86, 361.
(3) Domestic life: இல்வாழ்க்கை, 54, 130.

IV. மன்|னு, *v.* (§ 62) abide, 114.
மன்னா, unstable, 11, 16.

[T. 30: 'மன்னியசெல்வம், well-established prosperity.']

V. மன்|றம் (மன்று), *n.* a hall of assemblage, 23. [M. *mannu.* Comp. மனை, and s. मण्डप.]

மா MĀ. [Comp. s. मह्, மாண்; மான், மாடு.]

(1) *adj.* great [s. महा. See மீ, மேல், மிகு, மால், மாண்], 148, 296.

(2) *n.* mango plant, shoot, 41. [M. T. *māvi.*]

(3) *n.* an animal, 149, 152, 377. Especially *a horse.*

[N. M. K. 5: 'பண்ணமைத் தேறியபின்னறிபமாகலம், the worth of *a horse* is known after you have saddled and mounted it.'
கலிமா, 'a charger.' T. 46: 'காறுய்மை இல்லாக் கலிமா, a charger defective in its paces.']

அரிமா = சிங்கம், 198. ஆமா, சேமா, 377. [T. *māvu.* Comp. ஆ, ஆன். s. महा = 'cow.']

மாக்கள் = மனிதர் [for மக்கள், pl. of மக], 45, 96, 334.

மாசு = மறு, மை. [M. *māchu.* C. *māsu* (*mach*, மச்சை = மறு, 'wart'). s. मषि, मासिक.] = குற்றம், fault; spot, fleck, 128, 151.

மாட் MĀḌ, see மட். [M. Comp. s. मट, माडि, मालिका (மாளிகை).]

I. மாடம், a mansion, 361.

II. மாடு = place, and its inflexive base மாட்டு is used as sign of 7th case = இடத்தில், 161, 335. [G. 63.]
யார்மாட்டும், to every one, any one, 2, 14, 99, 168.

மாட்சி, see மாண்.

மாது MĀTH.

மாதர், 1. Women, = பெண்கள், மகளிர், 382.
மாதராள், 384.

2. Beauty, = அழகு, 73.

[This is pl. of மாது. M. S. मातृ. Hence the other meanings. Comp. மாதோ.]
Nig. மாதரே இடைச்சொல் காதல் வனப்பொடு மகளிர் ஆமே.

மாத்திரை [S. मात्र], a moment of time, 302; a limit, 242.
மாதோ, an expletive, = O lady! 355. [See மாதர்.]
மாந்தர் = மனிதர், men, human beings, 14, 30, 91, 257, 313. [S. मानुष. Comp. மைந்தர்.]

மாய் MĀY. [T., C., M., TU. S. माय, मार, मृ. Comp. மய, மை, மாழ்.]
மாய், v. (§ 57) die, disappear, perish: கெடு, 51, 285, 308, 359.

மார், மார்பு, = அகலம்: breast, 385. [M. *mārru*. Comp. S. मर्मन्.]
மார்பன், 387.
மாரி, n. = மழை, v. rain, 104, 232, 370. [M., T., TU. S. वारि, comp. मारि.]

T. 76: 'மாரி நாள்வந்த விருந்து,
A guest who has arrived in a storm;' = an urgent affair.

மார்க்கம் = வழி, way, 323. [S. मार्ग, मृग 'track.']

மால் MĀL. [√ = 'blackness.' M. T. *nal*. Comp. v. மலை = 'be confused.']
மால், Indra, 373. [S. माल.]
மாலை, n.
1. A garland, 393. [S. माला.]
2. Eventide: (6–10 P. M.), 393.

[In sense of இயல்பு, '*nature*,' see கலித். i. 9. (K. 1035.)
'மாலைக் கொளைநடை அந்தணிர்; வெவ்விடைச்செலன்மாலை ஒழுக்கத்தீர்,
O Brāhmans whose rule and practice are of the *nature* that, *etc.*; it is your *nature* and appointed duty to tread this fiery path.']

மாற் MĀRR, see மறு.
I. மாறு, a return, recompence: பிரதி, 98.
K. = பகை, enmity, 67. (T. 61.)
மாறேல், commence hostilities. [எல்.]
K. II. மாற்றார், foes, 3, 67. [M.]
III. மாற்று, v. (§ 62) deny, 98, 308.

K. மானம் (மாநம்) [S. मान, from मन्, = 'opinion'].

1. Honour: கவுரவம், 40, ch. xxx, 291, 294, 300.
2. Disgrace, 198, = அவமானம்.

மான், a deer, 378. [M., C., TU., T. Comp. மா.]

K. I. மி|கு [see மீ. Comp. S. महा. M., C. MIG, *miṭṭe*, *miṭu*. See also மெ, மெச்சு, மிஞ்சு, மீறு, மேடு, மேல். T.], abound, 193, 341, 346.

மிக, much, 31.

மிக்க, abundant, 134, 341.

மிகுதிச்சொல், presumptuous words, 346.

K. மிகை, greatness, 163.

[Jī. Chin. i. 252: 'காடுகவர் தீயின்மிகை சீறுபு வெகுண்டான், Like a fire that devours the forest, he swelled with rage at the *attack*;' (= *outrageous assault*.)]

K. II. மி|சை, i. (a case-ending) = over, above; on, upon, 21, 22. (§ 251. G. 63.)

ii. *v.* (§ 57) suck, feed upon, 259.

[In T. we find *min-çu*, *migu*, *miç*, *mī*, *mīdu*, *mī|rru*, *miṭṭu*, *migal*, *mēl*, *mēn*, with root idea of 'excess.' M. *micha*, *mī*.]

III. மிடி, *n.* affliction, 56. [M., C. = 'a tap.']

IV. மிடுக்கு, tightness, 93.

மிடுக்குற்று, holding fast. [Comp. இடுக்கு. T. *miḍa*.]

V. மிடை, *v.* (§ 57) be closely packed, mixed up with: நெருங்கு, 80. [M. *miḍa* = 'knot.']

[Jī. Chin. i. 250:
வேல்மிடைத்தவேலி, 'a hedge (compacted) of spears.'
தேன்மிடைத்ததார், 'a garland dripping with honey.']

VI. மிதி, *v.* (§ 64) trample on, 61. [M. *meti*; from S. मृद्.]

VII. மின், மின்னு, lightning, 8, 269. [Comp. மீன். M., T., C., TU.]

மின், a termination of plural imperative. (G. 84.)

மீ MĪ.

I. மீ (see மிசை, மேல், மெய், மிகு), above.

மீப்போர்வை, an external covering, 42.

மீப்போர்த்த, covered over, 47.

மீக்கூற்றம், eulogy, praise; authority in words, 53. [See கூறு.]

[*Ēl.* 2 = மேம்பட்டவார்த்தை : மேலாமெம்படியானசொல் : not = புகழ் !
N. N. 22 : 'மீக்கொள் உயர்விழிவு, glory and disgrace.']

II. மீ|து, 115, 389. [M., T.]

மீதாரு = மேலிட்டுவரு, அடர்ந்துவரு, throng, press on, 60.

மீதாடு, move over the surface, 115.

மீன், *n.* (I) a star, 113. [C., M. From மின்(னு), 'sparkle.']
(II) A fish, 375. [S. मीन.]

மீள் MĪḶ.

மீள், *v.* (§ 70) return ; redeem.

மீட்டு, (*as adv.*) in return, 70.

[The verb has two forms : *int.* மீள(ு)கிறேன், மீண்டேன், -வேன், மீள ; and *tr.* மீட்கிறேன், மீட்டேன், மீட்பேன், மீட்க. M. *vīḷuga.* C. *mīḍu.*]

மு MU. The idea is *precedence.* [M., C., T., TU.]

I. See மூ : 'old,' and 'three.'

II. Root form of மூன்று, 'three,' 24, 190, 200. (§ 173.)

முக்குற்றம், 'the three faults :' these are காமம், குரோதம், மயக்கம், 'lust, wrath, and mental confusion.' See B. I. S. 1636–1661.

முகை = அரும்பு : bud, 45. [See முகிழ்.]

முகிழ், a bud : அரும்பு, 262. முகிழ (G. 93). [S. मुकुल. Comp. C. *mugaḷu.* M. *mugil.*]

முட் MUḌ. [From முடி, 'a crown, knot :' *finis coronat opus !* C. MU|GI. M. S. मुच्.]

K. I. முடி, *v.* (§ 57) [= முகி] come to an end, be successfully accomplished, (க. வ.) 190, 250.

v. (§ 64) accomplish, 62.

II. முடு|கு, *v.* (§ 62) hasten, 238. [M., C.]

III. முடை, *n.* ill odour : நாற்றம், 48. [M.]

IV. முட்டிகை, a jeweller's small hammer, 208. [M. *muṭṭi.* C.]

V. முட்டு, *n.* a hindrance : இடையூறு [M., C., T., TU.], 238, 250, 288.

v. (§ 62) butt against, 64. [Comp. T. 31 = குறைவுறு.]

முகம் [S. मुख], face, 198, 260.

முகம்புகு, come before a man as a suppliant, 303.

முத்தம், முத்து, a pearl, 224 ; 45, 146, 399. [S. मुक्ता.]

முத்தரையர், wealthy persons; செல்வர், 200, 296.

[The precise meaning is doubtful. It may be முத்தர் + ஐயர், 'venerable ascetics,' *who have obtained* முத்தி. Again it may be 'lords of the three lands,' i.e. பாண்டிநாடு, சோழநாடு, and சேரநாடு.

BOUNDARIES OF THE THREE KINGDOMS (BY AVVAI):

1. The *Pāṇḍi-nāḍu:*

'வெள்ளாற்றினதெற்கு, மேற்குப்பெருவெளியாம்,
தெள்ளரம்புனற்கன்னிதெற்காகும்—உள்ளரன்
ஆய்ந்தகடற்கிழக்கன்பத்தறு காதம்
பாண்டிநாடெல்லைப்பதி.

The bound of the territory of the *Pāṇḍi* land lies south of the *Veḷḷāṟṟu* (="the white river:" Pālār). To the west of it is *Peruveḷi* (the great plain). Its southern point is *Kanni*, (*Kumari*, Comorin,) with its clear stream. On the east lies the sea, explored by the spy. It extends 56 *Kāthams* (560 miles).'

2. The *Çēra-nāḍu:*

'வடக்குத் தலம்பழனி, வாழ்கிழக்குச்செங்கோடு,
குடதிசைக்குக்கோழிக்கூடாகும்—கடற்கரையின்
ஓரமதுதெற்காகும் ஓர் எண்பதிங்காதஞ்
சேரநாட்டெல்லை எனச்செப்பு.

Paḷaṇi is its northernmost place. The most eastern *Çeṅkōḍu* (="the precipice:" Trichengode). At its western limit is *Kōḻi-kūḍu* (="hen-coop:" Calicut). On the south is the sea-coast. Declare the bound of the *Çēra* country to be 80 *Kāthams* (800 miles)!'

3. The *Çōḻa-nāḍu:*

'கடல்கிழக்கு, தெற்குகரைபொரு வெள்ளாறு,
குடதிசைக்குக் கோட்டைக்கரையாம்,—வடதிசைக்கு
ஏணாட்டுப்பெண்ணை; இருபத்துநாற்காதம்
சோழநாட்டெல்லை எனச்சொல்.

The sea is on the east. South is *Veḷḷāṟṟu* that chafes its banks. Westward is *Kōṭṭai-karai* (the fort-bank). On the north is the river *Peṇṇai* (Peṇṇār). 24 *Kāthams* (240 miles) is the bound of the *Çōḻa* land.' Its capital was *Uṟṟaiyūr* or *Kōḻi.*]

முந்திரி (முந்திரிகை), a vine; *caju*-nut; a minute fraction: $\frac{1}{320}$. [See இம்மி. M.] 346.

முய் MUY. [Comp. S. मुष्.]

I. முய|ங்கு, *v.* (§ 62)=தழுவு, கூடு, புல்லு: embrace, cling to, 220, 391, 392. [Comp. S. मुह्.]

II. முயல், *v.* (§ 70) use effort, be active [comp. T. *moyu*], 288,=முயற்சிசெய்து, 326, 365.

III. முயல், *n.* (=*the active one*), முசல், சசம்: a hare. [Comp. S. शशी. M., C. *mola.* T. *mosali.* TU. *muyera.*] 176: used for களங்கம், spots on the moon's surface. See மாசு.

முரசம்=பேரிகை, drum, 100. [M. *murachu.* S. मुरज.]

முரண்=போர், war, 149. [M. Comp. முர, முரடு.]

முரி, *v.* (§ 64)=முறி: break, 123. [C.]

முலை, female breast, (nipple,) 85, 378, 389, 397, 399, 400. [M. *mula.* C. *mole.* T. *mola, molaka.* Comp. மலை, முளை.]

முல்லை, jasmine, 45, 287. [C. T. *molla.* M. *mulla.* Comp. மல்லிகை. S. मल्लि.]

முழங்கு, *v.* (§ 62) sound out, thunder, 100, 146, 392. [T. *morra, mrōy.* M. முறை, முறுமுறு. S. मुहुर्, 're-verberate.' முழா=M. *viṛa*=விழா, 'a drum; feast.']

முழு [comp. முறு, முற்று] entire, 399. [M. Comp. முடி.]

முழுமக்கள்=கீழோர், கயவர், மூடர், 358.

[In T. 9, 87, the word is used ironically=புரைபடாதவர்.]

முளை, a germ, 367. [M. *muḷa.* C., T. *muḷ* and *moḷ.* From முள், 'anything pointed.']

முற் MURR. [See also முன். The idea of முறு, முற்று is 'thick, rough, violent.']

I. முறி=தளிர், a tender shoot, 16, 317. [Properly 'a fragment.' M. MURRI='*break.*' T., C. MURU, *muri.* Comp. முர, முரி.]

II. முறு|கு, *v.* (§ 62) become intense, 171. [M., T., TU., C.]

III. முறு|வல்=பல், tooth, 45. [M.=*murruvēl* (*vēl*='lance').]

IV. முறை, a course, turn, time, order; justice, 56, 99, 110. [M. *murra.* T., C., TU. Comp. வழு, வரி.]

V. முற்று, *v.* (§ 62)=முதிர், be accomplished, 231; become mature, 19.

n. maturity, 237. [T. *muvaru.* See மூ, முழு, முதிர். M.]

முன் MUN. [M., T., C., TU. from மூ. Comp. முதல், முந்து. See பின்.]

I. முன்=before. முன்னர், முற், முன்னை, 190.

With rel. part. 'before they pass away,' 22.

முன்னே, (*adv.*) before, 5, 326.

Sign of 7th case: 51, 117.

அவைமுன்னர் = in presence of the assembly, 325.
முன்னர், in front of, 16, 92.
முன்னை, (*adj.*) belonging to the former, 107. [Comp. மேலை, and ஐ.]
முற்படு, present itself, 237.

II. முன்னு, *v.* (§ 62) design. [p. I.]

III. முனி, *v.* (§ 57) detest, dislike, 92, 208, 316, 338.
முனிவு, 366.

மூ MŪ (மு) = 'before, in front, chief.' [Comp. மு, முது, முதிர், முதல், முகம், முன், முந்து, முற்று, முழு. M. C. D. G. p. 226.]

I. மூ, *v.* (§ 64) grow old, 351. [Comp. தோறும்.] Ever as they wax old.
மூப்பு, age, 52, 55, 92, 326.

II. மூக்கு = nose, 59. [M., T., C., TU.]

III. மூ = மூன்று, three, 100: the மேல், கீழ், and நடு, heaven, hell, and earth. [M. *mūn.* C. *mūr.* T. *mūḍu.*]
மூன்று, 114, 250. (§ 172.)
மூவர், 363.

IV. மூழை = துடுப்பு, அகப்பை, a ladle, 321. [Also முழி = முகழி = முகவை, from முக, 'draw water.' M. A. C. *moge.*]

[So B. I. S. 3872:

'आत्मानं नैव जानन्ति दर्वी पाकरसं यथा।

They know not the soul, as the ladle knows not the taste of food.']

V. மூகை = ஊமை, one dumb, 158. [S. मूक. Lat. *mutus.*]

VI. மூடு, *v.* (§ 62) cover, 24. [M. Comp. முடை, முடி.]
மூட்டு, *v.* (§ 62) kindle, rake up, 224.

VII. மூடர், fools, 316. [मूढ from मुह् = 'stupid.']

மெய் MEY. [Comp. மை. See மேனி. M., T., C., TU. மேல், மீ, மிசை. Prob. from மே|வு (மெய்|வு).]

மெய், *n.* (1) body: உடம்பு, 59, 399; while it is in its body, 213. [Comp. மை and S. मय.]
(2) Truth, reality; true, 129, 315.
மெய்யாக, in sooth, 235.
In comp. மெய்ஞ்ஞானம், 'true wisdom,' 311.

மெய்ம்மை=உண்மை, truth, reality, ch. xii. [s. सत्यं. See B. I. S. 6715-6746. வாய்மை.]

மெல் MEL. [மென், மெற். s. मृदु. மெது, மெள். Lat. *mollis.*]
மெல்ல, calmly, thoroughly, 135, 253; quietly, 53, 91, 254.
மெல், *adj.* tender, soft, 86, 394.
மெல்|லிய, 188.
மெல்|லியர்=எளியர், poor people, 178, 299.
மென்|மை, gentleness, 188: சாந்தம்.

மே MĒ. [See மிகல், மிசை, மீ, மெய், மேடு. M. In C. *mēl*=நல். In T. in all forms.]

I. மேல், above, upon, after, 193, 248, 326, 383; towards, 262. Sign of 7th case='on, above' (redundant in 22), 42, 61, 85, 113, 186, 256, 397.
மேலை, former, 31, 105. [Comp. முன்னை, and ஐ.]
மேன்முறை, former time, 56.
மேல், மேலோர், good people, 60, 303, 304. [Comp. கீழ், கீழோர்.]
மேன்மக்கள், 70, ch. xvi.

[From the root is formed a verb, மேம்படு, 'rise high' (which should be மேன்படு); and the noun மேம்பாடு (மேன்பாடு), 'dignity'=மேன்மை. (T. 8.)
In T. 2 மேன்மக்கள் are called மேன்முறையாளர்.]

II. மே|வு, *v.* (§ 62) love heartily, 217, 372. [M. (*mē*= 'above'). Comp. மெச்சு.]

III. மேனி=உடம்பு, மெய், body, 317. [T. *meyi*=*mē*; (மெய்) ='above:' மேன்=மேல். M.]

மை MAI. [Comp. மெய், and s. मय.]

I. மை, (1) 'ness,' as an affix=தனம், expressing an abstract quality, as in இள|மை.
(2) 'State, condition.' See மறு, அ, இ, எ, உ.
(3) =குற்றம், 'fault:' மாசு, 333, 347.
(4) =மேகம், 'cloud,' 142.

II. மை|ந்து=மயக்கம், bewilderment, 87. [See மய. Comp. மாசு. S. माय.]

III. மைத்துனன் [s. मैथुन] a relation by marriage [*boon companion*], 340.

மொக்குள்=(1) இளம்பூவரும்பு, குமிழி, a bud.

(2) நீர்க்குமிழி, a bubble in water, 27.

[√மொக்=மொட், anything spherical. M. *moṭṭu.* C. *mogge.* T. *mogge.* Comp. முகிழ், முகை, மொட்டு, கொப்புளம், பற்புதம். S. मुकुल.]

Nig. மொக்குளே குமிழி பூவின் முகுள் என மொழிய லாமே.

Comp. B. I. S.:

‘यथा जले नश्यति बुद्बुदो ध्रुवं।
तथा ध्रुवं नश्यति रूपयौवनम्॥

As surely as in the water perishes a bubble,
So surely perish beauty and youth.’

மோடு [முகடு. M. *mōḍi*] greatness.

=செல்வம், பெருமை, 358; opp. to எட்டை.

[Jī. Chin. xiii. 201: ‘மோட்டெழில், most beautiful.’]

மொழ் MOṞ. [Comp. முறை. M. T., C., TU. *nuḍi.*]

மொழி, (1) *v.* (§ 57) speak, 379.

(2) *n.* a word, 379, 382, 384; renown, 238. [Comp. T. 32.]

சின்மொழியார், the soft-voiced ones, 362.

ய YA.

1. Used often for எ.
2. Sometimes = S. स्.
3. Often euphonically inserted. G. 23.

யா YĀ.

I. யா, *v.* (§ 64) tie, bind, 214.

யாத்தார், close friends, 214.

யா|ப்பு, from யா, a ligament; imprisonment, கட்டு, 28, 277. [Comp. *Nīti.* 1.]

K. II. யா|க்கை [யா=‘tie.’ ? S. यम्. தொக்க உடம்பு in 37] the body, consisting of ligaments *etc.*, the *frame.*

யாக்கைநிலையாமை, ch. iii, 18, 27, 28, 30, 34, 41.

=உடல், உடலம், உடம்பு, ஆகம். [The common S. தேகம் and சரீரம் are not found here, or in K.]

Often written ஆக்கை.

III. யா as initial interrogative=எ, ஆ.

யா|ர்=who: எவர், ஆர், 2, 119, 127.

யா|ரும், any or everybody, 7, 22, 282.

யா|து, what, which? யாதும், anything, 71.

யார்யாரும், any people, 103.

யாங்கணும், everywhere, 120. (யா + ங் + கண் + உம்.)

யான் = நான், 'I,' 276, 389. [C. D. G. p. 255. M. *ñān.* TU. *yān.* C. *nān.* T. *nēnu.* Comp. என், நாம், நம்.]

யாம், pl. 'we:' நாம், 8, 132, 293. [ம் is a pluralising letter.]

யானை, elephant: களிறு, 3, 21, 198, 213. [ஆனை. (Comp. S. √या.) T. *ēnu|ga.* M. *āna.* C. *āne.* √ĀN, ĒN|*th* (TU.) = 'bear up.' A real Drāviḍian word.]

யாறு = ஆறு, a river, 150. [√ARR, அறு.]

வ VA.

1. ம is sometimes used for it: so in Tu. *amasara* = அவசரம். M. *varraḍu* = *varaḍu* = மலடு. வினை = மினை.

2. Inserted for euphony. G. 23. உடம்படுமெய், a consonant that aids combination.

3. A sign of the future. G. 81.

4. வ் is sometimes used (1) for S. प: पाप = பாவம்;

(2) फ: फल् = விலை;

(3) च: चहु = வெகு;

(4) भ: सभा = அவை.

5. வ் is sometimes inserted arbitrarily. In 51 தேய் + வ் + இடத்து, and தீர் + வ் + இடத்து, the construction is G. 153 = தேய்யும் and தீரும், and வ் is aoristic future.

6. வு forms nouns from weak verbal stems: அறி|வு. G. 94.

7. வி is added to any stem: கல்|வி, மனை|வி, கரு|வி.

வ VA (வா, வார், வர்), *come.* [M. *varu.* C. *bā, baru.* T. *va-ççu, rā.* C. D. G. p. 113.]

வரு (§ 70) come, arrive, 2, 4, 11, 30, 35, 55, with சேர்.

வந்தது, has arrived, 12.

வர|வு, coming, birth. (p. 1.)

வராமை, the not coming, 326.

தலைவரினும் [see தலை], 57, 79.

வாரா, they come not, 110.

[வருவாய் = 'income.' T. 21.]

K. வகை [from வகு ; comp. பகு] manner, 'as far as you can,' 36, 71 ; 'in the way that,' 384. [M., T., C., TU.]

வசை, a reproach : பழிப்பு, 111, 152. [Allied to வை, 'scold.' s. वचस्, 'abuse.' Comp. 119.]

['கன்றல்வசை = evil speaking.']

வஞ்சம், deceit, 172. [s. वञ्च्.]

வட, northern, 243. [s. उदक्. See வட-க்-கு, and இடம்.]

வட் VAḌ. [M., T., C., TU.]

I. வடி = பிழி, *v.* (§ 64) 1. squeeze out, 257.

2. Filter, make clear, refine, 163.

[K. Rām. I. xi. 88 : 'வடித்த மாதவ, கேட்டி! Hear, O great ascetic (who hast extracted the very essence of austerity)!'

In 279 is it அடியா or வடியா? *the recalcitrant,* or *that yields.*]

K. II. வடு = நவை. குற்றம், fault ; ulcer ; scar, 114, 156, 157. [Comp. வழு. M.]

வட்டு, anything circular: a worthless counter = அடியுந்தலையுமில்லாதது, 264. [Corruption of s. वृत्त? See வண்.]

வண் (வட்) VAṆ. [Comp. வள் = 'rounded, bent, curved, encircling.' M., C.]

I. வண்|டு [வள் + து], a beetle, a scarab of any kind, 73, 223, 283, 284, 290.

283, 290 are versions of the same. Notice the picture of the வண்டு which all these passages give.

II. வணங்கு / வணக்கு }, *v.* (§ 62) { bow. / bend.

[M. C. *baggu.* T. *vaṅku.* S. वङ्क्.] (p. I.) 336.

வணக்குதும், we will bend them. (G. 83.)

III. வண்ணம், way, manner (or beauty, grace, *ironically,* comp. 15), 50. [s. वर्ण. See வருணம்.]

வம்பலன், a neighbour : அயலான் (?), 87.

வய் VAY.

I. வய|ங்கு, *v.* (§ 62) glitter, gleam : பிரகாசி, விளங்கு, 391.

வயங்கொளிமண்டிலம், the resplendent orb, 22.

II. வயம் = வசம் [s. वश], subjection, 325.

வையவயப்பட்டான், he who was subjected to abuse: உட்படு.

III. வயல்=கழனி, a field, *generally of rice*, 367, 389. [Comp. வெளி, விளை, வளை. T., C., M., TU. S. वहिस्. T. *bailu*.]

IV. வயின்=இடம் [comp. வை, வாய்], sign of 7th case. [G. 63.]

V. வயா [? from வயிறு. See C. *basuru*].
=கருப்பம்; அதினுலுண்டாகியநோவு, 201.

[Found as வயவு, வயாவு, வயா.
In கலித். i. 29: 'வயவுநோய் நலிதல், suffering from childbed pangs.']

VI. வயிறு, belly, 121. [M. *vayarru*. C. *basuru* (? *basi*= 'ooze').]

வர் VAR. [Comp. S. वृ, वर, 'encompass;' परि. M. *vara*, *varu*. வரி. See also வ.]

I. வரை, *n*. [M., T.]

(1) *A mountain:* மலை. [Comp. வெற்பு. C. *beṭṭa*.]
With குளிர், பெரு, உயர், நல், கல், நீள், புனல், 71, 77, 154, 186, 223, 226, 231, 239, 283, 369, 387. *Note the variety!*

(2) *A bambu:* மூங்கில் (231 ?), 226 (? *extent*).

(3) *A limit* (of time or space), 24, 98, 130, 153. [62 note.] அளவு. [See வரி, *draw* a line.]
உளவரையால், to the extent of their means, 271.

II. வரை, *v*. (§ 57) 'refuse, reject:' so some read வரையாது in 98. But வரையான்=அளவிலுல். Comp. 271.

III. வரம்பு=எல்லை, அளவு, a bank, 188. 'Let these be your fixed rules of action.' [M.]

IV. வரிசை, order, 249; in the course of things, 18; dearer, 125. [T. *varasa*.]

V. வருந்து, *v*. (§ 62) suffer; take pains about, 31, 35, 155, 202. [Comp. S. वृषा. T. *varuṭu*. A. C. *bardu*.]
வருத்தம், suffering, 201. [M. Comp. வறு, வெறு. C. *bara*='famine;' *bari*.]

VI. வரன்று, *v*. (§ 62)=வாரு, as if from வரல்; கொழி, sweep *things* along, 369. [M. *varaṇḍu*.]

வருணம், caste: குலம், 136. [S. वर्ण. See வண்ணம்.]

வரி=புள்ளி, spot [see வரை], 198=புகர்முகம் : 85 'a line.' [M. T. C. *bari, bare.*]

வலவை=நாணிலி, a shameless person, 268. Said to be a priest of a demon temple. [Comp. இனியா நாற்பது, 3.]

வல் VAL, *power.* [S. बल्, and Āryan cognate forms. Comp. வள், வண், பெலன், பல். Also ஒல்லு. T. *valadu.* C. *balu.*]

I. வல் (வன், வற்), *adj.* powerful, hard, cruel, 331. [So வன்சொல் is opposed to இன்சொல். N. N. 18. K. 99. K. வன்கண், வன்கண்மை. *Ēl.* 23.]

வல்லூற்று, a spring in the rock, 263.

II. வலி, strength, 53, 85. Ch. iv. அறன்வலி, the might of virtue.

III. வல்|லே, *adv.*=விரைந்து, promptly, 4. [Jī. Chin. i. 236. T. *vala.* M.]

IV. வல|ம், the right hand side, 388.

V. வல்|லுதல், the being able :=is permissible, 309. [As from *v.* வல்லு. M. *vallu.*]

வல்|லை, thou art one able, 398. [G. 93.] வல்|லது, it hath power. [G. 93.]
வற்|று [வல்+து], a thing possessing ability, 343, 348.
வல்|லவள், a capable woman, 383. வல்|லவர், strong, violent persons, 279.
வன்|கழுகு, the cruel vulture, 48. வன்|காய், heavy fruit, 203.

VI. வன்|மை, ability : வல்லமை, திறம் (=சதுரப்பாடு), 313.

VII. வலை, a net, 331. [C. *bale.* T. *vala.* M. Comp. வளை, and வலி=' *draw.*']

வல்சி, food : உணவு, 328.

வவ்வு, *v.* (§ 62) snatch away : கவ்வு.

வவ்வார், they (can)not snatch away, 134.

K. வழ் VAṚ, *pass on, slip, glide by.* [Comp. ஒழு. M. பழ.]

I. வழ|ங்கு, *v.* (§ 62) expend, give, 9, 276, 277.

Used as a *v. intr.* and *tr.* (1) *be in use, pass current;* (2) *use, spend.* So செல், செலுத்து.

வழங்குமின், 6. [G. 84.]

[T. 21 : ' வருவாயுட்கால்வழங்கி, spending a fourth of one's income.'
T. 5 : ' வழங்காத்துறை, an unused ford.']

II. வழி, a way: நெறி, 311. [M., C. Comp. வரி and வரை.]

வழிபடு, be devoted to, wait upon, 309; manner, 102. [Comp. *Ēl.* 2: 'வழிவந்தார், men of undeviating obedience.']

III. வழு, *n.* a slip, mistake, fault, 253. [M.]

வழு|க்கு, *v.* (§ 62) slip, escape from, 71.

வழு|க்கு, *n.* fault, slip, 362.

IV. வழு|ம்பு, fat, 46. [M.] Sliminess, fault, 352.

V. வழு|துணை, brinjāl: *Solanum Indicum.* =வழு|தலை, கத்தரி, 264. [M. *varudina.*]

வள் VAḶ. [Comp. வல். S. वल्, बल. M., T.]

I. வள், *adj.* strong: வல், 198, or கூரிய, sharp.

II. வண்|மை=கொடை, உபகாரம், ஈகை, liberality, 269, 279.

வள்ளன்மை, liberality, 386. [வள்ளல்+மை. M. Comp. *Ēl.* 2. See N. M. K. 16:

'வளப்பாத்தியுள் வளரும் வண்மை:

Liberality grows in the flower-bed of abundance.' Here √VAḶ is well illustrated.]

III. வளம், abundance, 103, 367. [S. फल. M. Comp. வளர். Lat. *al.*]

[The commoner form is வளமை, as in the following (comp. 102, 119):

N. M. K. 79: 'சாவாத இல்லை பிறந்த உயிரெல்லாம்;
தாவாத இல்லை வலிகளும்;—மூவா
திளமை இசைந்தாரும் இல்லை;—வளமையில்
கேடின்றிச் சென்றாரும் இல்.

There are none undying of all that have been born;
there are no powers that decay not;
there are none that have attained a youth that grows not old;
there are none that have gone on in abundance that knew no destruction.']

IV. வளி, whirlwind, wind, 19, 108. [M. Comp. விண்டு. S. वा.]

V. வளை, a bracelet; and *by met.* a lady. [S. वलय. See வண். C. D. G. p. 460.]

பெய்வளாய், thou who wearest bracelets, 47. [G. 93.]

[N. N.: 'பொன்செய்ததிர்வளையாய்!
Thou adorned with twinkling bracelets of gold.']

VI. *v.* 'bend;' as *n.* 'a rat-hole.'

n. வளை|வு, 'a bend.'

[N. N.: 'மேருவரைக்கும் வந்தன்றுவளைவு, even to mount Meru came a twist.']

வற் VARR, *dry*. [Comp. வெறு, வரு. M., T., C.]

I. வற, *v.* (§ 66) grow dry, fail, 104, 232.

II. வறு, *adj.* empty.

வறு|மை, poverty, 95, 251.

வறு|ங்கோட்டி, ignorant assembly, 1, 155.

வறி|ஞர், paupers := வறியர், வறியோர். [G. 121.]

III. வற்று, *v.* (§ 62) dry up.

வற்றி, (the body) having become emaciated, 78.

வற்றிய, dried, 256.

[வறன் = parched land.
கலித். i. 8 : 'வறனுழுகாஞ்சில் = the ploughshare that ploughs a dry soil.']

வற்று, see வல்.

வன் VAN, *adorn*. [A variation of வண், வர்ண. S. वर्ण्.]

வன = அழகிய, beautiful, 397.

வன|ப்பு = அழகு (as if from a *v.* வன), adornment, grace ; beauty, 53. Comp. எழில், அழகு, and *Ēl.* 2.

[வனப்பு is used in a remarkable way in T. 78 :

'வனப்பாகுந்தீமை மனத்தினும் வாயினுஞ் சொல்லாமை,

The not uttering with mind or mouth an evil thing though seemingly beautiful.' (*Cor loquitur!*)]

வா, see வ.

வாக்கு = தன்மை, manner, appearance, 395. [Comp. T. *vāṭṭu*. It really is S. वाक् = 'speech.']

வா|ங்கு, *v.* (§ 62) obtain, receive. [Allied to வாய் ?]

பின்வாங்கு, draw back, 396.

வாட் VĀḌ.

வாடு, *v.* (§ 62) fade away, shrivel up, 269. [Comp. வற். M., C., T., TU. In C. *baḍu* = 'thin, poor.' In T. see *vaḍa* (வாடை) = 'hot wind.' (S. उदच्.)]

வாதி, *v.* (§ 64) afflict, coerce, 66. [S. बाध्, वाध्. Comp. வேதனை. C. *bādhe*. M. *bādha*, *bādhi*. பாடு, பீடு, பீடை.]

வா|ய் VĀY. [Comp. S. वहिस्, वास, वाह्, वा. M. C. *bāyi*. T. *vā*, *vāyi*. See வாயில் = வாசல் ; வை, வையம்.]

I. வாய், *v.* (§ 64) obtain, possess ; prosper.

In 58 எரிவாய் நிரயம் may be (1) 'the drear abode' where fire rages (G. 153); or (2) 'the place of fire;' or (3) 'fiery-mouthed hell.'

In 134 some say வாய்த்து ஈயில் = 'if possessing it you impart it.'

II. வாய், n. 1. PLACE, 279; under guard of swords, 362.

2. Entrance, 59; desire that has five inlets, 47.

வாய்க்கால், a channel, 218.

3. Mouth, 8, 59 (நாக்கு), 63, 66, 70, 156, 157, 396.

வாய்ச்சொல், 115, 321.

4. Beginning: நாள்வாய் = the morning, 207.

5. A sign of locative case: கைவாய், 59.

III. வாய்|மை, reality; truth. (p. 1.)

[வாய் = truth : सत्य.

K. T. I. 21: 'அவற்றுள் யாவோ வாயின, which of them are true?'

This is the title of ch. xxx in K. In this work மெய்ம்மை is its equivalent.

Comp. T. 78: 'துணிவார் தொழில் அகற்றும் வாய்மையுடைமை,

Truth, (reality of character) which makes to prosper the work you have resolved to do.']

K. வாரி = பொருள்வரவு, income, 370. [Comp. वार, वारि. ? From வா; but see v. வாரு.]

வார், see வ.

வால் VĀL.

K. வால் [வான். Comp. விள், பால், வாள், வெள். M.]

(1) Purity, 232; whiteness, 206.

வாலிது, what is pure, white, 258.

(2) Tail, 213. [M., C., T., TU. See வளை. S. वाल, बाल. GR. οὐρά.]

வாவல், n. = (வெளவால்), a bat, 261. [M. *vavvāl*; from வவ்வு.]

வாழ் VĀṚ. [Comp. வழ், பழ்; பிழை. S. भाग्य; वाह्. C. *bāḷu*. M., TU. T. *vāḍu* (ஆடு), *bratuku*.]

K. வாழ், v. (§ 57) live; live a prosperous life, 12, 31, 32, 40, 74, 96, 105, 106, 119, 122, 130, 192, 194, 202, 242, 264, 281, 288, 290, 296, 365, 383.

வாழை, n. the plantain (*Musa Paradisiaca*). ? 'The flourishing one.'

வாழ்|மின், flourish ye! 183. வாழ்|ப, they will exist, 289.
வாழ்|நாள் [see நாள்] = ஆயுள், 4, 22, 32, 330.
வாழ்|க்கை, 102, 288, 305. வாழ்|நர், 222. வாழ்|வு, 369.
இல்வாழ்பேய், a devil in the home, 363.

வாள் VĀḶ, *bright.* [M., C., T., TU. See ஒள், வெள், விள், வால். S. भा, भाल.]

I. வாள், *n.*

(1) Light, 176.

(2) A sword; the bright, keen weapon, 129, 191, 386.
வாட்கண்ணாய்! 358, 362. [But it may be ஆள் = 'husband.']

II. வாள் must be = 'speak,' though only found in the following negative forms:

வாளா and வாளாதே = சொல்லாமல், silently, 30, 325.

K. வான் [see வால்] purity, exaltation, brightness, 224.
வானம், *n.* [C. √BA = 'swell;' *bān.* T. *vāna* = 'rain;' *vānu*, 'fashion'] heaven, sky, cloud, 269; (p. 1.) 10, 38, 69, 80, 113, 125, 137, 142.
வானகம், heavenly world, 300. [அகம்.]

[T. 16: 'நட்டான், he who has established reputation.']

விசும்பு = ஆகாயம், the sky, 151, 176.
= விண்ணுலகம், heaven, 373.

[S. विपुव = 'the equinox;' विष्. In A. C. *visupu* = 'radiance.']

விசை, force, impetus, 152, 224.

[M. C. *bese.* T. *vese* (*vēyyu*). Comp. வீசு. Lat. VIS.]

விச்சை, corruption of வித்தை, 134. ஆரியமொழிச்சிதைவு = விஞ்சை.

விட் VIḌ. [T. *viḍ, uḍu, ūḍ.* M. *viḍ.* TU. *buḍ.* C. BIḌ. Comp. S. विडी. இடு, ஊடு.]

I. விடு, *v.* (§ 68) LEAVE.

Depart, pass away, 171.
Become, result in (with ஆய், ஆகி), 128, 188, 200, 357.
Prove to be, 107.
Renounce, abandon, 44, 45, 75, 109, 224, 225, 226, 373.

Send forth, 101; divulge, 230.

An auxiliary, 8, 28, 38, 72, 88, 97, 99, 189, 255, 356.

[Comp. H. B. § 254.]

[விடுபோக்கு, § 97 ☞.]

கைவிடு, abandon, 43, 76.

II. *v.* (§ 64) cause to leave.

(விடுக்கும்வினை=போகூழ் in K. 371), cause to depart; dismiss, 93, 143.

விடுப்ப=விடுக்க, when they dismiss.

III. வீடு, *n.* freedom, liberation; heaven: முத்தி, 59 note. (§ 190.) [In M.='house, freehold.' C. *bīḍu*, 'a temporary residence.' விடுதி.]

IV. விடர், a fissure, mountain-cleft: கமர், மலைப்பிளப்பு, முழை. [M.=விடவு. Comp. S. विदल.]

விண்(ணு), the sky, 226, 233. [Comp. வான். M. *viṇṇu*. T. *vinnu*. ? S. विष्णु. √விள் (விண்டு), 'expand.']

[Jī. Chin. i. 262: 'வேந்தன்போய் விண்ணோர்க்கு விருந்தாயினனே, The king departed and became a guest of the heavenly ones.']

K. விது|ப்பு, desire; eagerness, undue haste; trepidation, 370. (=துளக்கு in 371.) [Comp. விரு|ம்பு, விழை, விறை. M. *viduku*='be overhasty.' Comp. S. विधुर.]

வித்தகம் [S. वित्तक, √विद्]=ஞானம், learning, wisdom, 315.

வித்து, *n.*=விதை, விரை, seed, 38, 183, 315. [S. बीज. C. *bittu*. M.]

T. 80: 'துற்றின்கட் டூவிவித்து, seed scattered in a thicket.'

As verb, வித்து, வித்திடு=விதை, 243.

Jī. Chin. xiii. 164: 'உயிர் எனுநிலத்துவித்தி, sowing in the field of life.'

விம் VIM, *swell.* Comp. விண்.

விம்மு, *v.* (§ 62).

(1) Swell. விம்ம, tightly, 392.

(2) Sob, 394. [M.]

விய VIYA, *admire.* [வியம்='greatness.' S. वियत्.]

K. விய, *v.* (§ 66) wonder at, admire, praise, 267, 339.

வியப்ப=வியக்க.

வியத்தக்கான் = வியக்கத்-, he is one to be wondered at, 325. [G. 41.]
[T. 38: வியந்து = மெச்சிக்கொண்டு, 'extol.']

விரகு [S. व्रक] means; tact, 279.
விரதம் [S. व्रत] = தவம், vowed austerities, 57.
விரல் [√விரி], a finger, toe; claw, 123, 218, 237, 394. [T. vrē|lu. C. bera|ḷu. M.]

விர் VIR. [See விழ், விறை, விருந்து.]

I. விரவு, v. (§ 62) commingle.
விராஅஅய் = விரவி, being uncertain — mingling warmth and indifference—in friendship, 246.
விரவார், enemies, 88. [So விரவலர். N. N. 9.]

II. விரி, v. (§§ 57, 64) expand; expound, 164, 341. [S. वृ, बृह्. T., M. C. biri. Comp. பிரி, விள்.]
விரிநீர், expanding, blowing, 236.
விரி = விரியன், a viper, 240.

III. விரு|ம்பு, v. (§ 62) desire, love, 200, 221.
விரு|ப்பு, affection, 210. [M.]

விருந்தினன், a guest, 286. [From விருந்து, 'a banquet.' M. virunnu. C. and T. vindu. Perhaps S. विन्दु; the usual word is अतिथि = அதிதி.]

வில் VIL.

I. வில், a bow, 297, 395: [p. I.—See வள். GR. βιός = S. ज्या (Benfey).]

II. வில|ங்கு. [M.]
(1) v. (§ 62) stand off, recede, fail, 59, 333.
(2) n. a beast, irrational being, 76, 121, 315, 375.

III. விலை, price: கிரயம். [M. vila. C. bele. T. vela, viluva.]
விலைபெறும், will fetch a high price, 115.

K. விழ் VIẒ, *fall*.

K. I. விழி, v. (§ 64) open the eyes, 302. [Vulg. முழி, மிழி. Comp. விள், விரி, மினுக்கு. T. minukku. M. miẓi. S. मिष्, मील्.]

K. II. விழு, *adj.* excellent: சிறந்த. [Comp. மிளிர்.]

விழுச்செல்வம், 269. [So விழுத்திணை, 'high family.' T. 9.]

விழுமிது, விழுமிய = சிறந்தது, excellent, 133, 217, 228, [as if from a verb விழுமு.]

விழுமியோர், the worthy, 64, 159, 300.

In 329 விழுப்பிணி = a great, fatal disease. See 219: விளியாவருநோய்; and K. 776. [Comp. விழு = fall; வீழ், வீ.]

K. III. விழை, *v.* [விரு|ம்பு, வீழ், விது; S. प्रिय, पृ, प्री].

1. (§ 57) desire eagerly, 109, 339, 361.

[K. T. i. 18: 'இளமையும் காமமும் ஓரங்கு பெற்றார்
வளமை விழைதக்க துண்டோ....

Is wealth *a fit object of desire* to those who have gained the joys of youth and love combined?']

2. (§ 64) 330; but see இழை = go about to, scheme: சூழ். (Comp. T. 29.)

விழை|வு, desire.

விழைவிற்று, it is desirable, 233.

[In T. 95 விழைவு = பேராசை. And in T. 93 = வேட்கை.
'பொருளல்ல காதற் படுக்கும் விழைவு,
The eager desire that subjects (men) to the love of unreal things.' Comp. K. 351. விழை|ச்சு, *n.* = *lust*, in *Nīti*. 89.]

K. விள் VII., *open out.* [S. वि.]

1. விள்|ளல் = பிரிதல், separation, 76. [M. *viḷḷ.* T. *vir, vīl, vrīl.* S. विल्, विल्. Comp. விழ், பிள், விரி, பிரி.]

K. II. விள|க்கு, *v.* (§ 62) enlighten, 47; make illustrious, 132. [M. C. T. *vela.* TU. BOḶ-*pu.* (Comp. OḶ.)]

n. a lamp, 51, 189, 361, 371.

விளக்குறு, be a light to, 148.

[தெரியும் விழியிலார்க்கேது விளக்கு, what is the use of a lamp to a blind man?]

III. விளி, *v.* (§ 57). [Comp. விழ், இள்.]

K. (1) Perish, cause, 166, 198, 219, 266.

விளி|வு, a perishing, 166.

K. (2) 'Summon' (or 'dying' *with shame*), 253. [Comp. அழை. M., TU. *buḷ.* T. *pil.* Lat. AP-PEL-L.]

K. IV. விளை, *v.* (§ 57) grow, 367. [Comp. விள், வெளி, வயல், வள், வளர். M. *viḷa.* C. *beḷe.*]

விளைநிலத்து, 133, 356. [G. 153.]

v. (§ 64) produce, 218.

[Jī. Chin. xiii. 164 : விளையுள் = பயன், 'produce.']

V. விள, விள|ங்|காய், wood-apple (*Feronia elephantum*).

விளா, விளவு are the usual nom. forms; as *adj.* விளம் and விளாம், 103, 261, 328.

[This is the 'Gum arabic tree.' See Ainslie, i. 161. M. *viḷā.* C. *beḷavu, bēḷa.* Or *Aegle marmelos.* S. बिल्व (बिल्).]

விற, விறல் [from *v.* § 66, விற. Comp. இற. Comp. also S. वीर] abundance, 117; greatness, 348, 369.

Nig. விறலென்ப வலிவெற்றிப்பேர்.

வின் [மின்] VIṈ.

வினை, (*n.*) 1. action, function, 43: தொழில், கர்மம், செய்வினை. [M. *vina, mina.* TU. *ben.* C. *vinike.* T. *vin*, 'hear.' வினு = 'question.' Comp. S. विनय.]

வினைதீயார், men whose deeds are evil, 172 (= வினையில். G. 152).

ஆள்வினை, manly effort, 195.

வினைவினை = தீவினை, 3, 33, 58, 81, 101, 105, 265.

கடுவினை, 124. கொடுவினை, 124.

நல்வினை, merit, goodness, = புண்ணியம், opposed to பாவம், 51, 93.

அறவினை (see அறம்), virtuous action, 326, 332.

இறைவினை, 132.

பழவினை, old deeds, destiny, ch. xi, = ஊழ், 123.

முன்னைவினை, 107.

தீவினை, evil, demerit, ch. xiii.

2. Deeds; merit or demerit, 108.

[கர்மம், வினை, ஊழ்.

'எழுத்தினு னீக்கரதென் னூலொழியா தேத்தி
வழுத்தினன் மாறாது, மாண்ட—ஒழுக்கினல்
வோராமை சாலவுங் கண்டார் பெருந்தவம்
சாராமை சாலப் புலை.

It (destined effect of deeds done in former birth) is not removed by learning; it ceases not by thought; if you praise and pray it changes not; its removal is not possible by "decorum" (K. ch. xiv). Seeing this clearly, not to attach oneself to strict penance (K. ch. xxvii) is complete degradation.' *Ēl.* 39.

In T. 36: 'தான் உடன்பாடின்றி வினை ஆக்கும் என்பான்,

(*The fool*) who says that *fate* will do it without his own co-operation.']

வீ vī. [Comp. வீடு from விடு, விழு.]

I. வீ, *v.* perish, 106 : இற.

[So வீடு. T. 22 : ‘இம்மூன்றும் வித்தற வீடும் பிறப்பு,

The three are the seed : when these cease “birth” will die.’

‘பூளைவீபுரை மணிபுயற்குத் தேம்பிய . . . தாமரை,

The lotus which fades before the dew-cloud (light) as the flower (வீ) of the Pūḷai.’]

II. வீடு [see விடு], 59.

III. வீ|ங்கு, *v.* (§ 62) swell, 117. [M. T. *vāchu.* வீசு.]

IV. வீழ்=விழு, கெடு, be ruined, 14, 17; fall, 58, 300, 369.

[C. BIḶ. TU. BŪR-*u.* T. *vīḍu.* M.]

வீழ்(ந்)தக்கது, is ready (fit) to perish [தகு], 102.

வீழ்நாள், a failing day, i.e. the failure of a day, 22.

n.=வீழுது, the falling roots of the banyan, 197=விழுது. [M. Comp. T. 33.]

வெ VE, வெம் VEM, வே VĒ. [§ 131.*f.* T. TU. *bey.* C. *bisu.* Comp. S. वेग. C. *benki*=‘fire.’]

I. வெ|ம்=கொடிய. (G. 121.)

வெங்|களம், slaughter-house, 16.

வெங்|கருணை, savoury food, 207, 210.

[*Ēl.* 11 : ‘வெங்கோலன், a cruel oppressor.’]

II. வெ|டி, fear, 364 (வெரு). [M. ‘explosion.’ T. *vera.*]

III. வெ|ம்பு, *v.* (§ 62)=கொதி, glow with heat, 89.

[கலித். i. 10 : ‘வேரோடுமரம் வெம்ப,

So that the tree was dried up with heat to its root.’

Jī. Chin. iii. 15 : ‘கூற்றும் ஒளித்துலைந்தொழிய வெம்பி,

Blazing so that even *Yaman* would flee confounded and hide himself.’]

IV. வெ|ப்பம், heat, 68.

V. வெ|ய்ய, fiercely, hotly, 33.

VI. வெ|யில், sunshine, 171. [M., C. *bisil.*]

VII. வெ|ஃகு, *v.* (§ 62) desire, 17. (G. 92.)

K. VIII. வெ|குளு, *v.* [§ 56 (III)] be wroth, 64.

வெகுளி, wrath, 68, ch. vii. [M.]

T. 46 : ‘சிறிக்கறவி வெகுண்டுரைப்பான் பள்ளி,

The school of him who growing speaks in angry, passionate tones.’

T. 28 : ‘வெல்வது வேண்டி வெகுண்டிருக்கும் கோன்பிலை,

The unchastened man who desiring victory (in argument waxes wroth).’

T. 40 : ‘வெகுளிதணுக்கும் விறல், the power that restrains wrath.’

IX. வெ|ருவு, *v.* (§ 62) be startled with fear, 399. [வெருளு. M. C. *bedaru.*]

X. வெ|ந்தை, 289.

[Generally said to be a kind of grain; but seems= வெந்தது + ஐ, a cooked meal. See வே.]

XI. வெடி, an explosion; report; fear. [See வெ. M., TU. Comp. விள், விடு.]

வெடிபட, fear, 364: 'so as to inspire awe.'

XII. வெ|ருகு, a tom-cat. Infl. base வெருக்கு, 210. [§ 131. *c.* M. 'a civet-cat.' C. *bekku.*]

XIII. வெல்(லு), *v.* (§ 70) conquer. [M. *vellu.* Comp. T. *velayu,* and விளை. S. विजय.]

வென்|றி, victory, 315. [இ.] Opp. தோல்வி. [M. *venni, vetti.*]

வெள் VEḶ, *white.* [M., C. *bili.* TU. *boḷ.* T. VEḶ|I, VEL|LA. வெள்ளி = *Venus,* and *silver.*]

I. வெள், வெண், white, 217 [='useless,' in T. 32: வெண்மொழி. Connected with வீண். Comp. S. पलित; GR. πελ-, πολι-; Lat. PALL].

வெள்|ளறிவினர், the ignorant, 375.

வெண்|டலை, skull, 50 (note).

II. வெண்|மை = அறியாமை, ignorance, 269.

[Ji. Chin. i. 303: 'வெண்டலைபயின்றகாடு, the desert place where skulls lay thick.']

III. வெளி, the exterior. [M.]

வெளிப்படு, come abroad, be revealed, 88.

வெற் VERR.

I. வெறு, வெறும், வெற்று, *adj.* empty, *bare.* [M., T., C. *baru, bari.* TU. *varu.* Comp. வறு.]

வெறு|மை, poverty, 329. [Comp. வறு.]

II. வெறு, *v.* (§ 64) detest, 161, 172, 222. [M.]

III. வெறி [C., M., T.='intoxication'].

= வெறியாட்டு, Bachanalian dance, devil dance, 16.

= மணம், fragrance, 180.

IV. வெற்பு, a hill. [C. *beṭṭa.*]

வெற்பன், வெற்ப, O Lord of the hills! 142, 226.
[Comp. நாட, சேர்ப்ப.]

வே vē, see வெ.

I. வே, வே|கு, *v.* (§ 58) burn. [C. BĒ|*yu*. M.]

வேம் (§ 72)=வேகும், 35, 180. See வெந்தை, 289.

II. வேம்பு, the *margosa* (Port. 'Amargozeira') or *Nīm* tree: *Azadirachta Indica*, 112, 210, 239, 244. [Comp. S. निम्ब; but see C. D. G. p. 101. C. *bēvu*. T. *vēm*. See Ainslie, Materia Indica, vol. ii. p. 453 *etc.*; and Ellis, p. 235.]

III. வேர், *v.* (§ 64) perspire; fume with anger, 64. [Comp. வியர். C. *bevaru*, *bem*|*ar*. M. VĒR. S. स्वेद.]

IV. வேங்கை [M. *vēṅṅa*].

(1) The Kino tree: *Pterocarpus bilobus*, 180.

(2) Tiger: புலி, 300, 399='cruel-paw.' [S. व्याघ्र.]

V. வேல், *n.* a weapon, lance. [From வெல், 'overcome.' Comp. எய். (T. *vēy*.) M. T. *ballemu*. C. *balleya*.]

=வேலாயுதம், 213.

வேன்|மகன் = வேலைத்தாங்கிய பூசாரி, the sacrificing priest, 'the javelin-man,' 16.

வேற்|கண்ணள், she whose eyes are like a dart, 17, 44, 265.

வேகம் [S. वेग] wrath, 348.

வேசை [S. वेश्या] a wanton, 371.

வேதிகை [S. वेदिका] a raised altar, 96.

வேள் (வேண், வேட்), VĒḶ, ='desire.' [√VE. T. *vēḍi*.]

I. வேள் [√வேட்|கிறேன், -டேன், -பேன், -க. § 70] long for, love, 215.

II. வேண்டு, *v.* (§ 62) desire, pray for, 103, 109, 159, 187, 222, 300. [M. *vēṇ*, *vēl*. TU. *bōḍu*. C. BE-*ku*, BE-*ḍ*|*a*, BĒḌ|*u*. T. VĒḌ-*u*, *val*. Comp. WANT.]

Impersonal:

வேண்டும், is needed, 41, 220.

வேண்டா, is not needed (§ 110) 158, 167. [வேண்டாம்=வேண்டாவாம்.]

III. வேளாண்மை, liberality, 207. [ஆள்.]

IV. வேட்|கை, desire, 59. [M. VĒḶ|*cha.*]

[For வேள் compare K. Rām. I. xxii. 103 :

'வேட்டவர் வேட்டபின் வேந்தனு மேனைக்
கூட்டிய கீர்த்திகொ டுத்திலன் அல்லால்
ஈட்டிய மெய்ப்பொருள் இயாவுள எவ்லாம்
வேட்டவர் வேட்டவை வேண்டள வீந்தான்.

After the *lovers* were *wedded* the king distributed all his rightly-accumulated wealth; giving to all that *desired* what they *desired* to the limit of their *desires*, reserving only the renown he had gathered in the former days.']

வேழம், an elephant : யானை, 358.

[Anything hollow. See வேய், வேணு. M.

Nig. வேழமே கரும்பியானை கொழுக்கச்சி வேணு நாற்பேர்.

1. Sugar-cane; 2. ELEPHANT; 3. A reed; 4. A bambu. S. वेणु, वेत्र.]

K. வேறு VĒRR, *diverse, other.* [வேறு. See மறு, மாறு. M. T. C. *bēre.* S. भेद, भिद्; वृ. Lat. VAR.]

I. வேறு. This word is considered to be a finite verb, of the class of குறிப்புவினை. [G. 93; *Nannūl*, 339.] It is noun, adverb, or adj. with ellipsis.

(I) With ஆகு, படு, இரு : 3, 183, 210, 236, 266, 345.

(II) As predicate : 127, 264, 318.

(III) With அல்ல : 370, 371.

[T. 5 : 'வேற்றூர், a strange town.']

K. II. வேற்|றுமை=வேறுபாடு, distinction, difference, 75.

வை VAI, *place.* [M.]

I. வை=வயின=வாய், place : இடம்.

Hence வையம், the earth, 94, 109, 111, 114, 230, 238, 264. This is, perhaps, for வையகம் (அகம்), 80.

II. வையம், a chariot : தேர், வாகனம், 350. [S. वह्, वाह.]

[K. Rām. I. xx. 32 : 'வையம்பற்றியமங்கையர், the maidens who attended the *chariot.*']

III. வை, straw, 234. (TU. *bai.*)=வைக்கோல்.

[K. 435 : 'வைத்துறு, a stack of straw.']

IV. வை, *v.* (§ 58) abuse, 156, 219, 325, 356 : திட்டு : opp. to புகழ். [C. *bai*=வாய்='*mouth.*']

V. வை, *v.* (§ 64) place, put, 1, 39, 46, 293, 394. [M. *vckka.* Comp. பெய், பை.]

Store up (with ஈட்டு), 10, 273.
Keep in restraint, 122, 279.
Regard (as important), 50, 133, 163.

வைப்புழி=*வைக்குமிடம்*, 134. [வை + ப்பு. K. 226.]

வைத்தீர்! ye (who have) accumulated, 6. Finite verb used as participial noun:=*வைத்தநீங்கள்*. [Comp. 126.]

VI. வை|கல், see 39. [? S. वैकाल, from वि + काल='afternoon.' TU. *baiya*='evening.' C. *baigu.*]

1. =நாள்; hence வைகலும், *daily:* நாடோறும், 7, 39, 94, 105, 125. [K. 83.]
See especially 169. [Comp. நாள், பகல்.]

2. நாட்கழிவு or கழிவுநாள், the lapse of the day, or the passing day, 39.

3. விடியல், the dawn, 39.

VII. வை|கு, *v.* (§ 62)=tarry the night: இராத்தங்கு; be, spent (time), 169 [=போ, செல், கழி, ஒழி].

[In Jī. Chin. i. 76: 'அடிசில் வைகல் ஆயிரம்,
A thousand houses for lodging and food.']

வை|கும், it will tarry, 39.
வை|குதல், a halt, 39. [M., TU.]

வைரம் (வயிரம்) [S. वज्र], பூண், கிம்புரி, 358.

GENERAL INDEX.

THE END.

Clarendon Press, Oxford.

SELECT LIST OF STANDARD WORKS.

1. DICTIONARIES.

A New English Dictionary on Historical Principles, founded mainly on the materials collected by the Philological Society. Edited by James A. H. Murray, LL.D. Imperial 4to. In Parts, price 12*s.* 6*d.* each.

Vol. I (A and B), half-morocco, 2*l.* 12*s.* 6*d.*
Part IV, Section 2, **C—CASS**, beginning Vol. II, price 5*s.*
Part V, **CAST—CLIVY**, price 12*s.* 6*d.*
Part VI, **CLO—CONSIGNER**, price 12*s.* 6*d.*

Vol. III, Part I, **E—EVERY**, edited by Henry Bradley, M.A., with the co-operation of Dr. Murray, price 12*s.* 6*d.*

An Etymological Dictionary of the English Language, arranged on an Historical Basis. By W. W. Skeat, Litt.D. *Second Edition.* 4to. 2*l.* 4*s.*

A Middle-English Dictionary, containing Words used by English Writers from the Twelfth to the Fifteenth Century. By Francis Henry Stratmann. A new edition, re-arranged, revised, and enlarged by Henry Bradley. 4to, half-bound, 1*l.* 11*s.* 6*d.*

An Anglo-Saxon Dictionary, based on the MS. collections of the late Joseph Bosworth, D.D. Edited and enlarged by Prof. T. N. Toller, M.A., Owens College, Manchester. Parts I-III. A-SÁR. 4to, stiff covers, 15*s.* each. Part IV, § 1, SÁR-SWÍÐRIAN. Stiff covers, 8*s.* 6*d.*

An Icelandic-English Dictionary, based on the MS. collections of the late Richard Cleasby. Enlarged and completed by G. Vigfússon, M.A. 4to. 3*l.* 7*s.*

A Greek-English Lexicon, by H. G. Liddell, D.D., and Robert Scott, D.D. *Seventh Edition, Revised and Augmented.* 4to. 1*l.* 16*s.*

A Latin Dictionary, founded on Andrews' edition of Freund's Latin Dictionary, revised, enlarged, and in great part rewritten by Charlton T. Lewis, Ph.D., and Charles Short, LL.D. 4to. 1*l.* 5*s.*

A Sanskrit-English Dictionary. Etymologically and Philologically arranged, with special reference to Greek, Latin, German, Anglo-Saxon, English, and other cognate Indo-European Languages. By Sir M. Monier-Williams, D.C.L. 4to. 4*l.* 14*s.* 6*d.*

Thesaurus Syriacus: collegerunt Quatremère, Bernstein, Lorsbach, Arnoldi, Agrell, Field, Roediger: edidit R. Payne Smith, S.T.P. Vol. I, containing Fasc. I–V, sm. fol. 5*l.* 5*s.*

Fasc. VI. 1*l.* 1*s.* Fasc. VII. 1*l.* 11*s.* 6*d.* Fasc. VIII. 1*l.* 16*s.*

2. LAW.

Anson. *Principles of the English Law of Contract, and of Agency in its Relation to Contract.* By Sir W. R. Anson, D.C.L. *Sixth Edition.* 8vo. 10*s.* 6*d.*

—— *Law and Custom of the Constitution.* 2 vols. 8vo.

Part I. Parliament. *Second Edition.* 12*s.* 6*d.* *Just Published.*

Part II. The Crown. 14*s.*

Baden-Powell. *Land-Systems of British India;* being a Manual of the Land-Tenures, and of the Systems of Land-Revenue Administration prevalent in the several Provinces. By B. H. Baden-Powell, C.I.E. 3 vols. 8vo. 3*l.* 3*s.*

Digby. *An Introduction to the History of the Law of Real Property.* By Kenelm E. Digby, M.A. *Fourth Edition.* 8vo. 12*s.* 6*d.*

Grueber. *Lex Aquilia.* The Roman Law of Damage to Property: being a Commentary on the Title of the Digest 'Ad Legem Aquiliam' (ix. 2). By Erwin Grueber, Dr. Jur., M.A. 8vo. 10*s.* 6*d.*

Hall. *International Law.* By W. E. Hall, M.A. *Third Edition.* 8vo. 22*s.* 6*d.*

Holland and Shadwell. *Select Titles from the Digest of Justinian.* By T. E. Holland, D.C.L., and C. L. Shadwell, B.C.L. 8vo. 14*s.*

Also sold in Parts, in paper covers, as follows:—

Part I. Introductory Titles. 2*s.* 6*d.*

Part II. Family Law. 1*s.*

Part III. Property Law. 2*s.* 6*d.*

Part IV. Law of Obligations (No. 1). 3*s.* 6*d.*

Part IV. Law of Obligations (No. 2). 4*s.* 6*d.*

Holland. *Elements of Jurisprudence.* By T. E. Holland, D.C.L. *Fifth Edition.* 8vo. 10*s.* 6*d.*

—— *The European Concert in the Eastern Question;* a Collection of Treaties and other Public Acts. Edited, with Introductions and Notes, by T. E. Holland, D.C.L. 8vo. 12*s.* 6*d.*

—— *Gentilis, Alberici, De Iure Belli Libri Tres.* Edidit T. E. Holland, I.C.D. Small 4to, half-morocco, 21*s.*

Holland. *The Institutes of Justinian*, edited as a recension of the Institutes of Gaius, by T. E. Holland, D.C.L. *Second Edition.* Extra fcap. 8vo. 5*s.*

Markby. *Elements of Law considered with reference to Principles of General Jurisprudence.* By Sir William Markby, D.C.L. *Fourth Edition.* 8vo. 12*s.* 6*d.*

Moyle. *Imperatoris Iustiniani Institutionum Libri Quattuor;* with Introductions, Commentary, Excursus and Translation. By J. B. Moyle, D.C.L. *Second Edition.* 2 vols. 8vo. Vol. I. 16*s.* Vol. II. 6*s.*

—— *Contract of Sale in the Civil Law.* By J. B. Moyle, D.C.L. 8vo. 10*s.* 6*d.*

Pollock and Wright. *An Essay on Possession in the Common Law.* By Sir F. Pollock, M.A., and R. S. Wright, B.C.L. (Now the Hon. Mr. Justice Wright). 8vo. 8*s.* 6*d.*

Poste. *Gaii Institutionum Juris Civilis Commentarii Quattuor;* or, Elements of Roman Law by Gaius. With a Translation and Commentary by Edward Poste, M.A. 8vo. 18*s.*

Raleigh. *An Outline of the Law of Property.* By Thos. Raleigh, M.A. 8vo. 7*s.* 6*d.*

Sohm. *Institutes of Roman Law.* By Rudolph Sohm, Professor in the University of Leipzig. Translated by J. C. Ledlie, B.C.L. With an Introductory Essay by Erwin Grueber, Dr. Jur., M.A. 8vo. 18*s.*

Stokes. *The Anglo-Indian Codes.* By Whitley Stokes, LL.D.

Vol. I. Substantive Law. 8vo. 30*s.*
Vol. II. Adjective Law. 8vo. 35*s.*
First and Second Supplements to the above. 8vo. 6*s.* 6*d.*

Separately, No. 1, 2*s.* 6*d.*; No. 2, 4*s.* 6*d.*

Twiss. *The Law of Nations considered as Independent Political Communities.* By Sir Travers Twiss, D.C.L. Part I. *On the Rights and Duties of Nations in time of Peace.* New Edition. 8vo. 15*s.*

3. HISTORY, BIOGRAPHY, ETC.

Arbuthnot. *The Life and Works of John Arbuthnot, M.D.* By George A. Aitken. 8vo, cloth, with portrait, 16*s.*

Baker's Chronicle. *Chronicon Galfridi le Baker de Swynebroke.* Edited with Notes by Edward Maunde Thompson, Principal Librarian of the British Museum. 4to, stiff covers, 18*s.*; cloth, gilt top, 21*s.*

Bentham. *A Fragment on Government.* By Jeremy Bentham. Edited with an Introduction by F. C. Montague, M.A. 8vo. 7*s.* 6*d.*

Boswell's *Life of Samuel Johnson, LL.D.* Edited by G. Birkbeck Hill, D.C.L. In six volumes, medium 8vo. With Portraits and Facsimiles. Half-bound, 3*l.* 3*s.*

Calendar *of Charters and Rolls* preserved in the Bodleian Library. 8vo. 1*l.* 11*s.* 6*d.*

Carte's *Life of James Duke of Ormond.* 6 vols. 8vo. 1*l.* 5*s.*

Casaubon (Isaac). 1559–1614. By Mark Pattison. 8vo. 16*s.*

Clarendon's *History of the Rebellion and Civil Wars in England.* Re-edited from a fresh collation of the original MS. in the Bodleian Library, with marginal dates and occasional notes, by W. Dunn Macray, M.A., F.S.A. 6 vols. Crown 8vo. 2*l.* 5*s.*

Earle. *Handbook to the Land-Charters, and other Saxonic Documents.* By John Earle, M.A., Professor of Anglo-Saxon in the University of Oxford. Crown 8vo. 16*s.*

Finlay. *A History of Greece from its Conquest by the Romans to the present time,* B. C. 146 to A. D. 1864. By George Finlay, LL.D. A new Edition, revised throughout, and in part re-written, with considerable additions, by the Author, and edited by H. F. Tozer, M.A. 7 vols. 8vo. 3*l.* 10*s.*

Fortescue. *The Governance of England:* otherwise called The Difference between an Absolute and a Limited Monarchy. By Sir John Fortescue, Kt. A Revised Text. Edited, with Introduction, Notes, &c., by Charles Plummer, M.A. 8vo, half-bound, 12*s.* 6*d.*

Freeman. *The History of Sicily from the Earliest Times.*

Vols. I. and II. 8vo, cloth, 2*l.* 2*s.*

Vol. III. The Athenian and Carthaginian Invasions. 8vo, cloth, 24*s.*

—— *History of the Norman Conquest of England; its Causes and Results.* By E. A. Freeman, D.C.L. In Six Volumes. 8vo. 5*l.* 9*s.* 6*d.*

Freeman. *The Reign of William Rufus and the Accession of Henry the First.* 2 vols. 8vo. 1*l.* 16*s.*

—— *A Short History of the Norman Conquest of England. Second Edition.* Extra fcap. 8vo. 2*s.* 6*d.*

French Revolutionary Speeches. (See Stephens, H. Morse.)

Gardiner. *The Constitutional Documents of the Puritan Revolution,* 1628–1660. Selected and Edited by Samuel Rawson Gardiner, M.A. Crown 8vo. 9*s.*

Gascoigne's *Theological Dictionary* ('*Liber Veritatum*'): Selected Passages, illustrating the Condition of Church and State, 1403–1458. With an Introduction by James E. Thorold Rogers, M.A. 4to. 10*s.* 6*d.*

Greswell. *History of the Dominion of Canada.* By W. Parr Greswell, M.A. Crown 8vo. With Eleven Maps. 7*s.* 6*d.*

—— *Geography of the Dominion of Canada and Newfoundland.* Crown 8vo. With Ten Maps. 6*s.*

—— *Geography of Africa South of the Zambesi.* With Maps. Crown 8vo. 7*s.* 6*d.*

Gross. *The Gild Merchant;* a Contribution to British Municipal History. By Charles Gross, Ph.D. 2 vols. 8vo. 24*s.*

Hastings. *Hastings and the Rohilla War.* By Sir John Strachey, G.C.S.I. 8vo, cloth, 10*s.* 6*d.*

Hodgkin. *Italy and her Invaders.* With Plates and Maps. By T. Hodgkin, D.C.L. Vols. I–IV, A.D. 376–553. 8vo. 3*l.* 18*s.*

Vols. I. and II. *Second Edition.* 2*l.* 2*s.*

Vols. III. and IV. 1*l.* 16*s.*

—— *The Dynasty of Theodosius;* or, Seventy Years' Struggle with the Barbarians. By the same Author. Crown 8vo. 6*s.*

Hume. *Letters of David Hume to William Strahan.* Edited with Notes, Index, &c., by G. Birkbeck Hill, D.C.L. 8vo. 12s. 6d.

Johnson. *Letters of Samuel Johnson, LL.D.* Collected and edited by G. Birkbeck Hill, D.C.L., Editor of Boswell's 'Life of Johnson' (see Boswell). 2 vols. half-roan, 28s.

Kitchin. *A History of France.* With Numerous Maps, Plans, and Tables. By G. W. Kitchin, D.D. In three Volumes. *Second Edition.* Crown 8vo, each 10s. 6d.

Vol. I. to 1453. Vol. II. 1453–1624. Vol. III. 1624–1793.

Luttrell's *(Narcissus) Diary.* A Brief Historical Relation of State Affairs, 1678–1714. 6 vols. 1l. 4s.

Lucas. *Introduction to a Historical Geography of the British Colonies.* By C. P. Lucas, B.A. With Eight Maps. Crown 8vo. 4s. 6d.

Lucas. *Historical Geography of the British Colonies:*

Vol. I. The Mediterranean and Eastern Colonies (exclusive of India). With Eleven Maps. Crown 8vo. 5s.

Vol. II. The West Indian Colonies. With Twelve Maps. Crown 8vo. 7s. 6d.

Machiavelli. *Il Principe.* Edited by L. Arthur Burd, M.A. With an Introduction by Lord Acton. 8vo. Cloth, 14s.

Ralegh. *Sir Walter Ralegh.* A Biography. By W. Stebbing, M.A. 8vo. 10s. 6d.

Ramsay (Sir J. H.). *Lancaster and York.* A Century of English History (A.D. 1399–1485). By Sir J. H. Ramsay of Bamff, Bart., M.A. With Maps, Pedigrees, and Illustrations. 2 vols. 8vo. 36s.

Ranke. *A History of England, principally in the Seventeenth Century.* By L. von Ranke. Translated under the superintendence of G. W. Kitchin, D.D., and C. W. Boase, M.A. 6 vols. 8vo. 3l. 3s.

Rawlinson. *A Manual of Ancient History.* By George Rawlinson, M.A. *Second Edition.* 8vo. 14s.

Rhŷs. *Studies in the Arthurian Legend.* By John Rhŷs, M.A. 8vo. 12s. 6d.

Ricardo. *Letters of David Ricardo to T. R. Malthus* (1810–1823). Edited by James Bonar, M.A. 8vo. 10s. 6d.

Rogers. *History of Agriculture and Prices in England,* A.D. 1259–1702. By James E. Thorold Rogers, M.A. 6 vols., 8vo. 7l. 2s.

—— *First Nine Years of the Bank of England.* 8vo. 8s. 6d.

—— *Protests of the Lords, including those which have been expunged, from* 1624 *to* 1874; with Historical Introductions. In three volumes. 8vo. 2l. 2s.

Smith's *Wealth of Nations.* With Notes, by J. E. Thorold Rogers, M.A. 2 vols. 8vo. 21s.

Stephens. *The Principal Speeches of the Statesmen and Orators of the French Revolution,* 1789–1795. With Historical Introductions, Notes, and Index. By H. Morse Stephens. 2 vols. Crown 8vo. 21s.

Stubbs. *Select Charters and other Illustrations of English Constitutional History, from the Earliest Times to the Reign of Edward I.* Arranged and edited by W. Stubbs, D.D., Lord Bishop of Oxford. *Seventh Edition.* Crown 8vo. 8*s.* 6*d.*

—— *The Constitutional History of England, in its Origin and Development. Library Edition.* 3 vols. Demy 8vo. 2*l.* 8*s.*

Also in 3 vols. crown 8vo. price 12*s.* each.

—— *Seventeen Lectures on the Study of Medieval and Modern History, delivered at Oxford* 1867–1884. Crown 8vo. 8*s.* 6*d.*

—— *Registrum Sacrum Anglicanum.* An attempt to exhibit the course of Episcopal Succession in England. By W. Stubbs, D.D. Small 4to. 8*s.* 6*d.*

Vinogradoff. *Villainage in England.* Essays in English Mediaeval History. By Paul Vinogradoff, Professor in the University of Moscow. 8vo, half-bound. 16*s.*

Wellesley. *A Selection from the Despatches, Treaties, and other Papers of the Marquess Wellesley, K.G., during his Government of India.* Edited by S. J. Owen, M.A. 8vo. 1*l.* 4*s.*

Wellington. *A Selection from the Despatches, Treaties, and other Papers relating to India of Field-Marshal the Duke of Wellington, K.G.* Edited by S. J. Owen, M.A. 8vo. 1*l.* 4*s.*

Whitelock's *Memorials of English Affairs from* 1625 *to* 1660. 4 vols. 8vo. 1*l.* 10*s.*

4. PHILOSOPHY, LOGIC, ETC.

Bacon. *The Essays.* With Introduction and Illustrative Notes. By S. H. Reynolds, M.A. 8vo, half-bound. 12*s.* 6*d.*

—— *Novum Organum.* Edited, with Introduction, Notes, &c., by T. Fowler, D.D. *Second Edition.* 8vo. 15*s.*

—— *Novum Organum.* Edited, with English Notes, by G. W. Kitchin, D.D. 8vo. 9*s.* 6*d.*

—— *Novum Organum.* Translated by G. W. Kitchin, D.D. 8vo. 9*s.* 6*d.*

Berkeley. *The Works of George Berkeley, D.D., formerly Bishop of Cloyne; including many of his writings hitherto unpublished.* With Prefaces, Annotations, and an Account of his Life and Philosophy. By Alexander Campbell Fraser, LL.D. 4 vols. 8vo. 2*l.* 18*s.*

The Life, Letters, &c., separately, 16*s.*

Bosanquet. *Logic; or, the Morphology of Knowledge.* By B. Bosanquet, M.A. 8vo. 21*s.*

Butler's *Works, with Index to the Analogy.* 2 vols. 8vo. 11*s.*

Fowler. *The Elements of Deductive Logic, designed mainly for the use of Junior Students in the Universities.* By T. Fowler, D.D. *Ninth Edition,* with a Collection of Examples. Extra fcap. 8vo. 3*s.* 6*d.*

—— *The Elements of Inductive Logic, designed mainly for the use of Students in the Universities.* By the same Author. *Fifth Edition.* Extra fcap. 8vo. 6*s.*

Fowler. *The Principles of Morals.* (Introductory Chapters.) By T. Fowler, D.D., and J. M. Wilson, B.D. 8vo, boards, 3*s.* 6*d.*

—— *The Principles of Morals.* Part II. By T. Fowler, D.D. 8vo. 10*s.* 6*d.*

Green. *Prolegomena to Ethics.* By T. H. Green, M.A. Edited by A. C. Bradley, M.A. 8vo. 12*s.* 6*d.*

Hegel. *The Logic of Hegel;* translated from the Encyclopaedia of the Philosophical Sciences. With Prolegomena by W. Wallace, M.A. Crown 8vo. *New Edition in the Press.*

Hume's *Treatise of Human Nature.* Edited, with Analytical Index, by L. A. Selby-Bigge, M.A. Crown 8vo. 9*s.*

Locke's *Conduct of the Understanding.* Edited by T. Fowler, D.D. *Third Edition.* Extra fcap. 8vo. 2*s.* 6*d.*

Lotze's *Logic*, in Three Books; of Thought, of Investigation, and of Knowledge. English Translation; Edited by B. Bosanquet, M.A. *Second Edition.* 2 vols. Cr. 8vo. 12*s.*

—— *Metaphysic*, in Three Books; Ontology, Cosmology, and Psychology. English Translation; Edited by B. Bosanquet, M.A. *Second Edition.* 2 vols. Cr. 8vo. 12*s.*

Martineau. *Types of Ethical Theory.* By James Martineau, D.D. *Third Edition.* 2 vols. Cr. 8vo. 15*s.*

—— *A Study of Religion: its Sources and Contents. Second Edition.* 2 vols. Cr. 8vo. 15*s.*

5. PHYSICAL SCIENCE.

Aplin. *The Birds of Oxfordshire.* By O. V. Aplin. 8vo. 10*s.* 6*d.*

Chambers. *A Handbook of Descriptive and Practical Astronomy.* By G. F. Chambers, F.R.A.S. *Fourth Edition*, in 3 vols. Demy 8vo.

- Vol. I. The Sun, Planets, and Comets. 21*s.*
- Vol. II. Instruments and Practical Astronomy. 21*s.*
- Vol. III. The Starry Heavens. 14*s.*

De Bary. *Comparative Anatomy of the Vegetative Organs of the Phanerogams and Ferns.* By Dr. A. de Bary. Translated and Annotated by F. O. Bower, M.A., F.L.S., and D. H. Scott, M.A., Ph.D., F.L.S. Royal 8vo, half-morocco, 1*l.* 2*s.* 6*d.*

—— *Comparative Morphology and Biology of Fungi, Mycetozoa and Bacteria.* By Dr. A. de Bary. Translated by H. E. F. Garnsey, M.A. Revised by Isaac Bayley Balfour, M.A., M.D., F.R.S. Royal 8vo, half-morocco, 1*l.* 2*s.* 6*d.*

De Bary. *Lectures on Bacteria.* By Dr. A. de Bary. *Second Improved Edition.* Translated by H. E. F. Garnsey, M.A. Revised by Isaac Bayley Balfour, M.A., M.D., F.R.S. Crown 8vo. 6*s.*

Fisher. *A Class Book of Elementary Chemistry.* By W. W. Fisher, M.A., F.C.S. Crown 8vo. 4*s.* 6*d.*

Chemistry in Space. By Van't Hoff. Translated and edited by J. E. Marsh, B.A. Crown 8vo. 4*s.* 6*d.*

Goebel. *Outlines of Classification and Special Morphology of Plants.* A new Edition of Sachs' Text-Book of Botany, Book II. By Dr. K. Goebel. Translated by H. E. F. Garnsey, M.A. Revised by Isaac Bayley Balfour, M.A., M.D., F.R.S. Royal 8vo, half-morocco, 1*l.* 1*s.*

Sachs. *Lectures on the Physiology of Plants.* By Julius von Sachs. Translated by H. Marshall Ward, M.A., F.L.S. Royal 8vo, half-morocco, 1*l.* 11*s.* 6*d.*

—— *A History of Botany.* Translated by H. E. F. Garnsey, M.A. Edited by I. Bayley Balfour, M.A., M.D., F.R.S. Crown 8vo. 10*s.*

Fossil Botany. *Being an Introduction to Palaeophytology from the Standpoint of the Botanist.* By H. Graf zu Solms-Laubach. Translated by H. E. F. Garnsey, M.A. Edited by I. Bayley Balfour, M.A., M.D., F.R.S. Royal 8vo, half-morocco, 18*s.*

Annals of Botany. Edited by Isaac Bayley Balfour, M.A., M.D., F.R.S., Sydney H. Vines, D.Sc., F.R.S., W. G. Farlow, M.D., and W. T. Thiselton-Dyer, C.M.G., M.A., F.R.S.; assisted by other Botanists. Royal 8vo, half-morocco, gilt top.

Vol. I. Parts I–IV. 1*l.* 16*s.*
Vol. II. Parts V–VIII. 2*l.* 2*s.*
Vol. III. Parts IX–XII. 2*l.* 12*s.* 6*d.*
Vol. IV. Parts XIII–XVI. 2*l.* 5*s.*
Vol. V. Parts XVII–XX. 2*l.* 10*s.*
Vol. VI. Part XXI. 12*s.*; Part XXII. 11*s.*

Biological Series. (*Translations of Foreign Biological Memoirs.*)

I. *The Physiology of Nerve, of Muscle, and of the Electrical Organ.* Edited by J. Burdon-Sanderson, M.D., F.R.SS. L. & E. Medium 8vo. 1*l.* 1*s.*

II. *The Anatomy of the Frog.* By Dr. Alexander Ecker, Professor in the University of Freiburg. Translated, with numerous Annotations and Additions, by G. Haslam, M.D. Med. 8vo. 21*s.*

III. *Contributions to the History of the Physiology of the Nervous System.* By Professor Conrad Eckhard. Translated by Miss Edith Prance. *In Preparation.*

IV. *Essays upon Heredity and Kindred Biological Problems.* By Dr. A. Weismann. Translated and Edited by E. B. Poulton, M.A., S. Schönland, Ph.D., and A. E. Shipley, M.A. *Second Edition.* Crown 8vo. 7*s.* 6*d.*

Vol. II. Edited by E. B. Poulton, and A. E. Shipley. Crown 8vo. 5*s.* *Just Published.*

Prestwich. *Geology, Chemical, Physical, and Stratigraphical.* By Joseph Prestwich, M.A., F.R.S. In two Volumes.

Vol. I. Chemical and Physical. Royal 8vo. 1*l.* 5*s.*

Vol. II. Stratigraphical and Physical. With a new Geological Map of Europe. Royal 8vo. 1*l.* 16*s.*

New Geological Map of Europe. In case or on roller. 5*s.*

Rolleston and Jackson. *Forms of Animal Life.* A Manual of Comparative Anatomy, with descriptions of selected types. By George Rolleston, M.D., F.R.S. *Second Edition.* Revised and Enlarged by W. Hatchett Jackson, M.A. Medium 8vo. 1*l.* 16*s.*

Oxford
AT THE CLARENDON PRESS
LONDON: HENRY FROWDE
OXFORD UNIVERSITY PRESS WAREHOUSE, AMEN CORNER, E.C.